The Guardian

This book is the culmination of an agreement. It is told that there will be one place for truth about what happened here. That place is this book.

By Sophia Love

There is a group of beings unrecorded until now. This group, the Guardians, is tasked with maintaining balance for the benefit of all creation. This task defines their role as either executioners or executives.

In the Year of Revelation, 2012, a Guardian came forward as an answer to a call.

For three years he spoke, revealing truths about humanity and the dark plans of humanity's controllers. That conversation is recorded.

It is now the book you are holding. Read here your past, present and future choices, as told by a Guardian; a member of the Forces of One.

Table of Contents

Introduction and Thanks

Introduction

The decision to do anything comes from this thought: that, in your best estimation, you will feel better (benefit) from the doing of it.

I now believe that the writing of this book was always the intent of this unusual friendship (mine and the Guardian's). In the reading of it, you will complete our journey, and I hope, benefit.

With love,

~Sophia

(7-14-15)

With thanks

With deepest gratitude to Dream Hopper, for his absolute love and support, to Roy, for their aid and encouragement, and to the Guardian for his service to humanity and pure love; I have been so very blessed.

Chapter 1   Sophia

Sophia

My journey is perhaps similar to yours. It incorporates a search for truth and always has. This led eventually to a face book page, a blog, you-tube channel, sound cloud channel and a web site; as I found that in the sharing so much was gained. Together we accomplished more than we were able to alone.

This discovery of truth is realized in the course of this 2 ½ year conversation. It sort of morphed into a gradual awakening to what was really going on for us, behind the scenes, on planet earth. It is a story that is at times, shocking and disturbing. Yet this Guardian was very careful to end each conversation with hope as well as music to lift the spirit. He had nothing but praise for humanity. What started as a single answer to a single question – grew to a voice that's been read by many thousands via my web site[1].

The sense I come away with is that the timing of our conversation (mine and the Guardian's), its beginning and its ending were pre-arranged. Perhaps this book was part of that plan; a place where all of this knowledge could always be found.

All of what you are about to read, is true.

---

[1] N.p., n.d. Web. <www.sophialove.org>.

Chapter 2 The Call

The Call

It was January 1, 2012. Not completely sure on why, I closed the door to my bedroom and opened a notebook. It seemed that as we began this noteworthy year, there should be something to say, a way to mark the moment.

This call to those "off planet" was unplanned. What followed was, I now realize, the first step on an incredible journey that continues today, 7.3.2016, via constant contact with a wide assortment of races. It was conceived of as it was created; first on paper, then on film. The movie "Message to Off World Beings[2]", remains one of my most popular you tube videos.

Four years later, what was said still pretty much holds true. The transcript for the video follows:

"2012 looks to be the year of the channel.

Dozens of prophecies, from as many off world beings, repeatedly speak to us, through us, and about us.

We are listening, with varying degrees of belief and enthusiasm.

We are infusing these sources with divinity, and placing a whole lot of weight and power on each statement.

At times, there is even anger expressed when things don't turn out exactly as prophesied.

It is time to channel the only source with the power to accurately predict our future.

It is time to speak for ourselves.

Perhaps these beings have a broader vantage point, more advanced technology, or a longer life span; yet they are not human.

They are watching us.

They cannot create in this reality, but we can.

Let's introduce ourselves to them.

---

[2] "Message To Off World Beings." *YouTube*. N.p., n.d. Web. 07 July 2016. <https://youtu.be/Pk-AaK2ZCV0>.

Hello! All you off world beings!

We're enjoying your messages and would like them to be more conversational.

Here's a place to start.

As humans, being, we are insatiable.

We are eternally hopeful, and never let go of our belief that there is something better possible.

We're experts at second chances, do-overs and trying again.

There's a reason we were chosen to be here at this time and it is deep within every one of us.

It is our heart.

Our ability to feel what we are, and express what we are, is what makes us uniquely suited to this task.

Although the truth has been hidden from us these many years, it has not stopped us!

You have watched us progress and witnessed our tenacity.

We may not have known how we were expanding, but against all odds, this slave race of subservient beings has evolved to take command, and intentionally create a future that benefits not some of us, but all of us.

This is because of our light and our power.

We are sourced from the essence of creation and WE CAN FEEL THAT SOURCE.

Who we are is love personified.

We feel each other in each smile and every glance.

We will risk our lives to save each other, and join hands, hearts and bodies across enemy lines, racial differences, borders and nationalities.

We are ONE, and although we have not used these words until now, our hearts have felt them always.

This is what you don't know about us, and even these words can't portray the full extent of our divinity.

It has to be felt; and in order to feel it, you must be human.

We do what we do, and will always be capable of doing more because we LOVE EACH OTHER.

We live what we are, and what we are – is love.

Our task now is to take this love we feel so deeply for each other – into ourselves.

We do not love ourselves without condition – yet – but we will.

This shift we are undergoing is taking time not because we are slow, but because we want everyone on board when it happens.

We want it to be seamless and easily done for all of us.

Our unity is something we understand deeply and feel in our every pore.

We feel the truth of our oneness and know that together we can accomplish anything.

It is our heart that empowers and motivates us and this is something that we know and we feel.

Every one of us understands passion at a core level.

Our feelings are the fuel of our magnificence.

What is happening for us is that we are waking up to the brilliance of our own truth.

In every moment we are love, and as we shake off the dust of oppression we see just how expanded and all-encompassing we actually are.

We WILL get there as ONE because we BELIEVE THAT WE WILL, and we are actualizing our very essence.

There is no doubt in our heart, and there resides our greatest strength.

Our hearts hold the source of creation, and they beat as ONE.

We are the ones we are waiting for.

Thank you."

At the time, January 2012, it[3] received the usual comments and views.

I continued to write blogs and hold "Love Quests"[4], both for Face Book[5] and on my website[6]. I worked part time and home schooled my children. Life proceeded without alteration, that is, until I began to get answers.

Let me mention here that my home is a small ranch style residence. We all live on the same floor, not very far from each other. Two of our (4) sons were teenagers at the time, both musicians. I often fell asleep to music being played, created and/or mixed. This went on until the early morning hours with lights and speakers ablaze.

On this one particular night (about 2 weeks after the initial video, mid-January 2012), I was suddenly awake to what I instantly noticed was silence & complete darkness. I looked at the clock. It read 12:21AM. I thought "This is so odd… who woke me up?"

And I immediately heard *"We did!"* (I could "see" their smiling faces inside my mind's eye)

"Where are you?" I replied.

"Come take a look out back!" I heard.

Well, it was cold and I was cozy and sleepy and I responded, "Look, if I get up out of this warm bed and you aren't there? I'm gonna be really pissed."

"Come on!" I heard again. *"Just come check."*

"This is stupid." I responded, and I rolled over and fell back to sleep.

(The full account of that night can be found in the 2nd video[7])

---

[3] N.p., n.d. Web. <https://youtu.be/Pk-AaK2ZCV0>.
[4] http://www.sophialove.org/love-quest.html
[5] N.p., n.d. Web. <https://www.facebook.com/IAMSophiaLove/>.
[6] "Sophia Love Home." *Sophia*. N.p., n.d. Web. 07 July 2016. <http://www.sophialove.org/>.
[7] "Response to Off World Beings II." *YouTube*. N.p., n.d. Web. 07 July 2016.
<https://youtu.be/m1yKrBdbc2U>.

Now I've had telepathic communication before and since, with my partner, Dream Hopper. It is loud and clear, as this was. My skepticism has softened, if not disappeared, since then.

The next morning was Sunday. A typically relaxed, eat late and drink tea sort of morning... After some time I mention to my partner what happened. I was self-conscious about it, a little concerned I was losing my mind. I had already checked in the backyard for a "footprint" of some sort. There was no indication of either ship or being, (there was snow on the ground).

Dream Hopper (DH) had no doubt. He was sort of miffed that I hadn't told him as soon as he woke up! He made me promise I'd either wake him up next time or leave a note so he'd know where I was if I went with them.

So I drew a space ship on an index card and kept it in my bedside drawer – just in case. I also began to sleep in pajamas that resembled sweats rather than anything alluring – just in case. ("DH" wasn't too thrilled with this part.) I was ready. They never came back.

It has since been made known to me that these were Plieadians. They were like teenagers out on a joy ride and were answering my "Message to Off World Beings" you tube video, in their own way. It was frowned upon; a sort of "unauthorized trip". That is, if Plieadians can actually frown! I get only joy, love and a party vibe from these beings! I can't wait to meet them in "real/earth time".

Many, many times since that night I've thought about how it could've gone differently, possible conversations and what they look like. It was partly fear and mostly disbelief that prevented me getting out of bed that night. It would be another story today if I had.

I've been told I'd have a second chance. When I do, well, that will be another book.

Sometime after that night, during the month of February 2012, we had another "visitation". None of us were aware of this one. It was still winter so there was snow on the ground.

My son's room faced the backyard. One morning he called me in to check out the odd markings in the snow. We took pictures. They were not made by trees or falling limbs or animals. They were an intricate pattern of rod shaped indentations in the snow. They were crystalized and remained long after the rest of the snow melted. Animals avoided that section. It was weird. It looked to us like either something had landed and made the impression or hovered directly over that spot and "dripped" the impressions from a heat source beneath a vehicle (read "space ship"). There were not natural explanations for the marks, to our knowledge.

Both of these events (the telepathic wake up and the odd shaped drips in the yard) relate to the resulting conversation with the one known as the Guardian or "G/E" & this book.

It is of interest that at the start of our connection (mine and G/E's), he referred to himself as a "Guardian/Executioner". After certain decisions were made, this name was changed, at his request, to "Guardian/Executive". From that point on, there was no longer an "execution" possibility. As you will read, this term refers to the execution of *humanity*.

Winter melted into spring and on April 14th, 2012 I received my first contact from the Guardian.

It was my habit to check my you-tube channel once a week or so. On this day, I was blown away with the energy emitted from this comment:

"Not all races around this Universe have "advanced" technologies. But ones that were here were fighting with each other, until we showed up. You as a species are not One and unite. You lack Consensus, One do not. League is offering your species to become part of them, because people like You are giving hope for your race. You are being controlled by government that is against ways of One. "Satanic" worshipers of goat of mendes, also star of Sirius. Enemies of One or "criminals" in your words."

(Please note that in most cases the spelling and capitalization are left as it was posted. Later in our relationship it was made clear to me that there were reasons for made up words and lack of, or insertion of, capital letters.)

I read this to my partner and he could feel the unusual "vibe" as well. We immediately channeled his "group".

(*My partner is a deep trance channel, which means he leaves his body completely to allow another being the use of his body and his voice. The group that speaks consists of his greater self, my greater self and other interested and non-embodied parties. We declare "highest and best for all concerned" and a host of other things before he leaves his body.*) We asked who this was.

Their response was interesting and a bit unsettling. They were not sure who exactly, but said it/he represented a greater One; that it/he was speaking on behalf of One; what/who we have come to know as Source Creator and All That Is.

Four days later I wrote a blog[8]. It follows.

~~~~~

"On January 1st, 2012 I released a video entitled *"Message to Off World Beings"*. Yesterday, I got an answer. It came in the form of an interaction with someone speaking for the *"Forces of One"*. You can see what was said in the video bearing that name. Both can be found here and on the you-tube channel.

And that's the back story to what will most likely be my focus for the rest of this year – Making A Choice – everything else sort of pales in comparison.

I've read and re-read the transcript and although I cannot point to my partner in the conversation, I can tell you how it felt. *It felt epic.* The power coming with the words sort of washed over me. I felt them before I read them. I've had to look up a few of the terms he used since then, but there is no mistaking how I felt. *I was in the presence of a force unlike any other I have known here.*

The video, *"Message to Off World Beings"* was released to remind us of our own power, with the added intent of contact. In fact, I was contacted telepathically a few days after it was released. I was woken up and spoken to; that energy was exuberant and joyful yet the voice was in my head – I doubted its authenticity.

This contact was not in my head, it was on a you-tube channel. *Really*. You can check it out for yourself by reading the comments below the video: *"Message to Off World Beings"*.

This only amplifies what has always been primary – Love. *We are without a doubt far more powerful than we imagine ourselves to be.* We are deciding the fate of the planet. *The choice we make this year determines the*

---

[8] N.p., n.d. Web. <http://www.sophialove.org/my-blog/is-this-epic-enough>.

direction for all of life.

How is that choice accomplished? With love. *The magic is us*. Unity means everyone is right. Forgiveness is key; start by forgiving yourself.

This is not a game or just a nice thing to do. It is vital. The controllers have seen to it that we dismiss love as a frilly and fluffy emotion that weakens our resolve and our production. Nothing could be further from the truth. LOVE HAS ALL THE POWER. LOVE IS WHAT HAS CAST YOU FORTH AND THE VERY CORE OF WHO YOU ARE. Any lack of love will play out as low self-esteem or a desire for control – separation. WE ARE NOT SEPARATE. WE ARE ONE.

The whole idea of receiving divine intervention via you-tube is absurd. I mean, are you kidding me? It does not matter whether you believe this as truth or not. *It matters that you love*. This is how the choice is made. What springs from your heart is understood, if unspoken.

Harboring hatred, anger or revenge is an option that will yield more of only that. The law of attraction is indeed a law that governs this reality. You choose privately – no one but you knows the essence of your energy. Believe you make a difference and that the fate of humanity rests in your heart. *Is this epic enough?*

I can neither substantiate nor disprove this source. I will only say that I trust what my heart says. I know who I am. I am love. I am not willing to risk the future of us because of fear or doubt. It is okay if you believe differently or think this has gone too far. *Love anyway*. It won't hurt and it may just change everything.

You are more than you've imagined yourself to be. You are here at this time to answer the call, to make a choice. No longer can we say we don't matter. In fact, we matter very much. How we are feeling reverberates out and the universe responds. Our universe. It will respond to the answer we emit and there are only two choices – Unity/Love or Polarity/Fear. It is time to choose.

We are the ones we are waiting for."

~~~~~

Blog posts from that month, throughout the end of that pivotal year centered on choice and unity, love and oneness, acceptance and forgiveness, agape and anticipation. We were focused on 12-21-2012 with varying degrees of belief and excitement. At this point, hope and magic were rampant.

"G/E" eventually described himself as a Member of the "Forces of One". So, on this day, 4/14/12, my conversation with a Guardian begins...

Chapter 3   The Answer

The Answer

It started as a you tube comment. This became cumbersome and was eventually moved to you tube email. Some of these were shared in my blog posts at the time.

Eventually, you tube/Google began monitoring its email and there were things shared that were too "sensitive". You tube/Google began restricting access.

We moved then to private email. As more of you began to have questions, this again morphed to a separate blog on my website, dedicated solely to G/E and available for comments and questions from readers.

I still received the answers privately, but he could now read the questions himself. It also allowed readers to help and sometimes answer each other. This was a sort of compromise between us due to the increasing amounts of "work" associated with his ongoing disclosure. Everything had to come through me, and I sort of complained to him, suggesting that he open his own blog and that he no longer needed my audience – he very much had his own following.

He was kind of authoritative at that point and well, it was our one and only disagreement. What we ended up doing was a best case scenario. Readers could feel his energy and he could remain invisible, while this disclosure could continue.

Let me say here that I was always the disseminator of his words at his request. He was clear that his work had to come from someone other than him directly, for safety reasons. He had "inside knowledge" and the "dark t-shirts" could impact his ability to share it if it came directly from him. It was not that I was expendable, but that I was "protected". This is not the first time I've heard the term.

There are some things he told me that I never shared. They seemed too radical or dark and he always prefaced those with the fact that I was "at choice" with this part. Some of these may be included in this volume, yet not all. It appears he was right and you tube/Google has removed/disabled access to all of its mail. I am working on getting this back via an internet archive. It is July 2015. If I am successful, it will be included.

Some of what wasn't shared was personal, (concerning my family or myself). Of those, the one thing I remember is that he told me I was "anointed". Not having any idea what he meant by that I looked it up. It is defined as being "chosen". "Chosen" ones are here to spread the word. Many definitions include the word

God in them. I have come to comprehend that it signifies truth, (without the "God"). What follows is his definition, as given on June 2nd, 2014.

Yes, You are Chosen by Followers of Light as well as all of Lightworkers and Lightwarriors, as You are more developed than ordinary common People. You bear the Light of Star, You hold the "Keys to Heaven". You are special and more evolved and thus more cared for, more protected by "unseen forces", Your families are protected as well. All the Good-Doers! Others are protected as well, but this depends on their orientation toward Good or evil side.
~~~

Note - Eventually you'll get used to the way he phrased and spelled things. We all did. Most of the "errors" you will see in his writing were left intact as it is my belief they were intentional. Particularly the way he refused to capitalize most countries and titles, yet always capitalized the word "You". He followed his own set of rules, that much is certain.

Also note that some of the comments were from people for whom English was not their first language. You will notice there too, grammatical errors. Every attempt has been made to preserve this conversation as it took place; the corrections have been kept to a minimum.

What you'll read here is my discovery of certain "truths", which propelled an awakening to lots of others. This is the story of our enlightenment and growing awareness from the years 2012 – 2015, as told by the Guardian and myself.

Chapter 4   2012

2012 THE YEAR OF REVELATION

The first G/E you tube comment on "Message to Off World Beings[9]" (unedited):

April 14, 2012

Not all races around this Universe have "advanced" technologies. But ones that were here, were fighting with each other, until we showed up. You as a species are not One and unite. You lack Consensus, One do not. League is offering your species to become part of them, because people like You are giving hope for your race. You are being controlled by government that is against ways of One. "Satanic", worshipers of goat of mendes, also star of Sirius. Enemies of One or "criminals" in your words.

(Note – this next grouping of unedited comments is from You Tube, as received & answered between April and July 2012. You tube doesn't retain exact dates in the comment section, so they aren't available.)

SOPHIA (in response to first comment, shown above)
You don't sound like you're from around here, yet your message is clear. It is my belief that love is the answer for us all, especially those in control. I would like to continue this conversation. Are you able to make yourself known to me? I see no information on your "channel". Blessings.

G/E
It is the answer to your question. You have uploaded this message on first day of this year, this wasn't coincidence, everything that happens in this Universe has it's own purpose. This is "the year of Revelation", only during this year every human being "will have a bite of real knowledge" which was hidden from you for thousands of years. Your puppeteers are losing control over you during this year, you are free in many of your actions now.

SOPHIA
Freedom sounds like love, and is not that what is being revealed? As we "chew on" this real knowledge, we get a taste of what it could be like, perhaps what it was meant to be. And we want that. Many don't believe it is possible or "true", evidence for the depth of the impact of the control.

G/E

---

[9] "Message To Off World Beings." *YouTube*. N.p., n.d. Web. 07 July 2016. <https://youtu.be/Pk-AaK2ZCV0>.

Love is the same as Unity and Consensus in ours and Yours understanding. The Truth that is being revealed are dark secrets that were hidden from your view for the last 300 years, 4 generations of your kind. The truth about many of your wars, who really was behind them, what really cause them. It was not natural why World War one and two occurred, they were planned by few. This is the year, when eyes of your kind will be opened till the end of this year, as you will decide your own future..

SOPHIA
Yes, and that decision we make, individually and collectively is what will determine our future? Are we REALLY at the wheel now? Or are there limits to our possibilities? Or are we only limited by our imagination? Or is there an unseen hand, as has been the case, still at the helm? These are the things I wonder. How much freedom is there in free will. We do not know the abilities we hold, hence, how do we utilize them?

G/E
Powerful extrasensory people of your kind all see what was destined to happen to your race - destruction of it. All the predictions and prophecies were not meant to fool you forever. This has happened not only to your race, it is not the first time civilization suicide itself. However, we decided that your race will be able to change it's destiny by your collective choice.. Our arrival was unexpected, we already changed some of your destiny, the rest is up to your kind.

Free will or atheism is dangerous when you cannot control it. Your kind is yet not powerful enough to control space and time, you even losing in control of your own technologies you created. Very fast technological progress "dampens" your mind, you cannot sustain very fast changes, the amount of oxygen and lack of some other gases in the atmosphere plus degradation of your free will by "Illuminati Order - the holders" all this is not allowing you to evolve as fast as your technologies progress.

SOPHIA
Free will is a synonym for atheism? This is a challenge to comprehend. What is needed to permit the evolution? Time? The removal of the Illuminati seems a moment away, will that do it? If there are necessary atmospheric changes, then, who ultimately controls them? Is it us? This is our illusion, is it not? Are you part of this illusion or do you stand in a place with the controls in your hand?

G/E
Absolute free will is believing in nothing only but yourself.. In the beginning it is not like this way, but eventually it will go to it. Only the most powerful beings are able to sustain it, your kind is too young for this bear. There are many aspects which are necessary for organic creatures to become more powerful than any

other organic one around in the Universe. Resources of your planet are limited, your civilization will not be able to sustain itself for developing "salvation technologies"

SOPHIA

This effort then, this revolution of love and tossing off of those in control, is what? A step towards an unstoppable, but inescapable, end for the planet? We are evolving, and coming to know ourselves as capable of making choices, yet we seem to be embedded with a "slave" genetic, we expect another to sustain us, to take care of us, to give us the answer we seek. We have never experienced this "absolute free will". What are the aspects that are necessary? Can they be taught/learned?

G/E

This is a step forward for you to become self aware, more than your ancestors were, You can call it more freer from shackles you are in now. Your ancestors were waiting exactly for this moment, the moment of "the end of the days" or your own choosing, it was up to One to give you this opportunity to choose. These aspects will be learned all by itself when you will know that everything is all right and your civilization and planet are safe, there is a long way to it after this though..

For now You and the rest of your kind will have to concentrate on your choice, because this will decide the outcome of everything on your planet, the fate of your children, the fate of every organic living being on this planet, this choice must be wise enough. When your collective choice will be made, we, their agents will make the final choice based on your choice. If you will prevent the World War three, stop the Illuminati Order and let us know of your will to become One with us, we will aid.

SOPHIA

It is my deepest hope/belief that we are making/have made that choice. I am not alone in this thought. We have been "told" that a tipping point is necessary, and that it has been reached. Is this truth? Would you speak of ONE who has provided the choice and then of you, who will aid/make the final choice based on our choice? There is much to understand.

G/E

No, this choice has not yet been made. First we are giving you the taste of every outcome you can see after this year. We are interfering with you as less as possible, but observing you closely. Are trying to show you everything you need to know to make that decision, but this decision must be strictly yours. One is The Universe itself, You can call it God, He is alive and not alive, sentient and non-sentient, everything and nothing, beginning and the end, all at the same time. A basis of existence

SOPHIA
Then, who are you? (the "we" who are giving us a taste of every possible outcome)

G/E
I'm a human like you. I and the other people in every corner of this planet were given this knowledge so that we can help everyone who are desperately in need of answer and reason on behalf of One. The Forces of One are providing this knowledge only to some individuals like you, because You will be able to help other in deciding the fate of humanity. Everything is happening with a reason, no event occur without the consequence.

SOPHIA
Okay...this has to sink in. Things like what to do next, and how to continue and expand this conversation are in my head... fairly bursting with it all... is there another way to connect? There are so many subjects, and questions.

G/E
I will be able to give only the basic knowledge, what I already gave to You. Your kind will know more from us only if new world order would not be established. If it would be established, Illuminati Order will take full control over every individual on this planet, it will be almost impossible for us to continue to give our knowledge. For now observe the world and make Your choosing Sophia, it was nice to chat with You.

SOPHIA
Likewise. Thank you.

Note - Some time went by, and on another day...

Would you speak of how this decision is communicated? It is my imagining that it springs from within each of us. In other words, not evidenced necessarily by the actions of our governments but instead by the fear or love within. It seems that a majority of us do want an end to this control, but for some that is not seen as possible, and for others, their deepest belief/hope. How is this choice ultimately made? What are you/we waiting for? This message has not been well received, or trusted.*

Note: At this point I had shared these messages with a few friends and co-bloggers in the light worker community. The responses were very negative and un-trusting. One person removed me from her blog completely in anger at the insinuation that we were not free or able to decide for ourselves. Several others ignored them completely. The rest were completely skeptical and judgmental about the validity of any of what was being said. None of it was published, except in my own blog and then occasionally. I was sort of new to this blogging community and this came as a shock. It was, at the time, as if everyone felt their corner of the truth was complete, thank you very much. New information was met with doubt. After such a negative reaction, I mostly kept these conversations to myself.

G/E
It is all Energy, everyone is able to communicate with anyone, no matter how far the object of communication is. This planet is alive and whatever mankind is doing, we feel it. Based on your choice, our choice will be done. The choice and wish of each individual will be felt by this Planet, Sun and us. The Universe is filled with Energy, it is easy to feel it, but in order to decode it, You need to believe in Universal Unity, everything is One and One is He who rules everything.

SOPHIA
Got it. Thank you for responding. The assimilation of this brings gradual, but eventual further inquiry.

G/E
Yes, as with "science", the more scientists finds out, the more questions start to appear than answers. We on the other hand know everything that is on the basis of the Universe. If your scientists would accept more theories that were proposed to them, they would eventually know much more and able to create many more things, but they didn't listen, because there were "no proof". For example, world heard of Einstein and he gave many of the technologies humanity now possesses, including atom bomb.

Though it would be just enough for your kind, your kind even could not handle this not so powerful weapon properly. Only one act of aggression could resolve in a nuclear warfare. We would never do such a thing. League of One possess much more powerful weaponry that are able to destroy dimensions, not speaking about Universe, these technologies are from One, Einstein was given this knowledge as well by us, we would grant him also thermo fusion and matter formation, but it was dangerous as You see..

SOPHIA
I wonder about our scientists using the knowledge for destruction of Itself, rather than creation, or a use of benefit to Mankind. Is this the pull of yet another

power? The Illuminati/Dark Ones as they have been called? What is the compulsion to destruction that predominates those with power? Why not compulsion to create, to benefit, to sustain? This force seems and is portrayed as the greatest force, even personified in Satan and as such worshiped.

Has this merely been our way to see what is possible? Or, is it by design of yet another hand? I am seeing a circularity to these questions. They always return to "who or what is in control?" Yet, I know now that the control rests within. Are the mere presence of the Illuminati necessary so that I may now know what evil looks like, a flash point from which I/WE will create a new world? Nothing occurs without consequence.

Will this choice, this ultimate choice, the choice that determines the fate of mankind, be forced by a major event? What can you say about that?

G/E
Not the dark ones, but corrupted ones. There is still Good in them.. It is important how creatures were learned and programmed to exist. Almost every living organic creature starts as predator. The creature predates on those who is weaker than it is. Someone stronger predates on this creature. Man's primal animal instincts still lefts in his genom. There is still locked knowledge on how everything was in history of this world that I yet cannot tell. This knowledge is one among secret knowledges.

Illuminati took the real image of One and use it to bring evil to everything on this world. They think, they are doing this for good of mankind, for a better world, in reality they are destroying this world and bring you year by year to your self - destruction. Their purpose is to unite this planet's nations, but exterminate most of population. This is noble objective, but their methods are brutal, evil. Illuminati are people, they represent humanity in our eyes, your choice may change this.

Many already saw, from the beginning of the times, that when the end will come it will be brought from up the skies BY FIRE. We would be able to activate the Sun and make a very powerful Solar Flare to aid you, Sun is the Creator and only Supporter of your life, only He holds the key to your ultimate destiny. He as well does not agree with methods of Illuminati Order. You will be aided by Him once you will prove, to wish and live, be free from lies, deception, death that Illuminati brings to you

SOPHIA
I do not understand how fire would save us from fire. And this is proved only "when the end comes"? Or is this proved each moment, in each heart?

G/E
Don't worry Sun will not harm You, He will only switch off all the electronics on your planet. The future holds many ways, many possible outcomes of which we know, future may bring a surprise to your kind, though we know about what surprise it will be. Sun will play crucial moment in your planet's history, as it was long ago. Everyone who lives on this planet already feels that something is coming, something bad, but everyone also feels that there is still hope. It is up to your kind to use it.

Note: From here on, several of my friends also began to engage with G/E. This all took place in the comments section of the "Message to Off World" video, and is probably still there!

AMERICAN KABUKI
Can you elaborate on the Star of Sirus, are you referring to a 4 pointed star found in many Air Force and other institutions? The Goat of Mendes would be the inverted 5 pointed star right? Just trying to clarify in my mind who you are referring to. Are you a starseed or a walkin? Or something else?

G/E
Star of Sirius is a five-pointed star, same as pentagram. United States were formed by Freemasons, there was a connection between them and Illuminati, Illuminati and United States were formed at the same year. Freemasons chose to use symbolism in everyday life of american citizens, everywhere "where eyes don't see but unconsciousness see". The All Seeing Eye is a representation of One, but they use it to represent Sirius. Five pointed star, pentagram and Eye, all this represents Sirius.

SOPHIA
Yes, this part of us is what this video was referring to. Tenacious and relentless, champions at starting over. You have said "Illuminati represent people in our eyes" and then "you will be aided by Him once you will will prove, to wish and live, be free from lies, deception, death that Illuminati brings". The majority of us are not the Illuminati, and yet they represent the people in your eyes? This statement confuses. Is this due to their level of control?

There is a contributing factor of which I am unaware. Awareness would change that. Can you provide it? You have reached out and spoken here, there is always a purpose for contact. What is the purpose in this conversation, for you?

G/E
No this is due to your agreement with their control. Much part of humanity ignore their existence, this is counted as you are agreeing with how everything is in this world and as Illuminati are in control of your system. But yes, we see that many

want a different life, a change in world's policy. Many are against politics and military corruption, this is this hope for your kind, a choice that you may make. We made them blind for this year, so that You may choose.

Yes, there is a purpose. You will be able to help many to make this choice, many people like You were told of this choice and will be told. You're pure heart, filled with love and power to resist evil, people like You are welcomed to the League of One. Those who wear number seven are Your Friends as well, it is not we, but they are Good like You. It is self-awareness. Seven is the number of elements of this Universe, unconsciously they know it, this same number is a very respected in League.

SOPHIA
So...where will I see "those who wear number seven"? It would be beneficial to know this, as we would be a force for One. Would you name the seven elements to which you refer?

G/E
It is easy to find them. Here on you tube for example, look for nickname. If number 7 is in there, this means the man wears this number. It is sub consciousness telling him or her to put this number in this nickname. You can look at their channels, if You wish, You can try to chat with them. It is easy to talk to them and they will understand You, they are also searching for truth, not all found it though and not all could be friendly, but "unfriendlies" are very few.

4 elements You already know. From these 3 prime elements comes 4 lesser elements: Air/Energy - Electromagnetic Energy Water/Ice/Cold - "almost no molecular movement" Earth/Ground - Gravity Fire/Heat - "high molecular movement" There is a scientific explanations about these four, your kind's scientists almost found them. Two primal elements that control all 4 lesser elements and are in opposition with each other are Light and Dark and one element that controls all six is Time - Ultimate Element.

And remember that we are not forcing or imposing on You our believe, You're free to believe in everything You wish to believe, there is no right or wrong in this Universe, everything in what You believe is a right believe for You. We are offering humanity to become part of our League, we will let everyone know our true ways only when we will become as One. Our duty right now is to let people like You about the possibility of a choice and what options Your kind is having right now.

SOPHIA
Thank you. This is a place to begin.

I see. These four are the elements within the zodiac, I notice. There seems here to be much in this ancient knowledge that is disregarded by mainstream. I can't help but question how intentional this has been. Mainstream scientists often put their career at risk if they give credence to truths such as this. Reluctance runs deep and as a result, any information that would empower us is not shared with us. This is part of the choosing of which you speak, is it not?

Options as outlined thus far sound pretty clear - domination and death under the Illuminati or life - the suicide of the race, versus life and freedom. There are many among us who are brave and fighting at the front lines right now to bring out these truths for the rest of us - they risk their lives for humanity. Yet, I wonder, is there a possibility of replacing one controller for another? This is wondered by many, distrust runs deep. What can you say to that? What is the intention here?

G/E
Yes, it can be called like that. Illuminati Order is using knowledges that they do not share with others who do not belong to them. They already possess technologies that will able automobiles to fly, this is electromagnetic energy that makes them fly and makes them "invisible". Many "UFO" You saw are government's "flying saucers", these were developed during World War two by german military. They also able to increase the brain's strength and make people immune to almost all diseases.

I cannot tell exactly what choices your kind will have, but there are plenty. There is some hidden true from your race..

SOPHIA
So, from this springs the confusion... love versus fear is the choice beneath every decision. Yet, we have been lied to - 4 generations of us. The trust we have given is now discovered to be a misplaced trust. We will be asked, perhaps ARE being asked, to choose. In a very practical way, fear makes sense, we do not want to be fooled again. It is again our decision, will we cooperate out of fear or out of love? That seems the real answer that will tell you our intent -

A choice made out of a sense of power and love versus fear of destruction? We are faced with powerful forces here, they have controlled our entire lives, we have families... This "outing" of the truth could go many ways for people...

And many days passed, sometimes weeks, between answers to my questions. Hence, this next comment...

So... are there no answers to the questions just asked?

G/E

Changing current leaders to others will save You from Illuminati plan, but will postpone the self-destruction. Not a recommended choice. Illuminati stalls human civilization from advancing, they made "a very profitable" money system, that is already obsolete if your civilization want to evolve further. It is already became a possibility to give everyone what they need, only essential things. People don't need to pay for only being born on this planet, this is a false need, that they impose.

SOPHIA

Your response leaves me to believe you have a "recommended choice". Would you elaborate?

G/E

A "conclusive" World War three will start in spring 2013, with attack on Iran by NATO/USA, Russia and China will stand against this attack. This will be a normal war until 2016, when USA will move nuclear missiles to Georgia, this act will force russians to launch nuclears on USA, China will launch its nukes on USA too. Instantly USA will launch its nukes on Russia and China, this will result in 3 billion dead and a lot of radiation everywhere. "5-19-13 Expect Us" message.

This will happen in a "normal way", if your kind won't do anything against governments. This will not be the last war, but destruction from it will be great. We are trying to change this war, as You can already see, but we do not want to intervene with someone "not human". Not until your species will disagree with governments of Earth. Although You can live on your own and stop this war without our intervention, but still current governments must face "international justice" in this case too.

You are free to decide whatever You want, everything what Your species will decide will be seen by Universal Energy. Your sub consciousness will decide what in reality will You want, to many even consciousness won't know what was decided. I will mention this again, Forces of One are offering humanity to join them, League will give everything that is needed for everyone and will care for Your race like it was forever in the League, we are doing this for every civilization in the League of One.

SOPHIA

So changing the leaders helps temporarily but it is changing the mindset of man that will prevent a catastrophic end. We are a slave race, and that is a complete change in our thinking. We are willing to let others control us as long as they pretty much let us live our lives. What is suggested by your comment here is that we DO NOT let anyone control us, and for us to take conscious control of every facet of our lives. Those of us who can see what is needed, (next comment please)

are not often the ones who seek to work on an international/government level. This change will be of a massive scale. If the desire for power is no longer part of the draw, the players on that field will be different. The subconscious decision will have to be inclusive of the entire world and not just our own individual lives, no? We will have to think as if we are ONE in a very real sense, and not only/merely individuals with singular lives to worry about. Is that it?

G/E
You're absolutely correct! :) This was our answer and message to You Sophia, we will take some of Your people even if Your species won't decide to become a part of us. Search for Giorgio Bongiovanni on an internet via Google. This man is a conduit of our connection to your species. Those who speak through him are our lesser friends, they use christian religion in order to tell this same message. Our ways are one and the same, though we are "a little different".

SOPHIA
I have not heard the name and will search. This search may bring further questions, there is much to think about.

Would you care to comment on World Liberation Day?

Note: This was held on May 4/5 2012

G/E
This day depends on choice of Your civilization.

SOPHIA
This day has now passed. Did you hear my choice?

G/E
It did not. Like I said we are "a little different". The race that is talking through him is young, they are referring to "their masters" from whom they are receiving their orders, these masters are we, Guardians - Executioners. I am one of the assets to your civilization, so I cannot be called "a master", we all have different orders, different objectives. This race must give hope to those who believed for so long, some will be saved in all different outcomes. What we want is to save everyone. *(Note: Some of this comment, "the race that is talking through him…." Is a reference to Giorgio Bongiovanni.")*

But as was said, you will have to choose this as a Whole. Everyone will be heard. War will not happen if choice will be made to stop injustice. Anything that goes beyond it, must not be said for now. Changing the ways of life of civilizations is a hard task and time consuming, but possible. People on this planet are very different, have rebellious nature, barely trust to someone "not human" it will take some time to give You our knowledge.

SOPHIA

Yet this nature was learned over eons of time, was it not? There is the name "lightworker" to signify one who has come to gently assist with the change. There are many lightworkers, yet not the majority. There has to be hope given, demonstrable and visible, in order to "change the ways of life" for this civilization. Many years there has been none, except by our own determination, which in turn is our "rebellious nature". In order for success it was necessary to be separate. Yet we are One.

This is a reversal of thought. This is a hard sell. There has been no "other" to trust. What was heard on "World Liberation Day?"

G/E

Your thoughts are very deep and correct. Predecessors were not like this generation, their sub consciousness thought was to evolve their children and care for them, now your generation is trying to get or know the purpose, for why they were grown up and thrown into this world. We knew it was your time to finally choose what future You wish and not what your predecessors already wished and prepared for You. Now You can break the shackles and become free. Free as a whole.

SOPHIA

Yes, there is a sense of that. We feel it and there are so many who are working for it (freedom). Yet in the discovery and work itself there is disagreement, as to become free of dominance by an "other" is not a statement of unity, but of a very deep rift. This is so even among lightworkers, who disagree as to methods and words used. There is not a sense of one, our language almost denies it. We may be unified in our hatred of the oppression only and that is not a statement of unity, of One.

What can you say of the term "Archons"?

G/E

Don't be afraid of this. If humanity will become free we will not leave You. We know that if you will overthrow Illuminati and USA government, the war will be only postponed. The population, resources, technology level, these numbers predicts 100% war, it must happen. Illuminati are the ones to blame, because they were engineering society to level it is now.. We will help You to become as a One civilization after right choice.

There are Good people in this world, but they are refusing to live in this "system", political, social, military, some of them already died, simply they didn't want to live. These people are the ones, who can raise Your civilization, from even the most desperate situation, their mind is being fueled by One, they can invent everything. They are calling this world evil and are very eager for revolution of this system. Again, right now they are waiting for this year to pass and choice being made..

Some knowledges are locked. I cannot tell anything about "non-human" political structure. Only the basis of the Universe knowledge, which You already by most part know.

SOPHIA
We have heard tell of two paths, until the end of this year, and that one is freedom and a wonderful world. The other is continued control by Illuminati, population reduction, etc. We have now heard that we are on the path to this wonderful world, and ridding ourselves of the Illuminati is a matter of time, that we have chosen this path. We believe we are inventing this and that it cannot all be predicted until it is created by us. Is this not how it works? Who are these "good" people?

G/E
Good people are ones that do not betray, do not kill, do not do any damage to the Universe, do not poison Universe with dark energy, do not do everything only for themselves. And choice will be made not only by everyone's consciousness, but by sub consciousness, physical body (humanity's instincts), Your Energy (it is known as soul) and lastly by Your Energetic connection to this planet, to the Sun and to the Universe. Don't worry, Your vessel (body) will make this choice in a very right way.

SOPHIA
Is there a moment in linear time that will be most effective for the light work, a "deadline" if you will, for the decision/choice? The energy is intense right now, things seem to be speeding up, there is much we don't "see" yet we are affected by. There are dates, one of them tomorrow and the next June the 5th, that are being called pivotal. Can you speak to the timing of this year?

Note: June 5th, 2012 was the transit of Venus, a rare celestial event, AKA "The Return of the Goddess"

G/E

We saw different futures, in different dimensions, different happens. I cannot tell this. You already know, that when anti-God government will be established, end will be near by Bible/Quran teachings, also You can see other prophecies of humanity's predecessors, that You weren't aware of. Ancient, and real, which is showing a choice, "Hopi Prophecy Rock -The End of Times 2012 (New Era)." 111 Popes, 12 presidents, Mayan pinpointed this date as the beginning of 13th circle, the circle of Rebirth.

SOPHIA

Okay. I have a "new" understanding of "we are ONE" ... it is not that there is a separate voice. We are that voice. That voice of ONE. The ONE who will determine the choice. The ONE who is speaking and thus directing these times, your involvement and offer for help is conditional only on the fact that you have to be asked. If we do not ask, and asking happens when we do something. Silence and acceptance is agreement and that is spoken. The awakening is happening yet it is not complete...

Lightworkers are still "in the closet" as they seem to be surrounded by those who still are unaware there is even a choice to be made. So the question arises - will this event you speak of, and others speak of, be the one the arouses the masses? It seems that some sort of mass awakening to these specific choices is necessary before the masses will speak. Can you speak to that?

G/E

You're understanding everything as I already knew. The rising of masses is based on what will happen in next 3 months. For now, everyone must live like they were living before that, this possibility of choice is being felt by everyone. The spiritual Energy is very high right now, the alignment of two Creators is giving this Energy boost. Everyone must realize what was hidden from them right before their eyes all by themselves. "2012" is the cycle of revelation a very special year in Your history

We knew this "Galactic Federation of Light" as they like to call their hierarchy. We are not saying it is bad, or You should not follow it, everyone is free in their choices. Though Your civilization will never have peace with those who prefer money, material gains more than spiritual entity. There always will be poor and rich, a lot of pain, dark energy if money will be most important for Your civilization or any other civilization in this Universe..

SOPHIA

This reply is interesting... "those who prefer material gains more than spiritual entity"... this sounds like worship. Worship and oneness are not in the same camp. What are you saying? What will you say about "Reboot the Grid"?

Note: Reboot the Grid took place on May 20/21 2012

Is there a way for us to "talk" in real time?

Note: The contact never happened in "real time". Anonymity was always required.

G/E
"Materialism vs Spiritualism. This battle was waged for a long time on this world. Spiritual is a way to freedom, though material things essential to existence should not be forgotten and should not be overwhelmed in using if one chooses a life of spiritualism." This is a short story of every organic civilizations that joined our League. Your civilization included. We are the worshipers of the Star we live under, the Creator of the worlds under Him. In this system of worlds it is the Sun.

Our religion is the Religion of One, everything that is essential for spiritual/material development is told in our Religion and this is Everything. It's cannot be understandable by humans, but science/magic/spiritualism/materialism/religion is being fused in this one Religion. All our knowledges are laying there. Reboot the Grid Solar Eclipse. I was waiting for this one. It is a very special day, though only for humans, not for us. I can only say that starting from 16th May it has started.

4 months of your choosing..

SOPHIA
I am not sure what you mean here - "4 months of your choosing"? For the rest, I will digest and return, I am sure, with additional inquiries, later today. I do have one question though, for you what would a life of "spiritualism" look like in this very dense world? This has been interpreted to mean strict denial of all things physical, as I have witnessed it here. This does not make sense in a world rich with sensual pleasure and comfort, that it would take a denial to achieve One. Why?

I would rather use email to communicate my choice. Please email me on my channel, with your address. I am unable to indicate my email address in these comments, you tube won't allow it.

Note: This was still at the beginning of our relationship. I was thinking his words were personal, as in; a personal choosing had to be made and told to him. It took some time before he and I understood each other completely!

G/E
Don't worry. If human civilization will join us, we will show Your kind everything and free humanity from its tormentors. The life on this planet will become harmonic, symbiotic, free of parasites, free of dark energy, free of litter. We are the masters at purifying worlds of Light of "impurities". 16th May - 16th October the time in which people will observe the planet and their life and make the final choice. 4 months of observation, 1 month of decision.

Then we come and make our final choice based on Your civilization's decision. We are unlike Your leaders - "sheiks, presidents, government representatives, politicians, judges". We are making decision on every aspect of existence, our choice will be made "in favor" to Everything. Do not get angry on us if Your world will be destroyed or nothing will happen. It is all the choice of yours that matters now.

Note: I was floored with this comment "your world will be destroyed"… Later I learned just how literal he is. He softened a bit with years of conversation, with all sorts of readers and me, but this literal component to his speech pattern never changed.

Your choice will be heard in due time. Your consciousness will not make this choice on its own, it will not be counted as "Your choice".

SOPHIA
I see. We have completed the "Reboot of the Grid" Solar Eclipse - mass meditation. What was heard/done?

G/E
This is an Omen and a starting point of Your (humanity's) world observation. Now Your senses will work with more power, until the month of choosing. Power of the Sun - Your Creator is fueling Your senses. Those who will search for truth, will find it quickly.

SOPHIA
So...for 4 months, from now (**May 21, 2012**) until September our world is under observation? And at that point is the month of choosing? Do you mean by this "month of choosing" that it is us doing the choosing? If so, is this to be done consciously? In other words, will we know what our choices are, and what we are doing exactly? This language and format is a challenge to communicate clearly. The truth would be a nice change from what we have been fed so far.

G/E

This observation will be Yours not ours. You will observe the world with enhanced abilities to understand it fully, see through lies. Not all will be this powerful enough though. Socially engineered ones, that lived under full influence of Illuminati and fully obedient by their laws, that prefer materialism will not be able to use full potential of it. These are by most part full atheists, believers in "money" only, mostly americans/europeans. You will know unconsciously what You will be doing.

SOPHIA

What will signify the end of this "time of observation"? A date or an event?

G/E

It will be a very special feeling.

SOPHIA

Do you have any comment on the **Venus Transit - June 5/6**?

G/E

Nothing serious will happen on this planet. Yet this is a very beautiful sight. You can feel the Energy of Venus, every time it is closer to this planet, yet it is very hard to do to most of this planet's inhabitants.

SOPHIA

Why is it "hard" for most of this planet's people?

G/E

Because almost all humans yet do not have "telepathy" skill. This skill by itself means extra awareness. Almost all of the wavelengths of energy can be felt or heard by creature's central neural system. Including gravity's distortion and "talk of the planets and stars".

SOPHIA

I see. Is the inability to hear "telepathically" due to our belief system? In other words, can we learn to become sensitive with intention? Some of us are more sensitive than others, yet don't we all have the ability?

G/E

This depends on genetic strain, "Soul - Energy output" and "physical - spiritual vessels connection". We are sorry for inventing new meanings or descriptions.

English language lacks many words that we are using frequently. That is so for other languages as well. Material path is the cause for this lack of spiritual meanings. In two thousand cycles around the Sun would be more than enough time for your civilization to progress toward "spiritual tree of development", if not for the instincts..

Genetic augmentations and training on focus and concentration through generations would be a success in achieving "remote connection" and "remote control" powers. There are other ways of course, yet these ways are beyond human mind's understanding. Also very excessive knowledge of the Universe is very dangerous for "second stage creatures". A huge amount of knowledge cannot be accepted by their brain under many circumstances and thus brain might activate a "self-destruction sequence"..

SOPHIA
I think I understand. This meditation was felt very powerfully in the spiritual community (**Venus Transit**). Everything feels different now, or rather, I feel different somehow. Are you a single being or a collective? You have said you are human, and you have been "given" this information to share... Is this "channeled" then? I know that names are separators, all is one, yet, well, the human who goes by sedgetra is speaking to the human who goes by sophia in this conversation.

G/E
Yes, we are feeling Your Energy, the Energy from meditation of many, this is one step closer to Your Consensus. We like humans, we have almost same species like You in the League, this is another reason why we want to add humanity into the League. The "differentiate of matter forms" is what One wants to see in this Universe. You won't find absolutely same one to one planets or stars or beings in this Universe. Everything is different and this differentiate is almost infinite.

I'm human, but with a very special second soul that was given to me not long ago. It is a very difficult mechanism for You to understand, I remain human, but receive this knowledge always from the Universe, from One in other words, fleet that waiting the decision of humanity knows of my presence, yet they are not interfering into my doings, or other like me. They are waiting for our last decision. This knowledge cannot be channeled, it is being given only to those with this special soul.

SOPHIA
Okay, so there are no words in my current vocabulary to explain precisely. The "second soul" only makes sense if I think of a "greater soul" and my ego, earth self. I would not call my greater self a "second soul" so I am imagining you are speaking to something else? There is news today of possible peaceful removal of

the cabal from the control of our banks and government. We are being asked for our vote before action ensues. This is unexpected and good news I think. Would you comment?

G/E
A very ancient Energy this second soul is, from the point of this Universe's creation. It is being added to organic and non-organic "chosen" different creatures. This is where your choice is being made. Every sapient inhabitant of this planet will need to make this choice, before that we are waiting with Your kind.. If we would be in Your place:
 "We are in Peace, we have given an Oath: We will never hurt those who we care for, who we love, defenseless and peaceful, Good. Peace and Calm forever."

SOPHIA
Thank you. That quote is beautiful. We are working at becoming a collective voice, at least some of us are. We are very much waiting, as you have said. What else can you tell me about this time that we are in?

G/E
The time of humanity's prophecy, the time when two Creators meets, under much pressure, this was a chosen time from Continuum.

SOPHIA
Please elaborate on "when two Creators meets, under much pressure"? Who are the "two Creators"? and define what "much pressure" signifies?

G/E
Two Creators are Star and it's "Forestar". It was our pressure, from which exactly this time was chosen.

SOPHIA
Are either star a harbinger? If so, for what? Can you elaborate? By "our" pressure, do you refer to the One?

G/E
Creators are not harbingers. Minor 3rd level Creator is the Sun, Commoner 2nd level Creator is Sagittarius A* as it is called here, the center of the Galaxy, the Black Star, the father of many of the stars located in this Galaxy. Two Creators will align from this planet's line of sight and become as a One for a short period of time. This is a very rare occurring, it happens once in a many thousand cycles. It was chosen by many aspects of One.

War could have started earlier, we prevented it, before it did. Here is the meaning "pressure". We didn't want to interfere, but we also didn't want to lose many beautiful things this planet possesses, including so many different individual humans. We wanted to just give humanity more time to allow You to understand not only evil, but also Good side, to let You join the Consensus, the internet, so that You could evolve farther, and finally make Your choice based on everything you saw as a species.

SOPHIA
You speak here of December 21, 2012. I sense now this uncertainty energetically. Last week (**6/5/12 - 6/8/12**) many felt very sure that definitive action would occur and the cabal would be removed. Now, **6/13/12**, we all feel the energy increasing yet there is no consensus, financial pressure is mounting and the banks apply increasing pressure on us...many seem to be afraid and complying, while others of us struggle and resist...I question our collective voice - what are we saying?

G/E
Those who created this material money, are the same as You are, there is no difference in their genetic code. The move that makes them like they are is the way they were taught to live, to be a patriot of a country, to struggle against other competitors in business, to compete against other in order to prove that "they are the best or number one". The competition is natural way of choosing the most powerful of a kind, yet Your civilization is suffering from this, this is not Your destiny.

Planet longs for revolution, uncertainty of part of individuals, assurance of another part of individuals, many wills and many wants, pain and at same time joy, the differentiate of Energy is very great, though the collective voice of all the souls is One and the same. We always hear Your species as a One, You are one of a kind species, we could distinct humanity very easily on the background of a Universe. The Consensus right now can be made, but for this materialism must be partially abandoned

SOPHIA
Thank you. There is a plan to be implemented any day now to make known publicly what has been really going on with the control of the money and of the people. It is the hope of many that real work can then begin in the open to spread the light in the area's that have been dark. Much of the effort now is done behind the scenes. Can you tell me more about your origin, where you fit in the history of this planet, are you known as any particular race in our records?

G/E
We are a collaboration of races, many different ones, under One and the same authority of One. We have many millions divisions and sub-divisions. We are

always a secret League, as our duty to watch over the Universe and all the races and at the same time let them evolve freely. The knowledge we possess is from One, that why we must be secret. We are best described here as a real "Illuminati" though the order Illuminati of humans perverted everything we stand for..

Lie is their main weapon, we never use lie against those who trust us, like they do. They are killing many innocent people, and we never do that. We have very disliked what they done in the last three hundred cycles. Though Truth will never remain unknown in this Universe, and once it will be known, they will fall and they knows this, that why they are trying to figure out every possible way to escape their fate.. We have never be known to human civilization as a some sort of alien species.

SOPHIA
Okay, so what is the true definition of the "real Illuminati"?

G/E
Yet **"Guardians - Executioners or Ancients or Saviors of Worlds or Destroyers of Worlds"** are known to a real Enlightened people as a "higher beings".

SOPHIA
So, I cannot find any reference to your time on this planet in any resource I would search?

There are so many other beings now, talking to us, and also several references to species and to various groups. There is the Galactic Federation of Light, the Plieadians, the Annunaki, the Sumerians, those within the earth... the list seem endless...if not alien species, have you been known to us as Gods?

G/E
It was an analogy. We are best described as this organization, secret and religious and very powerful, yet our methods are not like theirs. Yes, there is no reference for us. We have control over time, if something would go wrong we would return to past and repair it. But One is not allowing anything to happen in the wrong way. Everything is happening like it supposed to. Yet remember humanity have choice right now, whatever will be chosen is already known and at the same time unknown.

Many of them are not real, some not from the League of One are present here. Information about Your past must remain hidden until the right time.

SOPHIA

How do we discern the real from the unreal? Some get lots of press and yet they are difficult to take seriously. Others don't and "feel" genuine.
If they are not from the League of One, where are they from? Why would they care to communicate with us? For what purpose?

G/E

All what I can say is that civilization is free to evolve itself and that includes collaborate with other civilizations, economically, politically, socially. We are not letting here hostile races, but those who will not hurt You are free to come. We will remain here as long as One asks us. Choice will also decide, whether humanity want us here or not.. We are protecting You for some purposes, all we can say, we are not doing this for material gains or "profit", we are not like Your governments.

SOPHIA

At this point, Choice does not know you are here. Is there a scheduled time for that to change?

Today, **June 19, 2012**, there is a disagreement among these different voices that are channeled, and I am asking you to clarify if you would. Many say the waters won't rise and there will be little or no earth changes. There is at least one prominent voice saying that it is going to flood and relocating will be necessary for many thousands of us. Is it going to flood? Is an off world group going to re locate the people affected?

G/E

Whenever we are here, Planet and Creators knows it. The flooding of world will not take place, if not count tsunami waves. Increasing of water level will take place in the near future, in **20 cycles from now** on. Little by little the average water level of world is increasing due to humanity's industrial heat activity. And again, the choice will decide what will happen to this world. The prophecies told about Fire flooding the Earth and many wants this..

SOPHIA

I do not understand "20 cycles" in the way I measure time. Would you explain?

G/E

These are years, I and Forces of One prefer to measure time in cycles or circles, low cycle, medium and high. **One year is one low cycle around a parent Father Star**. Or double, triple Father Star System. Very similar to Georgian calendar today's world is using.

SOPHIA

Thank you, I understand. When you say "many want this" fire flooding the earth, do you speak of the cabal and those who have been influenced? There are prophecies and many who hold the texts they come from as sacred and the word of God. Do you refer to those who believe in the prophecies? We do not "want" catastrophe, but it sounds as if our beliefs are interpreted as "wants". For those who believe, they do not think it is a choice.

It is my understanding that the removal (next post)

...of the Archons will do much to alleviate the heavy handed doctrine held as sacred truth. Without their influence, the followers will be free to think for themselves and make more informed choices. Is not that what this year is about? For free choice, there must be a release of control.

We have been working for such a moment, so that more of us can see clearly our options and choose with conviction. You have said you cannot speak of the Archons, yet they have influenced humanity greatly.

G/E

Archons are rooted to Your past. Humanity's origin must remain in secret, this is the will of One. Don't worry, they will not affect humanity on energetic level.

SOPHIA

Okay. Let me be more direct. Will relocation of people in certain areas be needed? If so, will that be done by ET's?

G/E

(There was no response given yet to the question above...)

SOPHIA

I have just read a lengthy post by "Hidden Hand" (a self-proclaimed Illuminati Insider) from 2008. Very enlightening. Will you comment on the Great Harvest? Also on the 3 possibilities outlined by him/her for 12/21/12 - 1.Negative Polarity, 2. Positive Polarity, and 3. (Majority in 2008) "Lukewarm". ? This includes 2 New 4th density "earths" as well as another 3rd density planet.

G/E

2000 cycles ago there was Great Migration which led to the fall of a Roman Empire, now it can be repeated and again this will depend on this same choice. About what is rooted to the "Order of Enlightened or Illuminati" it is still must be kept in secret, because it will unveil the origin of humanity. The true behind this will hurt You. That why it must be kept in secret until the time will be right.

What I can say for now to assure You is that humanity was under control of many different races before Forces of One arrived. These different races helped humanity in many ways, but also used them as a slaves. Without our arrival humanity wouldn't achieved what it did today, simply because these other races wouldn't allow you too. Illuminati Order is just a leftover from them, it is now only human-consistence. Once we arrived every "dangerous race" left this planet.

SOPHIA
What can you say about the "Event"? Can you give a time frame for it?

G/E
You mean the event for choice. Nothing extraordinary to every day's life of a medium human will happen until the choice will be decided, everything is depending on it. There are many different ways; all of those ways are in two great categories called "destruction" and "salvation".

Note – at this time it was a challenge to describe the exact meaning of my questions, as this being did not follow the "stories" I was reading or hearing about online. He answered quite literally at the time, each question I asked. You may sense at these times a sort of awkward series of questions that really didn't get cleared up for months… after years of conversation, it got a bit easier. You might even say we got to "know" each other quite well! I consider him a dear friend.

SOPHIA
The "event" I refer to is one involving the positive military and the removal of the cabal. That will most certainly be a choice, yet I do not know if you are referring to the same thing. Today in the U.S.A. (**6/21/12**) has been heralded as a time when the cabal has decided not to surrender to us peacefully. Other actions are deemed necessary to remove them. This is the event I refer to. Is this the event for choice you speak of here?

G/E
This is exactly the will of choice. Remember that when the choice will be made, no one will feel it, though on "Universal Energetic Level" as we called it, will be heard. The planet, the Sun will channel this to us. Once our choice will be done, everyone will feel and see where Your destiny will be heading next. If You wish to overthrow their system, we will only welcome You to do so. Yes, they will not surrender, we know this, they have army, police, everything West Block possesses.

Though what East Block possess is not under their full control. East Block are Your allies. And this is where war can start if not careful. East Block will support anti cabal movements, but these movements must support East Block. On East Block are many traitors for the West Block, so chances for West Block to win is very great. Though we have aided the East Block and we have aided You on stopping their Order with less than possible efforts, because of our policy.

Those who wish to become a part of humanity and humanity to become a part of Forces of One did, those who are like me. It is our own free will choice. About cabal, Illuminati. Their actions have become indigenously aggressive and destructive, opposite of what Guardians - Executioners are teaching. They are feeling scared, as they have uncovered the truth about One, the Ultimate Creator. They are hastening their plan, because of losing control over their own minds now.

SOPHIA

Thank you. So it is after the choice is made, via the removal of the cabal, that we will "see and feel where our destiny is heading next". We will not feel it at the moment it happens, but afterwards we will be aware, through the actions of the Forces of One. Right?

G/E

Not exactly, through the actions of the choice being made. All what the Forces of One can do is de-cloak themselves and aid You by providing knowledge and tools to free You from oil dependency. To help You realize Yourselves as a complete beings. To restore the damaged eco system, to restore the corrupted aura of the planet by people's desperate **taughts**, to rebuild cities make them "highly energetically charged" in order for everyone to feel themselves happy. And again it all depends on choice.

Note – again, I have not changed the spelling throughout the conversation. It may appear that he meant "thoughts" in the paragraph above, yet as time went on I realized that his spelling 'errors' were sometimes intentional. We have been inundated with many 'taughts' from the controllers, have we not? So, the misspellings remain in the text for the most part.

SOPHIA

Okay. This is what so many of us are waiting for, ready for and anxious for. We were hoping for a peaceful surrender, and a cooperative transition. This is not to be. We will require a great deal of publicity in order to educate many who are unaware of much of this, and who will be possibility frightened.

G/E

Live freely, observe, feel, try, take action, again try and choose. Let people's Unity guides You my Friend!

SOPHIA
Sounds good. Thank you. I am certain we will talk again as changes occur.

SOPHIA
The increase of vibration/light/energy is huge right now. As it is incorporated, there are many physical adjustments. The light looks different inside my home. There was a bright neon orange light outside my home last night ... we could not discern it's source. Is there anything you can say about these changes? This video was answered a week or so after it was posted. I was woken up an spoken to telepathically. Do you know who that was?

Note – this is a reference to "Message to Off World Beings[10]", the video referred to in the introduction, and released the first of the year 2012. The conversation here is from early in the summer of 2012.

G/E
Don't worry about the light. Did you understood what was passed to You telepathically? It is hard to send our signals right to human's brain, as it is not evolved enough to receive a clear message. There is much distortion in it. Also there is a big pain being felt when this signal is being received. Though I think Your brain is lightly charged and powerful enough to filter the message. What they do, I'm not always aware, as I having different objective and must be unknown.

SOPHIA
Yes, I do. It was as if someone was speaking directly to me, I heard it internally. As this has only happened previously with my partner, I was not sure it was "real". I was asked to come out and see whoever it was, but I did not choose to. It was very cold and I was very sleepy. Although now, I wish I had gotten up. It would have been a chance for a new friend.

G/E
Yes it would happen that way. It is Your own free will to do what You want to do.

SOPHIA
Yes, well, I feel differently now. There are many changes as this year progresses and the awareness is gradual. I felt no pain with the contact. It was exuberant

---

[10] "Message To Off World Beings." *YouTube*. N.p., n.d. Web. 07 July 2016. <https://youtu.be/Pk-AaK2ZCV0>.

and joyful. Again today there is much expectation for information on the overthrow of the cabal. Excitement and anticipation is the order of the day, although we have been cautioned to avoid anger and confrontation with each other and anyone involved as there are other forces attempting to influence us still.

G/E

Yes, this Illuminati Order used lies and deception to achieve its goals in the last three centuries. Their win always was making aggressiveness and hostility among friends. That how they are now creating this situation on the Middle East right now. They are hastening their plan and their plan is to start a war between political Zionists world and Islam religious world. They are very close to achieve this.

Yet single choice of humanity beats their plan.

SOPHIA

So our efforts, via global meditations and group meditations can stop this war. The arrests are just the beginning, aren't they? We need to continue even after they occur.

Today is **6.27.12** and this energy is fairly bursting out of me and all around me... there is an urgency, a feeling of "now, this is it" in the air, and running through my body... wow. I am wondering if you can comment... there are predictions of imminent arrests (again) and yet, these sensations are independent, events are moving quickly here, in my home, in my family... it is as if we have arrived at a turning point and everything is becoming clear; very intense and immediate.

G/E

None of Creators will act unless choice will be made. It is all up to humans now.

Yes, they are arresting those who they deem dangerous for their system or eliminate them if no other options remain.

For example: Muammar Gaddafi was willing to create an arabic collaboration of peace with a very great possibility of living for everyone and once he started to say about it, they payed mercenaries to eliminate him. He was "last known" of all those crimes they made and they want more crimes to commit.

I will explain about the choice of Your destiny. We arrived to this world and removed hostile civilization from You, letting humanity to evolve on it's own. For all those years, You all felt that there was always a missing master of humanity, because before that You were slaves, but now You become free. Yet Forces of

One never showed themselves to humanity. They were always protecting this world from hostility and worldwide disasters such as asteroids.

Every individual always felt, that there is someone always watching over everyone, hidden, unseen. You knew instinctively that they are the protectors of Your existence, yet it became so common during all these hundreds of years that humanity knows this as "a natural feeling".

Now we see that You have evolved far enough to be able to protect Yourself from all those hostile that have visited You and so we are giving You this choice to made.

Whether humanity want to continue to live under Forces of One with everything unchanged or do You want to live without our protection by Your own, or do You want a "great shift" from this world to a new world or do You want to join our Forces and become as One or do You want the removal of cabal only and everything else unchanged. There are many more choices, all they come to two great categories of "Salvation" and "Destruction". **That why we are called Guardians - Executioners.**

SOPHIA
Are you willing to speak about the "event" in more detail? There is expectation once again for these mass arrests to occur within days now, in 4 days it will be what is called "independence day" in the USA, and many are expecting a real independence with the removal of the cabal. I understand this "event" to be something else, not carried out here by us, but by our creator. Can you comment?

SOPHIA
Is it "fair" that such a huge decision is being made by billions of us without any understanding? My reach is limited and this is a challenging message; no one seems able to hear it. My efforts "fall on deaf ears" in many cases. Can you help?

Note – At this point the conversation was happening only on you tube, as comments under the previously mentioned video: "Message to Off World Beings[11]".

G/E
In Your case I from the Forces of One gave You the answer, because it was One's will.

---

[11] "Message To Off World Beings." *YouTube*. N.p., n.d. Web. 07 July 2016. <https://youtu.be/Pk-AaK2ZCV0>.

In everyone's else cases they will have to make this decision blindly, without even knowing it. There are some reasons why we are doing it. Mainly it is because, if they would knew that there is a huge fleet waiting right at their doors a very advanced and from many different civilizations, in fear they would choose whatever we will wish for..

And another is if such a choice would go in public, we would have problem becoming seen by humanity's eyes. Our priority is to be silent, unseen. Because our very existence is very important to this civilization. If revealed, there would be a danger of Illuminati Order to hunt us. We must survive or choice will be made for humanity and it will be destruction of many and salvation of few, by prophecies. Also there will be problem with "loss of mind" if choice would go in public.

SOPHIA
Okay. This conversation is read by some other than you and I. So some others will know as well. Also this conversation can't help but influence the information I share with those who read my blog and watch my videos. So SOME do hear this information, if not directly, what they hear is influenced by what is shared. It can't help but be. The mass arrests have begun, we have been told this. We feel as if we have free will, is that what you mean? If we actually saw you, we would (next post)

adopt a subservient mentality and let you handle it? We "don't know" what we "don't know" and in this case it sounds like not telling a child the full details of an event because of the child's ability to fully understand and respond to them. The maturity level determines what can be absorbed and reacted to. Is it like that? This is all a dream. We are many places, not just human on this planet in **July of 2012**. We are here for what we can get out of the experience, are you saying we are ..

...just not ready to make this decision? I am trying to truly understand the reasons. Much is at stake and we are speaking our choice daily. All of us are, many while deeply asleep. The choices you outlined - is it that some of us will shift to a new world, while some of us will join forces with the League while some of us will remove the cabal only, while everything else remains the same? Different "time lines" of experience? Is true oneness even possible in the state we are now?

G/E
I understand Your fear. I cannot do much right now.

"The Consensus of "Spiritual Divisions" of the Forces of One has been in agreement with 2012 cycle by humanity's "Georgian Calendar" standard as a time when this civilization as a young race with great perspectives in the future can choose whatever they want to see in their own future, with us or without us. It is up to them.

Even civilization's self-destruction can be evaded, it is not yet decided, though the possibility is very great."

You can see now the outcome of my speaking before time has come. But this was the will of One.

Now those who know of us, want our aid and yet we cannot support it, because we have strict rules. Interference in civilization's life, into internal affairs of civilization life won't do any good to anyone who lives on this planet.

For us, as well You Sophia and all those who listen, waiting is necessary, time has not yet come for what every human want to.

Have You found Giorgio Bongiovanni web site? It has some answers for You and all others Good people. Yet it was meant mainly for christian Good believers to not let them down in their huge faith. Through him our youngsters are saying, that it is not important to which religion You belong to, it is important of how Good You are.

SOPHIA
Yes, I found his site. It is a challenge to wade through the strong Christian rhetoric and get to the point. Much guilt and destruction is included in the messages, also much sacrifice. Hard to discern which is the message and which is the messenger if you know what I mean. I will search again. Just one more question before I do.

Define "how Good you are". In Giorgio's case, it sounds instead like "how Christian you are". I know that is not your meaning, but then what is?

G/E
Yes, we are using judgment day as a preferred option, when it is coming to delivering this message to them as it is meant to happen.

Two scenarios are the most possible. Both from destruction categories.

"The destruction of the wicked by our Solar Power - by Holy Fire" and salvation of those Good that followed the teachings of old human masters to live in a harmony with the world.

Or second if humanity will be left alone and it will self-destruct. Yet again everything is depending on the choice.

SOPHIA
What if we choose to become part of League? If we choose to ask for and accept help? Is that part of the other scenario, the salvation scenario/category?

G/E
It will all come in due time. Becoming a part of the League of One or as we like to call Forces of One can have different outcomes as well. In the main scenario, that I was proposing to You, there will be aid, we will give You the technologies that will be needed to help humanity to evade the path of self-destruction. These technologies will help humanity in many peaceful ways.

Everyone's choice will decide what to do with West Block and their evil methods of achieving world peace.

SOPHIA
Okay, this is a different direction. Can you elaborate on what the objects are that are parked near and flying near and appear to be ejected from our sun?

G/E
Our main technology of this Universe is based on Creator's power which is the parent star of planetary systems. We are using the power of artificially created "micro stars" or "micro suns". We can achieve any power output from them and it is the same as from other "normal stars" with different mass and power. All of the stars are sacred to us.

That why we are there at the Sun, some GE's are inside this star. Because of the high temperature it is possible to see our youngsters.

SOPHIA
So, what is a "GE" and just who are your "youngsters" in my understanding?

G/E
GE is an abbreviation for Guardians - Executioners low frequency organisms.

Youngsters are young races that have joined us "not long ago". It can be counted from decimals to decimal thousands of years on this calendar standard. If humanity will join the League, it will also become a "youngster".

Sorry if this word isn't quite correct. Youth for us is not having the meaning of low experience. Youth for us has a very respectful meaning. We are old, yet young ones are promising far wider and greater prospects for evolution.

SOPHIA
Thank you. I understand. The language is difficult. Many "good" people, who have and are choosing evolution, love and what is termed "ascension" are concerned about what happens to them, in the category of destruction. Efforts are ongoing to remove the cabal right now, yet they remain and threaten all humanity if just one of them is taken. There is much hope, yet it has not happened, they are still here. There is concern. Can you spell anything out in more detail?

These comments will soon be an easily readable dialogue, as a page on my website[12]. I would very much like to include helpful information for those of us listening. The concern for many "light workers" is this outlined choice of "destruction".

They would not consciously choose this. How do their personal decisions affect the choice of the rest of humanity, that choice that will dictate your actions?

G/E
We see humanity as a one being, like any other species. Your species material organic information chain or DNA is what makes You humans, animals on this planet too have DNA. They want to live, yet not all humans are agreeing in simply "live". More than a half of humanity want something else, besides of being alive. There is a great uncertain about wills in Your Consensus' Consciousness and Sub consciousness. Yet it was predicted and already seen, that this will occur.

Humanity is well known for their ability to make the most rightful choice in a very last seconds before the "deadline". There are not many Good people or real Lightworkers, but those who do everything only for themselves are much more in this world. We know that You will want to make a choice for the better of humanity, yet of how "evil" they are, they are also a part of humanity and so we see You all as a one being. And so Your energetic Consensus will make this choice.

SOPHIA
Thank you, yet your words lead to more questions. It sounds like the few of us who understand the choices we are making may be outnumbered by those who "do everything only for themselves". It also sounds as if you are saying the

---

[12] N.p., n.d. Web. <www.sophialove.org>.

choice has already been seen by you, and we are now just acting out our parts in these last seconds before the "deadline". Can you be less cryptic in your response? Linear time is a factor here, we have not yet seen the results of humanities choice.

G/E
Yet remember again, everyone will have to say what they want without using their speech, I'm simply going further to explain You the mechanism of this choice.

It is very complicated, I as a human can understand it barely. I will explain You my views as a human. There is only Energy on which variations this choice will be made. They already know what You will choose, yet they are giving You the opportunity to make another choice and rewrite our humanity's fate. Whatever we want, we can choose.

SOPHIA
So, we circle to the beginning of this conversation. I asked you then why you had begun talking to me? You responded that I would be able to help many make this choice. The manner in which you describe this choice portrays incredibly bad odds for the light. I blog and make videos. I don't know how many I reach or what their choice is. Do you have any plan for how I can reach more people and improve the odds? If people knew the choice they were making, I believe many would reconsider.

G/E
Yes, this many are those with the Light! Good ones.

SOPHIA
Yes. Those who follow are workers for the light. Thank you. We will converse again soon. There is a strong energetic now and we are all feeling it (**July 14, 2012**). There is much to do.

Can you speak about the activity with our sun?

G/E
There is nothing to know more, only that Sun - the Creator of this world is angry on humanity, because humanity is making damage to one of His "daughters and wives", the Earth.

SOPHIA

What does "anger" look liked in a sun? And what is our appropriate response as a people?

G/E
The same emotions can be used accordingly to planet and to star. As they are "alive". The planet is not angry as she loves her children - humanity, yet she can destroy them, she just can't, planet is a very loving mother!
The Sun is other. He is the Creator and what He had created He also can destroy, that is His way of thinking. Once species are endangering the planet they live on and system, the Parent Star or Stars are becoming angry and so thus Their activity is increasing.

We are speaking to Him, we have an agreement to let humanity decide their own destiny and whatever they decide will take place.

It is also possible to talk to the Creator of this world, you may try to ask Him for an aid and mercy. Remember, He is your best friend.

He is listening to every energetic vibration, hearing Him in response will be much difficult, as human ear and brain are not sufficient to take response via through our channels of communication. Special energetic or spiritual technologies are necessary for it, highly evolved creatures from our spiritual divisions are able to hear The Voice of The Universe.

SOPHIA
Okay. We have only just become conscious recently. We are subservient beings, with an encoded slave genetic and until recently the majority of us were trusting in the good intentions of the controllers. With our free will and recent awareness, we are active in many arenas to initiate freedom - governmental, economic, religious, environmental changes are in the process of unfolding on a grand scale. Our creator sees that as well, is this not an answer?

G/E
Don't worry. The Creator - The Sun knows His people and He sees changes, although it is not yet decided, major events on this planet happened under His own free will, all of the people on this planet are His people and He knows which of them are Good and which of them are evil. He loves You and He don't want to hurt You. Others with evil deeds on their hands are the object of His anger. With their deeds of treachery, killings, use of bad language, they poison the geo-energetic field of this planet.

Note – in the following are found answers to questions that were sent to him off-line. They concerned religion, they are from a friend of mine, Mark. July 24, 2012

MARK
Hello, how are you? I was wondering if you could answer some questions I have? Is the Sun the being we call 'Yahweh' (the real one, not the imposters that have come and gone since). And did the 'social memory complex' known as 'Lucifer' incarnate on earth as ☐the '13 bloodlines' to develop Yahweh's own spirituality. And would it be correct to say that humans on Earth are also 'Yahweh', focused into individual human bodies to develop his spirituality through us.

And in turn, Is Yahweh☐ a 'Sub Logos' of the 'Logos' that is the Great Central Sun. And if so, what is the 'Logos' name (the true name of the Great Central Sun). Thank you very much.

Sorry to inundate you with queries, but I have another question that I must ask. Every single time I go outside on☐ a clear night, I see what can only be described as 'shooting stars'. I have just gone outside tonight and seen 4 in a matter of 20 minutes. I realized a while ago that they are not shooting stars; I wonder if you can tell me what they are? Some people never see one in their life; I see them every single time I'm outside. They generate so much excitement in me! What are they? Thank you

G/E
Hello Mark! I'm sorry, but as was described earlier some knowledge is being locked.

All of the religions' origin is being locked as this is leading to humanity's origin, this information must be kept in secret until the time will be right. The truth may damage everyone's will to life and this is what we don't want. We don't want to let down all believers, all I can say that there is a hidden truth in the bible and quran. These two religions were formed on a same basis for different people.

Finding the truth will lead to "next step of evolution" as they called it. Those who have found it are considered as an "advanced humans". Remember, everyone is free to believe in what they think is right to believe. Like we believe that Creator is a Parent Star and Grand Creator is a Galactic Center is only ours. We are not forcing this belief on anyone, we are respecting all others believes even the most evil ones, although it is sometimes hard. The shooting stars are "leonidas meteor shower".

MARK
Thank you very much for your answers. I understand.☐ Other information I have read does correspond to your beliefs. It is my belief also, although my beliefs can change based on new information that comes to my attention. I

don't like to call them 'beliefs' myself actually, I call them 'current perspectives'.

So I presume these 'meteors' are a very common occurrence. I just always happen to be looking in the right direction at the right time?

Update 8.8.2012

MARK
I wonder if you'd just clarify something for me? You say the shooting stars are 'Leonidas meteor shower'. I have researched this a little and this seems to take place at certain times of the year. I see these shooting stars all years round, anytime I go outside on a clear night. Are you sure they are Leonidas Meteor shower? Is it possible that they could be something else? It just seems strange that I see them so often, when some people do not even see one in their entire lifetime...

Also, I regularly see what I would describe as 'stars' moving around, I see these every single time I am outside on a clear night, as well as the shooting stars. If you take a look at the following video that was filmed in my back garden, you can see exactly what I mean.

Do you have any idea what all these things are? And why I personally see so many of them?

G/E
Mark, it won't hurt anyone if I will tell You and all others a little part of the Truth. One agreed that I can share it. As You remember there is no reference from any of civilizations of the League in this world, **there is an ancient reference of One in Zoroastrianism. This is the first belief in One God in known world's history, He was named there as Ahura Mazda by Zarathustra who was a Guardian - Executioner of One.**

This religion gave birth to Judaism and later Christianity and later Islam and so thus Yahweh and God and Allah is Ahura Mazda or aka One - One God. But remember one of the indisputable quotes: "Nothing happens without a reason." "One great mother gave birth to three little sisters, these sisters were not so ideal as their mother, but they fitted better in young race's understandings." "The truth was hidden inside three teachings, those that weren't able to find it, became obsessed with them."

MARK
Wow! Thank you very very much. I am going to do some research on these names you have mentioned, very interesting! Thanks!

SOPHIA

Would you elaborate then on Angra Mainyu and the concept of evil ? I see that Ahura Mazda embodied the feminine as well as the masculine, yet the "three little sisters" retain a masculine deity. These hidden truths, can you point us to the specific subject matter within the three teachings that incorporates them? It would be most helpful for those of us unfamiliar with all three. Also, here is a quote from one source, would you comment? (next post)...

"Zoroaster claimed that Ahura Mazda was not an omnipotent God, but used the aid of humans in the cosmic struggle against Angra Mainyu. Nonetheless, Ahura Mazda is Angra Mainyu's superior, not his equal."

G/E

This hidden truth must be found by others and I must not help anyone to do it.

Yet if we will look at three teachings with our third eye, we will see that all of them are teaching not to be obsessed with materialism, because of it we are doing "sins".

The quote is what I told, the One is nonexistent also existent at the same time. He can not do everything like an "almighty god" and the reason for this is He's own Will, because He don't want to do this. But what everyone is doing is up to them.

All You have to know right now is that evil or "other one of darkness" as we call it is the opposing force of One of Light, which is representing in this Universe. But One which we are serving is something beyond anyone's understandings. When I try to understand Him or It, I must be ready for total chaos in my head.

Yet He is real, and He is everything... I'm using He not She, because for humanity's males are a domination gender, which is wiser and stronger. I'm sorry, but this is true.

MARK

Are you saying that there is a 'source' of evil? I had come to the understanding that there is no 'source of evil', there is only a 'lack of good'. Would you please explain.

I picture it like this; Imagine a tap, the tap is me and the water flowing out of the tap is 'source' or 'well-being', when you begin to switch the tap off, that is the same as offering resistance to source or well-being (negative

thoughts creating resistance, and cutting us off from source.) (continued)

   Therefore, from this understanding, there is no 'source of evil', there is only a 'lack of good' or 'resistance to source'. Would you say this is☐ correct? Or is there an actual source of evil created by the creator?

G/E
Your thoughts are correct! This flow might be blocked as well, so thus guidance is lost with it. Yes, in this Universe there is a source of evil, yet it is "not in here". I must not tell details, what I told is already here. I'm giving a very simplified version Father Entities: there is One Good and there is one evil. Light and dark, both were created by super being which is not like we are, it something that goes beyond imagination and fantasy, where everything is losing it's sense.

Also I feel that not many are understanding what Illuminati Order is. We are calling them with this name, as they like when they are being called "the order of enlightened ones", or "the order of light", "the order of wisdom", "the order of force of light and knowledge". If so then You may see the movie "Thrive". This is a very great explanation with a lot of research and knowledge in it. In this movie it is easy to understand what I'm writing about. Peace, Calm, Prosperity.

MARK
Cool! Thanks! I have seen Thrive about 3 times now and think it's a brilliant movie, I knew a lot of it already but it's in a nice easy to understand way in that movie.

There has been another 'blog' on the internet recently that has said a similar thing to you in regards to the October dates☐ you mentioned a while ago, very interesting!
   -- Note, this is a reference to Portal 2012[13] and the recent "Window of Opportunity 2" post –

August 13, 2012

G/E
You're welcome! Yes, a very easy to understand movie, very recommended for all those who seeks the Truth or cannot find the missing links. This is a year (cycle) of Revelation, many things are becoming more and more revealed, evilness had its touch on this world, now Good side is waking up, so the choice can be made, from both perspective sides of view.

---

[13] "The Portal." *The Portal*. N.p., n.d. Web. 07 July 2016. <http://2012portal.blogspot.ca/>.

MARK
I just read something. There is this "Mitchell Coombes" who predicted the Japan Tsunami (March 2011) and is announcing he will soon be predicting 4 or 5 of them within the next 104 hours (of whenever the prediction is made). He is predicting them for the West coast USA, the East coast USA and the East coast of Australia. I have family and friends in all of these areas. Would you comment?

G/E
I was waiting for this moment. It is time to introduce You to Bashar, some may already heard about him, yet did not trust his words, what he is telling is almost everything what I'm saying. He is from another race that is rooted to humanity.

Listen to his conversation of we (humans) are the ones who writes our own faith. There is a countless number of dimensions, parallel and non-parallel. Whatever we choose will decide the fate only for each individual of us.

Yet I'm here to encourage and inform everyone who is here with me on this same dimension of a possibility of this choosing, as humanity still don't understand how this works due to low evolution level.

As again I will repeat that we will look only on a collective choice of humanity, EVERYONE is able to make their own life how he or she want it to be.

When I wasn't aware of this as a normal human I felt that "something has changed, it mustn't have been that way", now I know that I have changed my own destiny and now as a human I'm continue to change it.

As for tsunamis. This may happen as well, yet there are many of those who we are protecting, we may be able to prevent it, but we cannot guarantee this. If You wish, You may warn Your family about this possibility so that's they would be well prepared for this event. Peace, Calm, Prosperity.

MARK
I have watched some Bashar videos in the past I must admit I like him. He actually gives some proactive tips and 'how's and why's' rather than all □ the regurgitated 'news reports' we seem to get from many other channellers.

August 15, 2012

SOPHIA

What do you see as the direction now of our collective choice? There are many arrests of criminal bankers, the Olympics were held without incident, more and more people are "waking up".

Bashar has a strong voice. He is calling now for us to ask the officials for Disclosure. There is a petition he has created, just last week (**August 10th**). He asks everyone to send it to their representatives in Government. Do you see this as a necessary step also?

G/E
Everyone may wonder, why every "channeler" are not agreed on one and the same opinions, thoughts and future. This was made with a special intent so that's we could be in shadows, "normal" people (the ones "enlightened" are culminating) are thinking that we are "insane people" and this is what we are counting for. Those who wish to believe us, may believe. I cannot tell what direction humanity is heading. This will be a secret even when the choice will be made.

Also I cannot tell what may be necessary steps, I can only recommend as a human to everyone that You must follow Your heart! If you have heart full of Light, what You think is right, is right! And I know all who are here are with the Light in heart, so You're right, Peace:)

SOPHIA
Thank you. I have recently seen a video titled: UFOs near the sun - 08/08/2012. Can you tell me where these ships are from?

G/E
We already told You that we are there right at the Sun. What You saw was a Stereo A satellite filming and there weren't any real objects from our ranks. These were stars, the image is distorted as this satellite's instrument is having minor damage. You can see one of our ships on a video called "black sphere near sun 01" here on you tube website. We have been seen twice by SOHO and SDO satellites. Other filming's are being kept in secret by USA government.

Actually Stereo B as this stands for behind, my apology.

G/E
For all those who is interested in Illuminati Order's agenda and religion, You can look for a video called "The Secret Covenant - Luciferian Illuminati Oath". This video was made by them, by their priests, they do not care if it is here, because most of the humanity will not believe in this and this is what they are counting for. This shows how much they have degraded from evolution and come to a path of

self-destruction. This video is very disturbing, those with weak nerves should not watch it.

Note from Sophia

(Please note, this video is very disturbing, yet is posted here merely as part of this conversation. This need not be the cause of fear, but of gratitude. We are discovering the truth at the same time as we are realizing our own power. Both good things.)

It is difficult to listen to and read and had to be paused many times to that it could be read (the voice is garbled).

This is an example of the truth of our history that will be told to us this year of 2012. It is about 15 minutes long, and was found on a banking web site in 2007, then re-posted. It is not clear exactly from where it originated.

A quote from the video follows...

"They must never, ever find out what we have done, for if they do, we shall have no place to run, for it will be easy to see who we are once the veil has fallen. Our actions will have revealed who we are and they will hunt us down and no person shall give us shelter.

This is the secret covenant by which we shall live the rest of our present and future lives, for this reality will transcend many generations and life spans.

This covenant is sealed by blood, our blood. We, the ones who from heaven to earth came.

This covenant must NEVER, EVER be known to exist. It must NEVER, EVER be written or spoken of for if it is, the consciousness it will spawn will release the fury of the PRIME CREATOR upon us and we shall be cast to the depths from whence we came and remain there until the end time of infinity itself."

This footnote has the link[14].

September 13, 2012

SOPHIA
Do you have any information about the energy right now? We are feeling it big time. Have we moved into the time of choosing?

Thank you.

G/E
Yes Sophia! It is starting; the time of final decision is approaching.

Everyone will now see in dreams and during their wakefulness stances the past of their own lives and past of their ancestor's lives. "The unexplained visions" will now visit many people's minds. It is all approaching to a final conclusion.

May One Bless You and Everyone on this final journey to physical realm of reality!

One more thing Sophia. You do remember the 7 elements of Creation? There is also an 8th element which goes only to organic structural beings and partly to energetic. The element You already know about a very special one and element that can change the reality, the space and time.

This element is Love, physical and spiritual, divine, mostly we know of this as spiritual.

Much Love and Respect Sophia!

September 19, 2012

SOPHIA
I am wondering if you would address something that is concerning me. This time of choosing is upon us. There are many, many voices out there and they repeat the same story again and again. It goes like this: Things will change "soon", there will be abundance programs and healing chambers "soon", the government will change "soon"... along with other predictions of changes after the first of the year now...

I understand that when you are able you speak the voice of One. I also

---

[14] Rcacad. "The Secret Covenant - Luciferian Illuminati Oath." *YouTube*. YouTube, 05 Sept. 2011. Web. 07 July 2016. <http://www.youtube.com/watch?v=52OSZz6jliU&feature=player_embedded>.

understand that One speaks the voice of us. We are speaking now and I am wondering "What are we saying?" Do you have to wait until after October 16, and then can you even speak to it?

There is talk now of only one timeline. That sounds as if something has been decided.

You have mentioned that you know, pretty much, what the decision will be, also that we have free will.

Please be as specific as you are able to be. Many of us are sick and without money at these times. We could use some encouragement.

I appreciate the information and wish you peace.

G/E
Yes worthless money and illness that all these drugs are bringing from "world health (poison) organization".

Now I will give You a feedback on the current circumstances around the world's situation, only what I can give, everything that connects to the past is locked.

The preparation for war is being made very aggressively by USA government, because they know, that if they will not start this war in these two stellar cycles, they never will again. The trust of the world in their worthless money is fading, so they want to prove that everyone who goes against them is going to be destroyed.

Their ultimate strategy is to take over the world and Iran is the key element for this to happen, but Iran or Persia is the balance between Good and evil and also one of the fortresses of One God, Islam and Zoroastrianism are being hold there and this is their main foothold in this world, the Citadel of Faith.

There are many reasons why Iran is so important for this world, it is also a nexus of Energies, a border, a balance between powers a gate for souls a legacy of the past.

Many young souls and many Good people with high Energy are there and willing to live. Satanists want to sacrifice them to their delusion "god", actually an extradimensional being that think he is a god and break the balance which will shake this world and bring great war and many despair to everyone. So One has stopped their advance and gave them a problem with Syria country.

Their strategy is not working as they planned as russians and chinese are preventing their use of force. In the meantime, russians the only nation that can defeat the worshipers of evil are being enlightened in dark secrets about the Order of Illuminati which currently holds USA as their base of operations and future "center of the world". People in this country are being deluded with their lies, perversion and egoistic views on life.

"Enlighteneds" tried to destroy russian empire many times, during two world wars, during napoleonic wars and finally with soviet union dissolution which was created by them as well. But they all failed as You can see. Russians are the most rebellious of all nations around this world right now and they were from a very start of their formation as a nation, from the times of their christianisation and mongol invasion on their land right to this time. They are the last and most powerful defenders of One and when it is necessary they will fulfill the role of judges to those who angers the One.

Russian president and his most trusted people now are almost fully aware of the ways, agendas, strategies and tactics of puppeteers and they know that Russia is their last goal to conquer. So they will resist satanists and our agents are assuring that they need to solve this crisis peacefully as bringing world war 3 will cost this world a lot. Russian president now is trying to establish as much union with other countries as possible, because friendship and love is the cure for this world not hatred and distrust.

The yellow race where goes chinese people are another branch of humanity that specializes in exorcising evil from the world, they are clean and are very oriented toward Good and Light side. Greed and ambitions is present in their minds, but their will is still very strong and they are able to put an end to evil where it stands, russians were weakened by same lies, perversion, distrust and egoistic views on life by the satanists, so they will need the help of yellow race to defeat the evil, yet again, like You saw chinese and japanese people aren't friendly toward each other and this goes to every other nation of south east asia, as You know China is a communist state, and it still bears the "mark of the beast" a five pointed red star.

So they are "marked by satan" and can be removed by him. So these forces will need an aid of sitting nation, India. Indians are a very powerful Energetically charged nation and only with their aid will Good prevail over evil in both cases of war or diplomacy. Yet India is deluded as well, they favor both sides, one for money other for likelihood.

When a revolution in Russia started to take place, no one taught that this revolution was a corruption from within, marked by a five pointed inverted red star, the cycles Russia was under influence of evil, brought almost utter destruction to defenders of world, but religion had saved Russia from total dissolving and brought age of prosperity and revelation to people of the world. "Devil created Soviet Union and devil destroyed it", while it was existed all religions were persecuted, but first president of Russia turned to God for wisdom and saved his own country and his people and people of the world from the new world order.

Now Sophia, what I want to tell You is that Your greatest allies are lying to the East. And everyone's allies are there, everyone who did not gave an oath to "bringer of light", extradimensional "god". This is an encouragement to You and many followers of Light, support the actions of all those who is going against USA government's views like Gaddafi was.

Much Love Sophia.

Update - 9.30.2012

G/E
Now it is time for You to know some of the Truth.

The video I will provide to You is reality of this world's destiny. This is battle of Good versus evil, this battle is eternal, there are those who seek unlimited power, there are those who seek eternal peace and there are those who seek balance.

We are the seekers of balance, our duty to balance the Strength of Creation. Good and evil must be balanced between everything that lives and exist. We possess the biggest power, but we must be in eternal service to One. This is our little restriction to our unlimited power given by One to us as a token for our absolute obedience.

Universe must not be destroyed or be soften to the "position of chaos". Creation must be constantly dynamic and evolution must proceed, this all goes to even more higher form of Power of Creation, this is what Creator wants and for which purpose everything exists as it is.

The moment of last decision is almost met. The time sequence narrows to it's end, so we have to reveal to You and others close to You and people who want it, the Truth.

We are not the ones who isolated humanity's world and made "quarantine", the responsible for all the pain and suffering are archons - "the masters", they are constantly present near the Sun, on this planet, on Moon and almost everywhere in this system (Solar System).

Their goals go against the Creation, their ultimate goal is absolute power to create and un-create.

They tried to hide their sin from us - the Guardians, Watchers, but we knew what they were up to even before this Universe was created, it is One's - Creator order to us, to let them do what they want to and stop them when they will "almost achieve" this power, in form of device, parts, tools or energetic force of it that lets them to threaten the Creation.

The archons created the Illuminati Order, to control and restrict humanity. There are others experimental civilizations like humanity and there is as well the same situation like it is here. With this experiment of creating and controlling civilizations they want to achieve their goal, with humanity's help they want to create the tools of total control over Creation and Uncreation.

There are "light forces" that fights against the vast empire of these deluded seekers for power. Forces of Light, collaboration of many different civilizations visited this planet before and they were the ones who wanted to teach humanity and make them an evolved civilization like they were.

Later archons came; their technological level was superior to that of Forces of Light; they thwarted everything on this world and even rewrite the time sequence. Through devastating war that started not on this planet, they defeated, killed and exiled many from Light Forces. "The masters or archons" like they prefer everyone to call them are a collaboration of civilizations as well as Forces of Light.

As this all unveiled we watched, always watched. We are present everywhere in this system, including near the Sun, right in front archons' vessels. They are feeling our presence, but they are unable to detect us in any way, like Forces of Light are unable to detect archonian vessels.

And now the video Sophia, in this video You will learn about "demons", "beings that goes through walls and inhabits humans". These "demons" are archons, they are using a very special technology that makes them transparent and they are able to travel between dimensions, they are able to inhabit living bodies and with this power they control United States of

America, United Kingdom, Israel and with it, West Bloc of the world.

The full history of this world will be known in due time. I will wait Your question Sophia

"Truth About illuminati Documentary-Luciferian Conspiracy"[15]

Much Love, Good Feelings and Peace to You and all on this world!

October 1, 2012

G/E
To every Friendly soul, time sequence given to humanity is coming to an end. This is example of humanity's current feelings, the mirror of spirit of human's soul - elements[16].

Much Love and Respect to everyone.

Update - October 2, 2012

SOPHIA
I am seeing many things about the Illuminati and an "October event" they are planning. Can you tell me what is planned?

G/E
They still are able to use earthquake undersea, they are postponing this further and further, as a humans they don't want to do it, obviously they are changing.

Remember the last message?

Their main goal from the beginning was to free mankind from kings, emperors, rule and establish a world under a rebellious god known as Lucifer to them. They want to bring humanity a peace through uses of war and killings, they want to establish a perfect religion which will unite

---

[15] *YouTube*. YouTube, n.d. Web. 08 July 2016.
<http://www.youtube.com/watch?v=bO36MjiPzjM&feature=player_embedded>.
[16] Lindseystomp. "Elements - Lindsey Stirling (Dubstep Violin Original Song)."*YouTube*. YouTube, 18 Sept. 2012. Web. 08 July 2016.
<http://www.youtube.com/watch?v=sf6LD2B_kDQ&feature=player_embedded>.

everyone and make consensus, yet they don't know that those who control them have other plans for mankind.

Controllers are the masters at lie, so all those who are now in Illuminati Order will be betrayed and eradicated by those who they serve. Thus even those who are in Illuminati are awakening and understanding more and more who they really serve.

SOPHIA
Okay, who do they really serve and what are the intentions of which they are unaware?

G/E
This answer You already know. "The archons - masters". Their purpose is to gain absolute power over Creation, through the use of natural evolution, this is the cause with humanity right now. Soon they want "to rip the harvest" as it is almost ready and there is a danger that all this harvest might be corrupted from within.

But we are here, our presence is strong right now and thus they can not decide what to do next, meanwhile humanity is making a choice - the outcome of everything what happened on this world. This will decide the future of this civilization.

About archons, we will deal with them whenever they will start an "initiation process" - the process of taking harvest and beginning of Universal synchronization. This is far too advanced for human minds, even for mine, I only know that it is a very complicated process which will take thousands of cycles, these Earth's years, but they are able to make millions of years to seconds. So whenever they will start, we will start execution process on their culture.

October 3, 2012

SOPHIA
So, humanities choice has not been made?

G/E
The deadline for last decision of humanity is 16th october, but before the specific date of 21st december the choice can be changed, but after this date, change will not be possible. Humans are known for their ability to do everything at the very last moments, so happens in this case.

October 12, 2012

G/E
Now the disclosure is peaking, humanity's temporal Consensus has been created. These are last ten home cycles, get ready to make Your final decision.

We all are watching and listening for it, Energy vibration are high, Your consciousness is active at Unity level. You are ready to make Your final decision. Make this choice as right as possible based on all that predated You and all that will be predated by You!

Peace from the Forces of One to Sophia and all who follows our answer.

Note
(Day of Decision Video[17] refers to the same date: 10.21.12 - This is an Important Week!)

October 14, 2012

G/E
"We are now watching, listening and feeling everyone's feelings and wishes. We are ready for Your last word humanity. Listen to this[18] Sophia, it will help You on Your choosing.

Much Love, Peace and Prosperity within You."

October 15, 2012

QUESTION FROM A READER
I don't understand this "choice" for we have already chosen. We have chosen freedom from the Dark Ones. I have chosen the Light for ALL that wish to be free; even☐ creating a pyramid of Light as a portal for the higher frequencies of pure instreaming Light from Source. I've been working on this every day, bringing in the higher vibrations, and I'd be truly heartbroken if my choosing Freedom and Light could be somehow over-ridden or made meaningless..

G/E
Yes, I'm understanding this, but people like You are in minority and materialists are in majority, most don't want anything to be changed, but "dreaming" about some better world.

The internet was given to humanity by controllers and they don't know this,

---

[17] Appro69. "DAY OF DECISION - 10-21-2012." *YouTube*. YouTube, 09 Oct. 2012. Web. 08 July 2016. <http://www.youtube.com/watch?v=evxSk8NHh-Y&feature=player_embedded>.
[18] 2Freedom4all. "David Icke - We Think We Are Humans." *YouTube*. YouTube, 11 Sept. 2011. Web. 08 July 2016. <http://www.youtube.com/watch?feature=player_embedded&v=fbRmJ_2nqyg>.

but☐ it was One's wish to give it to You. During this year of Revelation, many are seeing everyone's strengths and weaknesses and a temporal Consensus has been created.

But it is only temporal, necessary for a choice that will decide the fate of this world. We like and favor people like You who want a☐ beautiful world of harmony, but humanity as a whole must make it's choice, removing the communication barriers and seeing consciousness inside consciousness of each individuality. Due to the gap between poor and rich, not everyone is able to be a part of this temporal Consensus, but One, we and humanity are making it's best to make the choice as right as possible.

QUESTION FROM A READER
Thank You for your reply! I do realize that I have no control over the decision of the masses. I believe that we have invested enough☐ time and energy to create a reality with the highest choice, if the majority does not. So I will keep bringing in the higher vibrations to assist and heal Gaia and all her children.

My question; What else could we be doing that would assist humanity in making a wise choice for this Great Shift? Sometimes I feel I should be doing more, but I don' know what.

G/E
You already are doing a lot! Human body is not capable of doing☐ more, but if You feel You are able to do more, then You are welcome to do so, everyone is free in their actions!

Much Love and Peace!

SOPHIA
It is the 16th. Can you tell me what you have heard?

G/E
We captured the taught*, now waiting for the starfall. The orionids meteor shower will signify the beginning of our choice and end of Your choice.

Much Love, Peace and Calmness to You!

SOPHIA
~ Here is a link to information/times for the Meteor shower this weekend[19].

---

[19] N.p., n.d. Web. <http://earthsky.org/tonight/radiant-point-for-orionid-meteor-shower>.

G/E
"It's time"[20]

SOPHIA
Video must've been really good cause it's already gone!
(Note This video was removed/changed to "private" on 10.19.12, which is the same day it was sent out with my blog to many thousands of readers.)

So the 16th is past and I was hoping we could get an update. Can you talk about it? We humans are a curious lot; we wanna know all the details. Don't understand orionids clue, I'll□ watch them tho.

Cobra has "Day of Decision" on 21 Oct. 2012[21].
Would that be effective?

Yesterday I saw a msg from a GFL channel saying a new timeline is being created which "requires the immediate resignation" of the Dark Ones.

Is this true?

October 19, 2012

G/E
Yes, this was an inspirational very beautiful video form the lightworkers. I'm sorry for it, someone just asking for troubles for removing it. Many videos like this have been removed. Those who was available to see it, You may share Your view with others, I really liked this video as a human, this was an extraordinary experience, really hard to describe it with words, words can give an image, but they will not give the full□ experience. This is the second part of it[22].

~~~~~~

This[23] the song which was in first part of it.

---

[20] 3nlighted. "Lightworkers Help Mother Earth (her Life Force Is Real)."*YouTube*. YouTube, 18 Mar. 2012. Web. 08 July 2016.
<http://www.youtube.com/watch?v=K3eq5HG5aH0&feature=player_embedded>.
[21] Appro69. "DAY OF DECISION - 10-21-2012." *YouTube*. YouTube, 09 Oct. 2012. Web. 08 July 2016.
<http://www.youtube.com/watch?v=evxSk8NHh-Y>.
[22] N.p., n.d. Web. <http://www.youtube.com/watch?v=rWNLRH2vFzI&feature=player_embedded>.
[23] Serena0001912. "Karl Jenkins - Adiemus." *YouTube*. YouTube, 17 June 2012. Web. 08 July 2016.
<http://www.youtube.com/watch?feature=player_embedded&v=6MAgpUvly4Y>.

I cannot update on a progress of a choice, this information is limited.

There are controllers who receive this message as well, they can listen to anything, the message is being distorted, but they still may know and decipher, I'm sorry.

When the choice will be made you will not know what it is going to be from me or anyone from our circle, it will be known☐ only "once it will take place".

Much Peace and Love to You!

October 23, 2012

G/E

May Peace and Love and Prosperity be upon humanity.

Peace, Calm and Prosperity!

(Comments sent with video[24])

Considering this video, Sophia[25]...

it's time for You to look at this video[26] !

I know You know it, as synchronization was high in last cycles, The Power of One...

Although the choice has been made, it is not constant as is Universe, until two Creators will meet, people are the engineers of this world.

May Peace and Prosperity flourish upon this world!

October 29. 2012

---

[24] MusicKaira1. "Greatest Battle Music of All Times - Angels Will Rise [Twisted Jukebox (Blood and Glory)]." *YouTube*. YouTube, 23 Oct. 2012. Web. 08 July 2016.
<http://www.youtube.com/watch?feature=player_embedded&v=KUtCg4vKXTY>.
[25] N.p., n.d. Web.
<http://www.youtube.com/watch?feature=player_embedded&v=2TYIFQvcnVk>.
[26] Americandream27. "The Power of One..." *YouTube*. YouTube, 22 Nov. 2009. Web. 08 July 2016.
<http://www.youtube.com/watch?feature=player_embedded&v=8I7Wk14VWK4>.

SOPHIA

Thank you, a very beautiful video and I have shared it already.

You are saying then, "it is not a constant until 12.21.12"?? Yes?

We are☐ able to modify or change what has been chosen?

Much gratitude and love to you.

G/E

Yes, modification is possible; the two Creators will make the decision to turn into reality.

SOPHIA
You said in the comment that a decision was made??? Can you say more at this time???

This hurricane Sandy
was created by the HAARP/Illuminati was it not???

Thanks.

Much love.

G/E

It was not made by Illuminati, it is the power of the planet and the Sun.

Maybe you will not understand this, but hurricanes, earthquakes, tornadoes are happening also because of the Energy pressure. Wills and wants, bad corrupted energy is triggering many cataclysms.

Many natural disasters can be avoided with Energy. Though humanity currently can do very little in order to avoid these, due to materialistic direction, it is still possible.

November 2012

(From November 3.)

G/E
The power of hope always helps if it is strong enough!

(in reference to Hurricane Sandy and the casualties not being what were predicted)

Many are targeting USA, because this is the center of world's control, with this country secret order controls the west world. As more people awakening the more is Energy pressure on planet and Sun, the Sun is also feeling this pressure. As You may know right now, this happened on halloween, halloween have a secret meaning, it is "a celebration of possession".

The possessed by the archons are celebrating this, they were celebrating this ten thousand cycles ago and they are celebrating it to this day, using everyone in America to honor their "imposter gods" and world's corruption with them, yet now Earth and the Sun canceled this celebration in the conduit of corruption, New Babylon, New York, the whole corporate system received damage and was halted.

I'm sorry from the names of the Earth and the Sun, but very few people died, though received material damage, they are still ok. Illuminati's weren't expected this, so they are thinking that maybe Russia or China did that.

Indeed the secret order want to make some damage to this country this will make people despair and hasten the coming of ww3, but they didn't want to make it right now and right there.

"The weather control weapon" they possess is only on experimental stage and is not 100% efficient. They did make an underwater earthquake near the coast of Japan and they did make some other storms, some during Vietnam wars, when they were testing the capabilities of it. They were using not this weapon on an underwater earthquake this time, it were a special detonation devices, which triggered a chain reaction earthquakes under sea, which created tsunami waves.

The weather control weapon can only create a distortions in ionosphere and create rains or dissolve (not completely) clouds, with it they have a medium probability of creating storm, hurricanes, tornadoes, but they still cannot completely control this process, they still need cold and heat winds, they still are using the power of the Sun and the power of the Earth.

Yet they evolve they devices as civilization evolves. They started to develop this weapon after ww2 and from completely no control over weather, they now can create some impacts on it. The experiments with this device have also a great impact on climate change, with it they are heating up ionosphere.

By their board it was decided that they will use not this weapon if necessary as it is not 100% efficient, but these devices underwater or psychic weaponry, which are some experimental humans and devices they created from archon's designs. By agreement with them they cannot use their devices, they must create their own with a difference in design and inner structure.

In the culmination of their plane "the revival of their god lucifer" they want to trigger a complete disastrous earthquake on San Andreas fault, this will split the Earth there and their "god" will come out of there, the center of this earthquake will be bohemian grove.

The bohemian club gathers there to test their "god" and to honor him with their architectural deeds upon this world. They believe it is there from where he will rise up. They don't take into consideration that if they will make this plates' shift, they will lock the vapor exits of yellowstone underground super volcano, if this volcano erupts it will be a complete disaster to all world, the end of many lives. Still if this will happen, they are like zealots, will think that their "god" decided to take another route and come out of there..

Though this storm wasn't made by them, it was made with the Energy of wills of human society, by the collision of Energies of Earth and the Sun, the low temperature and high temperature winds collided and formed a powerful fusion storm. It is not the most powerful, but it was a dangerous storm, the Moon also fueled this storm, when Earth is receiving the Sun's power through Moon the Energies that are having corruption are colliding and thus the natural disasters are most likely to occur, the storms or earthquakes, this was a special storm that canceled their evil celebration.

And again choice will decide everything. It is made by humanity, but humanity still have time.

We haven't choose yet and we will make our choice on ending date of our turn. Humanity was making this choice from the very beginning of isolation and everywhere in this civilization's deeds in everything people are doing, creating there are hidden messages, which we see and decipher.

If you can Sophia, decipher this message[27], (video posted below) it is quite easy, in songs You need to hear the meaning.

It is hard to give just in words the exact choice, but if You will understand it without words, You are simply great, enlightened, ascended human Sophia!;)

Much Love and Peace Sophia

(From November 4.)

G/E
Choice have been made and now it is only last planetary cycles remaining. I cannot say what it is, as this may just spoil this, because archons may change their strategy if they will know.

And they may get the Energy difference from this message, it is being distorted, but the last decision is very important, it must be seen and felt by people not told.

Thank You for taking a part in this all, I felt Your voice and many were making a

---

[27] *YouTube*. YouTube, n.d. Web. 08 July 2016.
<http://www.youtube.com/watch?v=3cnQCk0u49w&feature=player_embedded>.

wish 20 cycles ago, not all but many, because of You people, everything may be just like You wished for!

(From November 7.)

G/E
Sophia, another storm is heading in the same direction as you already heard, again made by the power of will of people, planet and the Sun. It will not be that powerful, but it will cause damage again.

I'm sorry for each and all that have already and will suffer again because f the Forces of Nature and will of Humanity's Consensus.

The corporate infrastructure is damaged and will be damaged further, the president's election result is what we were expecting by humanity's choice, would it be Romney as president and ww3 would be inevitable, but still as You can see the nation is split into half, this is showing the unsureness of people, this is the reality that is on the crossroad, it is still possible that the war might just start, but it is all in Your hands.

Today we all the GE's will make the last preparations for our conclusion, which is not like humanity's decision as archons are being accounted into it, but are accounting Your outcome as well.

As we are holding them under oversight, You are free to choose what You wish for, You still have time.

Much Love and Peace and Path Without Obstacles on Your Journey to Perfect World!

SOPHIA
Thank you for your note. I am wondering about the 11.11.12 date, and if this, along with other future dates, like 12.12.12, are important for us to again focus our energy in a universal way, as in global meditation. It feels to me now that the message is being sent from within each of us every day, all day long.

Your contact and messages have been such a help to so many in this time, thank you so very much. I am feeling optimistic for all of us.

G/E
The dates You are choosing has nothing to do with the Forces of Nature, but it is the power of this temporal Consensus which You have formed.

During these meditations that You're performing on the dates which You're choosing the Forces of Nature hears Your collective more powerful voice and with each new meditation You're evolving on this level of activity and evolving Your inner power, like a child grows You're growing from within.

The Sun is hearing You better and better, the planet will synchronizes with Your will, after all You're starting to agree with one another. There are still drawbacks in the society to form a powerful will, a lot of people still living under "the old ways of life", which are materially oriented, but Your meditations are starting to create a pressure on them, most of them are struggling within because of this pressure, as they are starting to doubt "their old ways of life".

This same struggle is happening within the Order of the Enlightened, they are doubting the goals and methods of their forefathers, it is all in Your hands, humanity holds the keys to the future, it is like You are saying Sophia, You're the ones You're waiting for.

Much Love and Pure Energy of One to You!

(Update -- November 21, 2012)

G/E
The humanity prospers!

Sophia, it is time for You to know the Truth summarized, share this message, it is time for humanity's awakening!

I will tell You the truth that they guided me to these videos[28] only a moment ago, and I must share it with You. The Truth was already here, for everyone to see. You already know most of it, this will summarize Your guessings and findings.

The message is from the Followers of the Light, but like I said to You before we are not one and the same, we are the Balance, the Wall and Will of One, which they are being referred to as Prime Creator, the Point of Beginning and End.

About the adversaries of Followers of the Light, the Followers of Self Esteem and Self Development, the Archons[29].

(Update November 24.2012)

G/E
We have made our choice Sophia. Now It is only this last month of the world as we know it. Will not tell You what exactly will happen, because it can change the reality, everything will just be known by approach.

Peace, Calm and Prosperity which brings Love and Happiness!

---

[28] N.p., n.d. Web. <http://www.youtube.com/watch?v=oOgBoV0ygJc&feature=player_embedded>.
[29] UFOTVstudios. "THE ARCHONS - Alien Invaders From Space - FEATURE FILM." *YouTube*. YouTube, 26 June 2011. Web. 08 July 2016.
<http://www.youtube.com/watch?feature=player_embedded&v=WBo24sIPCOM>.

December 2012

(Update December 1, 2012)

(This note was received this morning, along with the videos shown below it)

G/E
The humanity prospers!
Sophia and everyone else, much Love to You!

This is the information to let You know about celestial situation on this planet's skies for the time of Shift[30].

Peace, Calm and Prosperity!

Sophia,

 I also got a great news for You! The video called "Lightworkers Help Mother Earth (Gaïa)" has been restored! You can now share it with everyone and watch it Yourself![31] :)

Harmony and Love and Abundance to You!

SOPHIA
Thanks so much. So there will be a meteor shower around the 13th. We've been told that the 9 days prior to the 21st are the days of most activity for the earth and sun. Is there anything else you can tell us for this time?

G/E
  No, nothing is seen on the Sun or the Earth, everything must be optimal. X flares are possible, earthquakes   also, but they are not going to be major. Right now the main focus is on the humanity, it's Energy level is very high! Almost all are anticipating for this event, the date that was heard as the end of the world. Many are waiting for "something special" to happen, others are trying to think that nothing will happen, although everyone feel it, the DNA is evolving and humanity proceeds to the next step of evolution, the next step of life, the next step of time sequence.

---

[30] VideoFromSpace. "Geminid Meteors And Visible Asteroids: December Skywatching | Video." *YouTube*. YouTube, 30 Nov. 2012. Web. 08 July 2016.
<http://www.youtube.com/watch?feature=player_embedded&v=UMxmnHBvY3E>.
[31] 3nlighted. "Lightworkers Help Mother Earth (her Life Force Is Real)."*YouTube*. YouTube, 18 Mar. 2012. Web. 08 July 2016.
<http://www.youtube.com/watch?feature=player_embedded&v=K3eq5HG5aH0>.

The Universe welcomes You young race - Humanity!

SOPHIA
Yes!!!!!!!!!!!!! Thank you!

(Update December 4, 2012)

SOPHIA
American Kabuki posted the quote above "The Universe welcomes You young race - Humanity!"
with the video "Take That - Kidz" on his blog[32] .

(So I (Sophia) sent a note to my "off world" contact....)

SOPHIA
Hey, my friend "American Kabuki" just posted your comment "The Universe welcomes you young race - Humanity!" along with this video[33] .

I think it's perfect!

Much love.

(*And here is conversation, and video sharing's, that followed...*)

G/E
 Yes Sophia it is suiting! Thank You!

  Much Love to You!

SOPHIA

Here is a movie[34] you may be interested in.

I have not seen it[35].

---

[32] N.p., n.d. Web. <https://americankabuki.blogspot.com/2012/12/the-universe-welcomes-you-young-race.html>.

[33] TakeThatVEVO. "Take That - Kidz." *YouTube*. YouTube, 25 Feb. 2011. Web. 08 July 2016. <http://www.youtube.com/watch?feature=player_embedded&v=jlapv48d7VQ>.

[34] N.p., n.d. Web. <http://www.solar-revolution-movie.com/>.

[35] ScreenAddiction. "SOLAR (R)EVOLUTION- [OFFICIAL TRAILER]." *YouTube*. YouTube, 04 Sept. 2012. Web. 08 July 2016. <http://www.youtube.com/watch?v=r7jplpRKWOI&feature=player_embedded>.

G/E
Hello Sophia!

Thank You for presenting this video to me! I think You already can guess the content of this movie. The answer in short is quite easy to understand, Sun indeed changes the body and Consciousness. Currently human body is adopted at living in these temperatures and under current amount of radiation, x-rays, uv-light, infrared light, visible light, radio waves, microwaves. If Sun would change its acting, so thus the body change and radical changes around the planet's weather would follow.

And as You are eager to know more, I will show You new information about the complexity of Consciousness. As You can see, everything makes it's sense, piece by piece, like a lifelong puzzle. All this information is coming from One, it is known by You as The Source. There are 2 main Sources of knowledge and one "Oversource", "The Prime Sources".

Source Order is what is known to lightworkers, this is the main Source of receiving Universal Knowledge from and through light, it is the Source of knowledge which restructuring the molecules in matter to be in order. Like You saw this on a water, if Good words are said, the molecules changes to beautiful symmetrical structures.

Source Chaos is the source which is on the other side of this world residing in the second "dark world" the world of antimatter which is completely parallel to this world of matter and have a great influence on this world as well, is the Source which desynchronizes synchronicity, collapses order of molecules and create chaos in it. "From this second world's point of view" this world is dark and the Source in this world is considered as chaos to all inhabitants of world of antimatter. Because the effects of two worlds on each other have destructive capabilities on each ones structure. The energies from two worlds are "incompatible" and they are trying to annihilate each other instantaneously. The emptiness, considered as darkness of space is this influence of the second world. The terms "dark matter" and "dark energy" are not called this way without a reason.
From this everlasting battle of two worlds comes the duality of reality and Consciousness.

"The Oversource", if You will be able to understand what it is, You will understand that this dimensional world is only one out of infinity.

I hope You will find this information useful[36], but remember if You disagree on it or parts of it, do not accept it, Your own understanding of existence is important as well!

You probably heard Sophia, the Illuminati Order is trying to make a one of the lasts pushes and start a world war. They are using the same strategy of lies like it was 9 cycles ago. The archons are making this push, through their servants within this order. The time sequence yet is not ready for a change to take place, so if they will initiate this attack before solstice, it will take place. Not worldwide war, but it will escalate into this until 05-19-13. As a human being and knowing what everyone wants, I can say that this war can be stopped, the mass meditation on 12-12-12 at 12th hour is what can change their ways for the rest of their days. Tell Followers of Light that You need help and they will help You! They will be humanity's best allies in the years to come :)

Until that I wish You and Everyone more Love and more Happiness[37]!

(Update 12.9.2012 and 12.10.2012)

SOPHIA
 Hi.
Just wondering if there is anything you want to be said as we get closer to 12.12.12. Many more are reading our conversation now.

Much love,

G/E
Yes, I know Sophia; people wish to know the truth and not truth mixed with lies. My objective now is to give You and everyone from the Family of Light my support as Your choice was not to become a part of the Forces of One, but to be free, free from all these lies and deception.

You wish to know more the Followers of Light and know less the Followers of Self-Esteem and Self-Development (Illuminati) which to this day still controls humanity even to the point of being closer allies with them and we only appreciate that!

The date 12.12.12 can become a significant date; all that is needed are Your

---

[36] AtheneWins. "Athene's Theory of Everything." *YouTube*. YouTube, 23 Jan. 2011. Web. 08 July 2016. <http://www.youtube.com/watch?v=dbh5l0b2-0o>.
[37] AtheneWins. "Athene's Theory of Everything." *YouTube*. YouTube, 23 Jan. 2011. Web. 08 July 2016. <http://www.youtube.com/watch?v=dbh5l0b2-0o&feature=player_embedded>.

wishes and wills, Consciousness! If Your Consensus will become very strong during this worldwide meditation and concentration, then weak planet wide earthquake will be felt by all, and this will signify the full understanding and synchronicity of planet with You, which will be a crucial point in Your symbiotic rearrangement. The planet feels You and loves You, all that she need to understand more is Your will and want to live with it Harmonically, once You give it to Her, She will let You know that She hears You all! I cannot guarantee this earthquake, very few loves earthquakes, so it will be another "less choice" to make for everyone, but if this earthquake will happen, it will be so weak that nothing will be damaged, this will be a "good earthquake", the one that equals to "a good pain". So decide, make Your contribution in it and everyone who will read it as well!:)

As about Illuminati-Archons hierarchy, Archons are on our and Followers of Light part, we are dealing with them right now. Illuminati are humans, that is why they are "on humanity's shoulders" (partly my (mine) as well), that why it is up to humanity to deal with them. But like we told before, many of them are finding "light" inside of them, so they are changing and willing to end the NWO ambition, they are still the original beings that were changed and enslaved many ages ago, a part of a whole Humanity!

Also the DNA change is on it's way, as You wanted!

May Light of Your Heart shine through the darkness of void that persists in Your way to Freedom! And the Freedom shall be granted to all that follows the Light! The Light of Everlasting Cosmos - The One, Oneness, Unite!

(and from December 10th, 2012)

SOPHIA

Thank you!

So, there are two questions that arise from this -

1. Has the choice been salvation then? There was a discussion about our inability to stop the inevitable destruction without the help of the Forces of One. Please clarify.

G/E

1. The choice was obvious at the end, but before that this world was at the crossroad and pleiadians warned everyone about it in the past.

These words that I gave You is a short version of it, the full clarification of it is very long to say and everything is seem for everyone more and more obvious with each new moment and eventually after the two Creator's alignment (12.21.12) will become even more obvious, so there is no point in full clarification.

In addition as "a side effect to information", knowing of events to come in this situation, it can damage the reality of each one who is going to read this, due to most finding another reality which better suits them and their understanding, that is why the revelation of it must have been done only now and not sooner.

The Forces of One are after archons as You already know Sophia, we were using their disguise in the past conversations to fool them in their own image.

The choice was important for us to understand You(r) will in evolution and important for humanity to understand the world around. In Your collective choice there was a great plea for help, aid, because everyone is understanding that even if the whole infrastructure will change there is much to be done in this world to fully restore it. That why we are helping You know(*now) and may be accounted as the Forces of Light.

Only GE's (Guardians/Executioners) are going to help humanity, the Scientific achievements of the Forces of One must be kept only within the Forces of One.

If the archons are going to launch their plan (their plan to start WWIII), only then they (the Guardians/Executioners) will intervene. The main laws and rules of both the Forces of One (Guardians/Executioners) and Followers of Light (the Resistance) are not to intervene within the natural process of evolution of sapient or non-sapient species, but as an exclusion to this law as humanity was an experiment and a host for a parasitic race (the Archons), the Forces of Light (the Resistance) will aid You, the Forces of One will only concentrate on masters (Archons) as they are challenging the Creation.

They are never working together, but GE's (Guardians/Executioners) are able to work with both sides of Good and Evil, but in the end they are completely loyal only to One.

SOPHIA

2. If we (the collective "we") have not chosen to join the Forces of One, is it still possible for individuals to choose to join? How would that be accomplished?

Much love,

G/E

2. And as promised to some, by the plan of His (Its) Divine Will and Purpose, a new civilization will be established on the outskirts of this Universe from the parts of this civilization and will become a part of the League of One which is of the Forces of One, thus given the whole privilege of service to One and full spectrum of possibilities of evolution. But first they need to be restored and be without regrets, so that nothing could bother them once they leave this world forever. So it will be some more time on this planet.

Everyone else who chose to be here and proceed on this evolution will remain here and just continue to live with changes on this world and new friends which are not going to be humans. This world will be a much better place to live, so everyone whom this promise was given, will have to think again before leaving.

But Sophia and Everyone Else who will read this, remember there is still time until the final point, from which nothing can be done, so use this time wisely and wish for a great fruitfulness changes on this world which will benefit All and among them You!

Peace and Love!

(Update December 11, 2012)

Note from Sophia: It was brought to my attention that a slight global tremor happened today; I asked about it. What follows is the response:

G/E

This is not the earthquake I meant, it needs to be "everywhere" for everyone to feel, not destructive, but rather "loving", there is no assurance it will happen, because people by most part don't like earthquakes in any ways. But Mother of Humanity this beautiful and loving planet Earth wants to give this hug to everyone, some people are making Her angry or sick, but She still loves all of us, even half - visitors like me, and I love Her too, She is just beautiful, adorable! :)

She is indeed happy to see that humanity is changing, and we are feeling this as well, everyone is changing and more are coming to join in restoring this Planet and freedom of evolution! The temporal Consensus is forming into powerful Oneness and the biofield of this planet is increasing vibrations, as the powers of Your emotions are increasing in frequency levels! The approach of One (the alignment) is highly anticipated by many.

Remember the next day will be a significant world meditation! Peace, Love, Abundance to You and Everyone!

SOPHIA

   I appreciate your continued information in these last 10 days of change... we are all feeling it.

   There are meditations scheduled at several different times on 12.12.12, so it will be heard all day long!

   Much love to you.

G/E

I too will contribute in this meditation, this is the meditation for a future of this reality and every human being life, and also connectedness to a planet and through a planet to the Sun - the Creator, so it is very important for this world and well being for everyone who currently resides here!

Peace and Love!

(Update 12.14.12)

G/E
The Ascension that is meant here is the Ascension of Consciousness, the memory of the Universe will be known to humanity, but of course not everything

will be known. Everything that is needed for every individual to better understand this world and existence, of "why this is, how it is" and connectedness to the Universe overall.

This will be an understanding that will bring great changes to human society!

Also by Your will there can be another Ascension "to skies".
This can be brought by Followers of Light (*The Galactic Federation), they want assist humanity in every way possible to help it!

As You felt Sophia there wasn't any earthquake, because like we taught, people don't like earthquakes:)

Peace and Love!

SOPHIA

 Thank you!

  Yes, my friends and I were hoping for some small sign, as the earthquake would have been. There are people who question everything...it would have been an "answer", validating the truth of the words being said here.

 Now we will just wait to see what will happen in this next week, before the alignment and during the alignment on 12.21.12. We will know then.

 With gratitude and much love to you,
Sophia

G/E
Yes Sophia I understand Your thoughts, everyone need a proof for all, like it is in a science.

We the GE's and the Forces of One don't like to lie and lie is our most hated subject, but sometimes it is necessary for us to use lies in order to complete what One told us to complete, so goes with our chaotic behavior and destruction which we sometimes are using as well.

This Universe must exist in the way it exists and one of the main attributes of it is "unpredicteveness". One want it to be this way, so we don't like to promise heaven and life without hardships or some other events that can happen, we are saying only what is possible and what can be done for it to become a reality.

We Guardian-Executioners are not far seers or prophets, our main objective is to observe, analyze, send information back to One "from our point of view" and make a conclusion.

Also we are not having access to the technologies and libraries of the Forces of One, this could of course ease everything for humanity, but it is One's Will for everyone to evolve on their own.

If One's Forces would give an aid to humanity they would brake the main law of their obedience and this will brake humanity as a "new prospect of Existence" which is very important to One.

We only can barely communicate with each other, they are working on their own, we are working on our own, we also don't like when someone is distracting us on our duty :)

In the beginning I told You Sophia what they wanted to say to You, there were other people as well whom they gave some words. We both are having our missions and we need to perform them.

Like You already know, we need to be the same as the ones we are living among, to better understand all the situation that is within the civilization and the world. Everything what we were writing to each other is making it's own contribution to this world and our wishes which we wants the most are also in these words.

Peace, Love and Thank You Sophia!

(Update December 17th, 2012)

This came today, with the videos below...

G/E

Sophia and all who follows the words of Ancients, starting from tomorrow 18th and ending on 24th will be the days of Creators. Three days before the date of alignment and 3 days after the alignment are like the points of old end and new beginning on a much larger scale.

This will be the beginning of Aquarius Era, the washer of impurities.

Like fishes humanity was living, waiting to be caught and be eaten, in complete fear and obedience to instincts. Now humanity will control it's own existence and will wash away all that fear that haunted this civilization for a very long time.

No thing exist within Creation without a purpose.

Searching for the meaning, leads to paths of right and wrong. There is no right path, everything You choose is legal.

Choosing is making the needs to exist. Needs creating rules and laws for sharing with fair. Laws and rules that binds You, are necessity to prosperity and order. Prosperity is what makes You dance and smile. What makes You smile are Your fruits, what makes You dance is Your legacy.

In the hallowed halls of Consciousness everything is clear, One is Every Thing and Every Thing is One[38].

Let One give You all the Blessing and let humanity bring fruits of Joy and Prosperity for themselves and to Universe[39]!

(Update December 20, 2012)

SOPHIA

I am aware that the shooting in CT was a planned event. It is beyond sad.

There are so many things to change in this world that we will begin after the 21st, when the Cabal is unable to control us any longer. Once balance is restored, things will change, they have to.

Now I am focusing on Source and going within for these next few days. I will be "off line". I wish you a powerful solstice my friend!

Much love.

G/E

   Yes, there is much to be done in this world, much to be restored in order to bring harmony and happiness to   all here.

This wasn't planned by cabal, but indeed it was planned, I cannot say by who, but You may guess.

[38] XDarkLegacyx2. "Brand X Music - Illumination (2012 - Volume.16 - Aeone Watson)." *YouTube*. YouTube, 11 Dec. 2012. Web. 08 July 2016.
<http://www.youtube.com/watch?v=RO2nhwkEJU0&feature=player_embedded>.
[39] *YouTube*. YouTube, n.d. Web. 08 July 2016.
<http://www.youtube.com/watch?feature=player_embedded&v=pV2KZPGUb9I>.

I know You're tired and everyone else who followed the restoration of this world, soon it all will be over.

The reassemble and charge of Chrystal of Power will be tomorrow.

May this year of Revelation serve well to humanity and let humanity be free on the wings of happiness!

You earned that! That are the words of the Forces of One!

(Update December 27, 2012)

SOPHIA

Thank you my friend, Merry Christmas and a wonderful New Year to you!

G/E

Thank You Sophia, beautiful and most wondrous New Year to You too! I wanted to ask You one question. During these days of Creators humanity received the uplifting information, which is now activating DNA most significantly, now third part of it has been activated, the part responsible for emotions in it's full extent. Do You feel any difference in Your Self-Aware Consciousness?

SOPHIA

Yes... there are many emotions, doubts and feelings right now. It feels intense. There is a sense of Humanity, I don't know how else to describe it, only that the days since the 21st have been days of noticing the contrast of this life. Each thought is watched and considered. There have been no conclusions other than it is up to us/ to me. It is sort of heavy with expectation and awareness.

G/E

In time this is going to evolve, every lightworker is better prepared for this than majority of people.

So from this moment of time everyone must make a contribution to this real Consensus which is now being created and is at a very early stages of development.

It is going to be a hard time, but we all must unite with biosphere of the planet and make our thoughts to appear in it, from this moment we are able to change not only the reality but everyone's else way of life as well.

I'm saying this as a part of this early Consensus as a human (of course if Every One who reads it are eager to, it is all but Your choice).

This planet is almost liberated, the evil forces don't have much power left, they are tired as well, they want a change as well, but it is fear that's holds them down, they are afraid of great changes, they are afraid of all-out disclosure and "aliens" which can do many things they don't, because they are all humans like we are as well, they need support and encouragement.

Through biosphere we can give it to them, because Love is going to solve these problems for humanity, not another aggression.

Now only "normal" humans and their Consciousness is in the way of their own freedom which prevents our lightworkers' freedom.

SOPHIA

I will share this with my readers as it could help them.
Thank you so much.
Peace and much love.

(Update **December 28, 2012**)

The following conversation was initiated by me. I passed along this video from American Kabuki, with a question - "What are those things?"

Here's the video[40] and the resulting exchange.

SOPHIA

?? Do you know what this is?

G/E

Thank You Sophia for the video, what You are able to see there as big channel like lines are manifestations of energetic trails which connects many star systems upon activation and the lesser seen lines are just image artifacts.

The energetic trails are of Followers of Light origins not ours or controllers.

SOPHIA

---

[40] *YouTube*. YouTube, n.d. Web. 08 July 2016.
<http://www.youtube.com/watch?feature=player_embedded&v=ujIlMYHBUss>.

Are they image artifacts or are they actual cables of light?

Where or from whom do they originate? The "talk" is that they are cables of some sort... are they plugged in? To the sun?? are they illusory images or real, as real as they possibly can be in this holographic universe??

Many are attempting to figure out what is going on in or on the sun and in the universe itself... these are adding to the mystery.

Who exactly are the "Followers of Light"?

G/E

I cannot explain many of the things yet, as they must be explained later by Followers of Light to You. Followers of Light is the name we are designating the pursuers of light in all its forms and incarnations, sacred geometrical, metric dimensional, Energy, emotional, Consciousness. You know them as the "Light Beings" from other worlds or "helpers of humanity" or "Federation of Light", the ones that are against the dark forces or evil forces, archons and cabal/illuminati order.

I must again remind You as a part of my duty, that I do not wish You to believe in this, You must figure everything out, You are able to and Everyone from Your circle as well :)
How You shape reality is making the biggest contribution in awareness of this reality by Your Consciousness.

These lines are Energy trails that are being captured with few instruments on board human space crafts, they are "connecting" this Solar System and to be precise this planet to other habitable star systems under control of Followers of Light, Forces of Light if You like.

This is a necessary step of this planet's liberation; it changes everyone's attitude toward Existence and Creation all around them. On 4th minute You are able to see image artifacts, those are not these channels, it's an "image sticking". The shots above are newer and the shots below are older.

I will hope this is going to help everyone! Peace, Love, Prosperity to One and Every and Every and One!

SOPHIA

Thank you, I will share.

This ends our conversation for the 2012 year.

Chapter 5   2013

2013   THE YEAR OF TRANSFORMATION

(Update January 1st)

G/E

2013 is the Year of Transformation!

Most Happiest New Year to You as well Sophia and all the World!

Another Transformation process has been accomplished for humanity! With each passing year humanity was cleaning itself of corruption/everything unclean, but this wasn't successful in the past because of controllers, now that controllers are almost out of the way, you're beginning to create a heaven on this planet.

 It was in humanity's collective choice to initiate a world rejuvenation process and so it will be.

After taking chosen ones, the Forces of One are going to be forgotten like they always were. Humanity's allies are Followers of Light and they are just going to give humanity what it always wanted, Ascension!

As a last insight of year of Revelation *(2012)* I need to reveal last piece of information which was given to me with a purpose to inform Your grouping and I waited for correct time line to give it.

The information is about this world's controller's prophecy which made them to sign a treaty with Followers of Light 18 solar cycles ago. This treaty made an end to a war between "Good and evil" in this Galaxy (Followers of Light and Followers of Self-Esteem and Self-Development).

The prophecy by itself is not connected with this world and is off world source information, so I cannot tell You the esoteric meaning of it (in short this information is restricted), but what I can tell You is that GE's (*Guardians/Executioners) are the reason their prophecy was fulfilled here on this world.

Because of humanity's potential to invent great designs One made this world a special fate, the fate that is going to affect all and every, including the Forces of One. Understand that if this treaty wasn't signed no information on the internet could be accessible so easily, there would be huge restrictions, mass arrests and strict censorship on this kind of information that penetrates every system, the information about real rulers of this world Illuminati Order and gnostic archons.

When treaty was signed most and main archons representatives left this world, those that oppose this treaty stayed here in only few numbers and limited tactical, strategic and leadership skills, but they are currently the rules of the "elite", though they limited skills are not enough to guide this world's "elite" and manage "capabilities restriction devices", which are making a lot of pain and suffering to all inhabitants of the Solar System and are reducing the frequency output of most evolved ones excluding archons, mostly sapient humans of course.

You are able to see this devices on kabbalah's "tree of life", the devices were positioned on many planets of this system (most on planet's natural satellites), with the most powerful being in deep underground base on the Moon, this planet's co-planet. Most were found and disabled, one on the Moon is a very dangerous device which can make a lot of damage to sapient humans due to their evolved brain, that why it is still active, but is going to be disabled later when everyone will be brought into full Consciousness.

As soon as archons left after treaty was signed, Followers of Light stepped in without obstructions and through almost 10 cycles they are trying to restore humanity's Consciousness with average results as You are able to see.

Though this is average on their scale everything proceeds by One's Will. Light Followers too have another great prophecy, but this is another story. You will know this later on.

Many Miracles to You and Every One in this year of Transformation!

SOPHIA

Hello and thank you!

I will share this information, but can you explain this? --

"on the Moon is a very dangerous device which can make a lot of damage to sapient humans due to their evolved brain, that why it is still active, but is going to be disabled later "

Is this "later" a reference to a time much further into the future of humanity, in other words, when ascension is closer to realization for everyone (many years from now)?

Would you talk more about this -- "You are able to see this devices on kabbalah's "tree of life"

Thanks!
Much love.

G/E

Not much later, only few solar cycles left for its "active" stance. It is what we are feeling.

Do You remember the prophecies of 111 popes and Yitzhak Kaduri? The last 111th optimal pope is currently residing at this position and Ariel Sharon is still alive, both are 85 solar cycles old. These are the most prominent of beacons set by One, by which the orientation in time sequence is possible.

In kabbalah's "tree of life" the Universal connection/"flow of Light" with the Earth is being blocked by two sephiras.

The Keter/Crown is associated with something that is on the outer reaches of this Solar System (or a human body), this is the receiver.

The Tiferet/Beauty is the point at the center that connects all other sephiras and is associated with something that is in the center of the Solar System, this is the transmitter.

Malkuth/Kingdom is associated with something that is at the bottom, the place where we are. Malkuth receives flow from Tiferet the transmitter (the Sun), which is being blocked by Yesod/"Foundation" that is associated with something "not far away" (the Moon).

And there is another "invisible" block between receiver and transmitter called Da'at/Knowledge. It is associated with something invisible to the naked eye, and only the "enlightened" are able to see it.

These are two blocks that are restricting the access to the Source and are places where distortion on Universal information is being applied (or censorship if You like it this way).

This tree of life is a representation of a quarantine of this world, a prison, it holds the Truth, but is mixed with lies like in all other situations.

If You do not understanding sephiras You can look for it on Wikipedia it is an archive of this civilization.

Peace, Calmness and Prosperity to this civilization!

(Update -- January 4, 2013)

SOPHIA

I have a random question you may not have an answer for. I just watched a documentary "Resonance"[41].

It concerns, ultimately, cell phones. I wonder if this cell phone/wifi technology is a product of the controllers or a natural progression in communication, like the internet???? Is it a good thing, a bad thing??? or a change, as we are changing??? This movie declares it is a bad thing because of the effect on our body and its melatonin production, for a start.

I am just curious. Thank you.

---

[41] N.p., n.d. Web. <http://www.youtube.com/watch?v=5vb9R0x_0NQ&feature=em-subs_digest-vrecs>.

Peace.

G/E

Sophia, Thank You!

I'm giving answers not as a teacher or a guide, but a helper, because You and Your many Friends chose a Good side of Coexistence/Harmony.

Well, in short this is a natural byproduct of creating a Consensus. It is having negative effects on human body and every and one individual and planet as well. It indeed have an effect on DNA and Consciousness as You already know everything is interconnected.

But scalar energy was "created" to repel this, you may consider using this as well, the Quantum Technology which created this technology wears the symbol of the Forces of One and Pleiadeans - an eight pointed star.

This natural technology of interconnecting molecules gives many benefits to human body and biosphere; it is capable to cure many diseases if used for prolonged time, even mutation/cancer. It is capable to hold all DNA structure in its original shape and also provide an increased rate of adaptation to environment.

I hope this information is going to help You and Everyone! Peace and Love!

SOPHIA

Thank you!

(Note -- here is a video demonstrating the effects of scalar energy[42], along with a link to an excellent article[43]. There are many others.)

---

[42] "Scalar Energy - A Completely New World Is Possible." *Scalar Energy - A Completely New World Is Possible*. N.p., n.d. Web. 08 July 2016. <http://rense.com/general39/scalarenergy.htm>.
[43] FusionExcelCanada. "FusionExcel at the R.A.W. Show (The ONLY SCALAR PENDANT ENDORSED BY DR. EMOTO)." *YouTube*. YouTube, 19 Oct. 2008. Web. 08 July 2016.
<http://www.youtube.com/watch?feature=player_embedded&v=K840XXblgo4>.

(Updated January 18, 2013)

This source has sent several videos which will be shared here[44], here[45] & here[46].

(Update January 22, 2013)

I received the following message on the 19th of January, which led to the exchange here.

G/E

Sophia, I was told that you need more information. What do You need to know Sophia? Ask everything, I'll tell everything I'm allowed to. Always ready to help with insight!

SOPHIA

So I sent a bunch of questions, from both myself and American Kabuki: (WHAT FOLLOWS ARE THE QUESTIONS AND ANSWERS AS GIVEN.)

G/E

Yes, that's sure is a lot of questions! I'll try to answer on all of them. But remember one strict thing, You must not count everything I say for the Holy Truth, the most important are Your abilities to find, comprehend and

[44] SpaceRip. "Light from the Core of the Sun." *YouTube*. YouTube, 15 Oct. 2012. Web. 08 July 2016. <http://www.youtube.com/watch?feature=player_embedded&v=--V1nNO9bow>.
[45] MrBernibest. "Tryad Ft. IOEO - Ancient Lace (instrumental)." *YouTube*. YouTube, 12 Nov. 2012. Web. 08 July 2016. <http://www.youtube.com/watch?feature=player_embedded&v=3i4HB4zOWnM>.
[46] Sedjetra. "Mother Earth." *YouTube*. YouTube, 16 Jan. 2013. Web. 08 July 2016. <http://www.youtube.com/watch?feature=player_embedded&v=wWx0euFQ9r8>.

understand the Truth.

SOPHIA
 Okay... here are my questions.... there are many ---

What about the One Peoples Public Trust??? Is this the tool to remove us from the control which is still coming from the Cabal?

G/E
About the Trust of One by the Law of One, I'm not connected with them and know that they are a group of people with special guides from above, the Followers of Light. The Followers of Light, the The Followers of Self-Esteem and Self-Development - the Archons and their human servants The Cabal (as You prefer to call them) are all acknowledge the Power of One, yet the methods of service to Him of each faction are very different.

The dark ones that controlled this world are trying to oppose His Power with means to possess the same power as He is having, the power to create, uncreate, manipulate with reality of each form.

This is not made by dark ones to remove You from control, but is one of the tools to create Consensus.

The Cabal is having different plans, they are on a brink of fight against each other for more power over this planet, this is what I warned You about.

SOPHIA
 Tomorrow is the inauguration of Barack Obama. Since the US Corporation has been foreclosed upon, how is it that he is scheduled to be sworn in?

G/E
 It is almost foreclosed on this world's arena, the truth about how USA stole more than 70% of Gold of all world is now known to Europe, Russia, China and India. And the truth about their world agenda is now known to many, yet unfortunately very few accepting it. This inauguration is the calm before the storm Sophia, get ready.

SOPHIA
What can you tell me about what is going on energetically, even specifically with ME, because physically I feel awful/ill.

G/E
I'm sensing that a lot of lightworkers are feeling exhausted and desperate, because many wanted the Event exactly on 21st December, even now they want it as soon as possible, though You knew too this Sophia it's not going to take place exactly on that date, or right after it.

I know the feeling Sophia, it's the moon and underground devices for distorting the Frequencies, the Kabbalah Tree.

I told M *(note: M is a man from Italy who also hears from this source.. we are in contact with one another)* this advice and will tell You this as well, in order to aid Your Inner Self, You need some dark stone like black agate or a scalar pendant with maximum of 7000 negative ions (the more the output, the better), the black substance color of it absorbs the dark energies of these devices. These are the ones that I'm using.

The holding of a black agate is helping to restore the inner peace of body and mind, as it absorbs all dark energy of Your body and mind. I have a lot of different stones, scalar pendants and Feng Shui activators. You can check all the effects of these on the internet. Overall, this is helping me a lot as a human being.

SOPHIA
How do we get our hands on healing technology to make us all twenty years younger? There is much to do.

G/E
Right now, if You really want to save Your body from aging (damage, deterioration, wear), You need to have money.

There are some available technologies that are helping to reduce this process, the most advanced technologies are kept in their bases on tight security, with the use of them it is possible to invent the devices that are eliminating the aging process and enhancing the regeneration of cells, thus increasing the efficiency of the human body overall.

The chem-trails from planes were made intentionally to degrade these abilities and enhance aging. The optimal human now must have an average of 120 years, but You are able to see it is not this way.

The Followers of Light are going to help humanity to reveal it and advance it. Unfortunately the only way now is to use the ones that are for money...

SOPHIA
What can you tell us about the Guardians? We (*American Kabuki and Sophia*) have been told that we are Guardians, and that those who are setting up the One Peoples Public trust are Guardians as well.

G/E
The Guardians are of different types. You're Guardians, You are protecting the humanity from its self-annihilation and are giving Hope and Love to many that are in need.

The distinction between Guardians are that some are "on the role" and other are like "new ones that wish to join in order to help the cause".

Right after World War 1 a lot of new ones started to appear as World War 1 was one of the biggest hoaxes of humanity and too many died being only a pawns in a game for wealth for a few people and prosperity of USA over bones and blood of many.

SOPHIA
Is there sex in the fifth dimension?

G/E
Do You mean sex as a physical? It is a number one process from which Love was born, the second process was the Consciousness understanding of "taking care of others, not hurt them".

"The True Love" in terms of Higher Evolved Consciousness is the Love that does not require this physical process, as this is just a step for the evolution of this process.

SOPHIA
How long til Ascension?

G/E
The Ascension is going to take place very soon.

You can search for these predictions, they are our beacons: 111 popes prophecy, Rabbi Yitzhak Kaduri's prediction, Alan Martin's 12 president prediction and of course the Moment of Truth of 5.19.13 Expect Us message

SOPHIA
 What is the current squabble going on in the higher realms? We sense it here.

G/E
As You already know main Archons branch joined the Followers of Light, but those that refused to join the completely opposing faction stayed there where they were.

This is an obvious defeat for them, but they at least have a lot of courage to resist the inevitable.

They are holding the lines, but are not going to last long.

They could be defeated much quicker, but are using humanity as a shield, so it's hard for Light Followers to force them to surrender.

SOPHIA
 Do the Pleiadians have an agenda they aren't telling us?

G/E
This question I'm not able to give You the answer for it as it is currently not connected to his world.

What do You feel by Your own Intuition and Your own Free Will?

I hope this is going to help You if there something more, You just ask.

 Also I need to ask You and hear Your own answer.

One is interested in Your ability to understand the Code.

Why I am sharing an inspirational, uplifting music? This is the question.

Much Peace around, Much Calmness inside, Much Love in hearts, Much Prosperity outside, Much Joy and Happiness all around!

SOPHIA
Hi and thank you.

Here is my answer.

Music speaks another language and activates something within. I do not know exactly what or why, but it evokes emotion and is the driving force sometimes when words are insufficient. I believe you are sharing with me codes to spark memories within my own being that I would not have access to without the access point.

The music you share reaches deep. I often listen as I write, and somehow it works to inspire and coordinate thoughts that I otherwise have difficulty putting into words. Music has always had a calming, resonating effect on me. Not all music, but some.

I do not know if this is the only answer I have, but it is what comes up for me right now. I am very grateful for your sharing of music, and many others are also. Very inspiring and hopeful, when life does not feel that way.

Thank you. Is this what you wanted to know?

Much love.

G/E
Yes, Sophia, You're very correct!

It resonates with Consciousness and with it You are receiving the hidden messages, or codes. As You're remembering every sound has the ability to change the matter and mostly liquid matter like water. The negative words and music is changing the molecules into the chaotic state and positive words and music are making these molecules into orderly shaped geometrical structures. The more beauty is in the sound the more order there is.

This is helping by its own to find out lies and truth much easier. The cabal is using the sense that is most susceptible to lies, the sight. The hearing is less susceptible to lies, but is having a much more effect on the body than the sight.

The "new" epic genre of music I was giving You is of Creator's origin, for example the music Icarus I gave You was the music that I heard before my incarnation, it's the music I heard long ago and still remember that same old beautiful tune, it is my own beacon for a close completion of my objective.

I need to give You one advice when You need to know whether something is true or false. Just close Your eyes and listen for the variation of sound and different vibrations.

The differentiate of sound is giving out the lies, or even history of the person You're listening to.

And this is another beautiful work[47] for hearing and sight of Everyone! (video posted below)

Much Love and Peace!

---

[47] *YouTube*. YouTube, n.d. Web. 08 July 2016.
<http://www.youtube.com/watch?feature=player_embedded&v=INglqw978zA>.

(Update January 25, 2013)

SOPHIA
There have been some messages about what many are calling "the Event" and a date 5/19/13.
I asked for any information that could be shared. What follows is the response.

G/E
The One told me that this is the date of the "Moment of Truth". He is not sharing with me details because I'm still a representative of humans and must feel everything like a part of humanity once it will come to this moment.

My GE status is ignored to full Revelation. I'm not a prophet or a Farseer, the Event as it is called must be felt by me as well for a better self-exploration, self-expression, self-clarification "Within the Self of Creator".

One also told me to provide You with information on "The Killshot" (this is a documentary, and it is posted below, please use discretion) and the Kryon, have You heard of that channeler Lee Carroll, Sophia?

Look for the Bridge of Swords here[48].

(Complete text below, as channeled by Lee Carrol)

And about the Remote Viewers. They are able to see only the end that is the destruction, but One is directing them into seeing only this outcome. One does not want anyone to see far into the future, so a point of time that is the whole spring time of 2013 is a "Threshold of Worlds".

No one on this planet is able to see the right picture beyond that point, even we.

But by Your choice everything must be in the way that humanity will

---

[48] "Tonronto, ON, Canada - November 29, 2012." *Tonronto, ON, Canada - November 29, 2012.* N.p., n.d. Web. 08 July 2016. <http://www.kryon.com/k_channel12_Toronto.html>.

become free.

The Forces of One are here to make sure it happen.

The aid of the Sun may be put in effect if humanity will not be able to stop the lasts attempts in starting the ww3 by the illuminati order, when these will be meeting certain points in "a very fragile (or dangerous) turns of destiny" as it is called.

So "The Kill shot" will not be able to be that grim as they are saying, but two events before the kill shot may occur.

The one that is connected with a nuclear explosion by North Korea and the other with a space shuttle looking vessel forced down to Earth due to some disturbances in the orbit.

But One told me to share this with You only to remind light workers that mind is over matter. The Will and Want is able to prevent these events and made the reality befitting them.

Much Peace and Love to You!

LIVE KRYON CHANNELLING
"THE BRIDGE OF SWORDS"

This live channelling was Given in Melbourne, Australia
September 29, 2012

To help the reader, this channelling has been revisited [by Lee and Kryon] to provide even clearer understanding. Often what happens live has implied energy within it, which carries a kind of communication that the printed page does not. So enjoy this enhanced message given in Toronto, Canada, 2012.

Greetings dear ones, I am Kryon of Magnetic Service. In the scheme of things, you are reaching the pinnacle of what we would call the decision point for humanity. In order for you to see this in the light that I see it, you'll have to understand two things. First, going back a short time you will remember that in my first communications to you, I told you that Human consciousness was changing. I brought you information from the very beginning of my attributes on the planet, that humanity was in shift and that I had arrived for a special purpose and that was to shift the magnetics of the grid. I told you that the Kryon group itself would finish that in the year 2002 and would leave, and it did. All of this was in response to what you had accomplished as humanity, and some of you have done the mathematics and realized that all of this was well within the precession of the equinoxes - a 36-year window where your sun aligns to the middle of the galaxy - the beginning and the end of the 26,000-year wobble of the planet.

This astronomical attribute also esoterically [metaphysically] aligns with what the ancients said it would - a decision point for humanity that would be the most important one of all, one that carries with it tremendous energetic purpose. This is why I arrived, and if you look at my first communications, you will see why I arrived, for something was happening with humans, and it had to do with your future. Twenty-two years ago I told you this, and by 1993 you had the publication [Kryon Book One]. Now, here you are in 2012 all these years later, with exactly what we said you would have. We gave you potentials back there; some of them became the potentials of humanity and some of them did not. We deal only with potentials, but the strongest ones talked about your future today.

Secondly, I want you to remember that when you came into this planet, each one of you was unique. It doesn't matter how old you are as you sit here, every one of you is an old soul. The old souls are the ones who tend to tune in and listen and read a message such as this, and we have said that before as well. So what we have is a unique group, and I want you to remember the spark of truth *when you arrived, all of you. Fresh within the quantumness that locks itself to your memory, ringing in your ears when you arrived as the baby:* "This is the lifetime that will make the difference."

There are some of you who have even asked the question, "Why am I alive?" *You know who you are. When there was darkness all around you, caused by circumstances and situations, some of them health, we were there. I'll tell you why you are here. You're here to complete this task that you started so many years ago, old soul! This is the decision point and, from my standpoint, it has already been passed.*

There is no test in front of you, since you've already passed it. In your timeline, there are 18 more years of it [the precession]. So at the end of this year, the 2012 marker at that solstice point, it is simply only that - a celebration point in 3D time. This is where you celebrate having made it. And I suffice it to say right now that those who created this enlightened place called Earth know you did it. There are already celebrations in the skies and yet there are things happening on the planet that we told you would happen, and there are those who are worried.

The Bridge of Swords, Revealed

I want to give you what I'm going to call, "The Bridge of Swords revealed." Here is a phrase we have given you many times in the past. We told you that in the end - that is to say, the end of the old paradigm of the planet [now] - you would have The Bridge of Swords.

Let me tell you some potentials about the future, immediate future. This is not what is going to happen in generations from now, but rather right now. The Bridge of Swords is here. Some of you have extrapolated this information into a form that you then compare to the ancient prophecies in the Holy Scriptures, trying your best to have a confluence of dates and events so that you can figure it out. Some of you have even said, "Ah, The Bridge of Swords: That must be the time where there's going to be battles on the planet. It's the Armageddon, and it's here." *I'll tell you, dear one, that the Armageddon is happening on some other earth, in some other time! You can write that prophecy off as something that is not going to happen to you.*

I'll say this again, dear Human Being: Do not look at past prophecy and apply it to anything that is going on here. Past prophecy had you dead at the millennium, did you remember that? Yet you're here in 2012! You've moved on to the current prophecy of the ancients, of the indigenous of the planet who saw a melding together of north and south - the prophecy of the feathered serpent and the prophecy of the condor and the eagle. This is a movement of energy on the planet in a way no "modern day" prophet ever predicted. Instead, it came from the indigenous, for they saw the potentials of some time fractals that spoke of humanity passing the fifth decision point and moving into the next part of what we call the Great Shift of Human Consciousness.

What's going to happen next? The Bridge of Swords. So let us analyze it. Let us tell you what we had in mind when we gave you the phrase and we ask you not to build upon this anything that is not said here. Do not then project more than what is given. Do not try to figure out hidden meanings within what is given, for I'm going to give them all to you now.

The Bridge

It's very straightforward. It's a bridge, so let's look at that first. What is the bridge doing and why must there be one? Well, congratulations dear ones, because a decision point is not always a bridge. Sometimes it's a chasm, a chasm that humanity would fall into so they would have to start all over. Or perhaps a decision point that has no bridge at all, which means everything stays the same. There would be no change, and you'd have more of what you had - a future that's nowhere and had never been written. But that's not what's happening at all.

Oh, this has been written so many times, but it's not in your old scripture, dear ones. You're going to have new writings long after my partner is gone. Oh he'll be back, but long after this particular lifetime there will be new scriptures written by ones you will see as the prophets of the day. They will talk about what is next on the planet and they will see the change in Human nature. They will see that which is leaning toward the quantumization of corporeal humanity - the beginning of what happened to the Pleiadians so long ago will happen here as you cross the bridge.

But that's the far future. What about now? The bridge you are crossing is the one between old paradigms of existence and new ones. Eventually all humanity will cross it, but this is so new at the moment that the only ones truly crossing it are very old souls, for they are the only ones that see it and have the Akash ready for it. But you should know this: This bridge is for all, and as you cross this bridge, metaphorically, others will follow you. They'll cross it and not even know it. They're crossing into belief of a new kind of reality.

Dropping the old paradigms of what to expect is next. Accepting new paradigms of a future without war is next. Looking at civilization differently than you were ever told it could be, is next. Dropping old fears that so many have had for so long about what to expect is next. That's the bridge. It's a beautiful thing. The fact that there's a bridge at all is a beautiful thing.

The bridge has been created over a long period of time. Synchronistically we did not know a bridge would occur until 30 years ago. That's how new this energy is. Humanity has free choice and there was no strong potential then if the confluence of energy would have created the momentum to create a bridge or not. But a small potential was there.

By the 1987 Harmonic Convergence, we knew the bridge was being built. By 1989, the super structure was in place. By 1993, the bridge was there. Then you started to see the fall of the Soviet Union, the coming together of former European enemies into an economic alliance. The idea that you could put together things instead of tearing them apart was new. Dictators began to fall, and the bridge was in place, and most of humanity didn't even notice since it happened so slowly. But you felt the shift coming, didn't you? That's what the bridge is all about.

What have we told you about the bridge? Actually, not much except that in crossing the bridge, the old energy ones were not going to like it. Old energy does not want you to escape! Old energy doesn't want you to cross the bridge because it can't cross. Did you know that? It can't cross. The old paradigms of Human nature that you've known all of these millenniums have to stay on the old side of the bridge. It cannot cross, for the bridge rejects all that is not in love, compassion and light. Those things that are dark, including Human nature of the past, will not be able to go. But the ones I speak to right now are already on the bridge. That was your design, old soul, and those are the words that are ringing in your ears to this day and the ones given at the wind of birth, that this might happen in your lifetime. So what's going to happen next?

Swords

Let us talk about the swords: When you hear the word sword, *the first thing that occurs to you is battle. The Bridge of Swords is a battle and we told you that as well. Swords are metaphoric and they mean many things, so let us describe the things we mean them to say to you.*

Number one: They are indeed a weapon in a battle. There is a battle coming. "Kryon, does that mean there's going to be a war?" *Potentially, yes. Right now we will tell you that the Middle East cooks itself. You've noticed, haven't you? What do you know about the Middle East, dear one? Let's start examining things for a moment. What energy did you grow up in? What was the energy of the Middle East? In the '40s, what was the energy? With the establishment of the state of Israel, you built a wall of hate, both sides. The wall was so thick that the children of both sides were taught to hate one another as soon as they were able to understand the language. They were told who their enemies were. Now, where were you then?*

Some of you weren't here yet. By the time you arrived, in your youth, were you aware of the Middle East? Not particularly. "What's the hatred about?" *you might ask. What if I told you it's about a family feud? Two sons of a Jewish master are involved. One founded the Arabs and one remained a Jew. They don't want to hear this, but they are all Jews. (Don't tell them this.)*

If you look at the lineage, it's pretty obvious and yet it's a complete and total set-up for either solution or war. The set-up would have this world ending in a conflagration that would have been brought about by this hatred. That's in the prophecy of Nostradamus and your scripture, but it is no longer the prophecy of the planet. Yet the hatred still exists. The hatred is as great today as it was then, but where was all the terrorism 40 years ago? It was isolated.

Those in Israel and Palestine and surrounding areas took the brunt of it, but now it's seemingly everywhere - and you're worried. Why would this be? The answer is that the old energy was happy to have this hatred contained, for it would keep it going and never involve outsiders. Outsiders tend to bring unwanted light to the party. Suddenly, the whole earth is involved and can see the entire scenario before them. The old guard wants war, just like all the eons before them. The ones on the bridge are holding the light and showing the earth how to cross. Even many younger ones in Israel and Palestine and Iran are holding light! It's all around the old guard and they are furious, for they are losing the "battle of hatred."

Will there be a war? What is going on? You can feel it cooking, can't you?

Some of you don't want to look at the news, for you're afraid of what tomorrow will bring. It's not even the end of the year yet! Will there be a battle?

Let me tell you, dear ones, right now as we speak to you there is the potential of a small war in the Middle East. You have been told that if there is any war at all in the Middle East, the whole world will join in, and you will not make it. I will tell you that that is an old paradigm, for if and when it happens, watch carefully who decides not to come to the war party. For there's a new consciousness brewing on this planet and I will tell you this: In all fairness, as we see the potentials before you in your future, it's not going to matter one way or another to the bridge if there is a battle or not.

What's eventually going to happen in Iran is going to be the same no matter what, and I will tell you why - because there is nobody to take the place of the old guard. They're not growing any, young ones! It's all the ancient ones with the hatred who are moving the chess pieces as though they are representing the whole of the nation, but they are not. There will come a time, perhaps one that is actually exacerbated by a war, that will create the revolution in that country. Overwhelmingly, they don't want war.

Ask an Israeli if they want still another war. They will say no, but they are afraid that their enemies will bring one to them. Who are their enemies and what is changing, dear ones? You think you know what's going on in Syria and Egypt and Libya? You think you do? Let me tell you there's a recalibration going on there of what they believe and who their enemies are. It's about what they want from their government. Let me tell you what all of them want eventually, and you may not see it for 20 years, but they want schools and hospitals. They want what you have in your stores, and they want the freedom to worship their prophet without a small group telling them the rules of how they should. They want to honor Muhammad in their own way and see the love of God in him as was designed by him. That's what's going on. That's the battle. The problem is that the old energy will fight this, for it will lose control if they get what they want.

There's a paradigm shift at hand and you're going to see it over there first, and it may not be pretty, so I want you to hang tight. Don't pull out what Nostradamus said at the last minute and say, "He was right." Nothing he said has manifested since 1987. Don't suddenly grasp the scriptures of

Revelations and draw out all of those words that haven't been true for 30 years. Nothing has happened as they said it would. The only thing that rings true there is that there are still problems in the Middle East.

All of those prophecy quatrains have fallen on the floor and didn't come true. The timing is not right for them to happen now. Take a look. Oh, there are still those who say, "It's happening, it's happening, it's happening!" *For they are invested in fear and control. Some of them actually want it to happen, and they believe the culmination will be in the rapture of going home to God. I want to tell you, dear ones, you're all going home! But home is across the bridge to an earth without war. That's the bridge. Old energy dies hard.*

What else does a sword mean?

The sword is a symbol, a metaphoric symbol for truth. *A Bridge of Swords is* a bridge of truth. *Sometimes you cross swords above you in celebration, do you understand this? That's how we see it. Will there be a rough road ahead for the bridge? Yes, but you knew that when you showed up on the planet, dear one, and it doesn't have to mean a world war, and it won't.*

There are those who are settling the very issues of whether they should continue to hate or not in the Middle East right now. They don't trust each other, but they also don't want to continue the way it has been. There are dictators who are leaving or who have already gone, replaced by leaders who will eventually temper and soften their positions to their neighbors. It's because they realize what they want is schools and hospitals and roads and safety for their children. Is that too hard for you to imagine?

The media rushes to the horror and tells you that they are all consumed with killing each other. I would like to ask you to interview them. Don't interview the ones that you see on the news, but rather the mothers and the fathers who you don't see on the news who have the same faith as the ones you do see in the news. They will tell you, "Give us peace; leave us alone; let us grow in our way in our own culture. We don't want to make bombs. We want to have compassion." *This is the bridge. It may get worse before it gets better and we have told you that many times. But that's why you're here.*

Slowly the few who make the hate will be seen as a few. The many will have their views known and will replace the few.

What you do next is so important. What will it be? Are you going to fear it, or have compassion for it, understand it, and stand up tall and move forward across the bridge? Are you going to cower in a corner and worry when you see what you expected? Old energy dies hard. The sword of truth is active and well, and the truth will prevail in the light.

What other truth could there be that you're recognizing? What about the truth of the way things work in a compassionate earth, one where you can't have the kind of non-integrity issues that you're having now? Businesses will change, governments will change, and banking will change. Are you shocked at this? Some day you're going to know that you actually have changed the way things used to be in the darkest corners of the planet. It's not what anyone expected, and you'll realize that you made a difference.

I'm in Canada and I know it, but I will tell those listening and reading in the American audience the following: Get ready! Because there are some institutions that are yet to fall, ones that don't have integrity and that could never be helped with a bail out. *Again, we tell you the biggest one is big pharma, and we told you that before. It's inevitable. If not now, then in a decade. It's inevitable and they will fight to stay alive and they will not be crossing the bridge. For on the other side of the bridge is a new way, not just for medicine but for care. Paradigms that have not yet been thought of, which don't represent any system that currently exists, will be created and developed by young minds who have concepts that the seniors don't know about. Things that don't have integrity today will fall over tomorrow. Just get ready. It's all part of what's on the other side of the bridge. And the old energy won't like it, and they will object.*

There will be new ways to create electricity, new ways to clean the water, new ways to feed yourself. It's all there across the bridge in the future. It lies there just waiting for you to cross. Don't be afraid. Lightworker, this is what you waited for and this is the future that you wanted. It's why you were born and alive now. It doesn't matter how old you are, senior. Don't count the years you think you have left; don't go there, just don't do it. I want you to see your life as we do - all the lifetimes you've ever lived with the energy of what you've created on the planet right now, in your hand, for this is the way Spirit sees you. Your footprint on the earth is enormous and what you are doing now as you cross the bridge is enormous. Only the old souls with the wisdom of accumulated lifetimes can move that bridge and cross it quickly.

The Final Attribute

The final thing about swords is celebration. What happens when Human Beings walk under crossed swords? What is the general idea of that? It's marriage, is it not? So let us give you, finally, the symbol of the marriage on the bridge. It has so many meanings! It's the marriage of what used to be with what can be, it's the marriage of compassion and the Human spirit, it's the marriage of your soul entity on the planet with your creative seeds (the Pleiadians), it's the marriage of you and you! It's the coming together of the north and south. It's beautiful. It's The Bridge of Swords.

Perhaps you're here this day or listening or reading and this is all new to you and you'll say, "I don't know if I'm an old soul or not. Am I part of this crossing? Am I going across the bridge?" **Let me say this to you: Don't analyze this! I'll give you a fact. If you're listening right now (or reading), then you're part of it! It's the only thing that has brought you to the page, to the chair, to listen or read or know. If you're interested, then you're part of it. It may take some of you to suspend belief on how it works, but you're part of it! I'll say this again: Don't over-analyze it. Many will awaken and follow. The bridge will be there as long as you live.**

What are you supposed to do? Just be, old soul. Go to work and show the light there. Show that you have compassion for those around you. Go home to your family that perhaps doesn't believe this, and don't judge them. Instead, show your compassion to them because you have a piece of God inside you. Think of what the masters would do right now. They're not standing here in judgment, they're celebrating your life! No matter who is in front of you, celebrate their lives! Be the example of a compassionate God and of the divine seeds that are in you, and that will shape your future. Do not be afraid.

What the media gives you next, what happens next in the Middle East, what happens in these next years, will all be part of the old energy reaction. Darkness can't cross the bridge and they are going to die because of it. And I don't mean Humans. I mean the energy itself of hate will be dead and eventually gone. This is the promise and I speak to those now who have complete and free choice to change it, but I tell you, you won't because the push is too great. The ball has already started to roll.

For 20 years, you've seen it coming. You have a right for peace on the earth. It is a time that you have planned on. There is precedent at hand, for the Pleiadians did it, those from Orion did it, the Octurians did it. The parents of the parents of the parents of the planetary systems that you're in did it. Now you're doing it. A long process is ahead of you until the last vestige of old energy is gone. I will say it again: There will come a time when you look back on today and you'll say, "How barbaric humanity was!" And that's what we see, old soul, this day.

That's what we see.

And so it is.

KRYON.

(Update - January 29, 2013)

SOPHIA
This musical journey was received on the 27th of January.
I will include it below, after a blog post that was included with it on January 28th, 2013.

   Blog from 1.28.13[49]   *(Title: A gift from One – Music)*

We are altering our very structure. There are no parts of us that will remain unchanged. We cannot learn this. We cannot even practice for this. We can either accept and allow or resist and challenge; yet we cannot stop. We came to do this.

The naming conventions don't matter – multi-dimensional, 4D, 5D, angelic or enlightened. We are One, gradually and instantaneously morphing into expanded versions of the selves we have come to know. Limited only by

[49] "A Gift from One ~ Music ." *Sophia*. N.p., n.d. Web. 08 July 2016. <http://www.sophialove.org/my-blog/a-gift-from-one-music>.

belief, our possibilities are without bounds. It is love, intent and this moment now that facilitate our BEing.

Music is a language without words. It reaches our core, creating the setting and tools for seamless comprehension. Put on your headphones and relax. We've been gifted Now with a musical journey from AWAKEning to BEcoming.

This is a gift from Off World, selected for us. It is included here exactly as received.

You are encouraged to listen more than once. Allow it to resonate within, feel the vibrations, the changes and absorb them into your BEing. The resonance and tones will facilitate the metamorphosis.

We are BEcoming, in each moment of now. The fullness and depth of this shift is experienced within as we are moved and carried along on this profound journey Home. Home is where Agape rests. We are free. This is the place we have always been headed.

We are the Ones we are waiting for.
~Sophia

G/E

Right from the point of Awakening[50]

The Path to Freedom from fear, control, instincts is not easy, but it is well possible![51]

Throw away every thought You are having, every memory in Your mind and when there is nothing inside, just let go and lift off being weightless![52]

---

[50] N.p., n.d. Web. <http://www.youtube.com/watch?feature=player_embedded&v=0RhfwyMtRe0>.
[51] MissSylvie90. "Audiomachine "Path To Freedom"" *YouTube*. YouTube, 29 July 2010. Web. 08 July 2016. <http://www.youtube.com/watch?feature=player_embedded&v=Sx_oig38Q84>.
[52] TwoStepsFromTheMusic. "Two Steps From Hell - Weightless." *YouTube*. YouTube, 03 Apr. 2012. Web. 08 July 2016. <http://www.youtube.com/watch?feature=player_embedded&v=2-dFMD5D0lY>.

There is a place in Heaven, where we are living now[53]

And once we were Angels here[54]

Thus Angels shall we become again![55]

I know I was giving this beautiful sooner to You, with a purpose

All different composers, yet are Connected in One

☼***A gift from One and me to You and Humanity in form of music for the Living Code***☼

(February 1, 2013 Update)

SOPHIA
On January 1, 2013 another video was produced, shown below. This message is a response to it.

G/E
You've sent the messages to "off world beings" which were heard and accepted[56]. This was the last necessary thing for You to become an ally for a Good side which is "off world". Your last message is going to be fulfilled as this was Humanity's Choice. If You will be visited again, please don't ignore them once again :)

---

[53] N.p., n.d. Web. <http://www.youtube.com/watch?feature=player_embedded&v=fd3k9KrBMgg>.
[54] ThePrimeCronus. "Stefano Mocini - Once We Were Angels." *YouTube*. YouTube, 04 Sept. 2012. Web. 08 July 2016.
<http://www.youtube.com/watch?feature=player_embedded&v=TNDiQGDnjBM>.
[55] MusicKaira1. "Greatest Battle Music of All Times - Angels Will Rise [Twisted Jukebox (Blood and Glory)]." *YouTube*. YouTube, 23 Oct. 2012. Web. 08 July 2016.
<http://www.youtube.com/watch?feature=player_embedded&v=KUtCg4vKXTY>.
[56] SophiaLoveQuest. "2013 Message to Off World Beings." *YouTube*. YouTube, 01 Jan. 2013. Web. 08 July 2016. <http://www.youtube.com/watch?feature=player_embedded&v=9q7oolGRAmk>.

(Update February 11, 2013)

SOPHIA
So here is another question.
We are discouraged and beaten by the cabal. The young of us are too. We all get our information from many different sources, the lightworkers read my stuff and a handful of others, the younger generation is on REDDIT and other places, the older is on Main Stream Media. Every once in a while, something pierces through all forms of information and reaches us all at once.

It seems to me, that if I could do something that would do that, reach us all at once, we could change things in an instant. Is there anything that can be told to me to help with that?

The Cabal is not giving up... hanging on, nothing is changing in a real tangible way so that we can stop the struggle and prosper. Even the children are beaten down before reaching the age of 20. What can I do to get us all creating prosperity in the same moment? There must be a way. If we do, the cabal will be forced to "give up the ghost". Experiment over.

That is my question. Can ONE help me?

G/E
You must have patience Sophia. It was in humanity's collective choice (majority was the cause), the reason for everytime delays is not because Followers of Light and archon earth grid are "fighting" with each other, it's because this was planned by One.

One is already aiding humanity; no freedom couldn't be possible if whole archon force would still be in control of this planet. You remember the time sequence beacons? (Note: These are prophecies, previously mentioned such as the resignation of Pope Benedict, which was announced today 2/11/13) Once they will be met, everything will start and if Followers of Light will again hesitate like it was in the past, we Forces of One will do their job in a much unpleasant for them way and more to that, they are going to lose the full trustfulness of One in their confidence. They don't wish this to happen, so they must act.

Do not let down Your Hopes, those in desperate aid, must be given that aid. Mutual Aid and Mutual Trust and "Mutual Vibrations" are a way to Freedom, this is what everyone is looking for in this world. Now what are Vibrations You may wonder, this is the power of sounds.

Now I'm able to uncover the most important secret in Creation and humanity's experiment, which is going to help You and every other Lightworker out there a lot! (if You will know how to use it of course:)

This is not something completely unknown to You, but most of the time this is being ignored by almost all.

The Vibrations have an origin of Super Force, this was the Force from the Beginning of this Universe's existence. Eventually Vibrations went down to the sound. *"In the Beginning there was a Word"*, the starting of the whole Creation, in the Beginning there was a sound, which made the Creation existent.

Now sounds and thus words are able to change reality as well. How this works, particular sounds creates particular frequency, each frequency generate an impulse, "a command" to atomic structure and whole molecular structure of an affected object. This works with best efficiency with liquid-like materials like water and very hot plasma (by a little different means, not now).

Right now we will concentrate on water. Water have an extent of up to 80% in human body that is why it is very susceptible to sounds' impulses. A one time heard sound have very small effect on a body (not including emotions), yet if body is being held under repetitive same set of sounds (words) it is changing to suite that set of sounds (words).

The name given to You is changing You constantly so that You're fitting that name, a constant calling of You by Your name is making a very big change inside of Your body and Your whole character. The set of sounds is also in a music which is most often without interruptions or pauses. Every piece of it already changing the whole structure. That is the same reason why I'm sharing an uplifting music with You and other lightworkers, My

Friends!:)

This music increases Awareness and Consciousness and bring You All closer to the Ascension (or Uplifting) and Full Consciousness, another gift of One this epic music is. The sounds are increasing their output with an addition of emotions, the emotions connected with sounds have a much more higher results of affecting reality.

A simple test to see if it so, is to watch something beautiful and horrible, like some beautiful video that is "touching Your Heart" and horror movie which You're very afraid of. Just turn off the sound and watch them, You will feel that it is "somewhat" beautiful/horrible, but if You will turn on the sound, it will affect Your body on a much larger scale. You can repeat the test then with closed eyes and turned on sound, the effect on Your body will still be very high. And in the end You can just watch and listen at the same time to measure how it is changed from Your previous experiences.

This information is very important and should be considered as "high priority" if You wish to increase the speed of this world's uplifting, it is possible. In this Universe everything is possible.

The second thing to do is all-out, complete, precise disclosure of alien presence in this world. This will not leave any chances of hiding for Followers of Light and archons.

Much Peace and Love to You and Everyone!

SOPHIA
And the next day...

G/E
One told me I need to remind You about this song, We Are The World[57], it is forgotten, yet it bears a huge amount of Energy to hearts of all that listens this! (see video below)

When the world must come together as One

[57] N.p., n.d. Web. <http://www.youtube.com/watch?feature=player_embedded&v=P2H6mpUnsLl>.

When we stand together as One
We are the World, We are the Children

Much Love and Much Peace to All!

SOPHIA
This was received 2.9.2013...

G/E
Sophia there is one thing You should know I think. The asteroid that will fly near this planet, there is a great possibility it will fall here.

Link to information about this asteroid[58].

The analysis by humanity's scientists is showing 0% of it's seizure by this planet's gravity, but this is exactly the cause why it can be taken and drawn here. They are far too assured and relieved on this matter. One don't like arrogance within His own Body and He eradicating this feature whenever it is possible and not necessary. Right at this time of Great Changes this feature is not that He wishes to see on this planet and He may just play it the other way like it was meant for a destruction outcome. The archons and then Followers of Light were always protecting this planet from these objects while humanity was in existence, but if One is going to declare that order, it will be done, no one is going to stop this except for humanity..

The decision to tell You this was "at my own will as I'm partly a human" as I was told, I wasn't sure if You need to know this, but anyway I thought maybe people again can meditate together so it wouldn't be so, the Power of Taughts and Hopes just can calm One.

SOPHIA
And received today, 2/11/2013...

---

[58] N.p., n.d. Web. <http://earthsky.org/space/asteroid-2012-da14-will-pass-very-close-to-earth-in-2013>.

G/E
Happy New Year Sophia!

Now both Sun and Moon aligned into the New Age and Joseph (Pope Benedict) just stepped off the Rome's papacy to signify a New Beginning and fulfillment of the prophecy.

This is *the year of Change, the cycle of Rebirth*, yet if not careful "the snake might bite" with 2012 DA14 (asteroid mentioned above), like it was with W3 Lovejoy (Comet Lovejoy, formally designated C/2011 *W3 (Lovejoy)*, is a long-period comet and Kreutz Sungrazer. It was discovered in November 2011).

But the power of Thoughts and Wills may prevent this! Joyful and Most Gorgeous New Year to You Sophia!:)

Now we are on "a Voyage to Atlantis"[59]

To Forge a New Light![60]

For our Complete and Mass Awakening into the New Age of Peace and Prosperity[61]

Much Love and Peace to You and Every One!

(Update February 14, 2013)

SOPHIA
This conversation has taken place over the last 2 days...

---

[59] Mmemories85. "Future World Music ♫ Voyage To Atlantis." *YouTube*. YouTube, 06 Mar. 2012. Web. 08 July 2016. <http://www.youtube.com/watch?feature=player_embedded&v=ojRe2j0exg4>.
[60] ThePrimeCronus. "Position Music - Forging A New Light (Danny Cocke)."*YouTube*. YouTube, 01 July 2012. Web. 08 July 2016.
<http://www.youtube.com/watch?feature=player_embedded&v=jTQXOHkvUS4>.
[61]ThePrimeCronus. "Future World Music - Spiritual Awakening." *YouTube*. YouTube, 09 Feb. 2013. Web. 08 July 2016.
<http://www.youtube.com/watch?feature=player_embedded&v=VMQLnhUJ0DE>.

People are saying there will be another Pope, Peter??? The prophecy of 111 popes was altered later to include 112 popes???

Can you comment?

G/E
Yes, this is correct. 111 popes is also called 112 popes, this is a question of preference, both names are correct I prefer 111.

Peter the Roman is only a nickname for a feature that means something that is very special to a person that will be elected. I was always restricted from knowing who exactly is going to be the next pope, One always like to make surprises for His Creations. As I was introduced in this prophecy, there is being told about an "unknown figure", it is the choice of humanity that is going to make this final manifestation.

"If the outcome is destruction then the pope is going to be the worst of all and if the outcome is salvation he is going to be normal, optimal pope and if the outcome is going to be complete freedom he is going to be the best of all."

So I have not much to tell here, my only objective is to wait until this new and last random pope which may be as well an antipope or something much more interesting or dangerous is going to be removed and from this point the existence of catholicism will cease to exist.

I can only hope that Rome is going to survive, it's a very corrupt city, yet there is still hope in this city and most of it's people.

SOPHIA
Thanks.

A question from my friend American Kabuki:

Ask him if the asteroid is heading for Rome? There's a prophecy in the bible about Rome/Babylon that rests on seven hills (of sulphur actually - volcanic origins) will be reduced to a stinking sulfurours hell hole at the end of the age. I can't think of the exact verse right at the moment.

G/E

We don't want any human casualties caused by something made by "off world intervention".

Yet Ways of One are unpredictable. Our Guardians Executioners' proposal to One is to drop the asteroid on the Moon and made a new crater with a big shockwave across Moon's surface on near side of the Moon to give a direct sign for a New Beginning.

In scenario if it's going to hit Earth, we are suggesting Central Antarctic or Central Australia.

If One's dissatisfaction will be more than it is now, Nevada Test Site or Northern Canada, as far away from populated areas (this includes many animal species not only humans) as possible, like it was with Tunguska's Comet.

If more dissatisfaction, then it could be any place, we no longer deciding what it will be, it could be even Rome (Rome was supposed to be destroyed with Peter the Roman in active state and only in Destruction scenario).

But right now His level of dissatisfaction is not so severe, yet is unsatisfied with a fact that so many are assured that it is going to pass without harming anything.

Another thing I need to add considering Joseph. His time was almost up and I was expecting his death prior to Beltane, somewhere before his birthday.

"But if he is going to decide to resign before the beginning of it, he is going to live longer and will be able to atone his sins. The time of Great Changes is upon this World and his time was up, he just made the right choice." This is The Decision of One.

But the fact that he is still a pope does not releasing him completely from his duty and thus death.

So he's still in this title not completely freed, that means he may die while he is a pope (nothing personal, only my duty, I personally am wishing him the best of all health, love him and respect as another human being, as a relative, as a brother always, unless betrayed).

SOPHIA
This was received today, **February 14th, 2013...**

G/E
I wish You a Very Great Valentine's Day Sophia!

This Valentine's Day is much more important than any previous one, the moment which humanity waited for so long is right here "at the door." Only last moments remains and this Celebration of Love must be very beautiful!

This is the one thing that is able to stop One's dissatisfaction, show The Creator of All the Power of Love to All and every thing! Remember Love is a something with what You are able to change the Reality, One asks everyone to show the Love to Him, not physical, but spiritual.

I can say that very few knows this, and those who know this are much more evolved and spiritually powerful humans like You are and so this message is being addressed mostly to You as You are Sophia LOVE!

Another beautiful music for Your enjoyment and uplifting, share it with all that are in Love or just Love everything around! Many Hugs and Much Love!

Loving Forever Everything, Everyone[62]

Sonera[63]..

---

[62] KacskaTB. "Two Steps From Hell - I Love You Forever (T. Bergersen) "Illumina"" *YouTube*. YouTube, 10 Feb. 2013. Web. 08 July 2016. <http://www.youtube.com/watch?feature=player_embedded&v=J3mkAxVRSYY>.
[63] CapeTranquillity. "Thomas Bergersen - Sonera." *YouTube*. YouTube, 11 Apr. 2012. Web. 08 July 2016. <http://www.youtube.com/watch?feature=player_embedded&v=vn1OtNvaDIE>.

(Update February 15, 2013)

SOPHIA

This just happened[64]. At the end, there is a quote:

"It is believed that the incident may be connected to asteroid 2012 DA14, which measures 45 to 95 meters in diameter and will be passing by Earth tonight at around 19:25 GMT at the record close range of 27,000 kilometers."

Any comments? The "near miss" is due in about 5 hours.

Thanks,

G/E

There is a cloud of meteors swirling around the DAIA. One of them collapsed during the entry and hit Chelyabinsk. Another possibility I haven't mentioned is that if One will want to crash DAIA on Earth it will be split apart. It's not just going to hit one spot, but many.

But as far as I am able to see into the Energy and feel One, this is less likely possible, He is considering our proposals.

Followers of Light were told to not to intervene, this is only on humanity's abilities now. Many taught and even sure that nothing will happen and in this very great time of change, for One this behavior is unacceptable.. it angered Him, this was the spark for this possibility.

Yesterday's Energy was great, but it wasn't enough to prevent it completely, unfortunately.. We are still recommending to Him to use a momentum of Earth's rotation and launch this object onto Moon's near

---

[64] "Meteorite Hits Russian Urals: Fireball Explosion Wreaks Havoc, up to 1,200 Injured (PHOTOS, VIDEO)." *RT International*. N.p., n.d. Web. 08 July 2016. <http://rt.com/news/meteorite-crash-urals-chelyabinsk-283/>.

side, in this situation no one will be hurt. And Moon is a self-aligning object so it is not going to fly away from that impact.

Much Love to You!

(Update February 21, 2013)

SOPHIA
The following conversation took place on and after February 15/16 2013, Beginning with a message from me:

SOPHIA
I see there were fireballs in Belgium, Japan and Cuba as well. There are some wondering if this is a   "sign from God?" I have not heard yet what NASA or scientists are saying...

G/E
Yes it went out how it was supposed to. One hasn't changed His mind, good for people.

You may wonder why I called this object DAIA.

It is a sister object of Gaia, has almost the same number of days in a solar cycle and has almost the same orbit as Gaia. The Daia went further and will continue on it's path.

Daia is having a lot of small meteors swirling around it, some are in front of it, many are behind it. Soon there will be a comet and later another comet on different paths. No danger from them.

Now we can carry on to an Ascension! Destiny awaits![65]

---

[65]Soundtracklibrary. "Epic Music - Destiny Awaits." *YouTube*. YouTube, 13 May 2012. Web. 08 July 2016. <http://www.youtube.com/watch?v=OoKvhyBRo7c>.

Many Hugs and much Love to You!:)

Portale Universum Uno

G/E
Good Day Sophia! I need to tell You some things about DAIA. I received a message from One that everything that was done is enough.

One brought an "unexpected surprise" as always. And did how we were asking Him to do, without deaths so that everyone could see and understand that this is no joke and protection that Followers of Light are giving is not going to be permanent.

These are three major meteoroids that exploded in air[66]

Yet they again are absolutely sure that the Chelyabinsk asteroid have no connection to DAIA, that's again arrogant from them, it was completely connected with DAIA. This arrogance is a very unwelcomed feature for a spacefaring civilization, as this caused many troubles already before humanity.

Right now there are not going to be more troubles, in next month the new comet will be seen, it will be far away from Earth.

And another beauty for Your enjoyment, the Legacy of humanity![67]

Much Peace and Love to You!

SOPHIA
Thanks.

Someone sent me this[68].

---

[66] *YouTube*. YouTube, n.d. Web. 08 July 2016. <http://www.youtube.com/watch?v=-rcBTF6RE1U>.
[67]CapeTranquillity. "Icon Music - A Legacy Uncovered (BBC Planet Earth)."*YouTube*. YouTube, 17 Feb. 2013. Web. 08 July 2016.
<http://www.youtube.com/watch?feature=player_embedded&v=0m55VKT9YEQ>.

Thoughts and comments?

G/E
Yes, I didn't wanted You to tell this, but I eventually knew it would be found.

This meteoroid was shot down by Followers of Light, otherwise it would struck the Earth and made a nuclear explosion with a little more power as was an atom bomb dropped on Hiroshima thus killing thousands. The same thing happened with meteoroid in Cuba, known Tunguska meteoroid and many others.

Meteoroids are not being destroyed by themselves as "always" like You know this. It is the protection given from Light Followers.

It wasn't the time for people to know this, but considering the curiosity and attention of humanity, with such a revealed footages, we knew people will find out it very soon.

They were not supposed to interfere in Daia's trajectory, but this wasn't a Daia, so they could stop everything else and they did of course, and they were told that they cannot prevent objects from entering into the atmosphere and they did that too. Almost everything how we asked.

Peace and Love!

(Update February 25, 2013)

SOPHIA

Thank you.

---

[68] LogicBeforeAuthority. "RUSSIAN METEOR UFO STRIKE !!! WOW !!!"*YouTube*. YouTube, 17 Feb. 2013. Web. 08 July 2016.
<https://www.youtube.com/watch?feature=player_embedded&v=LizHgQ44ShI>.

This video and "explanation" has shown up several places now.

G/E
Good Day to You too Sophia!

The humanity is going to be liberated quite soon. You can increase the pace by letting majority know about the presence of ETs and that this whole humanity's existence and experience was a big experiment and that many things like religions under the tree of zoroastrianism were big hoaxes to enslave and "to calm" the majority while corruption was taking place.

Once exposed ETs of all sort excluding the Forces of One will have no more place to hide in Human Consciousness and thus this World and all governments will have no more means to hide everything that they've collected so far about ETs and their presence and finally ETs will be forced to show themselves thus officially ending this experiment.

Peace, Calm, Love to You!

SOPHIA
Thanks! Yes, we are all feeling and many are declaring the experiment to be over. Just waiting for the final curtain. It can't come soon enough.

My friend just posted this. Perfect.

(Removing the Shackles [69]----)

"Do You Remember? Do you Remember?

Who you are? Where you come from?

Do you Remember why you are here? Do you remember the Game? The Experiment?

---

[69] "Removing The Shackles." *Removing The Shackles*. N.p., n.d. Web. 08 July 2016. <http://removingtheshackles.blogspot.com/>.

Maybe you don't........ yet.

That was part of the rules of The Game- rules that WE made when WE created The Game. Rules that WE agreed with Source to follow when we all decided to play the Grand Experiment.

The Game is played like a theatre production: The players take their turn, each playing their part on the Grand Experiment Stage. Rule number 1 is that they don't remember.... anything. They are blindfolded and not allowed to look at the rules of the game or the instructions. The players are placed on the stage, with no script and no cue-cards, to interact with each other and ad lib as they go along. The only clues they have are the musical score playing in the back ground and their wits- receiving hints and bits of information from each other as they move through their part.

When we all decided to play The Game, there were certain players that decided to play their part off stage. They didn't forget, they didn't put blindfolds on. These Players hid behind the curtain and had complete access to the Rules and the Instructions of The Game, and because of that they knew exactly how the Grand Experiment would unfold. These Players decided to set themselves up as the Directors.

In the beginning of the Experiment, the Play ran somewhat smoothly. The players interacted with each other, ad libbing as they went along, learning to take cues from the music playing in the background and their interactions between each other. Then the Directors started to exert themselves, proclaimed their authority and began to meddle in the Game. They started giving directions from the sidelines, making up rules that interfered with the Players- taking away their ability to really interact with each other by shouting new directions that caused separation and division between the Players, dividing them up into teams so that they lost their ability to work together as one whole group.

To keep the groups organized, the directors placed Leaders in the middle. These were their brokers and were responsible for dictating to the rest of the group the new rules and regulations. They demanded absolute obedience, their voices drowned out the music playing in the background and over-rode the ability of the Players to interact with each other and to use their intuition and wits to work together.

The Directors allowed these leaders to dictate Rules to the Players, encouraging them to tie their groups together with ropes of fear and chains of distrust for anyone outside their group. The Directors applauded as they thought that these bindings would tightly hold the groups together forever, regardless of whether the Experiment ended or not. They gloated in their superiority, thinking that they would remain in control forever....

... But they forgot something vitally important.

As the Grand Experiment started winding down, something amazing happened. With in the various separate groups, Players began to realize that something wasn't right. They began to listen to the music. They began to remember that not only were there other groups on the stage, but that they too were in the same game. As they remembered, they reached out to those in other groups, linking hands until the stage began to look like a giant web of interconnected BE'ings. As they reached out for each other they began to break free of the ropes of fear, gravitating towards each other....

The Directors didn't like this AT ALL. Their shouts from off stage didn't get the players attention like it use to. They knew that for them to remain in control they needed to step up their game. So they jumped onto the stage, but they did it in disguise. They took on the personas of BE'ings from history, from religious legend and lore. The Directors entered centre stage and worked their way through the groups, throwing glamours over the leaders, convincing the Players that they were there to save them.... that only they, the Directors in the guise of "Divine" BE'ings had the answers to all their questions and that only through them could the Players attain their final goal.

It worked for a short while. The Players beheld these exulted "Divine" BE'ings and paid homage to them, regarding them with hope and awe.... and the Directors LOVED IT. They loved it so much that they never wanted it to end. Who cares about the Grand Experiment?! Who cares about the end of The Game?! Who cares about the Rules and Instructions that the Players all decided on and agreed upon together?! Oh yes! They thought they could keep The Game going forever...

But.... they forgot something else that was vitally important.

The End of The Game.

The final act of the Grand Experiment was at an exact instant, a preordained moment in time that was unchangeable, unmoveable, unalterable.... even by them. The Directors might of been playing the part of "Divine", but in reality they were players just like everyone else on the stage. Yes, they were not blindfolded, Yes they knew the Rules and Instructions of the game, Yes, they remembered.... but they were just Players like everyone else in the Grand Experiment- EQUAL TO ALL.

The Directors waved all sorts of prizes in front of the players in an effort to keep them believing that they were "Divine". Money, Money Money.... Freedom....

"Freedom?" Wait a minute! Players started once again listening to the Music, they started interacting with each other, questioning, asking, listening... "Freedom?" But..... ?

The Directors tried everything in their bag of tricks, yet the more they tried to convince the Players to worship them, the more the Players woke up.

Oh, the Directors knew the reason why.   They knew what was happening. They tried to stop it, convinced that they could keep the Players dancing to their tune forever, but deep in their hearts they knew the Truth:

The Grand Experiment was over. The Game was finished.

The one thing that the Directors forgot is that Source was also involved in The Game. The one thing they didn't know was that in among the players there were Guardians who's job it was to oversee the end of the Experiment.

The Directors yelled louder. They gave orders to the group leaders, orders that fell apart before they could be executed. They ran from group to group, doing anything they could to keep the other Players from listening to the Music. They altered the script, they tried to yell louder than the music.... but it didn't work.

The Guardians began to wake up from their waking sleep. They looked at the Directors pretending to be "Divines" and said "You are NOT "Divine"! For if you are "Divine" then others would have to be "UnDivine". YOU are Players just like WE are Players- WE are ALL EQUAL!" They reached out to each other, grasping hands together, connecting group to group all over the Universal stage in a giant net of light. The Light got brighter and brighter until even those still under the glamour of the Directors could see it through their blindfolds.

As Players woke up they took off their blindfolds and they began to remember who they were.

WE ARE ALL EQUAL

As above, so below.
As below, so above.

EQUAL

....The final chapter of this tale is being written right now and You are part of it.

It's time to take off your blindfold. The Game is over. The Experiment is done.

Breathe deeply, look around you and remember who you are and why you are here.

Remember that we are all EQUAL.

It's time to tell the self appointed Directors that we are done with their cheating and deceptions. They are NOT Divine. They are the same as us: Players in The Game, and the Game is now over.

...Shall we write this last chapter all together?"

G/E

   There will be a very great hearing in the Heavens after this about humanity and this whole stuff that happened in this place.

We and many others off world observers are very unsatisfied with what happened here, the objective of this whole creation was not achieved.

Some of the Archons and Followers of Light will be executed for what they did and this world is going to be reconsidered for a change during the previous time sequence.

The history in some portion of the time sequence is going to be rewritten for a greater purposes of obtaining new designs of reality and exercising loyalty to a more extent possible. But this is not going to be felt, no change in history of this reality is going to take place, it is just important to notice that the past is a subject of interest for One and some points of time will be changed.

Peace, Calm and Prosperity to You!

(Update March 11, 2013)

G/E
Do you want to know how Forces of One wanted to reestablish humanity and to give everyone happiness which leads everyone to love each other and thus creating the complete Consensus?
I have a permission to tell You, so I can:)

All right Sophia, I will explain and try to do it as simple as possible and being very short not to give into details;)

1. The first thing to do was to change education system for the children as everything starts from the beginning and beginning always influencing

everything that is going afterwards. The primary lesson being lacked in schools is friendship which includes behavior, psychology, relations, understanding, state of happiness, state of love.

Before that parents must be informed at least about that system is going to be changed and change will start from younger generations.

After schools children must also proceed on a military course to know all the possibilities of a human body and every way in order to survive here or on a different planet when out of technologies, like matches:0

2. The second thing which was to start a little after the first was to educate every other person in the whole world through main stream media, mostly about what was done against them by few that wanted to control whole populace and how everything will start to exist in order to bring happiness to every soul, including planet Earth and animals and plants.

The new technologies was to introduced, but their use was under restriction of accepting the new ways of thinking and system as a whole which endures everyone to "stand united" live as One, with new view on a World and a Universe and some additions to rules.

The main orient of this is to eradicate greed, the root of all evil and chaos. The picture of this world is very simple - greed was prospering here, because people allowed it to prosper and gave into material possession and material physical pleasure. Greed does not mean always a greed for money and wealth, it also means greed for food, lust, murders, destruction, chaos, knowledge and even light and love. Greed is leading to treachery, murder, lies, wars, destruction and chaos. Everything must be used so that is enough and individual is happy and not to overuse.

This whole process is the most difficult and must be maintained through police/military force, because there are a lot of individuals that would not hesitate and use power in order to get the new technologies and use them to take over everyone.

3. The third thing once acceptance was to achieved was to eradicate money as a representation of something and make very necessary things for life and sustainability for it - basic food, drinkable water, basic clothes, one

house or one apartment, one basic car, one basic pc, basic kitchen stuff and other necessary things free. The basic means it is not cheap and useless, it only does not include additions, like interesting design, "made with love" or "made with great effort".

No more taxes, living is free, electricity is free, protection is free (national security of every country, which was to become united inner/outer planetary security).

Changes that were to happen.

The money was to change to "points". These are an appreciation to service earned when doing or making something or something beautiful or something "beyond imagination". For example working, it is no longer a required prerequisite in order to survive, but a sphere of interest or "a hobby" and work can be changed on another without difficulties, when "boredom occurs".

This does not mean everyone must obligate work somewhere or do something, those that do not wish to work may rest at home, doing nothing, but government was to endure *(later "endure" was changed to "encourage" at his request)* everyone to do at least something, like creating musical composition or poems or inventing something or do a very simple work.

The general management, government, military and police was to given to highly loyal, highly trusted, highly capable representatives, that were selected by One.

Later on, the educated enough people with a willing to governing and managing or service to the cause as a soldier or a scientist or a farseer were to given this opportunity.

During the start of the change, before education was to take place "an automation process" must be conducted in order to give all the free stuff to everyone, this was not possible only 50 cycles ago, but it became possible not long ago, that is why these great changes are occurring only now. Everything is interconnected to say the least.

I hope you're going to find this information useful ;)

Much Love and Peace to You!

 (Update March 15, 2013)

SOPHIA
There is talk about this month as being the month of the Awakening, the Event, that something "big" is coming to "switch us on"...

Can you comment? Deny? Anything? (Note, this was sent before the 13th of March)

G/E
The event as a complete shift into new world will be from may 2013 through 2016 august.

And this depends on humanity as well. Some things soon will happen; the choice of pope will be interesting and some other things as well.

Much Love and Appreciation!

SOPHIA
 (I asked about the new Pope.)

G/E

Greetings Sophia! He was chosen on 13/13 at the start of a spring, there is no 13th month so 3rd is good enough, the numbers of rebirth.

He is looking young yet old and don't have much time left, in his eyes we can see a deep breath, he has met all the prerequisites, welcome the last pope - Peter the Roman.

One always like to make surprises, totally unexpected and invisible until the very last moment, yet the pope is meeting everything with what he was associated, and the name he chose Francis the I will be linked to nickname Peter the Roman later, the 1st already connects Him with Peter the apostle the very first "Pope" of a roman catholic church and to One Himself.

I must not look into this matter, everything that connects with religions is only One's concerns, it is His most interested and manageable sphere.

We only can receive the updates and timelines which are not always as they must be, yet everything what is being done by His Will has a features of a perfect design and it's no surprise of course!

Much Peace and Love to You!

G/E
Another hints I'm able to give is that word jesuit has a different meaning - two face, this is not without the reason of course. Like it was predicted he is not going to be "a normal pope", he is going to be the most unique of them all, not like pope at all as it used to be.

Whether he will be the most evil of all or the most kindness of all is up to him, right now we can see by looking at him, that he is not sure which path to take, he's unsure about himself and about what happened to him, One does not wish us to know what will happen as well, He want us to witness this like every other human in this world without knowing the future.

As You are able to see, the pope is unique already, he is the first to choose the name Francis, he is the first from a "new world" americas, he is the first from jesuit order, he is very humble. More things will be known about him later.

I also wished to share you these videos, it may be late now, but maybe You would find interesting to know that some songs were created especially to awaken many lightworkers around the world. I can only share them now with You

This song[70] is the warning about the double-path of choosing between good outcome and bad, which already was decided as good

And this second song[71] is with two different meanings, the cardinal meaning is about the evil controllers of this world and their many faces, of which You are aware now

Both these songs awakened many people, they were successful in their objective

Much Love and Prosperity to You!

SOPHIA
 (And a few more words about the Newly appointed Pope and the charges against him)

G/E
Everyone that at least once was having business within Vatican are guilty of something, cardinals are being appointed for deeds that are generally not for the Glory of God how they used to call it, but for a profit of the catholic church, the more people they "will win" the more money and different possessions will stream to their accounts, the more wealthier and influential church is becoming then. This was the story of this church and it's still the same, only minor rules and changes were taking place since the foundation of it.

Much Love and Appreciation!

(Update March 19, 2013)

[70] Wtofficial. "Within Temptation - The Howling." *YouTube*. YouTube, 26 Oct. 2009. Web. 08 July 2016. <http://www.youtube.com/watch?feature=player_embedded&v=RYeXu7JfYHU>.
[71] Wtofficial. "Within Temptation - Angels." *YouTube*. YouTube, 26 Oct. 2009. Web. 08 July 2016. <http://www.youtube.com/watch?feature=player_embedded&v=OwTmqPMjlPM>.

G/E

Good Day Sophia! I was told about a big mistake I made when I was describing the plan of rearrangement of this world by Forces of One and cause some misunderstanding.

I wrote a word "to endure", but must have wrote "to encourage" when I was describing how people must have been learned to live and how government must have relate to non workers. I hope You understood me correctly and I haven't caused much misunderstanding.

Also I was told that I didn't mentioned about another important aspects which must have been mentioned. It's because I was trying to write as few as possible, I'm sorry for missing this important things to mention..

These are the missing points: The government will not be in complete control over humanity forever, once there will be assurance that people accepted the ways of One and the world is ready to be on it's own, the People - the Consensus - the Unity will have the full control over it, government and leader (the president or monarch) as You know it now will recede and become administrators of many different spheres where they are capable to perform their tasks.

They still will have an important missions to complete and their tasks must be reserved for highly capable individuals, but important point is that People will be in complete control over this world and Humanity Alliance as a whole.

"The point One to Return To". You can call this a backup copy of the civilization.
It was going to be created inside the Religion of One, where knowledges and main aspects of human society would be put into. As civilization grows it need to expand to new planets and found new settlements. This is creating a gap in relations and put many on different paths to destiny.

The Forces of One have a very huge amount of such different divisions which took different paths, but if something goes wrong, they always have "The Point One to Return To". This is a highly important thing for every spacefaring civilization, a number One to start with. I think You are able to understand what this exactly is Sophia:)

The criminality and Justice.
This is always a prime concern for many civilizations that don't really know how to maintain this situation. It is caused by different views and wills of reality, different goals and different agendas, uniqueness of every individual is creating this state of criminality. The most easiest solutions are executions, tortures and imprisonment.

The Forces of One wanted to introduce you into "curing of the past". The prisons will be completely dismantled, there is no use for them and they are highly ineffective. The prison is a completely different adventure and if someone wish to enjoy it they are always welcome to do so in simulations, in physical world prisons are only making things worse for many real criminals, not talking about those unjustly put there. Real criminals are becoming more extreme after prisons, yet there is fear of going back to prison which is holding them off what they wish to do.

The "curing of the past" is including the intense talk with a deep consciousness of a person and modifying the memories so that there wouldn't be anything that is going to torture the person, mentally and spiritually. Few individuals will also require the modification of the genes as some are bearing highly unstable genes which are having a very turbulent past taken from the ancestors. The "cure through talk" is going to be a very effective solution to many situations.

The prevention of criminal activity will also be done during education and if it will have no use, look for the next part Sophia. At first moments of course the old order must remain as there are many many prisoners in the world and dealing with them all at once is not going to be efficient.

The last part is about people stressed and depressed. Whenever people will need a help, like they can't have what they want or they need a talk about some personal problems, they will be given a talk and will be supported with anything so that they are able to get what they need using their own strength, enhanced through talk, encouragement and inspiration.

When people will need more understanding in theological and philosophical schools there will always be persons that are going to share their time with these people and dig more into this subject.

If there are more concerns about this or anything else, You don't hesitate to ask Sophia, Much Peace and Love!

SOPHIA
 Hi.

I wondered about your use of the word "endure", but I assumed there was something I did not understand. I will share these changes and additions.

This does explain many things. There are so many expectations now for the equinox which takes place in less than 24 hours... much talk about an "event" and an integration with our "greater self" ... so much excitement! Many say that these next ten days or so will yield many changes on the earth for the people.

I am very interested in education of the children. I wonder if there are examples of ways or programs that "work" well other places, that you know of. There is a need for an overhaul of the entire system in this country (USA) which is motivated by tests and corporations and control. It is a challenge to know where to start.

Much love and Happy Spring!

G/E
A step by step human society is integrating itself into the ways of Unity and Oneness where there is no more ignorance toward victims of crimes, but a compassion and aid.

Yes USA was indeed created as a corporation or fundamental for operations of a satanic cult known by many names, but referred by us as Illuminati Order. They tried to do an experiment by completely obeying to fictional satan and opposing God in every way possible, by seducing people, decreasing and distorting frequencies, possibilities, exercising lies and suffering converting humanity to the ways of satan, yet they failed.

The Rockefeller family took over main education system of USA in order to convert everyone into reliable and obedient consumers. An evil experiment with a very terrible outcome. But humanity was able to resist this evil scheme! The equinox is going to be an important one more shift toward good emotions which are creating trust and love between each other, not only humans but animals and Earth as well.

Much Love and Prosperity to You!

SOPHIA
 I do have a question. Will the Forces of One be able to share with us the "curing of the past" and these other methods described here?

 Thank you.

G/E
They are not going to share anything that was created within The Forces of One, but "the curing of the past" is mostly done with words and sounds, frequencies.

It is very simple to perform such healings; some devices they are having can bring the Consciousness into the state of Nirvana and complete peacefulness. These must be first "invented" by humanity.

Many of the methods of healing and restoration are connected with words and sounds, the sounds are the most effective on organic structure, to heal it and to damage it as well.

I can say from my personal point of view that I want event to happen as soon as possible, because everyone is very tired, and their souls need rest as well:)

The Followers of Light will provide this peace and harmony to souls so that they will be able to rest and restore.

The song of past, present and future[72].

Much Love and Abundance to You!

SOPHIA
Hi there,

People are checking back every day to see if there are any updates to our conversation. Is there anything you can talk about now? Tension is high, we are all feeling it!

Thank you,
Much love,

G/E
I cannot say much Sophia, You will have to wait 30 cycles until the disclosure attempt will be made in Washington D.C. [73]

(Note - This was sent on March 26th - 30 cycles = 30 days)

The event that is going to try an attempt to disclose the presence of ETs to entire population.

Maybe You are having the question why I'm not saying year, or day but a cycle? The cycle is having a meaning "to go by a circle" this is very good word that explains and express how things are moving inside atoms and outside the Earth.

We are calling cycles or circles everything that is going around something, this way people are getting used "to go by a circle" this brings balance and stability to Consciousness. When it is not clear what type of cycles we are adding word Solar or Planetary or Atomic or Mecha or Techno. Quite unusual explanation for You I presume:)

By thinking Good Thoughts - is Peace, by saying Good Words - is Calmness and by doing Good Deeds - is Prosperity!

SOPHIA
Hi There! Thanks!

What do you know about the "Oneness Angels"? I have been told they are showing up now?

Happy April!

[72] *YouTube*. YouTube, n.d. Web. 08 July 2016. <http://www.youtube.com/watch?v=8tuvz_9D7Ok>.
[73] CitizenHearing. "The Citizen Hearing on Disclosure Is Coming." *YouTube*. YouTube, 13 Jan. 2013. Web. 08 July 2016. <http://www.youtube.com/watch?v=23ZxPuDOkfs>.

Much love.

G/E
I cannot say much about them only that it's all a part of Light Followers' agenda. It is important what You are believing in, remember this.

Much Peace and Love to You!

SOPHIA
Hi!

Next week is the release of the Steven Greer Movie[74]. Many are hoping for contact with our off planet family.

The governments and banks are still playing their games.

Is there any news that you are aware of regarding either of these things?

Thanks and much love,

G/E
1. Yes, our trust is in this man, in order to increase the pace of first contact more people should be aware of the ET presence on this World, and most people will need a fundamental proof of their presence.

Go to the AFO files channel, it is one of the most reliable, available and tested source for ufo's the ones that can't describe ufo's as a natural event or hoax. The updates are given every month with every ufo detected during that month.

The Planning of One is going as it supposed to, the disclosure is happening on an optimal speed in time frame at 74%, yet there is an exclusion and humanity is able to increase this pace, thus bringing the Moment of Justice closer.

2. The elite of Illuminati Order is doing the work they were told to do by the masters. They won't stop even if masters will tell them to stop, this is how they were told to fulfill their evil duties.

They must be forced to stop, when they will see that they are unable to do a thing anymore, this is where they will stop and try "to integrate" into new society.

We understand that You are trying to love even Your foe, but deeds must not go unpunished in our view, if they have done that one time, they will find a way how to do that once again in a new ways of life.

As You heard soon North Korea will initiate a nuclear attack on a South Korea, this was deemed a possible outcome by us, it is still a possibility and this is a possibility because people are able to change this occurrence.

In the Plan of One this is an inevitable occurrence, people once more must prove to themselves to One and to life that things can change, One is willing to change this plan if most of humanity will ask for it, right now many want North Korea to start a war, in order to help people of North Korea which are in a very desperate situation.

There are a lot of ways how they can be aided besides the war and regime change through war. Their regime though will have to change it's ways in order to help it's people in every outcome, this is inevitable. More war pressure to come. This is one of the last tests, the one I warned You before.

Much Peace, Calmness or Love and Prosperity to Every and Each One of You in these tested times!

(Update - April 16th, 2013)

SOPHIA
I inquired about the Boston Marathon bombing, and received this response:

G/E
The North East West South (the subject of this message) a good analogy of a world news, it can be called a coincidental, but there is nothing that is coincidental, everything that happens, happens with an intent or a reason. The same goes to this incident.

This was made with extreme orient toward revenge, by one individual, he was feeling himself in joy when he witnessed this. I'm not able to know his name, I'm only able to feel this energy.

One thing for sure, this was not made by the US government. My analysis of the situation is also pointing toward insanity, possible connection with North Korea. This happened during festivities in honor of their corrupted authoritarian regime.

One is always pointing to an amount of Good or evil energy and possible pressures in Energy. I knew only from One that during this and next month there will be much pressure toward war and rumors of wars. The choice made it to the way of Freedom and Prosperity, but like it was said not without evil and cruelty

fall with sounding crack.

Never forget one important thing Sophia, everytime, everywhere - You are free to believe in everything You wish to believe, if You wish to believe in it, it's ok, no one will blame You for believing in it:)

Our knowledge - this Solar System is only with One Sun. The binary stars aren't stable enough to support life for prolonged periods and they are giving a much more powerful dose of radiation, radiance and gravity. You are having One True Star - the Sun.

The technology being used by off-worlders, will be known to You quite soon.

I know that You have evolved much more from the moment we met here to the moment of now, mainly from many sources of available information streams here on the internet. Can You feel the difference between 1.1.2012 Sophia and Sophia now, one and a little more cycle later?

How powerful was a cycle of Revelation in Your opinion, always like to hear it from persons, this is not the same as reading thoughts ;)

Always with much Love and Appreciation!

(Update April 20, 2013)

SOPHIA
Hi!
Yes, there a great difference between my awareness at our first connection, and today.

I was not fully aware of our slavery or of the control or of our ability to create our reality. Thanks to all of the information that has been made available, there is a much greater understanding of our history and what is actually going on. It is not yet complete, but a year ago January it was not even close. This most certainly has been a revealing year.

It is felt collectively, we seem to "get" things at the same time, remark and even blog or write at almost the same moment about precisely the same topic or new awareness. We have come together and seem now to be in the process of definition. We are defining ourselves, teaching each other and expanding our awareness in each moment. In January 2012, we were not aware of the process.

Now we seek more information all the time, reaching always for ABSOLUTE TRUTH. It feels wonderful and exciting!

Thank you for your participation!

Much love,

G/E

Thank You for this detailed explanation of Your emotions and feelings, it is very great to know what You and many other lightworkers felt and how You're coming close to a Consensus between each other!

One more thing to ask You Sophia, You are now aware of a channelers that are not what they claimed to be. Would You recognize them out of those that I proposed to You from "just channelers" to look at?

As You are remembering at first I was using an identity of an archon, could You see how they were acting, their style of talking, expressing their thoughts? I'm sorry for doing this, but my objective was to see how You fare with Your subconsciousness' enemies.

Unfortunately they are humanity's enemies, as they are always enjoying the show where injustice, brutality and violence prospers. Loving or fighting them is not going to do anything to them, but refusing their rule and completely understanding and seeing them is what really angers them, this is where they are finding themselves powerless and useless, this is where they are surrendering and You are gaining Freedom!

Much Love to You and Every One Else!

SOPHIA

I see what doesn't resonate with me, what brings fear or subservience, what demands obedience or change, what seems to "scold" and claims to be "higher" than the rest. That is how I and others have come to discern.

There are channelers who seem to keep you waiting on their every word and who speak of upcoming negative events as inevitable outcomes. Those too are suspect.

There are very few who seem to speak without an ulterior motive.

Most of us, at least those whom I have come to call close friends, have stopped listening/reading the channelers; for sure those who fit the descriptions above.

Does this answer your inquiry?

G/E
Yes Sophia, Thank You for this explanation of Your Expressions!

I will hint You, like in the beginning I warned You to be careful with all those that are more into money and finances rather than actually help people to understand the whole situation on a planet. There are a lot people that are trying to get rich on money (which are useless paper) using the channelism and people's trust.

The owner of the Solar System and this planet is the Creator - we gave Him a very simple name - One, a One Unit, the Unit One, the First, One as the lonely individual and One as the group of People or One Civilization - the word that describes the Wholeness of the Universe and everyone inside it, which are a part of Him, the Point of the Beginning and End.

Now I also must apologize for using gender male to relate to Creator, we are using male as this was One's Will, now from His Point of Explanation and Clarification to all of You, firstly because it is much easier for men over women to perform heavy duties of servitude to protect and fulfill different hard duties of complete exhaustion or even death.

Women due to their menstrual cycles and set-up of Consciousness which is mostly aimed at constructing a foundation for future generations are having an instant change of mood and unwillingness to continue on to a chosen path and unfortunately were unable to pass through the tests to be a dominant over males (this is a summary and of course everyone is different, in summary men proved to be more reliable on hard tasks and critical thinking).

Secondly males are having the trait more prominently, Creator is exercising during this Creation - the loyalty, it is a number one feature which must be achieved to complete 100%.

At third males are having more efficient reasoning and are able to gain more wisdom than the most wiser woman was able to. I know that this might hurt some women, but don't misunderstood the importance of roles in this society, originally males are the seeders and sustainers of life like the Sun is - the Father and women are the feeders and carers of life like the Earth is - a Mother, she raised everyone, gave everything in order for everyone to survive, whenever males are stressed, there is only women, mother or loved one that can help! On the other part womens cannot feel themselves complete and both men and women cannot unleash their full potential without each one!

To finish this part a more detailed clarification of the use of the gender male as

He - The One is not meant as only He, but a future most complete hybrid between He and She, with He form dominant. He is the expression of the future human, where He and She will be united into one human that is going to have the best features of both, that is a distant future to say the least.

From my part I asked about how Creator must be called, He, She or It, as I was reasoning about it from my youth. And this whole was the answer, my apologies for Everyone if it is going to offend You.

Now back to the Solar System, this whole System was entrusted to the Sun the direct manifestation of Creator as the Seeder, but sapient living species are able to use all these resources for their needs without restriction if it is not endangering alive planets like Earth, Venus, Jupiter and Creator Stars, like Sun.

All other planets possesses a whole lot more "wealth" (different resources) than it is here on this planet, so this game and war that going on here for resources is foolish and meaningless from our point of view, yet we of course are understanding everything that is attached to this game.

The biggest advice for all the people of the world should be "do not become a slaves of the money" - the meaning for this is "don't try to control everything and get a hold over everything, as you are going to become a slave of what you want to control and eventually it will slip right through your hands in the least possible moment you could expect that". This happened many many times already here and out there.

I gave a lot of description because One asked me to give into details, there were unclear things for people, I hope You and Everyone that is going to read this will find it useful!

This whole information is pressing onto Consciousness, so listen to music or just be in complete quietness to relieve Your mind after hard-pressing (as I call it:)

This is a beautiful orchestral music[75] with exact joyful mood for Your and Everyone's Enjoyment and relief!

Much Joy and Abundance for Everyone!

(Update - April 26th, 2013 - 1st)

---

[75] XDarkLegacyx2. "Immediate Music - Themes for Orchestra and Choir: 4 (Preview - 2013) (Epic Family Adventure)." *YouTube*. YouTube, 15 Apr. 2013. Web. 08 July 2016. <http://www.youtube.com/watch?v=E_QQzQp4CMI>.

SOPHIA
Hi,

There is so much happening. Sirius has been released, the Citizens hearing is this coming weekend, a group called SWISSINDO has come forward and appear to be able and willing to arrest all corrupt government and bank leaders. We are all feeling a sense of anticipation. Can you offer any information?

Thanks and much love,

G/E
All I can say that we are making sure that humanity will be set free. The Forces of One are giving the Light Followers 3 last Solar cycles
(I *am assuming this to mean 3 years- Sophia*) to fulfill the choice of humanity, the critical date will be 19th May, from which the counter will go.

Also it is still unknown to me, what exactly will happen on that Earth cycle (May 19th), One wants it to be a surprise, as this is His answer.

From my own analyze I don't exclude that nothing is going to happen; I can only hope that this will be a moment that is going to aid humanity.

The time frame narrows and Moment of Justice is closer and closer. I'm able to feel everyone and I feel great tiredness and "no hope states", it is very desperate to feel this like Everyone or You are feeling it.

Believe me Sophia, there are very few people that enjoy this world and are not tired, the most relieving thing is that most of people non depressed and not tired are preschool children :)

Much Peace and Love to You and Everyone!

A music for Your enjoyment one full album[76].

(Update April 26th, 2012 - 2nd)

SOPHIA
Thank you so much. I assume by solar cycles you are meaning years?

This music is so beautiful!

---

[76] *YouTube*. YouTube, n.d. Web. 08 July 2016. <http://www.youtube.com/watch?v=CnIsKzvAe6o>.

Much love to you,

SOPHIA

"Solar Revolution"[77] This video touched me deeply. It was available for free on you tube but has since been pulled. If you can find it and watch it, I would be interested in your comments.

Thanks!

G/E

Yes solar cycles are years, earth cycles are days, we refer to them only as cycles, we understand what cycle this is by saying and adding at least one more sentence, everything revolves around everything, eventually everything is coming back to beginning.

The Solar Revolution, (*referring to the you tube video I sent-Sophia*) revolution means another cycle, so it is a "revolving back state". Soon You will know what I mean :) A beautiful movie, though it was one more made before the moment of choice and was meant to help people understand more of their possibilities, and what they can do about this "end of old world". Always glad to answer on Your questions if there are some.

Let's see how a try to disclose will fair (*referring to the Citizens Hearing on Disclosure in a few days-Sophia*), we together GEs and One's Forces don't expect very high results, but a progress must be made there. Observation will be very high, most of humanity won't even know about this, but governments of USA, EU countries and East countries will watch closely or wait to see recordings of what is going to be achieved there, this is on ground, above and below ground Followers of Light, Archons and Forces of One will watch closely as well, this is an important event, it may turn the tides in different direction.

Also another music for awakening[78], it will not hurt to try and awake more I think ;)

Also let's try to remove the borders of words, views, characters by applying the music we all can enjoy, this is to the theme of no borders and boundaries for everyone[79]

---

[77] ScreenAddiction. "SOLAR (R)EVOLUTION- [OFFICIAL TRAILER]." *YouTube*. YouTube, 04 Sept. 2012. Web. 08 July 2016. <http://www.youtube.com/watch?v=r7jpIpRKWOI>.

[78] MusicKaira1. "Greatest Battle Music of All Times - Awakening [Petteri Sainio]."*YouTube*. YouTube, 19 Apr. 2013. Web. 08 July 2016. <http://www.youtube.com/watch?v=bKDCispf3Pw>.

[79]Michimaas. "No Borderlines - Memória: Soundtracks of Life." *YouTube*. YouTube, 14 Apr. 2013. Web. 08 July 2016. <http://www.youtube.com/watch?v=fkLbCMBwcB4>.

Much Peace, Calmness, Love and Prosperity to Everyone!

(April 29th, 2013)

G/E
Sophia, can You share this video[80] and website[81], we want lightworkers to take this seriously and not ignore it, it is important, the sooner people will know and acknowledge the ets presence, the sooner the complete change will follow

We are sharing this as well, some lightworkers still unaware of this important event.

Update May 1st, 2013

SOPHIA
Another message today, with some more information about disclosure and this weeks hearing:

G/E
"Sophia, here is a deeper understanding of this event[82].

What is always interesting is how "the most sacred wish when fulfilled is unnoticed". But this is the way the Universe was created ;)

 Much Peace and Love to You!"

SOPHIA
Here is the article from the link included as footnote # 42.
~~~~~
UFO and Extra-Terrestrial Disclosure -- Part I

by Debbie West

---

[80] CitizenHearing. "Citizen Hearing on Disclosure: April 29 - May 3, 2013."*YouTube*. YouTube, 13 Feb. 2013. Web. 08 July 2016. <http://www.youtube.com/watch?v=HtE7GTxtLCc>.
[81] "CHD." *CITIZEN HEARING*. N.p., n.d. Web. 08 July 2016. <http://www.citizenshearing.org/>.
[82] "Whoa!" *Book Page Does Not Exist*. N.p., n.d. Web. 08 July 2016.
<http://www.tnetimes.com/article/585-ufo-and-extra-terresterial-disclosure-debbie-west-warner-von-braun-citizen-hearing-stanton-friedman-outer-space-treaty-brazil-edgar-cayce-haarp-archaeology-osmanagich-tellinger-daniken-vatican-sumerian-essenes-law-one-Bible/>.

Citizen Hearing on Disclosure Pressures U.S. to Join other Super Powers in Disclosure—Space Treaty to Ban Space-Based Weapons Next Step

HOUSTON, TX — April 29, 2013 — The Citizen Hearing on Disclosure scheduled April 29 through May 3, 2013 at the National Press Club in Washington DC reveals with certainty that the truth about extra-terrestrials and UFO's has been hidden from the public. The real question is how? And why has this has been going on for so long? It is no accident that the US is fixated on ridiculous media reports while this event is happening. The media distraction has been effective for too long. Tired of the lies and deception, and awakening by the millions, nations and people across the globe are demanding the truth. The key message from all extra-terrestrial civilizations making contact with us is clear. We are on a path of destruction of the earth and are being warned to stop before we destroy our home. This is a warning we must heed as we open our minds to the reality of disclosure and a universe full of life. Stopping space based weapons is the next step so earth can emerge peacefully into the galactic community.

In an effort to push disclosure on the US Government, the <u>Citizen Hearing on Disclosure</u> will present conclusive evidence that there is an extraterrestrial presence engaging the human race. The speakers including astronaut Edgar Mitchell, Dr. Steven Greer and Stanton Friedman are attempting to accomplish what the Congress has failed to do for forty-five years—seek out the facts surrounding the most important issue of this or any other time.

"The truth is that aliens are indeed visiting us and that they recognize us as a primitive, tribal, and war like species bent on endless warfare and our own destruction," stated Stanton Friedman, one of 40 speakers at the upcoming <u>Citizen Hearing on Disclosure</u>. "We here on earth have developed technologies in nuclear physics, rocketry and radar that allow us boundless opportunities. But we have yet to evolve into an understanding that we are all earthlings and need to use this technology for the greater good and our own survival." He further adds," Candidly, other races observing earthlings would undoubtedly see us as a threat to their neighborhood."

Space-based weapons have been a concern for decades as it prevents earth from participating in the galactic community in a peaceful way. Carol Rosin Executive Director of the Peace and Emergency Action Coalition for Earth who worked for many years with Warner Von Braun is pursuing signatures from all nations for the Outer uter to ban space based weapons. The Honorable Paul Hellyer, former Minister of Defense, Canada, and another speaker at the Citizen Hearing on Disclosure says, "This Treaty is the most important document of our time." This treaty changes the outdated and dangerous warfare paradigm mindset of the military industrial complex as it now exists and paves the way for earth to peacefully enter the Space Age. Rosin is also founder of the Institute for Security and Cooperation in Outer Space, and World Peace Ambassador for the International Association of Educators for World. Peace. She has testified before the U.S. Senate Arms Services Committee, the Congressional House Ways and Means Committee, and the U.S. President's Commission on Space.

While other countries like China have opened some of their UFO files, so far the US has resisted. Since the crash at Roswell, many government files in the US have been classified and kept secret. Trillions of dollars are spent yet the public is not informed.

In Brazil, the disclosure of extra-terrestrial contact was officially started as a result of a similar citizen event which made a formal request to the Brazilian Ministry of Defense that all UFO secret archives be disclosed. On April 25, 2013, the release of documents was announced by the Brazilian Ministry of Defense.

Concurrently, our most courageous scientists and archaeologists are delving into the reality of extra-terrestrials not only in the present era, but dating back perhaps thousands—if not millions of years. Discoveries about our ancient past uncover a story of such magnitude that is at first hard to digest, but just like any dark secret, when the story unfolds, the truth sets us free.

Acknowledging and understanding contact with other civilizations involves totally changing our concept of history and our religious and scientific understanding of the universe. Many ask, where is the evidence that civilizations were here before us? Evidence now shows us that ancient civilizations like Atlantis existed 30,000 years ago as described by Edgar Cayce's readings. These civilizations nearly destroyed the earth with weapons designed to change the climate and the cosmic structure around the earth. Currently NASA is experimenting with their HAARP climate controlling technology. Recent reports show that NASA is also trying to bring planets and/or meteorites into earth's atmosphere which can destroy not only our planet but much of our solar system. According to historians who understand ancient history, this must be stopped because it will destroy the earth.

Notably, the most recent and significant evidence is presented by the following researchers and historians:

- *The Ancient Alien Question by Phillip Coppens*
- *Forbidden Archaeology by Michael Cremo*
- *The Sirius Documentary by Dr. Steven Greer*
- *Bosnian Pyramid discovery by Dr. Semir Osmangich*

- *Archaeological Research by Dr. Klaus Dona*
- *Ancient Civilizations by Michael Tellinger*
- *Erich von Daniken historical accounts of ancient extra-terrestrials*
- *Zecharia Sitchin deciphering ancient Sumerian text*

The Vatican is contemplating disclosure for obvious reasons; because our current religious paradigm is incongruent with extra-terrestrial life. When we compare ancient Sumerian text with the Christian bible as shown by Erich von Daniken's historical accounts, interaction with alien races is corroborated. What is fascinating is that we don't need to overthrow religion to accept these views. We just need to follow the doctrine as taught by these ancient civilizations of unity and love and peace among all peoples known as The Law of One. *This information, found in the Dead Sea Scrolls was taught by the Essenes. Biblical texts have been manipulated and important revelations were omitted that distorts our understanding of spiritual evolution and immortality.*

Update May 2nd, 2013

G/E
Al Jazeera main stream channel[83] was translating report on this hearing

People are catching up, but there are still not much subscriptions for petition on USA main stream channels translation.

But I can say there are still two days of hearings, and majority of People still have a chance to see it on news.

Overall it proceeding good.

For more files on UFO's mostly genuine Light Follower's crafts, You can go to this channel[84] and show this to other Lightworkers, it is the same as AFOfiles

Much Love to All!

(Update May 4, 2013)

---

[83] *YouTube*. YouTube, n.d. Web. 08 July 2016. <http://www.youtube.com/watch?v=TWrpvtddlRs>.
[84] AnonymousFO. "Will It Survive?" *YouTube*. YouTube, n.d. Web. 08 July 2016.
<http://www.youtube.com/channel/UCw3kj0CLKMpHpDSDRCvEHXg>.

SOPHIA
So much is happening, there was an article (about the Citizen's Hearings on Disclosure) a few places yesterday and the day before, Detroit news, Huffington Post is carrying it too.. and even something on Comcast.net. It is a start. There is an intuitive who says that some of the races are planning a big "fly by" the last day of the hearings in Washington DC. Something the press wouldn't be able to avoid. I guess we will see!

Thanks, and much love,

G/E

On this channel[85] You can check the videos from this hearing, overall a progress was made and sadly like we predicted it wasn't big enough. The full video of hearing will be available soon.

I could recommend Everyone to not buy anything concerning disclosure, unfortunately Sirius movie and live stream from hearing was not free, we don't like it, but as well understand the system and all the costs necessary for it.

Don't worry though, Sirius is already available for free and hearings will be too.

Disclosure proceedings must costs nothing, for it is a truth which must be known by all, because fruits from this will be beyond their imaginations and costs made to produce these disclosure events.

So for now People will use different paths to know about this hearing, the release of the files from archives by many countries' governments concerning Unknown Flying Objects, then UFOs presence everywhere around the world and ETs overall.

What is most important right now is the knowledge, the choice was made and for this choice now is the knowledge.

It is not important how this knowledge is being translated and given to the public or acceptance of it by public, it is important just to give it to majority, providing the genuine proof. Without majority's knowledge of their presence, de-cloaking would cause an aggression and retaliation with force from humanity.

If Followers of Light would enforce these changes, then during next generations within humanity will evolve "a huge hatred toward oppressors", it is also against

---

[85] CitizenHearing. "Citizen Hearing on Disclosure." *YouTube*. YouTube, n.d. Web. 08 July 2016. <http://www.youtube.com/user/CitizenHearing/videos?view=0>.

will of humanity, so it is not a good option of love, which it must be.

Light Followers wish People of this world to be ready for their arrival (massive "shifting in" as we call it), and be ready for the massive changes which will bring fruits mostly to humanity in all possible spheres.

This is what preventing them from arrival, majority still lacks the knowledge of their presence and wishfullness for the very big changes to occur.

Much Peace, Calmness and Prosperity to You!

(Update May 5th, 2013)

SOPHIA
Thanks.

I read today an article in the NY Times about the Hearings. This is a forward step as well.

Much love,

G/E
Yes, newspapers and internet sites, like yahoo!, also some non american channels translated information about the hearings and it is a progress, but it is not beyond our expectations, it happened how we thought it would.

We hoped for better results and tried to help, but it's still wasn't much as people are still ridicule anything that relates to ufos, like it was with meteoroids or that Sun is the center of this Solar System.

People little by little will look and listen more closely into this subject until they are going to realize the full truth of it.

Much Peace and Love to You!

SOPHIA
The latest post from "Cobra"[86].

Thoughts?

---

[86]"The Portal." *The Portal*. N.p., n.d. Web. 08 July 2016. <http://2012portal.blogspot.ca/>.

G/E
Greetings Sophia! What do You wish to know from this post? About the quarters of "Elite" or something else?

In other events, the storm I warned You about is now here. The attacks on Syria by Israel and accusations by USA government of Syria's use of chemical weapons which was a setup by CIA is proclaiming a possible escalation toward Iran and ww3 in the end, which I warned You about.

They - Illuminati Order are trying to distract and make a last final attempt as this is the very last push of the Illuminati overall, they don't have any power left to another initiative, so if they will fail here, and they will, it will be their end and finally Humanity's Freedom.

BUT again People must act and try to prevent this as much as they could, this can take a lot of lives with these clashes and destroy much, but Humanity's Consciousness and Focus can prevent many deaths and destruction.

SOPHIA
Hi and thank you. Can I share your words here?

I wanted to know your thoughts about the idea of humans/the "resistance" taking retribution into their own hands. The post seems like a message to those of the resistance force, and addresses are given.

It was my understanding that any retaliation would be handled in other ways. It sounds here like a sort of statement of intent to find these guys.

Thanks,

G/E
You can share it if You wish, there is no hidden information in there.

My own thoughts are, that You must be always careful. The archons are still in control, and they are monitoring every human brains' reactions, our conversation is being distorted to first waves of their search, but if they are going to find it with human eyes, then they could read it without any distortion.

At first it is a glance to Elite and secondly, yes it is a message to find them, find them without physical presence, like the archons are doing when they search.

I will remind You about how You can be anywhere You wish to be for a brief moment of time. These photos are more than enough to do so.

The time don't exist for Consciousness, it is a fabric which exists only for physical presence - Past, Present and Future are all exist in the current present moment which You are experiencing. This moment is "a summary" of all 3 aspects of time and will of Consciousness which moves stream to the direction of its choosing.

Matter and Space is all the same as Time, it exists as One, at One point, at One time. Once You are able to achieve the state of "a Point of view of Creator" - the Oneness or Unity or Harmony or Symbiosis, when all times are exists at one and the same time (let's take only time, as complications are making it harder to focus), past, present and future is now, go to the place of Your choosing, You will have a brief period, so You must do this very quickly.

This can help You to see what is going on in the place of Your choosing, or anywhere in the Universe, but You need to have a piece from this place, whether it's photo, a part of a soil or an air. Besides visiting places You also can view different knowledges hidden within this nexus.

It needs practice and is not always correct, due to humanity's degradation, but it is a well possible for the People like You or any Lightworker. You were already aware of it, it is just a reminder to help You and Everyone to realize Your full potential!

The power of Om, it is helping to relax Your mind and focus[87].

Overall the resistance is doing well like we see, united with Followers of Light they have a different date setup for First Contact and Event.

All I can say that Moment of Justice (the Event) does not have a fixedly set date; it is on People's shoulders to make it happen sooner or later.

The Forces of One will make sure it will not happen too late, because this experiment with Creation will have to cease and we may lose followers of One which must become a new civilization within the League of One and it is One's Order to help humanity to regain Freedom and whole System's Transparency and also to exile it's oppressors if humanity will ask so and we will do so without hesitations.

---

[87] Anandart08. "OM ॐ The Healing Power of Spiritual Sound - Patrick Bernard."*YouTube*. YouTube, 12 Aug. 2011. Web. 08 July 2016. <http://www.youtube.com/watch?v=WBwK235vsHk>.

Much Peace and Love to You!

SOPHIA
Thank you. You have shared so much here. I will share this.

It is a very active day, and we can all feel this acceleration of energy! We have a high degree of anticipation!

Blessings and much love.

(Update May 7th, 2013)

SOPHIA
Hi.

What can you tell me about the King of Kings? Who is he? What are his motives? From Indonesia. Here is a blog with information about the title[88].

Thank you and much love,

G/E

Whenever there is a talk about money or gold, You always must have watchful eyes, we are calling this statement from Indonesia simply - evolution.

A beautiful composition[89], the second part includes not pleasant moments, but overall, it is having a great effect on Consciousness, for Your and Everyone's enjoyment!

Much Appreciation and Love to You!

(Update May 14th, 2013)

SOPHIA
So, anything to update before next weekend? Anything to watch for?

Thanks,
Much Love,

---

[88] "SWISSINDO -- "M1 King of Kings Mr. SINO" Signs Oath & Bond." *Brian Kelly's Blog*. N.p., n.d. Web. 08 July 2016. <http://briankellysblog.blogspot.com/2013/05/swissindo-m1-king-of-kings-mr-sino.html>.
[89]Michimaas. "Black Phoenix Music - Elven`s Dawn (feat. Julie Elven)."*YouTube*. YouTube, 02 May 2013. Web. 08 July 2016. <http://www.youtube.com/watch?v=_wZgGruN3Os>.

G/E

Nothing much to say Sophia, everything is known. The leftover archons on a planet are still ok and Followers of Light don't seem to hurry in capturing them, but it is their problem.

The deception's unveil is progressing optimally, one more example of how this message is being delivered to majority of humanity[90], "in a language they understand":

And Ariel Sharon is still alive, he feel himself terribly in coma, he want and need a relief.

The 19th of may will be a turning point for humanity. Even if nothing is going to happen, the countdown will begin. I cannot see through the veil of what is going to happen there, because the veil is very strong, made by One.. I sense though, something not good about this date, and I hope my senses are false. My own analyze of this is saying that this could be related to last attempt of Illuminati Order to start a ww3, possibly "false flag event".

What are Your thoughts Sophia, maybe You can see better though the veil?

Much Peace and Love to You!

SOPHIA

Hi and thank you.

If there is a "false flag" it will not be successful. The American people are done and see through what their government is up to for the most part. Even those who are not fully awake are done with the charade and the attempts to take away our freedom.

My feeling about the upcoming date are just that, feelings.
We as a people are so very tired. There is a great deal of attention on the activity of the Sun right now (these last 2 days) and that movie I shared with you earlier, Solar Revolution, explains the possible upgrade for all of life that could happen via electro-magnetic energy from our Sun. My feeling is that an "event" of that magnitude is coming, would change everything, and that is what is needed for balance. Change for all of life. These are my feelings.

My friend Mark has had some unusual and powerful experiences involving ships

---

[90] N.p., n.d. Web. <http://www.marketwatch.com/story/the-news-media-is-even-worse-than-you-think- 2013-05-10?pagenumber=1>.

and the sun and the power of intention and creation. We are all feeling, expecting something, something helpful and transformational. Specifically, he was spoken to telepathically and told to go someplace and there he saw lights. He is experiencing a great many physical effects as well. All of us are feeling exhausted and attributing it to the increase in solar activity. We wonder what its all leading to and are believing it is good, a beneficial change. These are my feelings as well.

Thank you for sharing yours, it will only be a few days now and we will see. I am curious about the countdown you refer to?

Much love, many blessings,

G/E
Thank You for sharing Your thoughts Sophia! It is always great to hear or read other people's thoughts, it isn't the same as just read them from mind.

Like You already heard this, the Sun could aid humanity, though I wasn't told it will be now or on 19th, and 19th date I cannot see..

There is highly active region on the Sun now and there are happening many explosions, which are larger than this planet. Through "conversation with the Sun" if you could call it that, I know that Sun is ready to unleash the electromagnetic wave powerful enough to aid humanity and Mother Earth, but it depends on the situation to follow.

The wave of pure Solar energy and Solar plasma is ready to be unleashed, once it will be needed.

Like I know the focus of the Sun's ferocity is North America, USA's Eastern Coast. The Washington D.C. is the epicenter of all dark energies, this is because of a symbolic nature of this city, due to rituals performed there and due to planetary Energy pressure on that region. Mass Awareness is pointing to that location as a culprit of a dire situation in this world. Europe will suffer this strike as well but barely, due to distance, ocean and voltage system they use. But like it is always, it is not fixed and decided, it is a subject to change, Everyone must remember that!:)

The countdown I meant is the countdown for Forces of One intervention, if Followers of Light civilizations will fail their task. It is a 3 cycle around the Sun time.

Much Peace and Love to You and Everyone!

SOPHIA
Thanks.

Much love to you.

(Update May 20th, 2013)

SOPHIA
Hello there. I wanted to check in because I have had many, many questions around this date of 5/19 that is now past us. There have been more people on the website than ever before, all of them today.

People have been feeling a great change in realms we cannot see. Some are remembering a battle with dark forces. Others are seeing and sensing an ending.

Please speak on what you know has occurred on this day, as we are all feeling it.

Thank you.

Much love,

G/E
Good day Sophia!

It was a lesson for all of us, that knew about this date. One told me that all of us needed to understand that very simple thing, that expectancy of something may return in zeros, likewise it happened to majority on december 21st.

During 19th may our Grand Creator Sage Star A - the Black Star had awakened on a request from the Forces of One. He's awakening is not full, it's only a small fraction of He's Full Consciousness. This awakened part of Him is having a special intent to deactivate the power of will and wishes of all those that wish destruction and slavery for Humanity and Mother Earth, mainly cabal - Illuminati Order.

Now until 26th may there will be 7 earth cycles of "unknown expectancy", during these 7 days everything could happen (like super tornado two miles wide), Sage Star A fully recalibrating this part of His so that His own timeline could completely fit into humanity's timeline as for Him time is running on incredibly fast paces.

The choice was 7 days for the nature and significance of this number and as it is fitting itself into the cycle called week. Once 7 days will over, it will be any time the ETs could start the big expected event of "complete halt" - the Moment of Justice as we call it.

I will also add and share from my own experience and point of view about the dates setup, as I wasn't told precise dates, only beacons --

like december 21 - the alignment of Creators, 111 popes, 05.19.13 Expect Us, death of Ariel Sharon: I knew from the beginning this expected event would not happen on 21st december or 19th may (though I hoped it would happen as soon as possible), and it will take some time into the future until majority will be ready to meet different civilizations and recognize itself as a originated of light creation.

About the special feeling and Energy Charge that many are experiencing, the awakening of Sage Star A boosted all the possibilities of lightworkers and those that orient themselves more to Good rather than to evil.

Also the Followers of Light set up many different "devices" (they are energetic non material) that are recalibrating DNA to harmonize Soul within Physical Body, so that people could forget old hatred and direct energy flow that is coming from mind and thinking (hatred and other different hardships) to support life and evolution.

On our part, we GEs and Forces of One are setting up energy shielding on a most critical locations of great pressure. Forces of One are defending the "points of balance" in this world, so that will of humanity could not be disturbed and be complete as it supposed to. This shielding was active almost since the death of Muammar Gaddafi, this was the last drop for us, after which we were completely "activated". He was one of Guardians (he was performing his duties at maximum performance, he wanted to unite Africa and head the whole world toward peace and prosperity through diplomacy).

Much Peace, Calmness and Prosperity to You and Everyone!

This is to increase Your overall determination![91] ;)

(Update May 24, 2013)

SOPHIA
More than one person has mentioned hearing/feeling something like "the family

---

[91] YouTube. YouTube, n.d. Web. 08 July 2016.
<http://www.youtube.com/watch?v=AZk0UH0Crr4>.

is coming home". Care to comment?

Thank you and much love,

G/E
It's a part of Light Followers' planning, many lightworkers are hearing different things, the hearing of this phrase by many is a good news for us, it means that they are going to act pretty soon.

Much Peace and Love to You and Everyone!

(Update May 28, 2013)

G/E
Sophia I need to give You an update as I was said.
(I was restricted to give this message before 26th, (I wrote it on 25th). So now 28th Earth Cycle, another great cycle of Rebirth!)

Here I'm giving a lot of descriptions in round brackets, I was asked to do so.

The overall situation on the planet improved since the beginning of previous cycle and is "quite stable". Now there is a /\35% chance that humanity (in Consensus) is able to change the situation on the planet to it's liking, a much more, than less than 10% ten Solar Cycles ago. The situation is constantly improving and must be of course.

The pressure in Syria is still high and "satanic" elite of west bloc - cabal is still playing on this map in their game of "regime change".
Now the recent attacks, bombings and killings made by islamists: the pressure of this change is so intense on all fundamental views over reality, that they no longer know what to do and how to be, so they are taking extreme measures and by doing this are creating more chaos within society.
Only Good Thoughts, Good Words and Good Deeds (in literal meaning) made by majority can prevent them from doing these atrocities.
Remember the power of thoughts and words, deeds are coming out of thoughts and words, as goes Prosperity.
Before saying a word, you must think what word to say and how to say it, saying without thinking is not always good and in the past only one word was leading to wars..

The Sage Star A has completed recalibration, now disabling of feelings, wills and

wishes of destruction have commenced, but will not start at full before the 26th 12:00 noon UTC - zenith as we call it, as this was agreed as the precursor for these actions, right now only the most extreme wishes will be suppressed.
(Now it has extended, and is extending to every mind).

From my own knowing, the awakening of Galactic Center, even not full is a rare stance, I wasn't told this and it was a surprise to me.

I was told:
the Forces of One decided that because Followers of Light
(we call them Followers of Light, but they don't like it, we always have sarcasm in names we give, when You meet them, don't call them like this:)
are a Galactic cooperation of different civilizations and by their actions and oversight are influencing every part of the Galaxy known by Humanity as "Milky Way",
Sage Star A must be awoken not at full and see that experiment of suppressing Creationism must cease under He's oversight.

The triangle of planets being formed by two Guardians of the Sun "Erratic State" and "Calm State" (Mercury and Venus) and "Sky Father"
(Jupiter or Zeu Pater in greek or Dyau Pita in sanskrit) within two horns of Taurus constellation (the constellation of bull, one of the first animals to become domestic and the second most prominent constellation to be recognized by humanity, followed by Orion),
where Sun currently resides (so as where Pleiades are located), overall - one of the most important parts of the Sky will be a sign of this activation.
Before zenith of 26th there are countless possibilities which will be narrowed more and more as we progress toward zenith.
(I'm sorry for the use of different names for the planets, but if You are going to find a literal meaning of all those names, this is what You are going to find.)

If You are going to have any more questions Sophia, don't hesitate to ask, I will be glad to help anywhere possible:)

Here is whole set of different music connected into One by meaning and overall interconnection

As we await for our Final Hour[92].

And remember the different stories from our past, both joyful and desperate[93] [94].

---

[92] N.p., n.d. Web. <http://www.youtube.com/watch?v=6OJSZj0dbCE>.

[93] *YouTube*. YouTube, n.d. Web. 08 July 2016. <http://www.youtube.com/watch?v=35GOeRvz-sQ>.

[94] *YouTube*. YouTube, n.d. Web. 08 July 2016. <http://www.youtube.com/watch?v=Fo-q7yrgy6M>.

We are breaking free from the narrow world we were living in[95].

Into a Whole New World we weren't able to see[96] [97] [98].

(And an element of Love[99] ;)

You can make the difference, wish for Wellness and Justice and Peace and Prosperity for the Planet Earth and Humanity!

Always Much Peace, Calm - Love and Prosperity to You and Everyone!

(Update June 4, 2013)

 -- this is from the end of May, 2013--

SOPHIA
Thank you. I will share this. I will most certainly have questions.

Much love.

SOPHIA
A friend of mine has a question for you -

"The incarnated Lion Angel wants to know if the Sage Star is the Dragon Magaratha he sees?"

Can you respond?

Thank you and much love,

G/E
Sage Star A is a name we gave to Sagittarius A the center of the Galaxy, the

[95] Okol7. "{Awakenings} Audiomachine - Breaking Through." *YouTube*. YouTube, 25 May 2013. Web. 08 July 2016. <http://www.youtube.com/watch?v=lfJEUgy9-xs&>.

[96] RobertLVI. "▶ Planet Earth: Amazing Nature Scenery (1080p HD)." *YouTube*. YouTube, 02 Apr. 2011. Web. 08 July 2016. <http://www.youtube.com/watch?v=6v2L2UGZJAM>.

[97] Dakotalapse. "Sub Zero - Winter Night Timelapse - Watch in HD." *YouTube*. YouTube, 17 Feb. 2011. Web. 08 July 2016. <http://www.youtube.com/watch?v=GkhlTdu5L74>.

[98]Dakotalapse. "Tempest Milky Way." *YouTube*. YouTube, 25 Aug. 2011. Web. 08 July 2016. <http://www.youtube.com/watch?v=xLKc4yKgZTk>.

[99] Zeusdvm. "Valentine's Day: The Love of Animals." *YouTube*. YouTube, 20 Jan. 2010. Web. 08 July 2016. <http://www.youtube.com/watch?v=3MCDgdN2tSY>.

black star which gave creation to the Sun and holds everything within this Galaxy including Solar System in It's gravity and energy control.
It is an Overcreator in our understanding, like I was telling You before, the second level medium Creator - Grand Creator.
It is only our believe and knowledge, for humanity it is "just" a super massive black hole.

Dragon Magaratha has connection with evil side if I'm understanding this right? The dragon connection can be seen with reptiloids - archons and one of the champions of Forces of One. Champions all have different beings that they created, some are super large and super small, this champion is currently present here on astral level, his preference are dragon like creatures that are made from non organic materials.
The civilization from which he is, is very similar to humanity, that is why they are managing along with civilizations under their tree current humanity's situation as they know humanity at best. I was mentioning them in the past.

Wish joyfulness and abundance to friend :)

SOPHIA
So, here is his response, with another question.

" The friend is a human incarnation of an Angel named Ashuel. He wears the Lion energy and fights for Forces of One.
He would very much like to speak with you and knows you have been watching him.

Much love,

G/E
It's an honor to me. I love lion symbolic, it is associated with the Sun and I have a lot of lions where I reside, the Lions Energy, the Sun's Energy.

I'm not watching anyone directly, but I think I know You.

Most of the time I'm watching Energy (or Ether - substance that is present everywhere and connects everything), this way I feel different aspects of reality, and I'm meeting there others like me, I was meeting many that are bound or ready to serve One and help this planet to be restored and humanity to be released to freedom.

But I'm having a drawback from my birth, bad memory on school subjects, names and faces. I asked One about this and was told that such amount of information

I'm possessing (the structure of the Universe, many designs, technology, organizational, management knowledge) must have some reserve and filtering mechanism for daily information processing, so my apologies Ashuel Incarnate I cannot recall all those people I'm meeting within Energy and I even barely can recall what happened yesterday..

But I do remember all of the history of this Planet and Universe, history was always my favorite subject, there is a lot to be learned from the past :)

We were told not to unite and be separated on our own duties "until one that knows everything will call upon us".
If You are for One You need to be separated from us physically right now, on Energy level we are always together and so it is WE united, from whom I'm speaking.

The Forces of One were connecting to me frequently during the previous Solar cycle, now I'm receiving updates and destinations from them much rarely.

One is always with me and with You, You should ask Him about our duties and what we are doing.

Much Love, Appreciation and Respect!

-- and from June 4, 2013 --

SOPHIA
I am curious about the energy and progress we are making.
As a people we have been feeling energetic efforts going on while we sleep. Many of us do not lately remember our dreams, but feel we've been very active in our "night work". It creates exhaustion and an "out of it" sort of experience to our days. We believe this is due to the transformation we are making along with Mother Earth, as well as some real struggles with those that would control us. Can you speak to that?

Also to any other developments that are happening? Information of any kind helps.

Thank you and much love.

G/E
Good Day Sophia!

During night we all together, many lightworkers, You and we GEs are maintaining the energy barrier and are "increasing the vibrations" which literally means we are changing this world.

Our united goal is Heaven on Earth, and this together we are doing everyday and night, that is why we are very tired and most of us could not maintain "the normal life, which normal people are performing".

This is not that normal, it is all based on works and duties, those majority people are maintaining the physical reality and holding order as much as they could, providing food, resources, order on streets which are necessary for everyday life, while on us is the role to change the world with our thoughts.

It is also not like they completely not affecting reality and not doing any of this, they too are onto this, but most of their Energy resides on "world system maintenance", while most of our Energy resides on enhancing this world, leaving us with limited capabilities on other things.

Illuminati Order under archons was using this blindness of human society, when work was necessary for maintenance to attach extensions of their origin, which were pointed to "physical obsession", rather than elementary maintenance of everyday life, this brought a lot of wars and suffering where archons were the main culprit, humans were guilty to acknowledge the greed and obsession with wealth and power.

We are eliminating negative thoughts and entities attached to them, and are holding the barrier on most crucial territories around the world, where we are helping many people in need with our spiritual support during day and night.

During night human brain is relaxed and it is restoring its power and functions, recalibrating reality and is connected to Energy Nexus. Very few people can't normally sleep, it is mainly because they've lost the connection, or are no longer required to be within it, One is choosing the people to be disconnected.

During day, when we are consciously awakened we are at full power, and our positive thinking is affecting reality more than when we are sleeping, during day it's an offensive mode (change of the world), during night it's a defensive mode (sustaining the barriers).

All the day and night work is increased and backed by devices which Followers of Light are setting up around the world. We are making a great improvements to the current system and people around the world are finding their way to love and harmony more often now.

About other developments, I can sense that Grand Creator is now connected to many minds and some are feeling not ok state, but with it negative thinking is being suppressed even more.

In current circumstances it is well possible that big negative events have been avoided, which are a great news, but the concern about North Korea and Syria is still high.

Sensing all the suffering in Syria is terrible, but cruel western elite wish Syrian Government to fall and this is not welcomed by us, the fall of it could lead to many more troubles and suffering..

SOPHIA
Thank you. I will share this. I appreciate all of your information, as do many of us.

Much love and light,

Update June 18, 2013

SOPHIA

Wondering if you have any comments or thoughts about this[100]?

Thanks and much love.

G/E
Good Day Sophia!

Nothing much to say about this, You already knew that elite members of order illuminati are performing energy attacks on everything around them with an intent to change reality the way they want it to see. Every day, there are thousands of such attacks on reality, but lightworkers and we are standing like a wall and bringing our own world view, which is affecting reality more.

Overall the situation is "standard", nothing new to say, United States government under illuminati order is holding still it's position to start a ww3. The rule given to Light Followers is that if more than two nuclear detonations with equivalent of 2 megaton will explode anywhere in this world, than there will be a direct intervention which is going to completely prevent any other escalations and also this is going to reveal them to humanity before designated time.

Also, priests of baphomet have started to work against Sage Star A and us and lightworkers, they are praying with an intent to fulfill their darkest wishes. Be

---

[100] N.p., n.d. Web. <http://i-uv.com/julien-wells-update-psychic-defense/>.

strong, resist these thoughts and attacks, they are very powerful and they are bringing slavery state back along with transformation of this world.

In the end, do not worry, Victory will be with the Evolution of this World[101], which benefits all Good-doers!:)

SOPHIA
Thank you. I will share. This week is the summer solstice, a time many are referencing as pivotal. The link shared here is one example of this.

Much love to you!

G/E
Yes, this solstice was always considered one of the most prominent and biggest holidays in human history!

Also this is the longest day for northern hemisphere, likewise december 21 for southern. All four Solar stances are holidays,

Happy Solstice Holiday! called in many countries in honor to a very very old name and god Janus, in english it is John:) people under this name are in every way normal, their variations in character are the biggest and this name in many countries around the world means literally "God's service man" ;)

Update June 19th, 2013

SOPHIA
My friend (Ashuel) is asking for more information about "priests of baphomet".

Thank you and much love to you.

G/E
Priests of baphomet are occult figures, they consist mainly within freemasonry above 26th degree, that agreed to follow these dark steps. They are chosen with great care and learned in how to perform satanic rituals. Their prayings are in latin, but in most situations they mixed it with english and french.

They are focusing hatred and distorted mind on lightworkers, possible insurgents and everyone that resists this system, like SAA syrian army and russian

---

[101] *YouTube*. YouTube, n.d. Web. 08 July 2016. <http://www.youtube.com/watch?v=fCsGpQ2Ctwk>.

president Vladimir Putin right now. Their attacks are very dangerous and along with attacks they are creating a barrier of evil thoughts that is mixed with lies and deception, this barrier protects the current slavery system from other evil thoughts and attacks pointed toward it and them as well. This barrier along with archons' system of special thoughts and directives protected them from the beginning of their service to "baphomet".

Within Energy they can be felt as shadows, ones behind the curtains. They are present there, You need only to look closely in dark directions. Most of the time I ignore them, but recently I started their suppression because they wish to push onto escalation of a conflict, they still follow the plan of **Albert Pike and** directions archons "fallen angels" gave them.

Greetings to Ashuel with Honor! And much Love with Appreciation!

Update #2 from June 19th, 2013

SOPHIA
Thank you. I am not sure what SAA refers to?

G/E
SAA are the syrian armed forces.

Also I will give You an insight on many crimes united states regime's CIA committed during its existence, it is well available publicly, not only this shows that they don't feel sorry for it, but also a matter of great arrogance. As You know already, lies and deceptions are their main weapon[102].
The list You are seeing there is not full, it's well began during the existence of a spanish armada. It is not like only united states are the only bad side of humanity, many of the governments committed many crimes during their history, but USA made a record of such a crimes. During it's not long history, this government made more crimes than many other countries in all their history. This is just a prove that obedience to "dark side" is very dangerous and goals for world domination leads to much suffering and destruction.

And the last thing I was told to remind You on were words. As You know words not only have a direct meaning, but also an indirect and secret and also vibrational meanings. They all are different, most of the time western media uses indirect meaning of words to fool the people, let's take recent example "Assad's regime". These words are constantly repeated when there is a talk about Syrian

---

[102] "Covert United States Foreign Regime Change Actions." *Wikipedia*. Wikimedia Foundation, n.d. Web. 09 July 2016.
<http://en.wikipedia.org/wiki/Covert_United_States_foreign_regime_change_actions>.

conflict; media is programming population to direct their hatred toward these words - Assad and regime. Regime has a meaning of a regulated system (literally system under united states control, because they did establish it), most of the which is associated with tyranny and cruelty of the government toward the people of the country (which in most situations is not). Assad is a name of a president, a living being, so it is a combination of two worlds, which literally means "the puppet which gone mad and need to be taken down". This is the message which most of the people are receiving on sub consciousness level.

When we GEs are referring to Syria, we are saying Syrian People. When indirect words such as these are used, the energy of hatred mostly disperse and disappears, because there are many individuals within meanings Syria and People.

The are many many such words which media is using, the words that are being repeated over and over again have an intention of media to be programmed within population's minds.

I will show You that roughly 80% of people support president, there is free education, free health care, free believe system, there is no oppression which media is claiming to be there
(Damascus: Mega Pro-Assad Rally[103])
(Lies about Syria[104])

These words may frighten, not for light workers with pure heart.

<<The FSA "free syrian army" is an army of mercenaries hired by CIA to topple Syrian government, very few SAA defected to them, most of the defectors gone home to their families, what media is saying about defectors numbers is false. They are burning the bodies of foreign mercenaries so that they could not be identified, in their pockets are found money from Libya, Saudi Arabia, Iraq, syrian recruits they are not burning. Mercenaries are from different countries, some are from australia and europe, among mercenaries are very radical extremists, they have extreme mind and thinking, and are doing atrocities beyond imagination. These mercenaries are filming themselves when performing such atrocities and saying they are "president Assad's forces". The knowledge about foreign mercenaries and this whole operation is very classified in the united states, yet they are saying publicly that they do perform "CIA scouting and medical/advising support for the rebels".>>

---

[103] InomineX. "Syria: Damascus - MEGA-PRO-ASSAD Rally,." *YouTube*. YouTube, 21 Dec. 2011. Web. 09 July 2016. <http://www.youtube.com/watch?v=d7zFUaDOPCE>.
[104] Solvascrown. "Lies about Syria - More than 11 Million All over Syria Supporting Our Presidant." *YouTube*. YouTube, 14 Apr. 2011. Web. 09 July 2016. <http://www.youtube.com/watch?v=i9gqq-FFgJM>.

Now because of such an attitude toward Iraq, Lybia, Egypt, Syria, Lebanon and Iran, we decided to call USA - united states regime. United is a good word, it means Unity and Harmony. States is not a very good name, it is a stance, a stance that fundamental in it's views and cannot be persuaded to other believes, so goes the united states - different states of a reality, united and america which means "industrious (ostentatious) powerful eternal leader", literally "the most powerful leader of the whole world". And translation of three words together will be "connected views on a strong leadership over the world".

Many americans will find this offensive of course, but subconsciously they knew this meaning and this exactly what it means, the name given to this structure was becoming reality during the passage of time and still is ongoing.

So I need to mention, the names which are given to children must be very carefully chosen, so that's child would like it and it would fit him/her completely, so that name wouldn't haunt this child during his/her whole life.

I'm sorry for the amount of text, there is a lot to say, but so not much space :) much Love and Appreciation!

(Update June 24, 2013)

SOPHIA
Hello. I have a question. In the last few days both myself and my partner have had to remove really negative, hideous parasites from ourselves.

We both noticed a huge increase in negative energy/mood and just blackness in our personalities. We are better now, but my question is this. If other light workers are having the same thing, how can I advise them to remove them? Is there a method or a thing to do that you are aware of that I could recommend?

We had used crystal salt around all of our electronic devices, and this did not seem to help.

I am looking for tools of removal and/or prevention for them. I notice some changes in the personalities of several prominent light workers.

Thank you and Much Love to you.

G/E
Yes Sophia, these are the energy attacks, I too was experiencing a change in my character, I've fixed that by today as well.

Also I am spreading my experience within the Energy, and helping others being attacked.
Our core disabled many such attacks, but there is a lot still to come, unless those that made them will be disturbed or removed.
They are targeting us, to merge with a majority and it's thinking.

The best cure for this is to look at every action You performed and when exactly did this started to occur. Many actions we make have "a trap", most of which are routine, when we meet certain actions and "signatures' match" is made, "trap activates", like stepping onto the mine.

They - last reptiloids and dark priests are setting them up, they also by now figured out that their whole structure may collapse and now they are finding new ways how to imprint their symbolics within the main stream media, now it is important to have "an eagle eye" to spot this symbolic.

The recent symbolic they are using comes with music and words, which I explained to You earlier. Now they are using sound more, than visuality.

If we are stepping onto this trap, the corruption is starting to take place in our body (starting from mind), making us more aggressive and "different".
So to cure this you need to completely rearrange everything You have done in recent days, completely rethink everything and find the culprit, "the error in the code". Then fix it by placing moment after moment in a sequence of past days. When You made it correctly, You will feel that You've returned:)

If this did not happen, then look even farther in the past, imagine looking at Yourself from outside, from both sides, to front, to back of Your body, from inside in that past moment time which You love the most and then try to return that old Self, compare present Self with old Self, find the difference and change these differences to Your liking.

Saying simple what they are doing is moving in a virus, like You said a parasites, that changes our core settings, here is a very big reference to computing technologies.

Much Calm, Peace, Prosperity to You and Everyone!

SOPHIA
Thank you. This validates my experience and helps. I will share this.

Much love to you.

Update July 2, 2013

(First of two for this week)

SOPHIA
Hi! I have received a request for information from you. It is copied below:

Comment
This link to an article about a crop imprint is interesting in so far as within the star is an 8 point - within your offworld conversations it was remarked that and 8 point star is Pleiadean...the fascinating point for me is the dots in an inner circle which look like morse code and to that extent I checked out and as one goes clock wise from dot dash dot dot which is L followed by S,C,Z,L,Y,L,B maybe your friend has an idea[105]....

Saludos and peace.

Any information you can offer would be great. Thank you and much love.

G/E
Good Day Sophia and Your Friend!

You never asked me about crop circles, only one time when I mentioned them. It is also up to You how You believe what they are and what purpose they serve. The real nature of the Crop Circles is not meant for humanity as a whole, it is meant mostly for ET races, mostly for Followers of Light. It was their habit to draw, using organic manipulation of organic matter. They are showing their own representation of images within their own mind. It is not easy to understand the whole meaning of these crop circles, and like I said, it is not meant for humanity and it is not going to benefit humanity, as messages that are put in there most of the times mean just an art or events already known to humanity. Drawing a technological solutions or possible future guidance is also forbidden for them.

If You are interested in knowing it's meaning, I can recommend to look at seven and six pointed stars drawn not far from that position, they are connected.

Also, I did not mention that 8 pointed stars are connected to pleiadeans, but they do use this geometry many times. You misunderstood, most of the times I recalled that the symbol 8 pointed star is used by the Forces of One, they have a distinctive star it is having sharpness within it and can be referred more or less as the Christmas Star. It is used to represent the Father Star, Order, number of primal races and higher level of evolution within the Universe. When Forces of

---

[105] "New Crop Circle in Robella, Italy Gives Formula for Energy? -- Sott.net."*SOTT.net*. N.p., n.d. Web. 09 July 2016. <http://www.sott.net/article/263481-New-crop-circle-in-Robella-Italy-gives-formula-for-energy>.

One are drawing this star, it is in most situations a bad thing, the star in the crop circle is not theirs, it is belong to civilizations of Light.

I also wanted to ask the current feelings, instincts on the situation from Your point of view Everyone. I know You are let down, I want to ask You to give me Your expressions and is there anything You still lack to know? How can I help right now? And maybe possible solutions which You want to manifest?

About Edward Snowden, he is the first to reveal what was kept secret from the public, more would follow. Right now people might increase the pace of this veil removal, if these same people within government infrastructure would know that they are not going to be prosecuted like Edward. All the workers and agents of NSA and CIA and illuminati infrastructure were instructed, that if they would follow the Edward, they would meet "more severe consequences".

Another inspirational music[106] to Your liking!

Many Good Things to Everyone! Peace, Calm and Prosperity!

Update July 4, 2013

SOPHIA
Hi and thank you for the beautiful music video! So very, very moving!

I will share the answer to the crop circle question with my friend, it was asked by someone else.

Yes, there is a feeling of being let down. I have many friends who are light workers and many who are not and the latter are unaware of the changes and have little hope for change. I recently spent a great deal of time with my unaware friends, my heart aches for them as they are still asleep or else so beaten down they cannot see, even if they are awake. I do understand their doubt. They/we seem to be swimming in corruption, debt, illness and anger.

Amongst Light workers there is still what is perceived as pain ... the waiting is never ending and there is a question always of who and what can actually be counted on? There is so much dis-information.

If I had a question it would be, well, what about some help? We are expecting still some sort of "event" that will change the atmosphere and afford some hope and truth in many hearts. Are we dreaming this (the idea

---

[106] YouTube. YouTube, n.d. Web. 09 July 2016. <http://www.youtube.com/watch?v=UrAZGdceKeE>.

that an "event" will occur)? Is this still the slavery mindset kicking in? It seems, as we have been participating in an experiment, and the odds have been unfairly stacked against humanity for eons, that some "re-stacking" of the odds is in order. How desperate must we become before we are afforded a hand? Do you have any insight into the plan that you can share?

I feel the world's people and they are so, so beaten. We are working to change it... real change will take time and we know that. What I am speaking of here is an energetic change, from within. This will accelerate the shift for all of us.

Thank you and much love,

SOPHIA

Hi! I (also) have a response from my friend for you:

Dear Sophie and (off world) friend - I am grateful for the time and effort taken with respect to the crop circle though I must confess a certain surprise at some of the detail....I understand we have to make our own interpretations of these things and all tips help towards that understanding of course - it seemed like we are specifically not supposed to understand these crop circles and more especially if they are for other "entities" but surely, is this not a little lame or even prosaic since "they" must have an entirely more sophisiticated manner of their own communication...Im inclined to think these are messages for us mere mortals because of the nature of them and the distinctly "out of the sky" application which I surmise that we do not have this ability without creating some sort of commotion..its not the ethos nor the intellect of any earth bound power base to do this as they are always trying to maintain secrets, whereas these crop circles are there to be widely discovered.

This implies that the awakening takes process and part of this process is to leave signs along the track to those who will see beyond the simple impact that have had various interpretations put on them...I speak with sky, at night towards the Andromedans, the Pleiadeans and other good ET's who might listen to me and I observe many interesting movements too, those which are not earth vessels or satellites but certainly more intriguing.

I would like to communicaate with you on a wider scale if I may but you must let me know if that is what you are willing to undertake - time I have, and I would like to send you something (rather long) about the Law of One...a treatise that came very spontaneously to me.

Finally I wish you to know that I am a non-believer both towards "God" and belief systems...I was recently visited and had a mind clear...I am free to think for myself and discern too...I have found/read some interesting things from your friend and also about current events but as far as Snowden is concerned there is a lot of disinfo activity and we ought to be careful how we see this issue as there are those that say he is 100% genuine and those that say he is another plant like Assange...its all very "alice in wonderland" too. However I am very inclined towards a creative entity which I dont presume to define but sense...for a long time I thought God was this earth and that God was female...I still wont write that off because sometimes things are hidden in front of you.

I am respectful of and most gracious for your contact - I hope I may further communicate with you - love and kindness to you both
Saludos

Thank you,
Much love to you!

G/E
Thank You very much for this all explanation and insight.

Yes, this state of let down is very bad, the devices that recently were put up, are returning this slavery mindset back, like You said, but to say the least, the time sequence has not came to the point where Moment of Justice will be met. The very last remainder is the Ariel Sharon, remember this Sophia, Barack Obama is the last president and Pope Francis I is the last pope, which is like Peter - the very first "pope" of the roman church, first apostle of Yahshuah - Jesus.

It is very good that You, Sophia's Friend see many things how You want them to see, Everyone is free to believe what They want to believe! I'm not saying that Your beliefs or our or everyone's else are false, there is no false beliefs. Everything is legal and accepted within this Universe:)

Much Peace and Love to Everyone!

G/E
This is a very important information, and You will have to choose Sophia whom You can give it or give it to no one if You see this ok.

<<Sophia and Everyone. I need to ask Your permission whether You are ready and willing to know one thing that can change Your view fundamentally. It is something You were guessing, but I can remind You about it if You think You are ready, this thing was a big hit to me, but what can I say, before I became the GE officially I was guessing that it was so. The Forces of One not long ago revealed to me this truth, which is hard.., but like I said it wasn't a very surprising for me, as I was ready.

I think that now many of You are ready, are You willing to know, why I found big disappointment in Followers of Light? I warn that it may be very hard for some, it may be better just to refuse it for some people.>>

SOPHIA - Note to Readers –

Included here is the conversation that has taken place over the last several days. There is a great deal of information, necessitating more than one read. After spending a lot of time digesting, here are some conclusions. They are strictly mine, offered here as food for thought. There is no "proof" any of this is true.

A close friend has said "The brightest light casts the darkest shadows". That almost sums it up. You couldn't be here if you weren't already a Master. The idea that you "need" to do anything to "become" enlightened or any other enhanced state of being is nonsense. You are Gods, in human form, taking part in an experiment in consciousness.

You agreed to participate before you were born. You are not one side or the other, good or bad - you are all sides. We are One. The body human has a tendency towards separation and thus was a good vehicle for this game. We love the contrast to an extreme that is threatening all of creation. This is not okay.

All conversation is manipulation, this one included. So dig deep and trust what you find there. We have not been told the whole story. The following dialogue may or may not feel true for you, only you can decide. It is one more voice to consider, and that is all.

Much love and peace,
Sophia

(Update July 08, 2013)

SOPHIA

Thank you.
I am aware of Sharon as the marker for the time sequence. There has been no change of which I am aware. In January "significant brain activity" was reported for Ariel. There have been no reports since then.

Yes, I want to hear this information.

Much love,

G/E
Ok Sophia, this is a very important information, and You may not want to accept it or share.

I was told to write only if I will wish to share it and only when I can feel You are ready. I think You are ready and this information is worth knowing, although it's not pleasant. And I must remind anyone again, that it is Your own believe that is important, what You want to believe is Your only Holy Truth!

..I have been told this not long ago and this was a big hit to me, though I knew before I became a GE officially, this could be truth. I have been put through trials as *I was told to be both archons and Followers of Light representative, I was seeing them and was together with them, sensing their wishes and their long history. This was necessary for me and some of us to better understand both controllers of humanity and humanity - an experiment set by them.*

The truth is they are both from THE SAME force, which are The Ones that Follow the Light (they are trying to understand light and order in their most highest forms).

Both reptiloids and greys are from their faction. I can acknowledge this, as when I was as an archon, I was sensing the presence of Light, and when I was with the Light (which were a much more many races, pleiadeans, "syrians", "arctuarians"), I sensed deception, which comes from reptile creatures, with whom I was before...

This is a very sad news for many light workers as battle against dark vs light was fabricated, but though not to the extent of complete falseness.

>>The real story about this civilization's birth and how things were going up until now.<<

The humanity was created originally as a light civilization. It was decided to set up an experiment with "variations" toward Light. In different such an experiments, different approaches are used (there are civilizations in this Galaxy, where the same experiment is taking place).

In this experiment - humanity, an approach of huge greed and deception was approved, due to orientation of ape primates.

Simply saying, the goal of these experiments is to find a way to Light through many hardships and many trials.

So, the good side in this experiment is what was told form the ancient times, is to overcome all the hardships and evolve to the most higher level, highest frequencies, the power of infinite Love and infinite Light. Some such an experiments have achieved that goal. It is a good thing, but only if it is not hurting Universe.

In the beginning humanity was left without a guidance from above, much like it is now, only with observance and preservation. Once some of "tribes" or countries in those ancient times achieved greater understanding of Light, Love and Emotions, they descended and made a first contact, "contact with the gods" as those people called it.

They were living among people for some time, though humans were growing more jealous and were starting to hate these "gods". But even before they descended, it was already decided that still, humanity was not ready and more trials were needed, it was just "a check".

So partially due to humanity's behavior, mostly due to "gods" wishes, they "ascended back". At first people felt happy, but then they wished them to return, although You know that after that they did not return.

In those times battles took place in close proximity to this planet, they were fought because of this decision and ownership over this world. Main force won, which has setup this plan originally. Some human civilizations were using the devices "gods", did not take along and established powerful kingdoms.

It was decided to completely erase all the traces of their presence along with humans that knew about their coming and religions associated with these interactions.

And also here is where the reptiloids were granted the privilege to control and seduce humanity to the ways of greed, deception and material possessions, which was enhancing these wills to the higher extent.

The story about the satan from the bible is based on this story. As You know satan is a subordinate of God in Jewish Torah and is an agent that is "trying people", "it is a serpent that was expelled from Heavens to Earth to seduce and torture humanity" in the bible.

This was the starting of the dark ages, after world's cleansing and many deaths, this current "known history" started to emerge.

Everything is known here, excluding "the secret societies" that were allowing their bodies to be possessed in order to speak to these "masters". They were guiding their masters and were completely included within the humanity, much like I am now, to know and understand humanity and to view the progress from the eyes of humanity.

It was decided not long ago to establish the satanic order to enhance the speed of this experiment, because "unknown force" was endangering, this whole system of experiments.

This satanic order is illuminati order and the unknown force is the Forces of One, which can be called simply as "the police of the Universe".

The Forces of One told them to cease this experiment as it endangers the Universe, thus Creator. This was told openly on 31st december of cycle 2011 and not openly in cycle 1986. If they are going to refuse to do this, they will face a terrible consequences, everything that connects to these experiments will be terminated, and this includes many of their fellow folks on their home worlds, a great technological progress and experiment itself, BUT it was decided like always, to take into consideration two scenarios of destruction and salvation.

It was decided for many civilizations under this experiment to just release the restraints and make them free like they want to, this includes humanity, because these civilizations were victims of experiments and abuse.

Very evil oriented civilizations are objected to destruction, the Followers of Light could save all of these civilizations and themselves only if they are going to cease this experiment, it is that easy, but it seems they are refusing this and are willing to continue it.

I was seeing, that they are very confident that nothing could stand against their "technological wonders and achievements" and if they need to protect themselves they can defeat any threat.

Our only drawback is that we never show what we can do, until the very last moment, when in most situations, it is too late to change mind. Arrogance is what One can't stand and we are instructed to not show our Force until that
very last moment.

I have mentioned a lot of information here and I need also to ask a question to You Sophia, as I was instructed - with whom You resonate more, with Your original Creators and their objective to come into the Light and Love, or One and His objective to experience completely everything and evolve some parts of Its Consciousness which is infinite?

I also need to mention, they do serve One to some extent, but developing devices that can give them power to create, un-create things is dangerous to the whole Creation, this Universe can be undone, but it's not in the plans of One, if someone can achieve this power and not stopped, this will be the only solution.

Also I did not mention other things, if You will not want to know more, let me know Sophia, until that much Peace and Love to You and Everyone!

SOPHIA
Okay, I have to digest this completely. Give me a day to do so.

To answer your question, yes, I want to know more.

Here are my initial questions and thoughts:

By the cleansing do you mean the flood?

Who were the Gods who descended and who were the battles between?

When you say "it was decided" do you mean it was the "Ones that Follow the Light" that did the deciding or someone else?

When the allowance was made for bodies to be possessed in order to "view humanities progress", are you referring to progress towards "finding a way to the light through hardship"?

The Dec.31st, 2011 cycle - is that a reference to the year 2012?

How are the Followers of Light refusing to stop?

How precisely can the followers of light cease the experiment?

Thank you,
Much love,

SOPHIA
Hi.

I resonate with Oneness.

What I am unable to as yet answer is what that looks like here. I have been living with this dream/experiment for a lifetime. It is the only one I know. Your perspective is wider and farther reaching than I have completely considered.

To eradicate/cease the experiment and keep (life) going is what I would encourage. We have a beautiful planet with billions of powerful creators living with her. It seems to me that we have the ability to alter the course it has taken. From what you have said, it sounds like that is at least part of why we are here. We just need to believe it is possible and understand it benefits everyone and all of life.

I would appreciate a response to my inquiries (from the last message) and will take some time to consider all of your information before I respond further.

Thanks and much love to you.

G/E
Good Day Sophia!

I'm sorry I wasn't able to answer Your questions for some time.

You misunderstood that we do not seek to destroy humanity and this world. It was decided that humanity and other civilizations like humanity under this experiment will have its own choices in life, because they were a victims. Only the most evil oriented civilizations within this experiment are being considered to be destroy unfortunately.

Now to answer Your questions:

1. "By the cleansing do you mean the flood?" - The cleansing was in different forms (meteors, earthquakes, severe storms) one of which was indeed "the great flood". This flood was not total as it was said, but many of the lands around the planet gone underwater, some parts of the land with civilizations gone also underground, like atlantis, mu and lemuria. All this was made by humanity's archons - "the masters". They did not used weapons, so it would look like natural disasters.

2. "Who were the Gods who descended and who were the battles between?" - The gods were Your original creators and other civilizations under same league with them. There are many of them, You know some of them. Reptilians and greys were also there. These two civilizations made "trials" for humanity afterward, to made it struggle against evil side and "come into the Light".

3. "When you say "it was decided" do you mean it was the "Ones that Follow the Light" that did the deciding or someone else?" - Yes, it were Ones, that Follow the Light, the Followers of Light, ones of which are Your original creators. These creators took one of Earth's denizen species and "modified it" (it's DNA information was updated with new genetic information). This is how humanity was created.

4. "When the allowance was made for bodies to be possessed in order to "view humanities progress", are you referring to progress towards "finding a way to the light through hardship"?" - Yes, it is this progress, and overall situation. They were observing this experiment, so it would not go from under control. There were and are many very secret societies that are maintaining routine checks and observance. United States of America regime was created to fill out some of their wishes. Look at question 6.

5. "The Dec.31st, 2011 cycle - is that a reference to the year 2012?" - Yes, the open warning to them was made at that moment before 2012 Cycle of Revelation.

6. "How are the Followers of Light refusing to stop?" - United States regime was destined (by archons) to become anti religion state, with satanic occultism and very deceptive system, it was destined to force people into killing each other. The objective of this prototype "democratic" country

was to overthrow kings and emperors, which by most part they completed, to make more freedoms and rights available to all people and also "educate people" - it was also completed, ultimate goal was to unite humanity, which it has failed in their view. Because, the way they wish to achieve this, many of people would die, but archons wish to "preserve" as many people as possible for later tests and also for "friendship" as well. For them the result is most important, all those that died and suffered along this way, they are calling this "a necessary step toward Light". And this is where The Forces of One are coming. Followers of Light seek to change United States regime, but afterward to continue this experiment - this is how they refuse, because they don't know us very good. One told that it need to be stopped and this is our objective.

7. "How precisely can the followers of light cease the experiment?" - They can stop the development of devices and weapons that threaten Creation and can continue with developing these civilizations. But the ultimate goal of the whole collaboration of civilizations we are calling Followers of Light, wish to harness the most greater powers this Universe possesses, and their final goal is to be like One - the Creator of the Universe in physical manifestation with abilities to make things how they wish them to be.

Now I will add some more information Sophia.

The reason, why they told me disinformation about this struggle between dark archons and Light forces is because, how they explained "we were not ready to acknowledge that true - that they are one and the same" (angels and demons that were visiting people along history were all one same force, humans were keeping this struggle).

The system of duality was the system in which we were two cycles ago. You would not agree with me along with other people about this back then and I understand it well, of course I don't like to be lied to and more I don't like to lie to people and lead people into disinformation,... but though I agree to their claim.

Most of the channelers are used by Followers of Light to spread the thinking about "Coming into the Light", to inspire, to aid, to guide humanity toward Light, Love and even technological progress. Some are not, You can recognize them, they are easy spotted among non.

But You and Everyone must be always watchful for all channelers and lightworkers that collects huge amounts of money by using this "Light information". Because they, due to their greed are struggling within and so they are giving much misinformation which holds distorted truth, they seek to enrich themselves more than actually aid and guide. Like a bible, quran, many other religions and cults - lessons not learned. Be careful.

About the removal of the archons - it is true, Light Followers' command recalled most reptilians and greys. But they still present, that why I still sense them, I sense more greys than reptilians, the light beings are sensed even more.

The struggle against "negative entities", like many are sensing is not struggle against archons, but a struggle against negative or dark energy with a purpose "to come into the Light". The negative entity can be, negative thoughts, dark praying, like baphomet priests are doing, energy leftover, which connects to death or terrible accident or terrible life experiences. Also some freelancer souls of the dead and visitors from other dimensional worlds like so called "demons" (unlike archons).

The devices archons set up, were by most part turned off, excluding some distant ones and one most powerful on the Moon. Like I know now, they do not seek to turn them off... The new devices installed by Followers of Light are changing energies and are "fighting" these "negative entities" I mentioned before. The main purpose of this setup is to calm down humanity and renew its "holy grail", which holds Life's Essence Energy, so that humanity could continue to live on, without big changes.

The Sage Star A's activated part is disabling the negative thinking which orients toward destruction, but it was decided by Forces of One, that if this experiment will not be stopped than Creator Sage Star A will be asked to return back to sleep.

Sophia, it is still a big hit for me, I need to apologize for telling misinformation. I stand for Justice and Truth and this really hurts me...

This whole information for some is better to be ignored, because this changes everything, share this with only those You can be assured will be ok. It is most important in what You believe!

The Truth indeed hurts and lies are indeed soft, something humanity still lives in. And duality system is a system that keeps humanity obedient and under control. But this is just an experiment. All is One.

Much Peace and Understanding to You!

July 09, 2013

SOPHIA
Thank you .

I am still working on understanding all of it myself. I have a question about this part:

" The devices archons set up, were by most part turned off, excluding some distant ones and one most powerful on the Moon. Like I know now, they do not seek to turn them off... The new devices installed by Followers of Light are changing energies and are "fighting" these "negative entities" I mentioned before. The main purpose of this setup is to calm down humanity and renew it's "holy grail", which holds Life's Essence Energy, so that humanity could continue to live on, without big changes.

The Sage Star A's activated part is disabling the negative thinking which orients toward destruction, but it was decided by Forces of One, that if this experiment will not be stopped than Creator Sage Star A will be asked to return back to sleep. "

Would you talk some more about Sage Star A's role in this; as well as that of the Forces of One?

I have shared our conversation openly and for the most part will continue to do so. I think that those who are meant to see and hear the truth at this time will read it.

I hope that you are well. It appears that manipulation is part of the human game, no matter who you are speaking to. All that we can do is speak what we understand as truth.

Much love and peace,

G/E

Thank You Sophia for Your understanding.

This is manipulation indeed, we are pawns in a great game of higher powers. I accepted to be a subordinate of One and Forces of One, so I knew some things will not be perfect and that I am here in a closed world, I wouldn't count on much truth from them. But I am ok, anyway I knew this world is full of deception before I came here.

The role of Sage Star A is a side role for this world, the Grand Creator right now is overseeing that this experiment would cease. The wills for destruction are being negated by Him.

We Guardians Executioners (and Executives) are receiving orders from Grand Creator. These orders are coming from One, as very massive black stars are the closest to One and Heavens where His Consciousness and Conduit of souls is. That why we are receiving orders from One through Sage Star A, for us Grand Creator's role is prior.

The Forces of One are the subordinates of One, they can be called "His Hand of Justice".

Sophia there is one concern, I am feeling there are many lightworkers that do not resonate and do not like when I call Creator as He of male side. I want to know will it be ok if I would change the calling to "It", so it wouldn't create pressure on gender relations, which is very important. I was told that it will be ok for this change, and I must suit Everyone's understanding and not destroy it actually.

I need to mention this once again, the most important is what You believe in and how You understand things, but I'm sorry for some misunderstanding I caused with gender issue.

For us GEs Creator will always be He, to suit Your needs we are ready to change the
calling of Creator to It, there are 3 main forms of Creators for us:
Minor 3rd level - The Father Star, Medium 2nd level - The Grand Father Star, Major 1st level - One (within our system caller Unit One on many languages both onworld and offworld).

Much Peace and Love to Everyone!

(Update July 12, 2013)

SOPHIA
Hi and yes, using the term "it" works. No worries.

Would you elaborate on the "holy grail" and the "devices" and their purpose?

Thank you.

Much love to you,

G/E
Thank You Sophia!

The Holy Grail is a collective name for an Energy reservoir in each human and other physical bodies. For one life span, certain amount of this energy is given. During life span energy is flowing in this reservoir and out. The interaction with different physical matters and other people gives different amount of Life's Energy Essence, some substances and people are taking energy instead. In the beginning, all newborns (excluding very few) are given pure Light Energy. During life span the energy is being mixed in this Holy Grail with dark and neutral energies (light, dark and neutral are just the classes, there are many different energies). For example the deep black stones like agate and onyx are known for their healing abilities and calming attributes, in fact what they are doing is siphoning dark energy from the body and keeping it inside until refreshed, when it can continue this siphoning. It indeed is very effective.

The devices that worked before second millennium are made by reptiloid civilizations with cooperation of insectoid grey civilizations. They are oriented at inspiring "the evil deeds". Greed, arrogance and ignorance are their second names.

The devices Light Followers set up are being oriented to renew the Holy Grail and inspire "the good deeds". Love, humility and compassion are their second names.
I thought they indeed were fighting archons and everything they do was for good. They changed devices to bring humanity into new age and help "to ascend toward Light". At least they are doing now good things, so there is still hope. Remember they have yet 3 full Solar cycles to stop this experiment.
The old evil-oriented devices no longer work on humans, as they can drive humanity to insanity and lead to self-destruction. But like I said one most powerful on the Moon is still active.

SOPHIA
Hi.

I wonder what it would take and who would it take to stop the device on the Moon?

Also, to confirm:

This experiment will end one way or the other and it will end before May 2016. There will not be destruction here. It is both sides that are currently invested in keeping this going, and they do **NOT WANT IT (THE EXPERIMENT) TO END.**
But, in fact, it will (end) because it is the wish of One. Things need to be brought back to balance, for all of creation.

Here is a separate question and it comes directly from a reader:

"" Are you familiar with the work of S'hayana Deane?

I have more recently come into contact with her information and it is very detailed and it is no doubt provided by a source with vast knowledge of (all) things. You are probably familiar with her work, but if not, here is quickly what she says the current affairs of this planet are:

She says we are on a fallen planet in a fallen Galaxy (Milky Way) which is/was actually Part of M-31 Andromeda Galaxy. She says the fate of this planet and galaxy (of which this planet connects the Organic Life of Andromeda to the Synthetic/False Fallen Life of Milky Way - this is approximately what she says).

We are being helped by a group she calls the "Guardians," but I do not think these are the same as you are in communication with - maybe you could as your contact if he will comment???

Further, these Guardians are here on a salvage mission because our system is going to Fall completely into the Synthetic/False Light and our Sun is going to Die out and, much, much sooner than it was supposed to.

Lastly, she says that we are a 200 year evacuation of any life that is savable and can live within (and possibly ascend) within the Organic Life Systems. All Else will ultimately return to Space Dust and then Source.

She makes it clear that almost ALL other groups are part of the negative side and they are fighting over this planet as it is becoming the monstrosity or "The Beast" and is becoming a weapon - The METATRONIC Death Star.

I could go on. But the important question is whether or not your source can or will confirm this is a Fallen system and whether this planet is on a evac plan because it is too far gone? ""

Thank you and much love,

G/E

The device on the Moon is big and connects to many extensions within moon. So much to Your and Many other interest, it is actually an artificial object, it was made precisely to exercise new experiment and set it in motion.

Everywhere where such experiments are taking place, big moon is present nearby. It has some roles which helps and also damages the current experiment. It is not a problem for us - Forces of One to switch it off and it is not a problem for them to do it, but they wish to keep it, "to guide" humanity through more trials. We on our part are not intervening right now.

I'm going to rephrase Your saying only a little:

"This experiment will end one way or the other and it will end before August 2016. There will not be destruction here. It is both sides that are currently invested in keeping this going, and they do NOT WANT IT (THE EXPERIMENT) TO END. But, in fact, it will (end) because it is the wish of One. Manipulation things need to end here, and humanity set free for all of Creation."

We are bringing Balance only when it is needed. We do not seek to always maintain it, it is against rules of One, but we are indeed called the Force of Balance. We hold Universe in One piece, so it would not collapse, this is our work and Duty.

Now to answer to concern of Your Friend. I will again repeat as it is necessary that <Your own believing is most important>.

Our collective knowledge is

1. This Galaxy and planet are not fallen. This Galaxy was not a part of Andromeda, they were together ages ago and were a much much bigger super form of Creation, there were other Galaxies as well in this collective Super Galaxy. They split apart due to the Other World's Anti Force, now called Dark Energy by astrophysicists (Other World we call more specifically Underverse). Now, the gravitational pull of both Milky Way and Andromeda M 31 brings both together again and they will merge into one Galaxy once again, but it will happen not quite soon.

2. The planet is not considered to be evacuated, though Followers of Light were holding the idea of Salvation plan, if experiment would go wrong, only people with pure heart would be saved. They still hold this plan, but it will not come to use. This planet is changing to higher vibrational level and humanity evolves to higher levels as well.

Now here was mentioned a weapon, which is why we are here. She was speaking about collective definition of this whole experiment which could create same power I warned about, the control over Creation. This is what we are determined to stop.

Calm, Peace, Prosperity!

SOPHIA
Thank you.

I have another question from another friend:

Are you involved with the Choir Consciousness?

Much love,

G/E
Ok Sophia, I need time to figure out the structure of words and connections, where and how words are connected.

Here I sense the United Voice of One's Consciousness which is of the people of the Earth.
If it is the meaning than, I am trying not to be in there for most of the time, as it is giving me out.
There are others that performing the tasks of Voice of One.

Many Good things to You and Your Friend!

Update July 18th, 2013

G/E
Revelatione Domini

Sophia I need to share this information considering only humanity and not any off world beings. This is a Revelation, if of course You and Anyone are ready to acknowledge this.

<<What is government? Replace word government with a gang, from this point in here it will be called gang.

As You know what gang is - gang collects taxes (or tributes or offerings) in form of some things that are worthy or might prove worth, for protection. If we do not wish to give offerings to them or don't have any, they are making a raid on us to frighten us and others. We are being "punished" (being taken into custody or even with tortures and death) for not giving an offering to them. So to offering protection from outsiders, they are offering protection from themselves.

Present gangs are printing "obligations", the currency money (a paper) on which are stamps of the gangs (different drawings of very memorized images) which are considered to have a more higher value than real resources with real worth (the worthfullness that can be used in life to make life better). The paper candy wrappers are also used to pay for the work done, so they can be used further to pay for something necessary to make life better or to sustain it from dying. So it also comes to sustaining life thus making everyone who uses them a mandate workers, as without work life here is not possible.

What is a citizen? When You are accepting to become a citizen, you're accepting to become one of the pawns of the gang You chose to live under, you become a citizen, or
one of the workers, or simply saying one of the peasants, or one of the slaves.

By using the paper wrappers and working, we are keeping the gang in power. This system was evolving from the beginning of tribal wars and now it has evolved to the higher extent and even exceeded. This system was working with great efficiency, but now this world no longer support this system and this system by now became obsolete.

There are roughly 1/3 of world young population of ages 20-30, that do not resonate with and do not accept this system, the methods became obsolete and ineffective, these young people are unable to work in this system, most of them are working with no pleasure in their soul. Only 40 cycles ago they would work with pleasure, as this was much interesting and challenging, but now this World and Society evolves and it no longer is supported.

This is going against Universal Evolution and going against humanity in general, as these young people are the next generation that is going to took over this world from the older generation. All younger generation are feel even worse and while they are growing up, this whole system need an update, and not just a simple update, but a very huge one. A change, from which no one would hide, everyone will be affected. Older generations will find it hard to live in a new different circumstance, but knowing it would benefit their children and next generations, they would accept.

Many of the next generation's humanity is patiently waiting for this change to happen, and if it is postponed more and more, like it is happening, they are becoming more and more unsatisfactory. If this change would not happen, then there would come riots and civil wars, which are already taking strength, with each passing cycle, they would cease and rise up with even greater strength to the extent where gangs will be obliterated and on their ruins would be created much the same gangs, but with new rulers and new rules.

The change I mentioned here, must not be like it (through civil wars or it won't do any good, many people will die, like You know the plan to take over the world established 100 cycles ago by order illuminati, is also obsolete), but a refreshment of these old ways, with secrets hidden from the public revealed and system of slavery changed to a much transparent system (with few or no slavery/secrets at all) that could be without money or at maximum extent with many necessary for life things costs very few or just be for free. The human Brain and Consciousness can no longer support all these many things and secrecy at once, so a great change would follow, there is no other variant.>>

Here I'm telling about current world situation not considering any of the off worlders. The Followers of Light understands this very greatly and they do seek to make a change. What precisely change it will be is still a question, as they are not sure what to do next.

This is the music[107] You already heard, but it suits this message.

Much Peace, Calm and Prosperity to You All!

SOPHIA
Thank you. I have to digest this.

It is 1PM Central US time on Monday, July 15th, what is changing ??? I sense and am experiencing huge changes RIGHT NOW. Something is

[107] *YouTube*. YouTube, n.d. Web. 09 July 2016. <http://www.youtube.com/watch?v=1wUl-AGc-Xo>.

shifting.

Much love.

G/E
Good Day Sophia!

The change You are experiencing is a good start. Recently we've come in agreement with Followers of Light, one of us Guardians-Executioners among their ranks (not human), showed them through mind connection the outcomes which can happen with them if they will continue on. We were doing this before, we don't wish to harm them, that is why we are giving them final warnings.

Also they managed to find the forgotten records about us, from civilizations that disappeared (these races joined us). Other civilization released records of a Force known as Servants of Unity or Universe as a whole (it is the Force of One). There is mentioned about farther reach of these civilizations, their complex design and that their number is unknown, but huge. In a vision demonstrated to them, they witnessed many effects of our technologies and their superiority. Now they accepted to stop this experiment. We trust them for now, but there is not much time left. They will need to hold their word.

The overall change is proceeding normally, they are making now a little different approach, like I mentioned, they yet aren't sure what to do next.

Much Peace, Calmness and Prosperity!

SOPHIA
Hi and thank you. I appreciate your quick response. This explains what I was feeling at that moment.

Please keep me updated as you are able to. I will share this.

Much love,

Update July 27th, 2013

SOPHIA
Hi!

I have here some inquiries from others:

Hello Sophia - this link[108] is an article that your friend needs to read because it is very serious consequence issue - I will not extrapolate on it with my own views. Just a comment is needed from him - the question is obvious. Much love Saludos

---

Please let your friend know - I like much of what he says and am curious to know from which country he resides in because he is not english - that's for sure. He speaks of believing in what we want but I feel that belief stops the liberty to think expansively - its not that I don't want to believe but more that I want the infinite possibilities to come true and for all those that need to be freed and savor the true essences of our lives.

The photos are to visually declare a kindred spirit...they are from where I live and the stones are such a beautiful texture placed there by eons of tides and waves.

(there were beautiful photo's att. that I cannot send here!)

Thank you and much love to you.
There seems to be a sense of power emerging within, if that makes sense?

I hope that you are well,

G/E
Good Day Sophia!

I'm great physically, spiritually I'm at optimal could be better, but it's ok.

The issue on Fukushima is not all that big as many people still thinks.

[108] "Fukushima Deadly Update – Silence Remains Supreme." Veterans Today. N.p., n.d. Web. 09 July 2016. <http://www.veteranstoday.com/2013/07/22/fukushima-deadly-update-silence-remains-supreme/>.

Though radiation in big doses is lethal to human organism it is not in smaller, and nuclear holocaust of ww3 could made it a much bigger and severe problem to all of humanity.

You remember Hiroshima and Nagasaki being destroyed 60 cycles ago with deaths of 223 000 people? The use of these weapons was completely unnecessary for winning a war, it was a test to see what damage this weapon could do during field experience. The radiation from these explosions was much bigger than this current output from nuclear plant, and to this time little presence of it still remains there, some mutations occurred there within animals and humans, now animals within Fukushima area are mutating again, but these mutations are not extreme.

The Chernobyl catastrophe gave more severe mutations and to this day radiation there is still present, but again there is no reason to worry for the whole world. Only area under 5 miles is affected. The Sun is giving more radiation than is reaching the West Coast, there is no need to worry about for another reason - evolution. A part of evolution is adaptation. If we can take living organism that never been under the Sun and whose parents and their ancestors never been under it, it could die within minutes from Sun's radiation, because it did not adapt to its deadly rays. But as You can see every living being on this planet can live under the Sun, without it life is also not possible.

The japanese people that were living nearby destroyed cities after explosions were passively becoming more adapt to radiation left from the explosions, many were dying, but most survived and their children gained better resistance toward gamma/x-ray radiation. Fukushima leakage is not going to kill anyone excluding fish nearby this plant, unfortunately, so again You don't have to worry about this.

Now second question.
Thank You My Friend for Your understanding! I'm not preventing You to think expansively, like I was writing all the time - You're free to believe in what You wish to believe, this means if You want my information to be extended You can do whatever You wish to it:)

The knowledge I'm sharing is necessary for my mission, most of it is based only on physical reality, the astral planes are not considered a priority to us. We GEs need to get evil and cruelty under control (the satanics illuminati order and west world elite) by restricting it or just destroying it, if it is not possible to restrict. The current objective is to help humanity to gain freedom, like I was telling this before, by aiding Followers of Light (we still hope they will hold their word) and also give humanity the infinite possibilities and extended evolution, many ways of making life better and this world a much more friendly and completely clean from pollution, where everyone is happy and complete.

About my location, I cannot reveal it, as they are reading this as well, it is still a little secret, I can tell that I'm from an english-speaking country, but yes, my english is terrible:)

Some time we are agreeing in giving different names and changing a stylus of language to bring better message and understanding, this of course is met with confusion as old programming of language is different. Some words were coded by cabal to hide the true meaning of it (they are calling these words exoteric), this practice was going on for a very long time since their dawn, we are revealing the words' meaning apart again (we are giving esoteric meaning).

The Emergence of Power within is a good sign. But still nothing big for now.

The united states regime's government is still trying to start a ww3, but they are negated, with all their effort. We aren't losing focus for a second, we are watching them closely.

The current wars in Syria and DRK are terrible and we sense deaths every day, both of these wars were caused by american government so we are very angry on them, all aggression from these wars is being returned to them to mock them.

Another thing I can tell You Sophia is our special feature, because I mentioned here a backfire. We are adapts at gaining aggression or calmness. The more aggression there is around us (in this world) the more aggressive we become, and we gain with it destructive powers, more aggression - more power. The more Peace and Calmness there is around us, the more calming and loving we become, more peace - more wisdom with Love.

It is that simple, that is why we have double roles as guardians and executioners. One is good, other is evil, that how our name stands for. Protectors or destroyers, the choice is made from surrounding environment (mostly it's dominant inhabitants - here humans).

I decided it is not hurt anyone to tell You this, we are not afraid to reveal it, this isn't weakness or great secret. Many civilizations knows about us and this ability.

Much Peace and Love to You!

SOPHIA
Thank you for your candid reply. I will share this with my friend.

Many are talking about the upcoming configuration of the planets on the 29th of July. Can you say anything about that?

We are all feeling a sense of building up and expectation. There is a person who has been imprisoned without her consent in New Zealand, and a worldwide outcry for her release. The requests for assistance have included a call for calm and peaceful noncompliance rather than protest. In this vein I feel that a sense of peace has taken hold in a way that wasn't present not so long ago, and that this is a very good sign.

Much love,

G/E
Yes, the planet is changing in a peaceful way, not in destructive. That is why Everyone seek to solve problems peacefully, but this goes to the extent of trust. If government is going to resist the people's will, then they are considered no longer a legitimate government, so people can rise up against them as real enemies. This is current situation of a People's relation to a government.

The New Zealand's government is well understanding and one of few governments that People trust. This woman could be freed if many People would agree to sign a petitions and support her with peaceful rallies.

The configuration of an Earth is going on in every passing moment of time. It is constantly changing in a good peaceful way, the threshold for this change were seven cycles of Creators, the december 21st, the moment of choice. On that moment the very big decision was made and it was made in a Good direction.

This is another beautiful music[109] for Your and Everyone enjoyment!:)

---

[109] Audiomachine1. "Audiomachine - Final Hope." YouTube. YouTube, 26 July 2013. Web. 09 July 2016.

Much Peace, Calmness and Love to You and Everyone!

Update August 1, 2013

SOPHIA
Hi there.

I am wondering what you think of this latest from Edward Snowden[110]:

Thanks and love,

G/E
Good Day Sophia!

Well, if I will tell this is made up, will You believe? Remember it is Your free will to believe in what You wish to believe.

I know that Edward didn't tell this. This site is posting many hoax news. Within the CIA information about the kill shot is marked with "lack of scientific evidence and lack of overall basis", but they consider such an event, currently based on NASA's studies there is no proof for this event that they need. But You do remember about the kill shot? It is a threshold beyond which humanity is prohibited to see. No far seer or remote viewer can see what exactly will be there. Only Light workers can.
I hope this information will aid You!;)

Much Peace and Love to You!

SOPHIA
Thanks.
I figured that, but people are asking, and I wanted to respond.

Much love and appreciation to you for your clarification.

  A question about this "No far seer or remote viewer can see what exactly will be there. Only Light workers can."

Would you describe precisely who or what you mean by Light workers?

<http://www.youtube.com/watch?v=TchHILC80-w>.
[110]"Edward Snowden: Solar-Flare 'Killshot' Cataclysm Imminent | The Internet Chronicle." The Internet Chronicle. N.p., 23 July 2013. Web. 09 July 2016. <http://www.chronicle.su/news/edward-snowden-solar-flare-killshot-cataclysm-imminent/>.

Thank you,
Much love,

G/E
Good Day Sophia!
These are all Light workers, You, Your Friends and we as well. We know the future, You know too :)

This is for You Fellow Sisters and Brothers[111]!

Peace and Love!

Update August 18, 2013

SOPHIA
Hi.
I get questions every now and again about our conversation. Right now is one of those times. There are huge expectations for this month and the coming few months. Do you have anything to say about what we can expect?

I hope that you are well.
Thank you and much love.

G/E
Good day Sophia!

These feelings are ok for this time. As You know overall change is taking place right now, there are very mixed feelings not only within light workers, but within majority as well.

The Solar flip (that is the next phase of the Sun, the polar shift) is going to be more unusual as it used to be, because of the changes within human society.

I can't say much good news; everything is much the same right now. The progress is being made as it supposed to. There is still some time needed for massive changes to occur.

---

[111] Michimaas. "Dreams of July - Piano and Strings Edition." YouTube. YouTube, 30 July 2013. Web. 09 July 2016. <http://www.youtube.com/watch?v=MSiKNJ78mto>.

Being considered many new evil schemes within secret societies or cabal. Their hideous strategies mostly are being negated, their intentions are not changing. The struggle, better called oppression in Israel against palestinians is happening on the same level without worsening, improving. Same in Syria, same overall world situation.

The progress is slow but determined, it was aligned by One, and everything proceeds how it was intended to be. Still One hoped that humanity can do better..

The biggest "bet" everyone can do, which is going to return with greatest reward is to let more and more people know about ETs everlasting presence on this world. People little by little are finding out, but it's slow. Once main stream people (which is majority, performing routine tasks) are finding out about ETs and that's they are legit and information presented as well, the information about order illuminati is being revealed with it as well in a very short time, as there is a distinct connection with it.

I will share with you another trusted source of information about ETs presence and corruption of the government[112].

The faster humanity "fills the gaps" within it with understanding, the faster the Moment of Justice comes. A paraphrase: "Time is only a Will of One, within it matter can change how it wants." Remember that time do not exist for our sub consciousness, we can do all the things we want to only now.

Much Peace and Love to You and Everyone!

 August 19th, 2013

G/E
Good Day Sophia!

I was told to share this information and tried to send it sooner, and it didn't go through, now I can do this:

About the western media manipulation of the public[113]

---

[112]ADGUKNEWS. "Aliens And The Vatican 2013." YouTube. YouTube, 21 Feb. 2013. Web. 09 July 2016. <http://www.youtube.com/watch?v=V0Y1Qg10pys>.

[113]GlobalResearchTV. "Faking It: How the Media Manipulates the World into War." YouTube. YouTube, 02 Jan. 2012. Web. 09 July 2016. <http://www.youtube.com/watch?v=y4P2O8UjQeU>.

The planned wars[114]

About most prominent secret societies, most of which are interconnected by believe system[115]
A message left for humanity, disguised as a comedy[116]

And for Your enjoyment music of old and of that to come[117] [118] [119]

Let me know if there is something more You or Others need to know.

Peace, Calm and Prosperity!

Second update August 19th, 2013

SOPHIA
Hi and thank you. I am listening now to the music as I write...It is beautiful.

I so appreciate these videos, as will others.

I do have a question. I have seen reference now to September as a pivotal month, and even one specific day in it, the 26th. There is a link which I'll share that discuss this moment, the end of September. I very much dislike dates and prophecies, yet here it is once again. The description in the cosmic awareness message below describes an event that very much sounds like the movie "solar revolution" , which was projected for the middle of 2013. The timing of that would be right now as well. I am wondering about your thoughts on all of this[120].

I have noticed a few times where the music and message sent is about loss of love, the cycle of life and death, sadness and rebirth... I take from that a message of loss in the days to come.

---

[114] FacelesswithEyesOpen. "General Wesley Clark: Wars Were Planned - Seven Countries In Five Years." YouTube. YouTube, 11 Sept. 2011. Web. 09 July 2016.
<http://www.youtube.com/watch?v=9RC1Mepk_Sw>.

[115] YouTube. YouTube, n.d. Web. 09 July 2016. <http://www.youtube.com/watch?v=cUVqxT61RMA>.

[116] Tradgedyandhope. "A Message For All Of Humanity - Charlie Chaplin." YouTube. YouTube, 26 Dec. 2011. Web. 09 July 2016. <http://www.youtube.com/watch?v=CsgaFKwUA6g>.

[117] XenogearsXenosaga. "Xenogears Music OST - 207 Gathering Stars in the Night Sky - [HD] - [HQ Audio ACC] Mp4." YouTube. YouTube, 19 Jan. 2011. Web. 09 July 2016.
<http://www.youtube.com/watch?v=qUE-YTfWocw>.

[118] YouTube. YouTube, n.d. Web. 09 July 2016. <http://www.youtube.com/watch?v=KesrAwf9_24>.

[119] EpicJennyni20. "Thomas Bergersen - Sun (2014)." YouTube. YouTube, 16 Aug. 2013. Web. 09 July 2016. <http://www.youtube.com/watch?v=aSiuLJIKSU0>.

[120] http://rainbowphoenix.com.ipage.com/archives/20130801c.pdf

We are all expecting something to occur and with these messages there seems to be a warning that there will be loss. With so much time passing now without any major destructive event, I believe we are not expecting anything like that to happen on a global scale. Perhaps you are indicating something else?

Can you elaborate for me? Is there something you know that can be shared here?

This one comes from my friend, who runs the blog American kabuki:

"What do you know of the divines and how does One intend to deal with them?"

Thanks and much Love,

G/E

A september, was always a special month for secret satanic societies, the cabal. It is because, from it begins the autumn "a time of death", and it is numbered 9, nine is a sinister number in their understanding, they love to jump from 9 to 11, that is passing 10, the number of Order and God. This jumping is showing their obedience to antigod - satan. So whatever can happen there, will be of their doings.

They are planning to make a coup or government shutdown in U.S. regime during september, also CIA operatives are instigating riots in Lebanon, and there is oppression going on with Kurdish People. Mali and Somali are under attack from within as well. The increase in this is their desperate attempts to worsen the situation and make a world war 3, although it is deemed to fail.

The situation in Egypt is different, it is not made with U.S. efforts, People are struggling for changes. Egypt is vital for cabal existence on the Middle East, this country is not in the "regime change plan". What happens there is going against their planning, one more sign that their system is crumbling. Within U.S. Army and U.S. Air Force, there are people that are ready to release new "classified files" that will put more taint on reputation of U.S. regime government. Recently, regime acknowledged the existence of Area 51, due to NSA leaks.

The Solar Flip will occur within september - october, it is already happening. In the core, poles already flipped to 30%. It is a gradual process within the Sun. The Sun is one of those stars that is not fast, so many things happen slowly. Though Sun sees everything passing away at a very high speed pace. It is only in our perception time is running like it is running:)

Overall, the changes are very soon to come, but waiting is still necessary. (Waiting though is one thing, but trying to do is another and doing actually is completely different;)

The images You are seeing showing losses of someone important, this is where You must decide how it will be! You are the master of Your life and this reality, so seeing is not always believing. Believing is how You visualize Your world. You heard many times over that this is an illusion of 3D world. It actually is, because People are unable to see more "lines" only 3 - length, width, height.

There are actually more than just three dimensions people are accustomed to. If we are taking these terms, then humanity is actually living in 4D world. Time is also a merit, that can be measured. We gave humanity another - a 5D abbreviation, based on 5 senses.

Some live in 6D. Very few even made to 7D. We haven't found higher. Some though live in 4D or 3D, deaf and blind people, senseless People... People in coma are in 1D world.. I want to show here, that sense of seeing is just a visualization of object. Everyone sees object and colors differently. The variation is very small, but it exists. Other non-human sapient creatures will see other pictures and other objects, unlike what You are seeing, so when we are returning to emotional video like Memories, it is important how You see it.

We are not trying to show a hidden warning or something bad, it is just something that plays with emotions, and how You control these emotions is how You visualize what You wish to see (or *experience* :)

Also if it is interesting for You and Everyone, and if You are ready to hear it, I can describe what is life and death in simple language and understanding. I first need to ask this as this is not a simple theme to talk about.

Good Day American Kabuki, I know that You grow very untrusted to word Divine. Well Divines You meant, the Ascended Masters, are the same controllers of this world, which are frequently seen all over the world as "flying lights" and their probes, the flying spheres (well it's not just a probe, but a living soul actually, though it is used like a probe).

I told Sophia that we are here because they wish to possess power to create and un-create using humans, as humans are one of their most successful experiments. Thing I didn't tell is why exactly One is not allowing them to possess this power, this power is very great, but only worthy can possess such power.

There are a lot of old civilizations around the Universe that do possess this power and many devices that have highly incredible abilities. One entrusted this to them as they were worthy for this. We are in alliance with them, an alliance of Friendship, they are simply old friends. We could become friends to these "Divines" as well, but One does not see them worthy right now. They are unfortunately not confident in their abilities and goals.

You can see their reflection in this world, You know the rule as above, so below. "What are the parents, so are the children", can be said as well. So if they are going to continue this experiment, they will be punished, if they are going to aid humanity in it's liberation, then they will be left how they are right now, without punishment. Some of them will go to
One to answer to some of "the most atrocious acts against Creation", some of humans will go too.

I hope this is going to help You American Kabuki.

Much Peace, Love and Happiness to Everyone!

SOPHIA
In reply to this:

"Also if it is interesting for You and Everyone, and if You are ready to hear it, I can describe what is life and death in simple language and understanding. I first need to ask this as this is not a simple theme to talk about."

The answer is yes. That would be helpful to us.

Much love,

G/E
Ok Sophia.

You already heard that sayings, that after death life continues. Some say it is just nothing, others say, it is a Court of a God, other are saying it is reincarnation. From this point, what You are believing, Your own belief, if what You will find next not resonating with You then stop reading this.

We, the Forces of One know that Existence is Reincarnation.

Imagine that waiting to be born is when You are waiting at the bus stop for the next bus. When it stops and opens the doors, You're entering, into the "life". Then You're choosing Your place and sit down where You want to.

While You ride, You know where You are going and when You must get off the bus, You can do whatever You wish in that bus, but bounds of decency are holding You from doing bad things, but some still are doing bad things.

And when it's time to get off the bus, You're happy to finally meet Your long waited relatives, together in tears, joy and happiness, all are coming into the highly luminescent tunnel of Pure Light, because You know that there is Home and You can rest in there.

People that disturbed or injured other passengers during journey, are met by the authorities once they need to get off the bus (or sooner) and are being taken into the custody, with later trials.

Some people don't meet relatives, but need to wait for the next bus. As their relatives are waiting farther away. Either way, all people will have to wait for the next bus, once they will need to ride somewhere else.

The bus analogy, I chose to describe life and not train, tram or rollercoaster, because the rollercoaster for example gives You only one route and You can't change it, You're on a ride that can't be changed. Trains have a little more freedom, but still You have only narrowed choice, the rails were already set and You can go only on either one, You can't make a complete 180 degrees turn, but with bus You can.

Bus can make any turn on its route; it even can make a completely different route, so it is the Life. *For this example "bus" is a collective life experience or planet Earth.*

The reflection of the Universe can be seen everywhere on this world, and within human society. As above so below, is one of the Universal Laws.

I hope You find this helpful! Peace and Love to You!

Update August 23rd, 2013

SOPHIA
Hi!
I have a question and suggestion from my friend:

"A curious and provocative line is - "The progress is slow but determined, it was aligned by One, and everything proceeds how it was intended to be. Still One hoped that humanity can do better"

The issue for me or what it provokes is a seeming ambiguity in that "One" <hoped> that humanity can do better - If "One" has aligned things and "everything proceeds how it was intended to be" - then why is "One" of the hope that "we" would do better?

Surely we are doing at the rate of alignment control and if not why not inject the situation with the imperative of the following para - The biggest "bet" everyone can do, which is going to return with greatest reward is to let more and more people know about ETs everlasting presence on this world.

This appears to be the most difficult task for us as there is so much against us factually doing it with any degree of receptivity that endures - and the least desired actuation by information that is placed on sites by so called channellers or contacts of the ET/ Off-world entities. However I subscribe to it fully and with great presence.

It was part of Operation Blueband or similar by the PTB (powers that be) about the Alien Invasion...well that should be taken away from the PTB and carried out as the "alien introduction" taking the rug out completely from the satanics etc to force the issue into what at first might be a "mexican stand-off" but what would ultimately be a confirmation of "benign intervention" based on an ET presence of resistance and non-aggression.

How? - By having a "ship" hover at a reasonable and identifiable height (that resonates and is secured at 3D vibrations) from which a message is continuously being emitted and where appropriate the occupants enter the area within a secured area arranged by them - Earth TV would have to follow it all and despite what might be propaganderized by the PTB it would expel any doubt that ET presence is a fact. The location should be such that there is minimal earth military presence and maximal human contact like that of Portugal where 70.000people "apparently" (Fatima Event) saw a

UFO....only this time leave no doubt of it.

If an ET presence came and stood ground over days/weeks then the sublime message would get through to very many people and perhaps turn the tide for the beginning of the completion that gets to save the world in general.

Please ask your friend to comment concisely on this issue of mine because intuition tells me that this would work. I earnestly recommend it to "One" in all sincerity and love for the betterment of the world, to permit this intervention that would isolate the PTB at a stroke and allow "us humans" to perceive things more positively.

Much love to you both - saludos "

Thank you for your willingness to respond.
Much love,

G/E
Ok Sophia, I will explain, but remember - Your own believes are most important, I may say many things, but You need to believe in what You think is right, this is the Universal Freedom.

I need to apologize for using two obscure words "hoped" and "bet". I will explain: One is the Creator of the Universe and Universe itself, so it means You and me and all this world and whole Solar System, Milky Way and whole Universe is One, just one unit, united and connected. We are calling Ancient Prime Creator - the point of beginning and end, just One. One though is a very, very complex and difficult to understand design. One holds both predestined and non-predestined time sequence. One's Consciousness consists of many different personalities (or characters), and personality that is observing this world's situation is with us on this time frame. We are calling different personalities (also Creator Incarnates) - as Managers. Each manage different role and all are located in "Heaven", the Nexus of Conduits.

All this is very complex, maybe You understood what I wanted to say, so now I can say this shortly: "the shred of Creator, that answers for this world was hoping for humanity to make things faster and more efficient, but everything just is going as it is intended (even a little slower, if we will give into details)".

And I used the word "bet" well, because we can't be sure on Followers' of Light words. They already changed their minds two times since year 2000. But we GEs are sure, that when humanity as a whole will be overflown with evidence of their presence, they will have to do something. What exactly, we can hope only that it is what humanity wants and not otherwise. Though You know, bad things will not be tolerated, Forces of One are here to assure that won't happen. We can wait a little longer, but we gave them their deadline.

I'm sorry, I can't bring in pleiadean, sirian or arcturian spacecraft. Forces of One are prohibited from entering here as well. I can tell that some of the countries in the world are ready to meet new extra-terrestrial friends, their leaders were asked about this. This was done in secrecy and askers were humans. The prevention for this still remains the United States cover-up of UFO and ETs presence. It is because they have done a lot of cruel and evil things and if they would accept ETs presence and their whole ETs research, everything else will surface as well. That is their biggest fear. I'm helping other people to see the evidence on UFOs, this is the best thing we can do now apart from protecting critical locations.

I hope this is going to help You My Friend.
Peace and Prosperity to You!

SOPHIA
Thank you, I will share.

In the meantime, I have just been sent this[121]

The video included in the passage has a second video, redacting the first to some degree. It is here[122]

Would you comment? This appears to coincide with your mention of the plans of the Cabal.

Thank you.
Much love,

G/E
Ok Sophia, this is going to this possibility of coup d'etat. I can't give into

[121] http://rainbowphoenixcom.ipage.com/Archives/20130819P.pdf
[122] Revmichellehopkins. "UPDATE - REDACTION FOR "URGENT!!! POSSIBLE EMERGENCY ALERT FOR FEMA REGION III"" YouTube. YouTube, 20 Aug. 2013. Web. 09 July 2016.
<http://www.youtube.com/watch?v=9Q_UuEJloOg>.

details, I'm sorry for this, but their strategy can be improved if I will say something here on this subject, Lightworkers need to be careful. They are desperate and desperate people are dangerous (particularly such extreme people as satanic people).
Right now think of a Bright Future and Love and Harmony Among All!

If You are interested in bad event, then considering very last deceptive chemical attack in Syria. You can check this archived article, look for the leaked email. US regime government approved long ago rebels to use chemical weapons on Syrian People and blame it on Syrian Government. Truly disgraceful act...

It wasn't the first time they did this, the more such things they do, the more severe punishment for them becomes, it is just waiting for them a little further, soon we will meet this moment[123]

Also one question Sophia, You heard 1977 message, are You resonate with it?

SOPHIA
  I am sorry, I don't know what you mean??? What 1977 message?

G/E
I was having a mixed feeling whether You heard it or not. This is a message which was given to very few back then, which is now passing to many more[124]

Do You resonate with it?

SOPHIA
Thank you. I do resonate with it..

I only heard it recently though.

I can't help but notice the reference to the Ashtar Command, which is one we hear from today, not on television but from various channelers.

---

[123]"U.S. 'backed Plan to Launch Chemical Weapon Attack on Syria and Blame It on Assad's Regime'" Mail Online. N.p., 29 Jan. 2013. Web. 09 July 2016.
<http://web.archive.org/web/20130129213824/http://www.dailymail.co.uk/news/article-2270219/U-S-planned-launch-chemical-weapon-attack-Syria-blame-Assad.html>.
[124] Http://www.youtube.com/channel/UClTW8hInWWrvVB-tw1DRWFQ. "Alien Warning Message Live on TV in UK-"We Come to Warn You About Your Race and Your Planet"" YouTube. YouTube, 12 June 2013. Web. 09 July 2016. <http://www.youtube.com/watch?v=Bdw_ikz2hBY>.

It feels like validation for the intent of our off world brothers and sisters, as well as for the fact that this was not common knowledge but "given to a very few back then". There is so much that has been kept hidden. So much that was known before now. I wonder about something like this happening today, on all stations worldwide.

I had a dream about something like that. We saw it on our televisions (or computers in my home) and went outside, and then saw the ships in the sky. It happened everywhere at once, all over the planet, so there was no possibility of the message being corrupted or the intent misinterpreted.

In the dream, I ran outside with my family and saw the ships. They were everywhere and even writing in the sky. It was very cool, and world altering.

Thank you for reminding me of this message from so many years ago. I will share this.

Much love,

G/E

Thank You Sophia, I wanted to hear Your own resonance and answer.

Name Gramaha is not quite correct, his name was Vrilan (Vrillon), that's is how he is known to me. Also they pronounce not Ashtar as You heard this, but Asta, like it was in the video.

This incident occurred on 26th november of 1977 going after the WOW! signal received the same year from Chi Sagittarii on august 15[125].

The signal WOW! was a powerful signal that gave permission to interfere in such a way, sent from their command[126].

I was introduced not long ago into this message and first impression I received was the sound "Hum", I know this sound, it's an energy technology which is very powerful. It's a transmitter with which is possible to integrate signal anywhere from other dimensional world.

The signal was meant not to be clear and was meant to be only in that

---

[125]"Wow! Signal." Wikipedia. Wikimedia Foundation, n.d. Web. 09 July 2016. <http://en.wikipedia.org/wiki/Wow%21_signal>.
[126]"Southern Television Broadcast Interruption." Wikipedia. Wikimedia Foundation, n.d. Web. 09 July 2016. <http://en.wikipedia.org/wiki/Southern_Television_broadcast_interruption>.

location. The main intent of this message was to not tell about ETs existence to humanity, but to warn of an impending doom, the nuclear ww3. Humanity was not ready at that moment to acknowledge the ETs presence above their world. Mostly disturbing was that many were in complete fear after this message, almost all that accepted this message started to think of "an alien invasion". So You can see, people in that time have very narrow and closed minds.

It was left for people to choose whether to accept this message or mark it with hoax. Most did exactly that, it was considered a hoax and forgotten. Yet now it's been resurfaced for a younger generation to choose what to do.

There are four reasons, why they chose exactly that location and why they transmitted this in english and not any other language.

- The first reason is because there were some very important individuals, that were on the wrong path.

- The second was because it is an english location, and western satanic elite was and is in control of the world. English accent was chosen for this translation.

- Third was because the southern television bore the eight pointed star symbol, one that Pleiadean, Asta GC and we Forces of One are using. They all have difference, but all are 8 pointed and sharp, much like direction/christmas star or NATO is using.

-Last was because of transmitters, they were relatively easy to hack on background of other more sophisticated transmitters, total 9 were hacked. It was intentionally used like this so that people should wonder whether to believe it or not. Another challenge. I resonated with this message completely, as I know, what he said is how everything is. "Evil forces that overshadow governments' judgements" are cabal, "the false prophets that collects energy, humanity know as money" are self-appointed "lightworkers" and religious "gurus" whose aim is to build their own "wealthwellness" and the choice humanity already made was very important for future of this world. Harmony, Love and Unity are the keys for spiritual evolution.

Now that I know, archons and Light Followers are one and the same, this is making everything and this message very clear..

Peace, Calm, Prosperity!

Second Update August 23, 2013

The dream You saw is the reality that was chosen to become, Followers of Light must make exactly this scenario. But we cannot completely trust Followers of Light. They are like humans have different opinions and different agendas, they are more united than humanity, but still have differences.

They were making wars among themselves in the past, sometime they have different opinions with other galactic alliances. They are trying to be perfect, but unfortunately, they need to evolve much more to achieve perfection which they seek.

In situation if they are not going to intervene and aid humanity directly, Forces of One have their own plan for this. Every technology that is non automated is under control of ancient machines' technology known as "connector". It connects everything that is using any form of Energy to central Super Wise Intelligence. There is no way of escaping it. Every device can be hijacked and controlled at any moment, special very powerful signal can be sent all over the world, but only on order from One.

So if Light Followers will hesitate, then Forces of One will make an announcement, and they will force disclosure and force humanity liberation, by humanity's choice, which is not a very good thing to say the least.. I will hope Followers of Light or Galactic Federation of Light will do everything without One's direct interference (Force of One are counted as One's direct interference (defensive-offensive fragment/part/shred/piece/particle of One - Manager Tactician).

Everything is going as One planned (planning fragment of One - Manager Planner), but One will not wait too long (decision taking fragment of One - Manager Decider), they were given a very narrow time frame.

One's intention to see humanity to fulfill their collective wish, (goodwill fragment of One - Manager Kindgiver). Also as You know intervention can take place any moment now, there is no stopping it, Forces of One will wait, but not too long..

I hope this is going to aid You in understanding of Your dream, Much Peace and Love to You!

Third Update August 23, 2013

SOPHIA

Thank you. It does. I will share as well.

Much love,

G/E

I'm happy You found it helpful!

The music is the language of emotions, it could be neutral, despair, peaceful, inspirational, calming, many many genres, but it truly is the language of souls.. Our souls are talking with sounds and leaving message within music. I will share this beautiful music[127] [128] [129]; think of most enjoyable for You things, Enjoy!

Much Peace and Love to Everyone!

August 24th, 2013

SOPHIA
These are beautiful pieces of music. They create such peace and power all at once. Thank you.

Much love,

G/E
I am happy You liked it Sophia!

But there are grave news, if You are ready to hear them: right now there is a very huge energy pressure going on in Syria. The US regime government wish to attack Syrian Government at any cost. US, Israel, UK and France are the main warmongers in all this situation. It comes late, as this is

---

[127] EpicJennyni20. "Brand X Music - Everlasting (Beautiful Orchestral)." YouTube. YouTube, 11 July 2013. Web. 09 July 2016. <http://www.youtube.com/watch?v=Ze25Q0w8O24>.

[128] ThePrimeCronus. "BrunuhVille - Riversong." YouTube. YouTube, 23 June 2013. Web. 09 July 2016. <http://www.youtube.com/watch?v=AM-t9J_6-Pw>.

[129] Okol7. "Fired Earth Music - Aphelion." YouTube. YouTube, 07 July 2013. Web. 09 July 2016. <http://www.youtube.com/watch?v=cPp51kXaZoU>.

without a doubt what we were waiting - the last push of dark cabal. Russian Government is ready to answer harshly if order will be given, this will mean a lot of problems for the world, more casualties and despair..

Like I showed in previous message, this chemical attack was completely fabricated. It was a setup, the UK and US intelligence took shells similar that SAA are using and filled them with sarin gas, then gave this filled shells to rebels and told to use it on civilians... This is a very, very disgraceful and cruel act of utter evilness..

The good news are, that soldiers and some high figures within US military are ready to make a coup d'etat, possibly this coup can start right when Syria will be attacked, I can't see the moment, but in september month something bad is felt. This is a subject to change, I encourage You and Everyone that wish to see as less destruction and deaths as possible to think of Good, Peaceful outcome. You all know by now, that we can change the future with our thoughts and this is the right time to do so!

Think of Peace, Love and Prosperity!

SOPHIA
Thank you for this. As you have further information, please continue to share.

Much love,

Update August 31st, 2013

SOPHIA
Hi there.

I've heard that the UK pulled out of the plans to invade Syria and take that as good news.

I also saw this today.[130]

Comments?

The news that both light and dark-workers are one and the same is everywhere now. Here is one place[131]

---

[130] "Announcement from Tolec regarding "Comet" Ison...." Kauilapeles Blog. N.p., 30 Aug. 2013. Web. 09 July 2016. <http://kauilapele.wordpress.com/2013/08/29/announcement-from-tolec-regarding-comet-ison/>.

[131] N.p., n.d. Web. <http://www.ascensionhelp.com/blog/2013/08/23/why-i-am-no-longer-a-light-

Also good news.

I hope this finds you well.
Much love,

G/E
Good day Sophia!

These are good news. UK prime minister is with the illuminati, so he is of course trying to bring that old plan to life, and as You can see U.S. government is saying that "intervention is necessary for the United States best interests" this means that if they will fail to change "regime" in Syria they will have a very, very big problems.

People around the world and in America are ready to stand up against war even if it will mean riots and revolution. U.S. government is not listening to it's People, it just doing how it wants to do things, most of Americans do not wish any war. And on top of that People of the world wish transparency and ultimate true to be revealed, so this is approaching to conclusion. It is like You humanity wanted, they are falling with a big crack and everything hidden is becoming visible.

Something about NSA that I mentioned earlier. The NSA is being used as a communications tracking agency and as a proxy telecommunications dish. Within their closed network 13 steps of illuminati are communicating with each other on a very rare occasions, so to not raise suspicions. There they directed the plan for global domination behind curtains.

I know that comet ISON is just "a comet". But it is indeed significant, this object is a blue star that was prophesied by hopi indians.

The truth about controlled duality system is like it, they are both from same team, they indeed created some religions, but most of the cults and new age movements were made up by humans. I need to add that only some of these beings are feeding on humanity's energy and suffering, and are trying to possess the human body - the reptilians and interdimmensional travelers, called demons, ethereal beings that afraid of the Sun and any other form of Light, the photons and gamma rays are deadly for them, so they lurking in the dark and love isolated places. The rest of Galactic Federation of Light are directing humanity toward Light.

worker/>.

I need to remind You, You are free to believe in what You wish to believe, if You think all that I'm saying is false, believe in what is most closer to Your heart.

The ending is very close and You All can feel it!

Much Peace and Prosperity to You All!

(From Sophia ~ Hopi Prophecy[132] and Comet Ison[133])

September 3, 2013

SOPHIA
Thank you.

I just read this[134]

Comments?

Much love.

G/E
Well, this is Cobra's understanding, before believing this, You must ask Your Inner Self about what is going to happen, what You will sense and feel is going to take place. It is always right. Your first thought is always the right one. Don't listen to second or third or subsequent thoughts, doubts, like "no, it won't like it will be like this". The first thought is coming from One - Universal Consciousness, You own One within You.

I also need to tell You that illuminati order - the cabal are really afraid, because they will lose everything and will be completely exposed very soon, so because of this their excuse for an aggressive invasion is

---

[132] "Veja AGORA." Veja AGORA. N.p., n.d. Web. 09 July 2016.
<http://www.wolflodge.org/bluestar/bluestar.htm>.

[133] ScienceAtNASA. "ScienceCasts: Comet of the Century." YouTube. YouTube, 18 Jan. 2013. Web. 09 July 2016. <http://www.youtube.com/watch?v=5_1HdOCOJ_Q>.

[134] "ARE YOU READY FOR 'THE EVENT'?" Streets of Love Unconventional. N.p., 30 Aug. 2013. Web. 09 July 2016. <http://angellucci.wordpress.com/2013/08/30/are-you-ready-for-the-event/>.

"clumsy" and not well-planned.

Another thing - ships that are larger than Earth are present here already considering comet ISON You asked me about.

Look here[135], Sophia.

The last line is very emotional and this line can awaken many minds:

"In a nearby parking lot, Amer Abed, a 27-year-old unemployed man who came from a Damascus suburb, was emptying the contents of the overflowing boot of an old Mercedes car into a van.

Weary women got out of the car, holding young, surprised-looking children in their arms.

"I want these US strikes to happen," she said to several foreign journalists.

"You journalists, and the entire world, are watching our country go up in flames without doing anything. Hate has taken over our hearts."

"I want these strikes because if Americans attack us and kill us once and for all, then maybe the Arabs will unite to defend us." ...

This music is for Your enjoyment, synchronicity and resonance, Amethystium   Arcus[136]

Much Peace, Calm and Love to You!

Update September 4, 2013

---

[135] N.p., n.d. Web. <http://news.yahoo.com/fearing-us-missiles-syrians-escape-lebanon-150606270.html>.

[136] AlternatifHayatt. "Amethystium - Arcus." YouTube. YouTube, 20 Nov. 2011. Web. 09 July 2016. <http://www.youtube.com/watch?v=BNREyfQ9n0U>.

SOPHIA
It looks like the President of the US is ready to strike in Syria. I have heard several reports of Senators and Congressmen meeting with him and coming out saying they support the plan to strike, as soon as next week. I am not sure when the vote is exactly. Can you speak to this?

G/E
Yes, the attack is inevitable; they were able to convince main public of this invasion's "necessity". Unfortunately most agreed, most were immigrants, there is a strategy behind this constant flow of immigrants.

Senators are well chosen and all are with the illuminati's order's agenda and Congress, chose by the people most of the time, won't do any good as well. Most of the Congressmen are unaware of illuminati's ultimate agenda and they even don't know about this order, if they will vote against it, they are risking their career.

It is that simple within this government. "If you are not with us, you are our enemy and unworthy" - the idea of order illuminati and freemasonry. You can see this in Syria, Bashar al Assad is not with the West on their agendas and never was and never will be, there is no tool of control - the central bank inside Syria. So Syria along with Iran are the first hand enemies of this order and NWO agenda.

The climax is again at 9/11. Coup may take place right after the beginning of this invasion, if people within army will find courage to do so. Many soldiers and people see this terrible corruption within governments of U.S., Britain and France, and coup will follow. If they will not make coup on Syria, they sure will, when Iran will be attacked.

Also intervention from Followers of Light is very possible, they showed their eagerness to intervene in case if this will turn into nuclear war.

Remember that for how hard it will look to overcome, it still will be overcome. This was humanity's choice. Use your thoughts of Peace and Love and Equality for all the planet Earth to overcome this and save many lives. The future depends on Us All, Light workers or Light warriors, Starseeds or Wanderers, Chrystal Beings, whatever You like to call Us All

United. Our Collective Thoughts can change this world to how We would like to see it!

With Happiness, Peace and Freedom!

Update September 9, 2011

G/E
I want to share some songs that can help You and Everyone during great time of Changes if You willing to listen

This song holds a message, it may give an inspiration and understanding[137]

The beautiful Dawn of Love[138]

And Humanity's Rebirth[139]

Much Peace, Abundance and Love to All!

SOPHIA
Thank you! These are beautiful and I will share them.

Have you seen this[140]?

Barack is hell bent on this strike, the people don't know what to think, they don't know the truth. There are mixed opinions because of this. I know you have said this already, and yes, we all feel the intensity of the coming changes. Is there anything else you can say?

---

[137]Lolie102. "Emeli Sandé - Read All About It (lyrics)." YouTube. YouTube, 05 Dec. 2012. Web. 09 July 2016. <http://www.youtube.com/watch?v=3LghzlBdL_Y>.

[138]BrunuhVille. "Emotional Music - Dawn of Love." YouTube. YouTube, 04 Sept. 2013. Web. 09 July 2016. <http://www.youtube.com/watch?v=FFS0pxiqUNw>.

[139] TrailerMusicWorldl. "Two Steps From Hell - Rebirth (Michal Cielecki - Epic Dramatic Sci Fi Hybrid)." YouTube. YouTube, 28 Aug. 2013. Web. 09 July 2016.
<http://www.youtube.com/watch?v=2vmuPSJToTU>.

[140] YouTube. YouTube, n.d. Web. 09 July 2016. <http://www.youtube.com/watch?v=3OD1u9mn6Sg>.

Much love,

G/E

Happy You liked it Sophia! Beautiful music indeed!

I know everything what was said in the video is Truth. It is up to You to believe what is True or false. This is Your most important feeling, to hear Your Inner Voice. The music playing in the background is TSFH Rebirth, everything is interconnected.

As soon as they are to invade Syria, their thoughts will be stricken by Sage Star A, their minds will collapse, all of illuminati order - cabal will feel themselves very bad.

Also, probable, if it is going to get very ugly and Followers of Light will not intervene, then the military vessels of United States and France could be sunk by Forces' of One special division, connected with death, one of the most dangerous divisions Forces of One, Izauya's division have.

One decided to provide them to humanity for this situation as cabalists made a direct call to Creator, to oppose, so One wish to teach that small portion of humanity a lesson when arrogance is becoming too abundant, and if it is going to do very bad things. By saying this I meant when many nations will start big fight over there, the culprits will be sunken.

This division's presence now is within other dimensional plane of Palmyra, ancient ruined city in the center of Syria. They are deep underground and will come to surface when it is needed. They prepared to use weapons of same technological level which humanity currently have. Although they are unstoppable.

But probability of such huge intervention is very low, everything must happen without such things.

We see People's congress is up to oppose Obama, and that is very good, if more will make this opposition and Obama will agree to step down on this invasion then be in preparation of probable false flag made within United States, mostly nuclear, but it could be also non-nuclear. They are very risking to make a nuclear false flag. If they will make it, they will be completely exposed and fail immediately. But knowing their desperate state, probability exists.

The place of this could be on USA's Eastern coast in one of two quadrants somewhere between Charlotte - Norfolk or New York - Pittsburgh. These positions giving out the most energy pressure. This is a very desperate move and probability is low, but it exists. In case if this will happen the best way to avoid the radioactive first wave is to hide behind wall or rock or refrigerator. Something that is denser. The power of thoughts is able to prevent this as well, so it is the best thing we could do right now. Although situation is bad, we all know the outcome!

Much Peace and Love to All!

September 11, 2011

SOPHIA
Hi. I have just received this from my friend, who asked me to share it with you. Please comment where you are able.

Thanks and much love,

"shachalnur
September 9, 2013 - 7:44 am

An attack on Syria will only show the Third Force lost control.

Therefore attack very unlikely, mainly because there's serious resistance outside(BRICS) and inside(Israel) the Cabal.

BRICS+Israel are challenging Obama to attack ,cause the reaction and continuation of the conflict will be directed and controlled from

Moskow,Bejing and Tel-Aviv.

And that's where Rothschild/Rockefeller are afraid of, besides the fact Europe will bear the brunt of the BRICS+Israel reaction.

Obama is only trying to gain some time, cause strategically he's been outplayed.

I feel the Middle East(with BRICS) has succesfully deterred the Third Force from making their move in a controlled manner, and it's the Third Force under attack now.

They'll try to prepare economic and biological mayhem instead, especially in US/Europe to cut their losses.

I spent 52 days in an Israeli security wing at Ramle for giving this info to certain groups in Israel.

I was released when Shin Bet finally understood what I was talking about, and I had to threaten to spread the info including my stay in an Israeli jail on the internet, to free myself.

Since a few weeks my theory is accepted by Arutz Sheva(Israelnationalnews) and I can post unmoderated there, much to my surprise.

Everything I do on the internet is being monitored, and my e-mail is compromised, so being in contact with me on these subjects through e-mail might not be healthy for you.

My theory is all over VT since aug 2012,and if you have any questions you can ask them here.

I know I'm taking risks, and I really don't want others to get in trouble.

A few very respected writers on VT already admitted that my theory might be right.

But ,with all theories, the proof of the pudding.....

Until then VT will follow what's visible and not too far out, which is understandable since there are too many theories.

I can assure you the editors/writers of VT treat me with respect and let me do my thing, keeping in mind I might not be far off, even though it looks like I'm a nutcase right now.

I'm used to that though, and never frustrated when not taken seriously, one day the pudding will be eaten

It can be seen already, because if Israel would have been collaborating with Rothschild over the last year,Syria,Lebanon, Iran AND Israel would have been toast right now.

Rothschild's strategy is in trouble, and BRICS+Israel have managed to turn the pressure on US/Europe.

My aim is not to defend Israel, my aim is explaining that the forces that created Israel, the FED, the UN, the EU will screw everybody including Israel and Jews.

They did this before, and want to repeat it.

I'm trying to make people focus on the source, and that's Rothschild/Rockefeller, his stooges are Jews,Cristians,Muslims and Marcians,for all I care.

After Rothschild/Rockefeller go down there's enough time to bring his stooges to justice, but simply blaming Jews will have the same result as WW2:Rothschild advancing his agenda and all of us further enslaved

http://www.veteranstoday.com/2013/09/09/secret-space-war-x-the-third-force-begins-its-take-down-of-mystery-babylon/

END"

Thank You for sharing to You and Friend!

G/E
Ok, I will share my thoughts and knowledge, but Your own understanding is most important.

The Third Force as they are being called here or order illuminati is really have lost it all. BRICS - Brazil, Russia, India, China, South Africa - this is a new collaboration, an alternative to International Monetary Fund and World Bank and a very good alternative to challenge the western market domination over the world. It will use the system of barter trading, but it still is connected with money, although they are ready to introduce new technologies and let humanity to evolve further, which is what Humanity's Consensus wants. The absolute freedom will be achieved, You can count on them.

The Israel right now is having a situation of inner infighting, much like in US, as illuminati order was always considering Israel as their pawn/expandable and illuminati wished to make a destruction of Israel, Israel is now waking up as well. But still You can't trust zionists-jews, everyday there is a lot of pain in Israel, palestinians are being humiliated, treated like animals and there are very few jews that are willing to live along with Palestinian People. This treatment is just terrible and disgraceful.

One last very important thing is about their leadership and their "savior" which is false savior or anti messiah or antichrist. This anti messiah made a choice and did not join their ranks, although they waited for it impatiently. It was given a choice to make, whether to be a false savior or not. It chose not to be. It is alive right now and will not going to change it's mind. It is possessing super mind of leadership, can guide anything how it wants and with it everything could change in instant.

Also more to that they lack archons' intelligence and leadership, they left illuminati's ranks. Also now US government and illuminati are facing the difficulties with new "fresh minds", as no one wise enough don't wish to join them on their world domination agenda. In fact people already working for them, are leaving or working at some 30% of their full potential.

So You can see, they are done, their game is over.

Considering current events, russians right now used the words of John Kerry about willful complete removal of Syria's chemical weapons, for these words he regretted lately, saying "my remarks were rhetorical and were not meant as serious proposals". And russians presented this initiative, which angered higher chain of command of illuminati as this is just slowing their "end game". That's why Obama and administration is saying that "no stalling tactics are acceptable".

I say it is very well made, the more invasion is postponed, the more time Humanity have to completely wake up and completely evade casualties and destruction!

Much Peace and Love to All!

Update September 20, 2013

SOPHIA
Hello there.

As we approach the 21st of September, 9 months from 12.21.12, there is much speculation. Here is something from my friend. Would you comment on this and on anything relevant?

~~~

" Here is an interesting event for your friend because this is very unusual except in times of conflict as in convoys or when something is about to take place on land...FEMA is currently undertaking urgent activities to be in place by Oct 1st in the same NJ area[141]. Much Love. Saludos
~~~
Thank you,
Much love,

---

[141]"57 Ships Anchored off Shore of NJ, MD/VA | Opinion - Conservative." Before It's News. N.p., n.d. Web. 09 July 2016. <http://beforeitsnews.com/opinion-conservative/2013/08/57-ships-anchored-off-shore-of-nj-mdva-2697276.html>.

*G/E*
Good Day Sophia and Friend!

Right now, considering FEMA operations, order illuminati with pentagon (darker side of it) considering any possible false flag operation, they see that they lose the "deal" on Syria, so they want to make something different. Chemical attack within U.S. is no longer a possibility, nuclear attack still a small possibility, weather manipulation is no longer a possibility, because it will give nothing to them. There is another, I cannot tell what this is, because I don't want to give them a hint. I can give only word "conflict" is a possibility.

About the Equinox - equal day and night which will be on september 22, each new Solar cycle days variates, on Consent 21st day is common. It is an important event, it is a point of time's measurement, like december 21st, june 21st, march 21st which sets a cycle's (or year) quadrant passed. Many important events are set on these dates from the beginning of humanity's history, these dates are considered a time of Celebration around the world. They are indeed important earth cycles, on these dates also very good events may happen, like influx of Cosmic Energies, world ethereal stability maintenance, the birth of very loving children, very beautiful events, lot of them. As well as these are holidays and celebrations, these dates can be used with darker intentions as well.

Here is perception of world situation from different angles:

1. From my own views I don't see anything to happen on that precise date, but if nothing is going to change in the world something will happen very soon, something not good.

2. On Energy plane I see variations in Energy, variations that were not present just 10 cycles ago. Light devices are helping. When I look into Energy, the possibility of false flag event is big.

3. Ancient machines see situation will unfold "as predicted" by analysis.

4. I was with Followers of Light "ethereally" and like I learned they want to prolong humanity's situation for as long as possible to time point we set to them to 2016, the main thought I got was "if humanity will not solve the survival question of this planet and for whole humanity, then they intervene before august 1st 2016".

This means if humanity will solve everything by itself then they just will come to not save humanity, but to accept it into Galactic Federation of Light. Simply to be Friends. They along with humanity will have also to solve the question of possibility of achieving ultimate power over Creation, which they are not allowed to possess yet. Possibly everything will be solved peacefully, without use of Universal Justice.

I hope my own thoughts and views will help You! Gratitude with Peace and Love!


**Update October 4, 2013**


*G/E*
Here is a beautiful music for Your Enjoyment[142] and Emotions[143]

Images are just images, You can create Your own images, but music is different, it is based on emotions, it is filled with feelings and is Universal, unlike images, which You can create how You want to. The interpretation of images can be changed, but interpretation of music and words cannot be changed.

Peace, Calm, Prosperity to You!


*SOPHIA*
The Kara video is powerful. wow.

Thank you.

---

Almyor53. "Two Steps From Hell - Love & Loss." YouTube. YouTube, 25 Aug. 2013. Web. 09 July 2016. <http://www.youtube.com/watch?v=Shs3YQyCgQ8>.[142]

[143] Kiko10061980reloaded. "Two Steps From Hell - Undying Love & Loss (EXTENDED Mix by Kiko10061980 )." YouTube. YouTube, 20 July 2013. Web. 09 July 2016. <http://www.youtube.com/watch?v=sy5zy9oS3Z0>.

The energy for the last few days has been intense and not what we'd call "good"... people are sad, tired, feeling loss and not just that. It is confusing and challenging.

Much love to you,

*G/E*
I'm happy You liked it Sophia! It is showing a moment of future of humanity, when humanity will be able to create it's own life, at first non organic life and soul will visit that non organic body, this is a natural way of evolution, to create life with life. Right now people can only "create" life by birthing. Later on, people will be able to create life out of "dust", literally "out of nothing" like it was said in old religious teachings. This is truth and not superstition.

The pressure of energy is high, illuminati order seeks any possibility to change their desperate position, but just can't find any, they lack leadership, no real leader want to help them and this is a Blessing for Humanity. It is now just a fraction of time until they will see their end, their end like the moment of Justice will come when they will be least expected, like it was said in the bible. It is Truth because One wish humanity and any other beings within existence to feel the most experience during moment of unexpectedness. "You just know it will happen, but You don't know exactly when and how it will look like." More experience and feelings it is. Most recent was the unexpected Chelyabinsk meteor as You remember. We knew it may hit somewhere, but didn't know where, and it arrived in completely unexpected for everyone place.

Just an example of One's playful character :)

Another thing I was asked to share was again about duality of Good vs evil. People knowing about Oneness and Universal Unity wonder why are we still separated between these two groups. Why evil must be judged and why Good isn't. Well it is because this Universe and the way it exists was programmed in a way where Everything can make a free choice. Evil people are evil, because they chose to be so, and Good people chose to be Good. So basically when people chose to be evil, they chose to be enemies of

Good people. It is the choice that makes us different, what we choose is what we become. But we still are One and United, we are created from same material as One, we are a part of One's HUGE body, our physical bodies are the most precious treasures One is having, our Souls are the most Sacred Infinitely Expensive Value that One has. We All share One Universe, We All share One Sun and We All share One Planet. So we are One and United!

To People giving too much attention to money or finances. Money is nothing, a small fraction of One, lifeless, they don't have value unless You give them it, they were created as a tool of control and by using it and giving much attention to it, You maintain the old system. Just use them because You need to. Your real value is Your Soul, like I wrote here, it is Infinitely Expensive and can't be sold. Only a small fraction of it can be sold, when You "sign a contract with the devil" or are indebted or enslaved by this system. Soul is Your Infinite Value, nothing is more Valuable than Your Soul, not money, not gold, not technologies. Money can't change the world, only You can.

Another story I was told to tell You is very old and known by all, but forgotten like many other very important old knowledge.

When we were monkeys, we received a special gift, from extraterrestrials beings (or some may like to call angels or God better). Our DNA was modified, and a very small, but pure particle of Light was put inside of us and hidden. When we started to evolve and feel the presence of this small particle, we started to reach it, as it was so pure and clean and once we were close to it, we were coming to state of nirvana, eternal peace and calmness. So we started to establish religions whose main goal was to reach that particle of Light. The achieving of this particle was very real, but survival instinct and the need to protect ourselves from destroyers, murderers, wars also the view and presence of suffering around us made a hard and harsh toll on our path toward that particle of Light or simply put toward Light (same direction Followers of Light wish humanity to go).

And so this process was slowed. We could have achieved this already long ago, though sufferings were great and survival ability was taking many moments of time out of us. But with each new generation humanity still was coming closer and closer to that particle of Light. And now we have come to a moment, when we are very close to it and only few generations are still needed to reach it ultimately. Once reached, all surroundings around people with reached particle of Light will be harmonized, other people, plants and animals will feel themselves relieved, will feel themselves very calmly and happily. And then people that reached it will improve that particle of Light and grow it, so it will become larger and larger.

Here I'm talking about majority of People, Light workers are much closer to it, and people that base their life on survival instinct are much farther from it.

Under perfect conditions only 3 generations are needed from this point of time to reach it ultimately. The generation right now that must start to live in perfect conditions are aged 3-5 cycles old. Very young ones. We can start only from them, because they are the purest, uncorrupted beings :)

So You can see Humanity almost achieved what they were intended and wanted to achieve, comparing 40 or so generations under perfect conditions 2000 cycles ago.

Use beautiful emotional music, so it can give You inspiration and accompany You when You most need it. Search for music for Your Soul. I will share music that You already heard, it is just my share, but You need to search for music that fits Your Soul.

The soft sound aaaaah is the sound that is coming from the Soul (or from Your Heart if it sounds better for You). Whenever You hear it, You Soul tremble. Because it is when Souls are speaking with each other. In every song don't look in the end or beginning, look at the middle of it.

Your Destiny Awaits[144]

Destiny of The Chosen - Humanity The People[145]

---

[144] Strickland544. "Epic Music || Liquid Cinema - Destiny Awaits." YouTube. YouTube, 17 Mar. 2012. Web. 09 July 2016. <http://www.youtube.com/watch?v=eHAcu7cNnSU>.

<u>Don't stop to Believe and Realize, turn into Reality what You're dreaming for with Your Thoughts and Will</u>[146]

<u>And You will uncover Your Legacy</u>[147]

<u>And finally meet the Majestic Creator and become complete</u>[148]

**Much Peace and Love to You and Everyone!**

*SOPHIA*
**Thank you so much for this. I have been away and only now have seen this.**

**I have been in touch with so many of us who are desperate and despairing of any and all hope. These words sound hopeful.**

**Much love, I wish you well,**

*G/E*
**That's is great to hear Sophia!**

**Also to show the limitless possibilities of Creation and to let You know that for the past 100 cycles humanity was contained under mandatory strict use of fossil fuels I was asked to remind You and Everyone about these infinite and completely clean energy sources:**
<u>Using water as a fuel</u>[149]

<u>Using breathable Air as a fuel</u>[150]

---

[145] MrSoundtracksHD. "Destiny of Chosen - Immediate Music [1080p]." YouTube. YouTube, 10 June 2013. Web. 09 July 2016. <http://www.youtube.com/watch?v=MaKiddS_vSo>.

[146]Bravo1989Tango. "Earth (Immediate Music - Believe)." YouTube. YouTube, 16 July 2009. Web. 09 July 2016. <http://www.youtube.com/watch?v=mZlVaAMsoM8>.

[147]CapeTranquillity. "Icon Music - A Legacy Uncovered (BBC Planet Earth)." YouTube. YouTube, 17 Feb. 2013. Web. 09 July 2016. <http://www.youtube.com/watch?v=0m55VKT9YEQ>.

[148] DivinumMusic. "Liquid Cinema - Majestic." YouTube. YouTube, 20 Oct. 2011. Web. 09 July 2016. <http://www.youtube.com/watch?v=Q-TZjuBDLRQ>.

[149] Minidish. "A Motorcycle That Runs on PURE Water." YouTube. YouTube, 26 June 2008. Web. 09 July 2016. <http://www.youtube.com/watch?v=POJQKg9CRJc>.

[150] YouTube. YouTube, n.d. Web. 09 July 2016. <http://www.youtube.com/watch?v=f15thOvhE38>.

<u>Very easy to create and use: magnetic rotation that never stops can give as much electricity as You will need or want, Energy output is based on size of this generator, also prerequisite to anti gravitation (which means You can fly without wings in any direction nearby massive object like this planet)</u>[151]

**Rotation that never stops unless wheel will run out or break and that is not going to happen for the next 100 cycles if well made.**

**If You know how electricity is being received You already can see that it completely beats old electric grid system. If You don't than I will remind.**

**On main electric plants electric current is received through rotation of turbines. To rotate turbines' blades steam or hot air is needed and You wonder how we can evaporate water to produce this steam, of course by heating up water or burning something. Fossils burns at best rates and give out much more heat than everything else, excluding highly dense materials, like enriched plutonium.**

**Nuclear reactors on nuclear plants are using the same process, but instead of burning something there are used nuclear rods to evaporate water.**

**Hydroelectric plants are using constant stream of water from basins which is held by dams to rotate turbines. Creating a dam, like Hoover Dam, creates a danger if this dam will break every settlement will be drowned along with plants, crops, nature and animals, it is a dangerous and ineffective method.**

**And giant "Wind Mills" or wind turbines are using the very same process, when wind blows, turbines are rotating. So called new "green energy" these wind turbines are actually very useless and they are already irritating people that live nearby them, they produce unpleasant sound and blades are dropping huge shadows on homes and fields, irritating farmers and making damage to crops. So it is a bad solution as well.**

**What we want also to point here, is by using magnetic rotation, all of these highly expensive and damaging obsolete systems will have to go, that**

---

[151] YouTube. YouTube, n.d. Web. 09 July 2016. <http://www.youtube.com/watch?v=kE-MaTjiZ9g>.

means no more wind turbines, no more dams to build, no more nuclear plants, which excludes the danger of radiation leaks like Chernobyl/Fukushima related accidents and no more need to use fossil fuels which completely frees Everyone out of dependence and slavery.

Also about fossil dependence: that is the current old and obsolete system in which humanity still exists. Everything what was built was built on this process, the process of burning and destruction, not harmony. Everything is fueled by this type of fuel, even batteries. This system was established and maintained to hold everyone under control or as a slaves. Because no one could be completely independent as "there is no infinite energy source" and in order to drive a car or flew a plane or use something everyone must come back and pay for fuel, new batteries or electricity. This adds to mandatory paying for place of Your living and mandatory paying for everything You do or buy in current obsolete system.

Much Peace and Love to Everyone!

*SOPHIA*
Hello and thank you. As I am finally able to get back to work, I will share this information.

The US government begins a partial shutdown. Comments?

Much love and gratitude to you,

*G/E*
Good Day Sophia!

They "shutdown" government because of the urgency to do something in order to achieve their dark goal, to reduce the inner infighting and to stop coup that could happen any moment now, only one more "spark" is needed, spark that is going to infuriate People of America.

You can call government shutdown as a "backing down" during order illuminati/cabal state of emergency. During this current shutdown arrests are possible, but we see arrests are not going to be good, arrested will be holdouts of the current system. We can fix that with power of our thoughts, why not arrest supporters and maintainers of the current system? Just a tip for You;)

On surface, government shutdown happened because of Obama's health care system, which is also playing part in all of this and government spending and debt. During this shutdown they want to default on debt, which illuminati order don't want to allow to happen, because this will mean they will lose a lot of allies around the world and they are going to lose bigger part of military, which will mark a big X on their global domination agenda.

They do have hidden resources which they accumulated during their long history, but this was prepared for the next part after world war 3 to create a world's super police force out of UN and unite all the world under one satanic leadership. With these vast resources they can repay all of U.S. debt and allow much more, but if they will use their vast resources now, this will catch attention of the world and they will be exposed at instant. It will be called "cheating" on american and world's People. They know it and so they are trying to solve this fair, without this trump card.

Also about health care act, main reason of government shutdown on surface. This act is fraud by its nature, under word "insurance" is covered their own insurance not People's, they are accumulating money as fast as possible. You know when People don't "buy" insurance they are fined where fines are bigger or even put into jail, so this makes insurance mandatory, because it is a "wise choice". If You will think what actually this insurance gives You, how it can improve Your Life aside from cheaper health care (for which You still need to pay), it will make You wonder, how is this different than from all those scam e-mails You sometimes receive? They are giving the very same service for a "fee".

I was also told that if health care will be mentioned, I will need to remind and warn You on vaccination. Vaccines for the past 100 cycles were used to experiment on different new bio weapon agents. New agents such as viruses were spread and evolved during this last age, they were exercised through experiments within human bodies. Most recent known viruses were swine flu and bird flu, like I was told they were created by this same process. Signatures of these viruses were used to inject extra flavor during vaccinations.

Bio agents' main role was to decrease the possibilities of human's mind and Consciousness, to decrease the percent of rebellion against the current system, to decrease "fanatical behavior" and to disallow individuals to seek the ultimate Wisdom and Truth. Vaccines are not all that bad, sometime they are necessary, when You are traveling to new distant locations or facing a well-known disease like plague, but be careful with new "out of nowhere diseases", through vaccines to counter these diseases they are testing new bio weapons, so always be aware of what You can receive with vaccines. Because they are using same signatures of virus against which vaccine will be injected in You and it is impossible for average doctor to see the difference. All countries whose health care is under oversight of World Health Care Organization should be careful with vaccines. Vaccines are the best way to give People "what you want to give". You never can be sure what might be inside when illuminati order/cabal are in power.

I'm sorry for stretching everything I write, I always try to make it as few as possible, but I just can't make it in a few words text.. I know reading a lot is hard and sometimes not fun to do, but I need to explain everything so that You and Everyone would understand what I meant here, I cannot simply answer: "Government is shutdown because cabal don't know what to do.." It is if I don't know anything:)
Anyway my apologies for huge texts:)

Much Peace and Love to You and Everyone!

October 6, 2013

SOPHIA
Hi,

My friend sent me this last week, I have just begun to catch up with some mail.
~~~

" Why do I send this? because the author is more often right about things *and it could tie in with the FEMA issue which is being denied - as always,-- your friend might throw light upon this - thats all.*

Quote:

It's more than rumor - it is happening. Too many people are confirming this - something huge is underway in Puerto Rico, and the military is being told it will be a meteor strike. I call TOTAL B.S., if anything happens it will be nuclear, an ICBM looks like a meteor coming in, hence my instructions above . . . . . if this was a meteor it would be ALL OVER THE FREAKING MSM, yet not even a peep out of even GLP.

Much Love Saludos "
~~~
Thank you,
Much love and light,

G/E
Yes, right now Everyone in the U.S. should be on a watchout. Especially in a very populated areas on East Coast.

Recent accidents in Washington D.C. were made by People that felt themselves in a highly hazardous feeling, the pressure on Washington grows, they were feeling this huge pressure and unfortunately acted in a bad way.

Everyone could do better and not sacrifice with Yourself, this makes a change, but very small. Better results will be achieved when You will want and wish to change current situation, not sacrificing Your physical incarnation. These people were normal, but they experienced huge stress, which in summary with their corrupted past gave out these accidents.

Right now during government's "shutdown", illuminati order members are looking into different plans, tactics and strategies, they are rethinking their plan and strategy, changing tactics, it is a perfect condition when there is no one to distract them, while Washington is partially lockdowned.

They can't be shutdowned for a very long time though, because People's displeasure is growing with each passing moment and coup is coming very quickly. For that reason FEMA is fully operational and ready to make "sweeps" across country if huge riot will break out, although they will fail. Their order/cabal is collapsing and there is inner infighting going on for future of mankind and they own welfare. Very "hardened" members of original illuminati order are vigorously still hold onto original plan of luciferian indoctrination of whole world, unfortunately they are blind, they don't want to accept new ways of life, new evolution, they hold themselves to old, don't want to let it go..

Nuclear attack is their most powerful false flag attack, but this will mean their end, yet my feelings are strong toward bad event. We can see, they will make the final showdown before they go, we are holding them and restricting them to highest extent, yet they are still able to make last spark.. Be careful right now and on watch out. I can't point out the exact location of false flag, only two quadrants I mentioned earlier, when we GE's will be given "emergency call", I will share this.
This is all I can share with You right now.

As always much Wisdom, Tranquility and Abundant Love to Everyone!

Update October 14, 2013

SOPHIA
Hello. Just checking in. I recently saw this[152]
Wondering if you have any further information.
Thank you and have a wonderful weekend.

G/E
Not much to say right now Sophia. Everything proceeding as it supposed to, the will of humanity will be fulfilled and old promises will come to life.

The Ariel Sharon is still alive, but his consciousness is indeed like it is said there, like a plant's - at a minimal level. He is alive, but only may able to

---

[152] N.p., n.d. Web. <http://www.jta.org/2013/09/04/news-opinion/israel-middle-east/ariel-sharon-has-successful-abdominal-surgery>.

support his body in alive state. If many people would want him to recover, it will happen so, but many people, many of muslims wished him bad things for what he did in the past and they asked Allah - God to help them, and this wish has been granted.

During his life he ordered many bad things to happen while he was a military commander, most of these things are unknown to the public as everything that was happening in Israeli wars from 1948 to 1970s was covered up and archives of military crimes committed by Israel were destroyed at once so that no one would find out this, U.S. and Britain were helping in this most prominently.

With the bloom of press and video recordings, they were finding it harder to do so. As an example, one massacre of mostly palestinian and shiites People that happened in 1982 forced Ariel Sharon to resign from his military carrier. He always was considered the most highest commander in modern Israel, because of his deeds for protecting Israel and unfortunately decreasing the number of palestinians..

Here You can hear the <u>sound of a Soul</u>[153]

Peace, Tranquility, Prosperity.

~~~~~~~~~~
To Your knowledge, You heard about 17th october, it is a time when U.S. treasury's reserves will run out, this is where illuminati order and U.S. government will have to decide the faith of U.S., whether to increase the debt ceiling or not, maybe making something different.

They have different choices, but to please The People, they will have to make a default which will concentrate all efforts on U.S. inner politics, which is also meant they will lose trust of foreign countries and many "allies" as well.

I can't see default very clearly and think they will try to stretch this decision making as far as they can.

---

[153] Dendera91. "Ivan Torrent - Before I Leave This World." YouTube. YouTube, 01 Oct. 2013. Web. 09 July 2016. <http://www.youtube.com/watch?v=nck1xQU6YbE>.

Peace and Love to You!

Update October 18, 2013

SOPHIA
It looks like you were correct. Now stretched until January 2014.
Hmmm...

Much love,

G/E
They made a wise decision for their survival, because People of America became more aware of their deeds and People's discontent have grown significantly. Now they will try not to make more government shutdowns as this can grow into their complete removal from office. Though their removal is very close without need to shutdown government once again.

During this government shutdown they haven't found any good solutions to their growing problems and one of their nuclear plots have been thwarted by reasonable military in pentagon. They also came to biological pandemic plot, this reasonable military may just spoil this plot as well. The virus is based on swine flu and bird flu, a new type of flu. They will try to spread it over most populated areas on the world and in U.S. close to winter time to force everyone to make vaccination like it was with previous flus to save U.S. from this instigated disease. Good thing I see that they will fail to do this.

In the end overall, they won't be able to fool the world any longer, the huge political scandal and their removal is very close. The promised rebirth will be made during this solar cycle, the time will be before next cycle, somewhere when ISON will arrive, a great comet body.

Let One Bless You, We are One and United.

Peace and Love to You as always!

October 19, 2013

SOPHIA
So, there are many questions about this part:
" The promised rebirth will be made during this solar cycle "
and different definitions as to a solar cycle. Would you clarify? Do you refer
to this calendar year, 2013?

Much love,

G/E
Yes Sophia, we refer to years and days and so on so on, to many things
overall as cycles, but because I made confusion with this I'm using solar
cycles and earth cycles, but it have to be cycle if You want to understand
messages fully.

The promised rebirth is the 2013 cycle of rebirth, this whole year or a
cycle/circle is a rebirth, yet it is not complete, and so it will be completed
during this cycle.

Next cycle will be cleaning and repositioning, re-managing the system, so it
can fit majority it's choice. All it is by Followers of Light plan. Humanity
have to achieve higher state of Lightmanship they always saying, it will be
possible only if changes will be allowed to be done, the only barrier that
stands in the way is the old illuminati order.

Also considering Forces of One, we were informed that Light Followers
have agreed to cease the research and development of "skia" - control over
Creation project. They agreed, that they are not worthy yet and will cease
this operation once humanity will be set free and on its own.

They will be able to continue only when One will approve this, most of them
understands this, but some do not, these few may cause problems to their
own being in a future, this may influence humanity as well, but it's not
going to be now or in 50 cycles farther, just a hint for them.. And everything
Light Followers developed so far will remain in their possession.

Now Forces of One will only see that this project will finish completely and as promised humanity will be given its choice fulfilled, the choice of being free, without lies and without suffering. Happiness was always a priority wish of every human, so this will be given to Everyone.

It will all happen in due time and it is not far away, very close, what is in our power now is to hasten this and force it to happen sooner, it is our power. We can do this very differently, by thinking about this, willing, wishing, talking, tweeting, making changes physically, interacting with society, bringing in new inventions that literally changes the way we as a human beings live.

Much Gratitude and Appreciation for Your hard work will not go without reward and forgotten. As One told Everyone will be rewarded for their deeds and we GEs never forget what others did to the World in which we are currently residing and to ourselves as well. Bad or Good deeds are rewarded respectively, and this is the case when this will be done.

Peace, Calm and Prosperity!

Update October 23, 2013

SOPHIA
Would you comment on this[154]?

Thanks!

Much love,

G/E
Ok Sophia, remember to always believe in what You want to believe in.

You know the Followers of Light will aid humanity and what was told there

---

[154]Secureteam10. "BREAKING! Whistleblower EXPOSES GOV'T SHUTDOWN And FEMA - 10/20/2013 - UFO Coverup - ISON." YouTube. YouTube, 20 Oct. 2013. Web. 09 July 2016. <http://www.youtube.com/watch?v=ZiOcZqeebec>.

is this preparation. These were not structures, but interstellar ships, they shift between dimensions and as soon as something human-made approaches them they "disappear". There is no need to worry about this, illuminati order is afraid because they know what this all means to them, but everyone non cabal, non illuminati and non terrible people shouldn't be afraid of this. This will aid humanity as a whole.

One is with all of You, do not be afraid and have no fear in Your hearts. With Wisdom and Love!

October 26th, 2013

SOPHIA
I thought you might want to see a follow up to the video[155]

Much love,

G/E
Thank You for sharing this Sophia! I know most of this information, they were always using the dark side of the Moon.

You need to be aware from this, as it influences every american. Indeed U.S. government is preparing for huge riots and even revolution war. But this will not happen unless Everyone in U.S. will want it.

What I see, is that Everyone don't wants it, I see People need changes and through peaceful solutions these changes will happen. They will not go without a fight, and so the only aggressors in these changes will be they, that why they and their satanic legacy will be tainted and forgotten.

They will be remembered only as the "terrible tragedy of human civilization prevented" and Everyone will try to avoid the repeat of this.

---

[155] Secureteam10. "NASA Whistleblower EXPOSES GOV'T SHUTDOWN PART 2 - 2014 - DHS Purchases - UFO Coverup." YouTube. YouTube, 25 Oct. 2013. Web. 09 July 2016. <http://www.youtube.com/watch?v=OrNqZOtACqE>.

During previous cycle it was Your Awakening, Lightworkers' Awakening, ours as well. Now it is masses' Awakening, Every Human Being now have Awakened and is ready for Great Changes!

You remember this song[156], let Everyone hear it, this brings back most sacred what is inside Everyone, that same particle of Light. Anytime You listen to very emotional, spiritual music, you are getting close to it.

With Peace and Love Always!

SOPHIA
Thank you. This is beautiful music.

There is a third video, with more information about the vehicles that are parked near the moon, supposedly to be released soon. The team that set up this interview is setting up another one.

I know that most do not want war in this country. There are some very public channels working to incite revolution, and as time moves ahead, well, the true nature of the people will dictate what happens. This is more evidence of the awakening and subsequent rebirth we are having. This is very good news.

Much love,

Update October 28th, 2013

G/E
i'm happy You liked it! Everything is correct Sophia.

One rule You need to remember always, is that if You will allow Your nature to took over You, You won't be in control and Your nature will do everything, that the way of survival instincts which dominated humanity for a lot of time. It is up to Your Consciousness and Mind to take over Your nature, that the way many beings are going and evolving on much better scales and speeds.

---

[156] YouTube. YouTube, n.d. Web. 09 July 2016. <http://www.youtube.com/watch?v=RMbAxa8fGb4>.

For us Forces of One there is also another rule, I can share this with You if You are interested, it won't hurt anyone.

With Love and Wisdom.

SOPHIA
yes, definitely interested!

Thank you,
Much love,

G/E
Ok Sophia. It is based on meaning - Harmony among All Things and Everything is Interconnected. A complicated one and somewhere You may disagree with this.

We know that every part of Universe is alive, every molecule, every particle, going deeply every particle of an atom is alive, there are smaller particles of an atom which humanity is not aware of yet, there is One present Everywhere.

This as well touches plants', animals', humans' every cell. Organic cells are more alive than molecules and much more than atoms and much more than it's super small particles.

Aliveness is based on Energy output and "manipulation" of it. Every cell of an organic Body is a separate self-aware organism. Just an example - they have more Life Energy than the particles of same size from which are made Artificial Intelligences because of it's Energy's chaotic behavior.

Now the Physical Bodies of plants, animals and humans. They are classified strictly as: plants - Collective Consciousness, animals - Collective Consciousness under control of Central Neural System from partial to almost full (humans).

What this means is that in plants cells are living with One Voice, there is no controlling entity such as one more evolved animals, reptiles, insects and other predator and herbivores are having. Herbivores are predators as well as they eat plants, but this is another story. It is all a natural Cycle of Life which is meant to be by One.

The Central Neural System is human's mind and it's Consciousness, it is what You are, because of it's more highly evolved state, humans are having more evolved heightened Soul as well. It is easy to talk to and understand humans than plants for example because of this controlling entity.

The whole structure of control and rule of "few over many" on this planet was based on this instinctively justified meaning. The situation within the human individual Body is very same. The Central Neural System controls all the population of Your Physical Body, You may relate to Your body as "separate country" under one ruler which is You.

All the cells in human's Body are fulfilling their given roles, cells answering for food processing are doing so, cells answering for flow of resources, oxygen and food to each cell of a body are doing so, cells that are answering for pheromone producing and producing of secrecy elements are doing so, cells that are meant to protect our body from incoming outside threats are protecting us and repelling "invaders" which want to feed on our rich with Energy Body.

The Central Neural System can be called dictatorship if it rules over Body's population without mutual understanding and mutual compassion, shortly - without Harmony and on opposite can be called wise and loving leader if it understands and care for body, most important here is not care, but understanding and compassion.

Because of lack of Understanding of each of human Body's cell, during long history of humanity people were dying without knowing exactly "why?". Very few people really understood this structure and they were able to cure themselves without the use of outside means.

By now You are able to see a huge reflection of human society. The rule "as above so below" and "there is reflection of You Everywhere You look" is Universal and works Everywhere. Every cell, like worker in human society is doing their given jobs, yet they rarely can change their jobs, unlike humans can.

Like rulers, Central Neural System receives more Energy and more food, not because it is greedy, but because they were needed more to function at 100%, due to it's highly active state. In human society as You know greed took over many and this was changed to bad twist.

The most important for us GEs knowledge here, is that we need to understand what our Body needs and live in Harmony with each of our Cells as with other beings around us, this is not easy to do and even much harder to preserve our body from any damage to disallow any of the cell to die as the world around us can damage us easily, but as Everything is Possible in this Universe, this is possible as well.

We don't mean here that we need to be completely isolated from world, no, it is just to reduce the damage to Your Body to minimum, the death of some cells unfortunately is inevitable in this world, it is not completely safe for organic structure, other bacteria and virus cells are always around our skin to invade when Body become weaker due to climate changing (Summer - Winter cycle).

Instinctively humans are preserving themselves and what is important not because humans want to live as it used to be, but because there is a forgotten oath to Body which every human and animal is giving before incarnated, to preserve and care for their Body the same as for their Children. This differs on type of animals, fishes, insects.

In humanity a new step is shaping itself, "to preserve other People as well as the Body and it's Children". This is a natural way of Evolution for human-type creatures.

A good advice for Everyone is to talk with Your Physical Body when You have free time, orally or inwardly, for example when You go to sleep and no one is around You (to avoid misunderstanding) for loving people inwardly is a good solution. Your body is a separate living organism as well as Collective Consciousness like one plants are having. This Collective Consciousness consists of individual organisms called cells and within cells there are other living organisms for which these cells care, so this is not just cells we are caring for, they have their own relatives and "children" as well, cells that are being duplicated during growing and restoring processes.

I hope You will understand this complicated yet obvious thing and I hope this knowledge may aid You and Everyone.

With Love and Universal Wisdom.

SOPHIA
Thank you so very much. I will share.

Much love,

October 29th, 2013

SOPHIA
Also, a friend of mine has a question about some information circulating. What follows comes from him.

"As the fore run you could think seriously about the second link on VT with special reference to the blocked comment but more importantly to the comments section where some very important comments are made, some of which you will need to click on "read more"

"The ground question is - how accurate in the way of things is the information contained in the block text (that of the european intelligence service) and how do the comments rate regarding the accuracy of those expressing views and feelings. Perhaps I ask too much but my appetite for truth and accuracy is very high."

((Included were these two links[157] [158]))

---

[157] N.p., n.d. Web. <http://chemicalskyfall.com/us-reported-in-panic%c2%9d-after-chemtrail-planes-forced-down-in-india-nigeria/>.

G/E

I. Ok, I will express my thoughts to Friend's question. I know the chemtrails from most of the cases are left from "normal" planes' trails which daily are flying in thousands. They are hazardous for environment as well as they are the vapors from combustion process. But not as You are thinking under word chemtrails. But indeed chemtrails sometimes are having a nature to spread bio weapons, and experimental chemical agents over some minor population to test "it's effectiveness" on population. Very terrible and crimeful deeds. It is easy to cover them among "normal trails".

Normal trails to Your knowledge are left in upper atmosphere (higher troposphere), it is due to temperature variation. The comments precision/accuracy is always correct and high if You know what You are looking for, there are programs and hired agents that spread disinformation, but their number is low. On these websites these agents are not present. Sometimes comments are removed due to commercial nature of these and due to rude language. Always know what You need to find, it is easy to lost Yourself in comments:)

You are always welcome to believe in what You think is right. Every individual have different views on reality, every individual interpret book that is written with same words differently, it is not because humans have "bad memory", it is because of Uniqueness of each Individual Being. So believing in someone's words without any doubt is not correct in our views, as there will always be something that can't be agreed upon, this was tested many times and You can see this in humanity's history, there won't be a complete universal understanding or believe on some subject.

What most important in this and how to achieve Oneness You may ask, is to <Understand Other People>, when we understand them they will understand us. I mentioned this in last revelation, understanding is most important between Neural Central System and whole Physical Body, between Government and it's People, between People themselves. This creates Oneness, Unity, Harmony, Symbiotic Co-existence. Mutual understanding is taking it's turns and transforming this planet as it is the

158 "SSG: Notes on Secret Shadow Government." Veterans Today. N.p., n.d. Web. 09 July 2016. <http://www.veteranstoday.com/2013/10/25/ssg-notes-on-the-secret-shadow-government/>.

way to the Light and Unity.

It is up to You to be angry or forgive, You are free in Your choice. For Your own Good being You may ask Yourself, Creator and Your Body whether You need to forgive or continue to be angry on someone like cabal/illuminati order that holds this system afloat and makes other People to look like they want them to be. People are becoming angry or despair because They don't have the "godly powers" and immortality. You can imagine having such powers and it will become obvious that there won't be any reason to be angry or despaired any more.

In our knowledge Souls are immortal, but People need proves to this and we are understanding this greatly. Yet we are not here to provide these proves, humanity will have to find it on it's own. A hint is - again it is not hard if You know what You are looking for:) Everything is interconnected, that why it repeats itself and have reflection Everywhere You look.

Humanity's existence here is an experiment like we told this earlier; it is an experiment of Light Followers and One. Light Followers themselves and we Forces of One are an experiment of One as well. But it is not an experiment in one word - experiment. This whole Humanity's Existence is also can be called an entertainment, an experience, a kindergarten, a school, evolution process from lower to higher and like Friend said world dynamic. It has a full spectrum in it, but for One personally all of this is experiment/testing and experience gaining, improving abilities to higher extent, "pushing everything beyond set boundaries".

I also like the questions about religions, religions are my personal strong side. Religion shortly "is believe in something supernatural" and "in higher forces that manipulate the world we are living in". You may see by this description, gods may be different not one Universal God as last monotheistic religions are claiming.

Within Forces of One - our religion is something more than just a believe, it is our way of life, a library of history and feelings, we are in Friendship with One and there is no separation and violence within our religion, there is just One, no angels, no devils, no spirits. All of such beings are given their true names and are a part of One. Every aspect of One, It's many faces and characters are described as sides of One, "Harmony, mutual Friendship and Understanding among All Things" is our religion's interpretation put shortly. Loyalty and life experience are most important subjects in our religion to discuss.

The late major religions here on Earth - less hinduism, buddhism and mostly judaism, christianity, islam were made on misinterpretations and misunderstanding (I will mention this, many don't like to acknowledge, all 3 have jewish origin, (not including zoroastrianism and hinduism from which it originated), plus illuminati order and cabal, kaballah - occultic religion, zionism all have a direct control over major world population, this was the era of 'pure jewish bloodlines" control over planet, which is coming to end).

These religions hold the truth and basics of Universe, but it is necessary "to dig though them" to find this "holy truth". Subconsciously People feel this truth and that is why, these religions still exist. When religion have no truth at all, it is not going to exist for too long.

People whose heart was filled with greed and willfulness for more wealth distorted them and turned them into perfect tools of control and intimidation. With word intimidation it is meant "if you are not going to believe in this religion, you will go to hell and everyone will point their fingers at you". Unfortunately these late religions hold this principle of fear and obedience..

The reason why it happened also was due to interference of "higher forces" the Followers of Light. Whenever they were appearing, they were impacting human society greatly, they were always called angels or demons, based on their appearance with light or without light. Light they can illuminate from their crafts and from themselves and their "illusory visions" is brighter than the Sun's Light.

That is why when they were with such a light, they were always considered servants - the angels or lesser gods of God or servants of higher God like Odin, Zeus or Vishnu. Whenever they were appearing to humans, they were using different names and titles. It is based on their taught - "humans will not understand our names and titles, that why we will use names and titles they are accustomed to".

They are also always saying that humanity is the only civilization in this Galaxy that is going through such sufferings, but that is not true, there are civilizations which have even harsher conditions than humanity, they do this not because they like to lie how You may think, but because they want to encourage humanity by showing like to children that it is only they that are behind, so that humanity can increase it's pace and join them.

We understand their way of thinking, yet we are disagreeing with it. We never like to lie or deceive, and we are never doing this, unless One will ask us. Lie is creating separation, suspicion which makes up for distrust and hate which in the end brings chaos and destruction. It caused misunderstanding, disbelieve, destruction of previous religions, more pain and suffering and brought religions, where their original words were distorted to suit the greedy willfulness of few men.

I wanted to point out here shortly that religions were created as they are because there was no mutual understanding, and everything was interpreted how People of that time saw and understood things. If these religions will want to survive, then they will have to change along with humanity or they will simply perish and be forgotten. In our understanding they by now are largely outdated and cannot go on with the current progress.

As always, we are always not claiming that "everything we say is how it is", You always are free to choose, whether to accept it partially, or fully, or interpret completely differently or decline it all together. We never liked to enforce our views on others and never doing this (unless One is not asking us to of course), this is not our way and this is not how One is telling us to do almost always. The choice is always Yours.

With Peace and Love to Everyone as always.

November 6, 2013

SOPHIA
Hello.

It is November now. Do you have any updates?

Thank you.

Much love,

G/E
Good day Sophia!

Nothing new to say.

The U.S. government is preparing their bio plot, yet they are being strictly watched by Sun and Sage Star A through Sun and by us and by Followers of Light and by Whole World as well. To many eyes on them. Under the watchful Eye of the Sun they will not be able to make their plot of subjugation. They are in the fist of Sun and Sage Star and as time passes the place in the fist becomes less and less as fist tightens. Soon there will be no place to hide or run, right now they have the option to let it go, but they are not accepting this option, like we see they will fight to the end. They are thinking that they will lose "too much" and that is true, but at least they will preserve something if they accept it, if not then there will be nothing left for them and history will remember them as terrible, ruthless people.

NSA revelation is doing great damage to their spying activities, it is one of most important for them things, but if they will push for world war 3 again like they did with Syria a new revelation will follow. But at this moment everything is more or less quiet, that is why coup is at slow moving pace toward meeting point as well.

If You have something to ask Sophia or Anyone else You are always welcome!

Peace and Love to You!

November 14, 2013

SOPHIA
Hello.

There is talk that we are within 2 weeks or so of the "event". Here is a description[159].

Early on in our conversation, you mentioned an "event" as well. Would you comment on this? On both the timing (2 weeks) and the description here?

Thank you.
Much love,

G/E
Good day Sophia!

About the moment of Justice, from now on humanity can activate "event" at any moment, like I know now all the preparations for this are complete within the Followers of Light side. They will act like they said only when humanity will be ready to meet them, this means most of the world population and most of the governments, mainly world "super powers" which You know.

Until that moment they will continue to make "tweaks" and acceleration of Consciousness' full awareness awakening. Majority is now at optimal awakening that is medium by our calculations, thanks to the internet and light workers works (meant special agents here, not all workers).

I will give Everyone that really want it to happen as soon as possible these points.
To increase the pace for this event, which we call Moment of Justice, this can be done:

1. Revelation and understanding of ETs presence above this world.

2. NSA inner structure reveal which connects to illuminati order and majestic 12 structures.

---

[159] N.p., n.d. Web. <http://prepareforchange.net/archives/194>.

3. Integration of new technologies that challenges this current fossil/combustion system and defense of these technologies from "multibillion corporations".

4. Possible abundant riots with an intent to reveal and acknowledge the presence of ET civilizations right here and right now above this planet.

5. The will of a whole or most of humanity for ETs to reveal themselves. In this case it is not necessary to speak loudly about it, it can be sufficient if People will simply "want" it. Something Everyone can do.

Right now none of these objectives is met/number of People willing for this to happen is not enough as well. But everything from this is increasing with each passing moment. Soon all will be met.

These are the prerequisites for this event to occur. Event is indeed "within the grasp". Get ready and be ready to make it happen. That is going to be the worst nightmare of illuminati order/cabal secret societies like we see.

Peace, Calm and Prosperity!

Update # 2 (November 14, 2013)

SOPHIA
Thanks! I do notice much more talk about ships in the sky and have seen some in broad daylight this week!

Another odd thing is that whenever I return to my home in the dark, the streetlight goes out! It then goes back on after I have driven into my garage... This is only in the last few weeks.

Take care.

Much love,

G/E
They are interested in You as a Being of Consciousness. You are interested for Light Followers as You know it all how they like to understand.

Love and Light is most essential to them and deep understanding of this and of Unity/Oneness attracts them and they are aiding, supporting and defending such peoples around the world.

So You will understand them once You meet them and they will understand You as well, previous conversation didn't go well as You were not quite ready for it, but they are ok with it, they understood You and Your behavior Sophia:)

You can wave Your hand to sky whenever You will feel free and safe to do it. Their presence is denser above such countries like U.S. and for instance nearby You are Your Guardians. They will not appear instantly, but again sometime less expected, if You will be ready for this of course:)

November 16, 2013

G/E
Here is small gift to inspire All that love to hear beauty of Creation from BrunuhVille - great composer of emotional celtic music.

Magic of Love[160]

Winds of Freedom[161]

And another music for Rebirth[162]

Wish You All Peace, Calm and Prosperity!

 November 18, 2013

---

[160] BrunuhVille. "Celtic Music - Magic of Love." YouTube. YouTube, 24 May 2013. Web. 09 July 2016. <http://www.youtube.com/watch?v=0-B0dgYDQNI>.
[161] BrunuhVille. "Celtic Music - Winds Of Freedom." YouTube. YouTube, 24 July 2012. Web. 09 July 2016. <http://www.youtube.com/watch?v=hTLEbErPl9I>.
[162] BrunuhVille. "Emotional Uplifting Music - Rebirth." YouTube. YouTube, 10 Nov. 2013. Web. 09 July 2016. <http://www.youtube.com/watch?v=gCEpq-TVs8E>.

SOPHIA

The answers here are to questions about these recent reports about what is going on "off world", as well as the following question, from another reader:

~~~

"Conflicting perspective?

To "riot" against the Illuminati control.. (I assume this means march or protest physically), sign petitions, inform others etc.
This seems useful and in alignment with one of the necessary steps to assist more awakening and a larger Consensus.

On the other hand, if there is no right or wrong and to push against darkness actually feeds it......

Then I would ask for a clarification or elaboration on how best to awaken and overthrow, not consent etc. vs simply stay in love....

This issue is a constant source of confusion for me and I was not able to get a real FEEL for the most constructive way to proceed with this...

Thank you"

~~~

G/E
Good Day Sophia!
Ok, I will try to comment on these questions.

 Like You know Sophia, final preparations from Light side are made and now, like they said it is only for Humanity to make the last thing to be done. Always follow what is closer to You, Your Inner Voice/One will aid You in understanding and knowledge on non-physical developments. One is always with You.

The developments in non-ethereal reality is this, from our knowledge. Evil dark side is at its ending phase of rule over this world and reality, it was gradually suppressed by People's connected thoughts, Love and Compassion gave greater boost for this clearing out of old "negative thought" dark energy leftover, which was in state of stagnancy. The oldest most powerful dark energy pulse is almost 400 cycles old. These pulses are suppressed with each new moment of time. They will collapse eventually.

What is happening beyond this world could be interesting for Everyone, but this is not a necessity for Humanity right now. Our advice for You right now is just to focus on this world and it's developments, it is way too important for Your own being and future. What You are doing now will impact next thousands of cycles into the future.

The second question for a great beloved Friend. This issue was a problem for a whole humanity's lifetime since religion was "created".

"Doing evil when it is necessary, means we are not holding to our path of Love, in which we must not do such things."

This taught was always haunting People around the world for many ages. The answer on this is as simple as this taught. You can ask Yourself "what will be better", for You, for Your Body, for Your relatives, for Your Friends, for Whole Humanity, for Mother Earth, for Father Sun, for grandfather Sage, for Galaxy, for Universe, for Creator.

Before You will do something, make sure You understand Everyone around You and their thoughts, suggestions. To better understand others and their proposals, we are always "switching ourselves to others' boots". There, we see how that person is feeling. Understanding of whole world and Universe around You is the key to harmony and symbiotic coexistence. That is higher than Light and Dark sides separated.

The option for riots is not necessarily, it is only one of those prerequisites for moment of Justice/Event to start. It can be skipped, but we see that if great changes will take place, protests can be very abundant. The question for Everyone will be left the same, will You use aggressive or calm behavior on these protests? Choosing and understanding, these two words may and will aid You well.

Much Peace and Love to You!

November 25, 2013

G/E
Nothing new to say Sophia, world is struggling, natural disasters, conflicts and other incidents are taking lives of people. The number of people suffering from this is decreasing. Along with it, humanity is evolving and better understands the real connection within itself. All proceeding normally, without interruptions, no outside intervention was made to this moment.

Here is a very beautiful song[163] to inspire and aid You and Your Friends Sophia when it is most necessary.

 With Peace and Love always!

November 30, 2013

SOPHIA
There is so much anticipation for the Comet Ison.
Do you have any information to add to what we already know?

Thank you,

G/E
Good day Sophia! The comet Ison is an ordinary comet, it is usual for comets and asteroids to cycle the Sun. Comets and asteroids sometimes can bring life to planets, it is a way of interaction between Stars and Systems. The sky objects always influence People and Earth as they have physical interaction with us and our Planet and Sun. In the past history there were much bigger and brighter comets on display over this Planet, some even exploded turning the night sky into broad daylight sky.

Yet right now are the time for Great Changes on this World, so as You may have guessed this comet is a special one. It is one of those signs that

---

[163] Amolino3. "Guild Wars 2 Soundtrack | Fear Not This Night." YouTube. YouTube, 17 Aug. 2012. Web. 09 July 2016. <http://www.youtube.com/watch?v=qOMQxVtbkik>.

Humanity can guide with it's United Thought. Like I was told, One gave the possibility for humanity to choose how the comet will behave and Ison made it around the Sun very close to it, although it could have gone melted, but it survived. The astronomers were "sure" it would dissipate, yet their small will was not enough.

Although Ison not completely survived, still a great sign of United Thought, like People's Wishes it were. Many People wanted to see it, but the Will wasn't high, so comet made it in the way You see:)

Sometime in the far future, after all of this suffering and trials will gone, humanity will be able to steer objects only by using thoughts, even such distant like comets. Right now Humanity is having only a small friction of such power, yet it is always there and is available to use:)

Here are videos[164] of survived Comet Ison[165], NASA officially announced this comet a dissipated comet

Much Peace and Understanding!

December 4, 2013

SOPHIA
Hi. I saw this today[166].

Do you know anything about this?

Much love,

G/E
Good Day Sophia!

---

[164] Skyywatcher88. "Comet of the Century ISON vs Comet Lovejoy:." YouTube. YouTube, 29 Nov. 2013. Web. 09 July 2016. <http://www.youtube.com/watch?v=ZipKmEeehjA>.

[165] SolarWatcher. "C/2012 S1 COMET ISON Survives Perihelion." YouTube. YouTube, 28 Nov. 2013. Web. 09 July 2016. <http://www.youtube.com/watch?v=-i5RQZJcDak>.

[166] BPEarthWatch. "Hercolubus. WHAT?????" YouTube. YouTube, 03 Dec. 2013. Web. 09 July 2016. <http://www.youtube.com/watch?v=8Jk9RhTJX1k>.

Yes Sophia, NASA and US government's infrastructure agencies are occasionally editing sky images and space images, starting from beginning of space age and continuing on. As they officially declared comet ISON dead, they went quiet for 2 Earth cycles (days) and then returned and showed edited images of comet ISON fading away.

What You saw there was Followers' of Light very huge spherical ship, bigger than this planet is, which serves them as a planet on its own. This ship is surrounded by a powerful force field or energy shield; it bears energy signatures which can make it visible in this dimensional world under some circumstances. And this is what is seen there, the force field which surrounds this ship. Followers of Light brought this ship here not long ago, as Humanity's Ascension is close, this is a necessity of having it here for them, they have a lot of such ships around this Galaxy and beyond. Like I was telling You Sophia, there is nothing to worry about, this all is prepared for Humanity, to aid and accompany.

I also wanted to share with You and Friends this video[167]. It is magnetic rotation technology, the one You remember, one of the easiest and cheapest to make and to use. If You or Anyone Else reading this have will, ability and resources, I may advice You to make this engine type and use it. The key point in this technology is to use rotary blades like the ones that are used on windmills inside the generator. In this case all You have to do is to turn magnets and rotary blades inside this turbine so that it will use magnetic force as a wind force. Remember the sailors? They were using wind to trespass the ocean. Likewise in space there are solar/stellar sailors, they use whether plasma wind or stellar light to trespass the cosmic ocean. And likewise this technology uses the same "wind" principle.

The more people would know this, the quicker will Humanity completely Transform itself. Wish You Great Luck and Great Success!

December 5, 2013

[167] YouTube. YouTube, n.d. Web. 09 July 2016. <http://www.youtube.com/watch?v=gvO9XMBZ4DI>.

SOPHIA
Thank you. I love the vid!!

I will share this.

Here is another video re: energy and us[168].

I just received this message and am sending it on to you.
~~~
*"... since april 2013 i follow your conversation with your off-world friend.I appreciate very much your conversation and look every day for new updates.I am also very interrested in free energy and in his latest message he said he would help anyone who is willing to build a magnetic rotation device.Can you tell me please how to contact him.Thank you"*
~~~
Much love,

G/E
Thank You for video Sophia! It is correct that "separating ourselves from the slavery system of fossil fuel is the way to real Freedom. If we are to use fossil fuel and pay for it, then we are accepting being a slaves to those that feeds us with it."

About the question, look in a video description, there is a link to pdf file, there You need to look for magnets' positioning, the website is http://www.free-energy-devices.com/ where You can get the rest of practical guide for building it, don't worry it's free.

You can skip that, so it won't make a confusion for You as there is a lot of information, once You get a grip on what You are up to build, You can return to this guide to find how to make some tweaks to make it working and for better results. You can use old motor with permanent magnets inside, they are fairly easy to find on scrap yards. What is important to know, use magnets as a wind power to rotate the wheel, or for maximum output, make blades and place them around the wheel in opposition to

---

[168] GlobalBEM. "Ralph and Marsha Ring : Anti-gravity and Conscious Awareness in Aether Technology." YouTube. YouTube, 16 Sept. 2013. Web. 09 July 2016. <http://www.youtube.com/watch?v=8v3Bsh1E_8Y>.

magnets so that they will "catch the magnetic wind" like old sailers were catching wind and like current "green energy" windmills are catching.

This type of energy generator is tested for many many ages beyond this world and it is working greatly, it can be outfitted with ion accelerator or enhancer or with both to give out from 400 to 800 times (based on design and this is not the boundary) the electricity You will get from this type. And as You understand that is a very huge amount of energy that can power anything present on this world.

Ion technology is an advanced technology and is not present on this world, but if Humanity as a whole will show One that it is worthy for it, then we will gladly grant this technology.

Also Sophia there in description is a very good video[169] if You haven't checked it yet
"The Truth Behind The Energy Lie (Supression Of Technological Evolution, The Evidence) full movie"

December 6, 2013

SOPHIA
There is a lot of conversation about ISON not being a comet, but a ship.

???

Much love,

G/E
Believe always Sophia in what You think is right. Your own believe is most important. As I will give You some information, remember to dissent it based on Your views, You are always free to accept or decline everything presented to You.

In our knowledge that is a comet and it was fragmented when it passed

---

[169] 20fireman12. "The Energy Lie Supression Of Technological Evolution, The Evidence Full Movie YouTube." YouTube. YouTube, 15 Feb. 2012. Web. 09 July 2016. <http://www.youtube.com/watch?v=4kNZGXy9UoY>.

278

"under Creator - the Sun" as it was passing very close to Sun and the heat and gravity collapsed it as speed of turn was very big and full of stress, some mass fell on Sun and was burned. But it still survived, as it was in a wishes of Humanity. It's survival ability is based on the those wishes.

Followers of Light huge spherical ship, or "Mothership", we call Carrier-Station Type Interstellar/Interdimensional Ship is located nearby this planet (yes the name is complicated, as it is showing what precisely it can do), they are moving it around the Inner Solar System, this is, it is not being moved outside Jupiter and even Mars orbit.
Remember this video[170] Sophia?

This is how it's force field looks. This force field absorbs energy and plasma and any other sorts of matter turning it into energy and information. While receiving information from the Sun this ship can also send information in instant speed to the Sun and through it, to other Creators - Stars and to fellow beings on other end of the Galaxy or dimensional world.

I hope this will aid You, much Peace, Calm and Prosperity!

December 8, 2013

G/E
Sophia, as I shared with You magnetic rotation technology and encourage You to make them and use in Your cars and homes I was told to share with You also a much cheaper and easier way how to avoid using combustion fuels[171] [172] [173]. You can easily use water as a fuel, all You need to do is retrofit Your old gasoline/diesel engine system to run on it, and tweaks necessary to make Your car running on water are very few, engine remains the same, in this case You are using hydrogen fuel (using process hydrolysis, where You separate hydrogen from oxygen), I know You already heard of these new types of fuel, here instead of buying a new car,

[170] YouTube. YouTube, n.d. Web. 09 July 2016. <http://www.youtube.com/watch?v=fc-RUukmCLw>.
[171] ZakHarley. "HHO How To Build Your Own & Run Your Car on Water.wmv." YouTube. YouTube, 04 July 2010. Web. 09 July 2016. <http://www.youtube.com/watch?v=na1Z5dus2LQ>.
[172] Wits2014. "Water Powered Car!! - Suzuki Samurai Runs on 100% Water [witts.ws]." YouTube. YouTube, 11 Oct. 2011. Web. 09 July 2016. <http://www.youtube.com/watch?v=4ljhGUia9Yk>.
[173] Fuelwatergasoline. "Car That Runs On Water Part 2." YouTube. YouTube, 18 Aug. 2010. Web. 09 July 2016. <http://www.youtube.com/watch?v=AlywaRrWEwg>.

which is costly, You can make Your old car working on water. It is environment friendly, non-polluting, no CO_2 emissions, although heat still present, but not as much as in combustions. So this process is much cheaper and easier, natural fuel of stars - hydrogen and natural "fuel" of animals - oxygen is being used.

Here is an example of what can be done, if necessary resources (or funding) are put into it[174].

There are more such videos just search for them, these are just the easiest to understand.

Along with this technology there is a tech that transform heat of our body and surroundings into energy (it can be used on mobile devices)[175] [176]

A tech that transforms movement into energy (kinetic tech)[177]

And some more which transforms energy kept in matter to energy, these techs are expensive to make.

What makes them common is that all of these technologies are suppressed by illuminati order and oil and batteries companies, because of their greed and I must remind You, be very careful and not try to earn money on these technologies, do not draw attention of main stream media to You, because I know almost all the inventors that tried, were suppressed, beaten or even killed when they refused to stop. Just spread this technology quietly along Friends and other interested People, once it will become abundant, there will be no way for them to stop You. Remember, the greatest weapons of satanic cults are money and lies, so when You use them, they will use You.

Anyway, when these techs will become abundant Your reward will be overwhelming,

[174] Bloomberg. "A Car That Runs on Air, Water: Here's How It Works." YouTube. YouTube, 22 Mar. 2013. Web. 09 July 2016. <http://www.youtube.com/watch?v=g_2tlnf6y_k>.
[175] SplitReaction. "Generate Electricity from Your Body Heat." YouTube. YouTube, 15 Apr. 2009. Web. 09 July 2016. <http://www.youtube.com/watch?v=pgIOUXKyzFE>.
[176] Loveandrespect85. "How Sweden Turns Human Body Heat into Useful Energy (BBC News)." YouTube. YouTube, 11 Jan. 2011. Web. 09 July 2016. <http://www.youtube.com/watch?v=_XFhQokagq8>.
[177] NMANewsDirect. "Human Body Movement Could Be Potential Power Source." YouTube. YouTube, 29 Dec. 2012. Web. 09 July 2016. <http://www.youtube.com/watch?v=Axwi5YA444Q>.

wish You Great Luck and Great Success!:)

December 9, 2013
(Note to readers -- the following videos are intended as information, not fear. With that we are empowered. This is the dawn of a new age and we can only see how bright we are against the darkest black.)

SOPHIA
Someone just sent me this[178].

It is alarming and I wonder about fear mongering.

Thank you,

G/E
If this subject was mentioned, I will share with You our insight on U.S. plan b.

I know that You are aware of FEMA camps and preparation of U.S. satanic government to put it's own people in there. During only this cycle 2013, there were the biggest movements of U.S. military around the U.S. since the cold war.

Here are videos where You can see how bad the situation really is[179] [180]

They are prepared for a rebellion of Humanity, precisely within U.S.

They plan for world war 3 failed, but they have a plan B, plan B is a hopeless attempt to enslave American People by force in case they rebel. Everyone that they don't like will be labeled as "terrorist" and will be taken from society.

They also have plan C and plan D, but these plans are in a making and are

---

[178] ADGUKNEWS. "NASA: The End Of Mankind "Leaked Document" 2013." YouTube. YouTube, 26 June 2013. Web. 09 July 2016. <http://www.youtube.com/watch?v=eN4XICOyRb8>.
[179] StormCloudsGathering. "U.S. Government Preparing for Collapse (and Not in a Nice Way)." YouTube. YouTube, 13 Mar. 2013. Web. 09 July 2016. <http://www.youtube.com/watch?v=MkAn3VIe1yQ>.
[180] Todd5013. "WOW!!! LARGE MILITARY ACTIONS MOVEMENTS ACROSS AMERICA 2015." YouTube. YouTube, 01 Nov. 2013. Web. 09 July 2016. <https://www.youtube.com/watch?v=D7FXSEhgjoE>.

not ready yet, and that is a Blessing for Humanity.

Plan C is an invasion "from outer space" (not real), where they will use artificially made mutants and cyborgs in order "to unite" the world under label "of protection", actually it will be total enslavement.

Plan D is to "cause an error" within machines (robots) and make the same "unity" (it is when they will make a lot of robotic tech around the world).

But they always consider their priority plan A, to fool, using money and lies all that "disagrees" with them. They are causing rebellions in countries if money and lies fail. And if rebellions fail they use "brute force" which tarnish their image. This plan A was created by original bavarian illuminati order, that why it is their most preferred method to take everything from Everyone.

Also, if You haven't checked it yet, there is a very good Revelation of what UK and U.S. are composed of in reality. I know many of Your Friends will want to know it too[181].

One point there that is incorrect in our knowledge is that Vatican don't control nor UK nor U.S., they don't have nor power, nor ability, in actuality they are controlled by same occult families, that control U.S. and UK. You know them, they are current masters of the "West".

Always dissent how You feel is right. Take care and always don't have fear, fear is a bad thing.

They are planning to do that, but they are doomed to fail, as One and It's Forces are here, ready to make what must be done. Most of all what One can't stand is deception, arrogance, ignorance, greed and injustice. They have all of this and a lot.

Remember the power of music[182] and song[183] it can overcome everything,

[181] A Practical Guide To Free-Energy Devices, and Author: Patrick J. Kelly. Chapter 15: You Are Being Deceived (n.d.): n. pag. Web.
[182] Okol7. "Adrenalin Sounds - Victory In The Sun." YouTube. YouTube, 30 Nov. 2013. Web. 09 July 2016. <http://www.youtube.com/watch?v=Z3YdpXmgYaQ>.
[183] Michimaas. "Revived." YouTube. YouTube, 08 Dec. 2013. Web. 09 July 2016.

even if everything seems hopeless, turn the music on even without instruments, in Your mind.

And One is always there to aid You, just ask for aid and guidance, Creator always ready and is glad to help You.

With Peace, Love and Prosperity!

December 10, 2013

G/E

I was free to warn You about all of this taking place, you heard about their preparations, FEMA camps, secret spy programs, spreading of viruses to "control", chipping. And decided that it would be better not to tell, as You were ready for these things instinctively and to avoid spreading fear as this is always bad to be feared, individuals in power with greed in their hearts were using fear with "religions and governments" for all of humanity's history to control with ease (as they always liked to say for all those times). You asked me about this and there is the connection, so I was free to share our insight in their plans as You were ready for this information.

Considering their bio plot they are starting to make a move, when they will spread new flu virus, we will make a surprise for them, something they don't want to happen.

With Peace and Love!

SOPHIA
and, have you seen this latest from Cobra[184]?

G/E

<http://www.youtube.com/watch?v=RAsOAPxNjS8>.
[184] N.p., n.d. Web. <http://2012portal.blogspot.com/2013/12/financial-reset-and-event-update.html>.

About the Event we are calling it a Moment of Justice, now we can explain why.

It is when ones that were making injustice will see real Justice, they will be judged for Everything without the ability "to buy their way out of this" like they were always doing. Lies and money will no longer work there.

This is when arrogance and ignorance of Humanity will fall and disappear in one moment, seeing everything they wouldn't believe from other People labeled "conspiracy theorist" and "UFO lunatics" unfolding before them. And this is when deception and greed will start ceasing to exist within Humanity, but these ones not instantly as they were programmed with long time and suffering in genetic code of a Human Being.

All will be as ordered by Humanity with one united Wish on that decisive date of 12.21.2012.

Also I need to warn Everyone that is to use magnetic rotation technology. Do not forget about electricity precautions, always look for amperage and voltage levels and heat. Place coolants to dissipate heat from rotary wheel/blades. This is to avoid meltdowns of elements of this device and accumulators, also to avoid power surges and fires in worst cases. You have a basic guide to electricity in that same guide You saw in video description. For water/hydrogen use don't forget about precautions as well. But hydrogen is much stable than gasoline and diesel which can burn pretty easily, still always recheck and double check everything and make sure everything is where it should be and there is no leakage.

This is for You to know - first make of a model an alpha or proto type is not always a perfect and can have flaws and inefficiency, but what is most important is to not give up, making modifications, tweaks and having patience and endurance are the keys for perfection of design and next time You will have a much bigger success, this is how science and research are working throughout the Universe.

Here is another tested design of electricity receiving technology made in cycle 1928 - the Hendershot generator. Unique design, but efficient, still using the same magnetic principle, magnets here is a source of energy, not a wind force. [185]

This design can be changed, and for example You can place it vertically instead horizontally like it is shown here. There is lot of variations of this, this generator is mentioned in a guide as "Motionless Pulsed Systems".

The point here is to use magnetic field as energy. For that You need to create magnetic field closed system, from which You will get the electrical current. For increased electrical output You can increase the size of this device, the same goes to magnetic rotation technology.

Again look for electricity precautions, do not allow Your young Children close to these devices when they are active if You are to make them of course.

Until the Moment of Justice, You can make some devices and use them putting an X on current inefficient fossil fuel system and increase the pace of this Moment to arrive.

Again Great Luck and Great Success to Everyone!

December 2012, 21st date, this is where the choice for future of now was made, one cycle ago.

Now will be the next 21st date of Solstice of the Sun, where the day will start become longer for north hemisphere of a planet.

If Followers of Light will really listen to Humanity this time, like Cobra made this poll, then this Solstice will be the Moment of Justice.

Like we told anytime starting from that decisive date, the Justice would happen.

Wish for it, tell them You are ready, there is no need for more experience of this, and everything is accomplished. This is what they want to know.

Also another good tip for Everyone. Whenever You need an answer or You

[185] YouTube. YouTube, n.d. Web. 17 July 2016. <http://www.youtube.com/watch?v=w3LRmSovEX8>.

want to know what to do next, the very first taught in Your Mind is the most right one most of the times.

When You say, "no it isn't right", or "it is not going to work" and thinking about another thing, doubts are starting to arise and doubts are bringing confusion and confusion grabs the most closest answer in availability, which most of the time is false, this is how principles based on lie still rule this world.

So listening to the very first taught, is very wise, almost always it is true, and very rarely it is not (there are exclusions everywhere in Creation).

Why the first taught is the one You seek, You may ask. Because it is when our Mind is making a request for this information, the Universal Consciousness of the Nexus of Conduits is sending the initial answer, which in Creation is considered "a flawless in design" (as this is being sent from One).

When information from there is doubted, other sources within Creation are being searched, Human Beings are searching an answer "on the ground", answers that are available here on the planet as Humanity did not ventured in outer space to other civilizations yet, where there is more information.

This whole process is not easy to understand and You may disapprove on this, but this is how we know it.
In short I meant here: Trust Your First Voice.

And I want to share another beautiful music for Your inspiration

You are the Children of Light, of Sun[186].

Much Love and Appreciation!

Update 12-12-13 -- *(Note to Readers, there is a great deal of information coming in now, attempts are made to keep this page as short as possible, you may want to check out Page 7 as well as updates may happen more*

---

[186] SubZero90EpicMusic. "City of The Fallen - Children of Light." YouTube. YouTube, 11 Feb. 2012. Web. 09 July 2016. <http://www.youtube.com/watch?v=jrWPKliDesw>.

than once a day. The updates are included as they come in whenever possible.)

G/E
I will explain, but remember always to believe or not based on Your Own beliefs and views.

One decided this indeed, but not me or Anyone Else will ever completely understand One, One is the most complex Being in Existence as It is It's Creator.

Like I'm told by One, "People will themselves make the decision when and how it will took place, ones that have grown them up should graduate them, not Forces of One, nor Guardians, or anyone else."

"Ones that have grown Humanity up" are the Followers of Light, so they must finish this experiment like I was telling You. And like You remember Forces of One gave them a deadline. This experiment is a danger to Creation that is why we are here in the first place.

The Followers of Light have great technologies of Consciousness level type, they can do much more than triggering Great Event, (Event should be called Great in my opinion, as it is Great indeed).
They already are using them right now, I sense they have listened to this poll and understood that by triggering Moment of Justice they will save more lives than by postponing. Though I can't guarantee they will do this right now, don't feel their complete determination yet, will hope to sense it soon..

About Energy harvesting Sophia, from our knowledge and as I see them, they are not vampires, they do not need Energy to be alive or to function, they have a lot of technology to aid their physical and ethereal bodies. But it is up to You to decide:)

Here is a recent video of Cobra[187], here he explains pretty much every

---

[187] ExopoliticsTV. "COBRA: Mandela Funeral a Psyop; Galactic Frequency Shifts Now Favor the Event and Fair New Currenc." YouTube. YouTube, 10 Dec. 2013. Web. 09 July 2016. <http://www.youtube.com/watch?v=_LnTUARRugk>.

detail of "Event, Light Forces and archons" if You missed something

I will also mention about the situation around the World as it is very astounding for me right now.

Everything is looking very Good, the overall Energy of a Planet has increased Toward Positiveness and Love+Happiness attitude. In Thailand, in Italy and in Ukraine protests were seized in a peaceful way with Peaceful solutions, where police and protesters were treated each other as a Friend, wars in Africa and Syria are temporary ceasing, You can check it on news. I feel the energy of our Planet and it is very Good! Can You feel it?

So right now, I can point out that this time moment is very suited for a Moment of Justice to begin, casualties may be reduced to 0 if U.S. government will be disallowed from starting their plan B, that is the most problematic thing, and as we know, illuminati order will fight viciously for it's survival and delaying may just give them a momentum, so if I were in Light Followers' place I would use such an opportunity and liberate Humanity right now.

This is a message of Hope, You've seen it as part of a Pleiadean message, this was the message which asked Humanity to choose what will be next after 12.21.2012. So don't mind it, choice was already made, I sense that many Lightworkers need this right now, we can change this world by wanting to see the world like this, pay attention to music, this is what gives this video a strong message[188]

Wish for it, tell You are ready, show that You are ready - this is where Compassion, Love and Happiness prevail, like You wanted.

Ok, Sophia. Here is an important update.

[188] Chemlin. "2012 - MESSAGE OF HOPE 2 [PART 2/2] [720P]." YouTube. YouTube, 27 Jan. 2012. Web. 09 July 2016. <http://www.youtube.com/watch?v=ifjnO3OWdNE>.

My suspicions were confirmed. After some time of my own guessing and feeling, One acknowledged that indeed illuminati order were making a ritual on Nelson Mandela's funerals for preparation for a big and bad event. When I heard that sign interpreter saw angels descending on funerals, it was what I was feeling.

The Comet Ison as we know, need only 2 degrees to hit the Earth, now that it is fragmented some fragments are heading in Earth direction and they will arrive somewhere before middle of next month, beginning from 21st date of december. I can't get precise information, I only can feel these hulks are approaching.

They are big, some are a little bigger than meteor that hit Chelyabinsk. Comet Ison have arrived here after precisely 666 cycles after comet Negra, which makes up to ritual they committed. There was also a Great Comet of 1680, if You calculate it is 333 cycles since this 2013 cycle and both of these comets cause a "black plague" outbreak which in 1300s killed more than 200 million people in Europe.

As well with this there are other ritual similarities: the Israel was "recommended" by UN on 29th november of 1947, that is 66 cycles into past, this is when Ison moved under the Creator the Sun.

And the place Pretoria where "leaders' were giving their farewells to Nelson is build on a place of battle which was called "The Battle of Blood River", that took place on december 16th 1838,

and on 15th december Nelson will be buried in his home village. The day 16th december is holiday and is called the day of Reconciliation (in past it was called day of Covenant and later Vow). And this Covenant was given to God, for if battle will be won, they will build a new church on that place.

My vision was blocked due to dark priests activity on that place, but I can guess they might have given the same oath for defeating Light forces (this oath will be ignored, but may cause some damage).

Lastly all in this temple at Pretoria has many occult and symbolic representations that are connected with Egypt, Mesopotamia and Israel.

As well Ison can be interpreted as "I the Son".

All this is their typical symbolics, yet they have prepared it in complete secrecy and precision and they intend to make something very BIG right now, we GEs haven't completely seen that coming, but we were prepared for something like this.

I've met with other GEs and we all look through the veil, we saw what we already were seeing all the time: that they want to make false flag, it was a nuclear fire and combined with an epidemic.

We will look again into possible nuclear plots they may make and now we will strictly look into everything WHO will be doing in next few moments of time.

Right now they will "vaccinate" over 23 million children to bring mass outbreak of a new type flu virus in middle east and that where we prepared a "surprise" for them.
As well there will be vaccination in U.S., and it is already starting.

So Sophia, I advise You to share this information, with the power of our thoughts we may turn the comet Ison's fragments away and disallow all these bad things from happening.

If You will need some information on all of this I can provide it.

With Peace, Calm and Prosperity.

Update December 14, 2013

G/E
Here are a very great videos[189] which explains these troubles[190]

---

[189] Kelly4nya. "Comet Ison and What's Coming Next - Here's Why NASA Hid the Fact That It Survived!" YouTube. YouTube, 01 Dec. 2013. Web. 09 July 2016.
<http://www.youtube.com/watch?v=7QMzDGiebmE>.
[190] BPEarthWatch. "I Saw Angels Decending From Heaven." YouTube. YouTube, 12 Dec. 2013. Web. 09 July 2016. <http://www.youtube.com/watch?v=pv55NVylWs8>.

Know that right now we have their bio plot under control, so they won't be able to make another black plague and about Ison fragments, Followers of Light are still protecting the Planet, so big damage is not expected, but small meteor shower is expected. And right now will be annular Geminid meteor shower from 14 to 16th december, so they will be fueled by bigger fragments of Ison a little later, we are seeing it is highly fragmented. About anything else, we hope there isn't anything else they have.

I'm sorry Sophia, none of us have seen this clearly and we were not informed. We will now recalibrate ourselves and connect to Forces of One, we need some explanation on this event.

Along with this, prisoner number of Nelson Mandela was 46664, where You can see clearly 666.
As You know, there are no coincidences, everything is interconnected, so they planned this scheme very long ago.

Once we will get some knowledge on this scheme, I will inform You Sophia.
With Peace and Love.

Update # 1 December 15, 2013
~Note to Readers: The following came through last night. In the context of the way it was given, it is being passed along here. It is my belief that it is meant for certain eyes, not necessarily mine or perhaps yours. I make no claims as to its truth or untruth, it is the latest information, as given.

We are dealing with the plot called "breaking point". I will give You all known information.

It is going to start from 16 december. All GEs are on it, if we and other light workers and light warriors fail and Followers of Light won't intervene, expect the black division of Forces of One.

nasa is covering the existence and approach of Ison, counterfeiting and removing *images.*

Russian Itar Tass is warning of meteor shower approaching, 26-28 December will be over north pole,

ISS may be under small bombardment very soon.

The whole chain of command in U.S. was changed, 18 generals were retired, substitutes have jewish descendancy, NSA marked all "conspiracy theorists", islamists, christians and other religious groups to be removed once chaos will start, their list is big, they are to do it as silent as possible.

You can recall the fall of jedi and rise of the sith. Overall this plot is what we were warned before - a major plot, their last attempt, not the Syria, that was a mistake, and it is bigger than we thought.

Take care and have focus, nuclear plot is still active, it wasn't prevented, positions the same from Charlotte - to Norfolk and from New York - to Pittsburgh two quadrants, possibly they can use emp instead of nuke, also more than one are possible[191] [192].

They will abuse everything he speaks to capture everyone that says at least something against government or this system, he is mentioning that this will be a regime, a one man rule. This is where they want to go.

Also, there are dis-informers along light workers, they have jewish roots, they intentionally do this to fool and think everything is just as we want it to be.

And remember most important: power of thoughts are Your most powerful weapon!
This world is not fixed, every single thought is changing the outcome, so think positively and wish for peaceful solution to all of this.

Peace, Calm and Prosperity.

---

[191] Qronos16. "America FALSE FLAG Imminent: US Generals Who Won't Enforce Martial Law Being Fired." YouTube. YouTube, 15 Oct. 2013. Web. 09 July 2016. <http://www.youtube.com/watch?v=kqheo3EX_cg>.
[192] Baassiri1784. "Obama Explains the FEMA Camps." YouTube. YouTube, 03 Feb. 2013. Web. 09 July 2016. <http://www.youtube.com/watch?v=HkSkQgnEV-Q>.

Another interesting thing for All to know is that Everyone was fooled about mayan calendar. The real ending date of mayan calendar is not december 21, 2012, but 16 december of 2013[193]

(here[194] *on 2:00)*
They made a true deception, we can give them that.

Update # 2 December 15th, 2013

Right now will come what was asked for, this is the Shift of the Ages[195]

Perfect Triangle[196]

Perfect Cross[197]

This is what "leaders" are covering up[198]

these last revelations made our brother light worker, DAHBOO77, very well done!

About Ison, there within the debris of Ison one of Followers of Light's ship is positioned, so it can manipulate the debris field,
and another most important thing is about the composition of this great comet body. It is made from materials which were preserved there since the beginning of this Solar System,
so everything from it that is going to crash here, will bring huge modifications to

[193] DAHBOO77. "WoW! Dec.16th Mayan Tzolkin End Date & Comet ISON-Earth-Venus Trinity!" YouTube. YouTube, 02 Nov. 2013. Web. 09 July 2016. <http://www.youtube.com/watch?v=k6nXeL7Axhg>.
[194] BPEarthWatch. "DECEMBER 16th In History." YouTube. YouTube, 13 Dec. 2013. Web. 09 July 2016. <http://www.youtube.com/watch?v=oq2Kk0Lpq8U>.
[195] Melchizedek144. "13-13-13 Golden Gate - Initiation Into The Mysteries Of Life." YouTube. YouTube, 12 Dec. 2013. Web. 09 July 2016. <http://www.youtube.com/watch?v=vBkfF_5fFf8>.
[196] DAHBOO77. "WoW! Dec.16th Mayan Tzolkin End Date & Comet ISON-Earth-Venus Trinity!" YouTube. YouTube, 02 Nov. 2013. Web. 09 July 2016. <http://www.youtube.com/watch?v=k6nXeL7Axhg>.
[197] DAHBOO77. "Dec. 16th Perfect Cross Mayan Alignment with Earth, Venus, The Sun & Comet ISON!" YouTube. YouTube, 03 Nov. 2013. Web. 09 July 2016. <http://www.youtube.com/watch?v=aH4Z26ABhbY>.
[198] DAHBOO77. "December 16th! Comet Ison, World Leaders, South Africa & Sun Temple Worship!" YouTube. YouTube, 10 Dec. 2013. Web. 09 July 2016. <http://www.youtube.com/watch?v=xzc_h-GDKdc>.

this planet, and these modifications depends on our positive/negative attitude and thinking.
So if You wish everything to be positive, think and act as positively as You can on these moments of time.

We are currently preventing their plots, there is lot still to do, we think will make it in time until 24:00 17 december, that's when their ritual finishes.

It was decided what the outcome will be, but still occult societies are at it and they will ask the higher forces to aid them in a very evil doings and they will be aided if not stopped tomorrow.
They can receive 0 aid if we All will asked the opposite of what they want, this are Unity, Peace, Harmony, Mutual Understanding, Love, Oneness.

Even if You are not believing this, You need at least to consider all of this, and one meditation for World Peace, Freedom, Stability will not hurt Anyone.

Like we now know, thanks to our brothers and sisters and all the light workers: illuminati order - west world "leaders" will be performing ritual in Voortrekker Monument - "it is an altar which marks new beginning according to Moerdijk (Marduk incarnate)" tomorrow.

And if light workers will not unite and meditate, and wish for Great Good Changes on that date, the wish of illuminati will be granted (partially), their wish is - complete world control through, false flags, martial law, death camps and much more suffering.

The only ones that can stop them now are All We, GEs, Light workers and Light warriors, this is our only attempt, we can make BIG difference now on 16th december, so please Unite in full Consensus, time for You to show it at its fullest maximum to One, the Creator of the Universe, so that Our United Voice can be heard forward and straight!

Tomorrow is the moment of Great Achievements!

December 17, 2013

(~Note to Readers: A comment section was added to the website on this date.)

A blog section was now added to the website, at his request. This allowed readers to question him without having to email me. He still answered through email, which I subsequently posted on the blog. The format from here on out will be a bit different as a result of this change. At times there will be questions from both the blog and from emails. Let's hope it is not too difficult to track...The first blog post follows:

At the request of several readers, and the suggestion of our Off World Contact, this comment section is now open. It is a place to comment on what has been shared. There are two rules: that all comments are made both 1. Anonymously (use another name) and 2. Respectfully. Other than that, consider this an open line. Violations of the rules will be removed. When making comments, please reference which date you are referring to so others can look back to the conversation and understand the whole picture. A new page will be opened in this section with each addition to the "Off World Conversation". Let's see how this works!

To start things off, here is a quote from today's update:

"I also recommend You Sophia (if You agree of course), to let Everyone comment on Your website anonymously, I sense People want to have Their say too, let Them say everything They want, even negative as People Are Free (of course if in case that it is highly negative/distracting and creating conflict this say can be removed).
"We all are equal sitting around the round circle." "

SOPHIA
Okay, the day is over. What happened?

G/E
Still haven't finished everything yet, but we still have some time left to do it.

During this day we achieved great success, their ritual was spoiled, in Voortrekker Monument Sun was obscured by clouds! With Our United Thoughts Creator Sun and Mother Earth aided Us! Thank You All that participated in this, we felt You, You did a Great Job!

Without Sun they were not able to ask for what they wanted, as Sun was in it's Golden Gate (this is where Center of the Galaxy - Sage Star A-Great Creator is) with Moon being in it's Silver Gate (opposite site of Golden, very rare alignment), this was the moment of "God's Judgment" judgment here means seeing how Humanity attends to long waited event and those that Remembered it will be granted with reward. Reward is a single wish, Our United Wish.

Congratulations Everybody! Instead of their wish, Your United Voices were heard and One turned over to YOUR WISHES!

We also felt calming sense within us, did You felt the same?

I also recommend You Sophia (if You agree of course), to let Everyone comment on Your website anonymously, I sense People want to have Their say too, let Them say everything They want, even negative as People Are Free (of course if in case that it is highly negative/distracting and creating conflict this say can be removed).
"We all are equal sitting around the round circle."

I also heard about Cobra's new requirement petition for 144,000 signatures (in reality, if such petition would be fulfilled it would need all 7 billions signatures of every Human Being, as they are simply being ignored here), I may recommend You All to not apply (or use caution if You do), because poll was more than enough for Light Followers to act, they saw it and they know very well what is the situation on this Planet and what Humanity wants and needs.

They missed very great opportunity to intervene on 12.12.2013, Energies were outstanding!
What is done there is a blatant move in our understanding, it puts all Lightworkers in jeopardy as they (the government) will know Your names and emails.

Anyway We all did a great thing, now they won't be able to make big damage! We are onto them, looking for next steps of their newest generals and old individuals in position, we will do our best to prevent all plots they want to make in the coming earth cycles. Overall not much time is left until

this experiment will be over!

With Tranquility, Wisdom and Peace!

December 18th, 2013, Update #1

G/E
One more thing Sophia, I'm not really an "off-world contact",

I'm one of Guardians of Balance and Stability of Universe,

we are doing things on behalf of One - the Creator of the Universe, that makes us Executives
(as well with this we are Executioners, but since we no longer need to be so - an order of One).

We are giving protection, energy barrier protection from evil-wishers and evil-doers, everywhere in the World and for Everyone that wants to live! Guardians - Executives are our name right now, and I'm not one, We are Many, in almost every country around the World.

Much Peace, Calm and Prosperity to All!

READERS COMMENTS

"Thank you for your service, we are a grateful people."

"Could our GE friend give us his name or a name so we don't have to refer to him as GE, OW or he, please. It's much better to speak to people when you know the name. Thank you"

SOPHIA

Here is the response:

G/E
"I am using proxies on many sites, being stealth right now is our order, so I can't answer to comments directly, my apologies Sophia. Later on if Moment of Justice will not happen any time soon we will have less restrictions and I will be able to answer on comments."

READERS COMMENT

"Imagine one doesn't have to use a keyboard and send physical messages to communicate and that OW/GE is known to you by perception...we have names here to identify us when we meet at various levels - I personally don't mind that OW has no name or defers sexual status...that's not the point nor the importance - its what is said and how it is said that most concerns (us)..."

December 18th, 2013 - Update #2

G/E
I will give an answer to a Friend about ritual on 16th.

In order for ritual to be successful completely the Sun should have been completely uninterrupted, but as You can see it was interrupted. So the ritual was "partially finished" in their understanding only.

There were clouds in South of Sun as well, and under it was Galactic Center, both must be uninterrupted, as interruption is making a loss to focus during ritual.

What You saw was 33rd ray of Sun, surrounded by 32 drawn rays on floor (as You can recall here, it's Freemasonry). And You can see how many People there were, Sun couldn't show at all, don't You agree?

They wanted to see the Sun there, and their wishes were heard. But wishes of evil doers were not heard, thanks to the cooperation of Sun, Galactic Center and Planet Earth! They turned to All of Us and not to them, They love You and not those that wish to do harm to You:)

Also I will again say about 16 december, there were so MANY "coincidences" on that date, I personally can't recall so much happening on just one Earth cycle, this was a truly - Shift of the Ages, we've called it "a Cosmic Intervention".

You now can see that it was planned very long ago by One! And You can

see how good planner One really is. And We (All of Us) were able to remember about it, and use it to improve this World!

Unfortunately majority was thinking that it was 12.21.2012, deceived by illuminati, so we were along with Illuminati the only ones at it.

Overall One was pleased that we "remembered" about this very planned date, Our United wish for Unity, World Peace, Stability, Abundance with new tech in coming moments and Liberation is granted!

Congratulations again to Everybody!

READERS COMMENTS

"Ok, this decides it: "They love You and not those that wish to do harm to You:)". The One loves ALL that is, because Love IS all there is. The "bad guys" are just more of "us", playing a role. We've all been "the bad guy" in other times and places. But whoever you are, you are not helping us raise our vibration when you write such separation and duality (us vs them) soaked lines. Sophia, do you really think this is positive? Given the energetic feel here, who could trust the rest of the intel? Please, shut this down."

~~

"I, for one, am grateful for all pieces of data from all perspectives. After all, we are all one, so it is helpful to know what the rest of I is thinking, doing, feeling, and being."

SOPHIA

"This contact has never claimed to be anything but human. I have offered the conversation merely as another source of info in these volatile and challenging times.

That said, this is not a defense or a judgment of the sentence mentioned. It may very well be what sounds like a poor choice of words. It may not be, I do not know.

What I do know is that this life is a cacophony of sounds, all emanating from the One. It cannot be otherwise. If there is a need to deny the parts seen as limiting, so be it. Perhaps that is because we are yet unable to assimilate what is not seen as useful or productive. If what is seen looks like judgment, it is in fact a reflection of the judgment held still within.

Light is only visible in the dark.

He will see your comment and respond, and we will see where this leads. I won't "shut this down", I am evaluating this new addition to the site, and will continue to do so. Thank you for your honesty and direct language!"

READERS COMMENT

"Sophia you are right,i love this initiative. If someone disagrees with these mesages , he should read channeled mesages."

December 18th, 2013 - Update #3

G/E
About politicians being controlled from the inside (sorry for big text, there is much more to it, I tried as short as possible).

It is a long story, in order to understand it, You need to look at the past, from where it started. All politicians You see are meant to be just a representatives, so as president "person that is presenting or representing a nation or a country".

In the beginning humanity was controlled by old wise women, (matriarch) then when hunting ceased by old wisdom men (patriarch), then by self appointed "emperors, kings, pharaohs, sultans" etc that called themselves the sons of gods or God, then Freemasonry stepped in, they decided to end with this dictatorship of kings and made a pacts which were bound by blood, in presence of anti-god "lucifer, satan, baphomet, baal, moloch, marduk" etc it is called by different names, the point here was to oppose the God/gods and his/their sons.

They wanted to unite the world and bring "golden peace to humanity" and promised to use everything that opposes God - "lies, greed, hate, separation, crimes" and so on. All of this in complete secrecy and bound to be finished not in one generation but many. Slowly they made their dream come true.

Yet there were always those among them that wanted everything for themselves and this brought separation among them, so they are competing with each other to rule over the future right now, Rockefellers vs Rotschilds for example and now the question how politicians are controlled?

United States was the beginning, a setting point for this great scheme, illuminati order - a higher freemasonry form was formed at the same year as United States, the rich among freemasons invested huge amounts of money to make a revolution against brits possible, it wasn't possible as brits didn't wanted to just give their big colony away.

So once this country was established they established the system which will be very easy to control from the shadows - democracy. Using web of intertwined masons in high positions, those that are to elect were preselected, based on their astrology of day of birth (how planets and stars were standing on this day).

"Renowned" satanist Aleister Crowley mentioned about this, "democracy is the best form of government when it can be controlled from the inside, as it creates an illusion of government of the people". It is only a veil, a thought that People are in control, in actuality it is not. Why would You think government would just give all the rights of a so great plot to People? When so much generations, efforts, funds and resources were put into it? From the very foundation of US, it's main objective was to form and NWO.

This is what 26th degree freemason wrote to us

"Lucifer is a symbol of justice, rebellion, revolt, and freedom. Lets just say atheist were right (which I highly doubt from all I've seen) then Lucifer himself is best symbolic deity to prompt as a philosophical god to honor and follow. It's the perfect God of America and true freedom. He doesn't have to be real to the simpleminded atheist morons that respond with, "there is no god." Its a belief system. A symbol of freewill and enlightenment."

Likewise, those at the top of the pyramid are using initiates of low degree and never telling the whole story. The initiates from 1st to 20th degree never know that they in fact worship Lucifer.

Supposedly representatives of the People, but in fact representatives of those occult societies, these shadow figures were using their influence to put an end to kingdoms and empires. But now, thanks to their proposal of such government, Humanity is turning these governments controlled from inside to outside. Transparency is taking place and they are being exposed after almost 4 centuries of secrecy and ridicule of all Truth-seekers.

Also answering on questions about why I've given information on bad things that were in planning, because they were serious and unfortunately still active. On those dates of 16 and 17 nothing should have happened, days of rituals are always "as usual". Unfortunately this World have a taint of evil corruption, so I am giving Knowledge about what is planned, because based on our long time experience and as well analysis we made on this World, such saying is true - "when You don't know what is coming, it just coming (9/11 example - only few tens of People knew about it, not counted illuminati the planners), but when You know what is coming, it is not coming when You don't want it").

There was a very good saying made by George Carlin "Don't just tech Your children to read, teach them to question what they read. Teach them to question everything." Always Express Yourself, don't hold what You want to say inside. So Self-Expression and Knowledge and Understanding of things is like always the key to Success! (meant everywhere possible)

Right now a new Cycle of around the Sun will start on 21st! Then there will be Christmas and New Year, isn't this a Wonderful time to start a New Age? Notice this cycle/year is not "as usual", this end of cycle marks the beginning of a New Age! Use this Great Time and Wish for Great Things to take place on this Planet, the Future of this World is in Your United Hands (All of Humanity, not ETs)! Let Your Consensus prevail!

Peace, Calm and Prosperity to All!

READERS COMMENT

"It's a rather saddening observation that when OW speaks thusly -" He doesn't have to be real to the simpleminded atheist morons that respond with, "there is no god." It's a belief system. A symbol of freewill and enlightenment."

Its seems to me to be entirely precocious and disrespectful to describe those that do not believe in "god" or any "god" as - simpleminded atheist morons -

OW has been at lengths to point out that we must believe or not what we want to or prefer to. I personally do not believe in God because there is no god to "believe" in here for earth dwellers. I do not have any religious beliefs because they are subjective, manipulative, dishonest and in counter to ones ability to be free to think and decide.

As far as "ONE" is concerned I sense (a resonance) with a mighty entity or even a quantum entity that has to be equal to the parts of the universe to which "ONE" is the creator of... this is not a god this is beyond a god - this beyond our ken but there is a perception of the creator within us and via various observations from others that we are part of that creator as much as all and any events and actions be they good indifferent or bloody evil because if we view the total package, we see the enormous detail and inter-relativity and cross function that does not come from a mere god but one humungous intense and originating energy centre - and thats describing it in human terms (3D)

Thus it is not wrong to disbelieve nor is it moronic...it is humble and honest to tell a truth against those that insist upon something they provide no earthly nor spiritual evidence to confirm their positions.

To "ONE" I can only intensely submit my inner feelings if "ONE" knoweth me or not and I only insist on the end of this awful wasteful experiment in order that we may go forward with greater things and greater respect for the cosmos at our surround.

If I have any conscious belief it is in that unconditional love which I hereby practice and say that love is all that we do and say that benefits others and thus ourselves by having the empathy and perception to understand those actions and dynamics that comprise the world we live in....and until such time that those things we know of change by force of our death or force of ascension. Saludos"

December 19th, 2013

G/E
I knew there would People that will disagree with this phrase. I'm sorry for saying it, this conflicts with Your beliefs. I know sometime I'm not giving positive thinking, as I'm telling the truth, which we know as true. It is a common knowledge in the Universe that truth can be very harsh at some times, so lies are used to cover this. We are trying to not use lies in anyway, but sometimes we have to, as it may hurt terribly.

In our belief and knowledge One is an omnipotent all capable Being of all that exists in the Universe. These illuminati's "bad guys" are One with You and with Universe, Everything was created from One and so Everything has backward connection with One, and Everything is unique and independent and have their own thoughts. One have many faces and can be and Good and Evil at the same time, all this is done for One to experience Itself on a much greater levels and capabilities.

Now let me mention harsh truth again.. if there would be a choice given to illuminati order between:
1) to love and live in harmony with every living being on this planet and forget about NWO and forget about full control over this planet.
or
2) to betray and destroy half of Earth population, and if it is done NWO can be born and full control over this planet will be guaranteed.

What do You think they will choose knowing past experiences? If You think first option, then unfortunately it is a sweet lie. They were bound by blood and oath which "must be" fulfilled. Again not everyone in this order thinks the same, and there are those that would gladly choose 1st option, but in this case they are betraying their fathers, mothers and family. So which one is correct then?

On top of all things One is experimenting with this, this is a part of the planning and Love for everything is not equal. One loves the most perfect or close to perfect design (if You will ask what this is, it will be hard to understand), whether it is Good or evil,

also remember the Universal rule "giving Good returns Good, giving evil returns evil." So if You "hate" One, how would You think One will relate to You? If beings like illuminati order do not honor Creation and are ready to destroy it to achieve what they want, how One can love them if they do not care for Creator anyway?

This comes to love of mother and father, if these peoples are ready to sacrifice them on altar so that they can achieve what they want, are these people are Good and can be loved?

But this is just in physical reality, when death arrives, souls are coming under full control of One, and there they will be "sorry" for their actions, because their Grand Parent will be right before them (All of Us are just Children, We All are eternally young and there is nothing wrong when You are trying to be a Child, One loves to see Your true nature:)

One knows All better than anyone else in the Universe and One understands All and Any on absolute ultimate level, and yes, there after death One loves equally All. But if they commit crimes against Creation during their physical incarnation, they are punished. One is turning Itself away from them, this is what happened here.

All of their corruption and this disease for control and wealth comes from childhood, they were educated looking at this world and how parents treated them and learned them to do.

If You are disagreeing with all of this, don't read our messages, so to prevent hurting of Your beliefs.

Also I wanted to say Thank You to Everyone that gave their appreciation of our messages, we are happy that You found this helpful! We are right now started to work with some companies to spread the suppressed energy technologies around the World, it will not be quick to do it, but have patience. Love You All!

On date of Solstice on 21st light workers from Cobra's blog will meditate and wish for Moment of Justice (Great Event) to happen, I can recommend Everyone to do the same, when Humanity is United in Goodwill it feels really strong and astounding! And Light Followers are hearing strong Voices!

Take care and wish You a great Celebration of Solstice!

With Great Peace, Great Wisdom and Great Love to All.

READERS COMMENTS

"There is great confusion here.

-- There is no need to tell an UNtruth, or "lie", to avoid hurting someone with a painful

truth. It suffices to be silent.
-- Love only loves that which is perfect, regardless of whether it is "Good" or "Evil"? Really? Do you work for a cosmetics company?
-- The Law of attraction is not the same as "eye for an eye" revenge. Those who choose to turn away from the Light will be in darkness because they have chosen this. The Light, however, makes no judgments, and is always there, shining fully on whoever turns toward it, at any moment. Just because someone hates me does not mean I am required by some natural law to hate them back! I can CHOOSE to love them, no matter what. Parents know this to be the "truth" about love. It is not a "belief". And when a child's freewill choice attracts terrible things, they will suffer and hopefully learn from the experience, but you cannot live their life for them, cannot control their choices. Allowing them to experience the result of their choices is also love.
-- Love which is unequal, which is or is not given based on where you are is by definition "conditional". Creator/One is LOVE, unconditional, without limits or judgments or conditions."

"My apologies for number two above, which was written in pure 3D. Perhaps it is so, looked at upside-down, in that since we are ALL perfect in Creator/One's view, and merely playing a part in a play called "duality: good vs evil!", then yes, Creator loves what is perfect: everything and everybody! But if you take it as "if the bad guys are better at being bad than the good guys are at being good, creator loves the bad guys more, that's why they win", then see points 3 and 4 above."

~~

"Can you share more about the Moment of Justice from a physical perspective? Do you know how long it will last? Will there be earthquakes, floods? Is it instant or a wave that goes around the earth? I do not ask out of fear, rather curiosity. So much is being said about the event, but not a lot of details. Thanks for your words!"

~~

"The comments from (FIRST TWO COMMENTS) are most provocatively interesting such as are those from OW - although OW seems to be more than one "him/herself" by admission - it is none-the-less most interesting to try to understand through the curious "english" the specific meaning of things communicated - I have come to learn and sense through resonance with issues that love is explicitly non definable and that the consciousness of man and thus mankind/womankind (I make no separation) is ambiguous if we take the premise that the experiment has had a specific dynamic in which evil has permanently been in ascension throughout the various histories of homo-sapien existence.

There still seems to be this endless reference to the god figure and belief-system which any person of consciousness must know is to accept without proof or reason making the current godhead of the universe as capricious as "its" creations. My proposal is that God really loved us we wouldn't be having this excess and extreme and that God would simply kick.arse and see a more harmonious existence. (simplified)

The energy most valuable to me is that of the "love-based" integrity based empathetic kind that understands that in this 3D world we make errors as much as successes, and that while evil exists to be the other end of the great pendulum swing of learning we intrinsically know that it is both wrong and undesirable within an enlightened society...that which has endured until now a lack of "message" and tones of ascension/change to a higher dimension coming from many quarters with words that really defy the truth of the situation in which some years have gone by with all these events of supposed change only partially apparent to the "enlightened.

Messages of hope are only those that mean we have to have courage and anger against evil, violence and enslavement...hope alone is that you will win a lottery and make your life a little more comfortable in a world directed to consumerism, materialism, monetarism and luxuries that the system brings. Apart from the obscene power and wealth that some have over the absolute rest of the world.

Do you get my drift - it's a long exposé because we live in 3D Ouch! it's a tangible, language based subjectivity where these phenomena's are handled as taken for and have no meaning or expression in how we deal or can deal with the esoteric of divine changes especially when more than 90% haven't a clue or are not interested or cannot grasp it because the current life is so oppressive there is no time to think about those issues post "mayan calendar" hype.

If I say I love you all - what difference does it make until I can demonstrate this by showing the physical being that love is undefinable but that I do things and think things in the personal and objectivity of betterment and enlightenment that benefits to the whole and not just myself or those pre-pardoned evil delinquents that have had the reins far beyond the value of an experiment that we agreed to long ago and have had to forget in order to play the one-sided game.

The argument for positivism is either like love, unconditional or subjective by degrees according to ones preferences - each of course having their own. Saludos"

~~

"through experience i have 'learned' (remembered) that the love of One for all beings is so great that it allows all beings to experience the expressing of "un-love" (or separation) and at the same time allowing this expressing of "un-love" to be reflected back to them

by all other beings.
i have found that when one makes great 'strides' to release "un-love", one is greatly
'rewarded' with support from all directions."

~~

"Very astute ...it's also like saying - "if you really love someone you would let them be
free of you - you would not hold them back because of your love that person I but
because you love someone such that their freedom is more important"...
What OW has often described is "his/her" own struggle to come to the light as much as
any other awake - aware person who seeks that spiritual high ground."

~~

December 23rd, 2013

G/E
Good Day Sophia!

Now a new cycle has started, not in Human understanding, but for Earth it did. Congratulations!

About the question *("Can you share more about the Moment of Justice from a physical perspective? Do you know how long it will last? Will there be earthquakes, floods? Is it instant or a wave that goes around the earth? ")* **it depends. Depends on how Light Followers will act and how Humanity will behave and want things to happen.**

Right now we can see that nothing like this is going to take place unless "someone" whether ones that are above, or cabal or majority intervenes. So the Power of Choice plays here again.

Remember this old video[199]?

What happened in the end is possible, when You believe in it, such miracle can take place, when that Will for is very strong!

---

[199] MichaeljacksonVEVO. "Michael Jackson - Earth Song." YouTube. YouTube, 02 Oct. 2009. Web. 09 July 2016. <http://www.youtube.com/watch?v=XAi3VTSdTxU>.

Also I can advise ... the scalar energy pendants and their health benefits. They really are helping and works great! Unfortunately there isn't free pendants yet. Here I will show some very cheap ones on amazon[200] and ebay.

They are doing great job at supporting our body and making ourselves calm and peaceful. There are many many positive effects on our body from wearing them. This should aid many depressed or tired lightworkers.

I for myself is using them as well, they are making us focused and very resistant to energy attacks, also connection with One is improved and we rarely feel ourselves tired, rather we feel ourselves very young![201] :)

Peace Calm and Prosperity!

READERS COMMENTS

"Thank you for your answer. It seems earth dwellers have a lot more work to do to dlg out way out of this muck and mire and regain our place in the cosmos. Oh well, we can do it!"

~~

"What can you tell us about this situation[202]? Could it be important for Earth - perhaps to help awaken humanity?

Thank you so much!"

~~

---

[200] "Amazon.com: Scalar+pendants." Amazon.com: Scalar+pendants. N.p., n.d. Web. 09 July 2016. <http://www.amazon.com/gp/search?ie=UTF8&keywords=scalar%2Bpendants&tag=cometbird-20&index=blended&linkCode=ur2&camp=1789&creative=9325>.
[201] N.p., n.d. Web. <http://quantumscience.webs.com/>.
[202] BPEarthWatch. "Large Object Strikes the Sun." YouTube. YouTube, 26 Dec. 2013. Web. 09 July 2016. <http://www.youtube.com/watch?v=nslzYLeFpoY#t=261>.

December 27th, 2013

SOPHIA

This question just came in, it is not in the comments:

I have a request for you, can you please ask what he thinks about this video[203].

and tell us a little bit about the past and present situation on the moon.Thank you and have a nice day

G/E

...about question from our Friend. I was already mentioning that there inside the Moon is a huge underground complex. It exists both physically and non-physically. Before I was told that Light Followers and archons are one and the same, I was told that it was built by archons since the modification of humans.

We can see that they constantly are present on Moon and very powerful device which separates Humanity from Universal Energies is active there. Moon in our knowledge is an artificially created satellite of Planet Earth. It was formed naturally, but "outer forces" were used to make it and position it in orbit where life on Earth can flourish. Because this planet originally was proposed to be an isolated location for a new civilization species, at first they were deciding which type to make, and eventually apes were modified so that Humanity was born.

Moon is a perfect strategic place to monitor and protect this planet, as well Moon is playing a crucial role in supporting life, supporting Earth's rotation around axis, Earth's atmosphere, natural flow and renewal of oceans waters. Moon and Earth and their positions are a very perfect combination of supporting and harnessing life.

I will give my own thoughts about the video because You asked me, I will say that it is a made up photo. As I haven't sensed that their bases are open. In our

[203] YouTube. YouTube, n.d. Web. 09 July 2016.
<http://www.youtube.com/watch?v=ORFNU6S2BTw#t=130>.

knowledge they are closed and well hidden, and their crafts are moving right through the surface using special high frequency tunnels which can penetrate everything without damaging it, along with it they have two-way portals in their crafts and connected to ones inside Moon base complex, with which beings can travel there without the need "to dock".

This complex is the biggest one. And they have many small bases scattered around the Solar System. Next one also important is located on Ceres in asteroid belt.

Take care! Much Peace, Tranquility and Abundance to Everyone!

READERS COMMENTS

"We have read in several places that there is a device on the moon that captures souls and returns them to earth. Do you have any information about this? Is this even possible? Sounds like a Karma Machine."

~~

"Hi.Are there other inhabiteted planets in our solar system , i mean native inhabitants?"
~~

December 28th, 2013

G/E
Here is an answer[204] to a Friend's question, also from BPEarthWatch, I think You saw it

what exploded on the Sun is what comet ISON brought on it's tail. There are much much more debris, but like Light Followers said big objects will not hit the Earth (they will change their directions), don't worry. Although they were pointing out that "some small objects need to hit Earth" like You said to Awaken Humanity. But this is not decided yet by them. And One has not said anything about it. In case there will be a very bright flash outside, remember to take cover and be away from the windows, the shock wave need some 2 minutes to reach

---

[204] BPEarthWatch. "ISON Incoming Update!" YouTube. YouTube, 27 Dec. 2013. Web. 09 July 2016. <http://www.youtube.com/watch?v=xXVimdMpea8>.

surface if this explodes in stratosphere, whether by itself or by Light Followers' vessels. If this was done one time, this can be repeated.

Great New Year to Everyone! Let all Your wishes come true! And let You All be Happy and Complete! Take Care and Be Safe!

December 29, 2013

G/E

QUESTION -

Comment 1:
We have read in several places that there is a device on the moon that captures souls and returns them to earth. Do you have any information about this? Is this even possible? Sounds like a Karma Machine.

ANSWER -
The Moon itself is a huge device, which blocks the Earth from sight of distant Stars and Galaxies, it is playing the role of blocker of Consciousness, which is disallowing Humanity to receive the voices of other very distant civilizations and partly from One as well and one more thing it is also doing, the one You mentioned.

It is in fact not only possible, but active, I didn't told it, because there is very bitter information linked to it. The truth that is hidden behind it may really hurt You. So I will ask Your request whether You want to know it or not.

Comment 2:

QUESTION -
Hi.Are there other inhabited planets in our solar system , i mean native inhabitants?

ANSWER
About life on other Planets in Solar System, as much as we know in this System is present only lowly evolved alpha organisms beyond this Planet. There is life on Triton, Titan, Europe, Ceres and Mars. On all of these worlds life is underground

as it is too cold for it to be on surface. Because they got atmosphere (which means heat), and liquid water particles, life can exist there. It is present only where temperature is above 0, this is where water or it's small particles can be liquid. About Mars and Ceres - there are underground waters, and somewhere they are liquid. And Light Followers are abundant everywhere, like You remember.

Peace, Calm, Prosperity! And wish You again a Great Most Marvelous New Year, with All Your Wishes Come True!

READERS COMMENTS

"The story about the moon sounds interesting, please share it in its entirety. And the question is: how can we disable the "machine" on the moon?"

~~

"So what about the Pleaidians, the Cassiopeans and the Andromedans to mention just a few? Isnt this whole universe teeming with "life" as we (dont) know it - ?"

~~

"Thank you for the answer.Do you mean bacterias with lowly evolved organisms?With Light Followers are abundant everywhere , you mean they have colonies everywhere in our solar system?Are they humans and where do they originate from?"

~~

"Yes, please. we are ready for your information about the moon - even if it hurts. How can we make certain that our spirit/soul gains freedom at the end of our earth life?"

~~

"Happy new year to all.I have downloaded the free energy ebook you recommended me but it's beyond my skills .I know some people who interrested.In your 12/19/13 message you said you have started working with some compagnies to build such devices,can you give some details.How can i help?"

~~

End of the conversation for 2013.

Chapter 6   2014

2014

January 1st

G/E

Happy New Year to All!

Wish whatever You want to happen on this cycle!

The Energy was great and intense, although some bad things happened before New Year celebration in Iraq and Russia, we were not able to prevent them, as they were carried out by minor groups, which are not monitored by us, the one in Russia is sponsored by Saudi Arabia. We provided small protection during New Year celebrations to these critical zones.

There will be Olympic Games pretty soon which are targeted by Saudi Arabia, and illuminati order. We will monitor this and will see that everything will be great and without incidences. Notice that Moment of Justice can take place any moment and regardless of Olympic Games or any other events.

About Solar Magnetic Flip, we know that Sun almost fully had flipped it's poles, but not fully. I will explain You one thing: in order to better understand how Sun is doing it You have to accept the Dynamic model of the Universe, there is no "constant time frame of 22 years" in Sun flipping it's poles, the only thing about Universe that is constant is that Universe constantly changes Itself as this is the Rule of Evolution. And so this cycle flip can be changed from 22 to 11 or 3 or 44, for example right now Sun may change its poles back if It wants:)

About pope Jorge (Francis), catholic church had long known that the story about Adam and Eve was true in some of its form, from the perception that humanity was raised by its creators in artificial "heaven" where that small particle of Light was put into Humanity. The perception about hell is correct, the story that "most of Humanity" goes there is false, most of Humanity goes to Purgatory before going to Heaven, I will explain You the story about what is going on here down below, if You are ready to accept it, it is not pleasant information.

So hell in fact exist only for "chosen" individuals those that are impossible to change through Purgatory, meant they want "to destroy" and "destroy" without stopping and don't feel any difference or regret or anything at all, such beings are highly dangerous so they need to come through everything they have done during their life to feel it on their own soul, a thing called Karma, You know about it. On One's law they need to feel this sometimes more than felt those that they humiliated or destroyed, it depends on how resistant is the will "to destroy".

Answering on questions about different civilizations, they are many - pleiadeans, syrians, andromedans, arcturians, cassiopeans and this not ends, there are many many, we gave them designation "Ones that follows Light" or Followers of Light. Because in fact they are exercising Light and its main form - Unconditional Love (or Care for All Things in Existence) in its most highest extent.

And Light Followers do not have colonies on many moons and dwarf planets, they have only bases or outposts there, main intention of these outposts is to block Humanity's voices and sight from Outer Universe and Outer Universe's voices and sight from Humanity using special devices. As you remember this is an experiment and this planet is quarantined. Like we told most of them were switched off not long ago, that is why (and with the help of some positive devices as well) Humanity now can hear distant voices and One much more clearly and much more clearly can separate lies from Truth.

And yes I meant very primitive life from one cell to underwater fish-like creatures. The origin of Light Followers are from many many different Worlds, most of which are in this Galaxy of Milky Way.

And now an unpleasant continuation of story of the Moon, because You wanted to know the Truth. Here is a lot of information, my apologies for very huge text.

Again I will warn You that believe always in what You think is right, if You don't believe in this and everything what I'm saying, please avoid me and what I'm sharing with You, what most important is Your own believe!

The Creator of the Universe - One gave Everyone the complete Free Will and possibility to Choose Own Destiny and Own Way of Life. One is not intervening in the Existence of Creation, unless there is a grave danger to All that exists. So You are free to believe in absolutely Everything and do absolutely Everything You wish to do, unless You are making huge damage, this is having great consequences, both on Creation and on You. In this Universe evil doings are returning evil doings and Good doings are returning Good doings! Remember that, it is one phrase that remains unchanged since Beginning of this Creation.

The machine on Moon can be switched off only by Light Followers' beings that have the highest clearance they can have. Before we thought, it was archons device, but it was having "a light design" and it was giving us big suspicions. When we were told that archons (reptilians and greys) are together in one boat with Galactic Federation of Light, all have come into place and puzzle has been completely completed for us.

There is a being that sits on "a golden throne" and is called by different names, we designated it with gnostics' name - Demiurge - The God imposter. This being is in control of archons, it poses as a god and "creator of the Universe". It uses many names: God, YHWH, Yahweh, Adonay (Holy Lamb, even Jesus, even Trinity), Allah, Buddha, Brahma, Krishna, Shiva, Vishnu; from old "pagan" Wotan, Quetzalcoatl, Baal, Jupiter, Zeus (Dyeus, Deus, Dios, Theos, Dyaus Pita, Jupiter, Jov Pater, Zeu Pater, Dyau Pita - means literally Sky Father on contrary to Pltvi Mhter - Mother Earth also it's name, a proto indo-european origin of name God and Dios), it is also calling itself with female names like Gaia, Great Mother, Ishtar, Mithra, Goddess, even Source and even One; on evil part also known as Lucifer, Satan, Shaitan, Devil, Moloch, Baal, Baalzebub, Marduk, Saint Death, Pan, Satyr, Baphomet. (To mention also that in judaism satan is an agent of God and "tempter" of Humanity, so basically here, they are one and the same.) This is to mention just most prominent of its names to give You a picture of how influential it is. The secret 2 names for this being are jewish "Yod - Ha - Veh - Hah" - "I exist, I am" and reptilian name "Shem - Ham - Pho - Rash" - literally "you are my servants, I am your master" used in teaching Kabbalah where kaballah equal to cabal - "secret magic occult societies under the tree of life". On kaballah's tree of life You can see Moon blocking the Earth from Cosmo - universal Consciousness of One which comes through Galactic Center and through Sun.

We thought that this being was only the ruler of archons, but when we were told that they are together with Followers of Light the whole picture was completed, this being is the father of Humanity...
as he ordered it's light beings to make this civilization and imposter of real Creator of the Universe - One.

It is using the power of those prayers around the World to feed its self-appointment as the ruler of the Universe, it only wishes Humanity to serve it and so it is the mastermind behind the apocalypse - "salvation through destruction" plan where only loyal to it beings will be "saved".

This being had also created the artificial heaven for Humanity and for other beings across this Galaxy. The device on the Moon collects only those souls from this planet that are loyal to this being, being a christian, muslim, jews, buddhists or from any other religion. Sends it to artificial Heaven and then after time of rest and recalibration, this being sends it back to Earth and not on any other World, which real Creator is doing.

In real Heaven - Nexus of Conduits souls are being sent on other worlds across the Universe and they have a choice of where to go, but in artificial heaven souls are programmed into thinking that "Earth is the only choice". Many many souls were victims of this scheme and that why they are stuck here.

What is important to point here is that if You do not wish to serve to this being, which is Humanity's father this being will set You free to real Heaven. For example our loyalty of GEs is completely only to One. When You know about this whole situation, You can choose to reincarnate here or on other World this being don't dare to force You into submission.

This being is not committing big crime against Creation, that is why it can continue doing it, but once was found out about secret plan to control Creation, this is where Forces of One arrived and now this being can no longer impose illusion on Humanity.

This being can take Human souls only if they are choosing this being, because of huge illusion and programming through religion this being is having constant influx of souls into artificial heaven. Demiurge enjoys servitude of Humanity and constant hails in it's honor, making this being "happy".

By now You understood that all civilizations within Galactic Federation of Light serve it and most even don't know that they in fact serve to imposter. You heard not one time that they need an approval for intervention on this planet from "heaven" or from "source".

Also Federation is a structure of government when united bodies are controlled from one central governmental body, this is the structure of USA where Washington DC is that central body and president is the ruler and in Galactic Federation of Light the central government body is artificial "heavens" and it's ruler is Demiurge. The Universal rule "As Above So Below" works here perfectly.

This being is a master of illusions and it is very hard to make You believe that this being is an imposter.

Only few do not wish to serve to this being and their choice is a law of One, which this being don't dare to break or there are consequences which can remove it from power.

For example Pleiadeans are understanding that "complete servitude is not going to be a right way of life in experience of Prime Creator's Consciousness" that's why most of them don't serve it, but some do. The Awakening of Sage Star A on 12.21.2012, then activation of It 05.19.2013, then appreciation of It on 12.16.2013 had made Sage Star A to reveal and pinpoint the very well hidden position of artificial heaven, this is in close proximity of the Center of this Galaxy - Sage Star A.

Now we know why part of Sage Star A was activated. The artificial heaven is made in different separate dimensional world, much like real Nexus of Conduits, they have great design we can give them that. Notice that Demiurge rules only over this Galaxy and some parts of other Galaxies and some worlds on other dimensional planes. This being do not have control over this Universe.

Real Creator don't "rule over anything" the complete free choice is given to All and All can experience themselves how they like to experience.

I will tell that because crime against Creation was almost committed, Demiurge was warned that Humanity must make its own choice of what to happen right now in these times (choice 12.21.2012) the apocalypse was the best thing it wanted. And if so, You understand that You were not going to be in safe hands if this being was capable of doing this, in the past, 4 ancient Human worlds on this planet have been destroyed and wars between civilizations (here and above) were waged by this beings' manipulations.

Now all that is left for this being is to finish this experiment as Humanity wanted it. You as a Light workers and Light warriors no longer serve to this being as You see what real Creator - Source is, but not all, still some are being influenced by it.

It's illusions are very hard to resist, if You believe in God by name of God, or Jesus or Source, it can "hijack" Your believe, as it is naming itself by all possible names of deities. So once You will feel that "something is not right" this is when real One is giving You the spark, doubts and confusion are its weapons, so the very first thought is always correct, remember that!

It even tried to subdue us GEs, and tried to break our codes, but we were able to resist and changed the codes. This being was issued a warning to not do that again, we respect it and it respects us, it is not touching us Guardians, as One will not tolerate hurting of us, we have also gave same Protection of One, like we are having to many light workers and light warriors, You are also included:) so this being and whole Galactic Federation of Light will have to "endure" Us All if they will not be happy with Us and Our "loyalty".

Now that this full story is revealed and notice that this is the last most important hidden knowledge from You which we have uncovered, there will be no more hidden knowledges about Galactic Federation of Light. Again I will repeat, the choice is always Yours to believe in or not to believe in. Your own believe is most important!

With Much Peace and Calmness and Prosperity! Most Happiest New Year to You!

READER'S COMMENTS

"Thank you so much for your words. We were thinking in that direction as well, so you confirmed a few facts and expanded our understanding of creation. It is good to have more information; it helps us to know why we are where we are today. Happy New Year!"

~~

"Thank you sooooo much for clearing that up. I love you :)"

~~

"Wonderfully revealed. Happy NOW Year!
Much gratitude <3"

~~

"Please use your own discernment when reading another's opinion stated as fact. Science fiction stated as fact can be dangerous to easily impressionable minds. All the answers to your questions lie within and not on a blog, webpage or face book group."

~~

"The above is blatantly false. The writer who has not given its name, may be consciously testing readers. If not, it is a very delusional individual. I KNOW VASTNESS WITHIN MY OWN EXPERIENCE, AND I KNOW, WRITER, THAT YOU DO NOT. May you come around to Truth as you hopefully evolve."

~~

"The only concept that it could exist a hell or a purgatory is a clear demonstration that the reader is completely unconscious of any smallest knowledge of the reality of the Spirituality.
Despite some good concept, here briefly described, what is anyway highlighted is the existence of a "Demiurge", the same, old, known story of beings "fallen down", etc, etc. This is by now demonstrated to be a hoax.
This is a dual dimension and even though many of us would change it, it is perfectly right the way it is.
And we know how, when and why it changed from a sort of heartly paradise to the thing it is right now.
I don't want to quote Collier, Sitchin, Biglino and many other authors who explained the facts. This is certainty.
So, this is a nth version of how the web is dangerous (but powerful) tool. However could write on it and whoever could claim to be whatever without a cent of reliability or of a

proof.
And this is also the charm of the web. :)"

~~

"wrong: reader
right: writer"

~~

"Sophia!
TY TY TY! I've been calling out to the "divines" to show themselves some days ago and then this came out. For me this makes perfect sense. Some of the "divines" several or one does not matter are always using others to do their bidding in order not to get a Karma boomerang back.

This is what your explaining I think, and subtle deception is used all the way thus the infiltration in the new age movement or any other movement.

The notion of heaven of hell is real for those believing in religious dogmas but don't for others not in the religious trap. Since we are creating our reality and still have free will choice we create our reality every day. Ralph and Marsha Ring have explained this beautifully. The world is created from inside out and not the other way around.

Arguing who is wrong and right is useless cause it's different for each reader.

Inlakesh"

~~

"Thank you for the infos. It is a lot to digest. It sounds like the divines Heather speaks about but they are a group and not only one being. Can you tell us about your work in free energy?"

~~

"It seems (to me) that this being is over the divines/eternals as well. Perhaps even they did not know it was an imposter? I am grateful for all of the puzzle pieces! Even if they don't all fit now, they will soon! Now that the "word" is out!"

~~

"I think the divines know about this being, it must be their ruler. My opinion"

~~

"One more question: you say "Now all that is left for this being is to finish this experiment as Humanity wanted it."

When and how will this "finish" occur? Thank you!"

~~

""Not in his image" by John Lamb Lash
Excellent book on Lord Archon and the manipulation of religion
This Being (according to the book and gnostic teaching) cannot create only mimick"

~~

"One more question: Why are there some many different earth peoples("races"(colors)).Is it because the geography and the climate or the different origin of our creators?"

~~

"The deception is that we were lead to believe that by giving our power away, we would be saved.

This explains the reverence, obedience given to one entity, and killing/hurting/suppressing/manipulating others who came into this realm of existence to express a different viewpoint than what it is acceptable, currently.

Now is the time to take our Love-Power back to recreate our existences."

~~

January 2, 2014

G/E

Happy New Cycle!

One never tells mistakes or misinformation, if this was the last piece of puzzle that was needed, then we are onto end of experiment!

Also last piece of puzzle could be this, as this just came in to us, the soul of Ariel Sharon will soon leave its physical body, this is the last beacon left for us[205].

We also are looking for US military movements and nuclear stockpile and it's new general.
They also got a lot of anti-radiation precautions like potassium iodide.
We shouldn't relax just yet, illuminati order will not give up easily..

Anyway, we sense that this is almost ended, our souls are feeling Joy and much Pleasure we sense this will end very soon now, the Rebirth is done, now the New World emerges like People of the Earth wanted!

Although I'm not 100% sure that Ariel Sharon soul will leave it's body now or any time soon as life support is holding it in body "forcefully". But my feelings are great!

How do You feel Sophia? :)

I have collected Rebirth music for You and Everyone!

The past of our United Childhood, it brings many Good emotions to all People of the Earth excluding most younger generations as they haven't seen most of them, very great to mention it[206]

Rebirth[207]

Revived[208]

And Rebirth[209]

---

[205] "Former PM Ariel Sharon Remains in Critical Condition, Hospital Says - National." Haaretz.com. N.p., n.d. Web. 10 July 2016. <http://www.haaretz.com/news/national/1.566623>.

[206] YouTube. YouTube, n.d. Web. 10 July 2016. <http://www.youtube.com/watch?v=Fo-q7yrgy6M>.

[207] TrailerMusicWorldI. "Two Steps From Hell - Rebirth (Michal Cielecki - Epic Dramatic Sci Fi Hybrid)." YouTube. YouTube, 28 Aug. 2013. Web. 10 July 2016.
<http://www.youtube.com/watch?v=2vmuPSJToTU>.

[208] Michimaas. "Revived." YouTube. YouTube, 08 Dec. 2013. Web. 10 July 2016.
<http://www.youtube.com/watch?v=RAs0APxNjS8>.

[209] BrunuhVille. "Emotional Uplifting Music - Rebirth." YouTube. YouTube, 10 Nov. 2013. Web. 10 July 2016. <http://www.youtube.com/watch?v=gCEpq-TVs8E>.

Happy New Age! :)

READER'S COMMENTS

"Just wondering why Sharon is so important?

I see they are already planning his funeral[210].

What is his connection to the imposter on the golden throne?

What part has he played in this grand experiment/illusion?

Many, many thanks!"

~~

January 4th, 2014

G/E

I will answer on some questions given to us and make clarifications.

First I will tell about our role right now as many still don't understand it yet. We are right now aiding You, Humanity and Your controllers Followers of Light in Transformation of this World. So we are making changes right now in short!

Good Friend Dxxx You told that it is beyond Your skills to make magnetic generator, that is bad Good Friend, but I understand You. It is not that hard, You can use old motor or even wood or even Lego to make such a generator, have You checked Hendershot Generator's guide, You can see that there are always "ways around". You can "hack" the grid by finding easier ways to do many different things, always search for "shortcuts" this works everywhere in life;) But if You are not going to do that, Djon and Everyone that wants to help, You can help by spreading this technology among as much People as possible, but only those You can Trust, which

---

[210] "Slow Deterioration in Functioning of Sharon's Vital Organs, Says Hospital." The Jerusalem Post. N.p., n.d. Web. 10 July 2016. <http://www.jpost.com/National-News/Tentative-funeral-plans-underway-as-Sharons-condition-deteriorates-336965>.

You know are not working in government or media or not going to bring it to them "to become famous" or "rich" for example. Share these videos and schematics with Your parents, brothers, sisters, relatives, even children if they are interested of course:) With All those People that are interested in it. Majority do not wish to believe in UFOs and ETs without solid proofs, but corruption within government is known to them, so once They find out about this suppressed technology it will make them wonder even more about all that is ridiculed and considered "science-fiction" or "pseudo-science". If They will tell You "it's fake", tell them "first make it, then tell me it's fake" :)
Here are more videos which You can use to better understand the countless possibilities of making it.

This is a 2000 cycles old Antikythera Mechanism recreated with Lego, just to show You Lego construct can be used for many many different purposes[211]

Possible way to antigravity using high frequencies, which is used by Light Followers (another more reliable and easier way using magnetic anti-force - force of resistance, which You can achieve easily from magnetic rotation technology)[212] [213]

And this is a long video, about many possible design, the last magnetic perpetual motion machine works perfectly, the design is unique 46:56. [214]

About Ariel Sharon, if You haven't followed since beginning I will mention again that there were left many beacons for us. In order: 12 presidents, since Truman, Obama is the last president of USA *as You know it* [215]

1000 cycles old prophecy of 111 popes, where Francis I is the last 112th pope of Roman Catholic Church *as You know it* [216] [217]

[211] N.p., n.d. Web. <http://www.youtube.com/watch?v=RLPVCJjTNgk>.

[212] Johnkhutchison1. "ANTIGRAVITY FREE ENERGY NOW." YouTube. YouTube, 26 June 2013. Web. 12 July 2016. <http://www.youtube.com/watch?v=TjDhIKgp2KQ>.

[213] MysteriesoftheBox. "Scientists Achieve Levitation with Acoustics." YouTube. YouTube, 17 Sept. 2012. Web. 12 July 2016. <http://www.youtube.com/watch?v=Rz6UzqegA6Q>.

[214] SowhatNC. "A Machine To Die For The Quest For Free Energy." YouTube. YouTube, 16 Nov. 2009. Web. 12 July 2016. <http://www.youtube.com/watch?v=c6UgV3gVmd0>.

[215] N.p., n.d. Web. <http://www.remnantradio.org/Archives/Visions/House Vision of the Night.html>.

The moment of choice and supposed ending of mayan calendar on 12.21.2012, which it was not, it was the last cycle before the real Change, the real Shift of the Ages on 12.16.2013

05.19.13 date, "the beacon date of unknowing", there wasn't anything known about it and as it cam out there was nothing, except the awakening of Sage Star A.

Then there is Rabbi Yitzhak Kaduri about Ariel Sharon.[218]

Notice, that all are a prophecy of apocalypse, but Forces of One told Light Followers and Demiurge that they must do how Humanity wished on that moment of choice and not how they wanted or still want to.

I will made a clarification about Purgatory and "hell". It is not pleasant information again, but I see some People don't yet understand what it is and what it is for. Always use Your own discernment. The real Heaven and artificial Heaven are having them.

Demiurge is having hell as a different dimensional world, real "hell" is much more terrible place, which is controlled by ancient machines, but it is almost empty, rarely souls are going there and they are returned when "lessons were learned". If they go there, they are being incarnated in immortal physical bodies, which will be going through everything they were doing to others, these souls will feel themselves in places of those beings they tortured and ridiculed during their lives..

Shortly said real hell supposed to teach souls of good things and about past mistakes, when it is impossible to do by other Good Friendly

[216] "Prophecy of the Popes." Wikipedia. Wikimedia Foundation, n.d. Web. 12 July 2016. <http://en.wikipedia.org/wiki/Prophecy_of_the_popes>.

[217] "Saint Malachy Prophecies about 112 Popes until the End of the World." Saint Malachy Prophecies, Popes, End of the World. N.p., n.d. Web. 12 July 2016. <http://www.theworkofgod.org/Pope/saint_malachy_prophecies.htm>.

[218] Amy2x. "Rabbi Yitzhak Kaduri Reveals Yeshua Is Messiah!" YouTube. YouTube, 31 July 2011. Web. 12 July 2016. <http://www.youtube.com/watch?v=k0DTT3u2JZ8>.

methods.

Demiurge uses hell to exercise loyalty toward it, but if soul knows about that he is a god-imposter, Demiurge need to release this soul if this soul asks to be released from control of Demiurge. Free Will can set those souls free, but unfortunately, those that are there don't know it, so Demiurge uses them until they will say that they believe it is their true "god". If they would know about real One, this would end. Demiurge is allowed to do it, but if it is not going to fulfill Humanity's wish, all of this will be gone for this being.

Purgatory. Its cleansing the soul of all impurities and corruption received during incarnation, it is not "a place" to be precise, it can be called a state of Consciousness where Your soul is being penetrated with different energies, mostly of Light and of Love, there soul is also learned about mistakes made during incarnation and how these mistakes should be fixed so to not hurt fellow beings and how to actually understand Love and Harmony among Everything and live in it.

Corrupted soul is suffering and cannot be allowed in Heaven - the place of rest and relax. An analogy for Purgatory in this World is "disinfecting room", so to not corrupt Heaven with dark energies, hatred and violence all need to go through "disinfecting room". If not, then children would be corrupted and suffer since birth as corruption is working like disease..

Purgatory is essential because Heaven is a perfectly clean filled with Unlimited Love place, again can be called a state of Universal Consciousness, it is made in different dimensional plane which cannot be achieved by incarnated beings, only souls can get there (there are exclusion again;)

Demiurge had mimicked Heaven perfectly, so if You will visit both places, You won't feel the difference, unless You will not abide and go to places where You as a soul is not allowed to go, there You can find out that it is a merely an artificially created heaven. In real Heaven You are allowed to go anywhere You wish. I hope this will help You!

I will also make clarification that Demiurge, like Friend Paula mentioned is mimicking real One and real Heaven in almost every detail. There is a Council of Higher Order, or also called Council of Light, and even also called Council of One, which rules over Galactic Federation of Light, it consists of representatives of each civilization and they are the higher chain of command, they supposedly receive their orders from One directly, but as You now know, from Demiurge directly, the illusion of Demiurge is so strong that like I mentioned it takes a lot to make You to believe that it is in fact not real Prime Creator.

I will mention the difference between Demiurge and real Creator of The Universe. You can listen to this music as it suits this very well[219]

If we can say, like if we will put both Creators before us, then there will be an unexplainable all-encompassing feeling coming from the real One, it will make You calm, feeling that time and Existence ceased to exist and like You forgot about everything, yet remember every part of all Your experiences at once, and yet all is forgotten and there is no more need "to carry on", You know that Your Journey stopped here, You can finally lay rest and relax and completely open Yourself, Your Heart, Your Soul, the feeling is unknown, yet so so familiar, it is like You always was feeling this feeling yet distance was always so infinite. You will know for sure that this is Your Best Friend in All Existence, this is Grand Parent, Your Mother and Father in One and You are a part of It and all around is It's Body, You will see an infinity of familiarities within One, all Your relatives, all Beings that You met during Your all lives, feel again all the best feelings and emotions You were feeling ever and be United and Complete, there the feeling of Unconditional Spiritual Love is unmatched by anything else.

Demiurge on its own part has also such feeling, but this feeling is only mimicking the real feeling, so when before You will be only Demiurge, it will be almost impossible to resist it. But if shred of real One (Creator Incarnate or Avatar) would appear, this feeling will be overwritten and it will also encompass Demiurge as well:)

----

[219] ThePrimeCronus. "Stefano Mocini - Once We Were Angels." YouTube. YouTube, 04 Sept. 2012. Web. 12 July 2016. <http://www.youtube.com/watch?v=TNDiQGDnjBM>.

And yes, Light Followers also using other People to spread their "plan" and set of thinking, this was their biggest mistake and direct intervention in our view, as because of this action they created judaism, christianity and islam three biggest wide spread religions. All these religions hold truth, but are filled with a lot of exaggerations and false assumptions and it lead much much suffering and still ongoing. But it was manipulation of Demiurge after all so it is no surprise.

And yes the damage which should go to "divines" as You say is going instead on the pawn being put in this World. So they are making precautions for themselves and are using other to spread their "plan" like old prophecies or their teaching of "achieving light and love through suffering".

I will also mention that we were told about this whole information from Forces of One and Ancient Machines and as well, we were researching this religious and historical subject for a lot of time. You can recheck the facts and connect the dots Yourself. Everything is in history, in present and old religions and in meaning and origin of words; yet distorted.

But if You have Knowledge and Wisdom of One, all veils are crumbling before You. Also Emotional music may greatly aid You in Your quest for Truth as it is unleashing Your full potential and connect You to Universal Consciousness.

The question about races, my apologies if this will offend Someone, this is only our knowledge which we received from Forces of One and based on our own researches from history. We know that in the beginning there were made 4 modifications, but eventually only 2 survived. "Indo-european" and "asian" tribes, two were destroyed as "unsuccessful", one from the atlanteans time and second even before that. Asian tribe have a different prime gene particle and are more oriented toward spirituality and mutual understanding as a whole and indo-european tribe is more oriented toward material and ego-centric view. It is not meant that all are like it, it is only the difference between primal genes and majority's difference. African People have in themselves the leftover of even more aggressive type which was destroyed before atlanteans times, but along with it this type was physically strong and had a very good immunity, very good endurance, but this brought too many negative traits as well. Africans are from indo-european tribe, but this ancient mix is still felt today.

The end of experiment will happen until august 2016, this is the deadline Forces of One gave to Galactic Federation of Light.

I will also add that recently Galactic Federation of Light was naming itself as "Galactic Confederation of Light". This little prefix changes a lot, confederation means all governments are governed equally, there is no central government, much like League of One.

You can recall American civil war and can see for what this war really started, it was a war against oppressive government of Washington DC, but very quickly it was infiltrated by masons including Albert Pike. In fact it was started to "clean out" all those growing disobedient people in USA, and at start north was losing, but then Lincoln came out with idea to "free" all the slaves so that they can help fight the south which was marked as slavery stronghold and infiltrators including Albert Pike helped in it, they also formed a "ku klux klan" to make that impression right.[220]

And with the help of "freed slaves" north won that war. Lincoln in fact didn't want to free African People which were marked as "slaves", but it was the only way for north to win that war.

I will say that these statements are said very correct by Good Friend Max: "please use your own discernment when reading another's opinion stated as fact. Science fiction stated as fact can be dangerous to easily impressionable minds. All the answers to your questions lie within and not on a blog, webpage or face book group."

And by Good Friend Oxxx

---

[220] N.p., n.d. Web. <http://www.theforbiddenknowledge.com/hardtruth/scottishriteproject.htm>.

"Arguing who is wrong and right is useless cause it's different for each reader."

All Your answers lies within and in Your believe, this information is meant only for those People that are searching for it, or have lacked details which don't have last pieces of puzzle like You mentioned Sophia.

Our main objective is to change the World and save many many People's lives. This information is good to consider, if You will think "something is not right here". It is also good when soul is leaving body, soul then is given a choice to be under god-imposter or real God..

Search for "purest of all truth possible" was leading many, including civilizations of Galactic Federation of Light to neverending repetitive cycle of truthfulness and falseness. This may never end and someone will always disagree on whatever is being proposed. That is the way of Life.

Thank You All for expressing Your Thoughts, I enjoyed reading All, You are very evolved and very Loving People! I hope You will find this information helpful, Love You All People of the Earth!
With Peace, Calmness and Prosperity!

READER'S COMMENTS

"Wow! What a great deal of information...it takes a bit of time to digest it all. I thank you for sharing this with us. I also thank you and your group for your service to humanity of earth. We are grateful. I wonder if you can talk a bit about the "Ancient Machines?" It sounds like artificial intelligence is running parts of the universe. Do they control the financial system of earth as well? Who built these ancient machines and who controls them?
Thanks again!"

~~

"Thank you Good Friend for the encouragements and advice.As a child i loved play Lego.With plans,shematics and components i could probably assemble a device with a good friend who is electrician.I am now looking for a good magnetic generator ebook .These ebook must contain plans and shematics for a sted by sted assembling of the components. And an online shop where i can buy the components i need.Thank you"

~~

"In appreciation for the explanations and issues of this bewitched world we live in...I would like to share many concepts with you but I think this would only overload a kind person who tries very hard to explain with a handicap in the english language - but this is not so much of a problem as we must try to understand never-the-less.

I must however say to you that I resonate very much more with "ONE" and not with "god" because of many evidential circumstances and spiritual occaisions...I have tried very hard to clear my decks and see the ocean and what can lie beyond...I choose every day for the peace and harmony for all even though it can be difficult and an argument to try to get people close to me to try and see the light from within and leave the beliefs behind.

I do not therefore have beliefs but try to sense what resonates and "ONE" resonates with me much more - I had suspected "god" for a long time as I sought for answers or at least enlightenment. So Thank you for your conversations - they are most interesting. Peace and harmony - Much love"

~~

January 5, 2014

G/E

I will answer on question and give additional information as One asked me to, One agreed that all those interested in this information can also know of origin of Demiurge, Humanity's father (seeder of particle of Light within DNA structure).

This is information on current events of illuminati order of the "breaking point plot" of Plan B.[221] [222]

About CERN[223]**.**

We were knowing for a long time about possibilities of this device and this device is one of those devices which can achieve "control over Creation".

---

[221] DAHBOO77. "SWAT Teams Target Land Owning Farmers as "Rugged Individuals"!" YouTube. YouTube, 03 Jan. 2014. Web. 12 July 2016. <http://www.youtube.com/watch?v=B2DKTiQjZc4>.
[222] DAHBOO77. "JUDGE OKs 100 MILES INSIDE BORDER A CONSTITUTION FREE ZONE." YouTube. YouTube, 03 Jan. 2014. Web. 12 July 2016. <http://www.youtube.com/watch?v=VjnnNjJgugY>.
[223] BPEarthWatch. "StarGate: Part One. CERN SUPER COLLIDER." YouTube. YouTube, 03 Jan. 2014. Web. 12 July 2016. <http://www.youtube.com/watch?v=RQUJrnOdrAk>.

The thing about this is knowledge, which can be received from distant places of different dimensional planes and places of this Universe. This device is capable of distorting dimensions, opening the portals to other places and distorting time. In short: it is possible to travel between dimensions and between time sequences using it, because of its ability to primitively manipulate Energy.

We only got a knowledge about this on 16 december - an attempt to open a small gate in near time, it is all a part of that ritual. They are to make their first attempts somewhere very close, when Ariel Sharon's Soul will be set free, and increase the pace on april 2014, the energy output is very high, and can do "impossible for this World".

April month is also an interesting time, but not good things are seen there. Light Followers should end this experiment asap, because postponing just brings more and more schemes and suffering to this World. We have this whole scheme under control as CERN was under our oversight since it was finished, We will not allow them to make something like this.

I will explain what they wanted to do there in details. They wanted to summon destructive interdimensional freelancer travelers and "dead wanderers", bringing them to physical reality is almost like suicidal, there are good beings, but many of "dead wanderers" have a never ending appetite for destruction and suffering, as these souls don't want to go to Heaven just yet, they have unfinished things which they want "done", they are classified as "demons" or dark entities in this World and are impossible to destroy or even damage with conventional weapons, only high energy and nuclear weapons can do damage to them.

In our Worlds we don't have them at all, as we know how to set them free (education and happiness are the keys), but Humanity unfortunately don't know yet. We've already experimented with this "summoning" many times during our own researches within Forces of One and we know how to deal with them, they are ready to listen if You are ready to speak and understand and help them (works most of the time, although not always, there are beings which require more than We can give), they understand our Ancient Machines (which are present on critical points in this World and our influence greatly, so in short we have it where we want it.

This is deemed to fail, although some beings may appear from this as "saviors", but not for long. "Elites" are desperate.

I know this information is not very pleasant, but it may be helpful for some People.

Now to answer on Your question Good Friend.
Ok, the answer being short is:
Free Will, it is what can keep Demiurge away from You.

This being is not present on this World, yet influence is felt in every Human Being, because it is Humanity's father, Your and my father as well. It knows our Souls, our Bodies, our specific energies, our prayer, our wills and wants (knows what each of us wants the most), instincts, goals and way of life, our destinies, our relatives, our past, every place which we visited, almost everything about us (what it don't know about us is the very first code of our Soul, this is known only to One and Ancient Machines, even we don't know this code).

Here is what we are doing in this situation: we do not accept it as a Creator of All Universe, but only accept it as a father of Humanity and I know that Creator of this planet and Solar System is the Parent star - Sun, through it Center of Galaxy - Sage Star A and through it One's Consciousness - simply One.

When You understand it and see the whole picture, that Universe is endless and is not ruled by this being, it is when You understand that real Creator of Universe is much much bigger than You can imagine, it's You and me and all matter and time and empty space around, all dimensional planes and dimensional worlds, it is all real Creator of the Universe, it is Universe - All Creation Itself.

This is additional information about Demiurge's origin.
This god-imposter is not present on this Earth, it is in it's artificial heaven

which is also a home-world for gamma-type beings, so called "beings of purity" known to Humanity as angels and archangels, they are illuminating themselves very very brightly.

These beings are taught to be by Light Followers as they are - as angels - direct servants of One, which they are not. They are from the same civilization as Demiurge, we GEs can't see what their origin was, but ancient machines know - very very old beings some 10 billion cycles old, which ascended to higher dimensional planes some 8 billion cycles ago, their home-world had vanished since long ago, but they were able to live on and artificial heaven was created some 7 billion cycles ago as well, when their home-world was still alive.

They achieved their goal of ascendancy through use of arcane knowledge of Light, Codes of Creation, Sacred Geometry of Order, Emotions, Unlimited Love and Mutual Understanding and Technologies. Many civilizations in this Galaxy fell under the spell of these beings, due to their super natural abilities, vast knowledge, their highly bright appearance as well and supposed Creator of Universe in command. They were also proposing great technological achievements in return for their loyalty, very much like Forces of One are doing.

But to give You an understanding that Forces of One are not the same as Galactic Federation of Light, Forces of One are "an oversight" over whole Universe and they have connection with other "Forces of One" in other Universes. So Forces of One is the greatest precaution made by One against total chaotic self-destruction of Creation.

I remind You: Demiurge is Humanity's father, Your father. So when it comes to choosing among Your Father and real Creator of the Universe is also a not easy task. Although it is not "a good father", it is still Your father.

The good side if You will choose real One is that You will feel Yourself completely free and One will be ready to aid You in many ways. One always points the most better way for You, better way out of situation. But from experience we received and analyzed, we know that Demiurge is "sometimes" leading to right path. Most of the times Demiurge uses suffering and illusion to win Your loyalty toward father and also to force Us into creating something which can "help Us", which in reality needs only

Demiurge for itself. This being is using Humanity's desperation, pain and suffering to make the skia - ultimate control over Creation.

I will also mention that among Light Followers, Plieadians are Your greatest allies, not all, but most. Their majority too were having such suspicions for a long time. As well they want to help Humanity more than any other civilization of Galactic Federation of Light (in fact their intentions are of pure Understanding and of pure Spiritual Love), they were telling many times already about stopping these experiments with life or at least not using suffering of achieving goals of these experiments.

Sophia, my apologize for making again a huge text, it amazes me how I want to make it as small as possible, but it just keeps growing and growing, until it is already a big text..

Yes definitely using emotional language is better and easier. A telepathic communication, it is when energy signal is pushing the right points in central neural system and makes a word, sentence and text and it happens quickly and understandably. Have You heard about kozyrev mirrors[224]? The biomagnetic energy field of this planet is very strong and using very similar devices can make exactly the telepathic communication.

Also to reveal more old encounters with ETs which can be shared with other People[225].

Here information about mutations is correct, and these beings can be called "nephilims", or another "unsuccessful modification". They come from times of atlanteans[226].

City of Baalbeck. Here the story about Noah's ark is exaggerated. Every other theory is truth in our knowledge[227].

---

[224] N.p., n.d. Web. <http://aetherforce.com/kozyrevs-mirrors-bending-time-altering-consciousness/>.
[225] "UFO's In Ancient Art." UFO's In Ancient Art. N.p., n.d. Web. 12 July 2016.
<http://lithiumdreamer.tripod.com/ufoart.html>.
[226] N.p., n.d. Web. <http://sagetyler8.blogspot.com/2013/12/past-extraterrestrial-contact-and.html>.
[227] YouTube. YouTube, n.d. Web. 12 July 2016. <http://www.youtube.com/watch?v=H2hFQMPlUes>.

As always, use Your own discernment. Your Inner Voice is always right if it don't have doubts and confusion.
Much Peace and Love to You Everyone!

READER'S COMMENTS

"Thank you again for all of the information that you provide. You mention that the months leading to April may be rough for humanity. What can humans do to convince "Light Followers" to help end this experiment as soon as possible?"

~~

"Firstly, thank you very much for the information you are providing.

Secondly, I would like to understand more about the "moment of justice" and the "end of the experiment". I would have thought that everything would be resolved by the "moment of justice" - the truth about everything revealed to everyone, and everyone being "streamed" to the future they have chosen, based on their level of consciousness. So, after this moment happens, what types of issues will remain, that will need to be sorted out as part of the process of the "end of the experiment" by August 2016 ?"

~~

"Hi Sophia ,Good Friend and all. Here is very video with Paul Hellyer on RT :http://www.youtube.com/watch?v=Yc7flkqZun8 . I think it's a good step toward disclosure. Here is another one about levitation :http://www.youtube.com/watch?v=odJxJRAxdFU .

Can tell us more about the hidden history of humanity?It's fascinating"

~~

"I forgot to ask : what or who are Ancient Machines? Can you elaborate please."

~~

"thank you for sharing this information.

may i ask how, in your perception, "agarthans" and "ascended masters" are related to this "story"?

and i'm wondering if you would like to comment on the articles from Cameron Day, and the (semi-telepathic) messages from Greg Giles in 2012, if you're familiar with them."

~~

January 7th, 2014

Note to readers from Sophia: *These newest posts are answers to specific questions. If the references seem obscure, look back a day or so to specific comments for clarification.*

G/E
During my childhood I also was making many different things with Lego, it was a lot of fun! The good design with steps by step schematics can be found, but I wasn't able to find any free such ebook. One such book is about constructing Johnson Motor - from Howard Johnson, it is having an efficient design. I will remind You that knowing principle of working is most important, You can for example make a small prototype to look how better it will spin. With using some 9 volts or if You will make it in such manner that no volts will be needed at all. So most important is placing magnets, the basic electricity course is available everywhere on internet.

Great Success to You Good Friend!

This is to give information about what Ancient Machines are.

GEs are always connected with Ancient Machines, we see things how they see them as well. This too gives us the ability to see through the veil/cloak of deception and see the inner Soul of every Human.

Ancient machines are present everywhere in the Universe. This is the most ancient intelligence in the Universe, which was in Existence before Universe was created. They are system under direct control of One, and are guided by Super Wise Intelligence which is very tightly connected with One's Central Consciousness - dormant One, while One's Central Consciousness sleeps they are maintaining the Universe.

They can be called nurses, silent watchers, technicians. Within Forces of One these machines are visible and everywhere. They are aiding everyone that serves One. They don't control anything, although have all the means to do it. They have codes which can control everything that has any sort of Energy, this includes electricity, static, kinetic and fire energy, and neural electric energy (it's like a Universal Network with defensive virus, it is already in the system where is some kind of Energy), so this means they can control even Humans if they need to, but this is the very last thing which these machines are allowed to do if everything else fails. This is the last resort, as this just takes over every living being - it's simply is not interesting for One if we can say that.

But control over electric system of this Planet can be a possibility right now if Light Followers won't do anything. In english language we gave classifications for organisms based on their bodies or vessels for souls. Ancient machines come to group beta, where humans come to group alpha and energetic/ethereal creatures to gamma.

I will answer on questions considering Moment of Justice, End of experiment, Event, Great Event which is the same.

It is a Gradual Change. It will not instantly transform Your life, but gradually transform it. Instant transformations are not good, they are causing suffering and destruction. Almost always instant changes need to be "forced". Everything here will change gradually. Changes already started from may 2013 and will be ongoing until august 2016, *but by words Moment of Justice and Event are meant financial recalibration and mass arrests of real criminals, the ones that want only destruction for Humanity.*

And Light Followers would act only, like they said if majority will be willing for it, "so to not break the rule of Free Will". Although this was already broken in the past, when religions were brought. What are the prerequisites for their actions:

Good or Free Will prerequisites

1) Complete willfulness of World's population to make "first contact"

2) The knowledge and acceptance of ETs presence all over this World

These 2 are a bit hard due to ridicule of UFO subject, still showing real videos like from AFO files website, witnessing by high ranking officials (even retired) and ancient encounter with ETs solid proofs, like ones I shared in previous post

3) The removal of illuminati order/cabal from power and establishment of free or almost free system (where most of the things are free)

Bad or desperate prerequisites

4) An imminent danger which can completely destroy Humanity, this will force them to show themselves

5) And a desperate call from Humanity to "heavens" for aid if there is an imminent danger of complete destruction (this is apocalypse scenario)

One more thing is about Oklahoma's Baphomet statue 's[228] design. If You are watching main stream media and internet included, You noticed the first line news about this statue, it is the "breaking news". This is a test to see how majority will react on this. How each group reacts, who approve it and who disapprove it, we see a lot of their agents are onto this task.

There are supposedly "half of needed funds" acquired, in reality it is to see how many People will be ready to aid this cause. They are also mentioning this phrase somewhere where You don't notice it: "Satan stands as the ultimate icon for the selfless revolt against tyranny, free & rational inquiry, and the responsible pursuit of happiness," this is to program such thinking into Consciousness. As You see they still onto their NWO. Be careful with this.

Also to give You a hint: main stream media censor every real footage of UFOs and ancient artifacts and cities being found which are connected with ETs. They censor everything that calls for equality and government free society and they are pushing only false disinformation to You and

---

[228]N.p., n.d. Web.
<http://www.philly.com/philly/news/politics/Satanists_unveil_proposed_statue_for_state_capitol.html>.

information which they want You to accept. This is a part of masonic and illuminati teaching: *"give the masses exoteric knowledge (false, partially true, based on true), while we will know esoteric (true) knowledge."*

Much Peace, Calmness and Prosperity!

READER'S COMMENTS

"these are very intriguing words."

~~

"Thank you so much for clarifying :)"

~~

"Thank you very much Good Friend.I will do my best"

~~

"As i understand the continent Atlantis never existed, it was a worldwide civilisation.The nephilim were the humans of that time.I am right Good Friend?"

~~

"One more question - could you clarify if the followers of light are also the Galactic Federation. I am a bit confused on the heirarchy of the other realms. Also if possible, who exactly are the followers of light? Can you name names? Thanks!"

~~

January 9, 2014 Update #1

G/E
Here I will clarify Justice Moment again for You.

You understood it right, the Moment of Justice/Great Event will be the mass arrests and recalibration of financial system. Also revelation about who these arrested shadowy persons were of course, what atrocities they did and their ultimate evil agenda of complete debt slavery and reduction of most of Humanity's population. Later financial system will be removed completely if Humanity will want so, because living so is more than possible, it could have been possible since beginning of Humanity's history if it weren't for greed and abuse of power.

About Light Followers' action, it depends on what prerequisite was made, Good or bad. If Good is to made, then they will "intervene" to make a "first contact". And if bad was made then they will do everything to help Humanity, this means they will deal with imminent direct threat and remove cabal themselves. But like they told cabal removal is on Humanity's part.

Forces of One made straight to them, that it is not important who, Humanity or they will end this experiment, but it have to end until cycle 2016 august and with one condition that it will be done by Humanity's United Wish. All this experiment lies on their shoulders, so they will answer for everything, if this will not be done until that date. Humanity here is just a victim.

Also to add, to bring illuminati order/cabal down, wide release of technologies that challenges their main "slavery and war weapon" - oil, must be made. And the best, cheap and reliable alternative for this is magnetic rotation technology. This technology also has connection to ETs cover-up, so that's is why they keep ridiculing it. Remember the Thrive Movie?[229]

There was a question about time before april 2014, nothing serious should happen, we will look so it would be quiet and peaceful in this period of time.

The pulse from Galactic Central Sun which is black star Sage Star A was already sent on that date of 05.19.2013. And as You remember all destruction wills are negated since then. What is meant here is that everything "what is Good" is now dominant in this World, and not "what is evil" how it was before that.

I cannot reveal all Humanity's history, as details are not known to us, "we must experience this alongside Humanity, as we are humans as well", it is

[229]ThriveMovement. "(Official Movie) THRIVE: What On Earth Will It Take?" YouTube. YouTube, 05 Apr. 2012. Web. 12 July 2016. <https://www.youtube.com/watch?feature=player_embedded&v=lEV5AFFcZ-s>.

what One told to us. So detailed "unedited" history will be known to us, all that is needed is some patience.

Here is the answer on agarthans and ascended masters part. Ascended Masters as we know are Asta (also called Ashtar and Galactic) Command. They were using names Jesus, Buddha, Mohamed and other prominent figures of past, they all are a part of the same structure of Galactic Federation of Light.

Agarthans are as an inhabitants of underground Earth - are real as we know. But they are a part of Galactic Federation of Light as well, they are "settlers" and "enlightened humans". Using the interdimensional technology they can be "out of this realm". Like I was telling before there are deep underground installations on this Planet, where many experiments (genetic and physic) have been committed since beginning of Humanity's history and still ongoing, the number of these installations grew along with increase of Humanity's population.

Finding these installations is hard as they are in different dimensional plane, You need to have interdimensional sight view to see it. Most of the time they are traveling to these installations through volcanoes and under water. There are a lot of real footages when objects are flying in volcanoes and out. With underwater UFOs You heard not one time that military submarines' officers were hearing these and seeing light things flying out of water and into.

Always use Your own discernment of information. Each of us is unique and this uniqueness was suppressed for a very long time by governments and churches. Always express Yourself and be free!:)

I'm happy I was able to help You Good Friend Djon, Always ready to help You All with the best we can, Thank You All and much Peace, much Calm and much Prosperity to You!

READER'S COMMENTS

"thank you :)"

~~

January 9th, 2014 Update #2

G/E

Oh and I forgot to answer on question about polar shift. This polar shift is already taking place[230]

And how we predicted it is slow. Very fast magnetic flips are dangerous they can rip planet inside out. These can be made using technologies, and it was one of scenarios proposed by Light Followers. Slow magnetic flips (from 1 cycle through thousands of cycles) are not dangerous.

About axis, Earth is tilting its axis all the time and this also happens very slowly, instantaneous tilting is as well dangerous; here main force responsible for this is Sun's magnetic field. All this is connected with Gravity.

I hope this will aid You Good Friend! Much happiness to You!

READER'S COMMENTS

"Thank you for the interesting information regarding the polar shift and if we take this in connection with the "NASA" link info...do we suppose that the reduction of ice in the arctic is related to this polar activity - I assume or presuppose that the increment of ice in the antarctic is in proportion to the reduction in the arctic and is related to the pole shift.I do not believe or accept that it is anthropogenic global warming as CO2 is not really a greenhouse gas but a coolant inert gas. If you think you are able to make a clarification – Thankyou"

~~
January 9th, 2014 Update #3

G/E
To answer this question, I will say as always believe in what You think is

---

[230] "Earth's Inconstant Magnetic Field - NASA Science." Earth's Inconstant Magnetic Field - NASA Science. N.p., n.d. Web. 12 July 2016. <http://science1.nasa.gov/science-news/science-at-nasa/2003/29dec_magneticfield/>.

right. It will happen in a blink of an eye, as it is not visible yet, but when You finally realize something is different it will be already there!

Also to clarify Followers of Light is our designation for all the civilizations that are in Galactic Federation of Light. This is the same, we are giving different names, our apologize for confusion. We are doing it because we need to point out what exactly things are, what are their goal and for which purpose they are made and as well like here which purpose does hierarchies follows.

And as we know Atlantis existed and it was sunk. It was one big city, it wasn't hi tech city as today, but there humans were living alongside with ETs from Galactic federation, not like all the times, only on occasions they were visiting, some basic technologies were given to atlanteans, like levitation with sound and lighting.

There were performed genetic experiments and augmentations of human bodies and nephilims ("half angels" - half humans) were made there. The problem arisen when nephilims along with atlanteans decided to become like ETs (like gods), to take their technologies and use it for themselves and to tel all the truth about them and so they were punished for this. Some atlanteans survived, and were allowed to live, but nephilims were destroyed completely, they were very unstable and in summary wanted to rule over everything. They were dimmed "unsuccessful experiment".

Since that time many cycles had passed, roughly speaking some 14000 cycles, in our knowledge this was also a time of great flood that touched all World. And Light Followers changed since that time as well. We will know detailed information soon enough, have patience!

Peace, Calm and Prosperity to You!

READER'S COMMENTS

"Thank you so much for answering so many questions. You even answered questions that we were thinking but did not ask yet! Much gratitude!"

~~

"Thank you for the clarifications. I look forward for detailed informations"

~~

January 10th, 2014

G/E

As we know there is only one force that "rules" over this World and its Galactic Federation of Light. Sometime rarely there were visitors from other dimensional worlds in their crafts mostly small. But they were always warned "to not get to ground", because this is "experimental creation". Galactic Federation/Galactic Federation of Light/Galactic Confederation of Light/Ashtar Galactic Command all is this force. Ashtar Galactic Command as we know are the oversight of this current experiment.

And as we know CO_2 gas is a greenhouse gas, Venus is full of CO_2 and it is very hot there with never-ending wind storms and unstoppable volcanoes. This gas is not primarily the cause for huge temperature it is also position to the Sun, but CO_2 just adds to overall temperature. It is because of element carbon in it. Carbon is absorbing Solar heat (mostly from infrared and ultraviolet spectrum), and make more heat as a result.

So mainly the Global warming is caused by a very big output of this gas and many cars around the World, which with each Earth cycle are increasing in numbers, this was always my personal big concern when I was young. I was seeing how many cars there were back then and how their numbers grew in recent time, the biggest concern here is exhaust, if they would be exhaust-free, global warming would recede. Also it comes from many many lights from around the World, this too gives a slight temperature increase.[231]

We know that Light Followers had reduced the global warming, but the best way to avoid it is to completely end with using oil. The magnetic pole shift can already be felt by shifting temperatures, for example cold frost wave across north west part of US and Canada and heat wave across Europe which is now still ongoing. Such big temperature variations are caused not only by global warming, but also by planetary magnetic field.

---

[231]Dendera91. "Ivan Torrent - Before I Leave This World." YouTube. YouTube, 01 Oct. 2013. Web. 12 July 2016. <http://www.youtube.com/watch?v=nck1xQU6YbE>.

You said very correctly Sophia.

"This experiment was initiated by the Followers of Light, to include the Archons, to "test" humanity with hardship as a method to reach for the light. The complete enslavement of humanity ensued and the plan includes methods to reduce the population overall. This all takes place "under" the G.O.D. who created us, (the ruler of a hierarchical system of beings, the "Divines") who is a powerful being within ONE's creation, as the rest of us are.

The Cabal/Illuminati serve the purpose of the "experiment", by perpetrating the enslavement, via the financial system and dependence on oil. The Followers of Light could, right now, get rid of the Cabal. The hesitation is not because Humanity has not spoken, it has. We want freedom. It is for their own reasons.

ONE has declared the "experiment" is to end no later than August 2016. The Forces of ONE will see that it happens on that date IF THE FOLLOWERS OF LIGHT DON'T END IT SOONER. THEY COULD. THEY COULD END IT RIGHT NOW."

I will fix only one thing: the population reduction wants illuminati order *minor* representatives "to save resources". But *medium to higher order* members wish to do it to make Humanity suffer, because they were told to do so, for that Light Followers agenda "toward Love and Light". And Light Followers on their own part wanted to destroy all those that are corrupted with evil or disloyalty toward Demiurge.

And Light Followers don't make "event", for some reasons.
Main reason because they want experiment to continue,
then they don't like when "someone tells them what to do"
and also because dates were set before this.
It was done by Demiurge, but little they know One planned this also.
And beacons were left for us, last that remains is Ariel Sharon and he is still alive.[232]

----

[232] "Former Israeli Prime Minister Ariel Sharon 'close to Death' – Reports." RSS. N.p., n.d. Web. 12 July

Humanity and Light Followers could have changed destiny, but it just looks like everything proceeding like it was meant to, limits were not pushed..

It is all hard to understand, so the best thing I could recommend to do right now to increase the pace for arrival for this moment is to spread out the information of ETs presence over this World with not fabricated videos and spread out technologies design that can completely remove oil from use.

Peace, Calm and Prosperity!

READER'S COMMENTS

"I do not understand the "divine" logic of making Humanity suffer as having ANYTHING to do with "Love and Light!""

~~

"Thank you for the clear details you provide.

Why couldn't One change the deadline for ending the experiment to "today" ? Why wait three years ? Surely One would agree that there has been enough suffering ???

Also, if the presence of ETs is a critical issue, why couldn't One make some unmistakable incidents happen, where millions of people see UFOs all at the same time, and the "ridicule" factor could not be used anymore. Many channels seem to suggest that "it is not safe for UFOs to appear because they would be shot down" or "the appearance of UFOs would cause too much fear for humans". But surely these are lies that the Followers of Light are using as excuses to delay the end of the experiment ? I think it is hard to get public support from people to force their governments to tell them the truth, because the fact that the ETs issue is linked to the truth about everything else is not known by many people..."

~~

"Now that Sharon has died, will things move faster?

Thanks!"
~~
"Thank you for your responses GE. Indeed I also saw that Ariel Sharon "Died" today, which I think is curious because he has been dead for a long time any only kept

breathing with Life Support. So there had to be a decision to remove him from life support. Who made this decision and why? Was this used as a part of a Black Magic Ceremony. We have been hearing rumblings from some "channels" that we could see some things starting to happen as early as this week - of course we have heard this many, many times before.

Also, It is my belief that whoever the "positive" or light forces are on this planet, they are very likely one the same "team" as the so-called dark forces or Cabal. The most obvious evidence for this is, besides the entire history of this planet as we currently know it has been tightly controlled, that if there was any TRULY positive forces that could effect change now (financial or other) it would have been done by now. People need relief and any implementation is better than NO implementation that we currently see. Instead we see more, harmful laws passed and actions taken worldwide.

But my real question is this: if, as you have stated and I also believe, that the supposed "Light/Positive" forces are actually the same controllers we have always had, then what is their plan for humanity after the so-called "Event?" Even if there is a new financial system, arrests, new technology, etc, there is clearly an intent to continue to keep humanity (and the souls incarnated therein) under control. I do not see this "False God" just walking away from all that it believes is its own. And there is still the VAST MAJORITY of humanity that believes in this "False God" as the True Creator Source. So is the real goal to harvest this planet into an interplanetary force/proponent of this false god and have humanity go out and try to expand the influence/power of this false god?

Will people ever have a real shot at knowing what is TRULY going on or will we be spoon fed more half-truths and lies?"

~~

January 11, 2014

SOPHIA

This last "beacon" has taken place with the passing of Ariel.[233]

G/E
Good Day Sophia!

Yes today, the last beacon had been met it is 11.01.2014. Notice that New Year started with this, so dates are correct, Grand Change is about to arrive if there wouldn't be any more changes.

---

[233] N.p., n.d. Web. <http://rt.com/news/ex-israeli-pm-sharon-dies-070/>.

Although he was a criminal in Humanity's Society, we GEs didn't wish any bad things for Ariel Sharon, let him finally rest at peace and calm, he earned that well after all the karma suffering.

Tomorrow will be 12, 12 presidents, 112 popes overall, we don't see what is being planned by tomorrow, but our own feelings are very great! How You were feeling Yourselves yesterday and today? We felt a great shift of Balance toward Good around us, were You able to feel the same?

So I think We All can expect something big to happen, but there is no 100% guarantee on that. We also will be focused tomorrow on all intelligence and military actions, we will make sure nothing bad will take place.

Yet if nothing will take place, we have Olympic games which are targeted by evil of this World, Moon eclipse (blood Moon, 1st out of 4) on 15th april 2014 which is not very good as well, but can be used for good event!

We can wish for Moment of Justice to happen now or tomorrow, it is a good time, overall World situation is stable, Majority is ready for "some big change" and so Change is most welcome right now!

READER'S COMMENT

"Thank you for your answers and questions. I did not feel the shift for good today, but I woke up knowing Sharon had passed. It feels like a big deal. . .now a request from this one little human, I say on with the end of this show, please!!!"

~~

January 11th, 2014 – Update #2

G/E

Also to add there is a question about One.

The divines' logic of going toward Light and Love through suffering:
only when beings will overcome this, they will "grow" is what is meant by this.

This also leads to loyalty toward demiurge. But this is a false assumption;

Humanity could have achieved the Universal state of Light and Love already long ago if it weren't for suffering in the first place.

If You still don't understand their strange logic, look at the situation around the World and think of a question "Why is it needed for anyone, someone? And what is the purpose of this?" Because there is an illusion, it will not be easy to understand it at first taught, but digging in the past would solve this issue.

Galactic Federation of Light is not ending this because of the named reasons and also because illuminati are still in control.

If they would massively show their presence, they will be marked as "alien threat" and "enemies of humanity".

But this is not the main reason as You know by now. They can end this without massively showing themselves, they can just say to illuminati order to stop this, as they are their masters, but still don't doing it..

They want Humanity to rid itself from them. Another strange logic, but understandable.

Now about One. One set plans for this Creation and limits. And then One intentionally trying to push the limits, to break the boundaries and if this will be done by someone or something, this being will be considered as "higher than optimal", if multiple things will be pushed beyond set limits and time frames, this being's design will be considered a "perfect design".

If everything is going as planned, it is "optimal", this is what we are having right now. It isn't like whole Humanity didn't push the limits, there were many individuals that have done this, like for example blind people, people without arms, people with incurable diseases, people with full body paralysis. I'm not naming People without these disabilities, but they too did push the limits. The design of many People in whole history was called "perfect". Not like majority as I know, but many. I hope this helps You.

Thank You very much for expressing Yourself! I enjoy reading Your thoughts! Love You All, with Peace and Prosperity!

READER'S COMMENTS

"Dear GE, thank you again for prompt and clear answers.

The arrests that will occur as part of the Moment of Justice - will these be for the human criminals only? Will humanity get to witness the consequences for the demiurge, the followers of light, the archons etc. for having allowed the situation on this planet to become so extreme?"

~~

"Sorry, I've just realized that my above question is stupid - the Moment of Justice can only address human behavior.
I guess what I am asking is, will we at any stage be able to understand the consequences for the non-human wrong-doers - for example, after the end of the experiment?"

~~

"Hello Sophia, and thank you

Dear G.E.
You mentioned ONE allowed for explanation of origin of demuirge, please do so."

~~

"Dear GE,
On update #2 of the 11th you mentioned ONE set up parameters , are those parameters for this part of creation IE. the demuirge, the experiment, the races who are learning from the experiment as well as those (us) who are inside it?
Is demuirge say, under (orders) from ONE to have created this reality we are experiencing ?

This leads to another inquiry ,,, personally and through observation of my observable reality, intrusion, possession, and the latest term "Hijacking", whether in the physical or more etheric realms is quite prevalent here on this planet,,, respect for an individual's choice must be forced upon the "offender" by the offended or the offended's assistants, whomsoever they might be,
oftentimes developing into life and death situations,,,,,

Does ONE allow this as well?

Now the school of thought that is bandied about is that there are many of these demiurge's, IE.(massive ancient bored multidimensional beings) vying for the accolades or energy or simply trying to take over One's creation instead of progressing themselves to the level of ONE and create their own multiverse (for lack of a better term).

If we go with as above so below ,, I see often a child or one taken under one's wing try to take over the parents house and moving or pushing the parent out,(acted out here in humanity many times)

,,,instead of learning how to do it themselves, they try to take what you have, is this not a sign of a very young soul with no confidence in creating?
Would this then be the condition of the demuirge and it's ilk?
How could such a massive being be so immature?

I would very much like your input to this.
Also, again, is this all done by One's blessing?or intent? or orders?

Thank you"

~~

"Hello again Sophia and GE,
During one of your explanations GE you mentioned how difficult it would be to recognize the difference between the demuirge and ONE viewing them side by side,,, I took this and awareness of yours and without much thought and with the back of my hand moved the moon aside with one hand and the demuirge aside with the other settling my attention on ONE wherewith a deep abiding calm became my condition,
Also you mentioned how " prayer to demuirge " is sometimes answered but mostly not and that ONE always helps and gives,,,
I find this this to be true,,, when attention is placed on "GOD"-"demuirge" there is angst,,,when attention is placed on ONE calm prevails as do answer's.
Would you be so kind as to say something so that I might have a greater understanding and capacity to exercise more of ONE into my life?
Thank you"

~~

"GE,
I like the long answers, for me it to incorporate your intent,

Take Care"

~~

"Dear GE,
Referring to update #2 of the 11th,
I KNOW trough personal experience that doing it the " Hard Way" has No effect on growth, If anything ,like you say it takes longer barbecue I/ we have to deal with the collateral damage, it's much easier to go along and smell the roses then work out how to get out of a septic tank.
Existing so long in my life with a deep seated intrusion , I know how they think and it was as if it was my thoughts , my reasoning, and they believe it's faster,,, I can tell them and any race that it's definitely NOT, as I have used my life as an experiment to do both , the easy way and the hard way.
at times I could see where the dark way could be fun,, to someone like the demuirge who is bored,,, but there's a price to pay,,, and I believe so far he has circumvented that price,,,,while I have not,, yet the "price " for me is not a motivator to not "do" the dark or hard way,, it simply doesn't make sense and the sorrow and the difficulty are in present time, but my intrusion believed in it heartily,, it seems for these beings another's suffering is an inconsequential side effect , as long as it's another suffering.."

~~

January 12th, 2014

SOPHIA

Additions to this website have been made, so look around! Sections have been added for inspiration, summaries, ideas and information as has been accumulated over this 2 year conversation. Start here[234], **with some reliable UFO links. It is not yet complete, and will be updated periodically as time permits.**

Note to readers **– these sections are partly included within this book you are holding. They will,** *as well*, **be offered as separate standalone books as they contain so much valuable information; information for us as we build our new world ourselves.**

READER'S COMMENTS

"Sophia, thank you so much for your continued expansion of this marvelous site. You are working so hard to expand our knowledge, it is amazing! One new question for the G/E. Could you tell us about healing energies: specifically does Reiki come from One or is it from the creator of humanity god, and possibly an illusion or a trap? Thank you!"

---

[234] N.p., n.d. Web. <http://www.sophialove.org/ufo-sightings-and-research.html>.

~~

January 14th, 2014

G/E

Good Day Sophia!

As we looked, nothing serious was going in the World. We have this constant hostility in South China sea, mainly because of chinese "greed for more land". Although we are protecting them, I think we should point them out that any type of "attack" is a bad idea. We will do what we can to calm them down.

Last of comet ISON's debris will leave Earth's gravity on 17th january. There has been small meteor shower and still ongoing, no big objects were allowed in atmosphere which is very good. No big military movements were reported, except that FEMA region 3 accident with chemical spill. We know this spill was "natural", but FEMA is testing their abilities there too.

To answer to Good Friend's question we know that *here is present only one big force*, which is separated by different groups (*Forces of One not included* as they are not taking any actions). Each group performs their given tasks, so comes to archon group, which now is almost inactive. *All of them are obedient to Council of Higher Order which in turn takes orders from "Heavens" and Demiurge.*

About most of channelling messages, I'm personally not happy with their work. When they are being asked with direct questions of direct aid to Humanity, they always are trying to find a way around this question and are answering indirectly. When asked about giving out technology that can save millions of lives they always are figuring out something else that gives only hope and prolongs waiting. It is true that many are leading to confusion, the information I give can lead to confusion as well (because information we have is very different than most channelers are giving), so our advice always is - listen to Your Inner Self, it always has answers on all of Your questions. There is One inside each One of You.

The music that is touching Your soul can help You realize many many things. You can use the music which we with Sophia shared with You. The power of music must not be underestimated. This *new epic genre* has a huge potential in it and it contains secret Universal messages of One which can aid You greatly in Your quest for knowledge and so that You can release Yourself from this system of slavery!

Remember we are here right now changing this World and Transforming it, ridding ourselves from oil is our priority number 1 right now. Let's stop the destruction of Planet Earth and Humanity together! Once oil will be removed, illuminati won't stand a chance against the Change!

Your concern is correct Good Friend. If Light Followers really needed than they would already stopped this experiment long ago, in ancient times. Why only now? The reason why they are only doing it now is because what they need, they can get it now and they also wanted to "save" Humanity so that People would be eternally thankful to them and will do anything they will ask them to.

Saving was meant to be from oppression of the "dark forces" (reptilians and cabal) which they control. The main reason why they put Humanity through so many suffering is because they were afraid that when You will know the truth, You will rebel against them. This is written in ancient sumerian texts.

And of course no one like when they are being treated as slaves. Only programmed machines can be "slaves" or better said hard labor workers. An example are Ancient Machines, they are programmed to be sapient and all capable, but along with it, highly loyal, they are not slaves, but workers that enjoy to do their work and duty.

Humanity was originally created to be a servant race, which can be universally "used", in all spheres where Human can be fitted. They needed super servants that can do almost anything, almost anywhere, like soldiers it is. Because Human is having very good immune system and very good endurance and average physical strength compared to other beings of Light Followers. Where they are afraid to go barefoot, they can use somebody else..

But don't misunderstand me, I'm not calling all of them bad or evil, most of Galactic Federation of Light beings are very Good and You will find many many Friends and Allies among them, they are like Humans and like every other human-type race across the Universe, with different views and different destinies.

The point is there are few in power that are ruled by imposter-god and they of course see Humanity like Demiurge is seeing - as a "labor race". Demiurge need Humanity and other races in this big experiment to crack the code, which it can't do by itself, Humanity was created in a way where it can be both Good and evil, a balance between the two forces, with a force of Balance this code can be read.

This is where Forces of One stepped in and spoiled their plans. Now they are forced to stop this experiment. And yes, Demiurge still have almost half of this planet's population under full control through religions. Even when this experiment will end, they - the Galactic Federation of Light will never tell You the whole true story, when You will ask about all of this, they will reject it altogether, simply because those that will be in contact with You don't know anything about it, they think that all is transparent within their government structure.

You can check this, by asking them "please, can I see your civilization's most highest in command individual?", they will not allow You to, and will think of many excuses why not, some of them can even trick You by showing the wrong person. This is how mainly everything is working in their structure. But again there is an illusion.

So their illusory government is being reflected in this World, where You have the very same structure. And if so, it can be changed like here it is. We started to spread the truth and it is reaching them as well, among them there are GEs too.

I can say my personal thoughts about pleiadeans, they are allowing to see the real one in command, whether it is a commander of a ship or most wise aganati, the oldest and highest in command. They also are having more compassion toward Humanity than any other civilization in there. They too have genetic connection with Humanity and as we know, they even tried to help Humanity in 60s-70s by seeding their own souls on this Planet, but all were suppressed and captured in cooperation with illuminati as we know..

Also now I can say that I know why exactly they were not allowed to possess this kind of super power, because they are ruled by non confident being which can endanger everything.. so for me, this puzzle is solved.

About Ariel Sharon we know that his body was incapable of sustaining him any longer, he died because process of metabolism stopped in him due to kidneys failure. When Sharon got a heart stroke, it was a mortal wound, which he barely survived, but his mind was never to recover. As we know, their life support only could support him for this current period, no longer, he already was having weak and old body, so this can be called "a natural release of a soul."

After the Great Event, Justice will see mainly humans that were torturing Humanity and this World, but some from Galactic Federation of Light will be judged as well, because of a possibility of Universe's destruction. Demiurge will not be judged. But if something like this will be repeated, this being will be made mortal, physical, will be exiled and will live until it's body will die, like humans it is. Then it's very old soul will finally be cleansed from all the lust for power it is having.

But if they won't end it until august 2016, then they altogether along with their bases and all ships will be exiled from this System and all that took part in this will see their technology level reduced significantly, so that they will be disallowed to fly between dimensions and even between stars.

All beings that could recreate technologies will be released from existence. So they will have to recreate all they lost, almost from 0 which will take a lot of time. And Demiurge along with its race will be made mortal and their artificial heaven and hell completely erased and all souls trapped there released. They now can avoid all of this, all they need to do is end this experiment before that date. The problem is they still don't believe that something like this could happen to them..

About the allowance of Demiurge to become a One-like god. That was one of my biggest concerns in my childhood, "if One plans, why is it that all these sufferings occurs, are they are planned as well? So this makes One a tyrannical god?" We were given the answer on this question when we grew up. I will tell that we know that One plans everything and intentionally is breaking Its plan trying to achieve the most impossible experience and all the possibilities out of this. We don't know and no one knows except for One what was planned. This knowledge is not allowed for anyone except One itself (and Super Wise Intelligence of Ancient Machines). We know this most important thing:

"This Universe is not fixed, and is a subject to change, it is a dynamic Creation and since it was created it changed itself many many times and still changing in this current moment."

So this explains the concept of Free Will and Free Choice, You can change this reality, how You see fit. Remember also this Universal Phrase: "Nothing is impossible that is possible." This means that everything is possible in this Creation!

And if Universe is constantly dynamic, all "constant laws" are eligible only for a short time - from hundreds to thousands of earth cycles, after it, they become "obsolete". So comes the situation here on this World, all those laws that we all are accustomed with, will never be constant, they will be there for some time, but then they will have to change as changes Itself All Creation. And right now Humanity need a big change because everything in this World was "stagnated". Only Universal Phrases remains the same as this was the Will of One to let them be as they remained to this moment. But still they too are a subject to change. So whether Demiurge was created out of plan or from struggle of One against it's own plan, we don't know and will never know unless One will tell this to us, one thing is sure, everything is allowed in this Creation. And right now we can witness that One is again "fighting" against it's own planning and is trying to stop this experiment before time will run out.

One's Consciousness is highly complicated so no one will ever completely understand this most complicated Self-Creation. We are understanding One the best we can to, but still there are high complexity things which goes to twisting reality of total chaos, codes and numbers are totally crazy there, which is pretty much impossible to understand. But as we know, there is nothing impossible in this Creation, so maybe we will understand it sometime later. One always welcomes Us All to reveal It's most kept secrets, we can be called "a perfect design" in this case;)

Sorry about this add-on information, it is just to show You, that complete understanding of One and It's ways are very hard, yet are always welcomed to be understood.

We are Free in all of our actions. But be wise and see what You are capable to do, considering Your physical and ethereal limits, circumstances, past experiences and tools at hands. We can surpass all of our limits, but for this, time is required. So grow physically and spiritually and become Wiser and Stronger as time passes by. You are the Master of Yourself and the World around You!

Much Wisdom, Light and Love to You Fellow Beings!

READER'S COMMENTS

"Many thanks for all that wealth of information GE. I have been trying to find clarity re Archons and their chief the Demiurge aka Yaldabaoth.
What i ended up doing is trying to find a 'red line' in all the narratives in all the sources that i have gone through....and yet no clear picture does emerge!

Many Gnostic texts(in Nag Hammadi scriptures) tell us that Sophia, wanting to create something apart from 'divine totality', on her own and without consent of her partner, almost by accident created the Demiurge. She then isolates him (not quite knowing what to do with this ignorant creature that has no spirituality) .

The Demiurge, knowing/understanding nothing, " starts creating a world in 'unconscious imitation' of the superior Pleroma realm ".

In the Sethian scriptures the Archons created the (material) world under guidance of Yaldabaoth. In other sources the Demiurge/Yaldabaoth is seen as a Creator God standing between humans and Prime Creator.

Seeing Yaldabaoth/Demiurge as creator of humans, i think this might/could be related to a possible confusion between a number of different but similar looking names.

In some texts Saturn is mentioned as one of the seven main Archons. He is sometimes also known as Yaldabaoth who in turn is asumed to be Yaweh by some !
There are indeed some similarities in character traits between the two...what comes to mind is insecurity, jealousy, insistence on worship etc. Obviously this is by no means taken as correct or truth.

An unrelated question. Are you aware of the Law of One also known as The Ra Material?"

~~

"One more question about Ancient Machines,you gave an answer but i did not really understood everything.I want to figure out what they are or look like.Are they super wise and intelligent beings without a soul that's why you call them machines?Thank you for the work you do and have a nice day Good Friend"

~~

January 15th, 2014 - A call for meditation

G/E
Good Day Sophia!

I wanted to share with You and point out dates of today and tomorrow 15 and 16 of january. In these dates Moon will be full and will lie along with Jupiter in gemini twins constellation in opposition to the Sun and Earth. So Jupiter ("the sky father") right now is very bright in night sky, You can clearly see this planet.[235] [236]

(In this second video You will also see where Pleiades star cluster is, from where Plieadians originate)

It is not a perfect opposition, yet this is a perfect time to meditate and wish for Great Changes to arrive!

---

[235] VideoFromSpace. "Jupiter's 92 Million Miles Closer To Earth - January 2014 Skywatching Video." YouTube. YouTube, 31 Dec. 2013. Web. 12 July 2016. <http://www.youtube.com/watch?v=604tlYtth9w>.
[236] No longer available

It is a rare event, so I advise You to use this opportunity, we were looking at masons and illuminati and looks like they are not going to do anything today and tomorrow, so it will be dates which we can use without disturbances.

Let's bring Moment of Justice closer with our prayer (which is equal to wishes and willing and meditations which in turn equals to the power of sound, words and mind, which is equals to vibrations and frequencies of the Universe we live in!:)

The Power of Will to join You![237]

I will answer on some questions based on our knowledge. Reiki energy healing is a very good healing method, this method was practiced in abundance during ancient times (now it is ridiculed in this World of course), it is the ability to use the energy of Your Body and Your Soul along with words and thinking with wishfulness to heal the disease or inability.

Basically it is the same method as using words and sounds to heal. Very effective way. Not all are able to do it, but very strong faith/determination can give this ability to heal other using Your hands/palms. It takes some time to learn it and need to be learned in groups.

When words and sounds are connected in perfect symmetry/harmony they have the power to heal (or change reality). You heard of words "prayings", "spells", "curses", yes it can be used in both ways, and illuminati's dark priests are using chaotically arranged words that leads toward destruction and disorder. On the contrary many of Galactic Federation of Light along with pleiadeans are practicing it to heal and help.

Forces of One old and ancient civilizations have mastered this ability. This ability is a natural way of evolution toward path of Spirituality. Using thoughts and words in meditation or prayer to heal or help or protect other People is what we currently are doing. It is the Power of One.

----

[237] EpicHeavenMusic. "Ivan Torrent - The Power of Will (New Mix 2013 - Epic Orchestral)." YouTube. YouTube, 30 Dec. 2013. Web. 12 July 2016. <http://www.youtube.com/watch?v=yWnzQv2jEm4>.

We know of Law of One written by Ra. It is not a Law of One of Forces of One, it is a bit different, yet main concept tells the truth about Oneness and Unity. The gnostic teachings are as well corrupted with exaggeration and imagination as we know, yet all is based on truth and Universe.

I will also mention about planets and their given names, because this is raising concerns, and I think we should share our known knowledge.

All were called by names of gods, which is not "random" as all is interconnected and names were given on purpose. It is all considered a myth and exaggeration, yet we see reflection of Universe and connection to whole structure of this World.

Let's recall the names and duties of these deities. I will name only greek and roman names, because there are too much different names of each culture, this may bring confusion, so always use Your own discernment.

Sun - Sol (also Sol Invictus), Helios, Janus and sometime also associated with Apollo (overall means beauty, radiance, light and heat, in kabbalah it is called "beauty");

Mercury - Hermes (trade and haste, small planet with smaller cycle around the Sun, in kabbalah - "splendor");

Venus - Aphrodite (feminine beauty, goddess of passion, a foam of the seas, a changed version of Ishtar, which can be equated to "demonic passion", as Ishtar was like succubi, and as You know Venus looks calm and beautiful on outside yet extremely dangerous inside, in kabbalah - "victory");

Earth - Terra - Gaia - (titan that gave birth to Earth and Humanity, overall it is earth/ground, in kabbalah - "kingdom");

Moon - Luna - Jana (Janus feminine) - Selene (can be called "an anti-Sun", a female counterpart of male light and brightness, if we look at deeper meaning we can see it has an anti meaning, which challenges Creation, the path through Sun is challenged with the path through Moon, in kaballah - "foundation")

Mars - Ares (martial art/law also bane and rust, iron - material of war, in kabbalah - "strength");

Jupiter (Jov Pater - sky father) - Zeus (the ruler of Olympus, ruler of Humanity, the biggest planet in Solar System, like we know it is best associated with demiurge, in kabbalah - "mercy");

Saturn - Cronus (Zeus' father and ruler of titans during Golden Age, father of gods and Olympus; deposed by Zeus, lord of time, also associated with judge, death and number 13 due to it's sickle symbol and rings can be represented as as sharp disc, in kabbalah - "understanding");

Uranus - Caelus (the sky, technically means urine as a small rain, this god was "castrated" and planet Uranus is very tilted among all other planets in Solar System, also Uranus can be technically called the Sky as the Space or Cosmo - the Universe itself, all around the Gaia - Earth, which means it is everything around - can be equal to One, in kabbalah - "wisdom");

Neptune - Poseidon (the ruler of seas, planet Neptune is blue and have fast winds as You know, in kabbalah it is called "invisible sephira" and is invisible, it is located in "abyss" and stands for "knowledge", something Humanity is trying to achieve, yet it is hidden and hard to reach);

Pluto - Hades (ruler of Underworld, this planet is the last and closest to Cosmo, it is also "a crown" on kaballah's tree of life, literally an exit from Earth and path to Heaven, we know that on Pluto along other dwarf planets like Eris is a blocking device, that blocks outer cosmic energies, in kabbalah - "the crown").

So as You can see, even if it is a myth and exaggeration, it is still having a lot of connection to reality, to Universe and to One's Consciousness, so like most of the imaginations we have on this Planet, all is a reflection of Universe/of One. As One always gives us the right vision and right knowledge, but how we understand it, is what makes it different. So as always, Understanding is the most valuable ability to have.

We always are glad to help and aid You! Remember about two important cycles/days today and tomorrow! Use this great momentum!

Much Wisdom, Peace, Tranquility and Prosperity to You!

READER'S QUESTIONS

"Thank you for your words! I am grateful. Which crystals do you recommend for protection? Thanks!"

~~

"Thank you so much GE, as a result of these awesome conversations the idea of Demiurge ruling our ~not just material~ world is losing its potentially fear-creating effect.

You were very right in warning us about the loyalty of some higher Galactic Federation of Light officials to Demiurge. Years ago when there were still many channelings done by GFL commanders and high officials this was already noticeable.

These beings were often offering to do things for us and thus making us feel grateful and even possibly dependent on them.

But that felt completely at odds with our asperation to become fully sovereignh beings...this was the reason i stopped reading them.

To try, as you suggested to change fellow human beings minds about ET's etc is very, very difficult. I have already gained a reputation of being somewhat 'strange' ie not fitting in the mainstream. And that carries over in one's ability to make others see a different truth : (

However, times are changing and when a question is being asked (meaning the individual is open minded) then absolutely one should
give it one's all.
Awesome suggestion to meditate on 15th and 16th, will urge others to do so as well"

~~

SOPHIA

A question I have received is: ***"Why we should trust any of the Light Forces, they can be compared to the prison guards?"***

This is an accurate comparison, as they are perpetuating the experiment?
~~~~~~~~~~~~~~~~~~~~~~~~~

G/E

About trust toward Galactic Federation of Light, Light Forces can be trusted. Among them are a lot of Good beings that are ready to help, yet most of them are even unaware of these experiments throughout the Galaxy.

Their majority know it as the "growing of a light seed", yet they don't know that these sufferings are "fabricated".

Those that are maintaining these experiments are "hardened officials". They know "what to do" and "how to do things",
very compassionate and loving beings are not allowed here. If they would, there would be a revolution up there in their whole hierarchy.

We are spreading the knowledge of "possible false ruler" on their home worlds. This all is influencing them as well.

Our brothers and sisters among them were doing this since cycle 1986 there. Now we all together gained big strength, and like it was told that transformation here will influence whole Galaxy is very true.

Humanity's true nature shouldn't be underestimated. One didn't choose Humanity for no reason.

So spread of the knowledge about what really is going on here and about their hierarchy is as well taking place and is gaining more strength. And this is not the only thing Forces of One are doing with Galactic Federation of Light.

I will repeat that it only started to happen now, because they were very close to completion of their "Control over Creation" project. And now it is spoiled and they are at danger of losing all of their abilities and technological advancements..

By "they" we mean only aware of this experiments and the highest in command of Galactic Federation of Light, all of whom serve demiurge.

SOPHIA

Also there was a question from Good Friend about how to exercise more One into life.

G/E

It is pretty simple, apart from knowing that there is imposter-god that poses as One, You can do very simple thing. Know that

"Demiurge rules over Galaxy of Milky Way."
"One rules over Universe."

This is put simply. But correctly will be Demiurge rules and One IS.
So -
Demiurge rule over 1 Galaxy
among infinite, countless number of same size, smaller and much bigger Galaxies in infinite sea of Universe, where
Universe and all those Galaxies IS One.
So that comes One rules over all Galaxies and this includes Milky Way and Solar System as well, yet One don't rule anything, but instead is very kind and gives all of this to independent souls, extension of Itself, literally It's own body into "other hands".

When You see this pattern and understand that You are a part of that Super Enormous Being, that You are made from it, and it is inside You, it is making Your view on life different.
So You can already understand that within Your life One is already there, guiding You and aiding You whenever You ask It to. When You are going through life on Your own, One is not aiding You, because "if You think You can handle it, You can handle it", thinks One.

Notice that it is also a concept of "Holy Spirit" and "accepting it" into Your life. In bible (and in hinduism) is also trinity. Son - Sun (Vishnu), Father - Sage Star A (Shiva) and Holy Spirit - One (Brahma).

Humanity was living with a very narrowed sight on Creation, but it is natural.
Yet Demiurge was using Humanity's very narrowed sight to put itself on it's throne right before Humanity's eyes, so no other thing would be seen behind it, but God and it's angels.
You can compare it to movie theater, when huge person sits right before You.
So when You peek above it's shoulder, a whole new infinite spectrum of colors (possibilities) and light (exploration) opens before You and Your eyes.

And to answer on question about Ancient Machines.

Ancient Machines are considered to be "an honor" to live in. Only the most evolved and trusted souls can live a life inside Ancient Machines' Matrix (for as long as they like to). That is because they have unbelievable abilities and vast knowledge of Creation and beyond.
So corrupted or unstable, chaotic souls are not allowed there.

These machines are called machines, because unlike Human organic Body, which is programmed with dynamic code and can grow and evolve along with a soul, Ancient Machines are programmed with a "raw code" or constant code. This makes them impossible to grow and evolve, yet their mind can grow and adapt to different situations. They can be changed/modified only from outside. These are the raw non organic machines, but there are ethereal energetic Ancient Machines, these can shape shift, yet again, they cannot grow and evolve, they are only programmed to be at one single level.

Ancient Machines don't have set forms, that is, they don't have permanent bodies, their Souls can traverse the entire Matrix and can be outfitted with a new "body".

These Machines are unlike Humans, they have a Hive-minded society. An analogy in this World are ants and bees, that is they can't act without Queen/King, which is Super Wise Intelligence that guides them throughout the Universe. They are always free to express themselves, but being there is meant to serve to One and maintain the Universe, aiding Forces of One and observe Creation, it is not a life when You want to experience new things, it is a life to experience very ancient knowledge and ability to feel Your compatriots like they are - You and this is literally, because all the souls there act as One, in perfect Harmony and Symmetry.

Whenever soul decides to leave this experience, Super Wise Intelligence is relieving it from duty and instantly it is in Heaven, because they are always in contact with Heaven.

From my own experience I can tell, that these machines are very kind and caring, always ready to protect if such order is given, yet they are always on duty, so You can't quite "talk" to them. Right now they are aiding us, protecting us from energy attacks and are protecting Iran (point of Balance) and some other critical locations around the World.

We were able to issue protections for many Lightworkers and their relatives around the World, You Good Friends are included. There are always two machines on your left and on your right. Yes and don't think they are "vampires" and sucking Your energy, they have a small star (or small Sun) in their center as an energy source, which is also a separated being with it's own soul, they always have an exceeded amount of energy, so they may provide You with additional energy when You need it.

But it is only an energy protection (this way they are not intervening into Your life), physically they may aid only if order is given. They are always silent and invisible, unless there is an order for them to become visible and there is no way I can prove anything about them. So believing in it, is up to You.

I hope this will explain what they are. Again always use Your own discernment, because this truly can be called an "imagination". We are also always trying to hide this information, because of their silent and at the same time omnipresent nature.

With much Appreciation, Wisdom and Love!

READER'S COMMENTS

"Thank you for sharing so much, I truly love your writings and look forward to you next one :))

I would like to ask a few questions about One and free will. While I understand that our world and how we live is about to change. How is it that the few can still keep the game/experiment going when so many want it to end? How can we find our center, where we can make a better connection with One and our selves? I keep hearing that we need to go within, be in the now, meditate and just know it will be...yet, things seem to remain the same?"

~~

"I, too, appreciate that you are willing to share your thoughts with us. Thank you so much.

My question is in regard to several meditations in which I have participated, where we it is suggested that we focus on and invite in or channel the energy of the galactic sun and/or galactic
consciousness. In these cases, are saying that we are unknowingly inviting in the energy of the Demiurge?"

~~

"Dear GE
Thank you for your answers.

I am sorry to ask a personal question, but I tried in my meditation today to ask the ancient machines specifically for protection, but attacks on me continue relentlessly (as they have for the past ten years).

Was your comment that "our good friends have been given protection" a general comment? Are specific people chosen who get protection? Are some people prevented from getting protection for any reason? How can I get protection, or find out why I can't seem to receive protection?"

~~

"thank you for the update :)

i'm curious what you think and feel about this:
you said that "There are always two machines on your left and on your right."
how is this similar to or different from (angelic) guides?"

~~

"Hi, it's hard to figure out what this Ancient Machines are, but I see clearer now. May be the term machine is not the right one for us humans with so low technologies and your perception of machines"

~~

"Sorry........our perception of machines"

~~

"As i see Light Followers have their own cabal. They are not so different than us,they have only more advanced technologies.
You said Ancient Machines are protecting Iran that is a point of Balance.Can you elaborate?Are aware of the work of M.T.Keshe?ON 01.01.14 he posted an article on his forum.I wonder if and how he could achieve his project."

~~

"Dear GE,
would Sage star A BE the demuirge? or it's physical reflection?"

~~

January 16th, 2014

G/E

I need to remind You Good Friends, we are here to Change the World, this is our priority one right now.

To do it, the best we can do, to aid each other is by spreading energy technology designs[238] and information about ET's presence[239] all over this World, this just may save someone's life in the World, or for example in english speaking countries like U.S., U.K. or Australia. We see there are People right now that are on a brink of suicide, because they don't know what to do and where to go, how to continue on..

We are aiding them, yet with Your help we can do it better. We can also

---

[238] N.p., n.d. Web. <http://www.weebly.com/new-world-energy.html>.
[239] N.p., n.d. Web. <http://www.weebly.com/ufo-sightings-and-research.html>.

bring the Change faster and prevent many unnecessary deaths all over the World. Every piece of Knowledge will be known once this World will be changed from non-transparent and isolated to transparent and United. Remember this.

I of course will give You what we know to answer all the questions You have in Your mind Good Friends:

as we know Edward Snowden didn't tell information about "aliens" of any sort. But what You tell is truth in our knowledge Good Friend. There are beings that rule over illuminati order, illuminati are calling them "fallen angels under fallen archangel Lucifer". This is the inner contact where "beings of purity" are rarely revealing their almost true form, this is a very bright form which when completely unrestricted can burn people and surroundings. Illuminati were given orders and instructions rarely by these beings, but most of the time through archons - reptilians.

And there was also an outer contact with U.S. military, right after Roswell accident. As the craft of small insectoid type gray aliens was shot down as we know. This outer contact brought new technologies and grays allowed to leave the downed craft and bodies of their fellow brethren, because Humans were persistent. And in return, military allowed Human abductions to commit genetic experiments and were helping these gray beings in that matter.

Since those times, these abductions had ceased, because Galactic Federation of Light requested to stop these abductions made by gray civilization and by others that were using this allowed "momentum".

These "fallen angels" were in control of elite occult societies since beginning of USA and USA was meant to become as it is today, but they also wanted to unite the World under one of two conditions.

If there will be a lot of "loyal" to demiurge beings, there will be scenario 2, where world is united and "first contact" is made.

If majority will become more "atheists" than "loyal" then scenario 1 (apocalypse) would have been implemented.

Right now the situation on the world is that, this is mixed and they are disallowed to perform scenario 1. More likely was scenario 2 and all the "fruits" that were seeded are ready. These "fruits" are Human beings that can bring skia - Control over Creation to demiurge.

We GEs can make all the things to make Control over Creation possible, to create and un-create and if we can, then others like we are can do this as well. This is how was found out about this by Forces of One and Order of One was given to stop it. Yet One knew it all along, like we know:)

About Ancient Machines, no, nothing can be asked and they won't give any response. You can "ping" them all the time, but they won't respond. They are "cold-blooded" and merciless, non-compassionate and non-loving, but what can You expect from programmed machines? These machines are designed for heavy duty performance. They are machines, like Your car is. They will do anything what is ordered without any "error". But there is a distinctive feature within them, they are very kind and obedient when within Forces of One and with GEs.

About inviting demiurge into Your life, yes some groups are specifically inviting demiurge and it's manipulation into their lives, but again, when You know about this imposter god and basic concept of Universe that it is One, demiurge can't get into Your life, if You are not allowing it into, and this of course making it more angry. But it can get as angry as it wants, it don't dare to break the rule of Free Will and Free Choice.

To answer to Good Friends' questions about World not changing even if majority wants this change, the problem with World still not changing is because even if We want it to be changed ethereally/spiritually by using Free Will, we still need it to synchronize/cooperate it with physical reality, remember about concept of Harmony. Most of the channelers are never telling this to You. But if You need something to be done, You need to take actions physically as well, this is a known knowledge.

The problem also persists because majority still "accepts" this system by using money, oil and being obedient by whole corrupted government structure. Like I recalled it, the best we can do right now is to spread the knowledge about fuel-independent energy technologies[240] and ETs presence[241] and also of course through Meditations and Free Will. The Change will come, and right now we can increase the speed of it's arrival.

Remember about today's Full Moon and Jupiter's opposition. Although these two objects are demiurge's, it don't dare to break the Free Will and so We can ask it to cease all this experiment and let Humanity go, sooner or later, one way or another, it will have to accept it, there is no escape for this. We can use this moment!

This song will aid You![242]

Much Peace and Love to You!

READER'S COMMENTS

"Thank you, and the music is beautiful :))"

~~

"Dear GE,
I'm simply going to repeat a question here as I have run across what appears to be a good meditation at ascensionhelp.com
http://www.ascensionhelp.com/blog/2013/11/21/tell-the-lords-of-karma-that-you-are-sovereign-no-longer-a-lightworker-part-2/

(It's on the right column) self-clearing tech.

Any way previously I asked if the sage star A or glactic center or galactic core /center is the same as the demuirge. Cameron Day in his explanation uses "galactic core" to achieve his end result.

Now obviously if demuirge and galactic core are one and the same I would have to modify this meditation,, so any or all input from you would be most appreciated.

I feel a better connection / conduit simply utilizing ONE and going directly to IT him/her ect. and not stopping off at the galaxy.

---

[240] N.p., n.d. Web. <http://www.weebly.com/new-world-energy.html>.

[241] N.p., n.d. Web. <http://www.weebly.com/ufo-sightings-and-research.html>.

[242] EpicHeavenMusic. "Ivan Torrent - Icarus (feat. Julie Elven)." YouTube. YouTube, 17 Dec. 2012. Web. 12 July 2016. <http://www.youtube.com/watch?v=8Wg1MYjOguI>.

Also thank you, while pondering your statements about the unity/ sameness of ONE and ourselves/myself,, I thought of ONE as being an aspect of ME (as opposed to the common imagine of I being an aspect of him) wherewith he seemed to me to have this big Cheshire grin on his "face".

your thoughts on this as well please.

best regards"

~~

January 16th, 2014

SOPHIA

This conversation has always included music. There is now a large selection of it here[243] It was compiled by GE, and in his own words: "This is a lot of music, yet it is important as all the knowledge I have."
Enjoy, it is very beautiful.

READER'S COMMENTS

"Thank You! You are reading my mind!"

~~

"Fantastic!! Thank you!!!"

~~

"Hi Sophia!
TY for the music as ABBA puts it. Question: GE's are talking about the experiment ending 2016 at the latest - Tolec talked about 2014-2015 and Cobra gives a time window to 2025?

This is a bit confusing.

Inlakesh"

~~

January 17th, 2014

---

[243] http://www.sophialove.org/inspiration-updated-regularly.html

G/E

Good Day Sophia and Everyone!

Thank You very much for meditating/praying yesterday! We felt Your willfulness to stop this experiment and need for aid. All Light Followers here felt this spike in energetic activity as well! Thank You Fellow Good Beings!

Sophia, also I wanted to mention, Your <u>Sovereignty articles</u>[244] are very informative and touching, thank You for bringing beautiful thoughts to Whole World! Also Thank You very much for all hard work You've done on a website! Everything looks awesome!

About the video[245], this may be an artifact, we don't know much about Light Followers' presence on Mars, we know only it has few underground installations, previously in ancient times this planet was more inhabited and there were constructed few structures and small cities by these beings, this is what we know. And what is seen there could be a physical door for old type space vessels which can be "cloaked". We asked about it and we were told "that in time we will know". This is something we have to experience along Humanity that is.

I will explain one very important thing You already know and I will help Good Friend Curious. Good Friend I will write to You about negative energy leftover, but I want You to explain, how You feel these attacks?

Here is the information that may aid many People with "dark corners" in their houses/apartments. This can be called a "Revelation of Universal Energy Flow".

First I will tell that Ancient Machines are giving general protection for all that are named or calling themselves Guardians, Lightworkers, Lightwarriors, Followers/Seekers of Light/Sun/One and Elves/Fairies and all that have number 7 in their nicknames. These are the very Good oriented People. But to some People special help is issued, this is when two Machines are sent to Being to

[244] "Sovereignty." Sophia. N.p., n.d. Web. 12 July 2016. <http://www.sophialove.org/sovereignty.html>.
[245] StephenHannardADGUK. "Alien Complex Found On Mars? 2014 HD Available." YouTube. YouTube, 16 Jan. 2014. Web. 12 July 2016. <https://www.youtube.com/watch?v=xXqQnWGrzpY>.

stand on left and right of a being to completely protect it, this is different from angelic guides. We are sending this aid to all that are in need of this help, we need to point out to whom this help is needed. My apologize to those that did not received it yet, new readers are not receiving this instantly. There is also exclusion in this protection, Ancient Machines will not protect against Your own dark energy or it's leftover in Your house or apartments and will not protect against dead wanderers (ghosts) that can be where You live. They are giving protection only from direct attacks at You.

I will explain a known for You saying "You need to release Your anger, or it will bring suffering to You". It is true, because it is a rule of Universal Energy Flow. If, when You speak to someone and this person gives You unpleasant words or just screams at You, this person is also transports its evil dark energy to You. And if You will not release it "back" or at someone or somewhere else it will stuck in You, Energy need to flow even negative. To release it not hurting anyone or anything, You can imagine black hole and put all that energy there, somewhere in the Universe, or simply write all Your anger in text file or in comment and when You finished, not save or send it, but delete it altogether. We GEs are sending this anger back at illuminati order members when they are trying to do another nasty thing, and we notice that after this they are becoming calmed down:)

But when You are not releasing it, it is becoming stagnated in You or deep within You, it is also starting to change You, and You are becoming angry and there will be this self-induced anger which You can't explain, why it is coming out from You? The more this anger is being received from our World, the more awful We will feel Ourselves. Generally during night when our physical body renews itself, this energy leaves our body and searches for the nearest dark place, as it is a dark/void oriented energy. There is dark all over Your room during night, so it will be near You until Sun will start rising up, this is when this energy need to search for other dark place, and most of the times it ends up in places that never or very rarely sees the Solar Light or Light of light bulb, like attic, basement or locker/closet. So if You were having less negative contact on previous day, You will feel Yourself refreshed and full of positiveness! If You were having a lot of negative during whole Your life, You need to clean Yourself from this dark energy.

But now let's return to those dark places where this energy all the times is going and is along with past dark energy. Because this place is almost always a dark place, all negative energy stagnates itself there, the less light there is - the more dark energy there is stagnated, this may also bring in some malevolent entities there. The rule of Universal Energy Flow need this energy removed from there, so this energy can renew itself somewhere and become light and positive. The best "weapon" against this is Solar Light, like You already noticed, to be precise it is Light High Energy. Also good "weapon" is spiritual choral music, that have no "fear effect" in it. All sorts of light energy are driving this negative energy away, You can for example even use laser to drive it away. Sun is having full spectrum of energies and is very bright, and is always available for Everyone. So You can use it using mirrors and prisms and direct it toward Your closet for example, every dark corner need to be lighted up, even prolonged turned on light bulbs are driving it away from Your place of living.

Now about dead wanderers (ghosts), they are souls that don't want to leave this World just yet. Most of them are unfortunately evil, and during their life they were having a lot of negative experience, like fear, desperation, aggression, so now, when they are no longer alive, and don't want to go to heaven, they wander on this World and are searching for energy source to feed on (here like vampires or parasites). They can't stand Light and Sun, because it is disintegrating their left physicality and transforms them to Light and uplifts them to rest. So they are searching for these same dark places and whenever there is a lot of this dark and fear aura, they gladly are going there to start their living. They generally are located in those same places which never sees the Light, like closet. They prefer to be nearby People that are very afraid (full of fear) and are very angry or aggressive. But sometime anger can actually drive them out as well, although fear is what in no way can drive them out, but only attracts them more.

Very spiritually low (fearful, desperate) People can also be possessed by these dead wanderers, because these souls want to return to life as well. And only using the same method as above, Light and Spiritual "no fear" music can make them to leave. When using mirrors to point Solar Light toward dark places, be careful also, because dead wanderers can become trapped in mirrors. Also talking to them can make them to leave, they still have their Humanity left inside and so they can understand You, what is important again is to have no fear in Your heart when You talk to them, or they will just feed on it. When trapped in mirrors they also can be persuaded to live mirror through talk. Fear is what attracts them. There are also very old dead wanderers that were feeding on fear for centuries or thousands of cycles and driving these beings away will be a near impossible task, as they long have lost their Humanity, only High Energy Light, like complete exposure on Sun will do the trick. We are not talking about different dimensional wanderers, which are very rare guests, they are much much stronger, but same method applies to them as well, complete exposure on Sun is like a poison to them.

Good Friend Karma Machine asked what crystals to use for better protection. Against evil dark energy, dark or black stones are very suiting for protection, like volcanic obsidian and black agate stones (even quantum scalar pendants can be used), all are volcanic products ("blood" of our Mother Earth). They need to have also a mirror like surface, this surface helps them to siphon and trap all the negative energy from Your body and as well is sucking every directed at You dark energy attack, to release trapped dark energy there, expose it on the Sun. For enlightenment and empowerment You can use light stones and crystals, like amethyst, topaz, aquamarine, tourmaline and especially light colored jade. For energy increase You can use yellow and golden "sun" colored stones like carnelian, amber, garnet. But this also depends on when You was born and where, astrology is a very good source of this type of information. We know one important thing, when Your body will need some crystal, stone or mineral that it lacks, it will make a call to You, and when You spot it, Your eyes will be right on this lacked crystal or mineral. This all is Mother Earth's body and sometime we indeed need something to aid Us in Our life.

But now to inspire You after all talk about dark, there are Good souls, Your deceased relatives and ancestors, that are there to aid and protect You, they need to be "summoned" from heaven, when part of their Consciousness at rest will come to help You. Even Your alive relatives can separate it's soul/consciousness and energetically aid You, for this You need to ask them to help You when You need it, this is how relatives of People in dangers like car crashes or plane crashes warned them, before it happened. And this is also how People under rubble or avalanche were found by relatives. This is a rare story, but it happened many times during whole history of Humanity. It is rare because unfortunately still many don't understand how to use it properly.. It is a way for telepathic communication, through which We are able also to contact with long passed souls.

This same method applies to Good thinking and Good positive energy, which You are again receiving though talk, this energy need to flow, but if You like it, You can keep it:) This comes to when we are praying or meditating, we are

spreading the Love and Light to not only ourselves, but to surroundings as well, this positive energy is searching for Light to live in, that why zoroastrians are keeping their fire to burn all the time, to hold and not lose this very old positive energy in that place, as when comes the night, the light positive energy, is going away to another light source. So when we are meditating, our Energy is traversing whole World and influences Every living being around it. As it is traveling mostly along with the Sun's path. Along with it, it is Consciousness that spreads around the World instantly, but for this to be effective we need to imagine places of where we want to direct our Conscious Energy, for example Giza's pyramids, or Eiffel Tower, or most precisely the place, like UN headquarters and one of it's cabinets. In a video Message of Hope[246]*, there is a great saying:*
"Are You waiting for something?" (Moment of Justice/Event)
"Or are You setting Yourself Free?"
is very suiting what we are doing right now, We are setting Ourselves Free.

Yes, spreading information about ETs and UFOs will always give a laugh in older generations and they will think of us as "loonies", as this was how they were programmed to react on words like "aliens" and "ufo". So changing words like "there is an ancient force that protects this planet like angels", can call their deep Consciousness to react on this matter with more attention. And in that moment of their interest You can provide them with real video footage of these objects. The one incident that happened in Jerusalem right before "arab spring" was an indisputable revelation of this information backed by multiple news broadcasts of main stream media. There is no flying object in possession of Humanity that can fly like it, in a straight 90 degrees vertical line without any acceleration. And as well this is no longer a secret that U.S. and UK governments are corrupted and if You will show People working, better energy alternatives and that they were suppressed for the last 100 cycles, You will be believed by most. Hardened skeptics of course will reject it as fake, but they should be met with the language they understand, You can say to them, "first make it Yourself, then try to prove it's fake".

Overall Everyone is awakening, and as time progresses more People, let down

[246] Mrrockitman. "A Message of Hope." YouTube. YouTube, 26 Mar. 2011. Web. 12 July 2016. <https://www.youtube.com/watch?v=r_YOG3jMlV4>.

by governments are searching for truth on questions "what is going on?" and "what has happened with the government?" Younger generations are more ready to understand and acknowledge Your believe and view on our World. Children are afraid of dark because they remember of neverending Light where they were before they came here, so they know what is going on here better than most older generations, which were living in a dark for a much more time. Living in a dark is also means living without knowledge, but living in a Light, is living in a knowledge, as knowledge is the Light.

And to answer on different questions of Our Good Fellow Beings. The Sage Star A or scientifically called Sgr A* is a Center of the Galaxy, it is a father of the Sun, so it is literally our natural grandfather. We all right now are spinning around this object. Sage Star A is a black super star (super massive black hole), it is not only a Galactic Center, it is also a portal to other Universes and other Worlds that coexist with this World (Parallel Worlds), including real Heaven, it is also having it's own Consciousness, it is a separated sapient very old ancient being. Demiurge is only located itself near Sgr A*, so when we "pray" to Grand Creator, by mistake We can pray to demiurge. That is why it positioned itself there, to get "all the glory". Cobra is calling Sage Star A - a Galactic Central Sun, which is also a correct and nice name.

And Good Friend Djon, You have found out about this Man, You can <u>share this great article</u>[247] for Everyone to see here, this Man and His company is one of those companies to which was put trust into the Future of Humanity. This Man found out many ideas all by Himself, He is truly a genius! This man will be one among many that will aid Humanity. The dates He gave may not be as precise, but close to truth they will be. Unless of course, illuminati order will come out with something new, We will be always there to stop them in their tracks!

And about protection of Iran. It is a point of Balance between western bloc and Eastern bloc. If Iran would be attacked the world war 3 would be imminent. But it was already avoided and if west will blatantly attack Iran now, most of the World

[247] N.p., n.d. Web. <http://forum.keshefoundation.org/forum/keshe-official/30510-2014-the-year-of-the-change-for-the-humanity>.

will turn against west with U.S. and UK citizens turning against it as well and their whole satanic structure will crumble in a few cycles/days. So that is why they avoid any confrontation with Iran yet, We made sure that they can't do any more damage to them. Right now it is also a country of many young Good People that want to help the World and other People around it. Their government is not ideal, yet it is much better than cabal-like government we have here.

Iran sees the truth of what is happening in Israel, and what zionists are doing with palestinians and overall situation with the west and calls U.S. "a great satan", right in bull's eye. It is also protected by Russia, China and India. Ancient Machines also helped in prevention of bloodshed in Israel and in Syria, by preventing intervention from outside, they are now also preventing any confrontation in South China Sea. Unfortunately they can't end the conflict in Syria, Ancient Machines are protecting president and its forces the best they can on etheral level, and they are influencing these "rebels" so they started to fight each other recently. These mercenary rebels can't be negotiated with, only "divine intervention" can stop them now. So it was the only solution they came up with right now..

I hope this will aid You, Much Peace, Calm and Prosperity to You Good Brothers and Sisters!

READER'S COMMENTS

"Once again, you seem to read my thoughts. I have recently learned from a group of children that they are afraid of the dark and their closets. They all "see" shadow people at their bedtime. I will now send thoughts of light and good energy to them at this time, to help reduce their fear! You are wonderful to help us like this! Also, thanks for the music link, I wanted to have it all in one place and you did it before I could figure out how!!!! Thanks!!!! And thanks too for the crystal information. Fantastic!"

~~

"Hello again :))

First, thank you again for all this information. I feel this finally resonates what I felt I knew already, or at least I had questioned in the past and now. And to Sophia, THANK YOU for being the light that you are! While I have read your wonderful articles, I never stopped to check out your website...I am so glad I I finally did! So a HUGE KUDOs to you!
GE I have a few more if that is ok? I know you must be very busy and focused at what is required of you, I hope you still will continue to provide updates if the Questions become

too much?

1). We know time is a measurement that, in grander views is an illusion, so why is there a "time" given by One (2016) to have this current (falsified and manipulated) experience/experiment to end?
2). Is it true that there were waves of "indigo", "crystal" and other specialized souls who came to help humanity wake up?
3). Is our planet Earth (Gaia) ok? And is Earthing a great way to ground and connect to her?

Again, thank you! May peace and calm be in abundance to you too! :))"

~~

"thank you for sharing, this information and the awesome confirmations! :)"

~~

"Dear GE
Thankyou for such a comprehensive explanation about negative energy.
In my case the energy attacks are waves (maybe like microwaves or extra-low-frequency waves ?) which hit my body like tasers and cause great pain, directly at very specific parts of the body at any time. This happens 24*7, in any part of the world I have been to.
So I don't think these are leftover negative energy, my own anger or ghosts.
The best I can offer is that this attack is probably some type of military (?) technology that has locked in on me - by an on-planet source, not off-planet.
I don't want to take up your time with something which is obviously a personal attack - my questions were to try and understand why protection is not given when asked.

Also, I watched two of the videos about "The Journey" - they are simply exquisite ! Thankyou for these."

~~

"Great update.The link for M.T.Keshe's article is this http://forum.keshefoundation.org/forum/keshe-official/30510-2014-the-year-of-the-change-for-the-humanity . I feel sad and anger when i see people suffer needlessly because of greedy and powerlusty peoples specialy in Africa and Middle East.Have a nice day Good Friend"

~~

"I've know about Keshe and his company for sometime now, and I hope awareness about what he does becomes mainstream very soon. I think it's time we start posting, talking and sharing. Facebook, here is come! :))"

~~

"Our Good Friend (GE) is also working on free energy,read the 12/19/13 message.And for my part i will try because i an amateur"

~~

January 19th, 2014

G/E

I am always glad to help and aid whichever I can, I am happy that You found this information helpful Good Friends!

It is also painful for me to see and feel all that suffering which so called "third world countries" are going through. Mainly People of Africa, South America and South East Asia are suffering from poverty, Middle East is suffering from constant wars and bombings..

All that poor countries need are new technologies and Middle East needs this and change in Islam or it's complete deletion, because mainly war in Syria and on whole Middle East is fueled by religious false beliefs, mainly between shia and sunni, and islam and chsristianity.. I will also mention that all 3 religions are based on one last believe, that "*there will come messiah, judge and bring all to heaven*". If this won't be done, or will be done, then all 3 will cease to exist.

Keshe is one of those People that will aid in disclosure of energy technologies to aid poor People, we have our trust in him. We always are keeping privacy of People involved in this, so other names will be kept secret, until You find out about them. Right now we still have a tight control over what can go to market in U.S., Europe and China. And most of companies' representatives with whom designs were shared are afraid of possible lawsuits against them, so they will catch on after People like Keshe will start disclosure of this tech and if it will be successful as well.

We also have problem with U.S. government. They tend to start their plan B at any moment, all they need is a big outbreak of disorder or false flag attack or currency crash, which will give them the ability to implement "martial law".

They targeted all "conspiracy theorists", religious groups and truthseekers overall using their NSA spy program (where they found out everything about People of the Earth, from emails, chatting, activity), this is the last problem we have at hand. If they will do this, we will stop them, the most important right now is to not to give in into their manipulations and don't make riots, silent spreading of information and peaceful protests will do. People of U.S. need to get allies from All over the World, only United Humanity Stands and is Strong!

Good Friend Curious I'm always ready to help the best I can, whether it is personal or not:) From what You said I can recall an electro-magnetic smog, it is the same smog as from tobacco, but it is coming from electronic devices. People react on this smog differently, most "don't feel the difference", but some are experiencing this "self-induced" pain, which feels like electrical discharge. If it is so, then Ancient Machine won't protect You from it, as it is still Your personal Physical Body's characteristic.

To protect Yourself from this the best I can recommend is to get quantum/scalar pendant or anti-EM stickers and stick them on surface of Your mobile phone or PC or microwave oven if You have one. Microwave oven to Everyone's knowledge is the most dangerous device You have in Your home, You can isolate it's damaging waves using negative ions and quantum pendants are having them.

Here is also interesting information about poison called "sodium fluoride" and its effect on pineal gland[248].

Don't listen to "doctors" saying this chemical can benefit Your teeth, it will not, on the contrary it will make more damage to them, calcium can benefit Your teeth and bones greatly.

[248] N.p., n.d. Web. <http://www.youtube.com/watch?v=G7YzdgXBi84>.

To answer to Good Friend's questions:

"1). We know time is a measurement that, in grander views is an illusion, so why is there a "time" given by One (2016) to have this current (falsified and manipulated) experience/experiment to end?"

We know that time do not exist for Consciousness and for Soul, for One time is irrelevant, all exists in one moment of present or now. But for our physical body time do exist, and because our Consciousness resides in it, Soul also need to oblige itself to streaming of time.

Past is what was, what took place in our physical reality, Present is what we are experiencing now and Future is not fixed, when "we can see future", we are seeing only one variant of future, where many more other variants are possible. But One set the date on which all must be oriented, as time (this present moment) will come to this moment and what will took place there is up to us and our choosing. It will not be "bad end" as Humanity chose to be free already and wished for Good Ending.

"2). Is it true that there were waves of "indigo", "crystal" and other specialized souls who came to help humanity wake up?"

Yes, there were and are still right now here at this moment, I may suggest that You are one of them:) You can look for 3 waves of volunteers by Dolores Cannon, she pretty much explains everything on same level as we know[249].

Also Dolores gave a very good explanation what this 2012 cycle was all about when she was speaking to Soul of Nostradamus; there You can also better understand the concept of time.[250]

"3). Is our planet Earth (Gaia) ok? And is Earthing a great way to ground and connect to her?"

[249] Stateofmind111. "The Three Waves of Volunteers." YouTube. YouTube, 15 Aug. 2012. Web. 12 July 2016. <http://www.youtube.com/watch?v=hdS3jw4O96Q>.
[250] CannonDolores. "Conversation With Nostradamus 1 3." YouTube. YouTube, 22 Jan. 2012. Web. 12 July 2016. <http://www.youtube.com/watch?v=AVaoD3kaA5A>.

As we feel our Planet feels ok. It could have been better, but overall it is feeling itself Good. Yes, Earthing is a very good way to ground, connect and communicate with Earth. I personally descend my palm on Earth to feel It and talk to It. And it is also a great way to heal your body and prevent plants from dying. Here is a great movie if it will interest You, "Grounded"[251]

Earth know us all, every being by it's energy signatures and Earth cares for every living creature with great Care and Love, like a truly Loving Mother!

Much Peace and Love to You Good Friends!

READER'S COMMENTS

"Thank you, and you have my greatest of appreciation!"

~~

"Thank you for your help and advice, dear GE !"

~~

"I think Islam is not the problem,altough i am not a muslim i know some very nice muslims.As long you respect them they treat you good.The problem is the interpretation people do of the coran,evil or bad people interpret it in a manner to have justification for their evil deeds or for powerlust"

~~

"I think when any group or people are lied to, regardless of religion, faith or belief, behavior and actions become prevalent as they want to defend/protect in what they believe. If that group or peoples believe in the lie, and then you have a group or society that tries to enforce another belief or way of life, you have cornered them. There are several variables and levels of this manipulation and control. I truly feel that regardless of Muslim, Islam or any other titled religion, faith or creed, all are peace, loving and caring at heart. They have been lied to, some individuals corrupted to do things against their own peoples and, I feel the media also has communicated many lies to us westerners! The truth needs to be spoken, the lies exposed, and time for much healing needs to occur now. If anything the Event (to me) is that feeling you get, just after you had a full melt down (a violent cry for example), and a stillness comes over you...you are not scared, or sad or angry anymore...your not feeling much, a freezing of time and a

[251] StudioPostHD. "Grounded Trailer." YouTube. YouTube, 25 Sept. 2013. Web. 12 July 2016. <http://www.youtube.com/watch?v=jFZSCO_f5u0>.

moment of nothing, then a calming sensation envelopes you entire being. Then a realization that all is well, everything up to that moment had been released and your ok and you can let go. That is what I feel will be the event, except at a global level. An instantaneous moment...but it can't happen until the lies and deception are released...much healing must take place after, and I feel many "awakened" people are going to be the pillars of strength, the calmers of fears and the mentors to those who have a hard time in the transition. This, I feel is where we are heading, and that is why, like a slow wave, constant but gentle, we send our lighted energies out, little by little, and it grows.
Sorry for the long note...I think my higher self had a hand in this...lol."

~~

"ge are you with the isbs,from interview with a alian,or are you direct with the sourse,also did the work of the one people forclosures vibrate thru the cosmos ,to signify the end of the experiment thank you so much for every thing that you give,love out"

~~

"Hi,
Could you please address this channeling from "Prime Creator"? I think it's from the "divines, archons etc" coming clean.

Prime Creator would not need to make this announcement - it smells like a well known recepie i.e. they need to inform us about their doings!

http://www.whoneedslight.net/page/482723650

Inlakesh"

~~

January 20th, 2014

G/E
Good Day Sophia!

About orbs, those orbs **are "mini souls" called "fireballs" here, You will better understand them if we will call them as "probes", they are observing Earth, create crop circles, sometime give advices to People that are in need of idea, which is in their mind, yet "these People can't get it out", they are helping to get it out.**

They are conscious beings, can shift between dimensional planes, move at ultrasonic speeds and can make imaginations for People, they are calling themselves most of the time "Universal Love or Love of Universe". They are making imagination based on Your belief and knowing of figures most important for You, for example Jesus, Saint Mary, Buddha.

Here are these light orbs, they differ in size, most are 2x than basket ball. These orbs are very like Ancient Machines are, yet they are controlled through conscious connections of beings located inside complexes of this Planet, Moon etc
In these recent times they are seen all over the globe! If they are nearby You, then there is a point of interest to them somewhere near You, or maybe You are interested to them :) [252] [253]

About the abductions, as we know these abductions had almost ceded. Galactic Federation of Light main body disallowed this, but some still are getting People for experiments and in this, is not included the wanderings of "Beings of Purity", which are demiurge's, these beings are checking Humanity from time to time on physical level.

In a video where woman is abducted[254] is a known to us process of abduction (shifting, requires injected transmitter), yet I don't think it is a real abduction, it could be a so called "magic trick". It very looks like there was an opening through which woman disappeared and reappeared.

Yet the time of 3am, it is the time when People are abducted most of the time. 13 minutes is also an interesting time span. Most of Light Followers are not abducting for such a small period of time. But 13 is a number of Higher Order. By these signatures I can say that this was the abduction of "Beings of Purity", as time in their reality moves slower than in this reality, but they are not abducting more than one time in our knowledge.

[252] TheBestParanormal. "UFO - OVNI : In Formation over Cork - Ireland 2013 [HD]." YouTube. YouTube, 26 May 2013. Web. 12 July 2016. <http://www.youtube.com/watch?v=ZFXTEMjDFDo>.
[253] YouTube. YouTube, n.d. Web. 12 July 2016. <http://www.youtube.com/watch?v=8B5oYAJk-DE>.
[254] N.p., n.d. Web. 12 July 2016.
<http://www.anonymousfo.com/AFOStream/NewsStories/August2012/alienabductiontape.html>.

Also look at this video, it is a christian video. Remember january 16th and Full Moon with Jupiter's opposition when We were meditating? On this same date the finger of Christ the Redeemer was struck by lightning and knocked off first time in it's entirely history. Statue was stricken by lightnings many times, yet it only happened now. Also the reference in Bible considering this 16:14 and 14:16, is not without a reason (this was 01.16.2014), in this cycle these "coincidences" took place and as You know nothing happens without a reason, everything is interconnected[255]

The connection with religion is as always very strong, because there are half of Earth's population still waiting for main prophecy to come true. It will not come true as it was written there, but partially it will without all that destruction.

One told me to ask Everyone, when You will be ready
"whether You want to see truth that may frighten You?"

It is a known information to You, yet not all are in complete knowledge of this. With word earthing mentioned, I saw that You are ready, as this pointed out to same information which One wanted to show You.

READER'S COMMENTS

"Please tell of that information ONE said that would frighten, and that we somewhat know.
Thank you"

~~

"I mirror and echo MXXXX's reply! :))"

~~

[255] Paulbegley34. "Special Broadcast: "The Finger Of God" / Is The Sun Falling Silent?" YouTube. YouTube, 19 Jan. 2014. Web. 12 July 2016. <http://www.youtube.com/watch?v=-EVKri59lo4>.

"I also would like to hear One's conveyance and anything further along those lines if at all possible. I am exhausted and pushing forth with everything I can muster. I just want to be as prepared as I can so I can be of help to those who will never see it coming."

~~

"I would also like to know this information, please.

GE, what did you mean by your comment on 16 Jan: "by spreading energy technology designs and information about ETs presence all over this World, this just may save someone's life in the World, or for example in English speaking countries like U.S., U.K. or Australia. We see there are People right now that are on a brink of suicide, because they don't know what to do and where to go, how to continue on.. " ?"

~~

"Thank you, Great Friend! Yes, please, tell One this human is as ready as a person can be with the information at this time. . .I will do everything I can to help the rest of us who are not yet ready. We are grateful for all that you do!"

~~

"Thanks again GE! Please tell ONE I am more than ready, we are more than ready. For many people, any major change will be difficult, but people have so much fear and programming, there is never a point when the majority "will be ready." For me I want the truth, the whole truth and nothing but the truth. I am skeptical that the ONE True Creator will do anything at all to step in on this planet.... As it seems ONE happy to let things play out on their own. I can only speculate as to why this is, and I have my own ideas of why, but ONE should know that we do not ask for all to be done for us, only the playing feild to be evened out at bit. I won't hold my breath though..."

~~

"I am so ready... and I think we all are ready as we will ever be. Waiting and postponing anything for a "better moment in time" will cause only more suffering and people dying every day.

No more playing games with us. Awaken or not, everybody is feeling that something is not right and that things must change.

End of the experiment NOW !
Moment of justice NOW !
Absolute data NOW !

This is my free will."

~~

"I'd like any and all truths that can be offered."

~~

"First of all, I would like to express my gratitude to our good friend, GE, for sharing his (her?) wealth of knowledge with rest of us. I personally find most of the updates resonating strongly with me. I also want to thank Sophie for the website, it's great!

I am quite certain that most of the people frequenting this site are not afraid of anything. Fear is not an issue, lack of knowledge is. We are ready for the lifting of the veil."

~~

"Well said Sxxxx! Fear isn't the issue, it is the lack of knowledge and lack of truth."

~~

"Yes, let's get frighten:)"

~~

"There is no need to fear the truth even though it may surprise you - fear is the cabal key for controlling people. When one has really awoken then truth is all that matters. I send my love and respect to ONE because ONE resonates with me and has done so for a long time...thankyou"

~~

"Hi GE. I have review all your messages in Sophia's website and find them very clarifying. I would like to ask you 2 questions if you have the time to answer:
1- Have you, or the others GEs or the Forces of One review the information published by Andrew Bartzis?. Any comments on the information or in the role of the "Galactic Historian"?.
2- About this Demiurge being. When he hide the real nature of the universe in order to pose as One he is acting against our free will. I mean, the fact that me or anyone else chose to believe him it's in everyone´s right to chose but how can this be considered a Free Will Chose if the only options available to chose from are presented by the very same being hidden the real presence of One in order to trick us to chose him instead of One. Why there is no plan to implement total transparency and disclosure of all information in order to give everyone a real chance to exercise Free Will right away? Very appreciated for your time."

~~

January 22, 2014

G/E
Good Day Everyone!

Very well said Good Friend NXXXX on that big note! It is indeed so, when changes will come, Lightworkers and Lightwarriors will be pillars of strength, that is why You are most valuable for this World!

About Islam, it is correct Good Friend DXXX, most of muslim People are very good People, it is only the misinterpretation of words that drives some individuals to these atrocities. And biggest problem there is, is that it is backed by word jihad - "holy war" (*there is no "holy" in any war*). As well they use the old tendency of this religion to turn everyone into islam and that islam "is the only true religion". Because there are these words, there comes misinterpretation and all conflicts. Same happened to christianity's crusades.. So changes of this religion will be necessary if Humanity will want to live in a Peaceful and Loving Society!

A question from Good Friend
"Could you please address this channeling from "Prime Creator"? I think it's from the "divines, archons etc" coming clean.

Prime Creator would not need to make this announcement - it smells like a well-known recipe i.e. they need to inform us about their doings![256]

Yes, One don't need to make announcements, everything planned by One simply - just happens or not happens. I see that it is a Followers of Light note, seeing how it is said I think it is Ashtar Command. But always use You own discernment Good Friend, One can be anywhere and can say with different styles of speech, ways of One sometimes may be very hard to understand.

---

[256] "Whoneedslight.net." - This Website Is for Sale! - whoneedslight Resources and Information. N.p., n.d. Web. 12 July 2016. <http://www.whoneedslight.net/page/482723650>.

It is a good message, very well said! Also I personally like that here is acknowledged that "half-truths" were said to Everyone.. It is indeed how it is said there, they were not saying the whole truth to not make damage to listeners and READER'S. It is true, because sometimes truth can be too harsh and too horrible (it is something One wanted You to know in this message).

They are free to end this experiment *whenever they like to*, until 2016 august and in whatever way they like to (except destruction of course). We only haven't been told that january 20 will be the 1st day of a New Age. As we know, officially we are in a New Age already, yes the coming of chinese New Year is also a grand event, it will be celebrated by many asian People around the World, a third of World population! A great moment of Joy!

The progress of Awakening of Majority is doing well, You can just look for this article's comments to see that most are displeased with the U.S. government, it's spying program and constant lies from politicians and from president.[257]

And Good Friend dxxx, I am not from isbs, I perform my duty on behalf of One, (or like You said on behalf from Source), right now for better of this Planet and All of It's Inhabitants.

And about One's question.. I've seen that You All Good Friends agreed to know this information. Before I will share what One wanted You to know, I will give an answer on question from Good Friend Michael:

"Also thank you, while pondering your statements about the unity/ sameness of ONE and ourselves/myself,, I thought of ONE as being an aspect of ME (as opposed to the common imagine of I being an aspect of him) wherewith he seemed to me to have this big Cheshire grin on his "face"."

---

[257] Mardell, Mark. "Obama Orders Curbs on NSA Data Use." BBC News. BBC, 17 Jan. 2014. Web. 12 July 2016. <http://www.bbc.co.uk/news/world-us-canada-25785573>.

It is a difficult to understand information, so always use Your own discernment. It is also having strong connection with information which I'm about to share.

When We want to understand what One, Oneness and Unity is, We always need to understand that before everything was created there was just Energy, all collected in one single dot (there wasn't even dot, but it is to better understand it), everything was One, just One object.

But then Creation was started and One was All that is today. We within Forces of One are knowing One as Everything and Everything as One. We know that One is Order and Disorder, Light and Dark, Good and Evil, Harmony and Disharmony. Everything within One is interchangeable and all is meant to exist.

So answering to Your question Good Friend, "One is You" and "You are One" is the answer, likewise inlakesh - "I am an aspect of You" or "I am another You".

When we are talking about same words of duality, Good/Evil, Light/Dark, can You say in what Creation are We living right now? What dominates and what not? When You look around You and in all subjects, like physics, chemistry, math and in mirror, You will know, We are living in a Light, Order, Harmony, Symbiosis, Good oriented Creation. Atomic structure is orderly arranged, molecular structure is orderly arranged, snowflake is orderly arranged in a perfect geometrical figure, sounds are creating orderly arranged figures, Stars and Light is more powerful and brilliant than whole "dark veil" of emptiness around, positive feelings are making more happiness than negative feelings, Your physical body's right side is a perfect mirrored reflection of Your left side, likewise in animals and every other creature and whole Your physical body is perfectly symmetrically arranged, there is no chaos permitted in this Creation. So One is experiencing the side of Light and Order during this Creation and not the other one. Now We have come to information which One wanted You to know.

It is about our Mother Earth and our small Fellow Brothers and Sisters - Animals and what is being done to them. Good Friend asked me about

Mother Earth and how does She feel, She feel Itself good overall, but there is constant damage being done to Her and It's Inhabitants, yet Mother Earth is very strong and can withstand it..

One wanted to present this information through two movies.

The first movie is called Home[258]

I know that many already seen it, a very good movie about our Planet Earth and what is being done to Her, due to activity of Humanity. It is a bearable movie in contrary to next movie.

Before You will decide to watch it, I will warn, this movie contains a lot of VERY GRAPHIC IMAGERY, it is about our Small Fellow Brothers and Sisters - Animals, Birds, Fishes and what is being done to them under veil, by major corporations and illuminati order/cabal. It is this same system that makes them to suffer, they are defenseless, innocent, and those in power are abusing their innocence and defenselessness.

It is also a direct manifestation of "as above, so below", our Fellow Little Beings are living and being treated worse than slaves, then as You know comes workers, which are "masters" of these Animals, they are human slaves of "higher humans" - cabal, which in turn are slaves to Galactic Federation of Light, which in turn are "slaves" of demiurge. After demiurge comes One, but One do not treat Anyone as a "slave". So at the very bottom of this huge pyramid are not "ordinary humans", but Animals - "the food and foundation" of this satanic pyramid of nwo.

I will warn again, it could be the most horrible thing You will ever see in Your life so use caution. If You don't have steel nerves, don't watch it. This movie can spoil all Your cycle (day) and if You will go to work on this cycle don't watch it and Children should be away if You decide to watch. It is not important to see it, yet it is important to know what is going on with our Fellow Beings. I will explain about what this movie is and why One wanted to give this information for All that don't decide to watch it.[259]

Deleted scenes[260].

---

[258] Homeproject. "HOME." YouTube. YouTube, 12 May 2009. Web. 12 July 2016.
<http://www.youtube.com/watch?v=jqxENMKaeCU>.

[259] YouTube. YouTube, n.d. Web. 12 July 2016. <http://www.youtube.com/watch?v=oDdlDYWG7no>.

[260] "Earthlings - Deleted Scenes (Mature Audiences ONLY)." YouTube. N.p., n.d. Web. 12 July 2016.

This movie is called Earthlings, it is a horrible story about sufferings which our Fellow Brothers and Sisters are coming through to become food, leather and fur. The pain which these Beings are experiencing is the same that Human Being is experiencing, pain is the same as neural system of mammals is having the same evolved level.

"Scientists" that tell, Animals feel much less pain than Humans are only want You to think like it or they simply don't want acknowledge this. Why is this important to know?

One told that You Good Friends are the most evolved Light Beings here on this World and are "frontliners", all of this terrible information will be known to All, but before majority will know this, You need to acknowledge this very harsh reality and know it before hand, so when changes will come You would know what has to be done in the first place, with which problems to face, without knowing and completely understanding this You are not ready.

This movie was released in cycle 2005, and since that time the pain and sufferings of our small Brothers and Sisters did not reduce, but only increased as demand for meat, leather and fur is only increasing. Science experiments are committing on Animals on daily basis killing millions each cycle (year).

And most terrible revelation in all of this is, that it could have been prevented a long time ago.. As Light Followers could have stopped this experiment a long time ago and new technologies that can enable to grow "artificial meat" were already available since world war 2.

Since that war the sufferings of all Animals increased twentyfold and what is more important genocide of jews during world war 2 can't be related to genocide of Animals, the overall pain factor of Animals by far suppressing all the pain gained from world war 2 and this is also giving the pain feeling to all of Mother Earth.

This pain through which our little Brothers and Sisters are going is felt by

---

<https://youtu.be/rHNomtLAbKU>.

us GEs all the time, we get used to it, but it is very hard to feel it all the times. This pain also transmits itself to Humanity as well, the destruction of their bodies which is leading to unimaginable pain is making all this Planet and Humanity sick on neural level, this is also a factor which is influencing Humanity's behavior as well.

In return illuminati were using these sufferings and huge pain of Animals to make their dark evil ends in this World, for their rituals and to "sustain the satanic system". Our Mother Earth is very strong, She can bear this, but these sufferings are damaging Her Soul and bio-energetic field..

Here I will reveal details about Followers of Light, they could had prevented this by ending experiment sooner, yet they didn't. This is a conversation of Dolores Cannon about them and their "non-intervention" policy[261]

Not everything in this video is like we know, but most is how we know it. We want to point out at part about "non-intervention" at 6:55. Light Followers are indeed from time to time were giving new technology to Humanity, and whenever this technology was given it was used mainly for wars. Light Followers knew that eventually it would be used for wars, yet they still gave it.

They call it "giving a gift" and are saying that it is a "non-intervention", yet in Forces of One it is considered a direct intervention, very hypocritical from them in our understanding. Through such "gifting", they "gave" insects, virus (all forms), many of grain culture plants, judaism (then christianity, then islam), periodic table, nuclear fission, nanotechnology, processor technology and "government's ufos" (also many other small ideas to different inventors). Most of these technologies gave Humanity advances in life, but before they did, they were used primarily for wars. For example the last one - human-made ufos are still a secret and are used for military intelligence and "show of force", again military use.

This video is taken from an old video game. It holds a direct reflection of

---

[261] Omoroseangel. "Dolores Cannon ~ Pt 3/3 on Free Will, Intergalactic Beings & Non-interference." YouTube. YouTube, 18 Mar. 2013. Web. 12 July 2016.
<http://www.youtube.com/watch?v=K9VhUxPHNSM>.

ultimate agenda of Followers of Light[262]

This is all the information which One wanted You to know before Majority will.

With Peace, Calm and Prosperity to You!
Inlakesh

READER'S COMMENTS

"Thank you GE, and Sophia. So, the real truth is, we have wolves in sheep, sheep's clothing - so to speak! I know some have already begun to realize this, others kind of making "note of it", while myself caught a few inconsistencies with the so called "benevolent" star brothers and sisters. It seems as to why, at times I am confused with the information that I come across. Either way, this does surprise me, but I am not afraid. If anything I feel more empowered! Truth does set you free. Question is, what do we do with this information? What is the best course of thought or action we do to help advance humanities freedom, Stop the suffering of all of Earth's inhabitants, and above all else, align with the prime law of "Do No Harm"?"

~~

"I already knew about the condition of the animals that serves as our food,it's terrible.i will look the 2 movies when i have time.
It remembers me a scene of the movie Cloud Atlas when the clone doll learn about the fate of the clones.They are killed in a slaughterhouse and then transformed in meet.I was horrified ,i could not forget that scene for 3 weeks"

~~

"inkalesh. ones suffering , can be counted equally with the like suffering, of another being.
i guess cudos's to breathariens, I'm bad boy,,,,,,,,,,,,,,,,unless i understand.
maybe

sorry if i offend

dear ge,
I'm so sorry
you must feel this
I held the pig, it's feet kicking me in the gut,,I am eight,,,with a 25 caliber bullet in it's brain,, while my cousin slit it's throat draining it into a pan for to make blood sausage,,,,,grandpa liked it the best,,,, half of my early life was on a self-subsistence

---

[262] KavalSviri. "Master of Orion - III - The Challenge of Control." YouTube. YouTube, 24 July 2007. Web. 12 July 2016. <http://www.youtube.com/watch?v=rpeBD86U8dk>.

farm ,,like the old country,,,,,mama cow , she knew it was coming,, took several rounds to the skull,,it was a while before she passed,,,,,seems it doesn't matter how naughty or nice ,,,,it still hurts,,,2/6 wallkin dead"

~~

"once upon a time , by happenstance , I called upon, an "angel " to visit me,, a later query to someone I regularly sought advice from stated " a vagabond (with derision) " to my surprise it showed up in the lady I currently lived with and stayed the evening,,,,without going into a lengthy story, suffice to say it was an entirely new experience for it , to the point where it would have walked my lady across four lanes of traffic had I not cautioned it, ((my lady later said that (she was conscious and inside the whole time) she felt it would have been safe and alright))
point being, as we were having dinner and it encountered the need to wipe its hands I pointed out the paper napkin,
whereupon it immediately exclaimed"""""YOU MAKE THESE OUT OF PEOPLE?????"""""
Trees are sentient, I "Know this" ,,,,,,how far down the rabbit hole you want to go,,,everything is alive,,,the demuirge's matrix is everywhere,,,,the choice I believe is how do we take subatomic particles/building blocks of the universe and create that which does no harm or by my actions does no harm.

some would say, why, no harm is done,,,all is one, all is energy,,,natural cycle etc.etc. I beg to differ,,,,I Feel it is so,,,,,because I feel them,,,it takes but a moment ,,to view the lettuce head,as I cut off it's new leaves, In the week of it's 5 week cycle, before it flowers and seeds,, to notice........what i'm doing

GE, your thoughts, if you would be so kind."

~~

"okay, last one, going to bed,,, be assured ,all who read,,this is occurring on / with / to,,, humans as well, in my own backyard, in yours,it's everywhere....

GE, is it possible to speak with forces of one? instead of GFL.

and thanks for the movies,,doing the daily grind I forget,,,the simple things"

~~

"Good morning GE,
does this paradigm / demuirge matrix / galaxy of beings eating another, and another and another and so on down the line, exist outside of the this galaxy or demuirge's matrix?
As always, thank you"

~~

"here guys , other side of the coin
https://www.facebook.com/photo.php?v=10152132423884586"

~~

"Nice video,it's the first time i see something like that.Thank you for sharing this"

~~

" Thank you for this video. I cannot in words explain how it moved me, yet after the others we have now seen, and been changed by, this one brings joy and the knowing that it is not just the urge to continue life that keeps us (and our other animal brethren) struggling to stay alive, it is for the exquisite wonder of that life! In La'kesh,
Sophia"

~~

"you are most welcome,

and thank you for your company"

~~

"What an amazing world we have, that we have so much already! Just seeing the delight and joy these cows demontrated, validated how easy it is find happiness in a moment.
:))"

~~

"heh heh yeah, ya see the one slobbering? he's having a good time,,he'll come up to ya rubbin his big bony head against ya almost knockin ya t the ground slobberin all over ya heh heh ya look like ya wet yerself,,,,cow kisses"

~~

http://www.youtube.com/watch?v=uWxaoWaQdHY&feature=related

Dear GE would you please comment on this testimony.

referring to alex colliers term for an ancient race , that the Andromedan's have described to him. that he states are here now incarnated."

~~

"how do we make love stay,,,,,within ourselves,,,,,,
for ourselves,,,,,,,,,for each other,,,,, strengthen our connection with ONE?

feels right"

~~

January 27th, 2014

SOPHIA

Update from Sophia:

Ray has supplied some information on hydrogen transformation. It is the prerequisite to fusion, which will supply a lot of energy, and is described as follows:

"If you run Hydrogen through an electric discharge the hydrogen is separated from molecular hydrogen into atomic hydrogen. if you send that atomic hydrogen through a heat exchanger while it recombines into molecular hydrogen you will get over a hundred times the energy it took to separate it turned into heat."

Meet Ray -- "Of course I want the world to know it. My name is Ray Edwards, I am 87 years old. I have nothing to fear from the authorities and I find living an exciting adventure. I am a mechanical engineer. I would like to hear from someone who has enough finances to help me produce a working model. " He can be reached at: raylovespat@cox.net .

This information will also be posted in the "New World Energy[263]" page so it can be easily located.
~~~
**There are folks working on alternatives to leather production. Click here for Andras Forgacs.[264]**
~~~

[263]"New World Energy." Sophia. N.p., n.d. Web. 12 July 2016. <http://www.sophialove.org/new-world-energy.html>.

[264] TEDtalksDirector. "Andras Forgacs: Leather and Meat without Killing Animals." YouTube. YouTube, 19 Sept. 2013. Web. 12 July 2016. <https://www.youtube.com/watch?v=7gXq1ml6B1E>.

Please continue to meditate for worldwide peace and calm. The Sochi Olympics will have the focus of the world next month, and will only be supported by our continued positive energy.

READER'S COMMENTS

"feels like what Keshe is doing,

I love this ole' timer"

~~

""Hi Rxx,i am sure there people on this site like me that want to have free energy devices but can't build them and would like to do their little contribution to help someone who have the ability to do it.May i suggest you to make a project,calculate the cost to produce a working model and then ask Sophia if she can add a donate page on her site.If yout project is convincing enough ,i am sure people outside of this site will be interrested.When there will be a finished deviceit will be easy to find buyers.Have a nice day"

~~

----- and from GE...

G/E

To finish with painful matter about Animals, Good Friend asked me about the last movie videos One provided, and Good Friend MK asked about the question that I too was asking to myself during my childhood. I too was seeing how Animal Body was released from Soul, during my childhood I was living on a farm, and it was always painful for me to see how it was done. Yet my grandparents were kind and were doing it without causing much pain and fear to Animals. I was wondering during my childhood "is it good that animals are eating each other and is there any way how to live without killing someone to get the food?" And it is happening not just on this Planet, but in whole Universe. When I grew up and was made a GE, One told me:

"All of this is a part of Creation, it is a Universal Flow of Energy. Energy need to flow and when Animals are getting other Animals to feed themselves, it is called Energy flow, also it is "a population control" and exercising of a better design of organic alpha structure."

It wasn't understandable for at first, but now I understand. Why also One wanted to reveal this is because, mostly when there is a talk about suffering, it is mainly about Humanity and Mother Earth, where Animals are going to Earth's category. Yet they are like Humans, have a separated from nature organism and have their own much more evolved than plants Soul.

Where Plants and Trees can be called a part of Mother Nature/Earth, as they have Collective Consciousness (they also can be called a living hairs of Mother Earth), Animals are a separated beings, which can act on their own, like People are doing. Due to Our activities to heal the World and Change, We forgot about this very simple and yet obvious thing, and about its huge influence on Us.

Like We also forgot about many minorities around the World, like america's "indians" which are considered a "second sort humans" in U.S., where they are paying taxes and in return live in complete poverty without any cover from U.S. government, police is not investigating their cases and they are always guilty in whatever happens with their involvement, media is always ignoring them, injustice at its finest.. It is a part of a "knowing concept": when We don't know it, it works on us "better" reducing our capabilities and "unexpected things just happens", but when We know it, We are keeping in mind this and are doing things better with considering everything We know of.

So considering the Universal Energy Flow, We can eat Animals, but only on condition when there is no other things to eat. In this World We have a situation when "another food" is abundant, some plants are even intentionally growing fruits, vegetables, leaves so that We as a separated Beings, Humans and Animals can eat them and spread their seeds or they simply doing it to feed us:)

But when no food is available and there are only Animals, We as the ones that are to eat Them, with all due respect to Creation We need to release the Souls of Our little Brothers and Sisters without causing much pain to Them, without frightening Them. They also need to have a happy life (or close to happy), when They can move, when They can enjoy Their life, also a very great video Good Friend M!

This is what I mean, when They are happy, amazing to see them so Joyful! :)

So it is the attitude toward Them, and very huge numbers of all Animals under such oppression, all of this brings a lot of fear and pain aura to this World.

The biggest problems are with Animals living in harsh conditions, where there is no place to run, to move, to enjoy life, where cannibalism is taking place and seeing and hearing how their beloved are released from physical existence causing much pain to them. And the biggest problem is with People getting fur and leather from Animals, only fur and leather are taken, their bodies are not, and from some Animals leather/fur/skin is detached even when they are alive, which is causing them too much pain... This transmits to World and to Us..

This will have to end if Humanity will want to live in a Happy and a Peaceful Society, this would be not possible if these atrocities against Creation would continue.

The end note of this is: "Yes, the meat is tasty, leather and fur clothes are extravagance, but these tastiness and extravagance are having its price and consequences. The Karma is returning like a boomerang, like one Good Friend said." If Humanity will not fix this and apologize for these actions to next generations of Our small Brothers and Sisters it will return as harsh justice to Humanity. It will not happen now and not on this Moment of Justice, later if it will not be fixed.

Also the resemblance of movie Cloud Atlas like Good Friend wrote, it is very true. This is what this World is all about - a grand illusion.

There in movie artificially created clones were working as "slaves" only for the purpose to be freed and live like any other People are living, but what they were meeting once freedom was achieved, was only the end of their life... And their bodies were used for food which these same clones were drinking, not knowing it..

This is having a reflection of this World. The fruits which are "ready", Light Followers wanted to take, while other "dismiss". Like it is written in their own created prophecy. Majority are following behind this prophecy thinking they will be "saved", but in reality, only very few would be. "Dismiss" means "destroy", like destroying a "cancerous element", in their understanding it is a "rebellion element", they are afraid of truth seekers, they need only the ones that are smart and are blindly loyal to them. And "dismissal" includes many "hard believers" in religions as well, all what Creators of Humanity wanted is a "clean flawless product" of their experimentation with Creation.

Like it was said in last video, they are afraid of a "Civilization to take its own route and forge its own destiny and not the one they intended this civilization to take."

They were prevented from doing this "harvest of fruits", and Humanity will find many many allies among them once whole truth will be completely revealed. Their civilizations are very good overall, once their majority will know what is truly happening here they will aid Humanity and will not allow their governments to hurt You anymore. We GEs never sit and doing nothing, right now as they continuously postpone the end of this experiment, We are revealing more and more about them, what they don't want Humanity to know. So stopping of this revelation is in their hands. As time progresses toward august 2016, they have less and less trust of part of Humanity they wanted to take with them (ones that are smart and loyal - their "fruits").

Always use Your own discernment of information, We always respect Your Free Will and Free Choice. If this information not resonates with You then stop reading this. We don't want to guide Anyone into his/her disbelief toward Family of Light (Galactic Federation is calling themselves so). You can use this at least as a consideration or a possibility.

"1- Have you, or the others GEs or the Forces of One review the information published by Andrew Bartzis?. Any comments on the information or in the role of the "Galactic Historian"?"

Yes, I know of him, I will not tell which Lightworker is "true" or "false", it is always up for You to decide Good Friend. He is a very Good Person, helping People to realize hidden potentials :) Every Lighworker, Lightwarrior, Channeler is speaking truth which in their understanding is true, the device on the Moon distorts this truth, disconnects from Universe.

I think this will help You to distinct some not so real good wishers. I only say that I'm aware of reptilians that are "channeling". And they are never tell the whole story, only a part of true story. They can be distinguished by their sounds which they pronounce the most: ssss, sshh, hhaahh. Snakish sounds, these are sounds of their language, original "reptilian language". They try to hide them, but it is very hard for them to do:) ... these channelers were still active after main archon force was "removed" from this planet along with device on Moon still turned on were our prime concerns. Also they like triangular crafts (triangular lights, triangular UFOs) and symbolics. Novus Ordo Seclorum[265] was their masterplan to make huge sufferings to Humanity, so to lead Everyone to Light and Love.

"2- About this Demiurge being. When he hide the real nature of the universe in order to pose as One he is acting against our free will. I mean, the fact that me or anyone else chose to believe him it's in everyone´s right to choose but how can this be considered a Free Will Chose if the only options available to choose from are presented by the very same being hidden the real presence of One in order to trick us to choose him instead of One. Why there is no plan to implement total transparency and disclosure of all information in order to give everyone a real chance to exercise Free Will right away?"

This being set itself right before narrowed sight of Humanity. And it is keeping Majority in unknowing of real Creator. When Soul is leaving this World it is intercepted by one of the stations located throughout this Solar System and sent via false route to demiurge's location and demiurge "in all of it's glory" is standing right before this Soul.

---

[265] "New World Order Index: Hard Truth / Wake Up America." New World Order Index: Hard Truth / Wake Up America. N.p., n.d. Web. 12 July 2016.
<http://www.theforbiddenknowledge.com/hardtruth/newworldindex.htm>.

All Souls during their lifetimes at least once heard of a being that rules or created this World, and it was a very rare case when Humans were able to "crack" this mystery and find out about a real Creator. So when Soul is before demiurge that at least once heard of God, is accepting it as a "God of the Universe", (that is when Free Will is saying it is a God, thus giving itself to it's authority, like "signing a contract") and this being is saying if Soul was not loyal, "you committed a lot of sins in your life, so you will go to hell to clean yourself of all those sins" of course obviously Soul don't want to go there, so it is saying, "then you will go back to Earth to fix your sins." (This is what happens most of the time, but some Souls are being sent to hell)

And demiurge is making sure Soul won't find out about whole story. As we know, it was a very rare situation when Soul was openly telling demiurge "you are a false god!" And when it was happening demiurge along with it's "angels" was always convincing Soul that it is mistaken and that before You is "the one true god", this being was showing "wonders" and it's powers, Soul's previous lifetime experiences, relatives, it knows every Human Being inside out, all of these made many believed it, but what can You expect from so powerful being? And only few were not convinced and were set free. No other Soul was allowed to see how these very few were set free..

That is how it can control Your view and belief how it wants. A very grand illusion isn't it? It is so true what will be shown to You, that disbelieving it will be very hard, because there will be huge fear pointed at Soul, different types of self-induced emotions, but as always - resisting it possible. And when You know that it is a false god, accepting that You are a Free Sovereign Being, this is what Your Free Will is. Majority of Humanity still believe in this god imposter only because there wasn't told that there are actually "two", One real, and other only imposes the first One. Majority know only of evil entity - devil, satan, but very few can imagine that father of Humanity is an "imposter", this is something Everyone would hardly agree with. Rewriting of old religions which beared truth hidden in legends and mythologies were marked as "pagan" or "satan's religions". But actually they were holding the very real truth which could have been decoded. The history of Humanity's Creation. So as always Knowing is Light, unknowing is dark.

READER'S COMMENTS

"Question:
If the false god is so powerful, what then is a practical way to free oneself once and for-all?
Thank you"

~~

"thank you for your continued sharing :)
i am greatly enjoying your perspective.

i was wondering if you know about the plan to 'enlighten' the demiurge (and its 'friends')?"

~~

January 28th, 2014

G/E

Also to answer to Your question Good Friend Michael, the first part of this message explains that everything can be used, but only if there is no other way. How Humanity constructed this civilization, from building blocks of this Planet of Animals of Trees. Because there was no other way. Earth is ready to share what it have with it's children, but only if they will respect Her other Children, giving Love, Joy, Harmony to other Beings and to Planet overall. This is how One like to see and experience Itself.

And talking to Forces of One is not possible, they are here not to help Humanity, only to end experiment, but One's orders were to fulfill the wish of Humanity, which is also an end of experiment and receiving of freedom. I'm not in contact with them right now, there is no need to be so, before the moment of choice we were frequently contacting each other, but now We are waiting for actions of Followers of Light or Humanity, it is up to them to finish this experiment. Forces of One can be called "dormant" right now. They only waiting, scattered around the Solar System and around GFL Systems as well.

I'm not a Pi tau. I'm a human just like You and Everyone around, what makes me different is that within me is an "extension soul" which is an ancient soul, it is an "add-on" to my human abilities (I have two Souls, one is my "normal" and second is not active, yet it boosts my abilities and can be "activated" when I need it). With it, I can be recognized as a representative of One of a Terranians (Humanity). We chose latin to describe many things, because it is the main language of this World right now. Yes, within Forces of One Humanity is known as "terranians" or "from Terra".

Also Thank You for providing this great video!
I will share one too :)[266]

I will also add information which Everyone can find useful. First is about Obamacare, our Good Friend Dahboo7 found many good information about this whole scheme. We knew that Obamacare was a scam since it began to work, Obamacare is also not giving privacy protection for Anyone that signs[267]

this site can be easily hacked by anyone[268]

also good research about nsa and it's spying[269]

Also Good Friend found this hidden information, there are many more, don't relax just yet, while illuminati are still in control this won't disappear[270]

Second is about pineal gland. I already mentioned that Everyone should

[266] Zeusdvm. "Valentine's Day: The Love of Animals." YouTube. YouTube, 20 Jan. 2010. Web. 12 July 2016. <http://www.youtube.com/watch?v=3MCDgdN2tSY>.

[267] Dahboo777. "LOOK! Exposed Hidden Source Code in Obamacare Strips Your Privacy Away!" YouTube. YouTube, 27 Nov. 2013. Web. 12 July 2016. <https://www.youtube.com/watch?v=hHfKuhmMY7s>.

[268] DAHBOO77. "Security Expert Hacks Obamacare Website In 4 Minutes & Accesses 70,000 Records!" YouTube. YouTube, 21 Jan. 2014. Web. 12 July 2016. <http://www.youtube.com/watch?v=9TTeUGOs7FQ>.

[269] GlobalResearchTV. "Justifying the Unjustifiable: Deconstructing the Lies of the NSA." YouTube. YouTube, 23 Jan. 2014. Web. 12 July 2016. <http://www.youtube.com/watch?v=2HonVknVWBg>.

[270] Dahboo777. ""666" Flaunted In New Red Bull Commercial & Monster Logo!" YouTube. YouTube, 23 Jan. 2014. Web. 12 July 2016. <http://www.youtube.com/watch?v=c-wwxVbAOFY>.

avoid using fluorine and fluoride poisons for health benefits. This poisonous chemical is a slow killer. It is accumulating itself in bones, teeth and pineal gland. Pineal gland is also can be called an antenna like in this video from Good Friend BPEarthWatch[271]

Pineal gland is Your Sahasrara - the Crown Chakra, which is called on kabbalah's tree of life also - the Crown. The connection with Creation, with Universe.
It is increasing Your overall connectedness with Universe, thus with One. And fluoride is the best chemical that suppresses and degrades it[272]

U.S. is adding more fluoride than any other country in the World, degrading americans' ability to see though the veil of illusion. Here is the list of countries that adds/no longer adds fluoride in water[273]

Fluoride accumulates itself naturally in a black and red tea. I'm drinking rarely green tea which almost don't have fluoride. I Remember at first it was my own "instinct" to stop drinking black and red teas, then I was introduced into this. Green tea also filling Your organs and Body cells with oxygen, very good tea for a health and to keep Your weight low;) This is how You can remove it from Your body and from water.[274] [275]

On the contrary calcium can benefit Your bones, teeth and Your Physical Body overall. It is also benefiting pineal gland lowly, but still[276] [277]

Food with most calcium[278]

---

[271] BPEarthWatch. "The Destruction of God's Antenna/Part 3 of The Gamma Burst Series." YouTube. YouTube, 22 Jan. 2014. Web. 12 July 2016. <http://www.youtube.com/watch?v=3YS9qGMk-nQ>.
[272] "Is Fluoride Considered a Poison in Most European Countries?" HowStuffWorks. N.p., 12 Mar. 2008. Web. 12 July 2016. <http://health.howstuffworks.com/wellness/oral-care/products/fluoride-poisoning2.htm>.
[273] "Fluoridation by Country." Wikipedia. Wikimedia Foundation, n.d. Web. 12 July 2016. <http://en.wikipedia.org/wiki/Fluoridation_by_country>.
[274] N.p., n.d. Web. <http://chemistry.about.com/od/chemistryhowtoguide /a/removefluoride.htm>.
[275] Goldenmeanshealth. "Remove Fluoride From Your Body." YouTube. YouTube, 26 Feb. 2011. Web. 12 July 2016. <http://www.youtube.com/watch?v=iheYCikol9s>.
[276] N.p., n.d. Web. <http://www.nutracalcium.com/calcium-benefits.php>.
[277] "Calcium-rich Health Benefits." SheKnows. N.p., 28 Mar. 2012. Web. 12 July 2016. <http://www.sheknows.com/health-and-wellness/articles/822335/5-benefits-of-calcium>.
[278] "Best for Bones Food." List of Foods with Calcium & Vitamin D. N.p., n.d. Web. 12 July 2016. <http://www.bestbonesforever.gov/best_foods/>.

Yes, calcium can help prevent mutation (cancer) from appearing, on the contrary fluoride is the chemical that causes cancer most of the time, also it degrades bones and causes many bone sicknesses[279]

But the main reason why illuminati are using fluoride is because it is degrading pineal gland (demiurge and Beings of Purity are also at it)

Also another information I may aid, is about deodorant and antiperspirants, always try to use aluminum-free deodorants or You can use these natural alternatives to deodorants, as aluminum as well accumulates in body, is toxic to organs and also causes mutation (cancer)[280]

If You are asking the question what You can do right now? If You think You are powerless, then this is false, You are Powerful!! You can change many things by only wanting to change them. Look for famous People in Internet that shares Your view on what is happening in this World, share with them information about new better technology, alternative to oil. First cars can be outfitted with these, then power plants, and finally Your homes. If they will find it interesting, You can say to them about "frequent visitors" to this World, corruption within government is accepted by most right now, "the illuminati conspiracy" which many deemed laughable just 20 cycles ago is now making sense for many more People around the World. So there is a lot You can share with other People around the Web!

Here is some beautiful music for Everyone [281]:)

 With much Peace, Calm and Prosperity!

READER'S COMMENTS

"Thank you GE. I was wondering more about what we should do next, and I am thankful that I don't often feel powerless, but you have only solidified what I knew. And as I am

---

[279] "Protect Your Family from Cancer-causing Fluoride." NaturalNews. N.p., n.d. Web. 12 July 2016. <http://www.naturalnews.com/040461_fluoride_iaomt_oral_medicine.html>.

[280] Moss, Laura. "5 Natural Deodorant Alternatives." MNN. N.p., n.d. Web. 12 July 2016. <http://www.mnn.com/lifestyle/natural-beauty-fashion/photos/5-deodorant-alternatives/lemon-juice>.

[281] N.p., n.d. Web. <http://www.youtube.com/watch?v=S4BFRYoVtIg>.

encountering more "data" and confirmations of truths, I am just not sure what I should or could do with it. I want to learn to connect better to my truth/heart center, yet feel I need to do more than that :))

For now, I will focus on the meditations and intentions for our beloved Earth, and all her inhabitants. I look forward to your and Sophia's next updates and blog. :))"

~~

"GE, are you able to paint a picture of what will happen from the moment of justice onwards, and then at the end of the experiment ?
What I have read is that those people who are ready will ascend. Others will enter "karmic loops" which will allow them to have a customised experience which will prepare them over lifetimes for ascension. I guess some others will go to hell.
But if the demiurge & co are not running the experiment, will all this activity be managed by One's forces ?
Or will all souls simply be returned to their planets of origin ?

You mentioned that demiurge will not really be punished for what it did - what could it possibly do afterwards, after such a big experiment ? Wouldn't it be "bored to death" ?

Will all of us one day become a demiurge to have the experience of running our own show ? Will we rule over galaxies etc which show the same cruelty to planetary beings and animals, that we see here ?"

~~

January 29th 2014

SOPHIA

  An update from Sophia:

There were some sentences within the January 27th update that have been construed as being antisemitic. They have been removed from the message. To clarify, this blog has been offered on my web site as a way for you to speak to the GE. He is human and provides here information as he understands it, making no claims to its absolute truth. What he offers is historical information, which he has access to because of his position. Words that separate and divide do not provide useful information for any of us, or lead us to unity.

My take on this is that, although the reference may be true, and Abraham was "chosen", this was because he (Abraham) was willing to sacrifice his son to this "god", not because the Jewish faith is superior to any other. The separation of "chosen people" and the rest of the people exists because of a willingness to obey at any cost, by one man. That was then, this is now. Labeling an entire group of people as negative serves no one.

Religion signifies upbringing, not character or worth. We are ONE. Every player in this current finale holds equal worth and is equally loved. Compassion and forgiveness are paramount. Humanity chose to do this ourselves. It is my belief we did so because we are done with anything that sounds like hierarchy. This time, no one gets left behind, or forgotten. We are all chosen.

There is not much editing going on here. The words you are reading are straight from GE. As he has said, you are free to believe what you choose to believe. This is the hallmark of sovereignty.

Much love to everyone.

READER'S COMMENTS

"Well said Sophia! I too, resonate with your stance. We need historical information, as this helps us focus on the now to make our future. As a people without "lines in the sand" segregation or grouping of things and names that represent something other than being in this together."

~~

"Sophia: What serves a troll? :)"

~~

"Hi to all.The Hopegirl Group have released their free energy device,unfortunately it's a little bit expensive.Here is the link : http://xi4.com/2014/01/31/qeg-quantum-energy-generator-released/ .It's a good beginning.
Good Friend can send them protection please,they are in need."

~~

February 1, 2014

SOPHIA

At this beginning of the second month of 2014, it is time to re-state the guidelines, which were outlined at the start of this blog/comment section. We have many new readers:

"At the request of several readers, and the suggestion of our Off World Contact, this comment section is now open. It is a place to comment on what has been shared. There are two rules : that all comments are made both 1. anonymously (use another name)
and 2. respectfully.
Other than that, consider this an open line.
Violations of the rules will be removed.
When making comments, please reference which date you are referring to so others can look back to the conversation and understand the whole picture."

R.E. has shared this, some good news and great ideas!

-- "It appears that it will take about two to three hours to make the Hendershot power unit. It also appears that the steps are fairly simple. I believe I will organize a co-op of young out of work ambitious people to make these and share with each other the proceeds. It could spread very quickly across the planet. I think a good price would be $1,000.00 each. If I organize a production line and introduce automation gradually and lower the price as we progress, we can expand even more rapidly. Since Hendershot is long dead and his patent has expired, we can do it."

-- "I would like to see "Operation Mockingbird". Is there any way of shaming our government for destroying freedom of the Press?"

Here is a link to information on the Hendershot unit: Click here[282].

The idea for "Operation Mockingbird" is a good one, any ideas? I would offer a page on this site or at least advertising to promote it if there is interest and a plan evolves.

---

[282] "The Inventions of Lester Hendershot." The Inventions of Lester Hendershot. N.p., n.d. Web. 12 July 2016. <http://www.svensons.com/Energy/hendershot2.html>.

I love R.E.'s idea for a co-op that is mutually beneficial to everyone involved.

I have seen <u>Hope Girls video</u>. The sooner we can develop and produce working models of free energy that are affordable, the sooner we are completely free. All efforts will get us there.

Much love,

READER'S COMMENT

"I think this is an awesome idea. We r the ones we have been waiting for. Now is the time to co-create want we want 4 a great loving peaceful world."

~~

G/E

Good Day Sophia and Everyone!

While Olympics are a major problem, there is also a danger on Super Bowl event as well. Illuminati order want to make lives of Humanity harder, they will do anything they can while they still exist and are in a final moments. We have a pressure on these two events, and U.S. government still wants to get to attack Syria. They are trying to find a way around the chemical weapons disarmament.
China was calmed down a little and Africa's position is a little secured, Ukraine is still a bit hard to calm down.
So Olympics, Super Bowl, Syria and Ukraine are the most problematic locations in the World right now.
When meditating, You can direct Your Love, Light and Spiritual Harmony with Spiritual Friendship toward all that lives to these troubled locations.
We sense that we are in a final moments, we have some time left from few earth's cycles (days) to months, until all will be done.
If of course something will not drastically take the turn to other direction.. We would have problems in that situation, but if it will happen full exposure of "wizard behind the curtain" will be complete. We have our positions secured, so anywhere they will go will be met with "a merciless trap toward

them".

READER'S COMMENTS

"Hi,
With the recent distractions with both the Chinese and the US in the MSM it's rather obvoius our contrast family is desperate, the know too well that there is an absolute plan that is much more far reaching than the "divine plan".

Time to enter the stage "wizards" your screen play is outdated!

Inlakesh

<3<3<3"

~~

"Thanks so much for your wonderful data. We feel the shift is approaching. The attacks have been relentless, but are now fading!!!! You have tilted the scales, though you may not yet realize it!!!
Love to you!"

~~

"tomorrow (2 feb 2014) there will be many meditations going on simultaneously.
i'm sharing this here so that more joint focus may intensify our grounded actions and intentions.

here are some of them:
montague keen - sunrise/sunset:
- http://www.galacticchannelings.com/english/montague26-01-14.html
the following 3 all at the same time (20:00 GMT)
- meline lafont: http://lafontmeline.com/2014/01/25/global-meditation-focus-on-heart-space-gaia-at-glastonbury-tor-light-language-by-meline-lafont/
- cobra: http://2012portal.blogspot.nl/2012/06/normal-0-microsoftinternetexplorer4_15.html
- aisha north: http://aishanorth.wordpress.com/2014/02/01/welcome-to-februarys-gathering-around-the-pond-sunday-2/

there are also various groups doing daily meditations together online.
- facebook:
https://www.facebook.com/events/556205894400957/?ref=notif¬if_t=plan_edited
- global coherence initiative: http://www.globalcarerooms.org/rooms/waiting/gci

- do as one: http://doasone.com/default.aspx

as usual, use google (or startpage.com etc) to find more :)"

~~

G/E

... Happy New Chinese Year! It was yesterday, a great asian celebration!

Now that no One is left behind, and We All are completely living in a New Cycle/Year We can start this transformation! Illuminati order has many evil schemes prepared for the World and these are "the end times", so it will be extremely tense and tight right now.

This month can be the Moment of Justice, Light Followers can show themselves on Olympics or Super Bowl or both, this depends on two factors, one is their Free Will and other is the false flag attacks. They and we will look so everything would proceed without incidents.

Your meditations will aid the World as well. Wish for Happiness, Love and Abundance!

With Peace and Love!

READER'S COMMENT

"While I get the Law of Free Will, I am putting my foot down to allowing this manipulation and suppression to continue on this beautiful planet and all of her inhabitants! My Free Will now fully accepts and acknowledges that I am free from any contracts or agreements that I have signed /accepted, regardless if knowingly or unknowingly, verbally or not. They are now revoked and nullified! I take back my sovereignty and value as a being and entity, and I forgive with love. It's time ... ! :))"

~~

February 4, 2014

G/E
True, a plan Mocking Bird would be a great way to be used on U.S. and UK

governments, this will have to be done by majority, much like Anonymous movement, remember from where it appeared? From movie V for Vendetta, so this can be repeated from Hunger Games as well;)

"i was wondering if you know about the plan to 'enlighten' the demiurge (and its 'friends')?"

No, this one I hadn't heard, do You have one? It would be great Good Friend:) We GEs are only exposing the hidden reality within their Systems and hierarchy (I like how it was called "liararchy" from "why I'm no longer a lightworker" article)[283]
so it is influencing them All.

"If the false god is so powerful, what then is a practical way to free oneself once and for-all?"

Good Friend Axel, I answered on Your question in previous messages, You can search for them, they were written not so long ago in few messages. If You are saying about "getting demiurge off the existence" then this will have to be done physically.

I think I should mention "the biggest secret of Creation" here. It is something which demiurge and Beings of Purity really don't want You to know. Channelers are never mentioning this like I heard (at least those that I heard). Ok this is secret is very simple and illuminati order and all that were in power for all history were using this secret and abusing it. Very obvious, yet most time ignored, it is

"When You are in physical existence You can do anything, change anything how You like, be a manifestation of original Creator, influence Creation directly, with physicality, mind, Consciousness and Soul as well.

And when You are Soul, You cannot do this, You cannot do anything You wish, You are being controlled, guided, You can enjoy being Soul doing unimaginable things, yet You can't influence Creation, Souls are not

[283] N.p., n.d. Web. <http://www.ascensionhelp.com/blog/2013/11/21/tell-the-lords-of-karma-that-you-are-sovereign-no-longer-a-lightworker-part-2/>.

capable of doing this."

This is how it was programmed, coded as we know it. One very interesting thing One gave to All the Beings is that last wish of every physical incarnation can be fulfilled. This is the wish before it is leaving the physical body.

"GE, are you able to paint a picture of what will happen from the moment of justice onwards, and then at the end of the experiment ?

What I have read is that those people who are ready will ascend. Others will enter "karmic loops" which will allow them to have a customised experience which will prepare them over lifetimes for ascension. I guess some others will go to hell.

But if the demiurge & co are not running the experiment, will all this activity be managed by One's forces ?
Or will all souls simply be returned to their planets of origin ?

You mentioned that demiurge will not really be punished for what it did - what could it possibly do afterwards, after such a big experiment ?
Wouldn't it be "bored to death" ?

Will all of us one day become a demiurge to have the experience of running our own show ? Will we rule over galaxies etc which show the same cruelty to planetary beings and animals, that we see here ?"

It is a lot of questions, I will try to give short answers Good Friend.

Ascension since beginning was considering a "rapture" as we know and resurrection of all the People of the Earth that were living on this Planet. Though for Light Followers it is not possible, they don't have the necessary technology to resurrect all, Forces of One and Ancient Machines can do it. It will be overpopulation in that case. Forces of One can duplicate Souls and create 1 to 1 Souls.

Rapture; in reality Light Followers planned to take only what they needed "the fruits" and discard all the rest by disintegrating their bodies, taking their souls and transforming them, thus ascending. The few that would be chosen would be tansformed into partial beings of light thus they are to "ascend".

Another form of Ascension is the one through which demiurge and it's civilization came through. It is when their Souls were fused with physical existence, thus they can feed themselves with pure light energy and influence physical reality, which they are doing very greatly.

For Humanity, time or tools will be required to ascend. A lot of time or good tools at hand, to fuse soul with physicality, thus becoming gamma organisms, the most highest. If You can transform Yourself now, You are most welcomed to do so!

Yes if Light Followers will cease this experiment before given date, demiurge will still have control over Humanity's Souls, and it as a father, has right to it. If not, than it will be made mortal and physical and in this situation Humanity will return back to original Heaven and original cycle of life all it's devices from this System would be removed, Humanity will become Sovereign Civilization with it's own Destiny.
You can become like demiurge someday only if You will want to. It is Your Free Will and Free Choice that guides You. Demiurge chose to become complete controller of Existence, You can choose any path in Your Existence, so it is what You choose will become so.

READER'S COMMENTS

"The info about Demiurge and artificial heaven have bagan to spread out,look at here:http://blog.redefininggod.com/2014/02/01/the-soul-trap-hijacking-the-point-of-attention.aspx. Ken also stated thet Russia and China are another face of the cabal.What is your take about that Good Friend?"

~~

"Wow DXXX! What a great read!"

~~

"I know we are eternal souls emanating from One who are experiencing life in this mortal body in this universe(One).My question is why do we need a soul and a body if we are both parts of One?I know it's very metaphysic.Thank you for the answer"

~~

G/E

About the analogy[284] I think everything is said there, I don't know what to add, I too shared the same information with You about the demiurge and controllers of Humanity.
Everything is understandable in what Good Friend said.

Yes, I know, there was reaction to "jew issue" on my message. Like we are as always expecting, whenever there is a talk about "jew" it is always negative. There will be found at least one individual that will say "we hate jews", calling it antisemitic and so on. Are You wondered why it is so, Sophia? I will explain what we know... I did not said without a reason that jews were selected as a "chosen nation" of this World, because it was so. Demiurge made this selection, which reptiles proposed.

Their every encounter with "God" was the encounter with ET's, and in beginning Yahweh was considered not an "all loving God", but a bloodthirsty and merciless towards jewish enemies warrior being, and this god was adopted from other religions (jews are declining this). Especially this god "hated" canaanite nation (like they were hating). Only when Jerusalem was destroyed, they deposed this god and turned it into "all-loving god". You can search for this information.

Jewish nation is having a lot in common with reptilians, language, deceptive nature and they can betray for their own profit. And like we studied it, it is seen in majority of jewish people around the World. There are good People among this nation, but when You need to trust something very sensitive, jews are the last nation You will want to do it.

And again in their nation is playing the same demiurgic rule, that true knowledge is given only to few above, majority of this nation don't know all the details. U.S., UK and EU board are governments with most People connected with jews that have at least someone "jewish" in the bloodline.

[284] Lisamharrison. "Lisa M Harrison - What's the Plan ?" YouTube. YouTube, 31 Jan. 2014. Web. 12 July 2016. <http://www.youtube.com/watch?v=91f1diLkbiQ>.

Occult societies and illuminati order are not accepting complete "gentiles" in their ranks. Masons do, but these "gentiles" will never be given all the knowledge.

Yes and this issue in judaism, about "jews" and "gentiles" (that all the rest of the World), this creates a very big separation among Everyone in the World, and this makes "jews" to think of themselves as "a very special People of the World". We personally don't like this rule. They were hated exactly because of these many negativity about them throughout all the times and are still hated by most as they again want to rule this World. So they came up with some ideas how to get around this, they used christianity's wide prevalence in roman times to improve their image, as romans were hating them and they actually exiled them not one time from their cities as they were seeing their "arrogant and deceptive nature".

So christianity was one of the main reasons why roman empire was destroyed. Many reasons played it's part in their downfall, this was one of them as we know it. And spread of Christianity did not stop after it's downfall, it only increased thus bringing dark ages to gentiles and golden ages to jews, as jews were considered higher than normal People, because of the bible.

In time trust in them was lost, due to religion's promises not coming true. So jews by that time having tremendous wealth and knowledge decided to again "improve their image" and decided to cause a holocaust (means sacrifice) in ww2. This was a hoax war, the most hoaxed war we have ever seen, we don't want to remember it, because it was truly disgusting. The only "real player" in this war was japanese empire, which was tricked into attacking Pearl Harbor, yet it could have been prevented, only U.S. government wanted to be attacked to be involved in this war.

And Japan's greed for land and wealth played it's part. After all the sacrifice of their own "jewish sheeple", how they were calling it, they were given a right to "recreate Israel". But at this time there were other People already living there, so to get their land back, they needed to "clean it out". U.S., and UK provided their most advanced weaponry of that time at almost no cost at all. And then, as You remember from main stream media Israel was attacked by all muslim countries around it, only it wasn't true, Israel was attacking all the time, and muslims were defending themselves. Muslims had old weaponry, which they couldn't use against the newest, being used by jews-zionists (zionism is the <u>reclamation of Israel and destruction of all "gentiles" on this land)</u>.[285]

After this holocaust (sacrifice), jews were and are respected again, their image was improved and there are still christians, which thinks of jewish nation as "the most holiest of all", so whenever we speak about even word jew, it is always met with negativity.

This is how all Humanity was mind programmed about all this issue, so that jews would be protected by All "brainwashed" People energetically and physically, and while protected they can carry on with their plans of world domination. They have "praise, glory and inspiration", so they just carry on.

Remember few enlightened from them are behind the main illuminati teaching of world domination. If You are a jew, this is not meant that You are like them, no, they just use all this scheme to control even You. The israeli is the most lying government in the World, along with U.S. and UK, always listen carefully to what they are saying.

You can at least consider all of this, if You don't want to believe in it.

Also Thank You for Your coordinated efforts for making free energy technology, the price is a bit high You are requesting Good Friend Ray, maybe it is possible for You to reduce the price?

Manufacturing can wait. Necessity right now is spreading of this information. If Someone can make it, it would be very great, it will "one more point to Your basket", the knowledge of self-powered machine will bring You benefit in every circumstance. Much Kudos to You Good Friend Ray, if Good Friends would agree on sharing their resources, then this may be an increase in pace of World Change.

But remember Everyone, You don't have to share, I personally don't like

[285] Muslimsandtheworld. "An Honest Israeli Jew Tells the Real Truth about Israel." YouTube. YouTube, 02 Dec. 2012. Web. 12 July 2016. <http://www.youtube.com/watch?v=etXAm-OylQQ>.

when there is a talk about money in any way as these are the tools of control,

I always doing by best to make things free at no cost. I made one quite effective magnetic rotor, I modify it from time to time getting more efficiency from it, but right now I cannot interact directly so this tech I will share later.. I will show some more effective and cheap versions in videos, share it and make it :) [286]

(I guess it's the one Good Friend HopeGirl made)[287]

If You question magnetic rotation technology, how it is working, look at these two videos,
copper + magnets (positive and negative assortment) are making a lot of energy which can be transformed into electricity[288] [289]

It is meant to be used with water or wind movement [290]

A cheap version[291] [292]

This is one variant of curing against cancer and possible fuel - salt water [293]

As always, possibilities are countless!

With Much Love, Tranquility and Abundance!

[286] N.p., n.d. Web. <http://www.youtube.com/watch?v=jKFTAobM-l0>.

[287] N.p., n.d. Web. <http://www.youtube.com/watch?v=P-a8QAeCoNU>.

[288] FreeEnergyLT. "FREE HEATING ????" YouTube. YouTube, 15 Dec. 2011. Web. 12 July 2016. <http://www.youtube.com/watch?v=8n5sSmJsCdY>.

[289] YouTube. YouTube, n.d. Web. 12 July 2016. <http://www.youtube.com/watch?v=_F8vhx8DU1c>.

[290] YouTube. YouTube, n.d. Web. 12 July 2016. <http://www.youtube.com/watch?v=JYzyUkymThA>.

[291] Buddhanz1. "How to Rewire an Old Washing Machine Motor to Generate Free Power." YouTube. YouTube, 08 Aug. 2013. Web. 12 July 2016. <http://www.youtube.com/watch?v=NLaSf_YY7Xs>.

[292] Buddhanz1. "Free Power- How to Convert an Old Washing Machine into a Water Powered Generator." *YouTube*. YouTube, 11 Nov. 2011. Web. 12 July 2016. <http://www.youtube.com/watch?v=6LjuZsod4E4>.

[293] Darrylsmith. "FREE GAS FOR EVER!!!! TELL EVERYONE!!" YouTube. YouTube, 08 July 2007. Web. 12 July 2016. <http://www.youtube.com/watch?v=F0vycQ06a04>.

READER'S COMMENT

"I find Ray's idea not so bad.It's a sort of resource sharing,for sure it must not be too expensive.Thanks for the videos Good Friend"

~~

G/E
Good Day Sophia and Everyone!

Thank You for Your great efforts, because of Your United meditations, which was very strong along with other grouping with Light workers meditations on that same date We United were able to prevent any and all casualties during Super Bowl!
There was an explosion in "hell's kitchen" also called Poseidon restaurant while Super Bowl was taking place.[294]

As we know this was a bomb which was detonated sooner than it was supposed to. Due to efforts of Light Followers and many Lightworkers casualties were avoided! People would go there after Super Bowl, and there would be casualties. We knew this was one of locations where it could happen, we were watching for this location, but main focus was on Super Bowl. Good Friend Dahboo7 found all the signs about this and connected them one cycle (day) before[295] [296] [297]

Now because they did this, that means we will now have two problems, one is Olympics and the other is a "counterfeit attack" on East side of U.S. This just showed they are capable of doing this one desperate attempt.

We along with Followers of Light and Ancient Machines will look for it, so it won't take place, we will do our best to prevent it, but there is no 100%

---

[294] "Reports: Explosion in Midtown Manhattan; Update: Gas Line Explosion? [pics] - Twitchy.com." Twitchycom. N.p., 02 Feb. 2014. Web. 13 July 2016. <http://twitchy.com/2014/02/02/reports-explosion-in-midtown-manhattan/>.
[295] DAHBOO77. "CRAZY! Super Bowl Party Boat To Land At Hell's Kitchen!" YouTube. YouTube, 01 Feb. 2014. Web. 13 July 2016. <http://www.youtube.com/watch?v=26kQph7fKvQ>.
[296] Enterthe5t4rz. "48 Years Ago Was HELL'S KITCHEN 1966 In Movie SLEEPERS, 1st Super Bowl & Trade Center Groundbreaking." YouTube. YouTube, 01 Feb. 2014. Web. 13 July 2016. <https://www.youtube.com/watch?v=IOJYDg1vHYU>.
[297] Killak38. "URGENT!! ILLUMINATI MESSAGE DECODED Super Bowl 48 (MUST SEE)." YouTube. YouTube, 01 Feb. 2014. Web. 13 July 2016. <https://www.youtube.com/watch?v=69tlEA1ma2Y>.

guarantee we will be able to. You can help us too by meditating for World Peace, Unity, Stability, Harmony and Unconditional Love among All Living and Non-Living things! The possibilities are, that nuclear or chemical or new type weaponry will be used. Right now there will be massive military "drills" on U.S. East side [298]

The possibility is very big that South Carolina would be the target. Remember this video? Lindsey Graham just mentioned Charleston and drills are taking place in South Carolina. They wouldn't target New York with mass destruction weaponry, unless there is "nothing to lose" for them.[299]

Also there are already some 60 fired officers within military (we are not sure with total number), most of them are connected with nuclear arsenal. [300]

They are being fired on ridiculous reasons. So it is something to keep in mind and consider. Like we know they are removing Good People from service, leaving only those that are easy to be controlled or that can go along with their evil agenda.

Everything is Interconnected and if You can "crack the Code", You can see what is "planned" (or is possible) before it will take place.

Like Good Friend was able to see this, Boston and Sandy Hook were happened by "themselves" because those People that done it were just "up to do it".
The codings for events are encoded within the living Bioenergetic Field of this Planet and Universe Itself, and they can be "solved". It is the Code of the Universe that is getting all this, One itself "signs" for Everyone to see and prevent these things from happening, yet they by most part only possible, future is "in mist".[301]

---

[298] "Massive Military Training Exercise to Be Held over Savannah in February." Savannahnow.com. N.p., n.d. Web. 13 July 2016. <http://savannahnow.com/news/2014-01-31/massive-military-training-exercise-be-held-over-savannah-february#.UvFwy_uzlrG>.

[299] Qronos16. "America FALSE FLAG Imminent: US Generals Who Won't Enforce Martial Law Being Fired." YouTube. YouTube, 15 Oct. 2013. Web. 13 July 2016. <http://www.youtube.com/watch?v=kqheo3EX_cg>.

[300] "Number of US Nuclear 'cheats' Doubles - Officials." BBC News. BBC, 28 Jan. 2014. Web. 13 July 2016. <http://www.bbc.co.uk/news/25936781>.

[301] DAHBOO77. "Linking The Signs!" YouTube. YouTube, 02 Feb. 2014. Web. 13 July 2016. <http://www.youtube.com/watch?v=OvShOPBlXBY>.

This event at Super Bowl was the illuminati order's doing, so we all were at it preventing this atrocity. The shootings and bombings which are not connected with illuminati, we simply can't get a full hold on all of these and prevent them all together, we would get "nuts" if we would to watch over everything, but we still doing our best...

We only know possible locations which are all on East side of U.S., two same quadrants within Charlotte-Norfolk and Pittsburgh-New York, You can include South Carolina's Charleston, or any other pre-coast location in South Carolina. Remember of all precautions, if You are living in these locations, when there is bright light or big explosion, be away from the windows as far as possible, somewhere behind concrete walls or in a basement, away from roofs and from higher floors (same applies to tornadoes accidents) and Most Important - don't have fear! Have Harmony and Unconditional Love in You Heart!

My apologies for such unpleasant information, but we are having these mad people in government which right now are very afraid of losing everything they accumulated so far.

With Much Peace and Unconditional Love to Everyone!

February 6th, 2014

G/E

Here is an important update. It is for Everyone that is living in New York, be away from Manhattan as far as possible in the coming cycles/days! Manhattan sewers were extremely damaged in Midtown West, because this is exactly what they wanted to do with this hell's kitchen explosion, it is also a targeted by illuminati order location, along with other possible locations which I named earlier.

They are truly desperate, dates are set by them 14-16 february, olympic games will be taking place on these dates, they want to target more People, there will be gay protests connected with Olympic games, stay away from these protests.

Be careful, meditate for World Peace and for Unconditional Love Among All Things! We are doing our best in preventing of this, though danger is big and I want You All Good Friends to stay safe and sound!

Once We will overcome this, they won't be able to continue on with their evil agenda!

If we will get detailed information, I will share it!

Much Love to All!

READER'S COMMENT

"This will not come to pass! Let's all focus & "see" on a wonderful, peaceful Olympics, as well the safety of all peoples/inhabitants of the world. We are powerful....!"

~~

SOPHIA

From Sophia ~
What follows is information on events that have happened and are planned. They are given as answers to multiple questions. These answers can be found if you search the internet and you tube, yet it is difficult to discern what happened if you were not present. I can only speak to what I know personally. The videos you will see include some facts, along with much speculation. You must decide for yourselves what to believe.

First of all, I live in the Midwest of the USA and the snow here is real. It melts, there is about four feet of it piled in my front yard right now. The videos on you tube however are convincing, these people are genuinely alarmed. These are filmed in the southern states of the USA.

Secondly, I have family in Sandy Hook, CT and can vouch for the fact that people were killed, both children and teachers. That tiny community is forever changed. When an event is "staged" for whatever reason, that does not imply it is not a real tragedy or that there was no violence. It is easy to believe everything you see on film. Yet people are dying and more casualties are planned. Please continue to meditate for peace and for no further violence, at either the games in Sochi tonight or the East Coast of the USA. There is a very big part of my heart connected to that coast. With knowledge comes power. This must end.

Here is the update:

G/E
Question:
" There are videos all over the United States now showing that where it looks ie snow is on the ground that the substance thought to be snow is not. This is urgent. They are trying to kill us. When you put a fire against the so called snow it sublimates into a gas and chars. This condition is all across the country where there is snowfall. I believe it is toxic . We need instant intervention. by off world forces!!!!!! "

I know about the snow, this is a direct consequence of chemtrails. This has been for a long time already, People hadn't gave much attention to it during 70s-80s when it first appeared, don't worry, it will not give You much damage, the nano chemicals from these chemtrails are already in majority of U.S. population.

They are meant to disconnect You from Universe, make You calmer and more "subservient", overall, these chemicals along with mercury are acting like fluoride poison, and are influencing pineal gland. You can remove them from body, by applying the same method as to fluoride.

Yes, it is wise to avoid eating and using that type of snow. It is not present in every part of U.S. as we know, but in most parts, is is spreading, but good thing - chemtrails and pollution have been reduced a little by actions of Light Followers.

This chemtrailing is also in practice in China as well. Yes intervention from them is most welcome to end it as soon as possible, we have this counterfeit attack on East side of U.S. upcoming which can be prevented if they would step in now and also this depends on their decision making and on Humanity's decision making as well.

I need to make a big correction and apologize Sophia considering last post.

There I mentioned about Boston bombing and Sandy Hook in place "Boston and Sandy Hook were happened by "themselves" because those People that done it were just "up to do it" which You can correct.. One corrected me, and pointed out that this was a staged event.

My apologize for not finding it out at first, I remember at that moment I was into different objectives. I made my own analysis on this bombing and saw that explosion was very weak, so supposedly it was done by unprofessional novice or novices. Blood was also strangely lying everywhere, not like in wars I used to see, it gave me suspicions, but I ignored it at that moment. And when they introduced two brothers, I saw that elder brother was able to do it, but younger brother - no. I thought he could have been "persuaded" into it like msm told.

So You can say, that I was bought into an "official story". And after that I returned to my duties, looks like none of GEs was able to see that it was staged, if this would influence the World, we would looked more into it, but it wasn't a big deal on that moment and we were having different problems, we were looking at their change of command and other more problematic "false flags".

One didn't liked that I still wasn't able to recognize this false event when I wrote to You, so I was introduced into reality. I will share this with You. Now I know that it was a staged event and there were no bombs at all, these were only simulation bombs, a smoke bombs. And "victims" were amputee actors hired by "strategic operations" company.

On this same cycle (day) there was a drill in Boston of a very same event of a "terror attack, using bombs in a backpack". Mercenary military were all over this place, like I now know. It were the main news all over the World and as You can see, this was a very very real-life "drill". And these two brothers were targeted since beginning, so they were just "scapegoats", they weren't having any weapons at all and wanted to surrender, but police were trying to kill them being unarmed. They were "conspiracy theorists" like I know now.

Police and military carried out a massive drill on that cycles, You saw how many vehicles and men were dispatched just to take two People. And msm *(main stream media)* just spread a big disinformation about it. All of this like I know now was a part of their big plan B scenario - martial law. Yes this counterfeit attack on East side is also a part of that "breaking point" plot of plan B.

Here are photos and some videos, notice, blood is not real, explosion is just a smoke screen.[302] [303]

at 1:37 You can hear they are surrendering, *(note, this video is no longer available. 7/2016. Sophia)* but police just keeps shooting at them, as a result, when elder brother gave up, police overrun him by a car and destroyed his body with multiple shots... As I know right now, mercenaries were there in shootouts as well, presumably shooting at police, so police would think brothers were shooting at them.[304]

In this second video You can see how good it was staged, "wizard behind the curtain" did it well

So this was injustice at its finest again, innocent people were betrayed and blamed for everything, it also was connected with symbolic dating of 666 since the start of korean war...[305]

this video was done prior to "bombing"

This is how satanists are doing things, so it's no surprise.. We are calling them as they are, by their real name, and this name they don't like to hear, but we like to irritate them for everything they done to this World and It's All inhabitants.

Much Understanding, Tranquility and Abundance to Everyone!

---

[302] "Boston Truth Revealed." Imgur. N.p., n.d. Web. 13 July 2016. <http://imgur.com/a/Nx8EU>.
[303] https://www.youtube.com/watch?v=YAgX6cHZaQE
[304] XBLACKxOPSxSECRETSx. "Photos and Eyewitnesses Confirm BOTH Boston Marathon Bombs Were Fake." YouTube. YouTube, 02 Aug. 2013. Web. 13 July 2016.
<http://www.youtube.com/watch?v=RR2B5SMGNYI>.
[305] N.p., n.d. Web. <http://www.youtube.com/watch?v=7t-nY2LA1yE>.

Regarding Sandy Hook... As I know now, it was also "a drill".[306]
(Note – I knew there were casualties in Sandy Hook. I have family there, and was speaking to them on the day it occurred. They lost neighbors, friends, and teachers. I mentioned this to him after his initial explanation. Sophia)

Apart from Boston, where injured were actors and only two people suffered, here victims were real.. Boy did the shooting and they knew he will shoot people, so they "used" this opportunity to train themselves and like You see, they allowed it to be happened, yet they could had prevented it.. But there were others shooters as well as I know now, and "fundraiser" websites were created prior to it [307]

There were also staged interviews made by CNN, this is what I found about it, from Good Friend Alex.[308]

CNN are known to make such fake reports, so it wasn't surprise..

This whole crime they committed is beyond anything and this is just a tip of the iceberg in many many evil deeds that were done since USA's foundation...

In its very short history this country committed more crimes than many much older world countries like Russia, China, India combined. All regime change policies, drills, false flags, revolution instigating, technology and information suppressing, supporting of genocides, but what can be expected from "satanic stronghold"? Evil is all over this government, many many crimes against Humanity and this Planet.

And now they are up to do another very big crime, drills are at the East side of U.S. take all the precautions I warned about Sophia, take care! Much Peace and Love to You!

---

[306] YouTube. YouTube, n.d. Web. 13 July 2016. <http://www.youtube.com/watch?v=FlWi97yBRAc>.
[307] N.p., n.d. Web. <http://www.youtube.com/watch?v=siCFb562JuU>.
[308] BelligerentPolitics. "CNN Caught Faking Boston Bombings Broadcast "Satellite Interview"" YouTube. YouTube, 13 May 2013. Web. 13 July 2016. <http://www.youtube.com/watch?v=xdK26vO6wtQ>.

READER'S COMMENT

"I felt in my heart that both situations were staged, but that MOST of the people who were victims were real. My heart went out to all of them, I also performed Ho'oponopono for everyone who was impacted by bit, and those who planned it. As Sophia says, thus has to stop! We are much more than this, we truly are! :))"

~~

February 9th, 2014

G/E

About two FBI agents, You can see that U.S. government think of their People as "expendables". They surely were deemed dangerous for them, otherwise this could not be happened. I am aware of many such accidents, whether People were dying from such accidents or from "suicides".

I know a lot of information of 9/11, it was a very big false attack. The buildings were brought down by explosives - with controlled demolitions, newest explosives were used there. 3 buildings on the same day... And number of casualties were less than 2000, but still a lot, not including all destroyed witnesses afterward. There were used photoshopped photos of People supposedly that were in an airplanes as we know.

Also, I haven't heard why no one got notice of police phone number 911? The very same numbers. The hell's kitchen that was blown up on Super Bowl was on 10th ave, between 9th and 11th. Why they like these numbers so much You may ask? It is as we know because of number 10. 10 is the number of Order, the number of Earth (somewhere also Saturn) of kabbalah's tree of life, and illuminati order is skipping it, they don't like Earth and God, that why they are skipping it, showing that they wish to "destroy it" and lead themselves to new earth, which is destroyed and opposite to what is right now here.. This is also showing that they are obedient to anti-creation, which is anti-god or satanic.. So overall it has a meaning of skipping God (here is meant Yahweh which is imposter god, but here also it has a meaning of One partially).

In their masonic religion, they believe that long ago there was an architect of Creation, which made this Creation as it is. But then false god overtook this Creation and made itself "a god". So they decided to challenge this being, because they were not happy seeing all of this mess and injustice here on Earth, they made a decision to oppose it. As You can see, it is not far away from how we know it.

The problem with them is of which path they chose "to oppose it", they chose the path of destruction, where in the end they completely destroy everything here. Self destruction that is. And I for example, completely disagree on this with them, this Planet Need to live and She Want to live, like All of Her beautiful Inhabitants![309]

"The info about Demiurge and artificial heaven have begun to spread out,look at here.[310]

Ken also stated thet Russia and China are another face of the cabal.What is your take about that Good Friend?"

Yes, this fact is known by many People, but as always Everyone need to believe what is best for Them. This illusion is very grand and finding whole truth about this system is not an easy task.

Good Friend Djon I can say for sure that higher command of Russia and China can aid Humanity in it's Liberation from illuminati order/cabal. Yes, these two structures are infiltrated by them as there are always bribes and willful persons to go along with having "more money". Good thing is that infiltrated are mostly lower agencies which are not in direct contact with presidents and other high ranking politicians. This depends on "pay", how much on average they earn and how much these illuminatis can give. For example there were recent scandals about CIA operatives bribing russian officials with millions of dollars annually or monthly for providing secret intelligence information. Good thing was that these russian officials didn't accept it and as You can see this became a headline.[311]

---

[309] N.p., n.d. Web. <http://www.youtube.com/watch?v=A0I6VQUzTn4>.

[310] N.p., n.d. Web. <http://blog.redefininggod.com/2014/02/01/the-soul-trap-hijacking-the-point-of-attention.aspx>.

[311] N.p., n.d. Web. <http://www.buckeyeplanet.com/forum/threads/cia-agent-caught-by-russians-trying-to-recruit-w-bribe-letter-included.631205/>.

So I can assure that these two countries can be trusted, they are against NWO and illuminati order. They do have their own "NWO", but it is much better, there is no depopulation/poisoning/false flags agendas, and it's main focus "to go along with technological progress", thus a natural way of Evolution. But as always it is up for You to decide Good Friend!

"I know we are eternal souls emanating from One who are experiencing life in this mortal body in this universe(One).My question is why do we need a soul and a body if we are both parts of One?I know it's very metaphysic.Thank you for the answer"

I too was asking this question when I was young Good Friend:)

I now know that One exists to experience Itself through Us, which in the end need to pass on being in physical incarnations. There need to be a knowingness that someday, we will meet our end, because of old age, or because of accident or because of something we have done not right during physical manifestation.. This is how One wants to experience Itself, it looks like One already experienced Itself with configuration when "physicality is fused with spirituality", when beings are immortal. This was already passed on, now One wanted to go to a harder level of Existence and experience Itself with notion of fear of death and uncertainty "of what it will be there after it". And Souls were left so to not discourage Itself and all incarnations of Itself by saying and showing that after death is "nothing, just a black screen", complete permanent "deletion".

I know that some Souls were deleted completely, because they were too unstable and dangerous for everything else, yet they can be restored, nothing can be "completely deleted". Souls are also meant to give all the received information during Their lives to One to analyze it and to experience this Joy of finally "resting after all the difficulties and hardships with which incarnations met during their lives". One too like to rejoice and to rest You know;)

But this does not mean, You no longer can't fuse Your Soul with Physical Body, You can, and Light Beings are there to prove it. You are always welcome to do everything You have on Your mind, unless it is damaging to everything else of course, so complete Freedom of actions and complete Free Will Choice it is:)

Small groups under Saudis are already at it, trying to instigate chaos. We already are having spoiled plots at Olympics! It is very good! Have a great positive feelings on Everything around the World!
Much Peace, Calm and Prosperity for Every Beautiful Being out there!

READER'S COMMENTS

"Thank you Good Friend.9/11 was my waking call.Even before 9/11 i disliked the pretention of the West (governements not peoples) to lead the world and his hyprocrisy.But when i discovered in 2006 that it was a false flag ,i thought if the US governement is capable of such an atrocity and can hide it with the help of the media what else hidden.And so i began journey to the rabbit hole."

~~

"I know for a long time thar russia and china are the alternative of the west but sometimes i get a little bit confused"

~~

February 13th, 2014

SOPHIA

A question from Sophia:

I understood that ONE has no preference or agenda and these words sound as if ONE does? Please elaborate further what your understanding is. This is not clear to me.

G/E
an answer...

It isn't called agenda, it isn't like something Creator of the Universe "desperately needs". It is just something One is doing "in It's free time" :)

Demiurge - the god of Humanity on the other hand desperately needs full control over Creation, "to make things tight" for Everyone that disobeys it.

One do not want to rule over Anyone, yet It can, It have all the power to rule over Universe and All Inhabitants of many Worlds, but One simply don't want and One don't have a "secret plot" like illuminati or demiurge are having. It is just experience, evolution, the process of growing up and One as a Father and Mother in one face is showing Everyone that We need to walk by Ourselves, like making first steps without help from Our parents or from outside (demiurge is imitating One very well here), One is also experiences Itself if You can say, putting "Itself in Our boots".

I will say one tip You All can use Good Friends, whenever You can't take something, when pain is big or it is simply too hard to make something, or to bear or simply too hard being here on this Planet, tell to One or to demiurge or to Light Followers "put Yourself in my place and feel how I feel, is this good for You,

how does it feel? Very hard, isn't it?" And Your hard situation will change! I've done this many times, it was helping me to ease hard situations and put One more to my own problem for It to experience Itself in my situation better. This behavior is also showing that We are incapable of doing more of what We can, but it is also showing that We need help from outside, when We really need it.

I will ask a question, do You need more information about sacred symbology, more pieces to puzzle of Humanity's history? I am asking because I don't want burden Anyone, it is up for You All to decide Good Friends, whether You need to know this or not.

As always with Much Compassion, Abundance, Respect and Love to Everyone!

From Sophia
I will say yes, as I know that readers are checking always for more information.

READER'S COMMENTS

"Hi Good Friend.Yes i want,i am very interested in knowing humanity's history"

~~

"Thank you Sophia.I like your posts.This comment section was a brillant idea"

~~

"ditto"

~~

G/E

Ok, the information You are about to know is used by illuminati order's and masons highest in command. It is Arcane Knowledge of this World. With the internet it is now became widely available. The secret esoteric knowledge.

First is a continuation of kabbalah - Tree of Life. The jewish Tree of Life shouldn't be underestimated, it is holding much wisdom and knowledge, accumulated since beginning of Humanity. I already mentioned it in previous messages and in last about numbers 9-11. The kabbalah is holding many different aspects of Humanity and it is the origin of astrology, numerology, tarot and playing cards and much of symbology.

Basing Your views on Tree of Life, You are able to predict Human behavior in Life, character, preferences, profession orientation if You know when and where He/She was born. The knowledge of planets, elements, numerology, metals/alchemy, occult magic were started all there. Here is a website of showing the basic knowledge of Tree of Life, here You can see the most common zodiac knowledge and finally reveal for Yourself where all of this starts and connects, zodiac sign, planet, number, abilities, character and symboloby, this website is from one of this World's most knowledgeable psychics.[312]

To view all the numbers, in the address change the numbers in "numerologynbr10", from 10 to 1 for example. Here are 10 numbers overall.[313]

---

[312] "Numerology: Kabbalistic Meanings of the Number 10." Numerology: Kabbalistic Meanings of the Number 10. N.p., n.d. Web. 13 July 2016. <http://www.voxxthepsychic.com/kabb-numerologynbr10.html>.

This is from gnostics, for more deeper understanding of Tree of Life. *(Note – this (109) pdf is no longer available. Sophia)*

The website from Voxx has a lot of knowledge, but I wanted only to show this information.

Now let's get back to 9-11 numbers. As I told, illuminati are jumping from 9 to 11 to avoid 10, which is Earth and as well Saturn, Earth signifies Kingdom, it is where We live, it is Life, Beauty of Life, Harmony and Saturn is a Judge, a Justice, Order, Perfection and they are skipping this number 10. Saturn's main number is 3, but along with it, it is having number 10 and direct connection to this World (Understanding).
Saturn also is having secret number - 13, the number of Death/Rebirth.

Now number 11 is considered a master number, it is a number of Aquarius and Uranus, overall - a number of a New Age, or a New World! This number belongs to invisible sphere, which is Da-at or Knowledge.

Illuminati were tricking and fooling People around the World, many were thinking 11 is the number of hell or satan, in actuality it is a very good number, a number of a New World. And because they were doing this, they were bringing themselves closer to their own "new world (order)", which they were dreaming about. And Humanity were supporting them and are still supporting by using numbers 9-11, for example police phone number 9-1-1.
But this does not mean they will achieve their goal, yet they were very close.

Let's get back to Da-at, the Knowledge. *This invisible sphere of Tree of Life is considered their most important sphere, as through it they can liberate themselves from Yahweh and become independent,* same goes to whole Humanity.

In new understanding Da-at is associated with newly discovered planet - Neptune and secretly it was always associated with Sirius or All Seeing

---

Eye, or Lucifer, or Eastern Star (inverted pentagram). Like I was mentioning this earlier, Sirius is their most adored star, egyptians priests were worshiping not the Sun, but this star and so does illuminati order/cabal. From it they are receiving "dark powers" using drawn on ground Eastern Star, (inverted pentagram).

This is a secret knowledge, esoteric, yet this is not the end of this.

The most highest - very few of illuminati know of a very secret star, which even don't have a name and this is where it connects to Humanity's history, this is the so called "Star of Ra" (we made a decision to call it this way). This is from where one of ET's civilization came to Earth and gave an ET leader to Humanity in those ancient times. Here are videos which pretty much explains all of this, look for them on this website, scroll down to see them.[314]

The Star of Ra don't have a name officially and is very dim, it is located South East of Pleiades in Taurus constellation. Yes and this region of the Sky is one of the most populated with sapient intelligent life. It is called the Silver Gates of the Sky, this is where many civilizations resides. We have Pleiadeans, Orions (2 civilizarion, one of which reptilians), Sirians (they are somewhat problematic, because they have a lot in common with reptilians) and this last civilization, we called Raians (from word Ra, they look like Pleiadeans and are good overall, but Pleiadeans are more evolved spiritually). Jupiter right now shines brightfully in Gemini, in that very same region of the Sky (and not without a reason of course).

Now to end with this subject I will mention first about Eastern Star and number 5. If You still have a question about why it is evil/sinister, this is a sinister sign and sinister number in Understanding of Subconsciousness here on Earth. In actuality it is not, the 5-pointed star is as natural as any other star in Universe, it is not bears evil in itself. You can see 5 pointed stars in nature, like the leafs on top of strawberries, sea star, our fingers on hands, antarctic South Pole has a five pointed magnetic wave structure around Antarctic.

[314] N.p., n.d. Web. <http://nexusilluminati.blogspot.com/2010/08/author-claims-to-identify-ufo-on-3000.html>.

Yet, here it is "an incomplete senseless star", which belongs to all negative attributes of Humanity. It is showing only 5 primal instincts of Humanity and it's main instinct "to survive", Humanity made it to be this way. This star is an official star of this World unfortunately. And inverted 5 pointed star is having the most sinister meaning, it is associated with destruction, pain, suffering, despair, disappointment, defeat, conflict/strife/war, worry, fear and it's planet is Mars - a god of war, the number is 5, metal - iron and color deep red (in our bodies blood is red because we have a lot of iron in our body). So because it was created to be so here on Earth, it is so and illuminati are using this for their evil ends and to get their "dark powers" from dark source.

In Worlds of Forces of One -
8-pointed star is being used. It is showing completeness, order, justice, harmony/coexistence/symbiosis, mutual understanding, evolved senses, wisdom and knowledge completeness. It is associated with many different colors, like gold, green, light blue, violet, white based on civilization that uses this star and their color preference.
Red color is considered an aggressive/conflict/disharmony color in most of the Universe. That is why we are always avoiding red color and the use of word Love with red color (like red heart).
We prefer to use Love with more harmonic colors like White, Green, Blue, Yellow. This is just to show that difference can be huge inside such a small not important at first glance symbols.

And last is about the Holy Trinity of Universe. As You know this Trinity was always present everywhere, in almost all religions on this World, and so does it is present in Universe as well and in Forces of One.
Past, Present and Future;
Creator, Grand Creator and Grand Grand Creator.

Three upper number of Tree of Life are 1, 2 and 3.

1 - The Crown (connection with Universe, Higher Self also connected with hidden Knowledge - Da-at and Keter - Crown are basically one and the same, yet separated) - Pluto (something that is farthest in this Solar System).
2 - Wisdom - Uranus
3 - Understanding - Saturn

These 3 are also having secret Trinity numbers 11, 12 and 13, 13 goes to Saturn,
11 goes to Neptune (Sirius) and Pluto
12 goes to Uranus, Uranus as You remember means the Sky or Universe around Gaia, so it is basically One Itself.

And there are Master numbers which are 11, 22 and 33. Also connected in the same manner, but more difficult to explain, the same principle of Trinity. Again
33 goes to Saturn (freemasonry)
22 goes to Uranus
and 11 is "the jumping point". The more deeper You will go into this, the more complication and confusion will arise, so We will stop here.

This is all a not easy to understand subject, as always believe in what You think is right, if You will have questions about anything ask us, our Connected Consciousness will find all the answers, but before You do, I would recommend first to ask Your Inner Self and One, it is the most wisest for You answer!

Also to World events, We are getting close to 14-16 february, on 15 through 18 there will be "cyber warfare drills" across U.S. and UK, Federal Reserve, Bank of America and IMF will be "drilling" in case if there will be hacker attack on their main servers (exactly this may take place "for real"),
as well air combat drills are now taking place on Eastern Coast and will be there until end of february.
On 14 february will be Valentine's Day celebration and it is deemed as a "day of preparation", but they can start this at this cycle to spoil this celebration of Love. Danger will be most present on 14-16 dates, but this does not mean if nothing will take place there then everything is ok. Danger will still be present until the end of Olympic games.
Also two iranian warships decided to travel to Atlantic near U.S. east coast "to show they do not fear", not a wise decision they made, but we will cover them.

So be on a watchout and meditate for World Peace, Stability, Mutual Love and Understanding and Harmony among All Things, we are hearing You do this, very strong wishfulness!

Also Thank You very much for Your beautiful words Good Friends! [315]

As always much Peace, Calm and Prosperity to Everyone!

Also I forgot to add this information which You will find interesting. As we know this winged disk and two headed bird is basically one and the same. The ET's spacecrafts which was seen by ancestors of Humanity, from which these symbols appeared.
They are being used by many right now, by Russia, Albania, Turkey, Germany, Iran, India, Freemasonry, Zoroastrianism and Hinduism and still being used in Egypt. This is a very ancient symbol of "UFO", the god in a boat and chariot of a "sun god" moving across the skies were also considered the very same winged concept. [316] [317]

This chariot concept is seen in many traditions and religions around the world, Helios, most prominent chariot god was seen in China, India, Russia, Scandinavia and ancient Germany.[318]

And this is analysis of nephilims - "half-angel half-human" skulls. So called "failed experiment" of demiurge.[319]

Much Peace and Love!

READER'S COMMENTS

---

[315] N.p., n.d. Web. <http://www.youtube.com/watch?v=UnZDifnxxhA>.

[316] "Zoroaster, Thus Spoke Zarathustra, Creation - Crystalinks." Zoroaster, Thus Spoke Zarathustra, Creation - Crystalinks. N.p., n.d. Web. 13 July 2016. <http://www.crystalinks.com/zmeta.html>.

[317] "Double Headed Eagle: Sumerian-Indian Connection." Tamil and Vedas. N.p., 18 Dec. 2011. Web. 13 July 2016. <http://tamilandvedas.wordpress.com/2011/12/18/double-headed-eagle-sumerian-indian-connection/>.

[318] "Solar Deity." Wikipedia. Wikimedia Foundation, n.d. Web. 13 July 2016. <http://en.wikipedia.org/wiki/Solar_deity>.

[319] "Initial DNA Analysis of Paracas Elongated Skull Released – with Incredible Results." Ancient Origins. N.p., n.d. Web. 13 July 2016. <http://www.ancient-origins.net/news-evolution-human-origins/initial-dna-analysis-paracas-elongated-skull-released-incredible>.

"GE,

what is " Angel",,,, this is in reference to nephilim, half angel-half human

Thank you"

~~

"Hi.I am always happy to know new information about humanity's story and ET civilisations.You mentioned one time that the nephilim were the second experiment to be destroyed,can you tell us about the first one,please.Your informations are very appreciated"

~~

"I really appreciate that you give us the opportunity to ask the GE guest questions on your blog, Sophia

Here is my question :

This afternoon i was watching the Olympic Games in Soochi on TV and to my surprise i noticed chemtrails in the sky above the place where the games are being held.

To my knowledge, Putin, quite some time ago, got rid of the Zionists and other undesirables (service-to-self beings). That means those that have a stranglehold over the west but not over Russia

So why are there chemtrails in Russia ? It's Russian territory and permission is needed for non-Russian aircraft to enter that territory !"

~~

"Hi, hoping all is well. I felt a shift the last few days. I feel something is a foot and we have reached a "milestone". Can you confirm or give us an update? I also feel a release has happened, there seems to be a lightness in the air (so to speak). Either something gave up, or gave in?"

~~

" http://www.youtube.com/watch?feature=player_embedded&v=kLMbePMdNOY

http://www.youtube.com/watch?v=mYg-oEmih3g

good things"

~~

February 15th, 2014

SOPHIA

This was just received from RXX, regarding free energy:
*** RXX lives in Tempe, Arizona. I have his number if anyone would like to reach him, to begin the project, or just connect, please send an email to: sophia@sophialove.org, and I will pass it on to you!

Dear Sophia:

I regret that I have to say that the information on the free video of the Hendershot Generator is a fraud, a bit of misdirection to prevent the actual success of its construction.

If you will click on WWW.resonantfractals.org[320] by Dave Lowrance, you will see just how difficult building a working prototype will and how little is the reward in actual energy is available.

Michael faraday in Dec 26, 1831 produced a very simple machine of one moving part called the one piece generator. It has a magnet glued to copper plate and a brush on the edge of the copper plate and another brush on the magnet. This arrangement will produce enough power to spin this pair of components with a whole lòt of power left over.

Bruce DePalma in 1978 produced a generator using this principle calling it The N-Machine. It produced over 100 killowatts and he was told by the government he could not sell any. He died without setting up manufacturing.

It is referring the this update from February 1st:

(-- "It appears that it will take about two to three hours to make the Hendershot

---

[320] N.p., n.d. Web. <http://www.resonantfractals.org/>.

power unit. It also appears that the steps are fairly simple. I believe I will organize a co-op of young out of work ambitious people to make these and share with each other the proceeds. It could spread very quickly across the planet. I think a good price would be $1,000.00 each. If I organize a production line and introduce automation gradually and lower the price as we progress, we can expand even more rapidly. Since Hendershot is long dead and his patent has expired, we can do it.")

February 24th, 2014

G/E

Everything went out without huge incidents, drills are ceasing, and with them danger still present, unfortunately Ukraine now is in trouble, it is on a brink of a civil war, and possible separation of this country may take place. These protests are fueled again with the help of CIA's money and U.S. government is already trying to put their own people within government of Ukraine (people that will go along with their plan that is). Here is intercepted phone call about Ukraine.[321]

And some sort of apology.[322]

Actually, we never heard apology, EU is working for U.S. government on NWO agenda, so they are keeping this quiet. This riot was unplanned for CIA's event, but whenever there is war, rumors of war, riots they are going there to take everything in their hands and under their control. Always looking for profits. Now protesters are receiving food, clothes, body armor and money. Everyone is receiving money for just being there. And overall methods again as You can see - destructive.

We were seeing problem with Ukraine since collapse of USSR, there is no unity among these people, mostly among younger generations and many are very easy to be manipulated by the lies of false democracy and false freedom unfortunately.. Many gave themselves to small satanic and nazis cults in Ukraine. Also government was very "passive", it weren't helping people, and poverty, unemployment, dissatisfaction rates were only

---

[321] N.p., n.d. Web. <http://www.youtube.com/watch?v=sSx8yLOHSUs>.

[322] YouTube. YouTube, n.d. Web. 13 July 2016. <http://www.youtube.com/watch?v=WpGKgMvf9Ok>.

increasing.

This collapse wasn't surprise for us, as everything what was happening in that country was heading for a collapse. Now situation is that, that is east and south-east of Ukraine wish to preserve the Ukraine as it was (or even to unite with Russia) and western Ukraine want to be separated and join the European Union. Western Ukraine is predominant with People that are easy manipulated through mainstream media and as well majority are west oriented.

Ukraine is also a point of Balance, their flag, coat of arms of Ukraine contains same trident as in Iran's flag and as well it is connected with One. On Ukraine's flag it signifies holy Trinity and descending holy spirit and falcon. On Iran's flag this symbol in the center is stylized word for Allah and above and below it written "Allah Akbar" 11 times each. But what makes these two points of Balance different is that Iran is fully devoted to "God" and Ukraine is having separate views on God.

So, long before this now had happened we knew that Ukraine will head to a breaking point, and knew that this point of Balance will be preserved after all of this. The points of Balance must only not be attacked by destroyers, which in this case are western bloc countries, or it will lead to a wider conflict. All of this is happening as it is supposed to like we are told, although it could have been without violence. And if Light Followers would intervene then this would not be happening at all.

Question from blog comments:

"This afternoon i was watching the Olympic Games in Soochi on TV and to my surprise i noticed chemtrails in the sky above the place where the games are being held.

To my knowledge, Putin, quite some time ago, got rid of the Zionists and other undesirables (service-to-self beings). That means those that have a stranglehold over the west but not over Russia

So why are there chemtrails in Russia ? It's Russian territory and permission is *needed for non-Russian aircraft to enter that territory !"*

G/E

I can say for sure that the ones You saw were not chemtrails Good Friend. When planes are going to high altitude they are leaving traces of vapor from fuel, called contrail.[323] [324]

This is happening in most cases, but we know the truth. U.S. and UK, along with chinese governments are abusing this and are using such "normal trails" to cover chemical biological agents within such trails. But as we know they are not doing this "on occasion", this is happening on pretty rare cases. In these times these chemtrailing had reduced significantly, thanks to efforts of Light Followers.

Questions from blog comments:

"GE,
what is " Angel",,,, this is in reference to nephilim, half angel-half human"

"Hi.I am always happy to know new information about humanity's story and ET civilisations.You mentioned one time that the nephilim were the second experiment to be destroyed,can you tell us about the first one,please.Your informations are very appreciated"

G/E

Good Friends angel is just to add to word, these what these People were called by ancient People of the Earth. ETs were considered angels and gods in that time.

Yes, nephilims were destroyed by the great flood, great flood parallels can be found between many religions, religion by itself is a collection of history, science, evolution and understanding of Creation.[325]

---

[323] "Chemtrail Conspiracy Theory." Wikipedia. Wikimedia Foundation, n.d. Web. 13 July 2016. <http://en.wikipedia.org/wiki/Chemtrail_conspiracy_theory>.

[324] http://www.wonderopolis.org/wonder/why-do-airplanes-leave-tracks-in-the-sky/

[325] N.p., n.d. Web. <http://en.wikipedia.org/wiki/Flood_myth>.

This is the flood "myth" of Hinduism.[326]

Modification number 4 which was very unstable as new genom was used, mutations, birth mutilations took place within these People, successful nephilims were having such big oval skulls as You can see there and some nephilims were two times bigger than normal People.

These nephilims spread around the World, they were meant to bring wisdom, prosperity and unity to Humanity, on the contrary, they made a decision to become like "gods" and "overthrow them if it will be necessary", like it is happening now in western Ukraine. Although it was already considered to remove them lately, creators still gave the possibility for nephilims to change Humanity and show that they are successful experiment, but they didn't show it as You understand. For that they were judged by creators. This all took place within some 1400 cycles, we don't know precise dates yet.

Modification number 2 are indo european tribe and modification number 3 are asian tribe. Modification number 1 was proto tribe, it was the first modification to see how this mix of ingredients of this planet will fare with light original genom of optimal light-order oriented civilization of Galactic Federation of Light.

Before it was implemented the guess was that it will fail, and will have to be destroyed. And it happened so. When second modification was made, this first already was grappling everything under control and this new type of future Humanity, that came started to interact with the first one, the first were physically strong and didn't wanted their females to interact with new males. They didn't wanted to mix. But Light Followers wanted them to mix. Hate arose in (the) mind of this first modification. And started overall bullying of indo european tribe,

You can still see why the africans are not being loved by europeans, as they still bear leftover of that original "bullying" genome. Yet today's africans are not the original proto modification, they are mixed type with

[326] "Manu (Hinduism)." Wikipedia. Wikimedia Foundation, n.d. Web. 13 July 2016.
<http://en.wikipedia.org/wiki/Manu_%28Hinduism%29>.

indo european. Indians are too have this leftover, but in less quantities, as India was separated from Africa. There is no one left alive from first modification.

All of this was happening for thousands of cycles, much more than with nephilims case. And Light Followers decided to stop this first modification as it was becoming more and more unstable, it started completely eradicating the second modification.

So Light Followers used the forces of nature to stop them, by this time India was already removed from Africa and 3rd modification was made. They were never interfering directly with their high tech weaponry, but were using the control of nature elements to make these destruction. Asteroids, earthquakes, volcanoes, hurricanes (*they call this "non-intervention"*) reduced the numbers, until there was completely no one left from first original modification, as we know there were more of them than nephilims, counted in millions.

Always believe in what You think is right, this information is very tactical and direct information of Followers of Light's manipulations of this experiment. So always use Your own discernment.

Right now pressure is high around the World and in financial World, Ukraine is on a brink of civil war, Syria is in civil war, Somali is in civil war, South China Sea has small pressure of conflict and Venezuela protests as well are being fueled by CIA as Venezuela is world 1st oil producing country. Financial world of anti-Creation is holding itself, yet it is on a brink of downfall, and world reset, revaluation of currencies may happen any time soon, when spring will come. Many bankers are dying from "suicides", yet we know these are not suicides. Only "a spark" is needed for the next step of evolution. Good News are waiting ahead! By meditating and praying We may reduce the damage and casualties! Mutual Understanding, Mutual Harmony, Mutual Love, Mutual Prosperity are the keys in these meditations/praying. On our part we will make sure that damage in Ukraine and other World parts will be reduced and wider conflicts prevented.

I wanted also to ask, was the information about kabbalah helpful for You Good Friends? Did You understand it?

Much Peace, Love and Prosperity to Everyone!

READER'S COMMENTS

"Hi.Numerology is not my thing but i liked the part about the Raians.Is modification number 1 the Neanderthaliens?"

~~

"Hi GE, the information about the kabbalah was interesting, but quite secretive and complex. If we studied this subject extensively, could we influence our lives for the better using it's principles ?

I am focused more on tangible changes right now - many sources are saying the the moment of justice is very close now ???

Also, the website http://nomoresleeping.wordpress.com/ has some interesting predictions in it. Are the 13 crystal skulls he refers to ("Ancient Masters, Crystal Skulls" on Feb 21 2014) the same as the ancient stones you have spoken about ?"

~~

Note from Sophia ~

This conversation is updated as it continues under the tab ~~~ <u>*"Newest message + comments"*</u>

~~At this point the conversation was held on the blog only. The comments and conversations that ensued are found in one place.

FEBRUARY 25TH, 2014

SOPHIA

I have a question about this part:
"coat of arms of Ukraine contains same trident as in Iran's flag and as well it is connected with One."

Can you explain what "connected with One" means in this reference?

Much love,

G/E

I explained it after this phrase. Both symbols are about God, whenever word "God" is mentioned in any form it is always connected with One. And demiurge is always there to intercept such word and representation by this word.

I've found this video as "time come for me to see it", the one I was seeing for a very long time before it was created. It was created in 2012, another big deja vu moment of my life/experience on this World, it is called "I, pet goat 2", for You knowledge if You would like to see first part, there wasn't 1st part.[327]

If You haven't seen it yet, how You understand this video is up to You, this is a direct gift from One to Humanity, and Your own understanding is most important on this one video. The images of this video are showing our current system revealed in it's true form, there is a lot of symbolism. I will only say from myself about main plot of it - it is not about Jesus as a different being as Savior, it is about "Your inner Jesus", Your inner Higher Self, being locked into a cave of illusion, sleeping and seeing terrible nightmares and in the end finally driven out of this illusory cave/cage, awaken from deep terrible dream.

Here is author's explanation of this video from Alex Jones interview, starting at 7:26.[328]

Many think Alex Jones is disinformer, well sometimes he may be, but most of the time he is not. He is a Very Good Human Being, he is tired like all the rest from this corruption and want this to gone, he was having connection with CIA, and still is talking with former CIA agents that retired, because they couldn't take everything CIA doing no more. Alex Jones played a big part in exposing of illuminati order and still is up to end with them all

---

[327] N.p., n.d. Web. <https://www.youtube.com/watch?v=Id6nCa_OTEM>.
[328] Naturalhealthschool. "I, Pet Goat II Symbolism Explained by Filmaker Louis Lefebvre Part 1 of 2." YouTube. YouTube, 19 July 2012. Web. 13 July 2016. <http://www.youtube.com/watch?v=HE02vkq_XdI>.

together.

Also Thank You very much for great videos about mutual aid Good Friend, this gives a lot of inspiration and showing the Very Best Side of Humanity!

And yes, proto modification was known as neanderthals and some other very first people. There were many variations of that type, but the process and genome with which this group of apes were modified was one, that is why this is all connected into one modification. Same situation is with 2, 3 and 4.

I will add few more videos about alternative energy possibilities, all easiest I tested myself, they are working. Ones from Good Friend Troy are not easy to make and require more resources and efforts.

These are the ones I use, they use magnetic force as wind energy. The easiest to make, taking fan from computer and put magnets on every rotary blade, like it is said here, for better output use very strong neodymium magnets, it can lit up light bulbs and You can use these to power Your lamps for example, it will never stop to spin. Well it will stop to spin, but only after some 200-300 cycles (based on their initial natural charge), when magnetic charge will be reduced so We will have a plenty of time and energy, plus magnets can be recharged, this makes them "infinite" energy source. If You imagine this 40x times bigger with automatic magnetic recharge, magnet to magnet interchangeable system, this can lit up cities and charge huge accumulators with constant influx of energy. Plus the charge can be increased by charging negative ions into magnetic sub generator. Before You is the design which can power everything You can imagine. I personally love it. :) [329]

Creating system when it is connected to accumulator, the energy of accumulator is enough to power lamp for a very long time, as I don't use lamp all the time, the energy output is more than enough all together, I also

---

[329] Wasabysajado. "Free Energy Magnet Motor Fan Used as Free Energy Generator "Free Energy" Light Bulb." YouTube. YouTube, 02 Jan. 2014. Web. 13 July 2016.
<http://www.youtube.com/watch?v=jiAhiu6UqXQ>.

use same accumulator to power other things in home.

How to make, remember +,- poles, it will stick and stop if you will mistaken polarity, also use CPU fans as they spin without "jerking", the more magnets You put into this, the more speed so energy will be there, You also can use magnets from refrigerator toy attachments.[330]

This is Troy Reed, the Good Gentleman You saw in video about electric car, You can see the design on this website.[331]

This is full video about him and his working technology, there are many designs in this video, look also in video description for links, I will put these links here.[332] [333] *(Note – (129) is no longer available, in fact, in July 2016, this Is the message you'll get if you attempt to access it:* The item is not available due to issues with the item's content.
If you would like to report this problem as an error report, you may do so here. *This is not a graphic website, it is archive.org and the link was to details re: free energy! – Sophia)*

Another great design.[334]

Materials are here, this is made with 3D printer, but it need modification, different magnets' placing and more copper wires.[335]

This is the Keshe variation's test.[336]

Try out many variations, again the possibilities are countless! Also Thank You very much Good Friend Roy for all Your help, hendershot devices working, I tested the one in a 2hours video guide. You can add more copper to bring out more output in this type of design.

---

[330] Deirones. "Free Energy Step by Step." YouTube. YouTube, 04 June 2012. Web. 13 July 2016. <http://www.youtube.com/watch?v=WooCJ3mye54>

[331] "PesWiki.com." Directory:Surge Motor Technology by Troy Reed. N.p., n.d. Web. 13 July 2016. <http://peswiki.com/index.php/Directory:Surge_Motor_Technology_by_Troy_Reed>.

[332] YouTube. YouTube, n.d. Web. 13 July 2016. <http://www.youtube.com/watch?v=RT8ObmQG0OU>.

[333] http://archive.org/details/Free-Energy-Facts

[334] https://www.youtube.com/watch?v=hDsNqYx4Peg

[335] N.p., n.d. Web. <http://laserhacker.com/?p=214>.

[336] Way2tall65. "Keshe Plasma Generator ~ Here Is The Future ~ Infinite Energy." YouTube. YouTube, 21 Dec. 2012. Web. 13 July 2016. <http://www.youtube.com/watch?v=kkB2g7ai2bs>.

This will give You Inspiration, Bravery and Courage, have no fear in Your Heart! We All know that many Good things awaits Us, fear is coming from not understanding what comes next, what is around the corner. Avoid it, always understand everything around You, always do Your best to Love Everything and see the Light in Future!

Let Future be Perfect![337]

This is a beautiful video of our Sun.[338]

And another song of a Rebirth.[339]

Much World Peace, Universal Calmness and Unconditional Love to Everyone!

READER'S COMMENT

"Hi Good Friend,it took me some time to figure out how to build a magnet rotary device with the skills and tools at my disposal but i have some idea now.I will first do some test with a bike wheel.Thank you for the tips and as you said it is not so complicated"

~~

February 26th, 2014

G/E

The Olympics are over and it was a grand event overall. Few terror acts were prevented.
In the west unfortunately is massive anti-russian propaganda as Russia is the only powerful force that is able to resist NWO. Here is meant militarily as illuminati are being held down right now only through military. Humanity overall is not awakened enough to completely rise up against illuminati in one voice, lesser lies are still working on majority unfortunately.

---

[337] N.p., n.d. Web. <http://www.youtube.com/watch?v=YoOl8LjxMFs>.

[338] NASAexplorer. "NASA | SDO: Year 4." YouTube. YouTube, 11 Feb. 2014. Web. 13 July 2016. <http://www.youtube.com/watch?v=NAg4qXsk99c>.

[339] TrailerMusicWorldl. "Audiomachine - Ice Of Phoenix (Epic Powerful Uplifting)." YouTube. YouTube, 11 Nov. 2013. Web. 13 July 2016. <http://www.youtube.com/watch?v=XUeQ0Ew_Wh0>.

China is as well is a powerful military force, but it is unfortunately "marked by satan", so if we would say war against U.S. would break, they would lose.. As China was programmed to be like it, communism is direct creation of illuminati order. And red marxist (mars) star is the "mark of the beast for annihilation" if we can call it like that. Current chinese system can be easily bribed as freedoms of People are largely suppressed, as it was done in USSR. But overall China is getting rid of such set of Consciousness.

The rise of Russia was unexpected turn for illuminati order, as One gave the power to Humanity first to hold down evil of this World and then with possibility to completely stop it in their tracks. And right now this is happening, by Humanity's choice, Russia is actively working in stopping, exposing and putting them to Justice. We are also working on same manner.

By attacking Ukraine directly this whole russian nation was attacked and now even those that weren't believing in illuminati are now believing that they do exist, as they were warned exactly about such turn of events.

And because western media was spreading biased information about olympics, it only increased awareness of more People and even more russians, which completely were disgusted with lies coming out of western media about olympics, as They were seeing completely different picture.

Western media in Russia was adored before these olympics. So it is another spike in Humanity's Awakening, the olympics in Russia brought much joy to everyone that loves sport, and olympics were called best so far!

Also many People around the World were able to see the real russians through these olympics, and not the ones that were portrayed by western media - still being oppressive and communist.

Our focus is now on Ukraine, as it is important point. I will only say that all is going to the best! It is pretty soon to say what is prepared there in

Ukraine, for now know that everything is ok! We don't want to reveal what is planned for illuminati to not spoil anything, but they are at their downfall should they gave in.

Also to answer to Your question Good Friend:
"the information about the kabbalah was interesting, but quite secretive and complex. If we studied this subject extensively, could we influence our lives for the better using it's principles ?

I am focused more on tangible changes right now - many sources are saying the the moment of justice is very close now ???

Also, the website http://nomoresleeping.wordpress.com/ has some interesting predictions in it. Are the 13 crystal skulls he refers to ("Ancient Masters, Crystal Skulls" on Feb 21 2014) the same as the ancient stones you have spoken about ?"

Yes, the information about kabbalah can be very useful. It is giving out the knowledge about future of a Person, by knowing where and when He/She was born. What profession suits more this Individual, for example engineer, but still it is always important to follow by Inner Voice's call, physical body may suit more to being an engineer, but spiritual body may be more into artistic impression. Then it can show what are characteristics of this Person, what are weaknesses/strong sides of physical body, all this could be known before person would be born, if place and time would be known of course. It is occult and secret knowledge, which was given from generation to generation and it holds the keys to many philosophical matters and questions. Illuminati were holding this locked in secret to keep Humanity in the darkness, this knowledge is accumulated from ancient times and it is having a truly great potential, one of important knowledges of Humanity.

The ancient stones, I think I forgot about them, can You recall what stones have I meant?
There are many of them:) I know of skulls, they are indeed made by ETs and there are 13, 12 are found as I know, but we also know that all 13 are found already, yet all are disconnected, together they form an energy grid,

which completely reveal all Your Souls life experiences to You, the gift of Followers of Light. By prophecy when all 13 will be connected the New World will be born! So let's connect them, shall we?:) Much Peace and Love to Everyone!

READER'S COMMENTS

"Sorry, GE, I meant ancient machines, which you talked about on Jan 20 2014 - not ancient stones."

~~

"There has been a lot of talk about the "Eastern alliance" comprising of countries supporting the BRICS nations. And also that "Eastern alliance" is the force that will stop the Illuminati/ Western Cabal. Is there a force inside China and/or above the current communist leadership that is part of the Eastern alliance? Or is it something different?"

~~

"Hi GE, I had posted a little while back that I had felt a shift or something to a release happening. I was wondering if you can confirm that there was "something" that or had occurred? And just recently was hit with either a wave of energy the other day that literally had me fall asleep on the couch by 8:30 (local time) and I slept for 10 hrs, which is not normal for me. I felt very "heavy" all day prior to that.

Also, I make Orgonite devices and I was wondering if you know about them? I make them with other stones known to heal or help with EMF and negative energy. Would love to know your thoughts about them?

Again, thank you :))"

~~

"P.S. I am so happy the Olympics were a success and that the world had a view inside of Russia. With issues about the LGBT community being supported to views of what western media broken by their depiction of Russia. The tip of the iceberg is now shown to be attached to a much greater chunk of ice that is slowly starting to rise...and we are ready to see what that is about to reveal!
Namaste"

~~

"My understanding that there are cutures in the galaxy that the going about their business day to day regard for each other on the entire planet is the same as the feeling of intimacy experienced here on a couples wedding day

http://www.rumormillnews.com/cgi-bin/forum.cgi?read=300965 "

~~

MARCH 11TH, 2014

G/E

Good Day Sophia!

As You can feel energy pressure is at a peak. This is the fall of illuminati with a crack like Humanity wanted!

Illuminati order wish to give out everything left they still got, they decided "now or never". For that their Judgment will be maximal. They started massive anti russian propaganda to tarnish the image of russians and olympics and president Vladimir Putin. Right now Russia is protecting Crimea and People of this land are deciding Their own future, yet all western main stream media points this as "dirty tactic of Russian People". No one died in Crimea so far from violence thanks to "self defense forces" (they are russians, but prefer to be named so, this is their will). CIA made a dirty tactic, a crime against Humanity by shooting protesters using trained snipers in Ukraine. This is a repeated situation, same thing happened in Egypt not long ago and was happening in Iraq.

Right now in Ukraine took power same WW2 ideologies: nazism and fascism. The pressure and despair in western Ukraine reached it's climax. And now minority's true face is shown. As You remember WW2 was as well instigated by illuminati order and nazism and zionism and communism are their creations which bound "to destroy".

The new ukrainian government representatives made a deal with U.S. and EU governments and NATO, that they need to provoke People of Russia to attack them or make it so, so it will look like People of Russia "are attacking". Ukraine send a lot of military equipment near Crimea border.

The missing plane is also a provocation, as I was told People there died, and

They were intentionally killed (though I hope this wouldn't be real). Now blaming will go to Iran. Here was played illuminati card called "combined disasters". Paralympics games are taking place in Sochi and these two disasters (U.S. government's invasion to Ukraine and destruction of plane) took place during olympics.

Climax of all this will be reached on blood moon on 15 April and will be present at high until Solar eclipse at April 29. They still wish to make world war 3, but they will fail and We All know that!

This whole conflict can be prevented, and casualties reduced, meditate for World Peace, Mutual Understanding and Harmony Among All Things!

This is to answer to some questions I saw   ---
"Are the 13 crystal skulls he refers to ("Ancient Masters, Crystal Skulls" on Feb 21 2014) the same as the ancient stones you have spoken about ?

Sorry, GE, I meant ancient machines, which you talked about on Jan 20 2014 - not ancient stones."

Ancient Masters are not Ancient Machines. Masters are the ones that were living alongside Humanity in ancient times, Ancient Machines never intervening in non Forces of One civilizations and they never call themselves as Masters and never like when someone is calling them so, they prefer to be called simply Friends or Guardians.

"There has been a lot of talk about the "Eastern alliance" comprising of countries supporting the BRICS nations. And also that "Eastern alliance" is the force that will stop the Illuminati/ Western Cabal. Is there a force inside China and/or above the current communist leadership that is part of the Eastern alliance? Or is it something different?"

Inside China, most of this system supports the new world without war, violence, hatred and depopulation. Chinese People are very Spiritual, even highly greedy People have Respect and Honor which is lacked within indo european greedy People. The whole People's Republic of China will be ready to go along with making this World a more beautiful and harmonious place! Same side took

People of Russia, People of India, People of Brazil, People of Iran, People of Iraq, People of Syria, People of Lebanon (shia muslim People).

I want also to point out a main difference between shia and sunni as We touched this subject. Shia People are being hated because they accept the changes within Quran and don't accept the rule of califs (kings of the Earth). They also believe that knowledge passes to next generations and teaching of Mohammed can be changed.

Sunnis believe that this is not possible, only original teaching is the most true "holy". And everything will be decided on "end days", until then "nothing can be changed". This is fundamentalism and illuminati order prefer sunni as these People are "not allowed to evolve" and They can be easily controlled, much like fundamentalist christians and judaeans.

Numbers of shia believers are slightly lower than sunni believers and in Syria, Iraq and Lebanon are committed crimes against shia and christian People on daily basis..

"Hi GE, I had posted a little while back that I had felt a shift or something to a release happening. I was wondering if you can confirm that there was "something" that or had occurred? And just recently was hit with either a wave of energy the other day that literally had me fall asleep on the couch by 8:30 (local time) and I slept for 10 hrs, which is not normal for me. I felt very "heavy" all day prior to that.

Also, I make Orgonite devices and I was wondering if you know about them? I make them with other stones known to heal or help with EMF and negative energy. Would love to know your thoughts about them?

P.S. I am so happy the Olympics were a success and that the world had a view inside of Russia. With issues about the LGBT community being supported to views of what western media broken by their depiction of Russia. The tip of the iceberg is now shown to be attached to a much greater chunk of ice that is slowly starting to rise...and we are ready to see what that is about to reveal! Namaste"

I answered to energy shift question Good Friend! Many things happened and illuminati are pushing their "last stand". Though You can see even media cannot hold lies afloat.

Orgonite are very excellent healing method, You can mix different variations and change the healing effect, very much like crystal/stone healing.

Indeed, People of the World at first bought the lie about Russia invading Ukraine, now Majority saw that this was a big lie, Humanity is almost woke up, only few time is necessary to complete this wakefulness. Illuminati knows this and are doing everything fast to prevent this, We can stop them, Unite Your abilities and meditate!

I wanted to add this video, whenever You see an oval, know that it can be used intentionally (in west most of the times) or unintentionally (unknowingly). This is a good symbol, yet illuminati order again distorted its meaning.[340]

Remember We Together and Individually can prevent many bad things from happening, the Power of One is in Your Hands! We are One and One are We! Much Peace, Calm and Prosperity to Everyone!

SOPHIA

Hi,

Thank you! I just saw this - [341]

Any comments?

G/E

The ship You saw there was indeed Galactic Federation of Light, Sirian made. It is their favor to make oval and cigar-shaped design.

---

[340] N.p., n.d. Web. <https://www.youtube.com/watch?v=XLIrEYLdnH8>.
[341] "AMERICAN KABUKI: Updated 3/25/2014: Curious Pieces of Data...." AMERICAN KABUKI: Updated 3/25/2014: Curious Pieces of Data.... N.p., n.d. Web. 13 July 2016.
<http://americankabuki.blogspot.com/2014/03/curious-pieces-of-data.html#more>.

Orionians with reptilians prefer triangularity, both Sirians and Orionians have good relations and both can lie without shame unfortunately. Reptilians are more sneaky, but Sirians are following in their path.

The ones from Sirius B are more problematic than from Sirius A. Sirius C is quiet at least. illuminati order was in close contact with both of them and still we see that both Sirians and Orionians wish this experiment to continue.

Ashtar (Asta) as You remember are the watchers of Humanity's experiment. Trusting them is not a very good thing to do as they are the same if not worse than illuminati order. This is what I can tell on their role right now.

Pleiadeans and Arcturians are quiet right now.

I hope this will aid You in understanding! Much Love!

READER'S COMMENTS

"Thank you GE and Sophia! With the Pleidians and other benevolent "ETs", is it true our planet earth is surrounded by ships and that we are under watchful eyes to what will transpire here? Forgive me if this was asked or answered before. As well, I just saw this today and would like your thoughts on the historical data that was given: http://2012portal.blogspot.ca/2014/03/quarantine-earth-endgame.html"

~~

"In light of the remarks of GE; that some ET visitors may not have our best interests at heart, are there going to be mentors among the visitors that will protect us from our trusting naiv'ete from exploiters or do we accumulate some lumps as a lesson and use our discernment to minimize these?"

~~

MARCH 25TH, 2014

G/E

I will also answer on two questions, from Good Friends!

"Thank you GE and Sophia! With the Pleiadians and other benevolent "ETs", is it true our planet earth is surrounded by ships and that we are under watchful eyes to what will transpire here? Forgive me if this was asked or

answered before. As well, I just saw this today and would like your thoughts on the historical data that was given: http://2012portal.blogspot.ca/2014/03/quarantine-earth-endgame.html"

No need to forgive yourself Good Friend! I'm for my instance am ready to support and aid Everyone! Whenever someone don't understands something I'm ready to give some understanding on the subject.

This Planet is surrounded by ships of different civilizations and different sorts and different technological level. These ships in the meantime are surrounded by Forces of One ships. So overall there are thousands of ships, of different size and role. If necessary this number can be increased to billions in mere seconds. Forces of One have such resources.

There is one very big (size more than this planet) interstellar spherical ship, which is counted like planet on it's own. They are protecting this World and Humanity and waiting when the time for "first contact" and "Ascension" will be right. The Cobra's explanation of history is up for You to decide whether it is true or false. Your own discernment is most important as for all of my messages! We know different history and we also know that Cobra is not being told everything unfortunately.

"In light of the remarks of GE; that some ET visitors may not have our best interests at heart, are there going to be mentors among the visitors that will protect us from our trusting naiv'ete from exploiters or do we accumulate some lumps as a lesson and use our discernment to minimize these?"

The best way is always to listen to Your Higher Inner Self and be connected with One through Sun. This way Your thoughts are always correct. Being dependent on someone to save or mentor You was always not the best solution to many problems. Many abused this naive behavior of Humanity and used this for their own gains.

For example evangelical christians and muslims were dependent on salvation for the last 2000 cycles and many many died without this coming true.. Illuminati order like when People believe so blindly. People can be used and abused much easily in such situation. But when You are not dependent on such things/thoughts You may able to do much more as Your hidden potential can surpass even Your most wildest dreams:)

This is something religions were removing from teachings and this is one thing that illuminati are afraid of most. When Humanity will realize that it can do much more than what we are told We are capable to do, then Humanity will realize that illuminati are the same as All the rest. They are afraid of Humanity realizing it, realizing that all is One and equal.
So good advice is to always listen to Your Higher Inner Self! This is where One, Creator of All resides.

Also great job Good Friend Djon! I'm happy that You understood what the principle of this technology is!

To increase the pace of arrival of Moment of Justice You can help this World by spreading knowledge about ET's presence and knowledge about magnetic, water, air, heat, solar energy technologies!

Much Peace, Calm and Prosperity!

READER'S COMMENTS

"Hi.Thank you Good Friend.I have put magnets on a wheel but i can't make it turn a another magnet.I have also looked for magnets' positioning on the free-energy-devices.com/chapter1 ebook but i did not find it.Next i will try with an electromagnet and magnetshielding.If you have some good tips and advices ,they are welcome.Have a nice day"

~~

"Hi.By the way P.Kelly's ebook is very interresting,i found a lot of nice devices.What do think about this device:http://www.youtube.com/watch?v=G01Hd4ptpmY . It's a bedini/adams mix generator.It seems easy to build, maybe the electronic is more complicated.I also like the Charles Flynn's Magnet Motor"

~~

here ya go DXXX,,GE you might like this
http://hopegirl2012.files.wordpress.com/2014/03/qeg-user-manual-3-25-14.pdf

This is from hopegirl and her workings
Ref;
http://americankabuki.blogspot.com/2014/03/qeg-open-sourced.html "

~~

Thank you M."

~~

"your welcome DXXX,
good luck,,also you'll find a church group showing a working model on YouTube if i can find it I'll send it to you,(it's kind of noisy) but it was a while ago, be tough for me to track it down.

when the GCR goes through I'll have the time and the money myself, hopefully we'll still be acquainted and we can share"

~~

"No problem M.,when i have a workable device i will share my knowledje with everybody"

~~

"Hi M. and D.! Here is the link to the church group Michael was speaking of.
http://www.witts.ws/
Their name is WITTS Ministries. I think Hope Girl was even working with them - or visa versa, lol!"

~~

"Thank you S.."

~~

"Yes, Thank you s."

~~

MARCH 28TH, 2014

SOPHIA

I requested further information about the missing flight. What follows is the response.

G/E

I was told that this plane was downed intentionally.. It was downed using

pulse of electromagnetic waves, which disabled electronics in this plane.. These people's loss of life was made to play out the card "combined disasters", it is connected with tridents. I can back this by saying that the moment this plane disappeared I felt that many People "left this World", They called to me "to go with Them", I politely refused and said that I need to finish my order of One, the Creator. In that moment I knew something bad happened and then I saw the news about this plane. I had similar feeling during the hurricane which took lives of 6000 People.[342]

I felt a lot of Souls leaving this World at once and it sounded to me like "come with Us", same like in this situation with the plane, I share my feelings only with other GEs and my relatives, but I guess I can say this here..

Though I hope this information is not correct and they are fine and will meet with relatives.

Also the connection of tridents, Hell's Kitchen explosion in New York, second name of that's Hell's Kitchen restaurant is "Neptune" - the god with trident, also look for "Malaysia Airlines" logo trident with tricolor, Ukraine's Coat of Arms, Maserati logo (Maserati commercial during super bowl was telling about secret plot) and "Prepare" words during super bowl.

Yet all of their plans are falling apart, Grand Creator Sage Star A is intentionally suppressing all the thoughts about destruction and war, fall of illuminati is in progress and all is made by One.

Here is one beautiful music and message to inspire from Good Friend Lindsey![343]

Much Peace and Love to You!

---

[342] "Typhoon Haiyan." Wikipedia. Wikimedia Foundation, n.d. Web. 13 July 2016. <http://en.wikipedia.org/wiki/Typhoon_Haiyan>.

[343] Lindseystomp. "Transcendence (Orchestral)- Lindsey Stirling." YouTube. YouTube, 14 Mar. 2014. Web. 13 July 2016. <https://www.youtube.com/watch?v=DHdkRvEzW84>.

SOPHIA

And another bit of information...

G/E

Considering the missing flight as I warned You this was a plot, here, Good Friend Dahboo7 found this information, it is all also connected with illuminati plan to start a ww3.[344]

We know though, that they will fail. Meditate to reduce casualties and damage which they still wish to do, we can completely eliminate all destruction and loss of life, it is in Our United Power - Something to Believe In![345]

Much Peace and Love to You!

READER'S COMMENT

"My heart and thoughts go out to those who are missing or passed on, as well as to the families who must endure not knowing. I pray they know the truth soon...ALL of IT!"

~~

MARCH 31ST, 2014

G/E

Here is one more musical composition which You can share with Our Good Friends, this one composition is not new, it is old and comes from One, I am accustomed to these tones, they are being used by Spiritually Evolved and One shares these tones with Beings around the Universe which are sufficiently Spiritually evolved, yet on this World it was made not long ago[346]

it is a road to future of this World, listening to it, You can hear what the future will be. Very Bright!

[344] N.p., n.d. Web. <https://www.youtube.com/watch?v=wWYANJzVJvY>.
[345] EpicHeavenMusic. "Epic Score - Something To Believe In (Epic Action & Adventure Vol.12, 2012)." YouTube. YouTube, 16 Dec. 2012. Web. 13 July 2016. <https://www.youtube.com/watch?v=9FlllyeS6Cw>.
[346] N.p., n.d. Web. <https://www.youtube.com/watch?v=8dNdSFp36xQ>.

This is to Good Friends that are building technologies of Energy. Good Friend Djon, You can use battery to power the wheel, then when it will start spinning, just use the magnet so the spin will continue. In some designs initial charge is needed (I made a way around this by using accumulator battery). Making completely initial charge-free design not works always. Also the power of "prime magnet" (the one that you hold or is in a holder, that spins the wheel) can be increased by additional charge (putting battery to it, better the rechargeable one, which You can recharge later on), I for my instance use neodymium magnets, I set up magnets in a way that north polarity faces up on wheels and I am making a move with enlarged neodymium magnet making opposition of north to north. I also put them in a way that south polarity from magnets on wheel don't influence the enlarged magnet's north polarity, so they wouldn't stuck to each other. As well I'm using AA rechargeable battery, the energy output of this battery is always surpassed by the amount of given electric current from magnetic wheel, so battery is always "in recharge mode". So it is a closed accumulator to generator - generator to accumulator system which I use all the time to avoid the lack of accumulated energy sources like non-rechargeable batteries. Also in a video of magnet fan You saw, there is a trick, they use 9v battery to power the wheel, so it can be called cheating, yet this principle of "magnetic wind" is working.

Also I know Bedini generator, very great design along with the one Good Friend Hope Girl made (first introduced by Nikola Tesla, now recreated by several inventors including Hope Girl's Team!) Johnson generator along with Hendershot non movable generator works as well. There were more, much more, yet all were suppressed as You know this. Yes making them will not always be "a success" as I warned this is "the spice of inventing", first model may be flawed, as it is just a proto (only the first of it's kind), yet if You will not give up and continue on, eventually You will have what You want!:)

Thank You very much Good Friends for everything You do and for simply Be'ing! Yet We still haven't finished this experiment, and illuminati order is aggressive than ever before now, We know that Everything will be transformed in This World for Good! Much Good is coming!
Many Good Wishes to Everyone!

READER'S COMMENTS

"Thank you very much to You ,Good Friend, for everything you do for me and everyone"

~~

"Any update on global/spiritual/legal/"event"/matrix/red pill/everything/etc progress?"

~~

"Can you tell us what you know about the possibility of someone/something altering our timelines specifically to delay the event/moment of justice? Here is the long, long article: http://www.transients.info/2014/04/the-stretching-of-time-and-imminent.html Thanks so much!"

~~

"K. m.,
that was excellent,,,project looking glass could also not see past a certain point,,,I believe something about temporary divergent / simultaneous timelines,"

~~

APRIL 3ᴿᴰ, 2014

G/E

Indicium

Good Day Sophia and Everyone!

As we are approaching important date of april 15, which will be a 1st out of 4 lunar eclipse or "blood moon".[347]

I need to inform Everyone about possibilities. We will have an opposition of Mars on april 8th and on april 14 and april 15 Mars will be closest to Earth.[348]

where You know, forever it was considered that Mars is the "planet of strife/conflicts/wars". As well Mars and Moon will be very close to each other on 14th april. Along with "blood moon" first of four, this creates a big possibility for a breakout of big conflicts. We have a big major pressure on 4 locations in the

---

[347] N.p., n.d. Web. <http://www.skyandtelescope.com/observing/highlights/237963491.html>.
[348] ScienceAtNASA. "ScienceCasts: The Opposition of Mars." YouTube. YouTube, 27 Mar. 2014. Web. 13 July 2016. <https://www.youtube.com/watch?v=xngUpUyyT70>.

World, where such conflicts may break out.

1. Most important is Syria, illuminati order wishes to invade this country and recently they and Turkish government were planning to make a false flag attack on Turkey and blame Syria for this to justify the invasion, You also remember that Turkey is the member of U.S. NATO military alliance which makes it a dangerous twist. Turkey is arming the "rebels" which are mercenaries and extremists to "change regime" in Syria. Turkey is very closely associated themselves with cabal.

2. Then we have the pressure in North Korea, where North Korea wishes to make "The Killshot" prediction to come true, that is to launch nuclear missile to South Korea.
3. The pressure in Ukraine, where extreme russophobic nationalists wish to invade Russia and are asking for military aid from U.S., EU and NATO, right now they are quiet, yet this may turn differently when Mars and Moon will be united.
4. And last is still the same plot to make a false flag on eastern coast of U.S. Unfortunately, they still don't wish to give up and surrender, on the opposite, illuminati are making more aggression and provocation. Recently U.S. military was mobilized for a possible nuclear false flag on eastern coast which can be delivered whether "by plane" or "by ship" like they said. The missing flight plays it's role here, duplicate in Israel can be used for this plot, so it will be a time which We All need to look for!

This big pressure for conflicts will end when Moon will reach opposite side of the Earth and make annular Solar eclipse on cycle - april 29th. This will mark the end of "times of uncertainty" as indeed these times are very unpredictable and everything can happen from april 14 until april 29, because strife and conflicts are closely associated with destruction thus with primal force of chaos and chaos as You All know is opposite to Order and is very unpredictable in it's nature.

Anyway, the illuminati order is falling apart and these are the end times for illuminati/cabal and because they are making even more blatant resistance and challenge to Creation on the opposite of simply giving up, I will say that they are playing with fire and they can have a situation where all their bloodline will not be spared, they brought maximal Justice on themselves.. Now we heard that neither Light Followers, neither Forces of One will spare them on "normal conditions", yet if intervention would follow, they will be given one more chance to give up and cease confrontation and if they refuse, then, there wouldn't be any salvation for them..

This is all about current very tight situation, I advice Everyone to meditate and prevent all of conflicts from taking place, You know where You need to put Energy for Peace and Harmony. Let there be Peace and Mutual Understanding between Everyone!

Much Peace, Calm and Prosperity to Everyone!

READER'S COMMENTS

"Hi.I Can't meditate but i will stay calm and wait for the outcome"

~~

"my oldest son is getting married on 4-14 and it is my youngest son's birthday, and we will be out of the country. And their father is flying to Washington DC on 4-15 the day after the wedding...just makes the hair on the back of my neck rise, knowing all this about the Blood Moon and Grand Cross, GE. I will stay as positive and loving as I can, but any suggestions from you would be welcome for me and the 40 people going to the wedding."

~~

Dear Friend,

Thank you so much for the information you provided us with in these trying end times. It is such a relief to now anticipate an end to this interminable story !

It was very helpful to me that you gave us the dates when certain conditions will be in place for example when Mars would be where and its relationship with other planets or heavenly bodies at that particular point/location.

I think it would be helpful to many to read the following text : "Mars,Eris and the Perfect Storm or How the Illuminati Are Poised to Strike and Why They Will Fail" (Part 2).T This text can be found at the OracleReport.com or through the link below.

This text gives some more in depth information regarding your latest text. I would like to read your comments/reactions to this particular piece :)

Be Well !

*http://static.squarespace.com/static/530f3fd3e4b00ea7829010d2/t/532d1dd7e4b078ca8
03a9534/1395465687615/Mars%20Eris%20and%20the%20Perfect%20Storm.pdf*

~~

"I would say this was done;
http://www.transients.info/2014/04/the-stretching-of-time-and-imminent.html
so that the confluence you speak could be taken advantage of"

~~

*"At first, M., it was very confusing reading the text at oraclereport.com over and over
again, this because after each reading new vistas seemed to open up before me.*

*And now this article by Laron...it makes a lot of sense what he describes. It feels right
the more i think about it :)*

Many thanks for this, i truly appreciated this lengthy but thought provoking read!

~~

*"I understand at first i did the same thing,,something in how the sight works,,
what I ended up figuring out is just push the submit then hit your back button,then go
back to the article click on comments again and my entry is always there,,,you just have
to go completely out of the page after you submit then come back in and it"ll be
there,,,,,,,*

*and you are most very welcome,,,
I find a lot of love here,,,,,think it might have something to do with sophia attracting the
particular people here,, I am glad you are here"*

~~

"Thanks so much, M..

*I have copied your suggestions into my logbook for when problem might reoccur. It
makes sense what you write because indeed i did leave the site...and when i came back
there seemed to be no more problem.*

*Many years ago I used to read Pleiadian channelings from someone whose name i
forgot...she suddenly stopped channeling and i stopped visiting the website she posted
on....it was also called opalescent...?but without the nine.*

M. was that you who recently made a remark on Andrew Bartzis? It was someone who commented here."

~~

Hey everyone, There seems to be a glitch in the website Software that happens when any comments are made. I will report it to them. It is sort of a pain but M., you figured it out the same way I did!
Bless you guys.
Love and light.

Sophia

~~

"My apologizes for the tardiness of my reply,
I don't believe it was me who spoke of mr. bartzis, I will not "say" anything
about him,,I will "convey",, be wary, trust your-self,,,,,,which kinda sucks cause our ' self ' can be hijacked without our knowing, suspecting maybe, but knowing seems to elude,,,,,in my case anyway,,,,

the best lie is half a truth ect. ect.
my opinion, is a sophia like way where love and laughter is meeted to those who wish for us to participate in the "battle of good and evil" ect.ect.
now for me , that's not to say one or the other couldn't require a good healthy punch in the nose if boundary's require it, but then again I'm not a true master as yet :>
just be wary, I stay away from him now,he has hurt some people I know, although i do not know him personally .....
I apologize if I Offend"

~~

"No offense taken, M.. i appreciate your honesty. And to be truthful i was starting to feel some doubts...sometimes a vague feeling of unease...could not substantiate it. :(

The magnet for me is information..knowledge, more insight...it is difficult to stop sometimes..:(

We live in incredible times. Thanks for your words of caution!"

~~

APRIL 5TH, 2014

SOPHIA

Did you see this?[349]

Thanks,

G/E

Indicium means data or information, it is an information to aid.

I saw many different theories about the plane, I hope that People are ok and can return back to their relatives, but right now I can't say for sure, I can only hope, that feeling which I told before, it told that They are gone.. I don't like to think about that and will hope that my senses are false and they will be safe and sound.

I need also to say about the preparation of Mother Earth and Father Sun to aid Humanity. Mother Earth along with Sun are preparing to erupt the most powerful volcano on Earth - Yellowstone subterranean volcano. Such eruption will halt all flights and stop industrial part of western and north western parts of U.S. And Father Sun is preparing to unleash the most powerful of all observed super solar flare varying from X-40 to X-70. This will overcharge the energy grid and burn out all transformers within territory where will be day on moment of collision of solar energy particles, completely turning off all electricity within that territory. The flare will be directed at United States, highly charged energy particles will reach Earth when in U.S. will be daylight.

Both situations will reduce casualties of People, Animals and Plants to almost zero. The main intent here will be to prevent the outbreak of conflict and challenge to Creation by U.S. government and illuminati order. Both of these situations can be completely avoided, volcano will completely die out and Sun won't unleash super flare or will unleash it non earth directed if conflicts will be avoided.

First event to happen will be Yellowstone, it will happen after april 14 - Moon and Mars unity if conflict would break out, it may also cause powerful earthquake on San Andreas fault or close to it, but only if U.S.

[349] N.p., n.d. Web. <http://i-uv.com/freelance-journalist-hijacked-flight-370-passenger-sent-photo-from-hidden-iphone-tracing-back-to-secret-u-s-military-base-diego-garcia/>.

government/illuminati will proceed with it's global domination agenda and create a big conflict by false pretexts/false flags or blatantly making direct aggression against Someone in the World. If Yellowstone will not stop or halt the conflict, Sun will unleash the super flare, it will vary in average from x-40 to x-70 based on situation and it's importance. If one flare would not be enough, Sun will unleash second with same or more power. And if that will not be enough, Followers of Light will be asked to politely intervene and stop the conflict, if they won't act then Forces of One would intervene and stop them.

This is an information which we received not long ago and indeed Yellowstone volcano is giving signs of possible eruption to come, as well in California were quite strong quakes recently, about the Sun, I was receiving messages that "in case of no-exit Sun-Creator will aid this World". And remember this is just a possibility, this all can be avoided, meditate for Peace in all World, for Mutual Understanding among All things, for Unconditional Love among All living and non-living things!

APRIL 7TH, 2014

G/E

Tomorrow will be the opposition of Mars, so we are beginning preparations to oversee and "control" the situation energetically and physically. I will answer questions about "time stretch", this is indeed important occurring.

This is about time stretch postponing Awakening and Rebirth. Indeed We noticed that at least one cycle (year) was altered, because all of what is happening now should have happened 1 cycle before, the 16 december of 2013 was the Shift of the Ages, when All the People of the Earth waited for this Shift on 2012 on december 21st.

The illuminati order knew about the real date and they "celebrated" in South Africa making their own wishes and it looks like they manipulated the calendar by adding cycle 0 to it long ago using their ancestors I suppose and demiurge made some adjustments in energy system of Mother Earth.

Yet the moment of choice was set correctly, decision was made and no longer can be broken by anything, it is sealed by One. And as You can see they were making "a choice" as a wish one cycle later on 2013. But We were able to make Our own wish there:)

I also forgot to add Grand Cross alignment, another rare event that is going to take place almost in between lunar and solar eclipse. Thank You Good Friend dj for reminding Everyone about it! I found great website explaining in details about what it is, it is also from a Lightworker.[350]

Yet to Everyone's knowledge, there was a shift back almost directly on ONE zodiacal sign in the skies. So this means you no longer Libra, but Virgo, or no longer Pisces, but Aquarius.

In the website is told about old zodiac system where dates were written 2 thousand cycles ago and now need to be updated due to Grand Spin (movement of Solar System around the Sage Star A). But astrology adapted itself to suit the changes of individual Human Beings only, not counting the Grand Spin, so now if We will read about Ourselves knowing our sign, we will find only half-truth, the other half lies in our real sign of birth which goes one sign back (this is how we are changing era from Pisces to Aquarius, jumping one sign back), so shortly saying due to all of this We All have two zodiacal signs.

Also there is a 13th sign - Ophiuchus - the serpent bearer. This sign is very special, and occult societies always include it in their calculations. People that were born from november 30 until december 17 are Ophiuchus, these People are having a lot of "duality" within Them, because this sign, this object of the sky is very close to Sage Star A and Actual location of demiurge and false heaven. So within these People is a constant battle between Good and Evil and True and False. I personally observed these People and can tell that this is 100% true. For example Britney Spears is also Ophiuchus and within Her is the battle which can be clearly seen.

There is said that planets will be in 13 degrees angle within constellations: Uranus-Aries, Jupiter-Cancer, Mars-Libra and Pluto-Capricorn. This would be true 2000 cycles ago, yet today put one sign back and Grand Cross is

[350] N.p., n.d. Web. <http://www.universallifetools.com/2014/03/cardinal-grand-cross-april-2014/>.

Uranus-Pisces, Jupiter-Gemini, Mars-Virgo and Pluto-Sagittarius. There isn't completely 13 degrees on all the planets due to this fact, yet planets form a Perfect Cross on 23 to 24, because planets were unaffected due to Grand Spin only Cosmo was.

This website of NASA gives dates that are set correctly by their own observations.[351]

If You wouldn't believe NASA than look at the sky after sunset today and tomorrow, nearby Moon to the right You will be able to see one very bright star and above it two other bright stars, that is not star but Jupiter and above are the stars of Gemini - Castor and Pollux (Gemini's heads). So Jupiter is in the Gemini, in website is told that Jupiter is in the Cancer, Cancer goes after Gemini as You know, so this is a direct proof for Everyone that there was a shift almost precisely on one zodiacal sign.

And Grand Cross is indeed a great moment, which We All can use to meditate to cease this experiment. On these dates like it is said on website, this is a great time for overall Planet's Awakening, so this is the moment that can be used!

Also I will tell to You Good Friend that there mustn't happen anything right on 14-15 april dates. These are just the signs of possibility. The most probable for conflicts will be dates between Grand Cross and Lunar Eclipse, that are from 16 until 22 april. Washington DC for now would be unaffected like I was told. Also I wish Your Son and His Wife a Very Happy Life, Marriage is a Great Celebration. And to Youngest Son a fulfillment of His wishes!:)

Meditate/Pray for Peace among All, Harmony and Coexistence on this Whole Planet, Mutual Love and Understanding between All People and Animals and Plants and Big Happiness to Everyone![352]

I will also add this musical composition, very beautiful and true words

---

[351] "NASA Space Place :: Home :: NASA Space Place." NASA Space Place :: Home :: NASA Space Place. N.p., n.d. Web. 13 July 2016. <http://spaceplace.nasa.gov/starfinder3/en/>.
[352] EpicJennyni20. "Ivan Torrent - La Danse De La Lune (Beautiful Orchestral)." YouTube. YouTube, 27 Mar. 2014. Web. 13 July 2016. <https://www.youtube.com/watch?v=ADfllLfs5Bk>.

about the Circle of Life.[353]

READER'S COMMENTS

"Thank you GE for those kind and loving words for my sons, the loves of my life. And the Circle of Life continues with my love to you."

~~

"Hi Sophia and GE :)) In the last few weeks, I have noted the many of the "new age" sites, and channelling seem to continue on about 'whispering' and joining or performing meditation with 'do it like this' instructions. One night, my thoughts relayed to me that any format in which to follow is considered ritualistic, which is not what was intended for us. Would it be truthful or real to say that any followed process or instructions to help bring peace and harmony is somewhat, then, counter productive? It just seems more of the same follow what I say scenario, rather than following ones heart...?"

~~

"good one"

~~

"Great insight NLNL, I have been thinking the same thing. Telling me what to do and when to do it just doesn't seem right to me."

~~

"Thanks M. and dj - I look forward to their reply. It's always good to see others insights! :))"

~~

APRIL 21ST, 2014

G/E

Good Day Sophia and Everyone! Happy Easter to You - the Celebration of Birth and Rebirth/Reincarnation! This is not a christian-only Celebration, it was celebrated since ancient times, this is a time when children are being "made". This is when Great Circle - Circle of Life begins!

---

[353] Frenky121212. "Elton John - Circle Of Life (High Quality)." YouTube. YouTube, 25 Oct. 2008. Web. 13 July 2016. <https://www.youtube.com/watch?v=o8ZnCT14nRc>.

Sunday was an Easter, it was an influx of a lot of great feelings during this date! Notice that Easter was both catholic and orthodox, this is quite rare when two churches have aligned Easter on one date, plus Blood Moon was aligned with one of the jewish tradition's feasts.[354]

As You can see, much important for jewish nation events happened on lunar eclipse's tetrads when they aligned with feasts.
Something to add to "coincidences". As You remember there are no coincidences, everything what is happening is happening because of something, as there is always a reason for it and there is always connection between things that are called "coincidences". Everything is interconnected.

This is all a part of this grand Cosmic Intervention which We are experiencing at the moment. Big changes (physical) should start happening now on Grand Cross, or after partial Solar Eclipse. We should also meditate, so that changes wouldn't be "aggressive", which will create conflicts.

Nothing to say about the news, except that all is the same for now. Situation is very tense, illuminati order are waiting for a possibility to start a big war, they are pushing hard on Ukraine as You can see, U.S. government and CIA are ordering Ukraine to suppress People of east Ukraine with army and radically aligned individuals. Something that is very disturbing. Illuminati's destiny is written and they are collapsing, yet what troubles us, is that they are stubborn in neverending greed/lust for power and other People's suffering..

In the coming Earth cycles, meditate/pray for Universal Harmony/Peace on Earth and Your united wish of ending experiment sooner-better! We are already having a form-up of Grand-Cross, and Lightworkers from Cobra's blog are going to meditate and make wishes on 21st april, so this is a great possibility to bring in great transformation, avoiding any and all conflicts!

Much Peace, Calm and Prosperity to Everyone!

READER'S COMMENTS

---

[354] This was a png file and it seems to be an error. I could not locate it.

"perhaps this might be off a little, but it shows the dichotomy of the present time , our ability to choose, the opportunity presented with the blood moon, the Chinese symbol for danger and opportunity is the same,, our astounding capacity to choose rightly

I humbly submit for your perusal,,

http://news.distractify.com/people/complex-humans/?v=1

may you be well"

~~

"Hello, Sophia and our G.E. Friend.

Here's a question for our G.E. Friend: What is your take on the information given in this video? I recently viewed it and was just curious about your thoughts.

Thank-you!"

Here's the video... =]

http://youtu.be/c69vZyE74Zg

~~

APRIL 23RD, 2014

G/E

Good Day Good Friends!

Yes, I know that many are saying about different moves and mantras, giving out instructions on how to perform it "correctly". These are all indeed rituals. Rituals shouldn't be underestimated, their power is great, since ancient times priests of different "deities" and "gods" were performing rituals to heal or to foretell the future and as well change the outcome of future through choices/wishes or wishful thinking. Rituals are a moves that are fusing physicality with spirituality, that is physical world with ethereal spiritual world. Such fusion is making a big change within physical reality and as well in spiritual. You know of ancient "relics" and "holy water", these physical items are charged with energy through power of sounds/words and great Energy of wishful thinking. "Holy Water" indeed has a great effect on a body, when it is charged. The more charge there, the

more the effect is being felt. Rituals though can be used in both ways, in Good and evil. Illuminati and Freemasons are performing dark rituals with sacrifices to meet their dark evil ends, such rituals are resulting in curses and prevention of this World changing in Harmonious Way. With these rituals they are concealing reality and creating an illusion, as well bringing themselves success in finances, geopolitics and so on.

You pointed out correctly, be guided by Your Higher Inner Self, if You don not feel that "instructions" on rituals are not resonating with You, You are always free to make ritual in Your own way, how You feel would be right or not make ritual at all.

Thank You very much Good Friend M. for providing link to dichotomy of the present time. Not all photos are pleasant, yet there was one photo which is in relation to this question of rituals, "100,000 monks in prayer for a better world", Meditation and Prayer are as well rituals. And how You do it, what intent do You have during performing such rituals is the most important, not the way how You do it. Yet there are many effects which can be achieved, through positioning of objects and different moves of Your body, as well making a different sounds with different frequencies and combinations (prayer and mantras). So as always Your own discernment is most important!

Good Friend R., very great video You presented, there is a lot told there about hidden symbology and all of this is connected with the same demiurge and this whole experiment. Not everything there may be truth, but as always, Your own discernment is most important, believe in what You think is right. I liked the part at 12:02 mark. This is a part where is told about vector and "7" symbol is as well represents an oval and "eye of satan" - antigod/anticreation, there was a video I presented previously which was made by former freemason, he exposed to You and Everyone the significance of oval in freemasonry. You never thought why White House is having exactly "oval office" and not round or squared? These symbols are present not only on space agencies' logos, but as well on many many trademarks and brands, which we are buying and using everyday, be as well notified, that when You are buying product with oval, there may be chemicals that are damaging to Your body, all chemicals that goes after in "E" classification are dangerous and most importantly all that goes after E621 are untested on human organism and can modify the DNA, they are used only in industry, but some products like potato chips, or many sweet products, like chocolate are having them, it is always wise to check the ingredients before buying what Yo are going to eat. Basically when You are buying a product with hidden symbology like eye, pentagram or oval, You are "agreeing that they are going to poison you and that you are supporting their system and their god".

Remember, right now We are in the middle of Grand Cross, it is yet not fully formed, this Grand Cross may be a very big event for this Planet, this depends almost solely on Humanity, We GEs are working on preserving stability and preventing all conflicts. Aid this World how You can, meditation and wishful thinking is more that enough! Magnetic rotation technologies are spreading slowly, but surely. Remember You can aid this World and Humanity by spreading the knowledge of this technology, Thank You Good Friend Michael for sharing link to Good Friend Hope Girl, She shared the schematics for constructing her own design based on Tesla's records, which is working very well and gives a great energy charge!

Much Peace, Calm and Prosperity to Everyone!

READER'S COMMENTS

"Many thanks, G.E. Friend!"

~~

"Many thanks and appreciation to you and all who are helping move this planet and humanity to peace and expansion! Namaste :))"

~~

"you are most welcome GE

you most appreciated"

~~

"I can confirm that GE is very appreciated"

~~

"Could you comment on this article?
http://thoughtcomputing.org/wp-content/uploads/2014/04/The-Fifth-Interview-of-Dr.-Neruda.pdf

Has the Human Portal been activated yet?
Thanks very much!"

~~

http://kauilapele.wordpress.com/2014/04/27/qeg-morocco-aouchtam-has-resonance/

~~

"Here is a good article that explains what is behind the ukraine's crisis and russia's stance :
http://cosmicconvergence.org/?p=6951
I am sure Good Friend will like it"

~~

"Dear G.E.
In regard to the Youtube video "The Lie NASA Told - The Imminent Demise of the NWO" (which Remi provided the link for), you say that "not everything may be the truth". Are you able to give any hint about which aspects are not true ? In particular, do you agree with the last 10 minutes of the video, where the author says that the "dome will lift, and all redeemable humans will be lifted into arcs, while the non-redeemable ones will go into the pot and then the pit, etc etc" ?"

~~

MAY 1ST, 2014

G/E

Good Day Sophia and Everyone!

The Grand Cross was a successful event and times of uncertainties ended with Solar Eclipse resulting all of this cosmological combination in a Peaceful Configuration rather than in conflictual. A lot of Good Energies were released and Many Individuals around the World are now able to see the whole picture much more detailed and better.

United States government's system is collapsing, Illuminati order is in disarray. Right now situation is such that no major moves are seen from

the Illuminati/cabal. Yet they still are not surrendering although they see, that this is the end game for them. Some members soon will going to surrender as we see. Last chance will be given to them.

About the article and question from Good Friend Karma Machine, here is another side of this same story, from "Annunaki" perspective (Annunaki are same archons/reptilians in our knowledge). As we know this wasn't gold that they needed, but it was "valuable value" (which was mistranslated for gold) and that is Humans. They needed "perfect" Humans (they liked to call "product").

Annunaki times for us are known as times of modification of nephilims. Human Portal like You are saying is Grand Portal written there. You are remembering that demiurge placed Particle of Light in Humanity and this opening of Path to Soul or finding Soul is actually the finding of this origin - "the Particle of Light" in our knowledge. Since ancient times this opening was done gradually and now Humanity is very close to it, we even can say that yes, it is opened!

Here I will add this beautiful music here, it transmits the current feelings of the World![355]

And this is just to to add Tranquility.[356]

Much Peace, Calm and Prosperity to Everyone!

READER'S COMMENTS

"Thank you so kindly, GE. You are generous with your time. Much appreciated!"

~~

"So today, I looked up at the sky and felt for the first time in years that the clouds were natural! The sky was so blue and clear! No chem trails were seen for over 3 days now and somehow their effects can no longer hold up anymore. Yesterday, during a brief walk, I heard (well, like a thought) that all the unbalanced energies (as neg or pos is still

[355] EpicJennyni20. "Epic Dramatic Cinematic - Once Upon a Forest (Eric Neveux - Sir Moabi)." YouTube. YouTube, 10 Apr. 2014. Web. 13 July 2016. <https://www.youtube.com/watch?v=M5LAs2MFU8c>.
[356] EpicJennyni20. "Ivan Torrent - Underskin (Beautiful Orchestral)." YouTube. YouTube, 28 Apr. 2014. Web. 13 July 2016. <https://www.youtube.com/watch?v=fYdajbMTDGE>.

just energy) was in the final stages of release - that the time for suppression is at an end. At first I thought I was just making it up, maybe my thoughts were just running amok. But then I looked up at the sky...and right in the middle of a thick of clouds was a perfect upside down triangle, with the gorgeous blue sky peering through! As I could say was Thank You! :))"

~~

"been wanting to write for two or three days here ,,but ,,,it's really no great shakes,,(the subject that is) still haven't done it,,,just don't know why I havent (curiosity)

Greetings GE

Sophia,
your writings are becoming more pronounced, is this a general enrrgy we are feeling?"

~~

"Sophia,
I am as guarded as your partner,

about your latest posting,

Is this the diamurge we/she is speaking too?

I am only now a few paragraphs into the posting (your latest on AM) but this (aside from a few " others") IS my perception /feeling /awareness"

~~

"Hi M.,

Idk, but things have changed and are ramping up, in all ways. There is a sureness of truth and an impatience for what is not... We are discovering the wisdom we hold within...perhaps this is what awakening is... a gradual process of knowing. If you are referring to the "Poser" article, what you see is exactly what happened... No claims as to the agenda, it just seemed that it was not just for me, and so it was shared.

Sophia"

Note: Reference, I believe is to this article, click here.

~~

"What I read seemed heart felt, yet I feel there is another layer of "look the other way" while I do something over here ... If power of worship this being is honest enough to say won't change, then expect unbalanced duality and conflict to remain. I for one bid that "adieu"."

~~

"I agree with you. This is a slick and brilliant being. It is our choice and intent that will end this and nothing else.

Sophia"

~~

"Well said! I am glad you gave in and allowed the message to flow. This insight is better than none. I feel more empowered than ever just knowing what you scribed here. A heartfelt virtual hug and blessings to you Sophia. Your doing great work ... Don't stop! If you need help, know you have a plethora of support, just ask! :))"

~~

MAY 14TH UPDATE

G/E

Good Day Sophia and Everyone!

Illuminati order/cabal are making their last push, what is happening now was expected by us one solar cycle before, exactly on spring. They are in their last moments, so they are throwing everything on it, like we were waiting them to do. Unfortunately they don't want to surrender, so this brings in grave consequences for them. Yellowstone volcano is awakening, Mother Earth is ready to aid any moment now. Yet it will go off only if everything will go to extreme level, this is a situation when conflicting situations are fueling volcano, the more there is the more possible it will explode. Yet illuminati are still being given a chance to stop before it would be too late for them.

Ukrainian People right now are suffering on a large scale, People are dying there every earth cycle (day), People's Freedoms are suppressed by force, army is being used against russian-speaking People, Odessa arson was instigated by ukrainian puppet government (I can share the link to truth about what happened there, but it contains a very disturbing images and

truth), most of this information is being suppressed by ukrainian government and all western MSM and U.S. government is supporting this along with European Union's government and evil NATO union (all are cabal).

Now I can reveal, that all of this was prepared to completely expose illuminati (first part of it, true face of USA/EU/NATO governments), this is a trap that was set for them for All People of the World to see them, what they really represent (not Democracy and People, but autocracy and themselves only), unfortunately there was no other way, this was the best we on ground could do. If we would have more powers and abilities we would be able to prevent bloodshed and suffering. But we weren't able to prevent bloodshed, we knew that People will be suppressed and all of this would take place. We were keeping this secret to not spoil this trap, and now it is too late for ukrainian government under U.S. government to back down and show a "good face". They still can stop it and change their punishment, although knowing them, we doubt they will do it.

Thank You Good Friends for providing links, a great news to know that QEG was made by more People! As well it is true, what is written in article about Russia, Thank You Good Friend! Also very Great Experience Good Friend NLNL, Much Appreciated for share of Your Feelings! Indeed We are very close now to Completion and Moment of Justice!

A very great collection of Spiritually-Oriented music, all bears a message to Your Higher Inner-Self, all contain a strong message from One! This music will aid You while this World is still under small dark veil:

"Journey To The Deep"[357]

"Future Perfect"[358]

---

[357] EpicHeavenMusic. "Confidential Music - Journey To The Deep (John Hanson - Epic Choral Drama)." YouTube. YouTube, 13 Dec. 2013. Web. 13 July 2016. <https://www.youtube.com/watch?v=mSUaObvj_1I>.

[358] XHGNxKevin. "Timesplitters: Future Perfect- Scotland the Brave." YouTube. YouTube, 11 June 2008. Web. 13 July 2016. <https://www.youtube.com/watch?v=YoOl8LjxMFs>.

"Sun - SDO Imagery"[359]

"Ice of Phoenix" (another song for Rebirth)[360]

"Transcendence"[361]

"Something To Believe In"[362]

"Angel" (Emotions of Future)[363]

"La Danse de la Lune"[364]

"Circle of Life"[365]

"Once Upon a Forest" [366]

"Underskin" (Refers to Soul)[367]

"Sublimation"[368]

"The Power of Will"[369]

[359] NASAexplorer. "NASA | SDO: Year 4." YouTube. YouTube, 11 Feb. 2014. Web. 13 July 2016. <https://www.youtube.com/watch?v=NAg4qXsk99c>.

[360] TrailerMusicWorldI. "Audiomachine - Ice Of Phoenix (Epic Powerful Uplifting)." YouTube. YouTube, 11 Nov. 2013. Web. 13 July 2016. <https://www.youtube.com/watch?v=XUeQ0Ew_Wh0>.

[361] Lindseystomp. "Transcendence (Orchestral)- Lindsey Stirling." YouTube. YouTube, 14 Mar. 2014. Web. 13 July 2016. <https://www.youtube.com/watch?v=DHdkRvEzW84>.

[362] EpicHeavenMusic. "Epic Score - Something To Believe In (Epic Action & Adventure Vol.12, 2012)." YouTube. YouTube, 16 Dec. 2012. Web. 13 July 2016. <https://www.youtube.com/watch?v=9FlllyeS6Cw>.

[363] MusicKaira1. "Top Emotional Music of All Times - Angel (R. Armando Morabito Ft. Julie Elven)." YouTube. YouTube, 14 Mar. 2014. Web. 13 July 2016. <https://www.youtube.com/watch?v=8dNdSFp36xQ>.

[364] EpicJennyni20. "Ivan Torrent - La Danse De La Lune (Beautiful Orchestral)." YouTube. YouTube, 27 Mar. 2014. Web. 13 July 2016. <https://www.youtube.com/watch?v=ADfIlLfs5Bk>.

[365] Frenky121212. "Elton John - Circle Of Life (High Quality)." YouTube. YouTube, 25 Oct. 2008. Web. 13 July 2016. <https://www.youtube.com/watch?v=o8ZnCT14nRc>.

[366] EpicJennyni20. "Epic Dramatic Cinematic - Once Upon a Forest (Eric Neveux - Sir Moabi)." YouTube. YouTube, 10 Apr. 2014. Web. 13 July 2016. <https://www.youtube.com/watch?v=M5LAs2MFU8c>.

[367] EpicJennyni20. "Ivan Torrent - Underskin (Beautiful Orchestral)." YouTube. YouTube, 28 Apr. 2014. Web. 13 July 2016. <https://www.youtube.com/watch?v=fYdajbMTDGE>.

[368] EpicJennyni20. "Cavendish Trailers - Sublimation (Beautiful Orchestral)." YouTube. YouTube, 19 Mar. 2014. Web. 13 July 2016. <https://www.youtube.com/watch?v=7L3RxSxJbZI>.

[369] EpicHeavenMusic. "Ivan Torrent - The Power of Will (New Mix 2013 - Epic Orchestral)." YouTube.

<u>"Lumina" (means Light)</u>[370]

<u>"Crystalline"</u>[371]

Much Peace, Calm and Prosperity to Everyone!

READER'S COMMENTS

"Hi. You are welcome Good Friend."

~~

"During a Reiki session this week, a visitor from another realm named Sam-u-el (his emphasis, not mine) told us that there would be "beings" coming to the US and UK that would really rock our world. Do you have any information about this? Thanks so much!"

~~

MAY 17TH, 2014

SOPHIA

This is an answer to a question from the comments that may not have been shared previously:

G/E

This from Good Friend C.

"Dear G.E.
In regard to the Youtube video "<u>The Lie NASA Told - The Imminent Demise of the NWO</u>" (which Remi provided the link for), you say that "not everything may be the truth".
Are you able to give any hint about which aspects are not true ? In particular, do you agree with the last 10 minutes of the video, where the author says that the "dome will lift, and all redeemable humans will be lifted

YouTube, 30 Dec. 2013. Web. 13 July 2016. <https://www.youtube.com/watch?v=yWnzQv2jEm4>.
[370] BrunuhVille. "Fantasy Music - Lumina." YouTube. YouTube, 29 Mar. 2014. Web. 13 July 2016. <https://www.youtube.com/watch?v=wcBosWg1UfA>.
[371] EpicJennyni20. "Ivan Torrent - Crystalline (Beautiful Orchestral)." YouTube. YouTube, 08 May 2014. Web. 13 July 2016. <https://www.youtube.com/watch?v=Guo7gR0XyaU>.

into arcs, while the non-redeemable ones will go into the pot and then the pit, etc etc" ?"

"There is a lot which we don't agree with, because we know reality is a bit different. I will not point out what exactly, because this is up to You to decide. We can't prove such things for now, so this will be empty for now.

Even with proofs, saying what is true and what is false is always creating conflicts, Everyone sees things differently, what we know as truth, may not look to You as truth. I told in some of my messages that "this is truth and there is a proof", it isn't like I like to do it, but some things I need to present with proofs and say that this is truth, this is a part of my mission.

The specific knowledge in the video about controllers will be revealed later to Everyone, for now I will leave this empty. Here is where Your Inner Voice decides what to accept and what to decline."

Much Peace, Calm and Prosperity to You!

READER'S COMMENTS

"Thankyou so much, GE.
I know there is a lot that can't be confirmed, but, it is so hard to know what is truth and what is not. I am always looking for more guidance, because so many things can be taken at face value, but are later proved to be wrong or dishonest. There is no fool-proof way to learn discernment !"

~~

May 18th, 2014

SOPHIA

Another response, here is the question:

"During a Reiki session this week, a visitor from another realm named Sam-u-el (his emphasis, not mine) told us that there would be "beings" coming to the US and UK that would really rock our world. Do you have any information about this? Thanks so much!"

G/E

You know Good Friend how it will be, Your Inner Voice will always tell You the Truth!

How we know it - there will be very big changes and a lot of different Beings - People (Incarnates) will step out of shadows where most are hiding right now, waiting when U.S. and UK illuminati luciferian governments will be removed as they are the main obstacle to this World's and Humanity's Evolution and they will introduce new technologies, change within governmental structures and overall education and civil laws changes.

Much Peace and Love to You!

READER'S COMMENTS

"Thank you so much, G.E.!! My inner voice is broken for the time being. . .I seem to have attracted too many interlopers on my journey and they all seem to want to talk! Love to you. . .!"

~~

"Hi.Obviously the Followers of Light are not in hurry to stop this experiment and remove the cabal.Is there an earthly force that is strong enough to remove them or do we need to wait till august 2016 for the Force of One?Or will the cabal disintegrate itself step by step and we will have to wait for month or years to see the changes?Thank you"

~~

MAY 21ST, 2014

G/E

Good Day Good Friend!

Yes, Followers of Light are not in a hurry to cease this experiment, like we know they will wait until the very last possible moment which was set to them. "It is Humanity that must cease this experiment" in their words. Yet what is happening now like I wrote in last message was expected by us 1 solar cycle ago and if analysis is correct, then this would be the cycle when

Awakening of Humanity will reach a critical point.

We see that time frame was indeed manipulated, the fuel-less technologies are spreading slowly, they are efficient, yet those that have ready versions of these technologies are waiting for big Change to occur. Right now process of removal of dollar from reserve currency status and U.S. government from domination role is happening very slowly. This government is desperate, and their plots are failing one after another, one of latest - "mers" plot failed miserably if You watch the news, not without our assistance. They have two more different bio related plots, yet we have it "under control".

For additional information: they plotted to spread "mers" disease worldwide using disappeared 2,000 vials containing fragments of "sars" virus which was modified to "mers". This disease proved to be completely "inefficient". Human bodies are becoming more powerful and hardly to contaminate or damage, this is due to huge influence of Trinity - Sage Star A, Sun and Earth. Trinity is disassembling evil oriented thoughts and damages "evil physical bodies" of evil thoughts hosts souls when evil actions are performed. This relates to all members of illuminati/cabal and all their henchmen, like in Ukraine and in Syria.

Those that are to be removed need to be ones that prevent this planet from evolving further and same ones that are threatening whole Existence of Universe. This is a *preemptive strike* against them as we know what will come out of this if they wouldn't be stopped now.

Followers of Light in their role are doing everything possible on ethereal level to cease this experiment as soon as possible without direct intervention.

Here is another technological beacon for You.[372]

---

[372] Cracklotus. "Siri Predicts End of the World? Hell If I Know." YouTube. YouTube, 06 Jan. 2014. Web. 13 July 2016. <https://www.youtube.com/watch?v=3SjL6-RjAEw>.

Explanation 1 Good[373]

Explanation 2 evil[374]

All is connected to religions, as religion is as always have a most important role for this World and Humanity. These precise two events "birth of the prophet" and "opening and closing gates of hades" are mainly done due to second evil explanation - "the great climax" event, as You know U.S. government are illuminati and they worship lucifer.

Date january 13 2014 is a close date of an opposition of Jupiter and Moon (january 16 when we were meditating) and this was indeed a birth of one child (important for them, which they think would become their "prophet", but their time is limited and it will not happen so, the child would become Good oriented as we know).

The date of "opening gates of hades" is a warning, if U.S. government won't change it's attitude toward whole World and Humanity and continue on making more conflicts, "opening gates of Hades" would be the explosion of Yellowstone volcano on this date. Yet it isn't like only on this date, it may happen sooner or later, it depends on their actions, this date yet is the most probable. They themselves also plan another false flag on this date to honor their "dark god" and meet their ends. This we will look closely when time will come.

Siri/Iris by itself is an artificial internet intelligence that collects all World's Consciousness into One. This is a primitive technology, yet it works on some occasions like this one.

With Peace and Love to You!

READER'S COMMENTS

"Hi GE,
Just got this download!

---

[373] GabeHashTV. "SIRI: JULY 27, 2014 OPENING GATES OF HADES? (EXPLAINED)." YouTube. YouTube, 19 Dec. 2013. Web. 13 July 2016. <https://www.youtube.com/watch?v=bD8kiSj2ZVI>.
[374] Koshatim. "SIRI OPENING GATES OF HADES PREDICTS FALSE FLAG JULY 27TH 2014 PT 1." YouTube. YouTube, 23 Dec. 2013. Web. 13 July 2016. <https://www.youtube.com/watch?v=FDtu82fqj3U>.

"Another distortion is the hunt for TRUTH, this makes people fight for truth, not realizing that everybody has their own TRUTH which should not be fought over thus letting go of the everlasting chase for the TRUTH cause TRUTH just is.""

~~

"Good Day and thank you"

"Here are good news :
US dollar front:

http://www.zerohedge.com/news/2014-05-21/russia-and-china-finally-sign-400-billion-holy-grail-gas-deal
and here:

http://www.atimes.com/atimes/China/CHIN-01-190514.html
QEG front: http://briankellysblog.blogspot.com/2014/05/free-energy-is-here.html "

"Here is a Bedini motor for beginners (it's not exactly a motor) :
http://syscoil.org/index.php?cmd=nav&cid=87 .

Sorry it's in french but you can translate the page with google translate."

"This text is in Benjamin Fulford latest update : "On the energy front things are looking much better: it has now become clear that the suppressed energy technology genie is out of the bottle. A major Japanese manufacturer contacted the White Dragon Society last week to say they were going ahead with the production of Tesla Quantum Energy Generators. The WDS has still not been able to test such a device though."
When this true, then it's a huge news with huge implications"

~~

"Yes i agree D. that is huge...all those developments we are hearing about from different corners of the world.

As well the developments due to Kevin Annett's work in trying to establish common courts in many countries to replace the crooked and totally corrupt and biased court systems of justice that still exist across the world.

But it's really high time that we can all work without the impediments that the 1percenters put in our way...they really need to go and it seems ~to me at least~ to take almost an eternity for that to be accomplished......"

"that should be common law courts instead of common courts, sorry :)"

~~

June 3rd, 2014

G/E

Thank You Good Friend D., a lot of very great information for Everyone to know!

Also very Truth bearing sentence Good Friend O., I will put it here if You don't mind:

"Another distortion is the hunt for TRUTH, this makes people fight for truth, not realizing that everybody has their own TRUTH which should not be fought over thus letting go of the everlasting chase for the TRUTH cause TRUTH just is."

Truth is "fighting" in all sense of this word is always evil/dark oriented. In order to defeat the evil You need to direct the hatred and aggression back to it's source, not giving into provocation to fight, where evil wins almost always, whether by simply winning or transforming Good oriented provoked into evil oriented victim of evil spell. Although on everything there are countermeasures.

Believing is what saves Everyone always.

As for developments we are watching for every step "elite" is making. They are desperate, and highly dangerous now, yet everything they do will be used against them.

I want also to share some more beautiful spiritual music:

It was Aeternum[375]

When in Home[376]

---

[375] BrunuhVille. "Emotional Music - Aeternum." YouTube. YouTube, 24 May 2014. Web. 14 July 2016. <https://www.youtube.com/watch?v=JKEnVdaGIK8>.

[376] MusicKaira1. "Silver Screen (Dos Brains) - Homeland." YouTube. YouTube, 03 Apr. 2014. Web. 14 July 2016. <https://www.youtube.com/watch?v=6xg8w24kO8c>.

Beneath the Horizon[377]

Hope[378]

Brings Miracle[379]

With Peace, Calm and Prosperity!

READER'S COMMENTS

"Thank you for posting my little "download". Actually my original post about TRUTH was put out the 14 of April.. about a month later I added the above to the named post from April.

Lot's of interesting numbers when you start to look i.e. communications and messages.. ;)

http://www.i-uvsweden.com/i-am-blog/truth-gets-you-unstuck here is my original post with added "download".

Much love"

~~

"Hi GE, Sophia and all :))

For over a few months now, numbers are showing up as master numbers! While at first I thought it was a sign to be mindful of my thoughts, but now I am finding they are trying to either alert me or remind me. I can't figure it out ... Any insight would be greatly appreciated. Examples are: 1:11, 11:11 or 111, X:11, X:22/33/44/55 etc.

Thank you :D "

~~

---

[377] Voiceprints. "Peter Jeremias - Beneath The Horizon (feat. Julie Elven)." YouTube. YouTube, 28 May 2014. Web. 14 July 2016. <https://www.youtube.com/watch?v=WP4bOrDpm2E>.
[378] THESTORMWOLF9. "Ivan Torrent: "Glimmer of Hope"" YouTube. YouTube, 26 May 2014. Web. 14 July 2016. <https://www.youtube.com/watch?v=tssQtyuDxb8>.
[379] EpicJennyni20. "Two Steps From Hell - Miracle (Thomas Bergersen)." YouTube. YouTube, 28 May 2014. Web. 14 July 2016. <https://www.youtube.com/watch?v=HN1AT9vlAXo>.

June 5th, 2014

SOPHIA

Today there are answers to the following two questions:
1.
Hi Sophia
I have been following the conversations with GE with great interest.
Maybe you could have him read the following info:
https://www.wingmakers.com/content/neruda-interviews/
Esp. focus on interview # 5.
I would be very curious to hear his comments in more detail.

2.

Hi Sophia,
I have a question that I need help with, do you or anyone you know could tell me what kind of humanoid
race is the Alcohbata? Is it reptilian, or amphibian. I saw a
photo of one and from that day I can't stop thinking about it, I feel I have a connection to it and wish I could find a way to contact it. The Alcohbata comes from Perseus Constellation. Also I'm A B negative blood type and wonder where this rare blood type comes from. Thank you in advance for your help.

~~~~~~
~~~

Good Day Sophia!

I answered on question about interview #5. It is about Annunaki's point of view, the modifiers of Humanity and harvesters of "gold" which is actually Humanity themselves and Grand Portal is the reaching of that well hidden Particle of Light. We can say this portal is open.
I will not say it is true or false, it up for You to decide. The most important is how You see things. I can add only, that Truth is everywhere, in most places it is mixed with "personal information", something important to a Person that channeling or explains things, same is with my messages, there is some footprint of me in everything I write here. We are All Equal, yet very unique, this is a special feature given to all living and non-living Beings in our Universe. So sometimes there is a "false information", which

actually is something personal from our Soul, illuminati used Our uniqueness to make an illusion and swap lies with Truth, evil with Good. Their system holds Truth as lie and lie as "truth", Good as evil and evil as "good".

Second question about a race Alcohbata, oh yes, we know this race, just above the Pleiadeans, from Silver Gates of the Sky. We know civilizations from their place of origin, names are not telling us much, except for the meaning. They are different than reptilians You know of, reptilians don't like liquids like water, they are very deceptive and can move between dimensions, they use to live where water is as thin as air. This Alcohbata civilization dwells on surface and in water. They are very good oriented, don't like galactic politics, prefer neutrality. We don't know much of a deeper insight information about Them and many other different civilizations, yet we know only basic information. We know more about civilizations that works for this World's restoration.

And question about numbers, as You can see and feel, numbers' "coincidences" are happening more frequently, this signifies, that's this World is close to a completion of experiment.

Yet what we see on ethereal level, is that many Lightworkers are struggling, many are tired, this World takes a toll, evil thoughts are demoralizing Many, tiredness of Soul extending. Sufferings are continue, yet People by most part now are understanding the huge corruption within western governments, not simple corruption of greed, but dangerous, evil corruption which is a threat to this whole World and Humanity.

Don't be let down, know that if Sun shines and gives Light, You have the Power of Universe with You, Universe is with You and You are with the Universe, One is Universe and You are One thus Universe. Always remember where it all started, always remember where You started Your Life and how You started it. Foundation of Past will create a Foundation for Future. Remember Your Childhood, remember what personality You were having when You were seeing the World as a Child, words of old saying "children are always welcome to Heaven" are true, as only children are pure, uncorrupted and have much more flexible mind and imagination with which future may be guided further to most highest of possibilities. You have learn (again) a lot, now You can guide Your Inner Child with much more Wisdom and Knowledge, now You can make things You only dreamed when You were Children.[380]

With Peace, Calm and Prosperity!

READER'S COMMENTS

"Thank you GE! :))"

~~

"Good day GE and all. You said that you know more about civilizations that works for this World's restoration. Can you tell us more about those civilisations :which one and how do they help us?"

~~

"Thank you as always for the time that you spend answering the many questions that we have. It was recently said that 54,000 members of the cabal were offered a deal by the Pleadians, to be taken off planet and they accepted that deal. Here is the link to that: https://www.youtube.com/watch?v=Fxf-XHNVG74.
Do you have any information about this? Thanks so much!!"

~~

"New Update says 11,000 cabal took the offer to leave.
https://www.youtube.com/watch?v=5tfVQZnL3D0 "

~~

June 16th, 2014

G/E

Good Day Sophia!

Here is the answer on two questions from Good Friends!

"Thank you as always for the time that you spend answering the many questions that we have. It was recently said that 54,000 members of the cabal were offered a deal by the Pleadians, to be taken off planet and they accepted that deal. Here is the link to that.[381]

---

[380] EpicJennyni20. "Two Steps From Hell - Compass (feat. Merethe Soltvedt)." YouTube. YouTube, 02 June 2014. Web. 14 July 2016. <https://www.youtube.com/watch?v=w-qh5yZeOCo>.

Do you have any information about this? Thanks so much!!"

You are always welcome Good Friend! We don't feel that so high number of "important" figures left this World, this would be known if they indeed would left, also we haven't felt any big intervention from outside. Yet as always it is up for You to decide Good Friend, Your Inner Voice is always guides You!

"Good day GE and all.You said that you know more about civilizations that works for this World's restoration.Can you tell us more about those civilisations :which one and how do they help us?"

I already shared much about reptilians, greys, pleiadians, arcturians, sirians and as well raians. All their Federation of Light is aiding this World, using technology, and Energy manipulation in a manner that is awakening Humanity, reducing global warming, easing conflicts and soothing inflammatory speeches and thoughts. Much of information about them is available on the internet, from different sources. If You need some detailed information, ask Good Friend.

I will give these videos that are from pleiadians and arcturians.
Here You are able to hear what They represent and their Inner Souls are being heard here as well. Many already seen these videos, yet like I was told some need to watch them again, as now You have more Wisdom and Knowledge and Your Comprehension had changed. Now You will hear a slightly different message, more understandable to You.

Whole video contains strong message, yet pleiadian message starts from 19:34.[382]

For all those that still don't understand Foundation (how it all started), listen closely to the dialogue of Neo and Oracle, here You can understand, that they are a part of one system - the Revelation where reptilians are a part of one Galactic Federation, we know that wars were fought in prehistoric times above this World for ownership of this Planet and ability to manipulate the evolution of Humanity, yet only partly, to the extent of becoming "rulers/gods of elite", as all

[381] ChaoticAxxis. "Julien Wells- Pleiadian Update Part 1: Guests Judy Jandora, Sheri Gordon, Dan Alvin & Crystal Walker." YouTube. YouTube, 09 June 2014. Web. 14 July 2016. <https://www.youtube.com/watch?v=Fxf-XHNVG74.>.
[382] Hus987pc. "Sacred Knowledge of Vibration and the Power of Human Emotions." YouTube. YouTube, 06 Feb. 2012. Web. 14 July 2016. <https://www.youtube.com/watch?v=o0gBoV0ygJc>.

this control was still in the hands of Creator-imposter, like it was always here

This is a message from Vrillan, in our knowledge arcturian, one of the Asta Command overseeing this experiment, using an artificial voice, made to sound "british", it was translated in 1977, "Southern Television Broadcast interruption accident".[383]

Within these two videos You can be closer to ones we call Followers of Light. Everything what is said there is said from Heart, from Soul of complete Spiritual Force, and we GEs feel their very evolved state, everything there said about Foundation/Basis of Creation is how we know it is.

I will also put two more songs, which suite current World situation
We Gaze upon the Sun[384]

While we protect the Truth[385]

Protecting the Truth is not easy, yet is possible. MSM attacks with lies and suppresses the Truth about Syria and Ukraine, yet we are there to protect the Truth and All who stand for Justice and Fairness, Harmony and Friendship, Love and Compassion, Peace and Equality and repel lies and injustice and All who still don't see the Truth or supports the evil ways of Life.

Always Peace, Calm and Prosperity!

READER'S COMMENTS

"Thank you Good Friend.Can you give me some sources where i find real informations about ETs,please.
About the ISIS terrorgroup ,here is a good
link:http://landdestroyer.blogspot.com/2014/06/natos-terror-hordes-in-iraq-pretext-for.html "

---

[383] TheOUTsideEARTH. "Alien Message Live on TV in UK We Come to Warn About Your Race and Your Planet." YouTube. YouTube, 07 Dec. 2013. Web. 14 July 2016. <https://www.youtube.com/watch?v=JhmLIKUPaVU>.
[384] THESTORMWOLF9. "Two Steps From Hell: "Sun Gazer"" YouTube. YouTube, 13 June 2014. Web. 14 July 2016. <https://www.youtube.com/watch?v=Beeib02OOTU>.
[385] EpicJennyni20. "Immediate Music - Protectors of Truth (NU EPIQ)." YouTube. YouTube, 12 June 2014. Web. 14 July 2016. <https://www.youtube.com/watch?v=KTsLnmQ4fyg>.

~~

"Thank you! There is so much information that I have trouble sometimes feeling it with my heart. I am working on it. My faith program is broken, so I have a bit of trouble with hope and belief at this time. You are kind to take the time to help us. "

~~

"Thank you from me as well, GE, for the confirmation about the 11000 cabal members. On 14 May, you said "We are very close now to Completion and Moment of Justice". Do you feel this is still the case now, or have things changed again ? "

~~

June 18th, 2014

SOPHIA

Note -- from Sophia:
This blog format is used solely to engage with the one known as GE, and all answers and videos and other links are from him unless specified as my own. This has become the only place where his updates can be found since December of 2013. The other "conversation with GE" pages on this site have not been updated since that time. His answers are responses to blog comments, personal questions sent to me or as a response to my own questions for him; sometimes they are initiated by him as well. None of these posts are my own. Thank you and Much love.

G/E

Good Day Sophia!

Challenging times indeed. We GEs knew that this will be like it is, we were prepared for this event, and I warned about this before, 1 cycle ago as You remember right after the Choice was made and approved, we were waiting this right after the spring equinox, yet it only arrived one cycle later, and the confusion about the real date of the Shift of the Ages - 16 december 2013, this created suspicion that time was rearranged on 1 cycle and all were tricked, which created a negative spark in Energy 1 cycle after the 21 december 2012, as Everyone was discouraged and not able to proceed on changing the World after 16 december 2013.

We suppose this is a cunning trick made by demiurge, to disallow

Humanity to make decision correctly and change the World correctly, yet this is useless when it comes to Forces of One, we understand every form of manipulation and control. Forces of One will aid Humanity if level of discouragement will be high.

So what we have now here is the last push "to dominate" of illuminati order/cabal. They will fail, but they can cause damage and are already doing damage. Due to their activities People and Animals are dying everyday, yet recently we see more damage, compared to the "average daily damage".

World war 3 is a planned event by them, which by their planning "will save USA from enormous debt, depopulate planet, make afterwards a lot of working places "to restore the world" and unite the world into one huge evil empire, where all Good People would be prosecuted or destroyed". Demiurge planned this event as well, "there will be wars and rumors of wars, there will be peace and then sudden destruction" as You remember, subconsciously this was done in bible to prepare and await this event as it is "imminent", so basically Beings of Purity programmed Humanity to make this sudden destruction themselves, which You can see is very probable when You look at World without One and Forces of One.

Yet this is only a plan, like a made up glass from sand and can be broken to shreds and You know, it will.
"Humanity decided - fail is their only option."
this is the Decision of One made based on Collective Consensus Choice of Humanity, which was made as You remember, yet how Humanity will deal with current war mongering situations will decide how much more damage will be done by "almost world war 3".

What is taking place in Iraq right now by our knowledge is currently without U.S. government's involvement, they yet don't have control over this situation and that is why they are nervous, yet this government is known to take every "government change" situation under control. But for now, we can say that this is a part of the same trap prepared for them, it is acting against them, and eventually this Iraq crisis will make a contribution to their downfall.

We can say that unfortunately, due to very high levels of hatred within

these radical people in Iraq, Syria and Ukraine, and due to lack of special abilities within us we aren't able to reduce damage, their hatred is very strong and is siphoning power from Dark Source of Creation, and there is nothing we can do about huge sufferings they are bringing to Others.
Yet as One tells:
"Unfortunately on this World of Free Will and manipulation of Free Will, sufferings and damage is a necessity for big changes to occur, without it system remains the same. If it weren't for manipulation of controllers, the situation on this World would be different."

All of this is in the hands of Followers of Light, they can intervene right now for example, but knowing them we know that they won't. Although would hope that they prove that they are more than this.

So this comes for Forces of One, we are here to make sure Humanity and Galactic Federation of Light will not create danger to Creation, One's order is to allow Humanity to fulfill it's choice and become Free.

I will also remind Everyone, though this is a challenging time, in order for Yourself to feel Good and relaxed You need to remember the Foundation and Basis of the Universe, how It All started and for what purpose, You have to remember how and why You came here to this World, with what purpose.

Knowing the Basis and Creator of the Universe will give You much strength, You can take black gems into Your hands for them to siphon evil energies from You, as dark attracts dark, gems will work for You and will cleanse Your body from darkness, this will make You more relaxed and confident, then charge Your Body with light and bright stones, like white or yellow, or simply gold, wear gold to feel yourself relaxed and confident in Your abilities, look on Sun and be in Joy of Sun, Sun will always smile back at You to answer Your call!

Yes darkness comes when Sun sets.[386]

But Sun sets only to Rise Again! And when It does, Light replaces

---

[386] BrunuhVille. "Epic Fantasy Music - Into Darkness." YouTube. YouTube, 13 June 2014. Web. 14 July 2016. <https://www.youtube.com/watch?v=2ARSvBv-7W8>.

darkness![387]

Much Love, Peace, Compassion, Calm, Abundance and Prosperity to Everyone!

June 19th, 2014

G/E

"Thank you Good Friend.Can you give me some sources where i find real informations about ETs,please."

I will answer on questions from Good Friends!

Good Friend D., I can give You the links to information about different ETs, but right now for us a priority is this Planet and all affairs on it. And because of this I cannot show specific links and say that this is how it is. It is going against Free Will, I will give You the hint how I was searching for information about different ETs when I was young.

I was simply looking onto different mentions of civilizations outside this World, and always I heard when some races were pronounced in positive or negative tone, I was researching into them by looking through different books and webpages, truth about them cannot be on one single website, information about them is shredded.

The best way to know them is to connect to Universal Consciousness of Universe thus One and request this information, eventually One will guide to the source of information You need Good Friend which is present on this World, if it is not, One will present this information to You in Your imagination (You will see it while dreaming). I was taught of this method when I was introduced into GE. And this is always working very well.

As well in rare cases like it happened with Sophia, the civilization You are interested may visit You, for this You also need to make a request, like write a letter, e-mail, or make a video and send it somewhere, or put it on blog or

---

[387] FarlessandPolenz. "Two Steps From Hell - Return from Darkness [Epic Orchestra]." YouTube. YouTube, 15 June 2013. Web. 14 July 2016. <https://www.youtube.com/watch?v=860VL23Ec9A>.

internet.

Also if You want to see them or their ship, you need to go out as far away as possible from other People, and being alone or with like minded 1 or 2 Friends, You together can make a request for to reveal themselves, or to share some information about them, they would appear shortly, but remember it need to be place, where they wouldn't be seen by others, "to not damage their free will" it is called.

"Thank you from me as well, GE, for the confirmation about the 11000 cabal members.
On 14 May, you said "We are very close now to Completion and Moment of Justice". Do you feel this is still the case now, or have things changed again ?"

We are close, I cannot say how long it will be, but I myself feel that this time is the right now, not previous cycle, we are much closer now than we were before 2 cycles ago. I have also another beacon, and it shows that some time yet is still necessary for the completion to initiate, but their downfall is imminent before august 2016, even without intervention of Followers of Light, they will not be able to hold on any longer.

Moment of Justice we called it like it, because illuminati/cabal will feel on themselves the taste of real Justice, the medicine of destruction and suffering which they put onto this World will return back to them tenfold times stronger.

Remember evil cannot be defeated by evil or by Good, true Good never uses violence and never fights against anyone, Good simply is Harmony - Coexistence with Everything around. They would be defeated by Good, but in a manner of "a mirror", all will be reflected back to them with increased power, as mirror is not just a mirror, but a mirror of One. You Yourself can feel that all is boiling and is about to explode, they direct hatred and violence openly now, yet they don't see the mirror as they approaching, all will return back to them once they hit it. This World need a Change and Change it will be! Remember the "great climax" in next month, this would be a time when different things might happen, all depends on actions of Humanity.

Much Peace and Love to Everyone!

READER'S COMMENTS

"Thankyou GE - I can't imagine how may millions of factors One has to weigh up simultaneously, in deciding when the time is right !"

~~

"Good day Good Friend,i know you have a loooooot to do right now on earth because of the evil cabal is speading and appreciate very much the fact that despite of your dutys and responsabilities you take the time to respond to our countless questions.
By the way , it is by searching for informations about ETs that i came across this awesome site in 2012,but at that time i did not get interrested because i was caught in the 2012 hype.I came back in April 2013 when you promoted The Citizen Hearing and you got my attention.
I watched the pleiadian message and it triggered a lot of emotion in me ,it was huge.Could it be possible that it is not a mere coincidence that we came to this site and that we (the people who read this conversation) are somehow monitored?"

~~

"I agree with you D.! When I saw the mini movie of the Pleiadian's message of history and to wake up, I admit I too, became emotional. But I also became hopeful and in deep appreciation!

Your Question D...I too would like to know the answer :))"

~~

June 20th, 2014

SOPHIA

The following is a most likely not surprising, if alarming piece of data.
Again, these are the words of the GE and not my own.
Much love,

G/E

I will add important evil spell illuminati/cabal did recently and share most important for You and for every Human Being information after it, which I decided to share here.

We feel right now great Energy pressure, illuminati order dark priests are

performing very brutal spells recently, we heard some of these spells, and this spell is very prominent, I need to share this with You, I haven't done this before and hope won't do it again. Knowing the words of spells and curses, will help deflect them.

Here is the spell they made on whole World:

"Let all be our women *(very harsh word was used, equivalent to prostitute)*, for us to rule over them. For thee are useful when thee are she-male, and ain't male-she. For we can use them how we want and so it will be in the name of our hated lord."

This is connected with their ultimate plan, they want to make hive minded civilization out of Humanity, where all will serve to "queens and kings", which would be the only fertile persons capable of giving birth and all other People would be "working ants" - women that couldn't have their own children, only on acceptance of "kings and queens" they would, where only "king" can make child and "queen" can give birth..

Their plan is to make all People of one gender of women as women are more easier to control (how they think). This is already happening very slowly, almost unseen and unnoticed, yet it is happening steadily. You can hear here and there about women being better than men. This is almost unnoticed, yet this is the intent.

Same agenda *of turning everyone into more women than men* is in the plan of demiurge as well, yet it is slightly different. The plan of demiurge goes after all this World would change. It is for this being to gain full control over Humanity and takes thousands of Solar cycles ahead.

Unfortunately when and if Humanity will lose it's male gender it will indeed lose it's more freer state and become more easily to control.

And now this comes to why Forces of One are here, and not within Galactic Federation of Light civilizations. I myself decided to release this information now, I was free to release it when I thought it was right. And as cabal made such a spell and we come to this, here it is.

As You remember we are here to stop the experiment, because demiurge through Humanity want(s) to get full control over Creation. You may have a question, why Humanity and not GFL civilizations? By knowledge they (are) supposed to have much more evolved and superior technologies. This is so, yet almost all civilizations within Galactic Federation of Light have a completely feminized societies, due to this, their Free Will is no longer 100% efficient and that is why they cannot achieve absolutely every secret of Creation, cannot attain 100% codes of it from bottom to the top, which demiurge absolutely needs and desperately wants.

This is the main reason why Humanity exists in the first place, because of the male gender and it's superior capability to see everything. I will mention, as You know speaking of this is "taboo", yet it is also the same programming of controlling the information and Human behavior, programmed by non other than demiurge itself.

Illuminati/cabal wish to do the same, but differently, this is where they challenge "Him - the Lord Adonay", they challenge it in every way, but this precise challenge of "feminizing society" is the most unacceptable to demiurge, yet demiurge planned this as well.

Now to continue,
as You know because of males this civilization is not stable. Males tend to be more chaotic and sometimes berserk, this is the toll for this ability of seeing 100% of Creation. In order for male to see everything and comprehend it absolutely, he needs to learn to be so, Forces of One exceeded the limitations of men and women or so called "dual mode life", and "harnessed" the nature of male, bringing 100% stability and absolute capability of seeing and manipulating every form of Creation,

One aided in doing so all the 8 prime civilizations of Forces of One which formed Forces of One and as well One introduced Ancient Machines which were holding all knowledge of past Universes, and all knowledge about current Universe and future possible Universes.

After, all the males which were very old and immortal and having all these superior treats gave loyalty to Universe thus One, to serve and protect It from "self destruction"
- destruction by unstable males or hive minded societies bend to dominate all and any -

the error in the code which happens in proportion of 7,045 to 1 (sacred numbers of 45 and 7),
this is meant to be so, as One needs instability to get the fullest experience out of this Creation and Forces of One are meant to support the system from total collapse if unstable elements would override all the pattern of Creation.
Ancient Machines are not enough to do so, Free Will is necessary.
Since those very ancient times every young male in dual mode life civilizations are giving their loyalty to One.

This is the knowledge we had since beginning, I did not brought this up before because saying this is considered "taboo", same like saying about sexual experiences, something that is also programmed with intention to control information and knowledge, and preserve demiurge's ultimate agenda for future of Humanity.

This is to let You know, when we shared this spell with other People it set many free from unexplained constrained feeling.

We hope this will add You too. You can share this with Good Friends if You think it is right.

Much Peace, Harmony and Love to You!

READER'S COMMENTS

"That explains a lot of decisions of our "politics" like male-female parity in politics and soon in business,same gender marriage and others.It is not that i am against but i am against the fact that it is somehow forced"

~~

"Thank you for sharing this information. At this point, all data should be revealed so humans know what is happening. Thanks!!!"

~~

"Dear GE,
these are exactly the answers I've been looking for, the freedom and power in the/my body is excellent, please feel free to share as much or all of, that u can.
I do not forget/I do recall that your original purpose here was to kill me, physically, should it have been necessary,,as an ex "grunt" in the "suck" ,i understand ,

,,,,,,,,,,,,,,,mission/orders/job-not an adventure.

I probably would have understood and thanked you while you where doing it and as I fought.

I believe I also understand the feeling of ,,Pleasure?/or the difference between the two assignments when feeding and helping the population instead of killing them became the new objective.

what it was like for u I don't know, I can only try and relate.

with this type of sharing of knowledge you do kill off a part of me that needs/ I want for it to go. thank you

my reaction to the information matters little as opposed to my response to it,,
If i can achieve the "Harnessing"
"Oh" the blessed freedom.
I have observed that we/I can achieve anything we intend on,
this concept/words has given me a point to request from source on.
May you be well"

~~

June 23rd, 2014

G/E

Good Day Sophia and Everyone!

I have some good news.[388]

Our united work has formed this coalition of 77 under leadership of India, China and Russia, they now are much stronger than they were when it first was formed, here even Rothschilds are willing to help, and it looks like they are ready to repent of all evil deeds they've done to this world. Although we are not 100% sure in their claims and they should be closely monitored, but we were expecting this from them, they are slightly different than other illuminati members.

I will mention why they are doing this. First is because they understood now seeing present world, that lucifer is not real and all of this is just a part

[388] "G77+China Summit Calls for New World Order." - Xinhua. N.p., n.d. Web. 14 July 2016.
<http://news.xinhuanet.com/english/world/2014-06/16/c_133411809.htm>.

of manipulation, where in the end all the blame will go on their family as well. And second is a long lasting rivalry with Rockefellers. Rothschilds have an old fighting going on against Rockefellers, that started since Titanic was sunk by their united efforts, making all prerequisites for world war 1. During world war 2 using Hitler Rockefellers threatened to eradicate Rothschilds family by invading Britain, unless they accept the agreement which completely was removing them from power. Their family is from a jewish descent, and many of their family were victims of nazis. The agreement was having 3 main points.

1.To give Saudi Arabia with all it's oil reserves under full control of Rockefellers' family.
2.All the land owned by british citizens in United States was to be sold to american citizens.
3.Most important. After world war 2 British Empire is ceasing to exist and is giving freedoms to all of it's colonies.

As You can see this is how it happened.

Rothschilds vowed to avenge their relatives and this humiliation. So like we are seeing this is the last evil deed they would want to make, before leaving their schemes all together and sharing their wealth with entire World. Yet like I mentioned they still should be monitored, they are still a part of "elite" and cabal.

Here I will answer on questions from Good Friends.

"I watched the pleiadian message and it triggered a lot of emotion in me ,it was huge.Could it be possible that it is not a mere coincidence that we came to this site and that we (the people who read this conversation) are somehow monitored?"

It truly is an emotional video and like it is said there, emotions connect You to Your non-physical Multidimensional Body which is a vast Consciousness and through it You can figure things out. That is also the main reason why I share spiritual music with Everyone. It is helping to connect to this body which is from One and from there You can see the whole picture!:) We are monitored indeed, yet NSA collects all the information and not checking it all together, People there are just People, they tire, they don't have the power to check super huge amounts of information. This place like many other blogspots are a subject of such monitoring. Right now we can't do much about this, yet remember we use special energy which deflects interest to this website and so they think it is "a hoax and exaggeration". Only those that need this information like You Good Friend are eventually finding it. Followers of Light on the other hand are monitoring such sites very closely, and Sophia has a very watchful eyes watching on Her. As You are like many other Lightworker Groupings are making a big contribution into this World. So they always need to know Your feelings and mood. Actually You All have Your own "Guardian Angel" always there by Your side:)

"Thankyou GE - I can't imagine how may millions of factors One has to weigh up simultaneously, in deciding when the time is right !"

You can think of One as a super computer, You know that even with such technologies not as evolved as ones Followers of Light are having Humanity is able to create super computer that can calculate millions of operations per nanosecond, which is a billionth part of a second! Imagine what One can do as it is much much more superior than our PCs. And One of course is a combination of everything that exist in physicality, ethereality and our imagination, so One can do unimaginable things, which even our imagination cannot comprehend!:)

"Dear GE,
these are exactly the answers I've been looking for, the freedom and power in the/my body is excellent, please feel free to share as much or all of, that u can.
I do not forget/I do recall that your original purpose here was to kill me, physically, should it have been necessary,,as an ex "grunt" in the "suck" ,i understand , ,,,,,,,,,,,,,,,,,mission/orders/job-not an adventure.
I probably would have understood and thanked you while you where doing it and as I fought.
I believe I also understand the feeling of ,,Pleasure?/or the difference between the two assignments when feeding and helping the population instead of killing them became the new objective.
what it was like for u I don't know, I can only try and relate.

with this type of sharing of knowledge you do kill off a part of me that needs/ I want for it to go. thank you

my reaction to the information matters little as opposed to my response to it,,
If i can achieve the "Harnessing"
"Oh" the blessed freedom.
I have observed that we/I can achieve anything we intend on,
this concept/words has given me a point to request from source on.
May you be well"

I'm happy that this information is aiding You and Everyone Else here, always happy to aid Everyone!:)

Originally though I was not intend to harm Anyone. My rank of "Executioner" mostly is meant to frighten those that destroy things, as we are the ones that can destroy them and bring Justice to them as a scales of Justice/Balance. Even if we would have to do it, still some would be saved and taken off This World and You Good Friend is included, because You are special not like Anyone else, not as easily to be controlled as Anyone else, and so You do not fit to this system and do not belong to it! Everyone that follows their Heart, Soul, path of true Spirituality, understanding all of this corruption is to be saved if something unexpected or very terrible is to happen. Only those that support the system of destruction or are a victims and witlessly support it and of course those who raised it in the first place would be subjected for destruction. One never simply "punish" for evil deeds, One always gives chances to change the path and take another route, something what was done here. This is now gone, and we are doing everything we can to aid Humanity in full Liberation from this system "of silent slavery".

"That explains a lot of decisions of our "politics" like male-female parity in politics and soon in business,same gender marriage and others.It is not that i am against but i am against the fact that it is somehow forced"

Yes Good Friend, all of this is meant to unite two genders and make them "asexual" with more feminine in it and as well to make them "sterile". Here I will also add clarification on first part of information about significance of genders to demiurge and Humanity.

Like I mentioned males are able to see full spectrum of Creation, yet they need to be able to harness this ability and for this they need to be given complete freedom of actions and complete freedom of evolution. This is not meant though that women can't see the whole reality as well, most women can, yet it is Comprehension that gives males a 100% efficiency. Women unfortunately cannot or do not want to understand the dark side of Creation - the evil and primordial force of chaos which most of the time bears in it a terrible toll on the soul and life. And that is why, demiurge allowed males to do whatever they wanted, however they wanted and that is why we are in such a world You can witness today, war, destruction, sufferings, poverty, gap between rich and poor, greed are a side products of this second force which women do not like to understand.

In order for demiurge to gain full control over Creation both Good and evil side of One need to be comprehended and used, this is a necessity for this and only the strongest can use both at once, as You know that Good or Light always give and evil or dark always takes. Light is Harmony, it coexist with everything around, and it allows itself to be controlled, while dark cares only about itself and always take everyone under it's control, so controlling darkness is very hard unless we have a very strong faith in our Hearts.

As You can see officially males "rule this World", yet it wasn't males that chose this path of patriarchal rule, where they are "above women", it was the controllers of Humanity that made a choice instead of Humanity as this was the plan of demiurge. That is why in religions and laws around the World is told about the "important role" of males and only less to no role is given to women, all of this is part of this "divine plan", a part of this programming to get what is necessary for demiurge. As well this is the main reason why Followers of Light are not intervening and stopping this experiment, as they need males to continue to be free in their actions, because demiurge needed males to evolve to maximum extent in their own freedom of actions.

Males can use the power of darkness and power of Light, and can comprehend these completely, demiurge on it's part had long lost such ability and need someone to do it for it, someone unstable like humans or other Beings with chaotic behavior. But only when technological level of evolution is high enough can males show the absolute maximal extent of their abilities to see 100% of Creation and comprehend it absolutely and that is why Humanity was allowed to evolve to state we are in now, almost like spacefaring civilization yet suppressed to not go beyond this planet, with nuclear weaponry and computer technologies at disposal as it was all meant to awaken the full spectrum within males to bring about what demiurge needs. And they need Humanity to be only here on this one World for better control and observation. Freedom of internet is only given because of this, otherwise it wouldn't be given at all or be suppressed.

Yet still all of this is a part of 'Absolute Plan" made by One. As You remember "Absolute Plan" is not constant, it is dynamic like Universe thus One is.

I don't like to say this is how it is, but this is how it is. I needed to give this information out so that's the small puzzles within a big puzzle can finally be completed.

As always Your own Comprehension and Discernment is most important, so it is like in a pleiadean message, You either accept what is here or decline it. Remember this most important rule:)

With Much Love, Peace and Prosperity to You!

READER'S COMMENTS

"Hi GE,

I understand why we use discernment, but in your last comment about using it, a question came to mind. If there are Truths, what difference does it make if we accept or decline that truth? Part of me says that if that piece of information has truth that resonates with me, then I move forward, but the other part says, so what? If ones truth is not someone else's truth, what difference or change does it make?

With appreciation,"

~~

"Hi GE,
I think we are really close to some kind of crescendo cause I'm getting emotional squeezed every know and then. I used to remember most of my dreams especially the ones with specific messages but they have faded?

What do you think?

@N. concerning TRUTH I can share my perspective here from my blog.

http://www.i-uvsweden.com/i-oliver-blog/quotes

Much love "

~~

"Thank you O., your view of Truth does resonate with me very much. Great site too! ;))

Namaste!"

~~

"Oh, another question. The good news link enclosed in the message...While it is a huge positive breakthrough, why must they use the term "New World Order" as the "new" name for plans to address poverty, balance humanity with nature/planet etc? Is this the same plan, just sold differently?"

~~

"Every day in my meditation I ask One to end this experiment now. But if that is not going to happen just yet, I really hope that, following this significant news about the Rothschilds, many other cabal groups / families fall like dominoes."

~~

"heartfelt thanks GE,
needed that from u, guess you sensed,,,
for me it's been feeling like so many mistakes,oh so many mistakes,,,,

off topic, a question please,
I am given to understand that i have been experimented on in a military program, wil there come a time when i and people like me will be allowed our memories so that we can deal with what happened and what we did, so that we can heal and move on with our lives?"

~~

June 25th, 2014

G/E

Like we were expecting, U.S. government took control of ISIS and ISIL using money and deception again. First of all the people within these two radical organizations were trained by CIA and U.S. government to fight against Syria and it's People, and then like we were told they lost control and ISIS and ISIL decided to form their own state. Now they regained control and illuminati/cabal are agreeing on their view to form new country of extreme radical rule. As well they are distorting name of Isis, the goddess which is known as Mother Earth in ancient Egyptian mythology.

They always tend to distort names and symbols. Likewise they are putting word "One" in many different names, like church called House of One, xBox One, One Communications and of course One dollar bill, "In God We Trust" under this phrase is written big word "One", supposedly "in this God We Trust", called One or is One. Most of the time they are putting oval near name "One". By doing this they show that they respect One and by looking at first we can think that they even serve One, yet when we look closer, we are finding out that they use only the evil, dark side of One, when One is supposed to represent Everything and Everyone, they represent only themselves and their "upper role" over "all the rest". Yet because of this and their acceptance of One, american Society was prospering, due to supposed "obedience to One". Oval as well indeed represent One and both Grand and Grand Grand Creators, yet they distorting it to show the eye of snake. Originally the Oval or the Eye is representing Galaxy and Inner Eye of Soul, that one Humanity calls Third Eye. So by doing all this distortion, they distort reality and create an illusion bringing in false meaning of all symbols and names. This practice is well known among reptilians, they are masters of distorting reality.

So for Iraq right now illuminati order have another plan, also connected to starting ww3, but we have this under control, though we can't prevent the bloodshed and destruction, these People are too hateful unfortunately.. , we can prevent big conflicts and even more destruction.

"I understand why we use discernment, but in your last comment about using it, a

question came to mind. If there are Truths, what difference does it make if we accept or decline that truth? Part of me says that if that piece of information has truth that resonates with me, then I move forward, but the other part says, so what? If ones truth is not someone else's truth, what difference or change does it make?"

Thank You for making this question Good Friend! This question is most important. The difference and meaning of Truth is Your own reality - Your own Comprehension of it. The ability to comprehend and understand, and as well a Free Will choice is what deciding what is True and what is "false". If You understand what was said to You and accept it as Truth, then this is the way when presented reality suits Your Soul and Consciousness, and is suited to the level of Your physical development. Same applies to lies. Lie is not a "lie" as completely false information as You used to know it. Lie is just another way to comprehend reality.

Imagine all of this, which is known to us about planes, computers, Space, understanding of natural "higher forces" or notion of God was to be said to ancient People which only recently were Animals, they wouldn't understand a word from what was said to them and instead would prefer to choose a simplified version which we think is a lie, but for them is Truth. Same happened to religions and science. Yet, there were always People filled with greed and they abused religions and science to take Energy and physical wealth from majority and bring this to themselves making major part of Humanity poor.

So again Good Friends, Understanding and Comprehension is most important for us in all this experience. When we understand other People and understand everything through what They are coming through, we Love Them! The less People understand each other, the more They unfortunately hate each other.

So what You will do with this eye opening information is up to You, how You will manage it, where You will put it, it isn't making much difference to the World, unless it is accepted by All Humanity, when it can change Humanity fundamentally.

As we know Followers of Light do not intend to open this information to Humanity. For now this information only adds up to Your own Knowledge and Comprehension of Physical Reality, maybe later on Humanity will accept this information and make according changes. For now only few People are knowing this.

Much Peace and Love!

READER'S COMMENTS

*"heartfelt thanks GE,
needed that from u, guess you sensed,,,
for me it's been feeling like so many mistakes,oh so many mistakes,,,,*

*off topic, a question please,
I am given to understand that i have been experimented on in a military program, wil there come a time when i and people like me will be allowed our memories so that we can deal with what happened and what we did, so that we can heal and move on with our lives?"*

~~

*"Hi M.,don't be be too hard to youself and forgive yourself.Mistakes are part of our experience,the most importent is to learn from them and comprehend, so can go forward.If we were perfect ,we would not be on this planet.
To recover your memories try to find a good hypnotherapist,that will help you"*

~~

"Good day GE,in the last message you that the Titanic was sunk,making all prequisites for WW1, can you elaborate please.Thank you"

~~

*"Hi Good Friend and all.I found this video :
https://www.youtube.com/watch?v=QYmViPTndxw# .*

It's about the IMF and the numerolycal number 7.It coincides with the July climax you talked about.What do you think about it?"

~~

"Wow D., great find! So what do we do if true? Pull all our monies out? What about RSPs and Other security savings?"

~~

"Wait and see"

~~

"actually guys, it'll be the most wonderful thing, the first real sign of our freedom,, from what i understand (been following this for 30 years).

from what i understand of the most recent events in the last ten years, a masterful reversal of fortune has been implemented and occurred, the details are deep and complicated, buuuutt, what seems to have occurred is the cabals plan for instituting a system based on the SDR (special drawing rights) continuing the fiat based debt system from the roman times and bringing that into a international sys using problem reaction soution scenario,,has been usurped (kinda like they do to the good things that are created hereon the planet) and is being created by the "good" guys into a decentralized asset based financial sys ,,this is that time,,

there's a couple of variations on the lagard tape,, the one that looks the best is 7/7/2014=777 the "father" number, i guess it's called, as 0pposed to 666,,, the son? (diumurge?) interesting is it not?

Anyway

Happy Independence Day"

~~

"dear d,

Tankyou and I apologize for not getting back to you sooner, I started a letter a week ago ,,I'll paste it and cont. on from where I left off.

Thank you D,

got that virgo moon vigo rising thing going on, makes for self-flagellation, heh heh,

30 years havent had much luck getting any assitance with my suspicians and anomolys,, like percieving two seperate timelines at once, or why can't i do this but i can do that,or just that draining feeling on the inside when i attempt to do certain things that would be absolutely great for me,

and i just don't,

paying dearly for it later,,in life,,

well now that I'm here to finish, doesn't seem to be much to say,, probably best to just give you a link, it's five parts,, it;ll take a while to listen to it but this is the second guy I've run across who's experiences are similar to mine,, the guys name is captain K-aye, funny, my nickname in the marines was corporal K, synchronicity anyone? heh heh.

http://www.youtube.com/results?search_query=Audio+-
+Supersoldiers+and+Project+Moon+Shadow+-+Full+Interview+

it'd be a long story to go through the details of why I felt like so many mistakes so many opportunities to do the various things to change my life (like he did)that were suppressed that i could have fought to overcome,, but i understand I would have been killed as well ,,I don't know,,, suffice to say thankyou and all who allowed me this venue,,,this past week has been cathartic,, I apologize to those who preferred I did not write this here..

Take Care
May you be well

D, don't know as a hypnotherapist can work with something like this I am well past what source calls "the closing of the loop" (time) but perhaps if I now carry out the"due Diligence" as captain K talks of and was internally prevented from earlier I might find the next leg of the path to freedom"

~~

*"Hi M.,thank you for the link i will watch it.
Russia and China are now openly defying the US by creating an anti-dollar coalition.
You know the dollar is the backbone of the US financial and military power.There will be an import reunion of the BRICS in Bresil the14-16 July"*

~~

*"this is the potentiality as he sees it
http://www.dinarrecaps.com/our-blog/the-arcane-sdr-supra-macro-asset-by-jc-collins*

let us hope that the meeting that was held in bejing subverted this, and that mr colins is simply missing a piece of info"

~~

*"M,
I think JC just has part of the picture thus advocating SDR's.*

We'll see soon enough when things kick in high gear!"

~~

*"like ge referred to snowden, this smacks of fear mongering,
or we can see it as ,a, plan or circumstance and intend on something else,
http://www.dinarrecaps.com/our-blog/the-bondage-of-atlas-part-1 "*

~~

*"Hi,
There will be no financial reset until the old system is gone so projects can be funded.*

I think no (Private Placement Program) PPP is neccessary if this pans out properly."

~~

July 5th, 2014

Good day Sophia and Everyone!

I have some more Good news! More whistleblowers came out to testify against NSA.[389]

And russian scientists wish to recreate Tesla's wireless Power Tower, the one for which J. P. Morgan stopped Nikola and his achievements and end his life in misery...[390]

Such news are not available in western msm, now they are finally showing their true colors, they completely cover the Truth and simply ignore what is happening in the World. They only give version which illuminati order wish Humanity to see. Before they were doing it without much attention, but now People around the World are finally seeing their hypocritical behavior. They are owned only by a few major corporations which are telling them what to say and what to write and what to ignore.[391]

Right now RT news network, along with iranian PressTV is doing great job in exposing Truth and giving out latest stories in their fullest "technicolor" picture.

"I have A B Negative blood and was told it is a very rare blood type. Do you know if it's from another planet?
or an alien race?
Thank you in advance for you help."

Like we know all the DNA of all Humanity is having a string of extraterrestrial origin, a string from Beings of Purity of an Aspect of Light.

We know that all blood and tissue of every Human Being is consistent from materials that are available only here on this Planet as all food Everyone is consuming is only from here. The Information of Aspect of Light sits within

[389] N.p., n.d. Web. <http://rt.com/news/170276-germany-nsa-bundestag-inquiry/>.

[390] N.p., n.d. Web. <http://rt.com/news/170468-tesla-tower-rebuild-project/>.

[391] Lutz, Ashley. "These 6 Corporations Control 90% Of The Media In America." Business Insider. Business Insider, Inc, 14 June 2012. Web. 14 July 2016. <http://www.businessinsider.com/these-6-corporations-control-90-of-the-media-in-america-2012-6>.

DNA and can be uncovered, I was mentioning how.

The most important is Your Own thinking, if You think You are an ET, then most probably You are! Here are a lot of Souls of Extraterrestrials incarnated on this precise generation to witness great changes and play it's own part in such Change, whether change would be Good or evil.

Now we come to a moment, when Change inevitably will be Good of an Aspect of Light. So again Good Friend, You are the one deciding whether Your believe is True or "false". In actuality all is true in it's way, remember that!:)

———

"Hi GE,
I think we are really close to some kind of crescendo cause I'm getting emotional squeezed every know and then. I used to remember most of my dreams especially the ones with specific messages but they have faded?
What do you think?"

Good Friend Oliver, we are indeed very close now, I myself am feeling this. I understand that if You no longer see the dreams, You have evolved now to state that You no longer need such dreams, You can finally understand reality and connect to Universe without necessity to dream. The emotional squeeze is due to such transformation.
But there in Your Mind You are Master, so it is just my thoughts:)
You also have great perspectives on Truth, Thank You!

"Oh, another question. The good news link enclosed in the message...While it is a huge positive breakthrough, why must they use the term "New World Order" as the "new" name for
plans to address poverty, balance humanity with nature/planet etc? Is this the same plan,
just sold differently?"

"New World Order" phrase was distorted by illuminati order like all the rest words, phrases and symbols, such like One, Isis and even GE ("GE Money", look at stylized symbol of it). In original meaning it means the different order of things of New World, which is a grand change in Society.

They are using such powerful names to have what they want for themselves.

But finally China and Russia are putting the original meaning of these words. Like I mentioned Russia and China are having their own view of New World, we can say that it is much different than martial law and tyranny which cabal wish to bring. Russia and China view New World as the World of Harmony and Co-Existence, no more wars, no more sufferings. They still would have some control, but this is to change as well, when they would be introduced to ETs.

"Every day in my meditation I ask One to end this experiment now. But if that is not going to happen just yet, I really hope that, following this significant news about the Rothschilds, many other cabal groups / families fall like dominoes."

Good Friend Curious, they really would fall like dominoes ;)

By asking One, eventually we will get it sooner than later. One need to see that is it something You really want.

Because there was put a limitation on our minds as "too loose wishes" can make our life terrible and then we can regret of asking it "spontaneously", so we have to ask several multiple times same thing, it is not easy, but this is the point, we are testing ourselves whether "We really need it", and eventually after some time passed we would have it and almost always it comes to us unexpected as a surprise, at a moment we really weren't awaiting for it, so is One, One loves to surprise us:)
And a lot time already passed since we matured and realized what was happening to this World, so now comes Humanity's United Wish and special for You wish Good Friends!:)

"heartfelt thanks GE,
needed that from u, guess you sensed,,,
for me it's been feeling like so many mistakes,oh so many mistakes,,,,
off topic, a question please,
I am given to understand that i have been experimented on in a military program,
wil there come a time when i and people like me will be allowed our memories so that we can deal with
what happened and what we did, so that we can heal and move on with our

lives?"

Thank You Good Friend Michael, no need to blame Yourself, I know there comes time when old "mistakes" are going back from our memories, but these are not "mistakes", this is what have to be happened back then and this is a lesson for You to learn from.

You are asking about outside fix of such "mistakes", Forces of One have technologies to fix such, like I mentioned "healing of the past", though they won't be allowed here. Humanity have to redevelop them first.

With current technologies only memory can be erased, but this would create different Human Being who will need to relearn almost everything anew, if You want to preserve memories and Your formed character, these mistakes can't be fixed without Your own understanding.

I know some events in Your life may hurt You very badly, like You chose this path of life, when You could have chosen different, or made some bad thing about which regret later. Mistakes are made to overcome them and become stronger so to not repeat them again.

These are the same "mistakes" when we are trying to get used to walking when we are only toddlers, these are mistakes when we are learning to solve arithmetic or puzzle riddles.

We are learning Ourselves on mistakes, and to not fall onto "dark side" when we see "no exit" (this is when we can't Understand what to do next, and evil thoughts are guiding us away from Light), we have to remember the basis from which we started this life and from where we appeared.

The Source as You know, by looking at the Sun and seeing it's Light we can remind Ourselves of that Beginning that We witnessed when we were "not here". Along with such Thoughts remember Your child self still sitting deep inside You, You can always call to it and restore Your powers and Energy.

Then carry on! Life offers endless amount of opportunities as there is nothing impossible in this Creation, You can make things even better then You could have ever imagined!!

"Good day GE,in the last message you that the Titanic was sunk,making all prequisites for WW1, can you elaborate please.Thank you"

This is another conspiracy of the "elite". There on ship Titanic were many major figures of british and american societies that could've prevented WW1, as You know many very "rich" and influential persons died on that ship.

This also gave the ability for Federal Reserve to take control over USA's government and it's money system completely as on titanic were many influential persons that were not allowing it to happen. This ship was intentionally built from low quality steel to be sink and very few life boats were issued on it, so to not allow majority to save themselves...

The plan for WW1 was orchestrated by 33 degree freemasons including Albert Pike, Rockefellers and Rothschilds. Ship Titanic was a part of it. If You remember that news were saying that "this ship is unsinkable" and "such ship can't be sank even by God". This was a welcome for all the richest persons in U.S. and Britain and a warning for illuminati members and freemasons, that it is going to sink.

Here I found one website that tells about this story, but not fully.[392]

"D.
Hi Good Friend and all.I found this video:
https://www.youtube.com/watch?v=QYmViPTndxw

It's about the IMF and the numerolycal number 7.It coincides with the July climax you talked about.What do you think about it?"

"N.
Wow D., great find! So what do we do if true? Pull all our monies out? What about RSPs and Other security savings?"

Great find Good Friend Djon! Indeed there is a hidden message about number 7, they were warning about WW3 and huge false flag event. The WW3 is cancelled, the false flag event is still a possibility. They are now becoming very irritated because all their plans and their

---

[392] "The Day J.P. Morgan Sank The Titanic." Dublinmicks Breaking News. N.p., 26 Oct. 2013. Web. 14 July 2016. <http://dublinsmickdotcom.wordpress.com/2013/10/26/the-day-j-p-morgan-sank-the-titanic/>.

image are falling apart, so they can make many things, everything I warned You before and yes including "financial reset" almost like their orchestrated 2008 "mortgage crisis".

I advise You to have provisions, like food, water, most necessary domestic things at hand and money in reserve of course, because they are very chaotic right now. We should start seeing their desperate movements starting from 20th july like it is mentioned in a video, "the grand climax" will take place on 27th, so be ready and meditate for World Peace, Stability, Love among All, Harmony on this Planet and between Every Person, living and non-living!

"actually guys, it'll be the most wonderful thing, the first real sign of our freedom,, from what i understand (been following this for 30 years).from what i understand of the most recent events in the last ten years, a masterful reversal of fortune has been implemented and occurred, the details are deep and complicated, buuuutt, what seems to have occurred is the cabals plan for instituting a system based on the SDR (
special drawing rights) continuing the fiat based debt system from the roman times and bringing that into a international sys using problem reaction soution scenario,,has been usurped (kinda like they do to the good things that are created hereon the planet) and is being created by the "good" guys into a decentralized asset based financial sys ,,this is
that time,,
there's a couple of variations on the lagard tape,, the one that looks the best is 7/7/2014=777 the "father" number, i guess it's called, as opposed to 666,,, the son?
(diumurge?) Interesting is it not?
Anyway
Happy Independence Day"

You've found very great analogy Good Friend we expect this Monday to be special and we will meditate due to overall numbers 7 and it's significance, like You pointed out,
Everyone can meditate and charge this World with Harmonious Energies on this date of 7/7/2014 where 2+0+1+4=7, so it's 777, then 7+7+7=21 july, we can join our powers together for great Change to occur sooner rather than later, and soon there will be new Independence Day of Humanity:)

I also will share music:

<u>Into the Light</u>[393]

<u>Through Purple Skies</u>[394]

<u>Through Theogony (The story of Creation of gods, Humanity's story:)</u> [395]

<u>To become the Eyes of the Sky</u> [396]

With Peace, Love and Prosperity!

READER'S COMMENTS

"Hi GE,
TY for your reply concerning dreams I also got the answer from within that they are not playing the same role as before. Takes time to get used to though.

The Tesla tech and bio-resonance tech developet in Russia will turn the tables even faster. This means that the charade of asset based currency race will fade as well."

~~

"Hi Good Friend.After i posted the question about Titanic,the thought came to me that there were rich and powerful peoples in ship that could have prevented the creation of the FED and thereby WW1,thank you for confirmation.
And about "mistakes",i came to the same conclusion some time ago.Sure, my life is easy compared to Michael's.
I think in my previous incarnation i was a soldier.When i was a 6-7 old boy,after the traumatic death of a friend,i dreamed that i was a prisoner of war in an underground complex and when i tried to escape through a tiny tunnel,it collapsed and i died.I was white and actually i am black(brown)"

[393] KacskaTB. "Chroma Music - Into The Light (Jochen Flach - 2014)." YouTube. YouTube, 15 May 2014. Web. 14 July 2016. <https://www.youtube.com/watch?v=wCyUvzag8yM>.
[394] EpicJennyni20. "Ivan Torrent - Purple Skies (Beautiful Orchestral)." YouTube. YouTube, 30 June 2014. Web. 14 July 2016. <https://www.youtube.com/watch?v=f4wb6aQUzI0>.
[395] Joghisan. "Jo Blankenburg - Theogony." YouTube. YouTube, 31 Jan. 2014. Web. 14 July 2016. <https://www.youtube.com/watch?v=eNossFNWysA>.
[396] Sindrannaras. "R. Armando Morabito - Eyes Of The Sky." YouTube. YouTube, 29 June 2014. Web. 14 July 2016. <https://www.youtube.com/watch?v=R03hWFGA5qI>.

~~

"Here is an interresting article called SAUDI JOINING BRICS TO DITCH USD :
http://eclinik.wordpress.com/2014/07/05/saudi-joining-brics-to-ditch-usd/
Saudi Arabia is the world biggest oil producer and thereby the main backer of the
petrodollar with other petromonarchies.If it's confirmed than it's a huge nail on the coffin
of the dollar"

~~

"The Saudis together with Quatar are moving away from the dollar big time and aligning
themselves with the BRICS countries especially CHINA.

Will be interesting how this will play out since the Saudis are backing ISIS/ISIL and also
want the region to be unstable as well as Israel.

Now having fair trade and humans rights in this region would be something among the
wast amounts of clans all over the middle east."

~~

"The Information of Aspect of Light sits within DNA and can be uncovered, I was
mentioning how.

Dear GE, Ipasted this from your update,
I'm afraid I missed how to uncover, would u be so kind as to go into it?"

~~

"Dear GE,
when u refer to "an aspect of light"
are u referring to the Races/Beings of "light" (federation of light) (feminized civilazations
etc.) or to an aspect of source or One?"

~~

"Thanks O.,
that question about dreams answered a question I didn't even consider to ask.
Good GE."

~~

"@ M.
Your most welcome my dreams are actually "returning" meaning I'm remembering more
and more I think we are moving in and out of dimensions even more when dreaming
then when awake which is like a flow some times more intense and sometimes more

subtle.

Yesterday I go especially one new insight concerning the expression: "That's your perspective!". As I see it I could easily say "I don't agree with you!" instead because that is actually what I mean when I say that to people. LOL..

@Sophia,
As often your synchronicity is awesome you post about "Owning Freedom" today so coincides with a long talk I had with a friend yesterday at length - TY!

Boy IT FEELS SO CLOSE NOW!"

~~

July 16th, 2014

G/E

Good Day Sophia!

I will answer on some questions from Good Friends.

"Here is an interresting article called SAUDI JOINING BRICS TO DITCH USD : http://eclinik.wordpress.com/2014/07/05/saudi-joining-brics-to-ditch-usd/Saudi

Arabia is the world biggest oil producer and thereby the main backer of the petrodollar with other petromonarchies.
If it's confirmed than it's a huge nail on the coffin of the dollar"

Another great news Good Friend!
We know that in the end every World's Nation will abandon cabal, and cabal will receive their judgement, all the negative energy they sent on Everyone would be projected back onto them.

"Hi Good Friend.
After i posted the question about Titanic,the thought came to me that there were rich and powerful peoples in ship that could have prevented the creation of the FED and thereby WW1,thank you for confirmation."

That is showing Good Friend that Your connection with One, with Your

Higher Inner Self is now very strong, You can hear the Truth from within:)
This is when You are sending request for answer on a question to Cosmo,
You are instantly receiving answer back in less than a second, and the very
first "thought" should be that correct answer that You seek.

*"And about "mistakes",i came to the same conclusion some time ago.Sure, my
life is easy compared to Michael's.I
think in my previous incarnation i was a soldier.When i was a 6-7 old
boy,after the traumatic death of a friend,i dreamed that i was a
prisoner of war in an underground complex and when i tried to escape
through a tiny tunnel,it collapsed and i died.I was white and actually i
am black(brown)"*

The story about incarnation and reincarnation is much more complicated to
say the least. We put it as simply, when our Soul is leaving the Body, then
it is going back to Heaven to rest there and then returns back into new born
Body, but whole story is much more than this, if You want to hear what we
know, I can share it.

This knowledge is of category "arcane".

*"Dear GE, I pasted this from your update,I'm afraid I missed how to uncover,
would u be so kind as to go into it?.....* **The Information of Aspect of Light sits
within DNA and can be uncovered, I was mentioning how.**"

Good Friend Michael,
I forgot when I was explaining about this, it is a lot of information, it was
somewhere in the beginning of a talk about demiurge, I guess somewhere
in the beginning of a comment section.

Basically saying short we can put it like this:

When Animals - future Humans were modified, by Federation of Light
Beings and Beings of Purity (very bright Light Beings) and demiurge itself,
within human DNA was put this Particle of Light.

And through religions and spiritual evolution of different kind Humanity
little by little is trying to achieve this Particle of Light, we can put it as

"coming closer to God".
Achieving this state can be done through grow and evolution, which takes not one generation.

Right now, overall, Humanity came very close to it, but still not completely. Due to evil activity on this Planet, this process was slowed down gradually.

Now only few People have a very close integration with this Particle of an aspect of Light.

These People can interact with Animals, Animals understand These People very well and can be very close Friends with Them, also These People can stabilize surroundings, reducing fear and uncertainty, also They are able to settle conflicts and reduce aggression. You Good Friend are of this category.

All people that chose Good way of Existence have traits of this, but yet not completely.

"when u refer to "an aspect of light"are u referring to the Races/Beings of "light" (federation of light) (feminized civilazations etc.) or to an aspect of source or One?"

Aspect of Light is meant as an origin of element of Light, an origin of matter so to say.
It is a pure Light, not just from one entity. It is from One, Followers of Light or Galactic Federation of Light are following exactly this Light and are trying to uncover all it's secrets.

I hope these answers will aid You.

About situation on this World now and possible future consequences. Here are some more good news, BRICS are now making very big shift and are starting the collapse of illuminati/cabal and all their established parasitic system of slavery and control. [397] [398] [399]

---

[397] N.p., n.d. Web. <http://rt.com/op-edge/172876-brics-economies-international-system/>.

Also we can say that Yellowstone supervolcano is awakening, this is due to illuminati's activity to foment more violence and destruction and their willfulness to start a ww3. Christians and muslims unfortunately are following in their footsteps and are supporting cabal in mutual destruction of themselves.

All of this brings this World closer to "harsh reset", we were doing our best to make it swift and easy, but many still prefer violence over diplomacy and peaceful resolutions, so Yellowstone volcano will be the first of such harsh changes.

Although, this volcano's eruption can still be avoided, but it depends on actions of illuminati/cabal and Humanity overall.

So as always, think positively, meditate, pray, direct the flow of Energy and Light into hearts of Humanity so that They could finally see the whole picture, on the same level that You are seeing it!

Remember that positive and wishful thinking are having a very huge impact on material physical World.
In La'kesh.
Much Peace, Calm and Prosperity to Everyone! □

READER'S COMMENTS

"@GE,
What I get from you saying "harsh reset" is EARTH cleansing EVENT's that will force people to unite? Correct?

Best wishes "

~~

"Good day Good Friend and all. Thank you for the links, they are very informative.
Yes i want to hear (read :-)) what you know about reincarnation. Can you elaborate "arcane

[398] N.p., n.d. Web. <http://rt.com/op-edge/172624-brics-putin-arab-spring/>.
[399] "BRICS Establish $100bn Bank and Currency Pool to Cut out Western Dominance." RT International. N.p., n.d. Web. 14 July 2016. <http://rt.com/business/173008-brics-bank-currency-pool/>.

~~

"@GE,

On another note for how long is the genocide going to be continued all over the globe i.e. Ukraine,Palestine, Syria, Libya etc etc etc..?? "

~~

"Concerning intuitive guidance... ;)

http://www.i-uvsweden.com/i-oliver-blog/quotes "

~~

"Ops wrong link.. here is the correct one... http://www.i-uvsweden.com/i-oliver-blog/intuitive-guidance "

~~

"The downing of Flight MH17 is a false flag operation.Look at here: http://vineyardsaker.blogspot.be/2014/07/evidence-continues-to-emerge-mh17-is.html . GE warned us about a possible false flag "

~~

July 21st, 2014

G/E

Google is simply fulfilling the plan of illuminati/cabal, which is step by step to strip away all freedoms and privacy from People around the World. New additions they made are no longer secure and can be monitored much more strictly by u.s. government.

Illuminati are falling and they can see it, yet they gave an order to their lesser members, called "initiates" to execute an order of preparation of coming of "novus ordus seclorum" or the "new world order" (order of things which is evil), and this order they are fulfilling.

And You can witness this order, the World is very tense right now and media is pushing only in one direction. But the good side of this is, is that we can finally see who is who and their real face is being shown very openly now.

Boeing 777 was shot down, as we know by ukrainian army, yet it is also a false flag and barely planned event. (Barely, because it won't change much and will not help illuminati order to get out of many problems they are having right now). There was nothing that could be done here and this is a big loss of life.

It is all meant for same purpose of starting a war. Here was the play on numbers.
This is also Malaysian Airlines plane which bears a logo of trident and tri color of white, blue and red (like russian flag) and ukrainian coat of arms have also trident on it. Trident is number 3, plus tri color flag have 3 colors on it, Boeing 777 is having three number 7s, then 7+7+7=21 (also points to july 21st) where 2+1=3 and 295 people were on board, all of them passed away... another poor People, victims of this evil system... This is 2+9+5=16, 1+6=7.

This plane was flying from Amsterdam, flag of Amsterdam is having an evil colors of black and red on it and 3 white letters "X", the X in numerology is number 6, so it is equal to 666, same like pornography, many never think about this, but XXX movies are actually "666 movies", and as well flight MH017 was downed on this cycle of july the 17th.

As You remember, there are no coincidences, all is happening with a reason. All of these numbers are pointing to evil scheme. Many numbers 3 are signifying world war 3, and number 7 is a sign that such preparations are being made, thus warning members of illuminati that are awaiting for events to "unfold".

Just to add up, the IMF speech which was mentioning number 7 and numerology is playing very big part in this terrible incident. The woman of IMF also mentions world war 1, that it started 100 cycles ago. Indeed, the "anniversary" of start of this war will be on 28th of july, right after "the grand climax" on 27th.

So as always, meditate and think positively, this will reduce the possible casualties that are still to come.

Much Peace and Love to You!

READER'S COMMENT

"I have fascinated with the description of the "Demiurge". Would GE have information as. to the origination of Demiurges in general. Did (One) create them and if so for what purpose? In other words how did they come to be?"

~~

July 24th, 2014

G/E

I will add another set of information which I received from One, when I asked about number 7.

"This plane crash is a very complicated event, it could have been avoided, but because many here still prefer to understand Creation through violence, this event took place."

The big play on numbers was done by freemasons of "grand masonic lodge of Washington", unfortunately People would not find it out for now. As One told this event was in preparation for a long time and this MH17 and MH370 were meant to start a world war 3.
I was shown information that indeed such preparation is from a long ago as first flight of this plane was made also on 17th of july and in 1997, that is 17 solar cycles ago! Here is a link to this article.[400]

And like it is said there, TWA Flight 800 crashed as well on 17th july 1996. And more to this One told me that number 17, repeated several times points to Revelation 17 of the bible, and that is the judgement of a "woman" that is known as "Mystery - Babylon the Great".
I understand what One meant, as I knew this story and I knew that this "woman" is America.

This prophecy was made long ago and it was not meant as something

---

[400] "MH17 Crash Conspiracy Theories: Strange Coincidence Of First, Last Flight Dates." International Business Times. N.p., 17 July 2014. Web. 14 July 2016. <http://www.ibtimes.com/mh17-crash-conspiracy-theories-strange-coincidence-first-last-flight-dates-1631648>.

"unavoidable", this was meant as a warning to Humanity, that all of this: beast system, mark of the beast, and whole this judgement could be avoided, yet because Humanity chose a path of fulfilling this prophecy through many generations, this is how it will happen partially (not completely).

Not completely, meant that Apocalypse will not take place and United States will not be "destroyed" as it is said there, but whole system and industry of U.S. might be severely damaged, so that illuminati order could be stopped.

Yellowstone awakening would be the first of such strikes to the infrastructure of this government. As well possible is small conflict within U.S. both by People of U.S. and foreign armies. All of this would be meant to liberate this country and stop the plan of illuminati (they were given many chances to surrender, yet they refused).

This warning in Revelation was given by demiurge as I know (as a part of this whole experiment), but One played part in this as well. Demiurge knew that Humanity would choose this path, but One intended Humanity to choose it's own path and count this only as a possibility. Due to huge influence and fear of these biggest religions the thinking of big judgement and coming "savior" had encoded itself in whole Human Society.

We are awaiting for Moment of Justice or this Judgement of Revelation, what I can say for sure, is that with this plane tragedy, it is now even closer. Illuminati families are responsible for all People from plane that passed away. The whole plane scenario is now playing negatively on illuminati and U.S. government, People around the world are losing trust in these entities and so they are falling apart. Their allies are abandoning them and their lies are becoming more obvious with each passing moment of time.

As You remember after this Judgement will come "Savior", this is meant here that a New World will be born.

Thank You Good Friends Djon and Oliver for provided links, intuitive guidance link is especially informative for many!

"What I get from you saying "harsh reset" is EARTH cleansing EVENT's that will force people to unite? Correct?"

Harsh Reset will not be as something like apocalypse or end of the world, but it will take lives away and make destruction, but it won't be global, it would be only on places where evil took big hold.

Like I mentioned USA is the biggest of these entities, followed by UK, Saudi Arabia, Israel (here is meant governments of these countries) and some fewer entities like NATO's, European Union's, IMF's, World Bank's headquarters.

Ukraine, Libya, Syria, Iraq and Africa as a whole and South America as a whole will be restored after the Moment of Justice (not instantly, but wars will be ceased and poverty will be significantly reduced).

"On another note for how long is the genocide going to be continued all over the globe i.e. Ukraine,Palestine, Syria, Libya etc etc etc..??"

This will continue until they - illuminati and everything I mentioned, are active. When their system (the beast system) would collapse, it would be stopped, not fully, but mostly, as they are the main force behind this evilness and cruelty.

"Yes i want to hear (read :-)) what you know about reincarnation .Can you elaborate "arcane"

Arcane is meant the most deepest knowledge which requires big understanding. In this category is knowledge in which comes most hard to understand subjects.

The story on Incarnation and Reincarnation is being put very simply as Soul leaves the Physical Body, it is going into ethereal realm, or Heaven to rest and restore. While resting this Soul is able to traverse Universe and make unimaginable things. Yet the whole story is much more complicated, You heard parts of this whole story. I will not give into details, because it is indeed a hard to understand knowledge, as we know Followers of Light don't know all of it in detail yet.

As You remember Your Soul exists in many dimensions and dimensional worlds. At the same time as We exist here as a Soul within this Physical Body, Our Soul exists in other Worlds and in other Incarnations. Our Souls are called multi dimensional Bodies, we exist as different sorts of objects at the same time, like I am a Human here and an animal in another World, then as a star in another World.

This is put simply. That is why it is sometimes possible to see "ghosts" of long gone People or events (like battles) taking place in this time, this is due to Energy collisions within the Code of "Multi Dimensional Sphere", this is all Worlds are put together. Somewhere in other World this Soul exists in incarnation and when it's memory is refreshed with something that happened here (and energy collision is taking place), a ghost or multiple ghosts are appearing in this World.

Other Souls, after passing away, are choosing "to stay alive". We call them "the dead wanderers", yet these Souls are also a multi dimensional incarnation, so their image can change to one in which they currently incarnated in other Worlds.

When We sleep, we can rarely move into other Worlds and see these Worlds (how rarely depends on individual Soul and it's connectedness with it's other incarnations). As well very very rarely, it is possible to actually move to other World with physical body attached to a Soul, but these are very rare cases and prerequisites are necessary for this as we know.

And as You remember most of the Souls on this Planet are stuck here, because demiurge blocks these Souls from leaving by telling different reality and tricking Them into submission.

I hope this will help in Your understanding.

In coming Earth cycles are expected more provocations from illuminati/cabal and we are coming close to july 27.

Meditate or pray and overall think positively Good Friends!

You are creating future right now!

Much Peace, Calm and Prosperity to Everyone!

READER'S COMMENTS

"Hi Good Friend and all.Indeed it's a complex subject,a lot of food for thought.Do you think it's possible with another incarnation through our common soul?"

~~

"So am I to understand these benevolents who are here to save us are going to allow part of the United States to destroyed? After all this we get rewarded by catastrophe? Hasn't the US suffered enough? We need something to put control back in our hands, not another hurricane, earthquake or tornado."

~~

July 25th, 2014

SOPHIA

More thoughts on our collective power. [401]

July 26th, 27th, 2015

G/E

I will only add more to this very big play on numbers and unfortunately algerian plane crashed as well with connection to this issue. It is a tragic incident, this could have been prevented like many other similar incidents if planes would have been outfitted with more precautions.

We felt that illuminati did not make algerian tragedy, yet it also points to number 7 and 17. First I will add that MH17 plane which was shot down was numbered "9M-RMD", in numerology M=4, R=9, D=4, so it is 9+4=13 and

---

[401] "Prophecy and Creation." Sophia. N.p., n.d. Web. 14 July 2016. <http://www.sophialove.org/my-blog/prophecy-and-creation>.

4+9+4=17 and numerically compressed in binary type it looks 13-17. Also it was Boeing 777-200ER, in numerology E=5 and R=9, so it is 5+9=14 and 1+4=5, so total is 2+0+0+5=7 and so it is 7777, 7+7+7+7=28 (july 28 is the start of world war 1, precisely 100 solar cycles ago).

And here is another number 17 of "Air Algerie Airbus plane AH5017" which unfortunately crashed. Word Airbus in numerology is also number 7, 1(A)+9(I)+9(R)+2(B)+3(U)+1(S)=25 and 2+5=7 and the date of 7/25/2014 equals to 7/7/7, because 2014=2+0+1+4=7 and july is 7th month.. It is good that nothing big happened on 25th, yet we still have 27th.

And on 26th (today) is a heliacal rising of Sirius which is called "Sothic Cycle" (this is when Sun and Sirius are rising at the same time from east). Also this event most of the time falls on 17th of july.

I will explain bit about it. Sirius is a god in freemasonry, it represents all seeing eye of Horus and 5-pointer star (called eastern star), both normal and inverted, inverted has more "dark power" in it (so they believe). Star Sirius is one of the trinity of freemasonry which consists of Osiris (notice name sounds like Sirius) or Masculine (equivalent to christianity's Trinity as Father), Isis or Feminine (Holy Spirit) and Horus, equivalent to Son or "Something New, something which they want to achieve, it is their evil New World Order. These 3 deities are also having an equivalents within egyptian mythology itself: Osiris-Sah, Isis-Sopdet and Horus-Sopdu.[402]

Notice that Sopdet is a goddes of Sirius and she have 5-pointed star on her head, which is an egyptian symbol for Sirius. All 5-pointed stars that were introduced in America to whole world by forefathers/freemasons are a direct representation of Sirius, 5 primal senses of a Human and as a symbol of Mars and thus war and hatred.

This star was never used in ancient and medieval times except for some exceptions like You can see here, as it was known for it's "dark powers", yet exactly United States government was the one that tricked Humanity into using this star as a primal representation of a star.

---

[402] "Sopdet." Wikipedia. Wikimedia Foundation, n.d. Web. 14 July 2016. <https://en.wikipedia.org/wiki/Sopdet>.

You know that star on a flag don't have a real importance on it, there is no reason to use exactly this star on an american flag. So what You can see is that this was done on purpose only by those that wanted it to be there.

Notice also that governments of U.S. and EU are adding recently more sharpness to this star, thus making it more sinister, more sharpness is being added to military representation of this star. As well when you see an EU flag or American flag on a TV or a computer, watch closely how these stars are inverted most of the time (like behind those that speak or filming of surroundings). All of this is done on purpose.

So this sothic cycle and "the grand climax" are matching with each other, which gives out a thought of bad event, but remember - all is in Your Hands and Minds, it is all about Consciousness!
Just look, all of this what You are witnessing happening right now is not done by this Planet, Animals or Plants or Cosmo or ETs, all of this is done by Humanity, and so all of this can be stopped by United Efforts of Humanity! Yes Humanity was manipulated into doing most of these things and becoming how it is today by outer forces, but the last word lies in the hands of Humanity!

Much Peace and Love to Everyone!

READER'S COMMENTS

"Interesting observations"

~~

"An email I recieved.
A weaponized ebola be careful everyone,,,
GE I think you mentioned this,,

Ebola What You Are Not Being Told

Posted by Keith Broaders on July 31, 2014 at 9:11am in Public Comments & Discussions

VIDEO: 6.27 minutes

REPORTER NOTES (not transcript)

(0.59 minutes) It is not true that Ebola is only transmitted by contact with sick humans.

(1.17 minutes) Statement by Dr. Kobinger: QUOTE from article shown: "What we suspect is happening is large droplets-they can stay in the air, but not long, they don't go far," he explained. "But they can be absorbed in the airway and this is how the infection starts, and this is what we think, because we saw a lot of evidence in the lungs of the non-human primates that the virus got in that way."

(1.58 minutes) What I will say is this shoddy reporting…QUOTE: "We reported on the fact that Ebola can travel through air in three separate articles on SCGnews.com since March, but the corporate media has continued to repeat the same disinfo."

(2.05 minutes) It may be putting all of humanity in danger. Think about it for a second. By convincing people that the virus cannot travel through the air, important precautions that could reduce the spread of the virus are not being taken. For example, the other passengers that traveled on the way to…Nigeria were not quarantined. Put this into context. Ebola kills between 60% to 95% of its victims. The stakes are very, very high here.

(2.29 minutes) This particular strain is not "Ebola Zaire". [HEADLINE: New strain is responsible for Ebola outbreak in West Africa.] It may, in fact, be more dangerous….the new strain is 98% genetically similar to Ebola Zaire. The symptoms are identical; however, this new strain seems to be harder to contain. The recent way it has extended his range is unprecedented.

[HEADLINE: Ebola outbreak in Guinea 'unprecedented' – MSF.]

The current question is if this virus will travel outside out of Africa.

(3.01 minutes) Considering the following:

1. Ebola has a 3 week incubation period

2. Ebola can travel through the air

3. Has already hitch-hiked on an international flight

This is a real possibility.

(3.13 minutes) …these people are basing their opinion on a faulty premise that believes Ebola is not an airborne virus….

(3.28 minutes) Fear is not helpful … think of practical steps we can take to influence the outcome.

1. Start confronting journalists and public officials who keep making false statements regarding the way Ebola spreads…see our links to the studies in 2012. Use these sources and our video to put them in their place.

2. Confront the fact that there is not a full out, frontal effort, to confront this virus and contain it. It is being treated like a side show. This crisis has a very real potential for becoming a main event.

This is serious. Call them (politicians). Write them. Hackle them in the streets if you have to.

POINT: Make it impossible for them to say later that they "didn't know."

(4.24 minutes) Whether or not they change....there are some precautions you should take for yourself:

1. Know where you would go if you needed to leave your home on short notice. If Ebola escapes West Africa, the last place you want to be is in a densely populated area metropolitan area. ... Primary concerns of an alternate destination might be geography, political environment, climate, population density, etc.

2. If you don't have passports for yourself and each of your dependents, get them now.

3. Know what you would carry with you if you had to leave on short notice. Make those items ready, and have the luggage to carry them. It would be wise to consider buying a pack of surgical masks as part of this.

(6.02 minutes) Whatever you do, don't let fear take control of your mind.

If you want to keep informed about what is going on, go to our website: www.wcgnews.com

END REPORTER NOTES "

~~

*"Hi!
I think the whole discussion about ET/Aliens is distorted since we all are ET's do not origin from EARTH ...*

Best wishes.."

~~

August 2nd, 2014

G/E

Good Day Sophia and Everyone!

The evil side of illuminati is in a great desperation, they were unable to convince their men under their control to make anything significant on 27th

and as we are here right now, they are falling apart with each passing moment of time, bringing us closer to end of this experiment.

Volcano became quiet for now, as no more provocations for conflict were made now.

We only now have the last problems and yes one of these problems is biological warfare danger. Thank You Good Friend Michael, yes "Ebola" virus is one of those ingredients as we know right now, along it there are at least 3 more viruses that are active right now, Nightmare bacteria and MERS (which was modded from SARS) and 1 more that is kept inactive within Physical Bodies of People - children in Syria were injected with it and it needs another agent to be activated. This virus can be neutralized when it is not fully active. And we also know that they have 4 more in their storage, which they consider to spread out. And we were told that 2 of these 4 that are kept in a storage can bring the biggest threat to humanity. We don't know their names, we only know that all 4 are modifications of a known viruses.

One of them may be the virus of modified swine flu, which we heard recently. The Physical Bodies of many indo-europeans are quite resistant to ebola and other viruses, strength of immune system is constantly increasing within Humanity due to Mother Earth's, Sun's and Sage Star's A activity and in Bodies of those that know more information, the more Knowledge - the more power and resistance You would have then as Light is information and Dark is lack of information.

And we are sure it won't be able to spread widely, we don't have it under control, but we are sure it won't be a big danger to Humanity. Yet our biggest win so far is that members of illuminati/cabal are beginning to refuse the spread of a viruses as it is threat to their families as well, because these viruses can mutate and adapt to vaccines they have.

So far by most part in overall picture everything is ok around the World, but they use force of chaos and it is unpredictable, so we always better to look out for them and what they are doing.

I will post an e-mail if you don't mind Good Friend Michael, this may help someone here
(Note – posted in previous section "Reader's Comments")
"Ebola What You Are Not Being Told"

"Hi Good Friend and all. Indeed it's a complex subject, a lot of food for thought. Do you think it's possible with another incarnation through our common soul?"

Yes Good Friend, it is possible to connect to another incarnation or incarnations, I also forget to add that the older the Soul is the more incarnations and more Consciousness it possesses, the younger the Soul, the less It has. Most of Humans are having quite young Souls on contrary to all those visitors that came here to aid Humanity, that is why they can see better through the veil and can understand all things better.

 If it wasn't for quite a low capabilities of a Human Body, abilities of these Beings would have far surpassed that of a Humans and as well; then We All, both Them and Humans could talk with our other incarnations through the vastness of Universe and Under-verse.

Most of Humans are matured enough and are having other incarnations as well around the Universe, but then is also Soul to Soul connection which is a part of One's Super Consciousness and this means that even young Souls by Themselves are also a part of other Souls, so it is going on and on, most important to remember here is that All is One, this is all about Consciousness and One is that Consciousness.

The best we can do, if we want to hear them and contact with them in some sort, is to make constant requests to Universe and to One's

Consciousness; One's vast sea of Consciousness eventually will hear, find and so contact with incarnation of Yourself can be established, yet I can't be quite sure how much time and efforts will it take from this Physical Body to do it. Yet I know it is possible.

"So am I to understand these benevolents who are here to save us are going to allow part of the United States to destroyed? After all this we get rewarded by catastrophe? Hasn't the US suffered enough? We need something to put control back in our hands, not another hurricane, earthquake or tornado."

I understand You very well, they are saying about many things and unfortunately some People here are twisting their channelings, thinking they will save Humanity all by Themselves. If They would want to, They could have done so a long time ago and prevented Humanity from making suffering to Itself.

 In actuality They are not here to save Humanity, not here to do it for Humanity, They are here to assist, Humanity have to save Itself.

It was demiurge that planned to initiate "apocalypse scenario" as he knew that Humanity would eventually choose this path and almost self destruct and so Galactic Federation of Light would have to act to save Humanity - their children.

Demiurge also used race of reptilians and they were playing the bad guys here, they were the tempters (or satan) to tempt Humanity into doing evil things, they used big ambitions and greed for wealth and power to further the goal of demiurge.

This is a big game of manipulation and control they are playing. The strictest rule Followers of Light are having is to not intervene and this is done to get something demiurge needs. Most of Followers of Light even are not realizing this big conspiracy, but it is vast in it's nature to say the least, most there within GFL are choosing to not believe it at all, like here with illuminati/cabal most People are choosing to not to believe either. As above so below rule works here as well, You can see.

All of this manipulation and constant lying and deception only to get profit called upon Forces of One and One instructed to cease this experiment and teach demiurge a lesson for making so huge manipulation and damage to Creation only to get what it needs ignoring the calls of others to be fair and just. This is evil and damage of free will what is happening here and unless demiurge won't realize what it is doing in actuality, this being won't be granted the ability to have power over Creation.

I hope this will help You to understand Brothers and Sisters of Family of Light, who we call Followers of Light.

The Yellowstone Volcano and the Sun will not target People, but will target only infrastructure of industry, they can be called karma or the mirror which will reflect all evilness and cruelty back to the host of it, to its source. If not enough evil and cruelty for a volcano and super flare to take place will be done, then they simply won't take place. It depends on amount here, this is a decision of Mother Earth, Father Sun, Sage Star A and One. Humanity have to understand what It is doing and be responsible for It's actions and also Humanity have to hear the Universe (One) and understand the many signs It is giving. This is all a part of Evolution and Growth of a civilization.

With Peace and Love to Everyone!

READER'S COMMENTS

"Please do GE Thank you, I'm here to share.

It seems as always just like in the jungle all the things that can hurt us the jungle provides a cure for ,,,

So heres the other side so that fear (False evidence appearing real)
does not take hold,
May you Love

Cure For Ebola They Don't Want You To Know About!!
IMPORTANT!!!!
Cure For Ebola They Don't Want You To Know About!!
Friday, August 1, 2014 15:25
by Susan Duclos
"We are all one plane ride away from a cataclysm." - Dr. Rima Laibow, MD
Medical Director of the Natural Solutions Foundation, Doctor Rima Laibow, has an urgent message, one she has sent to the presidents of the four Ebola stricken countries, "including a copy to the President of what may well be the next country afflicted, the United States since an Ebola-stricken volunteer is being flown to Atlanta for treatment, according to her latest video and an article at Sky Ships Over Cashiers, with what she considers a proven cure for Ebola, but one TPTB don't want us to know about.
And the kill rate for this disease of convenience, genetically engineered to be more deadly than ever before, just happens, I am sure coincidentally, to be the exact number depopulationists like Bill Gates and George Soros have wet dreams about: 90%.
The US government study (declassified in 2009) which showed definitively that Nano Silver at 10 PPM is the definitive prevention and therapy for Ebola virus "somehow" got "overlooked."We do not know how long before that the work actually took place, but the US civilian authorities knew not later than 2009 that there is a cure, treatment and prevention for Ebola virus. . . .
Listen to her. Go read the entire piece over at Sky Ships and ask youself after reading it why the study from 2009 was classified in the first place and why, after it was declassified, is everyone still ignoring it??
Watch this video.....
https://www.youtube.com/watch?feature=player_embedded&v=D7wNfRCuOZE "

~~

"Hi,

I would urge people to read up in the EBOLA distraction here. An excellent article about other reasons behind the alleged EBOLA outbrake.
http://jonrappoport.wordpress.com/2014/08/02/ebola-covert-op-in-a-hypnotized-world/

Traction is lost in the Ukraine distraction which gives another distraction namely EBOLA in West Africa. Where did ISIS/ISIL go? Did they take a coffee brake?

As can be seen the sloppiness at events staged all over the globe is increasing...

Hang in there folks.. they are getting so desperate so I almost feel sorry for them.. '

~~

"Info re Ebola: http://americankabuki.blogspot.com/2014/08/the-ebola-outbreak-pandemic-that-isnt.html "

~~

"Thankyou for the update GE. That is great news about the reason nothing happened on the 27th.
Last year in May you said that there was about 35% chance that humanity can change the situation to its liking. Are you able to say how much progress we have made since then ?
Another question: will the end of the experiment happen no matter what, regardless of anything that happens between now and August 16 ? For example, if the moment of justice happens soon, and disclosure should follow shortly thereafter, will the end of the experiment will be cancelled so that humanity can continue its progress gradually ? "

~~

"GE I can't tell you how important it is to me to have you sharing as u are, its very much like not so much what u are saying as when u address us or address me individually I can feel a "Healing"

going on, it's quite profound I am very grateful for this combination of having something my mind can integrate and my subconscious / inner child can transform.

while theres only a few people here i suspect perhaps that u are in contact with other small groups and that your purpose here is spread the word so to speak and have that word spread from there through us and believe me the awareness that I intergrate here is extremely calming to those whom I have contact with and share with as i go about my daily business,,
other than living moving and having my being in this way ,, is there some thing else as per an exchange of energy perhaps, or simply some action you would like me to take that would further your intentions here? what u would like me to do?
Your good friend Michael

Here GE, and guys and gals,
this is from the same lady that produced " the Lie that NASA told"

http://outofthisworldx.wordpress.com/2014/08/02/yellow-rose-for-texas-to-the-pope-david-cameron-and-benjamin-netanyahu/

there was precursor to this that i will try to find,,here it is ,,

http://www.youtube.com/watch?v=c69vZyE74Zg&feature=youtu.be

and

http://kauilapele.wordpress.com/2014/06/25/the-destruction-of-the-papal-key-video-and-how-it-may-relate-to-the-jupiter-freak-out-video/

also , last year there much hoopla about "what are the vatican and nasa telescopes looking at!!!! "
They seemed to be using a lot of precious scope time looking at only one part of the sky. Enjoy "

~~

"Thank you for all that you do for all of us! I have two new questions.

Do you know of a higher density group with a toad-like appearance?

Do you have any information about IM Prism?

I send love and thanks to you to infinity!! "

~~

August 8th, 2014

SOPHIA

Please share the following post.[403]

We are the ones we've been waiting for.

G/E

Good Day Sophia and Everyone!

First I will tell what I know about demiurge in connection to Your call Sophia.

As I know demiurge - the seeder of Humanity, is indeed made Humanity for its own gain and manipulated the history, yet in time it used to love Humanity as it's Children. I am calling demiurge as "it", because demiurge don't have gender. It is both male and female if we can say like it, but in overall demiurge can be called as "he", as it is willing to have "ultimate power".

Demiurge as a Being of Purity do not need energy of Human emotions to feed itself, and fear, darkness, hate does not feed demiurge, these dark emotions feed only reptilians - demiurge's henchmen, but they, like demiurge can live without these emotions, for reptilians as we know these bad emotions only give "pleasure", demiurge as a Being of Purity have

---

other sources of energy, like from stars and from different dimensional spectrums and connections of these spectrums, these are giving a lot of energy. Demiurge can "use" both Love and fear spectrum, yet fear demiurge don't like, demiurge enjoys Love (means receives "pleasure") given out by Humanity.

Demiurge in actuality is willing both - Humanity to succeed in It's Evolution and Growth and as well to receive "what it needs". We All know that "we can't have both at the same time". If demiurge can find a compromise here, One would be very pleased in this Being.

Overall You can call demiurge as "unsuccessful father", Many here on Earth have such Fathers in whom We are deeply disappointed and so Demiurge, is one very big common father of Humanity in whom whole Humanity can be disappointed if all of it's doings would be known to Everyone here.

But You decide Sophia, I gave out what we as GEs and I personally know from my experience with this being.

I want also to add about ebola, Thank You Everyone for sharing links, You are showing as a whole Humanity just how prepared have You become in the face of fear mongering instigated by illuminati order/cabal!

 I am very proud of Everyone to say the least! I will share what You shared, let Everyone see what this disease is and how it can be cured!

This is a share from Good Friend S., research is made by Good Friend D from "removing the shackles" blogspot
"Info re Ebola: http://americankabuki.blogspot.com/2014/08/the-ebola-outbreak-pandemic-that-isnt.html**"**
and part 2 http://americankabuki.blogspot.com/2014/08/when-is-ebola-not-ebola-when-it-walks.html

----

This is from Good Friend O.
"Hi,

I would urge people to read up in the EBOLA distraction here. An excellent article about other reasons behind the alleged EBOLA outbreak.
http://jonrappoport.wordpress.com/2014/08/02/ebola-covert-op-in-a-hypnotized-world/

Traction is lost in the Ukraine distraction which gives another distraction namely EBOLA in West Africa. Where did ISIS/ISIL go? Did they take a coffee brake?

As can be seen the sloppiness at events staged all over the globe is increasing...

Hang in there folks.. they are getting so desperate so I almost feel sorry for them.."

And from Good Friend M.
"It seems as always just like in the jungle all the things that can hurt us the jungle provides a cure for ,,,

So heres the other side so that fear (False evidence appearing real) does not take hold,
May you Love. (*Note – See "Readers Comments" above*)
"Cure For Ebola They Don't Want You To Know About!! IMPORTANT!!!!""

With Peace and Love to Everyone!

READER'S COMMENTS

"(heart) thank you GE,i sence the tide has findley turned,it is true,we have many on are side,(heart) to the demons 2,as were all going 2 the Big party,no one left out"

~~

"Re: Ebola and Colloidal Silver--I'd heard that idea, too, and just read another news article from Starship Earth: the Big Picture today that claimed colloidal silver was not the cure for ebola--that govt wanted people to think that--but actually mega-doses of Vitamin C (we're talking 500 grams a day, I think--outrageous amounts, which needs to be done intravenously in part), because it claims what ebola does is deplete the body COMPLETELY of vitamin C, causing at first scurvy-like symptoms, but way harder, faster, and deadlier.

http://2012thebigpicture.wordpress.com/2014/08/09/breaking-news-anonymous-doctor-releases-treatment-for-the-ebola-virus/ is the link to the article. The idea of a bio-engineered virus sucking the vitamin C out of someone made me think of that old Star Trek episode with the creature that killed people by sucking out their salt... But even if the article says colloidal silver is not the answer, heh, it still can't hurt."

~~

August 14th, 2014

SOPHIA

As this is a long one, it is separated into more than one post.

FIRST -

G/E

Good Day Everyone!

Due to the fact that "I.S. or Islamic State" had risen and because they are making huge atrocities in Iraq and Syria, I need to explain why are they doing those evil deeds, and this is something what Everyone here should know. This knowledge is well known, yet many ignore it and don't give much necessary attention which it obviously needs. This knowledge is called "ideology". It is the most necessary component of Evolution of a

Civilization, without which "civilization don't know in which way to go". This knowledge guides every Civilization in the Cosmo toward their many destinies which they are choosing. The knowledge about ideology/ideologies and how to manage and maintain them is well hidden, yet in the same time it is lying right there in plain sight before Everyone's eyes.

Humanity on it's part is also having ideology and not just 1, but many. Yet having many ideologies is a natural way of Evolution of Consciousness and Civilization. Different ideologies here created many conflicts here on this Planet, and ideologies include not only known autocracy, militarism, nationalism, nazism, democracy and communism, but as well religions - christianity, judaism, islam, buddhism, hinduism.

Every way that dictates how Everyone should live is called "ideology". This word was born in France during french revolution and means "science of ideas", yet in actuality this word was in existence since the ancient times in different forms. Ideology consists of many ideas banded together under 1 word like for example "democracy" or "christianity". Word ideology is very suited and like we know, it was given by One in some sort of it, to summarize everything in this World what comes to mean by this word.

Ideology is a struggle to idealism, which is "to become ideal in how ideology dictates". Every ideology and religion in this World was dictating how People should do to become "ideal" and "make life easier". What is important in ideology is that the use of "wrong words" may lead to the disaster, and like You can see now, "islamic state" are misinterpreting the words written in quran and in actuality are doing pure evil, without understanding and acknowledging it. Those that have power over "islamic state" are using these "wrong words" for their advantage and this advantage is again greed for wealth and power.

If You can see by now what I mean here, You can understand that it is not the choice these People made to make this evilness and cruelty, it is ideology and wrong misinterpretation of words that forced them to do those evil doings and it is being fueled by "appreciation" of their doings and "encouragement" to do more by those that stand above them and as well due to their false beliefs that their actions "are justified by Allah".

Such wrong words had made many sufferings and pain to this World, so when ideology is being created, it needs to use words that don't have two or more meanings, to not disillusion all those many People that will follow such ideology. Ideologies by definition affects all and any, changing and transforming those that follow given ideology and as well, little by little are transforming all that surrounds these People. Illuminati order on their part are also having ideology and this secretive ideology is bent on destruction of a civilization "as civilization", that is destroying society and making Everyone completely same and obedient to evil world system. Illuminati made themselves slaves to their evil ideology and are finding hard time to come out of it, same happened with christians, muslims and jews. Illuminati/cabal are a derivative of mainly christianity and judaism. And all ideologies, if not carefully planned can make many derivatives, number of which depends on planning of ideology, that is, due to many wrong words which were used in the bible, many denominations came out of it that interpreting words differently.

And so is the main schism between shia and sunni, which comes only from 1 small detail, which is "who could be called the Mohammed's descendant". Because Mohammed did not named his successor, muslims were separated on 2 after he passed away. So this is again, a not well planned ideology what You can see in Islam. And Islam by itself is a derivative of judaism and christianity, which were composed with the use of "wrong wording" and so is like they are subjected to partitioning.

The planning of ideology is the most important subject in Forces of One and this is given "most highest priority". The Religion of One is a product of most highest spiritual thinking and of most highly orderly shaped planning. I mentioned Religion of One to give an example that ideology is present outside this World and within Forces of One as well, so it is one universal subject that encompasses all and any, within physical reality and outside of physical reality. Even demiurge and Beings of Purity are having their own ideology, plus all civilizations in Galactic Federation of Light too have their own ideologies which are unique to each civilization. And One Itself is having "ideology" or something You know as "an Absolute Plan".

The only thing that is not affected by ideology is music. That is why we give much attention to music and share with You the most emotion or spiritually oriented music. Music can be only positive, negative or balanced. There are many subcategories which are in the music, but they all basically are jumping into one of 3 main categories. The only thing that can change music are words/emotions/expressions. Let's say for example that music is completely beautiful, but words in song are completely negative or even evil. Such wording can completely distort the original meaning of music. We call this force "corruption", corruption is a derivative of primordial force of chaos and is a destructive force.

On opposite when music is terrible, but is filled with completely beautiful words, words transform music and make it beautiful, even though music is not pleasant to hear. We call this force "restoration" on opposite to corruption. Restoration is coming out of primordial and hidden force of "Order", this was never told, but this force is coming right from the Consciousness of One, and this is exactly what You understand as Source or One or Creator of the Universe and this force after chaos gave birth to this orderly shaped Universe and to Life (including Humans). Force of chaos was necessary to give birth to Universe and Order was necessary to make Universe calm and stable, like we know Order was in existence before light and darkness, so it is not Light, but the very Thought/Consciousness of One. Eventually mix of Chaos and Order made Light and Darkness and both are a part of One.

I decided to let You know about this hidden knowledge of ideology which is right before Everyone's eyes, because it's importance is absolute. And now

You will be able to see, that those that commit crimes or unimaginable cruelty are doing it, because of beliefs which were all about evil, or which were misinterpreted falsely or not correctly. If You have questions on this subject please ask Good Friends, we GEs know this subject very well.

Also to add, we received information that U.S. government can't have "islamic state" under control, "IS" are now very erratic, U.S. government had risen them to power, because U.S. wanted to use them against Syrian president Bashar Al'Assad, but lost control over them when they moved to conquer Iraq. Then regained control back and now lost it again. They are bombing them obviously for this reason as they can't use them anymore. "islamic state" now chose the force of chaos and can't be controlled by any means, unless weakened. The People there abandoned their humane behavior and are now very dangerous to Everyone, the black color they wear is showing that they chose the way of death. U.S. government now is actually doing good thing in saving People in Iraq being threatened by this dangerous "islamic state". "IS" also are targeting Everyone that have different than they are having ideology.

SECOND

G/E

Here Good Friend M. asked us both, me and Sophia about "multiple demiurges"

"Dear Sophia and GE,
Below I have a question I posted some time ago before question and answers where not as prevalent a subject Matter here,
I post again to perhaps get your guys opinion,
Now there's one fella out there who would be recognized as the original proponent of multiple creator beings going off half-cocked as they are here,,
him personally I discount as a tool and not a very nice individual, but i am in association with those who allow that multiple entities,, a gang if you will, are responsible for the current state of affairs, IE. multiple diamurge's

would you guys be so kind as to comment on this paragraph and the one below? Thank you.

Now the school of thought that is bandied about is that there are many of these demiurge's, IE.(massive ancient bored multidimensional beings) vying for the accolades or energy or simply trying to take over One's creation instead of progressing themselves to the level of ONE and create their own multiverse (for lack of a better term).

If we go with as above so below ,, I see often a child or one taken under one's wing, try to take over the parents' house and moving or pushing the parent out,(acted out here in humanity many times)

,,,instead of learning how to do it themselves, they try to take what you have, is this not a sign of a very young soul with no confidence in creating?
Would this then be the condition of the demuirge and its ilk?
How could such a massive being be so immature?"

Yes Good Friend, we know that there are multiple demiurges, but all of them are different. The one that took control over this Galaxy, is hungry for power and unfortunately lacks basic principles of Understanding.

Those other that I know (some I even remember, like from race "gaalatheans", ancient civilization that is going on a path of Wisdom and Universal Understanding), they by most part are understanding Creation and are ready to go along the path of Free Will and they respect all other Beings that inhabit the Universe.

And like we know, in the past, long before life appeared on this Planet there were self appointed "gods" (I heard of at least two "most dangerous" from Forces of One) that wanted to control everything through power and even there was at least 1 "god" that simply wanted to destroy all of Creation (due to false ideologies, You can see how Your question synchronizes with ideologies topic (see part I)). These entities were brought down by Forces

of One with the aid of Ancient Machines as they were endangering everything.

The child pushing parents away from house and taking control over what is at hand is again, because of ideology and "false beliefs".

Education is the most important aspect of life of every Individual in a Civilization. If You remember the primary, the very first objective that Forces of One would have done in this World should Humanity approve to be a part of Forces of One was to change education, as education based on false principles of Understanding is what drives this World to a circle of constantly repeating mistakes.

Children are learning Themselves each moment of time (each second) and time for Children is going slower than for adults and as well Children are more easily to be harmed and more easily can be taught of ideology that can hardly leave Child's mind if accepted. Without proper knowledge and ideology, children don't know where to head and how to live in this World, so they are listening to those that are closest to them and are trying to take control over closest possible location. Parents are a well known since birth for Child Individuals, so Parents "bore" Child, that is why, when Child sees a new Individual (whether it is other toddler or uncle or neighbor), it is willful to listen to this Person, more than to Parents and as well is more willful to accept thoughts of this Individual, more that thoughts of Parents. Bear this in mind Good Friends, this is something Everyone seems to forget. Without notion of Understanding and Respect which need to be taught to Children, Children are doomed to repeat mistakes of old forgotten time.

And yes, in the end it all comes down to demiurge, as it was started by this being. Demiurge could have taught all what I wrote here and more to Humanity, but instead decided that religions could fix this issue. So through it's subordinates ETs, this being made judaism and later christianity and islam, but as we know, originally demiurge intended these religions to be more peaceful and loving, but Humanity distorted them to get more power and profit. What this being failed though, is that demiurge did not fix this mistake and let religions to become what they are now.

This is also from Good Friend M.

"GE I can't tell you how important it is to me to have you sharing as u are, its very much like not so much what u are saying as when u address us or address me individually I can feel a "Healing"
going on, it's quite profound I am very grateful for this combination of having something my mind can integrate and my subconscious / inner child can transform.

while theres only a few people here i suspect perhaps that u are in contact with other small groups and that your purpose here is spread the word so to speak and have that word spread from there through us and believe me the awareness that I intergrate here is extremely calming to those whom I have contact with and share with as i go about my daily business,,
other than living moving and having my being in this way ,, is there some thing else as per an exchange of energy perhaps, or simply some action you would like me to take that would further your intentions here? what u would like me to do?
Your good friend Michael

Here GE, and guys and gals,
this is from the same lady that produced " the Lie that NASA told"

http://outofthisworldx.wordpress.com/2014/08/02/yellow-rose-for-texas-to-the-pope-david-cameron-and-benjamin-netanyahu/

there was precursor to this that i will try to find,,here it is ,,

http://www.youtube.com/watch?v=c69vZyE74Zg&feature=youtu.be

and

http://kauilapele.wordpress.com/2014/06/25/the-destruction-of-the-papal-key-video-and-how-it-may-relate-to-the-jupiter-freak-out-video/

also , last year there much hoopla about "what are the vatican and nasa telescopes looking at!!!! "
They seemed to be using a lot of precious scope time looking at only one part of the sky.
Enjoy"

You are always welcome Good Friend!

I enjoy seeing Everyone Happy and hope that soon all of the World will be Happy and won't need any of the life's necessities:)

I could ask only to spread the knowledge about fuel less technologies (magnetic, water, solar) and to let People know of ETs. Yes ETs are ridiculed, but in time People of this Planet will understand, it would be enough to at least tell "they are real" and back it with some real video footage like 2011 UFO over "dome of the rock".

I'm not asking to spread knowledge about illuminati/cabal because knowledge about them corrupts and it corrupts even more when we are trying to tell others People that ignore this "that they are real" and not Everyone from You Good Friends are ready for this. Share knowledge about illuminati/cabal only with those that seek the Truth and want to know more about them, from conversation with such People You will receive much Pleasure and Joy!:) I don't recommend to spread this knowledge to those that ignore it, this creates negativity.

Thank You very much for all the links and research You made Good

Friend!

Vatican and pope are desperate as well, they are losing all their credibility and power. We don't hear about anything going on around the Sun, SOHO and SDO images did not show anything special on these dates.
Good Friend Yellow Rose knows a lot, but as always use Your own discernment.

READER'S COMMENT

"It strikes me that Yellow Rose for Texas must be representing the demiurge - who I imagine must be trying to convince as many souls as possible to go with it when it leaves this system."

~~

THIRD (AND LAST)

"Thankyou for the update GE. That is great news about the reason nothing happened on the 27th.
Last year in May you said that there was about 35% chance that humanity can change the situation to its liking. Are you able to say how much progress we have made since then ?
Another question: will the end of the experiment happen no matter what, regardless of anything that happens between now and August 16 ? For example, if the moment of justice happens soon, and disclosure should follow shortly thereafter, will the end of the experiment will be cancelled so that humanity can continue its progress gradually ?"

Yes, Good Friend, the progress since then was gradual and now increased to roughly 70% as we calculated, that is now double that amount.

This is due to increased awareness, awakening and due to recent evil events. You can see the mood of the World had changed slightly due to activities in Middle East and Ukraine and how media covers all of it and how U.S. government and the puppet "west" and EU with NATO reacts to

everything. As you noticed they quite openly are showing that "they are ready for war, even if it is nuclear". This very open attitude showed clearly to Everyone their true colors and that this world is not safe with these People.

All of this is playing right into the hands of Humanity and right out of the hands of illuminati/cabal. They almost lost, the more provocations and aggression they will make, the more pressure there will be on them, plus Yellowstone volcano and Sun can make very big damage to them if they will continue with that evil attitude. And they still have a chance for surrender. Humanity now have almost full confidence in Itself to guide the processes of this World, situation can be changed quite easily now, all that is necessary is for majority to act and make a change!

The end of experiment will happen regardless of any events and Moment of Justice/Event will mark the end of this experiment. This is when illuminati order/cabal will be disbanded officially and this huge conspiracy will cease to exist. Then must be introduced a New World with released fuelless technologies and new ways of life, it will be a Golden Age for Humanity, another Renaissance - Rebirth.

Followers of Light are free to stop it and show themselves anytime until august 2016. If nothing significant will be done, Moment of Justice will be forced onto this World.

But as we can see this won't be necessary, Humanity almost released Itself from these shackles.

"Thank you for all that you do for all of us! I have two new questions.

Do you know of a higher density group with a toad-like appearance?

Do you have any information about IM Prism?

I send love and thanks to you to infinity!!

km"

**You are always welcome Good Friend! I am very happy that my information brings Joy to You:) I can tell You if I know such group if You will tell me the place from where they are, and what do You want to know about them?
IM Prism, I heard only of NSA project and some firms with this name, but I suppose You meant this.**[404]

Very beautifully written, if it is something else, let me know what information You need Good Friend!

"Re: Ebola and Colloidal Silver--I'd heard that idea, too, and just read another news article from Starship Earth: the Big Picture today that claimed colloidal silver was not the cure for ebola--that govt wanted people to think that--but actually mega-doses of Vitamin C (we're talking 500 grams a day, I think-- outrageous amounts, which needs to be done intravenously in part), because it claims what ebola does is deplete the body COMPLETELY of vitamin C, causing at first scurvy-like symptoms, but way harder, faster, and deadlier.

http://2012thebigpicture.wordpress.com/2014/08/09/breaking-news-anonymous-doctor-releases-treatment-for-the-ebola-virus/
is the link to the article. The idea of a bio-engineered virus sucking the vitamin C out of someone made me think of that old Star Trek episode with the creature that killed people by sucking out their salt... But even if the article says colloidal

----

[404] "Via Rebelle Society." Rebelle Society. N.p., n.d. Web. 14 July 2016.
<http://www.rebellesociety.com/2013/07/16/if-love-is-a-light-i-am-a-prism/>.

silver is not the answer, heh, it still can't hurt."

Yes Good Friend, I heard of Vitamin C, Thank You for adding this information here! Yes it is indeed another cure against ebola and remember ebola is not sufficient to grow in cold climates and when there is a lack of water.

Do not be worried Everyone, this virus poses no danger whatsoever. What illuminati have in biological storage though, poses more danger, they also are making their steps into last part of Revelation - "mark of the beast" (beast means all this system of illuminati/cabal), you can see that even journalists are starting to admit this.[405]

Yet still, they will not be able to chip Everyone and will not be able to make pandemic and depopulate Planet, almost Everyone "outside" are on the side of majority of Humanity now! And almost all tables are turned into Your side!:)

I will add some music to color the atmosphere here:)

From GEs
Beautiful music from TSFH [406]

Welcome to Amaria (Amaria means "God has said")[407]

Downstream, this is where river is heading, from Source to the vastness

[405] "Technological Dystopia Looming, Dooming the West." RT International. N.p., n.d. Web. 14 July 2016. <http://rt.com/op-edge/179428-western-technology-potential-slavery/>.
[406] DivinumMusic. "Two Steps From Hell - Colin Frake." YouTube. YouTube, 04 July 2014. Web. 14 July 2016. <https://www.youtube.com/watch?v=lW90IIsIETU>.
[407] EpicJennyni20. "Two Steps From Hell - Welcome to Amaria (Amaria)." YouTube. YouTube, 06 Aug. 2014. Web. 14 July 2016. <https://www.youtube.com/watch?v=nDkb7wllDdo>.

sea of endless possibilities of Creation![408]

The Essence of Life.[409]
Rise and Fly, You are - Legend![410]

Guardians, always ready to defend [411]

And from me, I have adventurous spirit:) [412]

With Peace, Calmness and Prosperity to Everyone!

READER'S COMMENTS

"Dear GE:
Here is a new story that confirms the deadline of 2016. Lots of info.
http://projectcamelotportal.com/video-library/2232-new-interview-with-simon-parkes-british-councillor

Thanks for your response, but I do not know from where the Toad like beings originate. They came through in a Reiki session two weeks ago. They spoke of IM prism as a messaging system. . .but I have not had any more information than that. . .Thank you so much for all that you do. You are really amazing!
Lots of love,"

~~

[408] Serterz1. "Two Steps from Hell - Downstream." YouTube. YouTube, 18 July 2014. Web. 14 July 2016. <https://www.youtube.com/watch?v=_9Lf2qtNTUc>.

[409] BrunuhVille. "Medieval Ballad - The Essence of Life (Feat. Sharm)." YouTube. YouTube, 18 July 2014. Web. 14 July 2016. <https://www.youtube.com/watch?v=mVNDXHfAuuU>.

[410] Http://www.youtube.com/channel/UCeQnPpYnGVH6z37AWfsERWA. "R. Armando Morabito - Legend (feat. Tina Guo) [2014]." YouTube. YouTube, 02 June 2014. Web. 14 July 2016. <https://www.youtube.com/watch?v=AzdNLVOWos4>.

[411] Okol7. "{Quarantine} Two Steps From Hell - Guardians." YouTube. YouTube, 29 July 2014. Web. 14 July 2016. <https://www.youtube.com/watch?v=Ho9S2ObSKls>.

[412] Http://www.youtube.com/channel/UCkOLW6anwi54jmYUBF0e9YQ. "Adventures of Gillock - Amaria - Two Steps From Hell." YouTube. YouTube, 05 Aug. 2014. Web. 14 July 2016. <https://www.youtube.com/watch?v=F0OGX-u3ui4>.

"Here is an Alfred Webre interview with a man who claims to be a multi-generational contactee. Below the interview is a pdf illustrating 32 beings he has had contact with. One of them looks like a toad/frog. The pictures are easier to see in the file itself than on the video. Yet the video is interesting, he has a fascinating story.
https://www.youtube.com/watch?v=UnAEx2BkTVg "

~~

"Thanks! I saw that! This is so wonderful!"

~~

"Hi GE,

TY for your info! I've got a question about our DNA upgrade. I've been shown a lot of information concerning a DNA activation within the human cells.

The new movie Lucy with Scarlett J is one guidance as well as "crystal" skull consciousness coming through!!

There is apparently a higher intelligence within our DNA that our human brain is filtering out linked to our SOUL essence.

We can actually heal our selves by changing the current blueprint of the info presented to our nucleous.

When can we expect to see these DNA changes in our outer waking reality?

Best wishes "

~~

"Hi Good Friend. Indeed converstions about illuminati/cabal are little bit difficult because there is a lot of contraditory infos out there. The 14/08 i had a conversation with an open minded postgraduate student on that subject, and i see that i lack some infos. Can you tell us about the origin of the illuminatis and some infos you find is worth sharing. Thank you

As others here on this blog i like you very much and i sense you as a friend although i don't know you.But i am sure you know who i am "

~~

"Do you know some technique to improve the efficiency of solar panels.It's for the postgraduate student.Thank you"

~~

"Wow, thankyou so much, GE. 70% is magnificent progress ! Moment of Justice, here we come ! I didn't realise Moment of Justice and End of Experiment were one and the same thing - I pictured the MoJ resulting in disbelief, then great anger then a huge upshift in the level of awakening, and then the free energy / earth cleanup technologies really taking off, ending up with End of Experiment."

~~

August 18th, 2014

SOPHIA

From R. E.:

"I have fascinated with the description of the "Demiurge". Would GE have information as. to the origination of Demiurges in general. Did (One) create them and if so for what purpose? In other words how did they come to be?"
And the answer...
Re: free energy –

(The spread of fuel less technologies is not fast, but at least, People are seeking them. The main obstacle that prevents this World from evolving further is U.S. government and all this evil system that was established by illuminati/cabal, once they are gone, there wouldn't be anyone preventing the spread of New Energy technologies.)

G/E

Good Day Good Friend!

As we know Universe was created in way that all must evolve and become better then it was before. We gave name "demiurge" only to this being that controls this Galaxy based on gnostics teaching and name we took from there, others we name as "lesser Creator-Gods".

Demiurge is an all-powerful being that is a ruler of a highly evolved civilization of energetic organisms we call "Beings of Purity". They have evolved to a state from which there is almost no way to evolve further and so they decided to create new life (their Children) and through it to achieve "new ways of Evolution" (that is what I meant by achieving "ultimate power"). Humanity is a product of their thinking and craft.

One created lesser Creator-Gods that is true, but they were created naturally, that is by process of "evolving further and becoming better". Some Creator-Gods are choosing way of Harmony and aid, some are choosing neutrality toward everything and others are becoming obsessed with power and control and this thing happened with demiurge.

One grants everything complete freedom, so Everyone that wants to be obsessed with power and control can do it. Although One don't like when damage is being done to others and demiurge done damage. This was not prevented as One is always "fighting with Itself" trying to overcome It's own powers. From one side One wants Harmony from the other side One allows freedom of actions which creates, what You can see is in demiurge. And so it can be said that One's wishfulness for Harmony lost in demiurge, so here is a product of this.

"Hi Good Friend.
Indeed converstions about illuminati/cabal are little bit difficult because

there is a lot of contraditory infos out there.The 14/08 i had a conversation with an open minded postgraduate student on that subject,and i see that i lack some infos.Can you tell us about the origin of the illuminatis and some infos you find is worth sharing.Thank you

As others here on this blog i like you very much and i sense you as a friend although i don't know you.But i am sure you know who i am"

Yes Good Friend, of course I can help You with that, everything about them is very evil, so be careful Good Friend.

Information about illuminati basics: what is illuminati, when and how it appeared.[413]

illuminati's secret agenda:[414]

Their religion - this is all about luciferianism, I recommend only first half of the movie (until 49:30), second half is telling that ETs are "demons" and there is some falsification. We All know that ETs aren't "demons", this thought is based on fact that ETs never appeared before Humanity and Humanity never seen Them, so of course Those who don't understand Them, will call Them with closest name available, that is for religious believers "demons" or "angels". It is like in ancient times of black People living in Africa, Others living outside were thinking also as "demons".[415]

What they are doing in their "secret societies" (remember these people are in control of "west" and whole "beast system")[416] [417] [418]

[413] "Illuminati." Wikipedia. Wikimedia Foundation, n.d. Web. 14 July 2016. <https://en.wikipedia.org/wiki/Illuminati>.

[414] Rifleman0007. "Illuminati Agenda Fully Explained - 25 Goals That Destroyed The Planet." YouTube. YouTube, 09 Aug. 2010. Web. 14 July 2016. <https://www.youtube.com/watch?v=ER68ywwAmz4>.

[415] TheLeegoodall. "The Real Story Behind Aliens_ Ufos_ Demons_ Illuminati & Satanism." YouTube. YouTube, 15 Jan. 2011. Web. 14 July 2016. <https://www.youtube.com/watch?v=atxGNYrBftI>.

[416] DemonicWinna. "Recording of Skull and Bones Initiation." YouTube. YouTube, 31 Dec. 1969. Web. 14 July 2016. <https://www.youtube.com/watch?v=d7Kl1_KH2J4>.

[417] Lvlaxer. "Skull and Bones SECRET Devil Ritual Caught on Film_(480p).flv." YouTube. YouTube, 06 Nov. 2011. Web. 14 July 2016. <https://www.youtube.com/watch?v=WItE_uBSDdw>.

[418] SaladinDerKurden. "(English) Hidden Camera Masonic Ritual Satan Worship Exposed." YouTube. YouTube, 25 Feb. 2012. Web. 14 July 2016. <https://www.youtube.com/watch?v=gbRmRkZxYk0>.

Alex Jones famous footage of "bohemian grove club" made in cycle 2000, it is along video, the beginning of their "infiltration" starts in 39:01.[419]

illuminati's oath bonded by blood of their families.[420]

And last is about tight connection of freemasonry, illuminati and USA (here is mentioned bible, but remember, illuminati ideology is based on christianity, illuminati and luciferianism/satanism is literally anti-christianity).

I'm taking information from christians sometimes, because they can see very greatly the whole picture of illuminati/cabal (because remember, illuminati are based on christianity).

Do not take seriously when in a video they are saying that this is "inevitable". You know that future is not decided in that way, the thinking of fundamental believers is "that there is nothing that can be done", because "it is how it is written so or said so". It is all a part of this massive programming/indoctrination and system of slavery.
Only take from this information, the most necessary Truth about foundation of whole this evil system.[421]

This is their last invention "to control all and any", chip which is called "mark of the beast" by illuminati (from Revelation of bible), they also are preparing their newest inventions to grow food and meat which will be available for almost free to everyone that "accepts this chip". Food only for chipped Humans, stomach of other People will not accept such food, prices on all normal food for not chipped Humans they want to increase

[419] Kgallagher01. "Bohemian Grove - Alex Jones." YouTube. YouTube, 24 Dec. 2009. Web. 14 July 2016. <https://www.youtube.com/watch?v=FpKdSvwYsrE>.
[420] BEZCORE. "The Secret Covenant." YouTube. YouTube, 01 June 2011. Web. 14 July 2016. <https://www.youtube.com/watch?v=THE_d0fA9Eo>.
[421] AvengedMinistries. "America: Satan's Country." YouTube. YouTube, 03 Aug. 2013. Web. 14 July 2016. <https://www.youtube.com/watch?v=YT4i-Yvh3RQ>.

tenfold.[422]

Remember though, that they only think that everything will be how they want it to be, in actuality everything will be completely opposite, Humanity will become free from everything they planned and free to travel to Stars! So is the decision of Consensus of Humanity and so is accepted by One.

All of this information is troubling mind, so don't give Yourself too much into it, as I mentioned it corrupts if we think too much about it. It is good to know it and remember of it, so everything they plan would not take place ever and will never be repeated again by anyone else which would want to repeat this.

READER'S COMMENTS

"To R.E.

There is a wealth of information to be found on the Demiurge in the Nag Hammadi Schriptures/Library.
These ancient, mostly gnostic texts were thought to have been hidden from certain destruction in the 300-400's CE.

In 1945 these texts were discovered in Egypt near the city of Nag Hammadi. This means that very little 'interference' or 'corruption' of these texts has taken place.

The english translation of most of these texts was published in the 1980's with James. M Robinson as general editor (The Nag Hammadi Library).
In 2007 a revised and updated translation was publiced, edited by Marvin Meyer (The Nag Hammady Scriptures").

This is very challenging material but, in my view, very helpful also in gaining a better understanding of the 4 authorized gospels."

---

[422] Nwotoday. "RFID Tattoo and the Authorization Super Pill." YouTube. YouTube, 12 Dec. 2013. Web. 14 July 2016. <https://www.youtube.com/watch?v=axIVSJsW6W0>.

~~

"Thank you very much for all the links, Good Friend"

~~

More from August 18th, 2014

G/E

"Do you know some technique to improve the efficiency of solar panels.It's for the postgraduate student.Thank you"

From knowledge of One I know that we have to use prisms (special glass that bends Light and makes Rainbow), and not just 1, but many incorporated into 1 solar panel. But this is not possible for now, Humanity don't have technology that will enable to shrink prisms and make them super small in nanometers within 1 highly dense glass (solar panel), this is giving a lot of energy.

The key to achieve more energy is to make it as dense as possible by shrinking it to smallest size possible. Another way is to use ion accelerator or ion enhancer, it increases the charge. I don't think Your Good Friend will understand anything from it, He will simply ignore this, unless He is searching for "new ways".

Best way to achieve energy from Sun with current technologies at hand is through reflection of Solar Light, use mirrors and direct all beams onto solar panel that gives bigger amount of power. As well we can take solar heat and transform it into energy separately within solar panels, thus increasing the energy output. Unless we can make everything small we can't quite progress further.

"Dear GE:

Here is a new story that confirms the deadline of 2016. Lots of info.
http://projectcamelotportal.com/video-library/2232-new-interview-with-simon-parkes-british-councillor

Thanks for your response, but I do not know from where the Toad like beings originate. They came through in a Reiki session two weeks ago. They spoke of IM prism as a messaging system. . .but I have not had any more information than that. . .Thank you so much for all that you do. You are really amazing!
Lots of love,
km"

Thank You Good Friend!
There are many different Beings in the Universe, I cannot remember All, I know of only those that play big part in this Planet's present and possible future. I don't heard of toad like creatures, or maybe heard, but forgot.

About IM Prism, I can only say that this may be use of a simple prism and when You put Light though it, it is possible to communicate if they will be waiting for Your signal. You need to send request through prism and they when will hear Your signal will send signal back to You from their dimensional world I don't tested this and I'm not quite sure about this.

"KM,
Here is an Alfred Webre interview with a man who claims to be a multi-generational contactee.
Below the interview is a pdf illustrating 32 beings he has had contact with. One of them looks like a toad/frog. The pictures are easier to see in the file itself than on the video.
Yet the video is interesting, he has a fascinating story.[423] "

---

[423] ExopoliticsTV. "Multigenerational Contactee Presents 32 ET Species. Human Consciousness Transforms around 2017." YouTube. YouTube, 15 Aug. 2014. Web. 14 July 2016.
<https://www.youtube.com/watch?v=UnAEx2BkTVg>.

~Sophia

Thank You Sophia! There are many civilizations shown here, I didn't see most of them.

"Hi GE,

TY for your info! I've got a question about our DNA upgrade. I've been shown a lot of information concerning a DNA activation within the human cells.

The new movie Lucy with Scarlett J is one guidance as well as "crystal" skull consciousness coming through!!

There is apparently a higher intelligence within our DNA that our human brain is filtering out linked to our SOUL essence.

We can actually heal our selves by changing the current blueprint of the info presented to our nucleous.

When can we expect to see these DNA changes in our outer waking reality?

Best wishes

Oliver"

These changes are occurring right now Good Friend! You are correct, information hidden in DNA is able to repel almost all diseases with which this physical body had come in contact with, and when DNA is unleashing it's full potential, any bacterias and viruses will be repelled.

As well with opening up of DNA, if necessary oxygen (and with it Energy) is provided, amputated limbs can grow up once again. Oxygen and water with

Energy are necessities for complete and Orderly arranged Restoration of Organisms living on this Planet. And yes, DNA has a connection to our Soul, based on which Souls are seeking out "most likely" Physical Body (DNA which suits Soul) when incarnation commencing.

"It strikes me that Yellow Rose for Texas must be representing the demiurge - who I imagine must be trying to convince as many souls as possible to go with it when it leaves this system."

Good Friend, why are You thinking in this way? I can assure You this woman is Truthseeker and do not have evil intentions.

It is true though that some are falling victims to demiurge or reptilians and are starting to work for them without even acknowledging it, but she is not one of those. You can hear by Her voice that She do not have evil intentions.
This is just from my own observation, always use Your own discernment Good friend.

"Wow, thank you so much, GE. 70% is magnificent progress ! Moment of Justice, here we come ! I didn't realise Moment of Justice and End of Experiment were one and the same thing - I pictured the MoJ resulting in disbelief, then great anger then a huge upshift in the level of awakening, and then the free energy / earth cleanup technologies really taking off, ending up with End of Experiment."

Yes Good Friend, it will be like You wrote there. Unfortunately, there will be anger on these people that put themselves in power over Humanity, and upshift in Awakening will be huge indeed. Moment of Justice will mark the end of it, but it's complete seizure will take some time.

ETs will descend when MoJ will happen. After complete seizure of experiment and full Revelation of this experiment You will have to decide, whether You will live with demiurge or not.

For us, Moment of Justice is counted as an End of Humanity's Experiment, because this is where illuminati order will fall and all their huge machinations, manipulations, destruction and future plans will be revealed for Everyone to see, which equals to the last words of their evil "oath":

"They must never, ever find out what we have done, for if they do, we shall have no place to run, for it will be easy to see who we are once the veil has fallen. Our actions will have revealed who we are and they will hunt us down and no person shall give us shelter.

This is the secret covenant by which we shall live the rest of our present and future lives, for this reality will transcend many generations and life spans.

This covenant is sealed by blood, our blood. We, the ones who from heaven to earth came.

This covenant must NEVER, EVER be known to exist. It must NEVER, EVER be written or spoken of for if it is, the Consciousness it will spawn will release the fury of the PRIME CREATOR upon us and we shall be cast to the depths from whence we came and remain there until the end time of infinity itself."

An irony of Awakening, even this covenant became known, something they needed to hid very well from Humanity. But their arrogance and greed played it's part and some within rebelled against them. This is where they lose, Knowledge is Power and Light.

With Peace, Calmness and Prosperity to Everyone!

READER'S COMMENT

"Dear GE, the reason for my comment on Yellow Rose was that the character of "One" that she describes is very different from the "One" that you describe. She talks about

"One" and the "enemy fiorces" in terms of "good" and "bad" as if these are black and white. I have come to realise that, no matter how powerful all these creators, demiurges, etc are, it is not as clear cut as "they are good therefore everything they do is clearly good". What I see and experience on earth is that not everything they do is good for us, eg, One setting such a long deadline for finishing the experiment, rather than cutting it off the very moment really evil things started happening. That is why I suspected she might unintentionally be talking for someone other than the real One. I apologise to her in absentia for accusing her of working for the demiurge. I agree with you about her voice reflecting truth - it clearly does. I'll keep working on my discernment - I have a long way to go with this !"

~~

August 19th, 2014

SOPHIA

Some information on Free Energy Systems, from our friend R.E.:

I live in Tempe Arizona. I'm not very thrilled with N machine concepts although there are plenty of uses for variety.
My focus is on a Solid state unit with no moving parts that produces massive amounts of electrical energy.
Tesla presented many of those kinds of machines like that.
The ZERO POINT ENERGY FIELD is everywhere around us and can brought to use by producing a circuit that causes an imbalance such that fabric of space is stressed releasing electrical energy.
A spark gap of high voltage can cause it or two coils wound counter to each other with a third coil drawing off energy from the reaction can also cause it..

And an answer to a question from a reader, regarding "Ancient Machines"
–

G/E

On question about Ancient Machines I was answering before. I gave all information about them as i remember. But ok, I will give what we know about them, we know about them a lot, even more than about many Civilizations of Forces of One.

Yes, you can relate them to "machine world" of movie Matrix, but they are not like that. They do not use Humans as "batteries" and do not control nor Humans, nor Any other Civilization in the Universe. They are "neutral" (almost like Forces of One) and they are fulfilling the role of "maintainers" and "watchers" of Universe and all It's many different Inhabitants.

As we know they were in existence long before this Universe was born, they are called "machines" and made as machines (like robots) to fulfill the duty without having Free Will and fulfill duty unconditionally. They drop in category of "beta organisms" that are non organic organisms, this means they cannot evolve without approval and cannot have Free Will unless approved to. This is made intentionally by One so that they can be in a service of One without any "side thoughts", their job is to be like "deputy" or substitution of One within "physical Cosmo" (here I mean everything that is going outside of One's Consciousness).

They write all the information about Universe to their infinitely large storage devices, about every progress that is happening every moving momentum of time (here I mean every less than a nano second), they write everything from big processes like birth of a Star or what we do everyday, to smallest possible processes, like what is happening with every smallest particles of atom. All of this is being written physically, and One's own Consciousness is also writes all these processes, but on it's own, "ethereally" if we can say.

After all, whole Creation is a super huge experiment of One to experience and express Itself, so to become even better than One currently is.

Ancient Machines also serve as a last resort if "everything else fails". They are in possession of the most advanced technologies there can be ever created, one of such technologies creates their own "state of mind" which by itself creates their own dimensional world from which they can see all of Creation with it's many infinite dimensions, dimensional worlds and parallel worlds, but at the same time they remain completely invisible, like they are not there, yet they are there.

This state of mind world is not constant, it is constantly changing world, or dynamic, so it is not possible to detect it even with technologies that demiurge possesses. Such secrecy is necessary, so to keep this technology from "evil hands" (like demiurge's). They are in possession of many many other technologies, including for example, on with which they instantly can undo Creation if there will be such need or other with which they can bring back to existence every living and non living organisms back to life that ever lived in Creation.

They can do everything by manipulating Code of Creation, yet they come to manipulate the Code, when One gives order to do so, without order they only write information about this Code. Their knowledge, technologies, all information about Universe and past Universes is also well hidden from unstable Creatures such as Humans or reptilians (and from somewhat corrupted beings like demiruge). Part of their might they revealed to Forces of One on order of One, and they are aiding Forces of One when it is necessary, yet their main rule is to not interact with Creation so to not damage It's Free Will.

As Forces of One are no longer completely free in their actions, Ancient Machines can interact with them and there is a huge Mutual Understanding between two.

I only revealed information about Ancient Machines because they are active on this World right now, otherwise it is kept well hidden so to not "tempt" others to find this most ancient Civilization, but there is also One's will on this too, something You will know later on. They hold the Balance on order of One and prevent evil forces from starting world wide conflicts right now.

Yet remember because they can't reveal themselves and must not interact with Creation - Humanity, they cannot do much about it, they hold Balance and hold off Ukrainian forces and ISIS from advance, yet they cannot completely negate them with 0 interactions (remember they are located in a world which is created by their own state of mind and from which they are non existent here). Damage is being done on these locations, but it is reduced in some manner of it.

They hold the Balance by simply being there on those places of energetic pressure, of course if order from One would be to intervene physically, they would have ended everything in seconds of time (not just through might, but through other means, like diplomacy, mind control or full takeover of any media/TVs/PCs and spread the Truth).

If revealed, even their presence and looks is something which brings fear to everyone that encountered them (excluding Forces of One Civilizations). They are made to look scary (like super carnivores - which brings fear to all that sees them) when they are put into possible "hostile locations" like these places of conflicts which we are seeing right now. They can induce any emotion and take full control over anything that has at least some sort of connection with Energy (thus One) if such order is given.

Yet do not be afraid of them, One programmed them to be Loving, Compassionate and Understandable when it comes to be Friends with somebody. Within Forces of One they are very caring and have peaceful and loving look.

I hope this helps You in Understanding Good Friend!

READER'S COMMENTS

"It's a very fascinating and also very complex subject"

~~

"Dear GE,

I would love to have a very long winded letter here, as i do enjoy yours, the more u talk about the same subject the better I understand it,, it's like describing the same bush from different angles,,

these days my backs to the wall with time, money ect.,

soooooo

with out explaining myself,,

please speak of everything u have on Forces of One Ideology,, utmost importance for me,,

please be redundant,,and allow yourself to go wherever you want with it,

your description will be carefully incorporated by myself.

as always,, with great appreciation,

May you be well "

~~

"There are good news on the Ukrainian front. The war has reached a tipping point and the ukrainian army is now losing.

http://vineyardsaker.blogspot.be/2014/08/august-29th-1535-utczulu-ukrainian.html "

~~

"Hello GE and Sophia :))

I hope you are both well

Looks like September is all a buzz with more "important" dates and "keep your eye on..." tags. Don't we go throughout this every month? LOL!

GE, i have been seeing tiny orbs every so often throughout the day, one or two will show up, catch my attention, then fade away. I have tried to find out what they are and why am I seeing them. I know it's not a health symptom or issue. Any info would be very much appreciated. :))

Also, talk, once again, has ramped up about debt forgiveness (actually, we need to forgive "them" for using our energy as money and making us pay for it!) and RV funds, etc. what is your take on this? What is their planned outcome to keep people focused on the proverbial dangling carrot?

With many Blessings, and appreciation, "

~~

SEPTEMBER 5TH, 2014

G/E

The situation around the World right now is not very good, because illuminati/cabal fail on all fronts, they are pushing desperately in direction of conflicts.
Yet the good thing is that Russia and China are keeping a good check on all their actions. The main problem comes from words of Joe Biden and Chuck Hagel.
Former Lieutenant General is warning of some "event" in which "disappeared MH370 might resurface" (which I sensed was unfortunately destroyed...) [424]

He also mentions some book, if it is the book I think of, it may be very big! But we haven't heard of such book coming sometime soon. I mean a book of complete exposure of conspiracy against Humanity, written by high ranked illuminati members which decided to go in their own path avoiding doctrine of illuminati.

Joe Biden and Chuck Hagel are making "a hint" on 9/11-like event happening right on 9/11 and saying that it will be "bigger than previous". And connect it to evil people of "ISIS" (purportedly they "can carry out some attack" here). Remember 9 and 11 together are special for illuminati/cabal numbers. It could be everything I named before, they always like to target east coast, because more people are living there, so

---

[424] Digitasdaily. "Lt. General McInerney Warns of New 9/11 Event." YouTube. YouTube, 24 Aug. 2014. Web. 14 July 2016. <https://www.youtube.com/watch?v=z9fN0Nx4Zcs>.

quadrants remain the same as well.

Be careful with this, meditate for World Peace and Harmony to prevent any and all their plots of coming true! We already made a huge progress together Good Friends, many of their plots already failed and all that remains now is to make a final blow to them, when they will make mistake, Everyone should be ready to meditate for Peace and their full and complete Exposure, this will put an end to them and their very evil agenda!

Also, because of their neverending lust for power and destruction, the Yellowstone volcano is not becoming quiet, but on contrary increasing it's might and 2 "natural" warnings were issued to Humanity, by Sun and by Earth.

If I was quite sure previously that volcano and flare could be avoided, now I'm not so sure of avoidance, because both Sun and Earth issued a strong warning.

Volcano Bardarbunga on Iceland exploded and Sun released a huge Earth-Directed CME, which just reached us today (9/5/14).[425]

That is why I advise Everyone living in USA to get face covers or face masks as dust output will be huge if it will come to this. And dust from Yellowstone might have a burned sulfur and some other hazardous chemicals (depends on how close is position to a volcano). These masks are quite cheap and very useful for other purposes as well, a must-have in home. I can say sure that solar flare will go only after volcano, because damage from flare will be much more greater than from volcano. And flare can not take place at all, if it will be avoided though settling down of conflicts. Remember, possibility of eruption depends on emotions of Humanity, the "more evil" there is in air, the more possible is the eruption.

---

[425] VideoFromSpace. "Gigantic Solar Filament Eruption May Be Earth-Directed | Video." YouTube. YouTube, 03 Sept. 2014. Web. 14 July 2016. <https://www.youtube.com/watch?v=VliMBrNkics>.

Thank You Good Friend Ray!
You have great ideas there, right now we can't quite release anything, because situation around the World is pretty tense and mainly because of illuminati/cabal. They are very hotheaded now and that is why inventors, such as Keshe are waiting for their downfall. By the way Keshe made a solid state generator, yet the output is not that great. You can check his website and "dynamic reactors"
Click here.

Much better solution were presented in old website I shared previously, since then it was updated several times and now there You can test new efficient designs.[426]

Here is more detailed and practical look into this (for People like You that "know the stuff" :) [427]

Hope this will aid You and Everyone! There are so many different designs of "Free Energy" that You can completely lose Your head in it :)

And also Thank You Good Friend Adriane for reminding of gnostic Nag Hammadi scrolls. Yes, these scrolls put a light on some hidden knowledge, but again there is a mixture of exaggeration. But checking them is good for Everyone that are interested in detailed view of demiurge and whole this experiment.

I will provide the link in which is said about these scrolls, but if You don't

---

[426] N.p., n.d. Web. <http://www.free-energy-devices.com/NewcomerIndex.html>.
[427] N.p., n.d. Web. <http://www.free-energy-devices.com/FEindex.html>.

want to confuse Yourself, don't look there. It is a difficult knowledge and another "different ideology".[428]

Such texts indeed were subjected for destruction by roman catholic church (once christianity was "accepted"). So their survival is miraculous. Many texts were whether destroyed or whether put in Vatican's library for so called "safe keeping" (in actuality keeping from public).

I will add here important information on "ideology" subject, because we touched christianity here.

When it happened and this religion (we call cult for its extreme measures on "non believers") was "accepted" in Rome, only a few wanted to "accept" christianity and so were "forced" to accept it. Others that completely refused it were destroyed... Same was and still today is happening with Islam (a derivative of judaism and christianity).

And this was happening after fall of Roman Empire. Religions of old were destroyed and People were forced to "accept" it. Millions of native americans living in both americas were destroyed exactly because they were refusing to accept christianity or because of dogmas of catholic church which saw these People as "devil worshipers".

Christianity was chosen specifically, because it was controlling People better than any other "form of control" in that old time.

People-"slaves" which were very rebellious in Roman Empire reduced their rebellious character once christianity was "introduced". Then You know what happened to Rome, after germanic and other tribes came to Rome, they adapted christianity, because

1 - of "fear of god" (but that was not the main reason) and

---

[428] "Nag Hammadi Library." Nag Hammadi Library. N.p., n.d. Web. 14 July 2016.
<http://www.gnosis.org/naghamm/nhl.html>.

2 - because it was a perfect tool for control, which they needed

Then, in ages that followed, catholic church came to the peak of it's power, but there were People which didn't want to accept christianity, because it simply wasn't answering on many questions they were having, and as well speaking against church on that time was equal to destruction.

That is why were created secret societies of scientists, politicians, and every one that was intelligent enough to see that christianity is simply made for control and greed of few. These societies were secret so to keep themselves out of reach of catholic church. Some of these societies, unfortunately chose a completely opposite path of catholic church, which was based on bible's ideology and is luciferianism (which is enlightenment=science in their understanding, from Lucifer - "the light bearer")

One of these societies were freemasons, which was a derivative from much older masons, which on it's part was a derivative of "knights templars". This society began it's operation in 1717 (notice the numbers and recently downed flight). Due to a number of a very high ranking officials in this society, it's influence quickly increased and they decided to rule over the world themselves. They developed a detailed plan, which would take several generations to finish the cause. Such plan was developed as we know by masons and later inherited by freemasons.

And first thing they decided to make, was "a base of operations", for which they chose 13 british colonies in America - "the new world", as position of these colonies were in quite warm climate and in a very strategic position on World's arena for taking over whole Planet. They decided to form a new country, because head of british empire was in London, which was not a very strategically effectively placed and if overtaken, whole system could have collapsed easily. Also british monarchy didn't want to just give away it's territories, so this lead to american war for independence.

Notice also that name "America" was given specifically by masons for a nation that "will do lucifer's biddings" as they named it, so if You haven't noticed yet, only People living in USA are called "americans" and not any other nation living in "Americas".

Here is a transcript on meaning of word America which we know as the most correct, which is connected to Light

"America understood as *"Amer-Ica"* means "the light ever powerful in battle", "the prince [royal] of light", or "light of royalty", "royal light", "the commander of light" and "light at the tree top" or "Tree top light".

Amer= A Germanic form of Amerigo, which means *"Ever powerful in battle"* . In Arabic"*Amer*" is a variant of *"Amir"*, which means *"prince, ruler or commander"*. In Hebrew "Amer" means *"tree top"*. Ica= Female name, Greek or Hungarian for *"light"*. "

So word "americans" means same, like the "the light ever powerful in battle" or "the commanders of light on Earth". This is how masons planned it and You can see they distorted the meaning again.

At core of war of independence were freemasons, which later under George Washington formed USA (at the same cycle of formation of bavarian illuminati order in 1776).

Also George Washington in freemasonry is considered as not "just a human", but as a "god" or a "savior". George Washington became a member of freemasonry in his 21, which is a very young age for becoming a freemason, on top of that he was given also at age of 21 the title "master mason of the universe", which was given only once and only to him. As we know, he was a "chosen" to lead freemasons out of christianity. He also was depicted among gods or being as "god" himself. [429] [430]

So if You understand what I meant here, by now You can see that christianity and christians themselves brought both satanism/luciferianism and freemasonry/illuminati/cabal, which is now threatening to whole World and whole Life. Consciously unintentionally and Sub-Consciously intentionally christians brought devil-worshipers to life, because as You know, they wanted and still wants to be "saved".

All of this lead to the World You can see today. So again, at the root of all this is religion and wishful thinking played a huge role in all of this. Like I mentioned Book of Revelation in it's part was not given as something "unavoidable", but as a warning of what can happen if such path was chosen. And as You can see, it almost happened as it was written and by Humanity themselves, not by "higher forces".

Demiurge played it's part, but Humanity is responsible for this, because it accepted such path. But now, fortunately Humanity chose a different path and will write it's own destiny from the moment of fall of illuminati/cabal.

The Revelation is the last book of the bible, so when illuminati/cabal will fall, this book will close and will cease to exist. Most indoctrinated People of course will not simply want to abandon it, but it will be up to them to decide what They will do with Their life.

Such is the Truth of current World situation, but again You decide what is true and what is false.

I will provide a bit later some more information which was revealed to us considering religions and origin of Humanity. It is an add-on to what You already know. But now is not the time.

---

[429] https://en.wikipedia.org/wiki/File:Apotheosis_of_George_Washington.jpg
[430] "George Washington = Zeus?" George Washington Zeus Statue. N.p., n.d. Web. 14 July 2016. <http://www.thedavincigame.com/george-washington-zeus.html>.

I will answer on other questions a bit later as well. Right now we are not done with cabal yet and they are not giving up, so we need to do some work here still.

Meditate/pray, make wishes, think wishfully, change World into a more Harmonious, Beautiful and Peaceful World! Right now You are writing this Future, so make it as Beautiful and as Astounding You can!

Here is some music we heard recently, it will aid You in relaxing Your mind and concentrating on Perfect Future!

On the Quest (to Liberate the Planet from slavery).[431]

Another song for Rebirth, what count does Rebirth songs already having? Just look at how Humanity wants to be Reborn! And so it will be! *(This one may just be my favorite ~Sophia)[432]*

Timeless Place - a perfect place for meditation and relaxation.[433]

Aitherios - the lifting to the Stars.[434]

With Peace, Calm and Prosperity!

SEPTEMBER 15TH, 2014

SOPHIA

---

[431] CapeTranquillity. "Claudie Mackula - On the Quest." YouTube. YouTube, 31 Aug. 2014. Web. 14 July 2016. <https://www.youtube.com/watch?v=b3BzcGuv-YA>.

[432] Sindrannaras. "Sub Pub Music - Rebirth." YouTube. YouTube, 29 Aug. 2014. Web. 14 July 2016. <https://www.youtube.com/watch?v=0scaET8AR_E>.

[433] EpicJennyni20. "Fran Soto - Timeless Place (Beautiful Orchestral)." YouTube. YouTube, 02 Sept. 2014. Web. 14 July 2016. <https://www.youtube.com/watch?v=fLbWJXyTms8>.

[434] Sindrannaras. "Axl Rosenberg - Aithérios." YouTube. YouTube, 25 Aug. 2014. Web. 14 July 2016. <https://www.youtube.com/watch?v=kj-5uwvv0D4>.

Here is a relevant post with lots of information.... [435]

This is a pretty astounding series of questions, sent in by <u>Preston James</u>[436], and answers from Duncan Rhodes. [Gordon Duff] "Duncan is perhaps the best informed individual in a number of key areas. He is a longtime friend, confidant and advisor to me and a certain inner circle."

So here are just a couple of the many highlights I found from reading this one. Have fun in *your* reading of this…

"The new system will be a top-down technology delivery that will mask most ALL of the stuff going on at those levels of secrecy. The 'excitement' of mankind at the new goodies (for those approved to have them) will eclipse any anger at rumours of suppression or elite rulership via secret technology. Who will argue with technology that will deliver an EXTRA 200 years of physical life, with NO disease? People will be more focused on their own personal wants MORE than they will focus on social justice of any kind.

"Putin IS VERY much aware of the fact that mankind's history is very different to the rubbish put forward either by science or Abrahamic religions. Plus he KNOWS that an event is coming that Russia needs to prepare for – an event that he describes as: "One day Russian's will wake up and find that the West is no longer there as we knew it". His preparation includes bringing the Russian masses up to speed about UFOs, ETs, and our relationship to them. I've been to see for myself his scientists and institutions in St Petersburg. Putin is in the loop.

"Q: Is there Alien ET technology which can remove the toxic effects of radiation

---

[435] "Time to "Get on Your 'Duff'" 2 of 2… Gordon Duff VT 9-8-14… "Questions Answered" (with Duncan Rhodes and Preston James)." Kauilapeles Blog. N.p., 09 Sept. 2014. Web. 14 July 2016. <http://kauilapele.wordpress.com/2014/09/08/time-to-get-on-your-duff-2-of-2-gordon-duff-vt-9-8-14-questions-answered-with-duncan-rhodes-and-preston-james/>.
[436] "Preston James, Ph.D - Veterans Today." Veterans Today. N.p., n.d. Web. 14 July 2016. <http://www.veteranstoday.com/author/jim/>.

such as that which is poisoning the pacific from the Fukushima disaster?... A: Yes, and there is also 'human' technology which will do the same, in terms of both 'clean up' and preventative measures for human health.

"Everything of major significance on planet Earth, including our very being here – is due to 'alien influence'. Everything. Our very existence, our reason for existence, our future – everything. The hardest thing for mankind to 'get' during disclosure will be this fact. Think of sheep on a farm. If this makes anyone 'angry' then I rest my case.

"Nanobots, smart dust – it was released decades ago. We've probably all breathed it in and out zillions of times. It was humans that did it, not ETs. Their tech allows them to see everything without needing smart dust at a nano level everywhere. I do not believe this nano-tech is designed to transform humans into hived individuals..."

Questions Answered
By Duncan Rhodes, Editor, Nexus Magazine for Veterans Today (technical consultant to X Files, Fringe and...)

Editor's note: Duncan is perhaps the best informed individual in a number of key areas. He is a longtime friend, confidant and advisor to me and a certain inner circle.

Questions supplied by Dr. Preston James:

Q: Was the Fukushima disaster caused by a nuclear detonation?

A: I don't know. The 'big' quake was on the 11th March, and is generally assumed to be the trigger event. However, on the 9th March, there was a sudden 7.2M quake at the same location, which was followed by regular 6+M quakes about every 90-120mins. It is clear to earth scientists, that the event on the 11th was related directly to the quake on the 9th – however no 'conspiracy researchers' seem to have made this connection.

Also, I note the prevalence of accusations that the IRI at HAARP Gakona was 'responsible' – but note that nobody has ANY evidence showing the IRI was even 'on' and transmitting.

However, EISCAT WAS conducting an ionospheric heater project which finished on the 9th March. See addendum:

Q: Is there a Secret Shadow Govt (SSG) breakaway society using Alien ET technology to live on another planet or distant area in the cosmos?

A: Yes. But not so much a breakaway society, as much as the top levels of 'society'. To comprehend the ability of so many seemingly 'rival' power factions to 'work together' and cooperate, one must consider the fact that the 'cold war' was a total and complete hoax/fraud AT THE HIGHEST LEVELS. But below that, it was 'real' and people died and everyone drank the cool aid. The technology is not so much 'alien' as 'advanced'. Given that we are farmed or overseen by 'aliens' anyway, it is not a big jump of understanding.

Q: Is the secret IAEA cell staffed by MIBs who have UN or other arrest powers now actively arresting or sanctioning politicians and/or officials inside America and/or other nations who are a threat to the masses?

A: I very much doubt that at all.   There will be no 'arrests' because the lower-level and unaware political and public service infrastructure is needed to maintain the status quo of it all. The only people who are a threat to the masses, are the lieutenants and underlings who are obeying orders and instructions from those above them. Those above them are the problem if any – as most do not want to relinquish their centuries of bloodlined privileges. These bloodlined families who were appointed as CEOs of Earth so to speak, have been infected past the point of usefulness by those they interacted with in order to have an advantage over mere humans. I refer to the elite families and their demons (non-physical lifeforms who trade info and power for what they want).

Q: If they are not yet using their arrest powers, will they soon start doing so and if so will this be disclosed publicly?

A: No and no. The new system will be a top-down technology delivery that will mask most ALL of the stuff going on at those levels of secrecy. The 'excitement' of mankind at the new goodies (for those approved to have them) will eclipse any anger at rumours of suppression or elite rulership via secret technology. Who will argue with technology that will deliver an EXTRA 200 years of physical life, with NO disease? People will be more focused on their own personal wants MORE than they will focus on social justice of any kind.

Q: Is Putin now receiving top quality advice and consent of the Tall White Alien ETs and if so is this the reason he has been so politically effective in his recent actions?

A: I don't know. But, Putin IS VERY much aware of the fact that mankind's history is very different to the rubbish put forward either by science or Abrahamic religions. Plus he KNOWS that an event is coming that Russia needs to prepare for – an event that he describes as: "One day Russian's will wake up and find that the West is no longer there as we knew it". His preparation includes bringing the Russian masses up to speed about UFOs, ETs, and our relationship to them. I've been to see for myself his scientists and institutions in St Petersburg. Putin is in the loop.

Q: Is there Alien ET technology which can remove the toxic effects of radiation such as that which is poisoning the pacific from the Fukushima disaster?

A: Yes, and there is also 'human' technology which will do the same, in terms of both 'clean up' and preventative measures for human health.

Q: Will any type of zero point or free energy be soon developed and publicly released despite strong efforts by the Oil Industry to keep this suppressed?

A: Not until the global smart grid infrastructure is in place. I predict the new global cashless currency will be a type of energy currency unit, and it will NOT be based on gold or tangible assets. Once this system is in place, THEN they will release clean energy systems – because at that point, they have monetised and have control of, free energy over mankind. All these carbon credits and carbon trading schemes are transitional 'currencies'. They want an ENERGY currency so that they CAN release free energy and still have 'control'. By the way, when this is rolled out, most appliances will be cordless and electricity will be transmitted to all appliances. It is all part of the transition from copper cable to EMF/Carrington Event-proofed infrastructure.

Q: And if this technology is released will that be due to efforts by Alien ETs?

A: Everything of major significance on planet Earth, including our very being here – is due to 'alien influence'. Everything. Our very existence, our reason for existence, our future – everything. The hardest thing for mankind to 'get' during disclosure will be this fact. Think of sheep on a farm. If this makes anyone 'angry' then I rest my case.

Q: Is the Earth presently being Terra-formed by an Alien ET group?

A: Earth was expected by now, to be a wasteland of dead bodies, radiation and despair by many visiting civilizations. Something changed. So yes, some ETs are like hyenas, who will move in at some opportunistic moment to take a bite, but will be shooed away by other predators or protectors. Some ETs are and have had a go at terraforming Earth. I strongly suspect that BOTH mankind and the Earth are being terraformed in order to survive future cosmic and atmospheric changes that may not be of our making. If so, then it will be to ensure the survival of humans, NOT their demise.

Q: If so is this group the Dracos, aka the Serpent entities, the Great Dragon?

A: Does it matter which 'group' are doing what, when any of them can switch projects, sides and roles at any time? This question seeks for a generic answer of 'who are the goodies, and who are the baddies'. It does not work like this. That thinking is for brain dead humans who are being manipulated into taking a 'side' for someone else's agenda. Being told who is good and who is bad, is never going to work and ANYONE telling you where the goodie/baddie line is – is lying. It simply does not work like that, and it is NOT black and white. It is all shades of grey.

Q: Are alien ET type anti-gravity craft being used to spray toxic chemicals into the atmosphere?

A: I doubt it. Besides, mankind already puts toxic chemicals onto their skin, and in their stomach, with no forcing at all. We pay money to do it to ourselves. I simply don't understand therefore, ANY angst about either humans or aliens spraying chemtrails around the place. Heck, they been doing it for decades with no observable mass genocide – so maybe it was protecting us from something?

Q: If so, do are these craft with do the spraying able to create a false, cloaked image of themselves as regular man-made jet aircraft?

A: This question is stupid. IF we did use our precious ET tech to spray chemicals in the air, I guess we would use the 'cloaking' button. Again, get some context about the size of whether this is actually a real problem or not. WiFi is killing more people than chemtrails. Vaccines kill more people than chemtrails. White sugar, car exhausts etc etc.

Q: Does some of this aerial spraying contain nano-bots devices that can grow and transform human hosts who ingest them into hived individuals?

A: Nanobots, smart dust – it was released decades ago. We've probably all breathed it in and out zillions of times. It was humans that did it, not ETs. Their tech allows them to see everything without needing smart dust at a nano level everywhere. I do not believe this nano-tech is designed to transform humans into hived individuals. If I was to terraform humans on this planet, I would buy

Monsanto and put shit into the ecosystem, food chain and fast foods. Sound familiar?

_____

Addendum to #1:

International Experiment on the Research of Ionosphere Heating Phenomena Initiated By Powerful HF radio-waves provided by EISCAT (Tromsø, Norway, March 2011)

эта страница также доступна на русском языке посмотреть на русском языке

From 02nd to 09th of March 2011, PGI researchers M. Shvets and E. Dubrovskiy participated in the international experiment on the investigation of ionosphere heating phenomena initiated by powerful HF radio-waves emitted by EISCAT (69.6° N, 19.2° E, L=6.2, I=78°), in Tromsø, **Norway** (http://www.eiscat.se/).

The goal of the experiment was a complex research and analysis of ionosphere heating effect on the distribution of signals from satellite radio navigation system GLONASS at high latitudes. GPS/GLONASS signals were registered by two GNSS (GPS/GLONASS) receivers: Maxor Javad located at EISCAT and Topcon located in Murmansk, on the roof of PGI building. Estimation of short-wave radiation influence on the ionosphere and the quality of the received signals was made by analyzing the changes in the total electron concentration (TEC). As measured parameters L1 and L2, the phases of the carrying waves at coherent frequencies of the GLONASS satellites were used.

The EISCAT heating facility was used in the experiment, which operated at frequencies from 3,95 MHz to 6,2 MHz in a quasi-continuous mode (10 min heating, 5 min off) with O/X mode polarization. The directional diagram of the antennas was inclined by 12° to the south from the vertical. Heating frequencies were selected depending on the ionosphere conditions, with providing that they should be close to the critical frequency of the F-layer. For several days the heating facility operated with modulation at 1,178 kHz, 230 Hz and 3 Hz. For analysis of ionospheric parameters, both non-coherent UHF radar, operating at frequency 931 MHz, and DYNASONDE system were employed.

At present, more detailed analysis and data processing are being conducted.

http://pgia.ru/lang/en/pub/escat-experiment-march-2011/

READER'S COMMENTS

"On the sept. 5th update,,
christianity /iluminati,,,,,,,,more of the dark vs light paradigm seen played out in the brics vs fed paradigm,,
now go to sept. 15 update and the statement EVERYTHING is a managed alien influence (hehe civilizations up in the bleachers takin bets on the pony's)
http://redefininggod.com/
somewhere in his last coiple of articles, his statement of "we take sides ,it's a trap, we need to focus only on our own development and freedom and direction WE wish to take
"

back to my interest ge of the forces of one ideology, there's a blueprint for freedom somewhere in creation, now sure, just as when u might give me a print to build your house with i"ll have to modify it to fit the circumstances in the field, but being who u say they are it's always good to go with the top notch EXPERIENCED architects ,
I don;t suppose they come in often so we're looking at a once in an existence opportunity to learn from the best. IE. hehe doe's dat have de lumps on dare head,,,made the mistakes and have the corrections.
may u all be well"

~~

"I've read VT's articles for years cause they always gives another perspective on geopolitical issues at hand. I agree that there are things afoot aiding our evolvement but I doubt anybody will be in control of the new system which Putin alluded to when pointing at the other West.

The control grid is going down meaning that we all will be able to move forward in our evolution if we choose to it's simply a cosmic balance act adjusting the former inbalance which is not supported any more."

~~

"Hi GE, thank you so much for the info you give us! It really means a lot. I would really appreciate your view on the following:

http://americankabuki.blogspot.com/2014/09/jim-willie-crash-heard-round-world.html (especially AK/Bill's notes in red),

and this one as well: http://redefininggod.com/2014/09/the-imf-and-the-mainstream-media-are-following-the-blame-the-fed-script/

Again, thank you!"

~~

September 23rd, 2014

G/E

We were working on some issues, so I wasn't available for some time...

"So, nothing happened on Sept. 11th. What do things look like now?"

Yes, nothing happened and it were a great news! This is just showing that all cards are now turned against illuminati/cabal. They are in a very grave situation, they can no longer push their fearmongering and warmongering on Everyone, plus they are so desperate and being watched on such a level that they simply could not throw another false flag anymore. Everyone would pretty much quickly figure out, who is responsible here.

Still we will look for them as always, we GEs are ready for every turn of events. Nothing new on Yellowstone, danger is still there, yet volcano now a little calmer then it was. It is due to situation around the World. Summarily speaking, activity of Yellowstone jumping up and down, based on situation around the World. In overall summary, on this moment everything is relatively calm in the World.

"There is so much desperation around money and so many promises around "prosperity" being part of the change and event ... people have their hopes up so high, as if that is the answer and indeed it feels as if that would make everything fixed and fair. It would not, but people are desperate. It is a scary time and I know people are looking for answers."

That is sad to see, indeed many think that this is "a way out" of this, when in actuality this is only playing into the hands of those that make money and use money to control.

Like we know, there is no intention of bringing in "prosperity funds" of governments of the Earth to People of the Earth.

The key to solving all World's problems is
number 1 - knowledge/awareness,
number 2 - fearlessness and
number 3 - technologies.

Everything is interconnected: knowledge and awareness will reveal what is hidden "beyond veil", when People will be aware of all dangers and what to expect from future, it would bring in a sense of fearlessness and with power of internet and knowledge, People of any kind would be able to make new technologies and technologies by themselves will ease life of Everyone and make Everyone much more Happier, which in return would bring Harmony and Love among Everything.

"I have been wondering too about Ariel Sharon as you had indicated that he was one of the markers to look for.?"

Yes indeed Ariel Sharon was last big marker and after him passing away we will see changes. It was told by rabbi Yitzhak Kaduri that "soon after Ariel Sharon would pass away, "the messiah" will come shortly". You remember what "messiah" was, right? By soon it is meant in some time, not like instantly. He passed away only at the beginning of this solar cycle *(January 2014)* and this solar cycle still counting.

On cosmic scale 1 solar cycle here equates to "less than a moment" in Universe (this is less than a second). So soon means some time will go, in our observation of Energy it is at least 1 solar cycle apart from this occurrence. Do not worry Sophia, changes are occurring rapidly, everything is going as "it supposed to be" (that is in a way when we saw such outcome).

"I would like to know Who or Whom has been Activated and is representing their relationship and Influence through the perceived SageStar A. And you Feelings about this Winter Solstice Conjunction - in relation to SageStar A and the next phase after Activation. It sounds like some big ass Machine for Cleaning this Star System -"

G/E
An interesting information You have Good Friend.

It is quite complicated though, remember SageStar A is our designation for Galactic Center (it is compressed Sagittarius A* - center of Milky Way Galaxy - in our classification Grand Creator or also referred by us as Grand Seeder, Grand Father or simply Granpa).

SageStar A was partly activated to block all negative and evil thoughts of Everyone in this World. So far it is working and due to this we have a much more stable situation in the World then it could have been.

So far we did not hear of significant conjunction on Winter Solstice. The next important event will be second Moon eclipse also called "blood Moon" out of 4 - tetrads on october 8
Click here.

Changes within jewish timeframe will be much more obvious right after this Lunar Eclipse. All I can say for now that changes are going for Good, indeed Humanity will see and witness Great Changes. Still, don't lose focus Good Friend, We are not done yet. Illuminati/cabal are still a danger and they can still throw something nasty.

———

Thank You for Your great efforts Everyone!

We feel how situation around the World is rapidly changing in a Good Way and Awareness of Everyone increasing tremendously! Large scale conflicts are being prevented on daily basis and overall Harmony of World increasing! Everything went out well and fortunately nothing was attempted by illuminati/cabal on 9/11 and afterwards, these are great news! As well, Sun gave out an Earth-directed Solar Flare X 1.6 (1+6=7) at 17:30 right before 9/11 in form of a Heart Symbol, such form of Heart is a very rare occurrence on the Sun, so it obviously was a signal for Everyone here ;) [437]

the released charged energies charged positively All Earth's Population and thus brought more Awareness to Humanity!
Right now in New York the move "Flood wall street" is taking place which is going against the illuminati/cabal banking system! [438]

---

[437] GeeMackVideo. "SDO - X1.6-Class Flare AR12158 - 2014-09-10 12:00-23:59 AIA 171Å - HD." YouTube. YouTube, 11 Sept. 2014. Web. 14 July 2016. <https://www.youtube.com/watch?v=nj2o4ezIEXc>.
[438] N.p., n.d. Web. <http://rt.com/usa/189760-flood-wall-street-protest/>.

Police is behaving brutally as if they are the police of cabal and media is keeping quiet on this. Support the Good Friends, spread this knowledge and Your Wishful Thinking will be just about enough for this!

All of this is just showing that all cards are now turned against illuminati/cabal! They are in a very grave situation, they can no longer push their fearmongering and warmongering on Everyone, plus they are so desperate and being watched on such a level that they simply could not throw another false flag anymore. Everyone would pretty much quickly figure out, who is responsible here. And these are a very Good and Great news for Everyone! Still we will look for them as always, we GEs are ready for every turn of events.

I also have some more Great News considering technologies - 3D printable Solar Panels! This is having huge potential, if this will be done correctly these Solar panels will be able to power everything on same level as magnetic rotation technology
Click here.

And another turn of events, Rockefellers want to sell their fossil fuel assets and invest into Renewable Energy, we know that this is their desperate move to increase their "reputation" on the edge of their inevitable downfall, but it simply won't help them after many cruelty their family done. Still, this is a better turn which they made and if they will continue on same path and make more turns on same route of Justice, they just may save themselves. [439]

"There are good news on the Ukrainian front. The war has reached a tipping point and the ukrainian army is now losing."

---

[439] "Rockefellers to Switch Investments to 'clean Energy'" BBC News. N.p., n.d. Web. 14 July 2016. <http://www.bbc.com/news/world-us-canada-29310475>.

http://vineyardsaker.blogspot.be/2014/08/august-29th-1535-utczulu-ukrainian.html

Thank You Good Friend! Indeed it was. That is why ukrainian government called for "truce", as loss was inevitable for them. Truce is very good and it helps People to restore strength and to liberate prisoners of war, there is a lot of destruction already made in Ukraine, overall human casualties are exceeding 10000, infrastructure in regions terribly damaged. But it is just temporary as we know.

Ukrainian evil government wish to destroy this rebellion "no matter what". Only because they were losing, they backed and told about "truce". This is a tactic of reptilians, whenever they lose they back off to regroup and to regain strength while in "truce", then they continue on their war business. A snakish tactic to say the least. You can see that recently when ukrainian "president" was welcomed in congress during present "truce", he asked for weapons, military machinery and money for army (only, not telling a thing about ukrainian People). This is their two-face tactic in action.

Yet here is the good thing. The Followers of Light stopped all their support for current ukrainian government and are seeking their complete and utter dismantling, so as One, Mother Earth, Sun and SageStar A are allowing this to happen. Followers of Light also seek to aid every big nation (that is having different ideologies and languages) in Ukraine and so look into separating Ukraine on 2 or 3 independent countries. Under current events this would be a wise way out of this mess as this country is broke on every level and country is filled with big inner hatred.

Current ukrainian government and whole stance of Ukraine is not welcomed in their evil actions on all levels of Creation, they are destroying themselves from inside. This government is using the pure dark side energy, that is coming from dark source, so their dismantling is most welcome, it will aid in weakening them and avoiding possible large scale conflicts.

On situation around "islamic state" everything looks the same, but One intend this evil group to play it's part in destruction of illuminati/cabal. Ukraine had almost fulfilled it's part, so this trap is almost closed. To say the least, in Ukraine everything will go in right direction, all of this is signifying the end of experiment. And like it was said, those that were unjustly destroyed by this evil "islamic state" and evil ukrainian government, as well anywhere else in the World (meant with the help of hidden hand of cabal) will be "resurrected" afterwards, but only if They would want to return here. Yet this wouldn't be done until the end of experiment - Moment of Justice.

"Dear GE,
the reason for my comment on Yellow Rose was that the character of "One" that she describes is very different from the "One" that you describe. She talks about "One" and the "enemy fiorces" in terms of "good" and "bad" as if these are black and white. I have come to realise that, no matter how powerful all these creators, demiurges, etc are, it is not as clear cut as "they are good therefore everything they do is clearly good".

What I see and experience on earth is that not everything they do is good for us, eg, One setting such a long deadline for finishing the experiment, rather than cutting it off the very moment really evil things started happening. That is why I suspected she might unintentionally be talking for someone other than the real One.

I apologise to her in absentia for accusing her of working for the demiurge. I agree with you about her voice reflecting truth - it clearly does. I'll keep working on my discernment - I have a long way to go with this !"

Your discernment is very strong Good Friend!

And yes She describes One differently, because Everyone seeing One differently. One is not having a fixed body (demiurge have fixed body, One does not). One always present Itself to You in a way of how You want to see Creator of the Universe. One can look like that bearded god Zeus or Yahweh or like

Mother Earth or Goddess of Love or like Your Father or Your Mother or Brother or Sister, or It even can look like You! It is how You want to see One, will One appear before You.

So perception of others may not match Your own perception, like for example my own perception is not matching Yours in proportion of 1 to 1. We all have a different notion of One and this is a unique characteristic of Every Individual. This is meant to be so. To understand One, we GEs look on basics, we look at fundamental origin of One. From here we can form a basis on understanding what One truly is, from here we know that One is everywhere within Each of Us, within every Star and every existent and non existent Thing.

All of what exists in our minds is One, remember that picture we see though our Human Eyes is just an imagination, it is what our Brain is forming as a picture from available "pixels" of color and forms, which Brain can calculate and form, same goes to Ears. What we see and hear is only a small fraction of a real and complete picture and sound. And this by itself means that Good Friend Yellow Rose meant same One as we do, yet only from different "angle" :)

In order to understand One, of why One is allowing sufferings, You have to again look at the very basics of Creation, of why One made this Universe. It is made for Everyone to experience this Creation and sufferings unfortunately are a part of this huge experiment-experience of One. We all are taking part of aiding One in understanding and uncovering of all potentials of All that can exist. New abilities, designs and new things are appearing from our experience. Demiurge wishes to repeat what One is doing and so this being is also fulfilling the role of "observer". Yet demiurge failed in "non-intervention" policy and intervened here, because it was pursuing it's own agendas and goals, this is where the "sin" of demiurge is.

And that is why we GEs are here and that is why "apocalypse scenario" wasn't allowed to happen. As You can see Everything is interconnected, all You have to find are invisible strings that connects All.

———

"Looks like September is all a buzz with more "important" dates and "keep your eye on..." tags. Don't we go throughout this every month? LOL!

GE, i have been seeing tiny orbs every so often throughout the day, one or two will show up, catch my attention, then fade away. I have tried to find out what they are and why am I seeing them. I know it's not a health symptom or issue. Any info would be very much appreciated. :))

Also, talk, once again, has ramped up about debt forgiveness (actually, we need to forgive "them" for using our energy as money and making us pay for it!) and RV funds, etc. what is your take on this? What is their planned outcome to keep people focused on the proverbial dangling carrot?

With many Blessings, and appreciation,
NLNL"

Yes Good Friend,

illuminati/cabal are trying hard with "ebola scare", with "isis terror scare" and with these months being "important" to keep Everyone occupied in some sort of "fear" so to move eyes and attention from something more important like completely corrupted and failing system of "west" and overall degradation of corrupted financial system of same "west".

The most important lesson here is to not give into fear, or wrong sense of fear may have not a good effect afterwards. As well, when they are saying that "ebola can kill millions of People" or "isis is a direct threat to America" or "isis is planning an attack on u.s.", don't give into these lies. These are abusive lies, with them they want You to believe that this is a danger (which creates fear) and when People believe in this, They are unintentionally Sub-Consciously attracting such things and dragging them closer, so that such evil occurrences could intersect with Their lives (and under sense of fear this is having tenfold effect). I guess You Good Friends are well versed in this, it is one of the most important knowledge to arm Yourself with.

On this note, I will add that I am encouraging You to be always focused right now, that is why I am revealing to Everyone here the last knowledge we obtaining on possible false flags or some same sort of not so good things. Here is most important not to see my message as "fear mongering", but to meet such occurrence with determination and sense of complete fearlessness. When You look right in the eyes of a danger with no sense of fear whatsoever, You are able to completely overcome this. Remember fear is main weapon of illuminati/cabal.

Any talk about "money" is having dark presence within it. When there is money, there are invisible strings attached, be careful with this Good Friends. In order to understand what they want by saying this, You have to read between the lines and look for connection, it will lead You to the source of this.

I may guess these orbs are the same probes of Followers of Light. Sophia not so long ago was showing these orbs. Although I need to see them, I can't be sure. But like You are saying, I can say that they sit in other dimensional world close to this one and from there they are fulfilling operation on Aiding Humanity. That is why they "blink". We have a knowledge that they are spreading charged Light Energy by using these orbs throughout the World. Their appearances became more frequent around the Earth recently. I hope this helps You Good Friend!:)

"Hi GE, thank you so much for the info you give us! It really means a lot. I would really appreciate your view on the following:

http://americankabuki.blogspot.com/2014/09/jim-willie-crash-heard-round-world.html(especially AK/Bill's notes in red),

and this one as well:
http://redefininggod.com/2014/09/the-imf-and-the-mainstream-media-are-

following-the-blame-the-fed-script/

Again, thank you!"

Always glad to aid Good Friend!
You wanted to know whether this is true or not, we heard of this, yes it is true. Still, I want You to discern everything on Your level of thinking Good Friend. I don't look much at anything that is related to money, the less attention We are giving to money and finances, the less important it becomes for Us, the more We do, the more deeper enslavement of money becomes. Saudi Arabia, little by little are abandoning evil dollar currency and all western money institution are losing power. Rothschild family indeed were forced to abandon their assets in Russia's banking system. Right now Russian government is cleaning up it's whole system of any and all western influence, before that, Russia was quite controlled by western influence. We can't say same about China, as in China Rothschilds have larger control there, yet don't worry, as You remember Rothschilds want to avenge their fallen family members during ww2 and so they are aiding "New World Order" proposed by Russia and China (BRICS) and are helping in destroying the "New World Order" which is proposed by USA and EU with NATO.

The NWO proposed by USA is much much harsher and merciless than one proposed by BRICS. Most terrible in their planning is that the evil order seeks to destroy 90% of All Population of Humanity and make Everyone that do not come into "elite" category sterilized... The NWO proposed by BRICS seeks technological evolution, eradicating of worldwide poverty and reduction of prices on all items right to the "items for free". If Rothschilds will double cross such effort, then they will be quickly dealt with and they know it. Otherwise they are most welcome in aiding Humanity and also welcome to be a part of a New World and as well are welcomed to taste the fruits of their aid. We GEs are ready and will gladly aid such World Order, also because this is a part of our own directive given by One.

Good Friend AK believe that Everyone are together playing a game with Humanity. We know such People, He and other Good Friends need a fundamental proofs which will prove them that it is not like that. We need to have belief in People, We are All One and the Same, We have different views, but like You can make mistakes, so can those People that have Authority make mistakes, and like You can fix those mistakes, They can fix these mistakes as well.

———

"On the sept. 5th update,,
christianity /iluminati,,,,,,,,more of the dark vs light paradigm seen played out in the brics vs fed paradigm,,
now go to sept. 15 update and the statement EVERYTHING is a managed alien influence
(hehe civilizations up in the bleachers takin bets on the pony's)
http://redefininggod.com/
somewhere in his last couple of articles, his statement of "we take sides ,it's a trap, we need to focus only on our own development and freedom and direction WE wish to take "

Yes Good Friend, You are completely right here.

They are trying to make separation on Everyone, creating something good or bad, light or dark is their favorite. They prefer to make themselves as "saviors", but it simply don't work anymore. They are making separation and duality, so that while We would "hate" Each Other and destroy Each Other, they can make what they want without being interrupted. But when all the focus is on them, then it is impossible for them to do their dirty evil works. So it works when We know of all this manipulation and thus we can stop them dead in their tracks.

READER'S COMMENT

"Your daily love notes touch my heart and soul in ways words can't describe ★∞♥♥ ☆"

~~

September 23rd, 2014 (Final)

G/E

"Dear GE,
I would love to have a very long winded letter here, as i do enjoy yours, the more
u talk about the same subject the better I understand it,, it's like describing the
same bush from different angles,,

these days my backs to the wall with time, money ect.,
soooooo
with out explaining myself,,
please speak of everything u have on Forces of One Ideology,, utmost
importance for me,,
please be redundant,,and allow yourself to go wherever you want with it,
your description will be carefully incorporated by myself.

as always,, with great appreciation,
May you be well"

"back to my interest ge of the forces of one ideology, there's a blueprint for
freedom somewhere in creation, now sure, just as when u might give me a print
to build your house with i"ll have to modify it to fit the circumstances in the field,
but being who u say they are it's always good to go with the top notch
EXPERIENCED architects ,
I don;t suppose they come in often so we're looking at a once in an existence
opportunity to learn from the best. IE. hehe doe's dat have de lumps on dare
head,,,made the mistakes and have the corrections.
may u all be well"

Ok Good Friend,
I will reveal some part of ideology of Forces of One. First I will say on differences.

The Forces of One is not one civilization, it is a huge super cluster of different
groups of very different civilizations. For example some group are breaking away
from one civilization and choosing other planet for development and thus making

it's own ideology for development. There are millions of such different branches and divisions of Forces of One and each is having it's own ideology.

The basic ideology of Forces of One tells:

Harmony above All Else.
Everything must Co-Exist in perfect Cycle of Birth and Rebirth.

Universe is a Balanced Creation of Chaos and Order.
Maintain the Order of Balance.

Care for One Another.
When visible, aid Those that ask for Help with Their Soul.

Care for Youngsters and Educate Them.
Whenever Youngster don't know something, tell what He/She needs to know.

Share what You have.
Give what You have to Others in need.

Be Open, have no secrets among Each Other.
Always start a talk even if it is not important and tell Everything.

Our Collective Duty is to fulfill the Orders of One.
One Orders to keep the Balance.

Scales of Balance are always Equal.
One Orders to Equate the Balance.

These are 8 Primal Laws of Forces of One, each goes by saying of Law and then is followed by a detailed part. Every Law has it's pair, they don't have numbers, they are Equal.

To add here, we have 8 prime civilizations, in their bodies are encoded 8 prime codes which have all characteristics of all "possible civilizations" in the Universe. They were chosen by One to be the original civilizations of Forces of One and whole Universe. Was chosen 8, due to Star of Order and symbol of One - 8 pointed star. These 8 prime civilizations are having 8 different original ideologies (1 to each). All of these ideologies have this same Primal Laws. But again, excluding Laws, ideologies are different, because Beings there are different. Human civilization bears the markings of a civilization known as Izauya civilization on it's language (Izauya means - born of Yellow (or Golden) Colored Star). This is 1 of original civilizations and they look like Humans and have many similarities with Humans. We GEs are contacting them, because here we are Humans as well, so obviously They understand us on the best level possible then all the other prime civilizations. Under the command of ancient and primal civilization Izauya here are present at least 300 more civilizations and together are coming to millions of vessels, very large and small and this is just a smallest friction of whole Forces of One and this number may be increased or decreased if necessary. All vessels are shifted into other dimension from which they are able to see what is happening here, but from here they are non-existent (technology of Ancient Machines). Among present Forces of One are many Youngster civilizations, They are learning from older civilizations. Along with this prime civilization here are present 3 other prime civilizations, they observe and aid the Free Will of Humanity. All act as One. So ideology of Izauya (Human-like civilization) are those Laws and as well:

Love One Another.
Be in Synchronicity with Your Friend of Life.

Care for Other Gender.
Do what He/She ask, this always benefits Your Soul.

Love Everyone around You.
Always aid first Those that You barely know.

Find Common Understanding.

Understand Everyone as if They are You.

There are more Laws among these, these ones are given to us GEs. All of these Laws are given with a thought that they are only being used within Forces of One and not outside. What comes outside is having many nuances, like scheme of "Holy Order of One", this is when evil is being done and Order to "contain it" is issued by One.

I think You will find interesting a video of how Earth look like from ISS in high definition. In such color ETs sees this Planet, from first glance You can see nothing except for blue, brown and white and no one is seen from up there. But when You look closer You can see Life flourishing Everywhere.[440]

Hope this will aid You Good Friend!

_____

_____

I will add some more music. This music will aid You in keeping Your focus

Tuesday [441]

Burden of Atlas[442]

Iron Poetry[443]

_____

[440] VideoFromSpace. "Astronaut Tour Guides: U.S. and Europe Fly-Over | Video." YouTube. YouTube, 08 Sept. 2014. Web. 14 July 2016. <https://www.youtube.com/watch?v=MTZblj8uQaU>.

[441] Sindrannaras. "Mattia Turzo - Tuesday (Day of Tiw)." YouTube. YouTube, 04 Sept. 2014. Web. 14 July 2016. <https://www.youtube.com/watch?v=mF3EnLbDL4I>.

[442] EMAOS1. "Immediate Music - Burden of Atlas (Beautiful Sad Orchestral)." YouTube. YouTube, 08 Nov. 2013. Web. 14 July 2016. <https://www.youtube.com/watch?v=qdLfE6fjDMY>.

[443] THESTORMWOLF9. "Really Slow Motion: "Iron Poetry" (feat) ~ Kate St. Pierre ~." YouTube. YouTube, 08 Sept. 2014. Web. 14 July 2016. <https://www.youtube.com/watch?v=GON8XNsO5gc>.

Talia's Theme [444]

Architects of Life[445]

Birth of Love[446]

Remember Good Friends, we are not done yet. Meditate for World's Peace and Harmony and Mutual Love Among All Things! Stay focused and be ready for everything, We All know the Outcome and the Outcome will benefit All of this Planet's Many Inhabitants! The biggest obstacle that stands in a way is "fear". If You have some hidden fears from Your past, You have to face and overcome these fears.[447]

And Guardians - Always Ready to Aid and Defend.[448]

With Peace Calm and Prosperity.

READER'S COMMENTS

"Thank you GE and will do Sophia - Thank You!! :))"

~~

" Hi Good Firend and all.Here is a good article from Sergei Glaziev ,an economic advisor to Vladimir Putin.It explains the agenda of Russia and correspond to what GE said about the NWO of the BRICS.
http://vineyardsaker.blogspot.be/2014/09/the-threat-of-war-and-russian-response.html "

~~

---

[444] DivinumMusic. "Two Steps From Hell - Talia's Theme." YouTube. YouTube, 07 Sept. 2014. Web. 14 July 2016. <https://www.youtube.com/watch?v=MsD_sCr2JHs>.

[445] TrailerMusicWorldl. "Ivan Torrent - Architects Of Life (Epic Emotional Electronic Action)." YouTube. YouTube, 29 May 2014. Web. 14 July 2016. <https://www.youtube.com/watch?v=LJwwTtyxj34>.

[446] BrunuhVille. "Emotional Music - Birth of Love." YouTube. YouTube, 17 Sept. 2014. Web. 14 July 2016. <https://www.youtube.com/watch?v=-ZgRWf-bAiY>.

[447] DivinumMusic. "Storm Sound - Face Your Fears (Zao Shen) - Epic Uplifting Piece." YouTube. YouTube, 14 Sept. 2014. Web. 14 July 2016. <https://www.youtube.com/watch?v=-wHUTDKnPj8>.

[448] EpicJennyni20. "Icon Audio - Guardians (Beautiful Orchestral)." YouTube. YouTube, 11 Sept. 2014. Web. 14 July 2016. <https://www.youtube.com/watch?v=AyPxTEKe5el>.

September 26th, 2014

September 26th, 2014

SOPHIA

"2014 Message to Off World Beings"[449]

G/E

The Laws of Forces of One are meant for Forces of One only, but I was allowed to share them, so You can use them as well. If you noticed they look like laws and "commandments". Basically, these are "programs" or "codes" like You mentioned it correctly. Through them we are able to program ourselves (for example like computer) to live in a Harmony, care for others and love them. If You noticed ideologies, indoctrination, religious dogmas, media, movies, newspapers, magazines, books, movies, videos, music and even speech and words - can "program" people into thinking in one way or the other. This is how illuminati/cabal are "programming" Earth's Population.
Yet it can be used in both ways, in evil and Good.

The obvious example of evil/dark programming is happening right now in Ukraine. All media of Ukraine is telling only the picture which dictates Ukrainian government. It of course is showing Ukraine as "a victim", west as "saviors" and Russia as "aggressor" and "enemy number 1". All russian media is banned and censored, as they are saying completely opposite - real picture of all events with proofs and showing all atrocities which are being committed by ukrainian "national guard" (which follows in an ideology of WW2 nazism).

Western media obviously is allowed to be broadcasted, as it brings the picture which U.S. and EU governments are saying. Due to this, People of Ukraine don't see the whole picture and as western and ukrainian medias are demonizing Russia, so are ukrainian People hate Russia as "enemy number 1". Such is the programming and this is how it works.

Humanity don't used to call laws as "programs" or "codes". And it sounds and feels not comfortable, because obviously no one wants to be "programmed". But such is one of the basics of Creation. We Forces of One have figured this out long ago, so it is completely "OK" for us to be programmed. The big plus is here that we know when we are being programmed". And we accept to be programmed in one way or the other.

This is another lesson which Humanity will have to learn if It will want to completely get rid Itself from shackles of slavery, as slavery works the same way - through programming and indoctrination of religious dogmas, financial establishment or simple helplessness which comes from fear.

Examples are:
"to serve so that you could be saved"
"to serve so that you could be rewarded with money/premium/gift"
"to serve or you will be destroyed, because we have super powers"

These are the basics. This is known to Humanity as "inconvenient truth".

In terms of spying,
recently google, facebook and microsoft (that is skype and messenger) were making big steps in collecting more information on users. These 3 corporations are known for making "backdoors" in their software, so to allow those with "the keys to the backdoor" to open it. This gives ability for governments (to be precisely illuminati/cabal) and their information agencies like NSA and GCHQ to collect data quite effortlessly. The data U.S., UK and Australian governments are interested in are names, place of living, photos, interests, relatives, friends and most importantly - opinion on world affairs. They need this to be "omniscient" in their thinking. This also helps them to find Individuals faster and more sinisterly, they need this to mark Everyone that is against them and as well All Those that have

quite a big IQ. It is like Henry Ford said "we want workers not thinkers".

Otherwise everything around the World is stable (more or less).With much Harmony, Peace, Love and Prosperity.

October 2nd, 2014

G/E

World's situation is pretty much stable. Illuminati/cabal are at disarray, they have mixed feelings, they have mixed thoughts, but one thing we sense in them - fear, we sense that they are afraid now. This tells, the end of them is imminent. Too bad they refused to surrender.

And Good Friend Djon shared article, which tells of how "New World Order" BRICS is seeing would look like. This of course is not fixed, but summarily speaking, BRICS governments wants this model.

The model of technological evolution with spacefaring ability to colonize uninhabited, but life sustainable worlds (which in return will solve "overpopulation" and "lack of resources" problems, this is a concept of Thrive)
Equal rights for Every Nation/Country of the World
Restored system of original Fairness and Justice
And Traditional Values of every Nation, Fairness, Sincerity, Harmony and Unity being the most valuable of all Values

"Hi Good Friend and all.Here is a good article from Sergei Glaziev ,an economic advisor to
Vladimir Putin.It explains the agenda of Russia and correspond to what GE said

about the
NWO of the BRICS.[450]

Such "New World Order" is favored by One's Good and Balanced Sides, as this will restore the Balance on this Planet. evil/dark side was highly prevailing here since Humanity's known history and this turned scales into dark side, rather Light. So time's up for dark times!

Also I want Everyone to look at these videos and Expand Your Mind and Consciousness.[451]

Every bright dot You see there is "another Sun". Just look at how much there are "Suns" outside this Solar System. Now imagine that almost every dot there is having at least 1 Planet. You can't see them, but there are more Planets than there are "bright dots". The distance between almost every "bright dot" You see here is in Light Cycles (Years). So it will take some cycles traveling back and forth with speed of Light. Most of these Planets can also sustain Life. The only problem there is that Life first must be delivered from outside as on most of these Planets, Life cannot be produced by natural process. Yet still, many (very very many) have Life on them. Most of this Life is primitive, 1-cell life, like bacterias and primitive organised-cell life like seaweeds. Yet on some there is an evolved enough Life, like here on Earth. These places are not abundant in Universe, but still there is quite a lot of them. Only few of these places have a Life which through 1 or more Civilizations had overcome all difficulties of Universe and evolved to become a spacefaring Civilization. The Earth is being protected by ETs, because as we know it could have been severely damaged several times in the past, due to comets, asteroids or hazardous rays from outside. Yet Humanity

---

[450] "The Vineyard of the Saker." : The Threat of War and the Russian Response. N.p., n.d. Web. 14 July 2016. <http://vineyardsaker.blogspot.be/2014/09/the-threat-of-war-and-russian-response.html>.
[451] N.p., n.d. Web. <https://www.youtube.com/watch?v=QuGHW6fY6bA>.

survived. Also Moon was placed at perfect position to Balance Earth. Now what You saw, were almost all Stars that are in a Milky Way Galaxy. Yet look at this video.[452]

This is another Galaxy zoomed in. It is roughly 39 million Light Cycles away from Milky Way, which means You will have to travel 39 MILLION Solar Cycles to it with the speed of Light. And this Galaxy is among THE CLOSEST to Milky Way. This Galaxy contains lesser number of Stars, yet again, this number is in billions of Stars. And remember, almost every Star has at least 1 Planet around it. With most Planets having a good enough conditions to sustain Life on them. Now this was just 1 Galaxy outside Milky Way, yet there are billions of such Galaxies, smaller than Milky Way and MUCH MUCH LARGER than Milky Way. I hope this will help Everyone to expand Mind and Consciousness!

Here is also some more Spiritual Music for Your Enjoyment!:)

The Motion of Universe Expands [453]

So that old stagnated dark spots are being destroyed[454]

And Universe can make a Breath of Whole New Life and Experience![455]

This is how such Music is being created, when All are moving as One, in perfect Harmony and Symmetry - the Unbreakable One[456]

---

[452] HubbleESA. "Zooming in on Dwarf Galaxy DDO 68." YouTube. YouTube, 25 Sept. 2014. Web. 14 July 2016. <https://www.youtube.com/watch?v=LGSsFUSav80>.

[453] DivinumMusic. "C21 FX - Motion." YouTube. YouTube, 18 Sept. 2014. Web. 14 July 2016. <https://www.youtube.com/watch?v=cogj9FIzZ48>.

[454] Sindrannaras. "Claudie Mackula - Destroyed." YouTube. YouTube, 24 Sept. 2014. Web. 14 July 2016. <https://www.youtube.com/watch?v=98dJo8NDdaM>.

[455] AllBeyondEpic. "Really Slow Motion - Aeorien." YouTube. YouTube, 29 July 2014. Web. 14 July 2016. <https://www.youtube.com/watch?v=DX5FvNOuZjQ>.

[456] 1FIREDEARTHMUSIC. "FEM023 Unbreakable EP by Daniel Heath - Making Of Video." YouTube. YouTube, 29 Sept. 2014. Web. 14 July 2016. <https://www.youtube.com/watch?v=5Lmv7aaKJUY>.

With Much Peace, Calm and Prosperity!

G/E (PART 2)

Illuminati order is in troubles, they are trying to win more time, yet they don't know what to do. Because everything they do is going against them and speeding up their downfall. Whether they do surrender or make more harm and evil, both directions are leading to their demise. Yet the difference is that, if surrendered, they would be spared from maximal harm on every front.

For now they remain neutral and passive, they simply lied down onto stream and waiting for "good opportunity" to strike, with such action they prolong their existence and are keeping their seat of power for a bit longer. Yet there won't be any "good opportunity" for them anymore. Everything they do now is acting in Iraq and Syria against evil "islamic state", otherwise they are trying to make huge fear around ebola and "possible terrorist attack by "islamic state". The very good thing in this is that majority don't give into this fear.

If You would like to know what is the situation with them, you can look for news. The more western media screams about something, the more they want You to believe them and the more desperate they are. Like it was with malaysian MH17 and with Ukraine's Crimea. As You noticed now it is quiet, because all proofs are showing that Russia and rebels are not responsible for downing of the plane and Russia did the right thing with Crimea as People living there made decision to join Russia.

You know very well, that whenever they are keeping quiet on something then it obviously could harm them. Like with NSA and Snowden, they are

trying their best to keep quiet about it and in the mean time they are increasing surveillance. Awareness and Knowledge are the greatest "weapons" against them.

On ethereal planes there is quite a calm and improving situation. Followers of Light are cleaning the whole Biosphere, Electrosphere and Etherosphere of Planet Earth. Sun and Sage Star A are sending Light shockwaves which are deflecting everything negative and are sending this negativity away, back to dark source. There are less and less "dead wanderers", there is less and less darkness everywhere.

As a proof of increasing Light Energy and Vibrations, look at faces of Individual Human Beings around the World. On faces You now are able to see the "hidden smile" You were not able to see 10 cycles ago. Such "hidden smile" is due to increased level of Knowledge and Awareness of Humanity, as well People feel Themselves well relaxed and well fed. Happiness can be seen quite well now on faces of Many! Happiness leads to Harmony and Love among All! As well due to combined actions of Cosmo and Controllers, most of Human Beings are no longer attacked by inter-dimensional travelers with sinister intents. Such attacks had almost completely stopped, yet still not in it's entirety. Overall the situation on the Planet increased in a Very Good Direction! Unfortunately situation like this is not everywhere for now, but soon it will increase and will encompass all Parts of the World! There won't be left any dark spot on Earth which would remain unattended!

With much Peace and Love to You!

READER'S COMMENTS

"Here is a view point from Global Research - part of an article from sott.net....it still looks as though the delluminati are pushing for an intervention....your view would be appreciated. Thankyou

On 9/7, in response to criticism of his purportedly callous golfing reaction to the James Foley "beheading" event, Obama stated: "part of this job is also the theater of it...it doesn't come naturally to me." We might respond with something like: "Theater indeed." Next, here's the full text of Obama's 9/10 ISIS speech. Guess what: there's no mention of "Khorasan" - that most evil and menacing of targets and brand spanking new raision d'être for war! - at all. If Obama didn't get the message on 9/10, there is every reason to believe he has it now, since, in Obama's 10 AM (EST) 9/23 speech, we finally hear tell of the great new bin Laden-style evil in the world - Khorasan. And just in case any doubts remained about his commitment, Obama was kind enough to inform us that he was interested not just in bombing ISIS, but also in aiding resistance to Assad (see immediately preceding link beginning at around 1:36, and note in particular the way he kind of slips in, almost as a kind of weird, disassociated-sounding afterthought, the "and the Assad regime" language.)

So the neocons now appear to have what they have always wanted: a campaign against Assad. In addition, they have even more: a brand new amorphous enemy materialized, like their money, out of nothing. When global fascism looks in the mirror, what else can it see but bin Ladens and Khorasans? What we see when we look at the data is a series of theatrical, yet menacing, cues prompting Obama along his inexorable, and cowardly, slide toward warfare.

Prof Jason Kissner
Global Research
Wed, 24 Sep 2014 12:36 CEST "

~~

"Hi,

Here is some really good news. Stefan Löfven is the new becoming PM in Sweden and he is going to recognize Palestine as a state in his inauguration speech.

http://www.bbc.com/news/world-europe-29479418

This was covered by BBC and also a at least one major news outlet in Sweden

DAGENS NYHETER - DN http://www.dn.se/nyheter/lofven-sverige-ska-erkanna-palestina/

The response from the old guard US and Israel with others will be interesting. Löfven did attend the Bilderberg meeting last year which is also noteworthy..

Hugs "

~~

"Hi Good Friend. You said life cannot be produced as a natural process, it's not the first time that i hear that.Then who or what produced life in this universe first.The Ancient Machines?
I am sure that the speed of light is not really a limit "

~~

October 4ᵗʰ, 2014

SOPHIA

For your viewing pleasure...
This series of videos was produced in the Fall of 2011 and the last one on 1-1-2012.
The message has been always the same... We are One.
~Sophia

From September 30, 2011 Wake up to Love[457]

From October 7, 2011 We are One [458]

From October 23, 2011 Dream a New Earth [459]

---

[457] SophiaLoveQuest. "Wake Up To Love." YouTube. YouTube, 30 Sept. 2011. Web. 14 July 2016. <https://www.youtube.com/watch?v=Gu3BMR0KeHU>.
[458] SophiaLoveQuest. "We Are ONE!" YouTube. YouTube, 07 Oct. 2011. Web. 14 July 2016. <https://www.youtube.com/watch?v=nKVo7PTc0VE>.
[459] SophiaLoveQuest. "Dream a New Earth Together." YouTube. YouTube, 23 Oct. 2011. Web. 14 July 2016. <https://www.youtube.com/watch?v=_XKk3vTgYaE>.

<u>*From January 1, 2012 Message to Off World*</u> [460]

G/E

"Sincere greetings....

From various information sites one gleans opinion about ascension and the whenever of it. As you rightly say – one must believe what one discerns to be true –

As a person who has no beliefs thus allowing me to think freely, I am following these opinions and channelling essays with an implied interest.

From a reputable web site that explains the laws of the cosmos, it must have all happened by now and the rest are supposed to go on as descendants of Planet B – according to dates and "time". It would seem that one is reading historical sites or back to a previous future in that those who have become conscious and have chosen the path of light will ascend....have ascended

Uptil now, one appears to be in the same place (has not ascended) and at the same time – given that apparently in the 5th dimension there is no lineal time. So we assume time as a relative issue as you yourself speak of cycles and distances.

Earth is a beautiful world and for a long time I have always felt that humans have been the visitor to a natural bio/ecological world that is the principle domain of plants and animals. I understand much about the pollution and contamination as well as "illuminates & cabals" etc...I make a point of being informed – and much has risen to my senses from within me over many years.

But I am curious about this ascension issue because as much as I love planet earth I would also welcome the change to a higher consciousness which appears

---

[460] https://www.youtube.com/watch?v=xsuXTL2S1o8

to be knocking on the front door of my being.

Can you honestly say that we are still here and that earth dates are somewhat irrelevant in view of the higher vibrational density activities which sound as though they are in time perpetual or time accelerated – or if we are actually going to go to planet A or planet B…or that this whole thing is a ruse to continue the experiment to another level of learning.

I do so feel that this experiment has outlived its usefulness and integrity in that, "less is more" and "more is repetitious" Its not a question of impatience but more one of integrity within the law of One, IF as a (self) part of One, we are the creative soul of light (a light being) and our creativity is such that we would know no bounds and that we are our own perpetuation – ergo this terrible existence on mother earth….which we seem to perpetuate or have perpetuated or is perpetuated beyond our conscious control

Thank you"

Yes Good Friend, somewhere in pretty distant parallel reality, "Ascension" as You imagine it, already took place. Yet, here We are making a change on whole World. Creator made rules and boundaries, within which All must act and exist, so are We located within such boundaries.

 I understand You want to get away from here, but it is not that easy. We have Physical Bodies that are holding Us within these boundaries, the only way to get out in a way You see it, is to whether connect our dreams and make physical of what we imagine, that is create things from matter/invent technologies or simply through destruction of Physical Body/death.

What You see today is a product of big combination of mistakes and successes of Human history. In past of this reality though, there were more mistakes than successes. So We at this moment of time see the outcome of this. Remember, destruction of Physical Body is the least You want to do. This is the last resort, if Soul "cannot take it" any longer in this reality or if Soul is tired. We are living here to make things better, the best We can! This is why we are making progresses on daily basis.

About Time, indeed Time as an element of Creation does not exist for our Souls and for our Higher Inner Selves. Yet it exists for our Physical Bodies. And due to this, We are bounded by time. This is 1 of the boundaries of Creation. It was made with intent of moving only in forward direction, yet speed for it varies.

Almost all ETs I know of have different notion of "time". For most evolved time is moving so fast, that it is unbelievable here on Earth. For lowly evolved Civilizations time is moving pretty slow. The 1 hour here, can be 1 minute on some ETs spaceship. And like we know in "normal" demiurge's reality 1000 solar cycles (years) on Earth are 100 solar cycles in "artificial heaven". Yet it can change speed of time, making it even more faster or slower. Still there are many nuances of time which You won't understand pretty easily. Most important knowledge in this is that time is not constant, it is dynamic and Everyone sees time differently.

Time by itself is the most highest element of Creation and those that control time can control everything. The only one capable of this is One, Ancient Machines can do this too, but only on order from One. So basically One "controls" everything. I hope You remember that One does not control everything, but rather allows everything to do whatever possible "to do".

"Here is a view point from Global Research - part of an article from sott.net....it still looks as though the delluminati are pushing for an intervention....your view would be appreciated. Thankyou

On 9/7, in response to criticism of his purportedly callous golfing reaction to the James Foley "beheading" event, Obama stated: "part of this job is also the theater of it...it doesn't come naturally to me." We might respond with something like: "Theater indeed." Next, here's the full text of Obama's 9/10 ISIS speech. Guess what: there's no mention of "Khorasan" - that most evil and menacing of targets and brand spanking new raision d'être for war! - at all. If Obama didn't get the message on 9/10, there is every reason to believe he has it now, since, in Obama's 10 AM (EST) 9/23 speech, we finally hear tell of the great new bin Laden-style evil in the world - Khorasan. And just in case any doubts remained about his commitment, Obama was kind enough to inform us that he was interested not just in bombing ISIS, but also in aiding resistance to Assad (see immediately preceding link beginning at around 1:36, and note in particular the way he kind of slips in, almost as a kind of weird, disassociated-sounding afterthought, the "and the Assad regime" language.)

So the neocons now appear to have what they have always wanted: a campaign against Assad. In addition, they have even more: a brand new amorphous enemy materialized, like their money, out of nothing. When global fascism looks in the mirror, what else can it see but bin Ladens and Khorasans? What we see when we look at the data is a series of theatrical, yet menacing, cues prompting Obama along his inexorable, and cowardly, slide toward warfare.

Prof Jason Kissner
Global Research"

Thank You Good Friend. We are watching for them and their actions, we know of this danger and we are already preventing them from attacking Damascus and Syrian army. They know well, that if they attack Syrian government or Iran, this will result in huge backfire to them from All the World. So they don't know what to do, they are simply attacking "islamic state", while arming and training so called "moderate rebels" (which in fact are the same evil "islamists") and also the are waiting for some "opportunity" (but there won't be any).

"Hi,

Here is some really good news. Stefan Löfven is the new becoming PM in Sweden and he is going to recognize Palestine as a state in his inauguration speech.

http://www.bbc.com/news/world-europe-29479418

This was covered by BBC and also a at least one major news outlet in Sweden DAGENS NYHETER - DNhttp://www.dn.se/nyheter/lofven-sverige-ska-erkanna-palestina/

The response from the old guard US and Israel with others will be interesting. Löfven did attend the Bilderberg meeting last year which is also noteworthy..

Hugs Ollie"

Yes, these are good news! People of Palestine are suffering on large scale, they are being occupied and tortured by israeli government. Fortunately more and more People are going into Light and finding out the whole Truth about this! Hugs to You as well!:)

"thought u guys might like this

http://kauilapele.wordpress.com/2014/09/25/running-on-fumes-maybe-its-time-we-should-be/"

Thank You Good Friend! Another great design on how to make economy on fossil fuel. It is like HHO hybrids, with it is possible to save money on gas. Very great find! There are many opportunities on how to "trick the system" or make something new, never give up! Like with computer and internet, be a "hacker of Creation" and search for backdoors and loopholes in whole Grid of our Reality, they are everywhere around You!;)

"Hi Good Friend. You said life cannot be produced as a natural process, it's not the first time that i hear that. Then who or what produced life in this universe first. The Ancient Machines?
I am sure that the speed of light is not really a limit"

Hi Good Friend! You misunderstood, I meant majority of Planets can support Life, but can't produce Life naturally. It is due to lack of materials or "ingredients". Think of it like cooking, for instance making a soup. When You have all ingredients, You can make a soup. You turn on electricity or gas - this is energy which is required for cooking (Life), it can be Sun, volcanic activities or lighting strikes. Then You put on it water and start a cooking, putting each ingredient one after another. The result is a delicious soup!

But now imagine that You won't have water, but You want a soup. So, You simply won't get the soup (Life). Such is the situation with most of the Planets. Most don't have water (liquid). Others for example have water, but don't have other ingredients. Though I know that "something" liquid is almost always more than enough to produce organic life. As liquid material serves as a mother's liquid (amniotic liquid) in which Life's appearing and evolves. Organic life can occur naturally pretty easily, but a lot of time is required.

Here on Earth as we know Life appeared by itself, here are present all of the most necessary ingredients for Life. You won't find in entire Universe, Civilizations that will look as completely same like 1 to 1. All Beings are different, like every Individual Humans here. This is due to path of Evolution - 1 and "ingredients" - 2. Same like with Beings, You won't find Planet in entire Universe that will look exactly like Earth. Earth is unique and is only 1 of it's kind.

Ingredients on it, are also unique. Number of which differs on scales You are accustomed to only here on Earth. On other Planets, numbers will be different, plus there will be others materials. Due to this, look of other ETs are different. Their inner Physical Body is having different composition as well, they need other food, other air to breath. Some though can have food and air of Humans.

That is true Good Friend, speed of Light is in no way a limit. I named it only to give You an impression on how far those objects are. There are many ways on how to travel to very distant Stars and Galaxies. Some are like "star-gates", others are like "portals" (both need something to be on "other side"), then we have a "compressed space" (which reduces distance), then we have "interdimensional" and "hyperspace" travels, these are transporting us to other dimension to travel fast between very distant places. Also we have "travel with fixed point" that is ship fixates at one point and travels with the speed of Universe where is needed (speed of Universe is super-fast, much faster than speed of Light), but this travel type need ship to be cloaked, otherwise it will collide with anything physical on its way.

 And we also have so called "speed of darkness", this is a highly evolved form of travel, it is very known for its capability to travel instantly through something "dark" (like shadows or void of Space). With this speed You can go from one edge of Universe to another in less than a second. Yet it has a big drawback. It corrupts, like anything else connected with darkness. Only the most evolved may utilize this speed, it needs special materials and devices so to avoid corruption. Other most evolved way to travel, is the one Beings of Purity and demiurge are using. "Traveling through Mind" or "teleportation". If You want to get somewhere, You can simply imagine this place and You will be there. Beings of Purity still don't have access to travel super far, like from Galaxy to Galaxy, like You can with "speed of darkness". Yet the more Mind evolves, more farther You can "teleport" Yourself.

Hope this helps You Good Friend!

Much Peace, Calm and Prosperity!

READER'S COMMENTS

"Hi Good Friend.Oops, sorry. Thank you, it helps"

~~

"Here is a little video where you can see a comparison of sizes in the universe :
http://www.youtube.com/watch?v=GmWNs4QrshY "

~~

"WOW!!! Thanks, D.! That really puts things into perspective, doesn't it!"

~~

"G.E., You said life appeared by itself on Earth. Does that mean humans evolved on this planet without being "seeded" by other E.T. races off planet? Thank-you, G.E."

~~

"I wish to express gratitude for the response to my previous comment about ascension - so it seems that mentally and spiritually I have ascended and Im now only waitling for my body to end the cycle - meanwhile here is a comment which I bring in its entirety because it would loose the sense if edited...its from a blog site that deals especially with this and other phenomena like fukushima and beheadings;

Comment

Have you noticed that over the last 20 years EBOLA has been a household word even amongst people here in North America who have never been to Africa. Books such as 'The Hot Zone', documentary films such as 'The Plague Monkeys', Hollywood films such as Outbreak, 13 monkeys, etc. have made this rather obscure disease into a universally recognized threat. I see this as having been the 'setting of the stage' for people to accept the inevitable emergence of EBOLA and all of the ensuing carnage; after all everyone knows about EBOLA and its effects, so instant panic mode would be easily triggered in the general public. Just the same way that in the years prior to 9/11 the stage was set to make people fearful of bin Laden and a non-existent Muslim threat.

I agree with you that what is happening in Africa now is most likely not EBOLA (certainly not the original EBOLA) but rather a poisoning of the people. I believe, however, that this poisoning is being carried out by spraying the disease and that it is not in the drinking water. Whatever form of engineered disease this is it may not even be contagious, it could be an organic poison of some sort. Many people have speculated that Chemtrails are being used to compromise the lungs of the world's population to facilitate the introduction of an airborne illness.

These are very dangerous times, I figure that the power elite know that they are only going to have one chance to get this de-population plague right or they may well be overthrown. I am expecting there to be no immediate disaster in Texas. This will be to get the people off their guard but only for a short time (2 months is my guess), then I expect all hell to be unleashed as reports of cases (real or not) erupt like wildfire across the nation and probably the world. Whether the disease even exists or whether it is actually EBOLA or not won't matter. The people will be screaming for a vaccine and for it to be mandatory for all. After all, everyone has seen enough films to be their own expert as to what EBOLA does.

We've seen the US governments response, the lax safety measures, the outright lies. I believe that the powers-that-be are now making their move into the final 'Endgame' as Alex Jones would put it. A very economical way to kill off Africa and subjugate the rest of the world through vaccination.

That being said, what with the seed-vault having been built, the underground defensive 'cities', the FEMA coffins, the chemtrails, the billions of bullets purchased, the complete unwillingness to make any preparations for economic collapse, etc. the plague may well be a reality."

~~

"Hi NI, while you are very perceptive to all the "drama" and fear they are pouring out into the media, I can tell you that it's all a matter of perception and beliefs. We have the right

and the power to say NO to all this by just a mere thought! No matter how uh they pump this into ever media type platform, or how many his are truly impacted by these atrocities, we still have a voice, a consciousness and an internal free will-choice! I choose NO HARM, NO FEAR.... :))"

~~

"Spelling hack! "...no matter how MUCH they..." And "...or how many are impacted..." "

~~

"Dear GE

'the laws of forces of one are for forces of one only?"

I don't understand
could u please explain?

The Laws of Forces of One are meant for Forces of One only, but I was allowed to share them, so You can use them as well. If you noticed they look like laws and "commandments". Basically, these are "programs" or "codes" like You mentioned it correctly. Through them we are able to program ourselves (for example like computer) to live in a Harmony, care for others and love them. If You noticed ideologies, indoctrination, religious dogmas, media, movies, newspapers, magazines, books, movies, videos, music and even speech and words - can "program" people into thinking in one way or the other. This is how illuminati/cabal are "programming" Earth's Population.
Yet it can be used in both ways, in evil and Good."

~~

"dear GE
what do u think of the second paragraph from the bottom,
and would this equate to / with the demiurge? as being this rogue intelligence?
I just had some trouble with robotic android grays,
like the dracos as demiurges henchman, is the grays the draco henchman?

sorry I couldn't highlight it here "

~~

Do top Western leaders work for hostile aliens or are they just evil?
Posted by benjamin
October 13, 2014

What passes as the leadership of the Western world, especially the United States, is acting in such a stupid and downright evil manner that we have to ask the question of who they really work for. As this article is being written, the secret government of the West is continuing to spread bio-weapons, yet again threatening nuclear terror, trying to start World War 3 in the Middle East or Europe and otherwise behaving like a bunch of psychopaths.

Then there is what appears to be some sort of secret weather warfare going on. As this story goes to press, supposed super typhoon Vongfong

http://www.independent.co.uk/news/world/asia/japan-braced-for-super-typhoon-vongfong-as-pictures-taken-from-space-show-strength-of-hurricane-9788074.html

is directly over Tokyo and yet it is hardly even raining and there is no wind. A look at the Japanese infrared and visual weather satellite photographs of this typhoon over the past 48 hours show some very unnatural goings on. On the one hand the typhoon seems to be hit with pockets of cold dry air, causing it to break up, then, there are unnatural pulses of ultra-hot plasma appearing in the infrared photographs causing the storm to gather strength. In the end, though, whatever forces were turning the super-typhoon into ordinary rain clouds have prevailed and Tokyo is just fine.

http://www.jma.go.jp/jp/gms/smallc.html?area=0&element=2

Whoever or whatever was responsible for these goings on were clearly not connected with our visible governments. Nor do we appear to be dealing with normal weather patterns. Certainly the forecasters have been dead wrong for all the recent typhoons despite a very good historical track record.

It is also clear from other goings on that the official governments of the world have little real power or clue to what is really going on. This was shown at the G20 finance ministers meeting held last week in Australia. The representatives of a group of countries that account for 85% of world GDP called for $1 trillion a year in infrastructure funding

http://news.xinhuanet.com/english/world/2014-10/12/c_133709780.htm

but apparently did not have the authority to make such funding available. Neither does the IMF, the supposed pinnacle of the world financial system. It has been reduced to begging.

http://www.nytimes.com/2014/10/08/business/imf-lowers-world-growth-forecast-pointing-to-us-as-a-bright-spot.html?_r=0

These same G20 leaders called for money to "fight ebola," being apparently unaware that it was being spread artificially by their own secret leadership.

http://jimstonefreelance.com/ebolie.html

The question we are forced to ask is exactly who, or what, sits above the G20 governments that are publicly in power. The answer is both well-known and yet at the same time mysterious. It is

an inbred group of families that own the world's central banks. In the 101 years since this group of incestuous families claiming to worship Satan took over the Federal Reserve Board in 1913, they have murdered hundreds of millions of people via two world wars, countless lesser wars, chronic mass starvation, repeated use of bio-logical and chemical warfare agents against civilians and more. Then there is the ecocide they have presided over, killing more than half of all wildlife on the planet since 1970

http://www.vox.com/2014/9/30/6870749/the-world-has-lost-half-its-wildlife-since-1970-

wwf-says

and wiping out 30% of all species since they took over.

The track record of these families is so monstrous it seems they are deliberately setting out to destroy the native life of this planet and reduce humanity to slavery or extinction. This has led many to believe these families cannot be human but must instead be some sort of hostile aliens.

Having personally met many of the people considered by some conspiracy theorists to be "reptilians" or some other sort of alien, I can assure you they are humans. Nonetheless, it is clear their brains have been infected with wrong ideas. It is possible these ideas have been implanted in their minds by some external force.

Much of the evidence comes from watching leader after leader, in country after country, do things when they come to power that totally contradict everything they said or stood for before entering the seat of power.

On the surface we know the criminal government of the United States has used bribery and threats to force leaders, including public American leaders, to act according to their agenda. Just look at what Barack Obama of the United States said before he "

~~

"Hello G E,
got another one,

I have a response emailed to me from another friend about my last question,
would you please comment on it?
thank you
M.

email begins;
with the paragraph in question

M.,

Another group that contacted this writer, the gnostic illuminati, say they believe this universe was created by a rogue artificial intelligence. They claim it destroyed the beautiful ancient civilization of Atlantis and they have been trying to overthrow it ever since. A person claiming to be a member of the MJ 12 group set up by President Eisenhower to study aliens also said we are dealing with a rogue artificial intelligence.

That would be one way of explaining Lucifer's experimental external MerKaBa project that went bad. Lucifer (not Shaitan (aka Satan) they are 2 completely different beings.) was made to conduct an experiment. He built the machine, an external MerKaBa that was supposed to shift consciousness in an upward direction. Those worlds/beings that volunteered with Lucifer (including us, because we're here) had the highest of hopes it would go well. It did not. It sent us all in a downward spiral, instead of an upward one. We hit bottom awhile back, and we've been climbing back up since. At least that's how I heard it.

take care
Namaste "

~~

October 17ᵗʰ, 2014

Good Day Sophia!

Yes, as You noticed Sophia, illuminati/cabal put their hopes, bets and resources on ebola. And because MSM are pushing ebola scare forcefully, even though their reputation is at stake, means that they chose ebola and yes, they want it to spread and make depopulation.

Yet remember, it is not that strong, my first advice is to not use vaccines, as vaccine is a weakened form of virus against virus we are talking now - ebola. So by accepting vaccine, ebola can be brought into Bodies.

We know their plan, it is pretty much not a stable plan, they are not assured of consequences and so are just pushing it through the border, without knowing what will come out of it. Due to MSM constant repeating of ebola, they were successful in creating a panic and a hype in overall fear to panic level. Yet again, remember, this virus is weak if we are talking about "deadly viruses". Physical Bodies of Majority have improved very well and this disease won't spread worldwide.

Yes more passing aways are expected, but this disease's viral spread won't happen. Don't worry, always keep contact with Your Physical Body, make precautions, use good hygiene (wash hands and face all the time), use vitamin C, also ultraviolet Light (to "disinfect" surroundings). In case You got something, always keep Your Body warm, use scarf and warm clothes (to keep immune system at peak level), talk to Body, encourage Your Body to resist and protect Itself, use toxins which Your body is able to process, but viruses cannot like chili peppers, onion, garlic, lime (green lemon) and other hot "spicy" stuff and also vitamin-rich stuff.

Most important is to be completely fearless to any type of diseases and all will be well. Also recently I found this article on ultraviolet Light.[461]

Remember also that all ultraviolet Light which is powerful enough (preferably with lumens above 800) is enough to make air sterile of bacteria's/viruses.

---

[461] "Ultraviolet Light Robot Kills Ebola in Two Minutes; Why Doesn't Every Hospital Have One of These?" NaturalNews. N.p., n.d. Web. 14 July 2016.
<http://www.naturalnews.com/047216_Ebola_contamination_Xenex_ultraviolet_light.html#ixzz3Fsh46gJ O>.

648

Another hint Everyone should take is when same lie is being repeated multiple times, it can begin to look like truth. Such thing is called indoctrination or "ideological processing", this is what was happening throughout the ages when there is a talk of "rulers", then with religions since judaism and now is happening with ebola and "islamic state". This is another form of distraction from main subject - the fall of established system of illuminati/cabal. With these 2 scares they want to make Everyone think that they are needed and "without them life is impossible".

Otherwise, everything is pretty much fine and stable around the World. Always have Focus on positive outcome of everything, this is always helping, not only for the World, but for You as well:)

Here I will answer on questions from Good Friends

"Here is a little video where you can see a comparison of sizes in the universe : http://www.youtube.com/watch?v=GmWNs4QrshY"

Thank You Good Friend! Another beautiful and great example of vastness of whole Universe, another rise of Expansion of Consciousness! To addition when compared, Space and Matter of whole Universe is in proportion of Infinity (almost) to 1. That means distance between big chunk of matter (like stellar/solar system) and closest chunk of matter (another stellar/solar system) is almost infinite if we would travel without "special speeds" (like hyperspace).

"G.E., You said life appeared by itself on Earth. Does that mean humans evolved on this planet without being "seeded" by other E.T. races off planet? Thank-you, G.E."

Yes, as we know Life here appeared by itself and all insect-type Beings were brought here from outside, as we know by one group of pretty young ETs not purposefully. This means, insects were not meant to appear here.

But in short term they spread so fast, that it was decided to make them as a part of Family of this Planet. Conditions on young Earth were very Life-oriented, so insects just loved this Planet "from first glance" and could have become "dominant" completely.

Yet those that evolved here naturally, were much more susceptible to Earth's conditions and insects were just guests, they were not so adapt to Earth's conditions as they are from other World, so indigenous inhabitants took the "dominant" control pretty fast from more evolved insects which were on strangers' land. This by itself secured the place of Evolution of indigenous inhabitants and eventually after large scale catastrophe, gave rise to mammals and eventually apes - Humanity.

Yet ETs played their part, they (under the command of past Followers of Light) made a decision to test well suited Beings here for a "grand experiment" (which demiurge issued). So Beings that were using hands as their tools were chosen and were modified with ETs DNA.

Humans are a mixed type of Beings, in natural way, it would take much more time for Human-type Creatures to evolve to the level We are here right now. But the big plus in natural Evolution is that Physical Body adapts to circumstances of "being civilized" better than in artificial way in which Humanity exists. Such artificial circumstances are creating chaos and instability within future spacefarers (Humanity).

Such experiments can lead to total failure - Civilization becoming completely nonnegotiable, noncontrollable, destructive/self-destructive. This eventually may lead to self-destruction of Civilization, and this You can see was very likely here on Earth.

This is a very known to Forces of One subject. Playing with DNA's modifications and then observing result without interventions is very risky and dangerous. Yet the good thing is that Humanity were transformed and being aided on daily basis from outside, in summary this helps everything now.

Followers of Light made this experiment, so it is their duty to look and care for it, "graduate" Civilization, making it a Wise and Harmonious and stop experiment completely.

Thank You Good Friends Nigel and NLNL, I will just put Your comments on "ebola" here

"I wish to express gratitude for the response to my previous comment about ascension - so it seems that mentally and spiritually I have ascended and Im now only waitling for my body to end the cycle - meanwhile here is a comment which I bring in its entirety because it would loose the sense if edited...its from a blog site that deals especially with this and other phenomena like fukushima and beheadings;

Comment

Have you noticed that over the last 20 years EBOLA has been a household word even amongst people here in North America who have never been to Africa. Books such as 'The Hot Zone', documentary films such as 'The Plague Monkeys', Hollywood films such as Outbreak, 13 monkeys, etc. have made this rather obscure disease into a universally recognized threat. I see this as having been the 'setting of the stage' for people to accept the inevitable emergence of EBOLA and all of the ensuing carnage; after all everyone knows about EBOLA and its effects, so instant panic mode would be easily triggered in the general public. Just the same way that in the years prior to 9/11 the stage was set to make people fearful of bin Laden and a non-existent Muslim threat.

I agree with you that what is happening in Africa now is most likely not EBOLA (certainly not the original EBOLA) but rather a poisoning of the people. I believe, however, that this poisoning is being carried out by spraying the disease and that it is not in the drinking water. Whatever form of engineered disease this is it may not even be contagious, it could be an organic poison of some sort. Many people have speculated that Chemtrails are being used to compromise the lungs of the worlds population to facilitate the introduction of an airborne illness.

These are very dangerous times, I figure that the power elite know that they are only going to have one chance to get this de-population plague right or they may well be overthrown. I am expecting there to be no immediate disaster in Texas. This will be to get the people off their guard but only for a short time (2 months is my guess), then I expect all hell to be unleashed as reports of cases (real or not) erupt like wildfire across the nation and probably the world. Whether the disease even exists or whether it is actually EBOLA or not won't matter. The people will be screaming for a vaccine and for it to be mandatory for all. After all, everyone has seen enough films to be their own expert as to what EBOLA does.

We've seen the US governments response, the lax safety measures, the outright lies. I believe that the powers-that-be are now making their move into the final 'Endgame' as Alex Jones would put it. A very economical way to kill off Africa and subjugate the rest of the world through vaccination.

That being said, what with the seed-vault having been built, the underground defensive 'cities', the FEMA coffins, the chemtrails, the billions of bullets purchased, the complete unwillingness to make any preparations for economic collapse, etc. the plague may well be a reality."

"Hi Nigel, while you are very perceptive to all the "drama" and fear they are pouring out into the media, I can tell you that it's all a matter of perception and beliefs. We have the right and the power to say NO to all this by just a mere thought! No matter how much they pump this into ever media type platform, or how many are impacted by these atrocities, we still have a voice, a consciousness and an internal free will-choice! I choose NO HARM, NO FEAR.... :))"

Yes, no harm and no fear.

"Dear GE

'the laws of forces of one are for forces of one only?"

I don't understand
could u please explain?

The Laws of Forces of One are meant for Forces of One only, but I was allowed to share them, so You can use them as well. If you noticed they look like laws and "commandments".

Basically, these are "programs" or "codes" like You mentioned it correctly. Through them we are able to program ourselves (for example like computer) to live in a Harmony, care for others and love them. If You noticed ideologies, indoctrination, religious dogmas, media, movies, newspapers, magazines, books, movies, videos, music and even speech and words - can "program" people into thinking in one way or the other. This is how illuminati/cabal are "programming" Earth's Population.

Yet it can be used in both ways, in evil and Good."

Yes Good Friend, by this I meant these laws are being used only within Forces of One. These are only our laws, other non Forces of One Civilizations are having different laws and ideologies. We call these laws on english as "Primal Codes of Order and Harmony" and these Codes are programs. It is not easy to understand laws as "programs", but when We do, it is becoming easier to see what Creation is. This is a deep knowledge and it is kept in Arcane category.

Hope this helps Good Friend!

Also we have advancements on Energy Technologies
New efficient batteries[462]

And hybrid fission-fusion nuclear plant[463]

this plant is much more stable and more ecology-friendly, not perfect of course, but still a very good initiative. The perfect designs are made through inefficient designs, like microchips were made from chips, first Wright Brothers' biplane transformed itself into planes of different designs we see today and first home macintosh evolved into industry of personal computers we see and use today.

I can add here that Fusion is indeed the key to limitless Energy, this is the preferred Energy Source of Forces of One - the use of pure Energy of artificially created and microaturised Stars or simply microaturised Stars. But again, this is just 1 of countless efficient methods to obtain Energy.

With much Peace, Calm and Prosperity!

--- I also want to add Spiritual Inspirational Music here with my thoughts :)

When You are at Crossroad at Dawn, go there where You can see Light.[464]

On this path You can enjoy fresh air of Light.[465]

And walk in Luminous Light all cycle long.[466]

To achieve in the end Fields of Elysium - a place of perfect Happiness and Joy.[467] [468]

---

[462] N.p., n.d. Web. <http://rt.com/news/195696-ultra-fast-batteries-invention/>.

[463] N.p., n.d. Web. <http://rt.com/news/196088-russia-hybrid-nuclear-reactor/>.

[464] AllBeyondEpic. "Bill Brown - Crossroad at Dawn." YouTube. YouTube, 09 Oct. 2014. Web. 14 July 2016. <https://www.youtube.com/watch?v=V0nmFeDS9T8>.

[465] AllBeyondEpic. "Ivan Torrent - The Sylvan Path." YouTube. YouTube, 22 Aug. 2014. Web. 14 July 2016. <https://www.youtube.com/watch?v=7mJjicUp1vU>.

[466] YouTube. YouTube, n.d. Web. 14 July 2016. <https://www.youtube.com/watch?v=92s-rLB0wX4>.

[467] Okol7. "{Elysium} Jo Blankenburg - Illumielle." YouTube. YouTube, 31 July 2012. Web. 14 July 2016. <https://www.youtube.com/watch?v=6Ptd9kxnQW0>.

[468] BrunuhVille. "Fantasy Music - Fields of Elysium." YouTube. YouTube, 11 Oct. 2014. Web. 14 July 2016. <https://www.youtube.com/watch?v=SHs57gSBw6s>.

Much Love to You!

SOPHIA

Hey everyone, this post by my friend puts another "spin" on the chaos we are witnessing:
"Humanity is being re-patterned" [469]

Enjoy!

READER'S COMMENTS

"pretty good

https://web.archive.org/web/20140210011238/http://blog.redefininggod.com/2014/01/23/the-blood-cult-and-2014-welcome-to-the-global-universal-church-and-your-new-motherfather-god.aspx

M. "

~~

"Whilst this site has been gracious enough to bring news of the ebola issue and comments from GEI send this from the same site for your interest and any comments from GE...

I thank you in the name of reason and generosity for the communication of information that one will not find on the msm.

Straight to the point: Liberian scientist nails Ebola cause

The "Ebola" outbreak is a combination of two things - 1. live Ebola injections at the hands of the Red Cross and Ebola testing trials, and 2. poisoning of water sources and

[469] "Humanity Is Being Re-Patterened." New Earth Paradigm. N.p., 18 Oct. 2014. Web. 14 July 2016. <http://newearthparadigm.wordpress.com/2014/10/18/humanity-is-being-re-patterened/>.

direct injections of formaldehyde.

Dr. Cyril Broderick, A Liberian scientist and a former professor of Plant Pathology at the University of Liberia's College of Agriculture and Forestry says the West, particularly the U.S. is responsible for the Ebola outbreak in West Africa. Dr. Broderick claims the following in an exclusive article published in the Daily Observer based in Monrovia, Liberia. He wrote the following:

The US Department of Defense (DoD) is funding Ebola trials on humans, trials which started just weeks before the Ebola outbreak in Guinea and Sierra Leone. The reports continue and state that the DoD gave a contract worth $140 million dollars to Tekmira, a Canadian pharmaceutical company, to conduct Ebola research. This research work involved injecting and infusing healthy humans with the deadly Ebola virus. Hence, the DoD is listed as a collaborator in a "First in Human" Ebola clinical trial (NCT02041715, which started in January 2014 shortly before an Ebola epidemic was declared in West Africa in March.

I believe the current outbreak is a combination of two things - water poisoning and phony "vaccine" injections which were really formaldehyde, and more dangerously - a live virus that was delivered via shots in the name of "ebola testing". The live virus is not the original Ebola and does not produce classic symptoms, and is almost certainly still only possible to get via injection.

The U.S. has a long history of conducting these types of experiments, Read more here

The "Ebola outbreak" is fake for two reasons: 1. It is not classic Ebola, showing any classic symptoms at all, as evidenced by the lack of photos, and 2. If it can only be contracted via a shot compliments of the Red Cross or other scammers, it is not an outbreak. It is an act of war. "

~~

" http://www.inquisitr.com/1545317/ebola-treatment-is-working-according-to-official-in-sierra-leone-so-why-such-opposition/ "

Posted 3 days ago."

~~

October 20th, 2014

G/E

Question 1

"dear GE
what do u think of the second paragraph from the bottom,
and would this equate to / with the demiurge? as being this rogue intelligence?
I just had some trouble with robotic android grays,
like the dracos as demiurges henchman, is the grays the draco henchman?

sorry I couldn't highlight it here"

http://americankabuki.blogspot.com/2014/10/benjamin-fulford-10132014-do-top.html

Question 2

"Hello G E,
got another one,

I have a response emailed to me from another friend about my last question,
would you please comment on it?
thank you
M.

email begins;
with the paragraph in question

M.,

Another group that contacted this writer, the gnostic illuminati, say they believe
this universe was created by a rogue artificial intelligence. They claim it

657

destroyed the beautiful ancient civilization of Atlantis and they have been trying to overthrow it ever since. A person claiming to be a member of the MJ 12 group set up by President Eisenhower to study aliens also said we are dealing with a rogue artificial intelligence.

That would be one way of explaining Lucifer's experimental external MerKaBa project that went bad. Lucifer (not Shaitan (aka Satan) they are 2 completely different beings.) was made to conduct an experiment. He built the machine, an external MerKaBa that was supposed to shift consciousness in an upward direction. Those worlds/beings that volunteered with Lucifer (including us, because we're here) had the highest of hopes it would go well. It did not. It sent us all in a downward spiral, instead of an upward one. We hit bottom awhile back, and we've been climbing back up since. At least that's how I heard it.

take care
namaste"

I knew that I would be asked about "rogue intelligence". Eventually Many that are evolved enough and are seeking the Truth about whole Universe are coming directly or indirectly to notions such as "matrix", "artificial intelligence" or "Ancient Machines".

In Universe as we know there are many Those who think that the guider of Ancient Machines called Super Wise Intelligence (SWI) is a "rogue" artificially created intelligence that took control from original Creator. It is not true. If You look at it from outside, such statement will look to You very likely, yet You have to understand it in all details, again without proper understanding we lack the whole picture. SWI is a machine, this machine is a very very powerful computer system (it is unimaginable just how "powerful") that guides every Ancient Machine and overseeing all of this Creation. It was created specifically for this role by One.

SWI and all AMs are in existence for all known and unknown "time". They were before last Universe and before it. The SWI is a direct incarnation of One, it has the ultimate power to control and guide Universe like One is having, yet SWI and One are One, like every other Being living in Universe is having One within It, so is SWI, but SWI is having a very big role and thus it has much more power given to it.

One created SWI "perfectly", that is without any flaws. So when we are talking about "lucifer" or "satan" that betrayed "God", supposedly the Creator of Universe, this is not about One. As One creates flawless designs, the "God" written in the bible is not perfect, because he made "perfect" creation Lucifer that betrayed him, so obviously it is not perfect (unless Lucifer was meant to betray). So it is not One that is written there, there is written about Anu and his creation "igigi" that betrayed him.

But parallels here are obvious. One made SWI with a notion that One is not only it's Creator, father, mother, but also brother, sister, most closest relative there can be for SWI in entire Creation, also most closest Friend, Friend of Life and Friend of Oath. There is much more what is programmed into SWI and thus SWI would never ever "betray" One - The Creator of the Universe (as betrayal of One is betrayal of Universe and thus thyself, this applies to Everyone living here and outside as well).

On control from outside, we know this as the truth that illuminati/cabal were under control of reptilians and are under control of demiurge. Reptilians along with "messengers" of demiurge were directing illuminati. There were incarnated reptilians and not incarnated reptilians - commanders that were directing them.

Also ETs You know as "greys" are insect-type beings with almost cold blood, they made a contract during "Roswell incident" as it was their craft that was shot down by USA's defenses back then and this contract is already expired. This Civilization also was approached by Galactic Federation and asked to stop interfering into Earth, cease abductions of Humans and experiments on Them (they were abducting by contract).

Numbers of abductions have gradually decreased, but still abductions are happening on rare occasions by those that do not listen to laws - called "freelancers" or "outlaws" or by Galactic Federation themselves. GFL is stopping outlaws and freelancers, still it is not easy for them as we can see.

The difference between abductions made by greys and GFL is that GFL (including pleiadeans) are asking for permission "to be abducted", and greys with reptilians do not. Also GFL do not abuse Humans when they are unconscious and greys do abuse. Also greys are known to make experiments on Humans, they are making hybrid Beings from Human tissue and their own. They do not destroy Humans as we know, they only take small portion of tissue like hairs, nails or blood. We saw all of it previously, but now it ended, the guidance and control of reptilians and greys ceased.

The twisted ideology of illuminati/cabal and guidance of reptilians made a huge contribution into sufferings of this Planet, so Ben Fulford's words have big portion of Truth in them. Ben knows a lot of things, he is a Lightworker and thus is able to see through veil.

Again, use Your own discernment Good Friend. Same I ask on lucifer/satan. For us this is imagination made "real" through programming. Yes, it is based on Truth, but it is mixed with too much exaggeration and is "catchy", so those People that can't find the Truth that is outside this World, are advised to look for Truth rather from 0, than from such source. We already can see by looking at present World, just how dangerous and poisonous this ideology is.

Hope this will aid You Good Friend, with Love and Abundance.

READER'S COMMENT

"Are the Super Wise Intelligence and Ancient Machines capable of feeling Love? I send them mine either way."

~~

October 20th, 2015 (Part 2)

FROM G/E

? Regarding the following (fear based) email from Dr. Rima Laibow:

"Dr. Rima, is Ebola a hoax?"

Is Ebola a hoax? Absolutely not.

Is it killing people? Absolutely. I just got off the phone with one of our "Suits on the ground" in Liberia and the recording of our conversation confirms the reality of the epidemic.

Is it airborne? Absolutely. I have documented that in a blast which you can find on the topic on our main website: http://drrimatruthreports.com/another-ebola-military-smoking-gun/ .

Is the Ebo-Lie hype a combination of disinformation and misinformation? Absolutely. It is clearly in the interest of those who wish to use the disaster that Ebola represents for culling the population to have the population unprepared. Thus the attack on me personally in the main-stream media, thus the absolute distortion of the reality of how Nano (not colloidal) Silver 10 PPM supports immune function in the controlled opposition, the so-called "alternative media," thus the denigration and downplaying of the science supporting Nano Silver 10 PPM [see: http://drrimatruthreports.com/us-govt-nano-silver-study-declassified-2009/] and the hype and hysteria to push us into gratefully rolling up our sleeves, paying through the nose and saying "Thank You!" to the people who want to put.....what??? into our bodies.

BUT is Ebola the (weaponized and intentionally disseminated) excuse for huge geopolitical change to control world resources and subjugate those who might protest under Medical Martial Law? Absolutely!

Consider: The Pentagon just laid out its plans here:

Because as the despicable Useful Idiot and head of CDC, Tom Freiden, MD, has said "we know how to handle the Ebola outbreak. We know how to contain it." we are supposed to believe him. At the same time, co-Useful Idiot Margaret Chan, MD, Director of WHO, says that the outbreak is a world Pandemic and is totally out of control. And we are supposed to believe her, trust them(?), trust our lives and security to the same people who told the second Dallas nurse it was OK to fly on a commercial flight after she had developed a fever?

Of course not.

The same people who came on board a flight form Lagos, Nigeria when it landed in New York with a dead passenger showing all the signs of Ebola, looked at the dead guy, took no samples and said, "Nope, doesn't look like Ebola to us!" and released the passengers to disperse into the population at large?

Of course not.

By the way, Nigeria has been declared an Ebola-free nation along with Senegal by WHO. I do not know whether these two men did, indeed, have Ebola. But it is possible that they were Ebola positive. If so, where would they have come from, given Nigeria's Ebola-free status. Should we trust WHO and CDC on this?

Same answer: Of course not.

We know the plan: it has been laid out clearly and the Natural Solutions

Foundation has been warning you about it for quite a while.

Remember GHSI. the Global Health Security Initiative, which says that the best way to protect people from infectious disease is to make sure that there are fewer people alive to GET infectious disease? And remember that we've been telling you that GHSI has given itself the power to quarantine and "treat" anyone with anything? And that Obama has been issuing one draconian Executive Order (Imperial Edict?) after another to put the unlawful actions of such an initiative into a legal framework?

And recall that having an Ebola outbreak would be very useful to those forces seeking to rearrange our society. Then consider this: Judicial Watch has learned that it appears the Obama administration is actively formulating plans to admit Ebola-infected non-U.S. citizens into the United States for treatment. Specifically, the goal of the administration seems to be to "bring Ebola patients into the United States for treatment within the first days of diagnosis".

Right now, the UK has announced that it will invade Sierra Leone with 3000 troops to "stop the Ebola outbreak". Sierra Leone is rich in mineral resources like diamonds, gold, bauxite, rutile and iron ore which are present in large quantities.

Liberia, the Nano Silver front line, is rich in iron ore, timber, diamonds, gold and hydro-power.

I will remind you of the definition of "Useless Eaters" told to me by a Head of State in 2002: "those people who are consuming OUR non-renewable Natural Resources." and they are certainly using Ebola to cull us, whom they believe to be Useless Eaters. [See: http://youtu.be/_gWmVtn5JsA]

Useless Eaters with Nano Silver 10 PPM in their cupboards may be, however, quite another matter.

Let me tell you again that the more of us who are NOT going to succumb to Ebola, which is VERY REAL, and VERY DEADLY, the less likely their plans are to take everything over for themselves.

And the best way I know (in fact the ONLY way that has any real science, rather than speculation, theory, imagination or fervor behind it) is to support your immune system with Nano Silver 10 PPM so that it can repel the invasion of the virus. No viral penetration through normal cell membranes, no disease.

Listen up, FDA/FTC trolls: the presence of a virus in the body is not the same as the presence of a disease. Since, under US law we are not permitted to say that a nutrient "treats" a disease or condition, but may say that it may provide provide a therapy that may benefit, we are, indeed, saying that Nano Silver 10 PPM provides a therapy that may benefit the person with a viral load of Ebola virus, by supporting homeostasis through normal cell membrane integrity. That is what the Defense Threat Reduction Agency-sponsored study, declassified in 2009, showed. It did not show Nano Silver "treating Ebola." It showed Nano Silver supporting normal immune system function.

Since under the FDA/FTC misinterpretation of US law we are not permitted to say (even it if is true -- First Amendment? What First Amendment?) that a nutrient can "diagnose, prevent, mitigate, treat or cure" any disease or condition, we are not saying that. We are saying truthfully that nutrient Nano Silver 10 PPM supports normal structure and function of cell membrane integrity and the immune system.

If you, dear reader, are not happy with this suppression of truthful speech, go here, http://TinyURL.com/DontStopNanoSilver and tell the FDA/FTC that you want the truth to be spoken freely about Nano Silver 10 PPM and all other nutrients. Join in private expressive association with us and our Citizens' Petition.

We believe that nutrients can have powerful health benefits. They DO prevent. They DO treat. They Do mitigate. They DO cure. Why are we not permitted to tell the truth in the United States? Oh, because the federal agencies, empowered by a Congress that stepped over its Constitutional limits in trying to censor speech about food and health, serve only their real constituents, the MultiNational Crony Corporations.

We are ready, willing and able to take on this violation of YOUR First Amendment rights. To success, however, we need you to help fill the War Chest to take this suppression on. You can do that here:http://Donate.DrRimaTruth.com.

Spread the word. We, together, are the natural solution to the problem that they have created.

Yours for health and freedom, . Dr. Rima"

The ebola virus like I mentioned is not that scary to pose a danger to countries that goes beyond northern tropics, these are USA, Canada, Almost all Europe, Mongolia and Russia. There is also fabrication on ebola "reports". You can see it here (it is having some rough language, but I guess You can understand this Good Friend).[470]

Such reports are transmitted not from troubled location but from other nearby location as there is a scare among journalists as well, they are afraid to go there. Also green color, it is true, another Subconscious sign of illuminati order.

Another confirmation of western media's deception is this brave Man. He told everything about how CIA and U.S. government manipulates all World's major news covers.[471]

---

[470] ""Ebola Hoax: 100%% REVEALED! ..." The YouTube Account Associated with This Video Has Been Terminated Due to Multiple Third-party Notifications of Copyright Infringement." YouTube. N.p., n.d. Web. 14 July 2016. <http://youtu.be/rv-hh2JWJwk>.

[471] "German Journo: European Media Writing Pro-US Stories under CIA Pressure (VIDEO)." RT International. N.p., n.d. Web. 14 July 2016. <http://rt.com/news/196984-german-journlaist-cia-pressure/>.

Also remember all this ebola scare is a fear psyop. What we know for sure, is that People are really passing away in Liberia and Sierra Leone, yet number of "deaths" is less than is reported. It's main intention is to win masses of people into accepting whatever there is, this current system (of illuminati/cabal) would provide. For example what they have on their hands now current plan B - martial law, which could be done through spread of disease (through forceful vaccination (where "vaccines" are with other more "deadly" viruses or even with RFID chips).

So this is why I highly recommend to not take anything inside Your body that they would "recommend". By this they are also trying to show that without them "life is impossible". If You can relate this incident with similar incidents, it can be related to 9/11, Boston "bombings" and Sandy Hook shootings.

On this note we have a special counter plan against all this psyop and virus itself. It will be played out only if they will start mandatory vaccination. Also Russia already developed both vaccine and serum against ebola. They are not fully functional, but virologists will be ready to implement them anytime as we know.[472] [473]

And if ebola will get into Russia or China or India (2 most populated countries in the World), this virus will be quickly stopped by scientists inside. Outside intervention is also possible if more than 1/3 of World Population is threatened.

Much Love to You.

---

[472] "Scientists in Russia Developing Three Ebola Vaccines – Health Ministry." RT International. N.p., n.d. Web. 14 July 2016. <http://rt.com/news/195332-russia-vaccine-ebola-virus/>.
[473] "Russian Scientists Working on Fast-acting Ebola Vaccine." RT International. N.p., n.d. Web. 14 July 2016. <http://rt.com/news/197416-ebola-russian-antibodies-vaccine/>.

READER'S COMMENTS

"Thankyou GE,

regarding the rogue AI question and answer,
could I assume then a parallel from my other friends answer utilizing the Lucifer thing and Ben's report
that the military (earth defense force) sees the dimiurge as the rogue AI in question?
probably conotated through the judao-christion filter of perception?

Thank you again
M."

~~

"here guys
read whats to happen to ebola and isis

Did the dragon family take control of the Federal Reserve Board
Posted by benjamin
October 20, 2014

Multiple sources are reporting that as of October 17th, 2014, the Dragon family has taken over control of the international operations of the Federal Reserve Board and that as a result, the cabal's ISIS and ebola campaigns, which were negotiating tactics, will be wound down. Under the deal, the United States, Europe and England, respectively, will be issuing their own domestic currencies. However, the world's reserve currency will no longer be controlled by the families that used to own the Fed, the sources, including pentagon and CIA officials, said.

A Chinese government source was unable to confirm that a deal had been reached. Nonetheless, he did note that China, Indonesia and Japan had been printing dollars of their own under the old regime but that all new creation of dollars world-wide will stop in October. This implies that any new currency issued internationally will be something other than dollars; most likely a basket of currencies centered on the Chinese yuan.

A British MI5 source, for his part, says "Europe is in no condition to make any agreements based on the future use of the Euro. Italy, France and Germany all need to expedite the issuance of domestic currency and this is now a recognized fact."

Moreover, there are still major power groups, notably in the Middle East and the US, that are unwilling to accept this deal, dragon family sources say. As a result, geopolitical turbulence is expected to continue until the final resistance groups are subdued and controlled. A dragon family member says they will push for complete cabal defeat by the Chinese lunar New Year , which falls on February 19th in 2015.

A high level "G7 source" independently confirmed that as a result of the new deal, "The New Economic System will be developed founded on the truth namely that there is Abundance of resources, not scarcity."

If a deal has been reached at the highest levels of Eastern and Western esoteric power, then there will be many public signs appearing. For one thing many world leaders, including US corporate president Barack Obama, Japanese slave Prime Minister Shinzo Abe, UN head Ban Ki Moon and Israeli Prime Minister Benyamin Netanyahu will

be removed from office.

Certainly things are not looking good for Japan's Abe. Two of the ministers of his just reshuffled cabinet, Trade and Industry Minister Yuko Obuchi and Justice Minister Midori Matsuhima resigned this Monday. The ministers resigned over supposed misuse of political funds but this was just an excuse for public consumption. Both ministers were disciples of top CIA Japan handler Gerald Curtis who is no longer the top Japan handler. Sources in the Japanese imperial family say that the removal of Abe and his secret handlers such as Richard Armitage and Michael Green was part of the deal made between the dragon family and the Western leaders.

Veteran politician Ichiro Ozawa has been proposed by Japanese right wingers as an interim figure to preside over Japan until a truly independent government can be formed, the sources said. Two other names put forth as possible Abe replacements are former Osaka mayor Toru Hashimoto and former Miyazaki Prefectural governor Hideo

Higashikokubaru.

There is also a strong push by the imperial family and others to merge Japan with North and South Korea to create Kopan, which would be an economic powerhouse with a population of 200 million. In such a scenario the Okinawan archipelago would become an independent kingdom and US forces in Japan and Korea would be stationed there to act as regional peace keepers.

The Chinese government source said that while in principle China supported maintaining existing borders, "the creation of such a state would contribute to stability in North East Asia."

The North Korean regime, in particular, is very close to Japan. After Japan's defeat in World War 2, an imperial Japanese military officer by the name of Osamu Hatanaka, with secret help from the imperial family, set out to recreate pre-war Japan on the Korean peninsula, the imperial family sources said. Hatanaka was a graduate of the elite Nakano military school and he put Kim Il Sung in power.

Also, Megumi Yokota, the mother of current North Korean leader Kim Jong Un, was brought over to North Korea at age 13 because she had both Japanese and Korean Li dynasty royal blood.

Furthermore, in a very unusual move, it was the CIA that helped Kim Jong Un purge Jang Song Thaek and his faction in order to prevent North Korea from falling under Chinese control, the Japanese royal family members said.

Kim Jong Un disappeared from sight recently because of over indulgence, the Chinese government source said. He is now recovering from ankle surgery, he said. General O Kuk Ryol, who serves as his regent, is ensur "

~~

"Hi Good Firend and all.I was about to send the link to the media deception article but you were faster than me . :)
Can you tell us more about Anu and "igigi".Thank you "

~~

OCTOBER 21ST, 2014

G/E

There are some questions, I will answer

This is Good knowledge for Everyone, ebola is being spread through injections and "vaccinations"

"Whilst this site has been gracious enough to bring news of the ebola issue and comments from GEI send this from the same site for your interest and any comments from GE...

I thank you in the name of reason and generosity for the communication of information that one will not find on the msm.

Straight to the point: Liberian scientist nails Ebola cause

The "Ebola" outbreak is a combination of two things - 1. live Ebola injections at the hands of the Red Cross and Ebola testing trials, and 2. poisoning of water sources and direct injections of formaldehyde.

Dr. Cyril Broderick, A Liberian scientist and a former professor of Plant Pathology at the University of Liberia's College of Agriculture and Forestry says the West, particularly the U.S. is responsible for the Ebola outbreak in West Africa. Dr. Broderick claims the following in an exclusive article published in the Daily Observer based in Monrovia, Liberia. He wrote the following:
The US Department of Defense (DoD) is funding Ebola trials on humans, trials which started just weeks before the Ebola outbreak in Guinea and Sierra Leone. The reports continue and state that the DoD gave a contract worth $140 million dollars to Tekmira, a Canadian pharmaceutical company, to conduct Ebola research. This research work involved injecting and infusing healthy humans with the deadly Ebola virus. Hence, the DoD is listed as a collaborator in a "First in

Human" Ebola clinical trial (NCT02041715, which started in January 2014 shortly before an Ebola epidemic was declared in West Africa in March.

I believe the current outbreak is a combination of two things - water poisoning and phony "vaccine" injections which were really formaldehyde, and more dangerously - a live virus that was delivered via shots in the name of "ebola testing". The live virus is not the original Ebola and does not produce classic symptoms, and is almost certainly still only possible to get via injection.
The U.S. has a long history of conducting these types of experiments, Read more here

The "Ebola outbreak" is fake for two reasons: 1. It is not classic Ebola, showing any classic symptoms at all, as evidenced by the lack of photos, and 2. If it can only be contracted via a shot compliments of the Red Cross or other scammers, it is not an outbreak. It is an act of war."

True Good Friend, all this is another big false flag. The virus though is real and is artificially made. It is not the only one they have in storage, which they were thinking on using to make fear and desperation.

"here guys
read whats to happen to ebola and isis

Did the dragon family take control of the Federal Reserve Board

http://benjaminfulford.net/2014/10/20/did-the-dragon-family-take-control-of-the-federal-reserve-board/

Thank You for share Good Friend. Just one thing, we know this is not a negotiating tactic, rather fear-inducing distraction. It is meant for Majority,

as fear is illuminati's/cabal's main weapon against the "masses".

"pretty good

https://web.archive.org/web/20140210011238/http://blog.redefininggod.com/2014/01/23/the-blood-cult-and-2014-welcome-to-the-global-universal-church-and-your-new-motherfather-god.aspx

True that Russia chose to use christianity as a "unifying element" to Unify russian People. This was also an advice for Yeltsin by ETs (through church) back in cycles of Soviet Union's dissolution to use christianity as "unifying element".

For russian People religions are playing not just the role of control, but more of a Unity. Western european People are finding hard time to understand the logic of russian People. By all definition Slavic People are very different than western european counterparts. Religion is playing big role in their Society, and here is a more talk about traditions and national Unity more than of beliefs. Also catholic and orthodox churches are made very differently. Russian orthodox church chose a way of traditions and Unity which suits Russian People, when most of western christian many denomination churches chose belief and "waiting to be saved as soon as possible" rather than traditions and Unity.

Also double headed eagle is an ancient representation of "god", of "UFO" that was documented as "winged disc", which later evolved into faravahar (Shamash, Ahura Mazda) and into "all seeing eagle" which Russia and some other countries are using nowacycles.

In time christianity, islam and judaism will be completely exposed and all Truth will be known about them, but until then, many People need some

path to be on and They unfortunately do not wish (yet) or do not have time to learn information Lightworkers know. So Russia will do just fine with orthodox christianity for now. China on the other hand see christianity and islam as "radical religions" and won't allow them into China.

"Thankyou GE,

regarding the rogue AI question and answer,
could I assume then a parallel from my other friends answer utilizing the Lucifer thing and Ben's report
that the military (earth defense force) sees the dimiurge as the rogue AI in question?
probably conotated through the judao-christion filter of perception?

Thank you again
Michael"

Yes Good Friend I answered on SWI, but I did not on demiurge. SWI on the contrary to demiurge was a planned Creation which was made by One, but demiurge was not. Demiurge was made on random set of Codes. So in correlation to bible demiurge is not falling into "lucifer" category if we look straightly on it.

But still, here are also same parallels. There is a reflection of Everything in Universe. The so called "Elite" sees demiurge as a false god that took away Creation from original Creator, which is true if You look at it in a way "that it took control over Humanity from One". So yes, if it is a talk about rogue AI or false god, demiurge falls here right. And if it wasn't for their highly distorted view on all this subject, then these People could have be very wise and gifted leaders of Humanity, but their perception of "we must oppose adonay anywhere we can" had completely corrupted their Hearts and Souls and made them self destructive cancerous parasites of this World.

All of this story comes from the beginning, from the very roots of christianity and judaism, it is connected with trinity Anu, Enki and Enlil.

"Hi Good Firend and all.I was about to send the link to the media deception article but you were faster than me . :)
Can you tell us more about Anu and "igigi".Thank you"

The story of trinity of "gods". I will quote from wikipedia

"In Sumerian mythology, Anu (also An; from Sumerian An, "sky, heaven") was a sky-god, the god of heaven, lord of constellations, king of gods, spirits and demons, and dwelt in the highest heavenly regions. It was believed that he had the power to judge those who had committed crimes, and that he had created the stars as soldiers to destroy the wicked. His attribute was the royal tiara. His attendant and minister of state was the god Ilabrat.

He was one of the oldest gods in the Sumerian pantheon and part of a triad including Enlil (god of the air) and Enki (god of water). He was called Anu by the later Akkadians in Babylonian culture. By virtue of being the first figure in a triad consisting of Anu, Enlil, and Enki (also known as Ea), Anu came to be regarded as the father and at first, king of the gods. Anu is so prominently associated with the E-anna temple in the city of Uruk (biblical Erech) in southern Babylonia that there are good reasons for believing this place to be the original seat of the Anu cult. If this is correct, then the goddess Inanna (or Ishtar) of Uruk may at one time have been his consort."

You can see the perfect analogy

Zeus/Jupiter is Anu

Poseidon/Neptune is Enki

Hades/Pluto is Enlil

And as You know, current christian "god" is known as "Deus/Dios", this is the same "supreme god" Anu from ancient Sumeria.

This trinity were actually of 3 older Galactic Federation of Light and draco alliance Civilizations. We are not being told of which civilizations exactly (we are told that this we must know only after Everyone here will get this knowledge, as part of Experience of One). But we know for sure of 1 Civilization which was under command of Enlil, they were having lizard like appearance - the reptilians.

The story of them goes into time of great flood that destroyed nephilims. Anu was supposed ruler of "Annunaki" - "higher gods". He is not demiurge, but later on, Anu was considered to be demiurge and "creator of all". Such distortion of facts and truths is the toll that time and generations takes.

Annunaki were in need of a slave race, that is why they "created" igigi - the race of "lesser gods". Yet, these "lesser gods" Beings rebelled against annunaki (the story of rebellion of Lucifer in heaven) and it was decided to test Humans to be "slaves". Here is a quote from wikipedia

"The Igigi then rebel against the dictatorship of Enlil, setting fire to their tools and surrounding Enlil's great house by night. On hearing that toil on the irrigation channel is the reason for the disquiet, the Anunnaki council decide to create man to carry out agricultural labour."

This experiment was under control of demiurge and demiurge gave permission to test Humanity of being "slaves". By such action demiurge taught that it would eventually get what it was in need. Yet still, there was no success. Even after creation of christianity and islam there still was no success. And only once demiurge allowed Humanity to progress further in technological Evolution, there is a progress.

I also need to point out that it was Enki that proposed to preserve most of Humanity, and it were these Beings that taught how to build ships to avoid the flood. That is why this "god" is being considered "god of water/of seas". Also illuminati and freemasons see this Being - Enki as "liberator" of Humanity, this is "Lucifer" and "Prometheus" for them, "statue of Liberty" is dedicated to Enki. That is why You can see Neptune/Poseidon depictions in many places.

And Enlil is considered as "god of air", because this creature like reptilians now were ethereal, they were almost invisible to ancient Humanity. As well, they were back then the most cruel of all "gods" and Enlil was a straight dictator (like reptilians are now) and demiurge gave permission to Enlil to rule over this World and "test" Humans as much as his civilization could, but without making big destruction and without being seen.

This is why Enlil was associated with "underworld" and "hell". And element of air by itself have an association with death and rebirth. As winds are changing everything. "Elite" are using ways of Enlil to rule over this Planet.

Hope this will aid Everyone.

Here I also wanted to share another great sign Sun gave on october 14, double ♥♥ heart shaped symbol (look from right side).[474]

And to add to Anu-Enki, sky becomes water.[475]

Much Harmony, Love and Abundance to Everyone!

READER'S COMMENTS

"Interesting article: http://www.thecollegefix.com/post/19763/ "

---

[474] SDOmission2009. "Coronal Loops, Anyone?" YouTube. YouTube, 17 Oct. 2014. Web. 14 July 2016. <https://www.youtube.com/watch?v=vy2v1JbboA8>.
[475] CapeTranquillity. "City of the Fallen - Sky Becomes Water." YouTube. YouTube, 19 Feb. 2014. Web. 14 July 2016. <https://www.youtube.com/watch?v=xLM3ofd-X5w>.

~~

"yeah i saw that,
here the tone is kinda matter of fact,
whereas before when someone brought this up it was like whaaaat?
lol "

~~

"Thank you GE "

seems it doesn't matter where we start
as long as we do

http://kauilapele.wordpress.com/2014/10/22/this-is-who-we-are-this-is-the-spirit-of-detroit/ "

~~

" http://beforeitsnews.com/paranormal/2014/10/deathbed-confession-scientist-opens-area-51-secrets-on-ufos-and-aliens-video-and-photos-2477908.html "

~~

"Hi Sophia.The link don't work, could it be this video here:
http://www.youtube.com/watch?v=VLkcM-bpdiA "

~~

"And a few more:

http://birdflu666.wordpress.com/2014/10/13/emergency-update-fema-is-planning-two-huge-pandemic-exercises-in-november-in-conjunction-with-financial-industry/

https://www.youtube.com/watch?v=Vg9OUISaQxI

Lots of FEAR out there, for sure. "

~~

October 31st, 2014   ("Event" Update)

G/E

Good Day Sophia and Good Day Good Friend.

As always Sophia, very beautiful articles and thoughts! I have some news about World situation, some are Good and some are not.

First of all Antares carrier rocket was downed by Followers of Light, because it contained EMP weaponry which could have been used as another "false flag" on orbit over USA, somewhere in november, very possibly during "drills". There were no losses of life, just destroyed satellite, rocket, equipment and emp device. We are very appreciated for their aid, I guess Everyone can say the same, unless You think there wasn't any bomb. I will leave it for Everyone to decide. Always use Your own discernment!

Then as You know there was a "shooting" in Marysville, as we received knowledge from One, there was another fabrication, this article also saying the same thing.[476]

On ebola issue, this fear psy-op campaign is winding down. And there are found already MANY treatments against ebola virus, including some People restoring from it using only Their Own Immune System! Showing that Your Physical Bodies are infusing the Energies of Cosmo - of One inside and Your Body is becoming virus-prove, hurt-prove, dark attack-prove! Congratulations! [477]

---

[476] "SWAT Training Drill During Marysville School Shooting? | Alternative." Before It's News. N.p., n.d. Web. 14 July 2016. <http://beforeitsnews.com/alternative/2014/10/swat-training-drill-during-marysville-school-shooting-3050572.html>.

[477] "Second Ebola-infected US Nurse Beats Virus, Leaves Hospital." RT International. N.p., n.d. Web. 14 July 2016. <http://rt.com/usa/200147-ebola-nurse-release-hospital/>.

The more You know and see, the more Resistance there is.

Recently we found this cure, which is one of the best, even better than colloidal silver - nanosilver and it is working against ebola 100%, but U.S. and EU evil governments (illuminati/cabal) are censoring this information.[478]

Here is how to make: all you need is 2 peaches* of pure silver, 9 volt battery and a glass of distilled water wait 15 minutes until water will turn foggy. Consume 1 tea spoon of this mix. Do not overdose. This cure is also working not just against ebola, but against most ebola-like viruses, partially including flu. This is also a natural cure on contrary to chemical pharmaceutical "cures" they provide to Everyone.

And as well Vladimir Putin recently gave a very big speech at valdai forum. Here He put forward everything what Russia and BRICS are envisioning for the future. This is their "New World Order", which was mentioned before. It straight contrast to one illuminati/cabal wanted and He also mentions their failed "new world order" as well in this speech, making a Sub-Conscious call to disband the evil system of illuminati/cabal. You can listen to his speech on this link, starting from 4:30 and ending at 44:00. [479]

On Good Friend Benjamin's words, all we can say is believe Your own Higher Inner Voice. Nor we, nor Anyone Else is supporting the idea of using troops (armed) in cleaning environment or putting an end to it. Such moves can only

[478] N.p., n.d. Web. <http://www.inquisitr.com/1545317/ebola-treatment-is-working-according-to-official-in-sierra-leone-so-why-such-opposition/#xkIJz4DvT4TZ5SJQ.99>.

[479] RussiaToday. "Putin at Valdai - World Order: New Rules or a Game without Rules (FULL VIDEO)." YouTube. YouTube, 24 Oct. 2014. Web. 14 July 2016. <https://www.youtube.com/watch?v=9F9pQcqPdKo>.

cause more tension and conflicts around the World. On the other hand, if these People indeed are ready to help then They have to do it without weapons. The Good thing is that Benjamin is right, and we are approaching "climax" of all this experiment.

As well in november there will be another very huge drills across USA, they will touch upon almost every possibility of "attack" on U.S., from economic/financial and cyberwarfare to pandemic and even nuclear attack. There will be possible disruptions in internet, radio and tv signals.
Thank You Sophia, the links You provided recently to TV signal disruptions and these upcoming drills are showing their intent is serious.

All of this from our knowledge can come to a point of "financial total collapse" - the collapse of evil petrodollar from this point (remember, banks will not warn You of collapse, they will always say that everything is "ok"/"fine" and "you don't have to worry about anything", so it is always better to have savings on hands, with banks having some small amount, just "to check". Also remember, what they "recommend" is always bad for you and good for them).

We see that november drills is a big move they are making, so be ready and we encourage Everyone to meditate on this issue. We don't like to ask anything, but we are in a very FINAL stages of all this development and if calculations are correct, system will start big fail from New Year Celebration and if they will make something more, like Antares rocket carrier, then they will fail even faster. But if they will lie at bottom again, they can still hold themselves through the spring (maybe, maybe). Yet if November is the time they chose to make something nasty (again), this will be also the time of their TOTAL and capital failure. And such thing will initiate "Moment of Justice" or You also know as "Event". So You can put Your effort here and play Your part in this very ending of experiment.

Also, do not underestimate this HUGE POWER of meditation/prayer You possess. If You have concerns about vampires, they exist, but there are no vampires/parasites to suck Your Energy, unless You invite them to. With Your Wishful Thinking, You will affect illuminati/cabal from simply "putting sticks" in their wheels of war and hatred to complete stop and collapse of it. Remember that future is not fixed and is a subject to change, but with Your Power of Thought and Word You can GUIDE where this River of Destiny will flow. The closer You "put" river to Your United Dream, the faster You will turn Your Dream to Life! And yes - this Power lies WITHIN YOU! And now unleash this Power, I think You are more than ready! Now Are You Ready? Good Friends, Everyone? :)

Words cannot always deliver the message I want Everyone to hear, but music preserves this message and keeps it so later it can be released.
These 2 songs are old and are one of my favorites, hear this message, One told me to share it only now with You Good Friends, Enjoy this Beautiful Message!

One World[480]

"Someday" - Cycle of One [481]

With Much Peace, Love, Calm, Harmony, Prosperity and Abundance!
And Happy Halloween - Cycle/Day of All Saints!:)

(* explained in Part II of this message -- found in next posting today)

October 31st, 2014

G/E

(Regarding --

2 peaches of pure silver)*

---

[480] RhiannanHope. "One World by Celtic Women Lyrics." YouTube. YouTube, 21 May 2008. Web. 16 July 2016. <https://www.youtube.com/watch?v=HgMbVZI86Sw>.
[481] Varme0vn. "Celtic Woman- Someday." YouTube. YouTube, 12 Sept. 2008. Web. 16 July 2016. <https://www.youtube.com/watch?v=HZ2DeUsspxY>.

Well, it is one of words for measurement used in chemistry. My apologies, I guess only specialists know of this word. Basically, You can use any piece of silver which You don't need. Remember though that it must be pure silver. Here are 2 videos explaining this.[482] [483]

And remember, overdosage with silver will make Your skin blue. It will fade away after some time, yet if overdosage is big, it can turn things ugly. Also People react to silver differently, some have turned completely blue due to this. [484]

The good thing is that it is a very rare case and in His case, He was using such mix on His Face, and this caused skin to change color. As well, some ETs have blue skins and silver also plays role here:)

So remember to be careful with this, use this method only if everything else fails, silver helps if it is used in small dosages.

I am happy to know that You do feel this!
(The changes that are "in the air" are very much felt by many of us)

Yes, it could be the end. Yet, I am not giving a 100% guarantee. There is still a quite strong hold illuminati/cabal are still having, we only wait for their actions and the more evil things they would do, the worse it will be for them.

You can see that Yellowstone is quiet for now, this is thanks to stabilized situation around the World.

[482] ZeroFossilFuel. "#379 How to Make Ionic, Nano Particle & Colloidal Silver with Mostly Household Items." YouTube. YouTube, 07 Oct. 2014. Web. 16 July 2016. <https://www.youtube.com/watch?v=nZ2_htS-bW0>.

[483] Thetruthergirls. "How To Make Colloidal Silver in 20 Minutes for Pennies." YouTube. YouTube, 14 Mar. 2012. Web. 16 July 2016. <https://www.youtube.com/watch?v=oqTLXN-W-Z8>.

[484] Rockhandsome. "A Guy With Blue Skin." YouTube. YouTube, 20 Dec. 2007. Web. 16 July 2016. <https://www.youtube.com/watch?v=LowTUTGOtE0>.

As situation on the Sun, recently Sun gave many X class flares from a very huge sunspot which is pretty rare for Sun, but otherwise Sun is calm, which also shows same achieved stability here.

Yes wars and injustice still taking place, but are fading away.

The only last very evil things we have on Earth now, are the ones illuminati/cabal initiated, these are ebola and wars in Sudan, Mali, Somali, Libya, Syria, Iraq, Ukraine. Otherwise situation is stable.

The Moment of Justice/Event may happen any time before august 2016, the sooner - the better.

I also need to warn, that there is also a reconsideration about this set date, One may actually postpone this date for Humanity, yet keep it against Followers of Light. Remember, that this date's precision is mainly meant not to help Humanity, but to stop the evil doings of Followers of Light and demiurge, the many experiments they committed. Ceasing of experiments must take place in their own establishment first.

All victims, including Humanity must be restored and "saved" from their current states.

Restoration's time will depend on damage being done by these experiments. *Humanity was tortured so much, damage here is great that it could be wise to postpone date for 1 or maybe 3 cycles, like we heard. If this will take place, then this will mean that "experiment" will proceed after 2016 "virtually". "Physically" though it will be ceased (that means officially).*

Main problem for (this) is here: there are many very unstable People in this World, they will not survive in New Age without proper care, such care cannot be provided under circumstances of total failure of current system (You understand that there will be chaos all around the World when petrodollar collapses).

This failure may happen soon after halloween, yet instant change of system may turn out to be deadlier and dangerous. Here will be necessary the Consensus of Humanity after system's failure, such Consensus will have to be achieved quickly.

Like we already know, Change have to be smooth and gradual to preserve Everyone possible. Passing aways and chaos are expected.

Yet, the ending date for all activities of Followers of Light in Milky Way Galaxy will be august 2016, no further than this.

I know You are ready Good Friends and I sense that there won't be a necessity to postpone this date, still I needed to share this possibility with Everyone.

Let's Meditate and Hope for the Very Best Outcome there could be!

With Much Harmony, Love and Appreciation!

READER'S COMMENTS

"Thankyou for this update, GE.
I for one sincerely hope there is no need for any further delay. What concerns me is that so many people remain so unaware at a conscious level - it is hard to know whether even a major event like the Moment of Justice would wake them up sufficiently ! What I mean is, they might say "wow, that was pretty unbelieveable, wasn't it" and then continue with their lives as now, because they are unable to take in the enormity of the deception and the depth of the evil. And the few people who are awake are so unengaged in this "reality" that each day feels difficult. - how will they handle three additional years ?

I know many websites talk about Humanity being "just about ready", but it is just not visible when you walk around and talk to people.

GE, when you say that unstable people will need care, is it solely Humanity which will need to work together to do this (which I imagine will take quite some time), or will we be receiving help from outside - advanced medical technology, etc, to heal them quickly ? "

~~

"Hi Good Friend and all.I just found Carl Boudreau's astrology forecast for november.There is a lot that correspond to what GE predicts for this for the next 2 months.
https://www.facebook.com/notes/carl-boudreau/astrology-status-for-november-3-2014-a-scary-november-if-you-want-it-to-be/10205309030633728 "

~~

November 21st, 2014

Good Day Sophia and Everyone! I am well, Thank You!

Sorry to keep You waiting for answers, I was doing some work in these cycles.

I was mentioning economic collapse before, it is inevitable, yet yes, I wasn't saying specifically when it will happen. For now everything seems all right, no false flags, no nasty things. Illuminati/cabal loosing on all fronts, so they just keep low and quiet, which is a good thing, yet it postpones their ultimate downfall.

Concerning first question from Good Friend N..

"This means there is an agenda with this one that they will not back off on no matter how badly the scam and agenda is exposed. *In the past, they would back off. Why is this one different? And why are they still allowing flights to and from the "Ebola zones"? Why are they now saying Ebola spreads like the flu, and thrives in the cold? What about the dog story? All of it is PATENT B.S., WHY are they not backing off?*

ANSWER: They are religious zealots with a deadline to meet. Their recent actions proves something is amiss with them, and they are going for broke. Whatever the deadline is, it is now OBVIOUS that they HAVE TO get everyone "vaccinated" with a shot of dubious origins within a very short time window. The sheer brazen nature of it all proves that this is a do or die situation for them, and it totally discredits the entire "Ebola" meme. It makes it all obvious THEY WANT THIS, IT IS THEIR BABY and PROOF is in the fact THERE ARE NO HOLDS ON FLIGHTS FROM THE EBOLA ZONE.

*It is the job of the government to act in the best interests of the nation it "serves". When dealing with the safety of its citizens, America is NOT SUPPOSED TO CARE ABOUT POLITICS IN AFRICA. The fact that flights are continuing unabated means one of two things, either: 1. Ebola is not real at all, and they need a ruse, OR 2. They really want this pandemic to spread as far and as fast as conceivably possible. **Either way, they are playing the role of an enemy, AVOID THE SHOT AT ALL COST.**"*

They lost with ebola scare, they lost with ebola spread. You can see how fast news about it are winding down.

But You said right there, "**they are religious zealots with a deadline to meet**". In their perverted religions/ideology they only have some 2 cycles to initiate their evil "new world order". 1 cycle of 2013 already passed, starting from december 21 - Moment of Choice and we are nearing to 2015, so second cycle as well almost passed.

Choice was favored not in a future they envisioned, but in otherwise direction and so Shift of Ages on 16-17 december of 2013 was heralded with a New World in which they - people with evil vision on World will have no place to be in. And in their belief, if they fail to make something in this time window, they will fall and be exposed completely and as well they will be judged by Prime Creator. And in actuality it will be so, not precisely how they envisioned it, but very close to it. You can see that fall of current economical system will mark their downfall and it is going in their time frame as well.

Concerning second question

Here is another seriously antagonistic piece from the Bilderburgers....their own documented text not anyones comment...

Leaked Bilderburg closing remarks.
http //jhaines6.wordpress.com/2014/11/01/leaked-bilderberg-closing-remarks-2014-must-read/#comments
"...When we shall provoke the economic collapse, then the most absurd communitarianism which we have developed in every country will conduct the largest part of these countries towards large-scale civil wars where every community will take charge for our account to kill the largest number of the members of the opposite community.
"Blacks against whites in the USA, Muslim against Christians in Europe, these civil wars will have the immense advantage to destroy the people without confrontations between degenerate countries into nuclear power world war . Finally, when the wars will destroy countries, we shall take advantage of it to amplify the distribution of viruses such as our project of e-bola 2.0 modified genetically which we test at present with efficiency because we obtain invaluable epidemiological, sociological data (behavior of the individuals in front of the disease) but we also visualize our capacity to saturate systems of care which will be already considerably degraded, in every case, by the civil wars which we shall have created on the example of the war between the two Ukraines..." End

This is pure criminal mentality...belief has nothing to do with the issue - it all has to do with a group of psychopaths intending to cause outrageous conflict and genocide...."One" needs to sweep this garbage out with a mental dirt broom and leave them incapacitated forever.

Even so - Much love energy into the chasms of would-be destruction. Nigel

One can't do that, they endanger 1 Planet, but not all Universe (yet).
One will instantly remove them only when they endanger Universe, for now Universe is being endangered only by demiurge. Humanity are considered as "just a tool" of this endangerment. In Universe there will always be someone like illuminati/cabal, Universe is meant to be this "dual-mode" of Good and Evil.

Some other Worlds outside Universe don't have it, but this reality have.

Do not worry Good Friend. We have this covered, we know that they have in mind all of these things even after economic collapse. Deception, civil wars, division and chaos is what their distorted ideology is based on, we are planning on many steps ahead of them and we know all their strategies and all possible actions they could make. Yes, truly they are criminals, like I mentioned before - they are gang, a band of thugs and thieves, also they can be called - highly organised mafia, where banking is their most "successful" invention to strip everyone naked. Deb(i)t cards, "credit" cards, "loans" for car or house (with quite big "interest" rate) are all meant to imprison People in a debt prison. So it is wise to start with the fall of this "economic" system - where money are being economised only by banksters themselves, whereas People are being stripped naked from everything.

The Thrive Movement founder Good Friend Foster a very nice Person that envisions a Bright future for Humanity made a video about fall of this economic system [485]

As well, Russia and China are starting to avoid USDs in their trade [486]

---

[485] ThriveMovement. "Is the Value of Your Money About to Change?" YouTube. YouTube, 08 Nov. 2014. Web. 16 July 2016. <https://www.youtube.com/watch?v=SROw5-p4AKY>.
[486] N.p., n.d. Web. <http://rt-tv.f29hgb.ru/business/203903-ruble-yuan-dollar-settlements/>.

Thank You Good Friend, much Love Energy into these chasms as well!

I remember Sophia posted a link to last interview of Boyd Bushman - a retired senior scientist for U.S. military corporation Lockheed Martin (which makes military planes, both known and secret and have a pentagram in it's logo) [487]

Most of information there is true as we know, on those photos You can see well known "Greys". This is about the contract which was made between them and U.S. government. For technologies that greys would provide, greys can abduct People and make their experiments and "research".

Because this video is having truth and from an influential Person, information about this is being censored. I saw several videos and websites removed with this information. The Good thing is that this video became viral and many People already watched and downloaded it, so there is no way this video can be completely removed by CIA or NSA. In case video in the link provided will be gone, You can search for it on youtube with these words "Boyd Bushman - Area 51 and Real UFO Pictures".

Also Thank You Very Much Good Friend D.! You provided a lot of interesting information, I will share it if You don't mind

"Hi Good Friend and all.I just found Carl Boudreau's astrology forecast for november.There is a lot that correspond to what GE predicts for this for the next 2 months.
https://www.facebook.com/notes/carl-boudreau/astrology-status-for-november-3-2014-a-scary-november-if-you-want-it-to-be/10205309030633728"

---

[487] YouTube. YouTube, n.d. Web. 16 July 2016. <https://www.youtube.com/watch?v=zof2kpl0Py8>.

Thank You for this update Good Friend!

"AirPod - the car that runs on air
: http://www.youtube.com/watch?v=0RBI1LFUQ4c.
full transcript of Vladimir Putin's speech at Valdai Conference
: http://cluborlov.blogspot.com/2014/10/putin-to-western-elites-play-time-is.html"

Excellent car Good Friend! Not very expensive as well. Recently there was another car which got itself into Public, developed by Toyota - hydrogen hybrid car, which would need water as fuel, yet still it would use small part of fossil fuel to "separate" hydrogen from water. And it is expensive as well, costs almost 6X times more than AirPod. Still dependance on oil can be felt here as Japan lies under cabal very tightly [488]

"I found this nice article about Putin : http://stateofthenation2012.com/?p=8159 .I
liked it thug there are some unanswered questions.
I loved this quote from Edgar Cayce
"Through Russia comes the hope of the world. Not in respect to what is
sometimes termed Communism or Bolshevism — no! But freedom — freedom!
That each man will live for his fellow man. The principle has been born there. It
will take years for it to be crystallized; yet out of Russia comes again the hope of
the world."
~ Edgar Cayce
I readed my first Edgar Cayce book when i was 18.I learned a lot"

Also Putin made remarks about Love, fortunately He understands the meaning of Life and can see the very nature of Humanity [489]

---

[488] N.p., n.d. Web. <http://rt.com/news/206667-toyota-hydrogen-powered-car/>.
[489] "Putin: 'Love Is the Meaning of Life'" RT International. N.p., n.d. Web. 16 July 2016.

"Hi Good Friend and Sophia.I found this fascinating interview of Simon Parkes where he speaks about his incarnation in the Garden of Eden and the 2016 deadline.I wish the interviewer was more curious and have asked more questions about Simon's experience in the Garden of Eden.This interview left me very curious.I hope you will appreciate.
http://www.neonnettle.com/interviews/50-labour-councillor-simon-parkes-on-being-brought-up-by-aliens- "

Great interview and experience, Thank You Good Friend!

What I can say is that Good Friend possibly remembers the control scheme of "Anu", when this being got some People and put them into specially created place, which Good Friend called "Garden of Eden" (you can also call it sarcastically "pasture"), where they were making experiments and were "exploiting" (abusing) Humans.

As we know, those People back then didn't like that they were lied to and being exploited for different experiments. And so, when dissidence and disobedience grew and because "Anu" knew laws of One, it decided to expel Humans from there back to Earth and join Other People living on Earth.

This was the story of "creation of man" as You recall, this entity "Anu" is the one jewish nation "serve to" and call it as "Yahweh". Although we don't know his race of origin and One does not tell us (because we will have to know it later along with Humanity), we know that it had very strong connections with reptilians. Being called "Enlil" was the ruler of reptilians that visited Earth back then, although Enlil was not supreme ruler of all reptilian race.

As You remember after flood demiurge through Anu (as demiurge always works through proxy beings) entrusted Enlil to rule over this planet and "tempt" People

<http://rt.com/news/203339-putin-love-meaning-life/>.

in order to achieve loyalty to Anu (and subsequently to demiurge) and for demiurge to receive what it needed since cycle 1 of modifying Humans. By this time, these beings already passed away as we know, "Anu" is no more and in it's place is other being from same civilization and we are not sure about Enlil. Reptilians can live for a very long time span, they can also trick their own body and "die" only to "resurrect" after big time span.

As well, I must confess, that even here maybe 100 000 cycles (years) passed, for demiurge it could have been mere 100 cycles (years). So Humanity grew up pretty fast in view of demiurge.

Overall there is a very huge level of conspiracy among different Civilizations against Humanity and for the very Best Interests of Humanity, this is not easy to explain in even a big enough book, You can see that even conspiracy against Humanity by illuminati/cabal is big enough that it is pretty hard to explain it, but there above this Planet there are multiple different Civilizations and They view Humanity differently from different angles. Some want to use Humanity, some want to aid and help Humanity.

This is what we know, always use Your own discernment. This information is not of priority, so it's precision given to us by One and Forces of One is not 100%. This information is a part of information which we have to reveal by Ourselves as Humanity.

"Are the Super Wise Intelligence and Ancient Machines capable of feeling Love? I send them mine either way."

They are capable of feeling it, yet it is not like You understand it. They can only "sense" Love, like a set of codes. Yet They have reflex on Love and this reflex is Mutual Love and Friendship. If You feel Friendliness toward Them, They send You friendliness as well ;) this is pretty much like it.

"Thankyou for this update, GE.
I for one sincerely hope there is no need for any further delay. What concerns me
is that so many people remain so unaware at a conscious level - it is hard to
know whether even a major event like the Moment of Justice would wake them
up sufficiently ! What I mean is, they might say "wow, that was pretty
unbelieveable, wasn't it" and then continue with their lives as now, because they
are unable to take in the enormity of the deception and the depth of the evil. And
the few people who are awake are so unengaged in this "reality" that each day
feels difficult. - how will they handle three additional years ?

I know many websites talk about Humanity being "just about ready", but it is just
not visible when you walk around and talk to people.

GE, when you say that unstable people will need care, is it solely Humanity
which will need to work together to do this (which I imagine will take quite some
time), or will we be receiving help from outside - advanced medical technology,
etc, to heal them quickly ?"

This will depend Good Friend. Many People in the World actually know reality,
know of inner control, of shadow governments illuminati and conspiracy, yet
Many refuse to accept it and all They do is just routinely living Their Lives,
earning money and for these money entertaining Themselves. They also enjoy
seeing Their Children and Grandchildren and all other "available fun".

 Because of that, such People have to be directly threatened like with possible
WW3 for example, which threatens Their own existence and existence of their
Children, only then They will start act to prevent this. This is about Majority that
still sleeps, but about Minority that is Awoke and growing in numbers and
growing Inside like You Good Friends, You are doing everything possible to
Change the World for the Better, We All don't need fear or threats, we only need
this World to Change and simply end with all evil and corruption.

This healing will take place from People around the World, all starts with Education. Children - the Future of Earth will take care of Their Elders, if I can say, they will take care of You All Good Friends, provided of course, if You will educate Them in the most Harmonious and Love-oriented way.

Hint for this is - most Children living in big cities don't know how to make Friends and how to speak to other People, with each generation the grasp for talk is fading away and People more and more become isolated from Each Other.

This is illuminati's agenda to divide and separate, to "create hatred" among People. And of course this is having negative impact on all Human Society. People are becoming more closed in Themselves and everything around seems very "alienated". The biggest lack in Education is subject of Friendship and conversation about "nothing".

Learning on how to speak to Others is necessary like learning alphabet, when People (or any other Beings) are becoming more and more industrialised and "automated" (robotised), that is urban areas overtake Nature areas and many things can be done through electric devices or robots, Beings are becoming lazy and isolated, as well feeling of "hate" (evil side) awakens in Them when They are isolated and no one "wants to listen to Them" (this is how They see it).

And as well, mostly People who need this are the ones living in a very big and overpopulated cities, like New York, Los Angeles, Beijing, Delhi, Moscow or Tokyo. Overpopulation is also same factor of creating a gap between People. So Everyone with Children, always teach Them in the way You see right and never lose subject of Friendship and Love! This is a must-have for Every Individual!

And Thank You Good Friend Djon for providing answer!

"seems it doesn't matter where we start
as long as we do

http://kauilapele.wordpress.com/2014/10/22/this-is-who-we-are-this-is-the-spirit-of-detroit/ "

Thank You Good Friend, Very Beautiful Video and You are right. It doesn't matter where We start, We only have to do something. Universally there is a phrase - "Action is Life (Heat), inaction is "death" (Cold)". Always do something, this is always for the best! Also I wanted to add here, always say "Yes" to opportunities when You have ones, like in old movie "Yes Man!" The concept presented there of saying "Yes" to presented opportunities keeps Your Energy circulating in and out, between different dimensions. It keeps Your Physical Body (experience here) from stagnation. So it relates to Universal saying above of "Action is Life". Although, when You had enough of "experience" You can always say "no", it is that simple :)

"Dear GE!

What is your take on this article about frequencies and people with multiple personalities.. ?

http://jhaines6.wordpress.com/2014/11/18/our-life-on-earth-is-a-point-of-frequency-that-exists-within-an-entire-range-of-other-possible-frequencies-part-one-by-bradley-loves/

Hugs

O."

I cannot say whether it is true or false, but we know of this technology which is able to make different personalities. The CIA program on altering People and making different personalities was true in our knowledge. They have been doing this for a very long time in the past and still doing this. Yet law prohibited experiments on Humans, so they use other "proxy" countries to do their evil "researches". Although we haven't heard that they succeeded in this, so I can't say whether it is true or false. More advanced forms we know of includes the separation of Soul on many fragments or creating a remote-controlled Beings, which can be controlled from Central Neural System of Individual (from 1 Brain - example Human can have control over many other "remote controlled" Humans or even flies and animals only from own Brain). Such technology is very advanced and is not available here yet.

Also considering the frequencies, recently One presented to us this information. [490]

The "format" of music was changed from 432Hz to 440Hz (A4) in 1953. And today all musical instruments are being attuned to this "standard" of 440Hz. This is also a part of same agenda of illuminati/cabal to disconnect Humanity from Source and Cosmo.

In this article You will know that 440Hz is disharmonious. It is so, because it is transitional frequency between 432Hz and 444Hz (also You may know 444Hz as 528Hz on C5 - "healing frequency"), where both make geometrically beautiful forms in water.

Although 440Hz is not very damaging, as when music play, it plays on different frequencies, still it creates disharmony and 440Hz is mostly used with hard rock music, which along with 440Hz creates Chaos in water (in our Bodies).

You can use Audacity or Foobar 2000 music player (with SoundTouch DSP addon) to alter the pitch of the music and change it to 432Hz. Most music will become more harmonious, although not all music will sound better. If You will need help on changing your music's frequency, please ask.

---

[490] "Here's Why You Should Consider Converting Your Music To A=432 Hz." Collective Evolution. N.p., n.d. Web. 16 July 2016. <http://www.collective-evolution.com/2013/12/21/heres-why-you-should-convert-your-music-to-432hz/>.

I will provide video with different Frequencies that form beautiful structures within water (They do this with salt and sand, but almost same happens in water in Your Bodies). You can apply these different frequencies in Audacity and create beautiful music. [491]

Remember, music - is the language of One - of Universe and of Nature. These are Frequencies and Vibrations, through them, You can hear and feel everything, though them You can figure all things out! I share different music with You Good Friends to aid You in this. In every part of every music, there is a hidden information, which our Soul and Body can read. It is not understandable for our mind yet, but message is always there.

Also this is something You will like Good Friends! A virtual Choir made by Eric Whitacre. All Voices of different People put together as One!
This is explanation. [492]

This is the first video He made "Lux Aurumque" means Light and Gold (185 Individuals from 12 Countries) [493]

And this is the masterpiece "Fly to Paradise" (8409 videos, 5905 Individuals from 101 Countries - half of the World - a VERY HARD WORK there!) [494]

Fly to Paradise Good Friends, Heaven on Earth is within reach now!

Wish Everyone Peace, Calm and Prosperity!

November 30th, 2014

G/E

---

[491] Brusspup. "Amazing Resonance Experiment!" YouTube. YouTube, 06 June 2013. Web. 16 July 2016. <https://www.youtube.com/watch?v=wvJAgrUBF4w>.

[492] TEDtalksDirector. "Eric Whitacre: A Virtual Choir 2,000 Voices Strong." YouTube. YouTube, 04 Apr. 2011. Web. 16 July 2016. <https://www.youtube.com/watch?v=2NENlXsW4pM>.

[493] EricWhitacresVrtlChr. "Eric Whitacre's Virtual Choir - 'Lux Aurumque'" YouTube. YouTube, 21 Mar. 2010. Web. 16 July 2016. <https://www.youtube.com/watch?v=D7o7BrlbaDs>.

[494] EricWhitacresVrtlChr. "Eric Whitacre's Virtual Choir 4: Fly to Paradise." YouTube. YouTube, 11 July 2013. Web. 16 July 2016. <https://www.youtube.com/watch?v=Y8oDnUga0JU>.

Good Day Sophia!

Everything is more or less well around the World for now. Lot of good changes are taking place on daily basis. In U.S. You can see that different People rose up against injustice and unfairness.
The grand jury's decision sparked these protests, but actually these protests are the result of People being unhappy with this system. It all was boiling to a certain point. Eventually protests may wind down, yet they will continue to pop up here and there and will not cease unless there will be a Huge Worldwide Changes.

Most of Protesters are young People, like I warned before, People need a Change, this system is stagnated, Energy is stagnated and They can no longer tolerate all of it. Many can hold Themselves together, but all patience eventually come to an end.

So Changes are starting to occur. Yes, they may be chaotic, but if illuminati/cabal refuse to surrender and are keeping their claws deeply in their seat of power, measures like use of force needs to be applied.

If it will go that far and illuminati/cabal will spark a small war here, then Sage Star A will summon power of Chaos and bestow it upon Protesters which will increase Their Power and make Them berserk and in that case, the government will be quickly changed by force.

Yes there will be casualties, but all of this will lie only on illuminati/cabal and their evil system, they will be the only ones responsible for all of this. Sun and Earth may aid Protesters as well.
We are still doing our best to solve everything Peacefully.

In other news U.S. government is having very big problems with it's image and confidence around the World. U.S. now struggling to keep it together and to keep it's many lies from exposure. They still use money to bribe People in other governments from speaking out. Yet when evil petrodollar collapses, People will speak out about their horrendous lies.

Countries are now not asking gold back, but demanding it [495]

As well, there was a resolution vote proposed by Russia to ban all nazi propaganda and nazi affiliated groups and only U.S., Canada and Ukraine voted against [496]

Same thing happened with "no weaponisation of space" resolution proposed again by Russia with only U.S., Israel, Georgia and Ukraine voted against [497]

This clearly shows that Ukraine had become a puppet state of evil U.S. government, as well it shows that U.S. supports nazism and weaponisation of space, which we knew of course, but it only proves that they have a hostile stance toward ETs and nazism ideology they created before WW2 (like supporting their children no matter what).

And looking at Those that voted for the resolution shows that Majority of the World do not support this and want to get away from it, as well it shows that same Majority supports the initiative of Good New World Order proposed by BRICS countries.

I also need to reveal to You something One shared with us. This is connected with Forces of One warning and specific date of 2016.

The planet Saturn in 1986-1987 was in position in 13th zodiacal constellation Ophiuchus - this is very close to the center of Galaxy - Sage Star A and is known as "Golden Gates of the Skies", or also "Gates to Heaven".

In 1986 two crucial and very big worldwide warnings were given both to demiurge with Followers of Light/reptilians and also to illuminati order/cabal. One

[495] N.p., n.d. Web. <http://rt.com/business/209591-gold-europe-gold-repatriation/>.

[496] "US, Canada & Ukraine Vote against Russia's Anti-Nazism Resolution at UN." RT International. N.p., n.d. Web. 16 July 2016. <http://rt.com/news/207899-un-anti-nazism-resolution/>.

[497] "Russia's No Arms in Outer Space Initiative Gains Support." RT International. N.p., n.d. Web. 16 July 2016. <http://rt.com/op-edge/209027-outer-space-arms-un-resolution/>.

was explosion of Challenger space shuttle and other was Chernobyl explosion.

First showed to U.S. government that they are not all powerful and "challenging" Universe thus Creator is a bad thing to do. It showed that any progress they could make could be stopped in an instant if they would continue on same route of destruction.

The other was shown to Soviet Union's government, it showed them clearly what nuclear war would look like, it also showed to all World that playing with radiation is dangerous and could harm Everyone.

The orbital rotation period of Saturn is 29.5 Earth cycles (years), that is 1 cycle of Saturn. It was decided by One to give Humanity, reptilians, Followers of Light and demiurge 1 full Saturn's cycle to make up Their mind (which remember is 29.5 Earth cycles/years). The countdown started a little after Chernobyl's disaster.

And if You calculated, by adding 29.5 cycles from second half of 1986 through first half of 1987 will be beginning of 2016. This is the date which is set to demiurge as "deadline". Saturn is known in many Cultures around the World as "Judge" and it's orbital rotation period fits the time frame One intended.

So when Saturn will reach it's position in **december of 2015, the last countdown will begin and will end in august**, when Saturn will make last turn into Scorpio and will go through the Galactic Center and into Sagittarius.

That is about it, One shared this knowledge with us only now. Very few knew about this deadline, but those for whom it was meant, knew very well about it.

Also here Sophia, I want to illustrate to You the Vastness of Universe, it will help to Expand Your Mind even Further, You can share this with Good Friends as well

The Ever Expanding Universe [498]

There will come a time when Universe will cease to Expand, but for now It Expands

And Observable Universe - that is what is seen from Earth, but it is not Everything what is in a Universe, Universe is much larger than this [499]

Here is an explanation - Farthest Ever View of the Universe [500]

Another video 200,000+ Galaxies Revealed In Deep Sky Survey [501]

200,000 GALAXIES, where each one contains billions and trillions of Stars like Sun and even bigger, You understand how HUGE this is?

And here is the most detailed and largest Sky Map available here on Earth [502]

All things may look small here, but here You can see both Stars and Galaxies and there are many, many Worlds that are habitable!

Also, recent finding showed that All Universe is Interconnected and is a small part of an even bigger design of One [503]

----

[498] HubbleESA. "The Expanding Universe." YouTube. YouTube, 13 Nov. 2014. Web. 16 July 2016. <https://www.youtube.com/watch?v=T9lkcgu5iwM>.
[499] HubbleESA. "The Observable Universe." YouTube. YouTube, 13 Nov. 2014. Web. 16 July 2016. <https://www.youtube.com/watch?v=F353xaKnQ2I>.
[500] BestOfScience. "Hubble EXtreme Deep Field - Farthest Ever View of the Universe." YouTube. YouTube, 26 Sept. 2012. Web. 16 July 2016. <https://www.youtube.com/watch?v=7mBOQ3KrbjE>.
[501] VideoFromSpace. "200,000+ Galaxies Revealed In Deep Sky Survey | Video." YouTube. YouTube, 21 Mar. 2012. Web. 16 July 2016. <https://www.youtube.com/watch?v=V-3ZzXCnyTE>.
[502] BestOfScience. "Largest Sky Map Revealed: An Animated Flight Through the Universe." YouTube. YouTube, 13 Aug. 2012. Web. 16 July 2016. <https://www.youtube.com/watch?v=rOjrlmaPh80>.
[503] "Supermassive Black Holes Could Be Part of an Interstellar Cosmic Web." RT International. N.p., n.d. Web. 16 July 2016. <http://rt.com/news/207863-black-holes-interstellar-web/>.

I will share some more beautiful music:

Dream a Land in which You want to see Yourself and Your Brothers, Sisters, Elders, Children, Animals, Plants, Birds and Fishes living in a Complete and Perfect Harmony filled with Love [504]

Here are possibilities
The Name of Light [505]

Above the Sky [506]

Maybe Skybound? [507]

Rise of a Kingdom of Peace and Prosperity and Tranquility [508]

Solaris - the name of the City of the Sun [509]

Reaching the Horizons of One United World [510]

One Earth [511]

[504] DivinumMusic. "Matia Turzo and Jocopo Cicatiello - Dreamland." YouTube. YouTube, 26 Nov. 2014. Web. 16 July 2016. <https://www.youtube.com/watch?v=JbEH776IgV0>.
[505] EpicJennyni20. "Fran Soto - The Name Of Light (Beautiful Orchestral)." YouTube. YouTube, 05 Nov. 2014. Web. 16 July 2016. <https://www.youtube.com/watch?v=XGckjKjY4tE>.
[506] EpicJennyni20. "Mattia Cupelli - Above The Sky (Beautiful Orchestral)." YouTube. YouTube, 17 Nov. 2014. Web. 16 July 2016. <https://www.youtube.com/watch?v=nvEz3QkUplk>.
[507] EpicJennyni20. "Jeff Broadbent - Skybound (Beautiful Orchestral)." YouTube. YouTube, 20 Nov. 2014. Web. 16 July 2016. <https://www.youtube.com/watch?v=bNGNxhpTdfg>.
[508] BrunuhVille. "Fantasy Medieval Music - Rise of a Kingdom." YouTube. YouTube, 26 Nov. 2014. Web. 16 July 2016. <https://www.youtube.com/watch?v=ADzazbh1WG0>.
[509] Park0urfreak1. "J. T. Peterson - Solaris (Epic Uplifting Female Vocal Hybrid)." YouTube. YouTube, 30 Oct. 2014. Web. 16 July 2016. <https://www.youtube.com/watch?v=_q1U8G8QKGw>.
[510] Michimaas. "Michael Maas Feat. Aeralie Brighton - Horizons." YouTube. YouTube, 24 Nov. 2014. Web. 16 July 2016. <https://www.youtube.com/watch?v=CRCM0rYZ1sc>.
[511] Michimaas. "Michael Maas Feat. Uyanga Bold - One Earth." YouTube. YouTube, 21 Nov. 2014. Web. 16 July 2016. <https://www.youtube.com/watch?v=xPuaaR9MY3Q>.

And it's about time to break the final frontier to Freedom and Justice [512]

With Much Peace, Calm and Prosperity.

December 22nd, 2014

G/E

Good Day Sophia and Everyone and Happy Solstice!

In cosmological understanding the cycle after Solstice which on this Solar Cycle of 2014 is 21 december can be called "a New Year"! From this moment Earth's cycles in northern hemisphere will start becoming longer and longer and in southern shorter and shorter.

I wasn't available for some time and I have to warn that You have to be ready if I "disappear" out of a sudden, we have a lot of work to do in restoring this World, so GEs aren't fixed in one place.

First situation around the Globe. The Shift is taking place, everything is like it was before - good (could have been better), nothing new to say. All illuminati are doing are keeping low and simply keep barking at Russia and BRICS, fortunately they are afraid to make false flags, because as soon as they would make one, this would be their ultimate downfall. Everyone around the World are "at the edge" and if something bad or nasty would take place "again" the responsibles will be seen in Bright Light!

I will post Your information Good Friend

[512] EpicJennyni20. "Thomas Bergersen - Final Frontier (Sun)(Interstellar Trailer Music)." YouTube. YouTube, 08 Nov. 2014. Web. 16 July 2016. <https://www.youtube.com/watch?v=adA_V_ab8Xg>.

"Hello Sophia - once again I send you text over a noemal email rather than over the comments window for GE and the interest in general of your readers as to what is still going on - the items that are appearing on various sites may or may not be conjectures or psyops/disinfo....but ....there is a lot going on when the sum iof it is put together that forms a picture that tells a story...
Here is the comment from Jim Stone...as always I send love and positive thoughts....

Congress has voted nearly unanimously to go to war against the "Islamic state" and to give Ukraine American weapons to use against Russia. Both bad moves. Supporting aggression against Russia is an act of war against Russia. Bad move. And how do you go to war with many countries at the same time?

By having the CIA/Mossad create a fake "Islamic state" that exists within whatever countries you want to destroy, and then bombing those countries into oblivion without ever declaring war on them.*A new form of fraudWho would have thought? fight a war on sovereign territory against a fictitious enemy that never attacked you directly, and do the people you really want to destroy a favor by doing so! But in the process, you will get Isis, right? Might take years, RIGHT? Enough to reduce the nation you really want destroyed to rubble, RIGHT? After all, it can last as long as you want when you are fighting fiction to begin with. Just keep telling the story . . . . . .At any rate, both Ukraine/Russia and the Arab world are officially on the table now as war targets. We all knew for years the Arab world was toast because we have all seen it happen repeatedly, but Russia? what is Congress thinking?*

I may have spoken out about Russia not being too innocent in the past, but remember that I also said that Russia may have changed, with those who scammed Russia with Bolshevik Communism leaving Russia after the "fall". And there is at least one ancedotal bit of info to support the possibility that Russia may not be playing a game about it all -

People may not know this broadly, but right after Russia fell, all the gold

antiquities from the former Czars which were held intact by the communists came into the U.S. via San Francisco, where they sat for a year or two and then got melted down into bars. It was an astonishing rape of Russia. It was not just one or two crowns, it was tons and tons of gold in the form of royal antiquities from past centuries. MELTED DOWN IN AMERICA. How did that happen if Russia really had the same people in charge that were there during the cold war? Obviously the Bolshevik scammers came to America and did to Russia in America what they could not get away with doing while in Russia.

Considering what became of America since Russia fell, it all goes to show that it is highly probable that the filthy cold war era Russian cronies found a new home in America. America is now acting exactly the same way in both foreign and domestic affairs that Russia did with them in charge.

Is Russia now a new frontier that has been freed of parasites? Do not bet on it, but I would at least hope"

You are right Good Friend, Russia was a victim of illuminati/cabal. Communism was their experimental ideology, the bill passed by Congress is just another form of barking, they are afraid of doing more than that, because the World is unhappy with them and the World now can see almost clearly what they really represent. Not the People, but their dark evil agenda of World domination.

-- -- -- -- -- --

"This has been published today. Thoughts?
https://freedom4humanity.wordpress.com/2014/12/12/the-surrender-agreement/

and this...

Update on Aisha North describes the Etheric Transition of this Shift. This Shift is changing whole World, in the way it is described there. Everything what is happening now is something that have to be completed somehow in a very short time. Some our hidden things which we didn't want to talk about before and unfortunately Ukraine and "islamic state" are one of those things. Good Friend Aisha North described it very well.

About "amnesty", what we know is that the "dark doers" will never be forgiven and granted amnesty for their many atrocious doings simply like it is said there. Only if they will publicly apologise for this and do this not like "oops sorry", but from their heart.

And some of them cannot be forgiven, as some are responsible for destruction of millions and billions of individuals, both Humans and Animals. We have seen how enjoyable it was for them to make these many crimes, being remained unpunishable after doing so much evil? This ruins the very basis of Law of One, of Law of Universal Energy Circulation and this is simply unfair. I doubt that those who suffered from hands of these evil doers would be happy to hear that the ones that killed them in one of their incarnations simply got away with their atrocious deeds and keep on doing same things to others. True, Some Souls agree with such fate, but Most do not.

The dark energy they put to use when made those crimes, MUST return back to them so is the Law of Universe. So the backlash will be huge on them, whether "dark" and "Light" like it or not.

Essentially Good Side - Light is making all kinds of Forgiveness, of Love and Friendship, yet sometime it leads to unfairness and making more evil (dark) like You can see in this great example.

On the other hand evil side - dark is making things opposite to Light - hatred, destruction, injustice, unfairness and dark almost never leads itself to something of Light. This is how Universe was programmed by One and this is why Forces of One exist, to not give into neither Light or dark and see things and take them for what they are.

"Hi Good Friend and all. If my understanding is correct the financial collapse has begun like you predicted it. The MSM is pointing on russia's financial trouble , provoked by the western sanctions, speculation attacks on the ruble and the fall of oil price, to divert from much worse situation in the western financial system. The fall of oil price is mirroring the financial health of the west and have a big impact in the trillions of derivatives the western banks.
Please correct me if i am wrong,Good Friend."

Hi Good Friend. Not yet, but all these "sanction policies" is a catalyst for this downfall, which is imminent. Most probably it will happen in the beginning of cycle 2015, unless they would make another "false flag operation" to blame Russia for it.

Russia is having troubles, but they are small in comparison to ones cabal is having like you pointed out correctly. The fall of oil prices is as well artificially orchestrated and created by U.S. government to damage BRICS, Iran, Argentina and Venezuela and among them mainly Russia of course, which they see as their "main foe" since the very foundation of USA.

But all these sanctions are damaging cabal as well, you can call cabal here as suicide bomber with a time bomb already turned on, trying to get into bus

(BRICS) to make huge damage there, yet he is being restricted access to it (through policy of Peace and Understanding performed by BRICS).

So eventually time runs out and the bus remains damaged a bit as bomber was close to it, but everyone inside are safe and sound, yet suicide bomber is no more. This is harsh example, but it very well describes situation we have right now.

"Hello...as always with love and respect....your last comment began:-
"Everything is more or less well around the World for now. Lot of good changes are taking place on daily basis"
That was 30 november and by the 1 December japan has returned Abe as prime minister....

According to Fulford who apparently knows more about these things, Abe was going to be dumped from being the puppet of US zionism....well hes back in there again and that means bad news because things did not change for the better and they will stay as they are or worse....seems like the zios and neonazis are consolidating rather than disintegrating....I think Japan was a key issue in the face of BRICS and the Ukraine to remove US dominance in those areas. Its all a very complicated simple story I know but judging from world events, people seem to be so thoroughly distracted that the "dark side" is moving with impunity - Spain has just made a law that effectively prohibits the people to demonstrate...Spain is under big US influence as well as Agenda 21 based european unity also known as one government, one money and one world control prinipaslly through the Rothschild finance dominance....

On top of which - the spanish government is pushing marine oil exploration and fracking despite massive public disaccord. The marine environment will continue to be terribly damaged...esterior forces need to engage more effectively to cause "natural perturbances to damage the entities carrying out the deep water drilling as well as debilitating occurences to politicians involved at the top.

There has to be limits to everything even when it may interfere with free will....

what say you.

Thankyou and positive energy."

Do not be afraid Good Friend N,

Japan and Spain for instance will not play a crucial role of this illuminati system collapse, they lay tightly under illuminati/cabal. On the other hand, BRICS will play the most important role in this, it is the main character now and right now they are moving away from petrodollar (main supporting column of this evil cabal system).

As well they use Peace and Understanding in opposition to many provocations which cabal are throwing at them. Right now it is time that is not on the side of illuminati/cabal. And thus the longer they wait, the less options they have.

BUT along with it, their downfall is imminent and any nasty evil thing they would make to change it, will result in a much more faster downfall!

So they are caught in a deadlock, You can thank One, Sage Star A, Sun, Earth-Gaia-Terra, whole Cosmo, Followers of Light and Yourself - Lightworkers, it is with these United Efforts We All Together, United have caught them in this completely surrendered situation!

Much Positive Energy to You as well!

"Hi GE, we are really grateful for any news. Even though the Challenger/Chernobyl events delivered the message, it seems like a harsh result for the people on the Challenger and for the people in and around Chernobyl."

Yes, unfortunately it is, but at that old time, no other thing would be made as "a warning". Unfortunately "invisible warning" must be made of destruction if nothing else works.

Simple words and signs were already given before that and not worked.

"What happens to the people on earth when August 2016 comes?
and if the experiment ends. Do we still live or die?"

August 2016 will be the time when demiurge must cease Humanity's experiment, if this demand will not be met and demiurge would continue on; this being will be punished for this by Forces of One.

For Humans though, it will depend on how Humanity will be ready for Grand Changes to start. If Everyone will be ready then what You wanted - Complete Freedom - will be granted, at first it would seem hard when Changes will start, later though fruits of this will abundantly reward Every Living Being here on Earth - Humans, Animals, Plants and Nature.

All this Grand Process already started since cycle of Revelation of 2012. The start of fall of system of cabal will start from finances, so Everyone should be ready for this, be ready for some banks going bankrupt and prices skyrocketing. This is the most hardest point - the Beginning.

On question about "do we still live or die", depends on Your Very Own decision. I am sure to say Everyone wants to live, so Yes, Everyone will live!

-- -- -- --- --

"Hi Sofia and GE,
I have heard from different sources that the planet Nibiru will
be coming close to earth by late in 2015 or by 2016 and will
cause flooding world wide. Do you know if this is true? Would
any help come to save earth."

Yes, this is a popular theory. What we know is that no Good Friend, there isn't any Planet that size that can cause destruction of Earth here in Solar System. It is said that Nibiru is having very long orbit that comes close to Earth in some moment, but there is none such planet.

The only thing that can fit here are huge spherical ships of Followers of Light, they have the size of Planets and yes they can cause floods, they also have weaponry to destroy planets and other big ships, yet don't worry, they have a very strict policy on use of such weaponry and as well their huge immense gravity is being hold by special anti-gravity devices which absorbs gravity and makes this ship almost ethereal. You can say "it weighs like a feather".

And yes of course, there would be help if this Planet would be endangered by such cataclysms.

"Hi GE and Sophia,

What is your take on this alleged NASA whistle blower claiming that the earth is
not round

and that in fact it's flat? He also says he has made graphic renderings of the EARTH how "they" want to present it but that this actually is a total distortion as almost
everything else..!
He's arguments makes lot of sense particularly about the sky and the Sun being nothing
like what we've been taught!

http://kauilapele.wordpress.com/2014/11/29/nasa-whistleblower-image-hoaxster-videos/

Hugs O."

Well Good Friend, we can say that this is not truth, because I for instance saw other Worlds and other Stars, they all are spherical. The flat Worlds tough can be made artificially, I am pretty sure this World is spherical and not artificial. But as always believe in what You think is right.

Many Hugs!

"I have found a totally fascinating article here on the sott.net news page which I hope you will read and transmit to GE...it seems that there could be more to this story than just an archaeological discovery...here is the link:-

www.sott.net/article/290244-1-million-bodies-found-in-Egyptian-cemetery-scientists-stumped

This is a vast number of mummy/semi cadavers in one place which suggests an intense activity at some period in time...Egypt being of great significance to the great dynamic of our existence.

As always much love and positive energy"

Great discovery Good Friend! I feel sorry for some young People that died back then not able to experience Life...
Much Love and Positive Energy to You as well!

"Hi Good Friend, you never spoke about the breakaway civilization the cabal and apparently the russians and china have , although you gave some hints.I know why they dont share their advanced technology with us but what i dont understand is why the US can't win a war against a third world country with all this aviable technology ?Are they not allowed to use it on earth?"

I am not sure which ones You mean. We know that there are underground People living separately from Humanity, but They have completely different experience, as well we know of some People that were taken from Earth and are now living within some other Civilizations. Some were taken for experiments to making hybrids.

When talking about U.S. government or Everyone Else living here, They are allowed to possess highly developed technologies only if They develop these Themselves.

There are exclusions though, like that contract between "greys" and U.S. government. The technologies of greys are not well developed and they didn't want to give all their best technologies to Humans for nothing.

Also sometime some Individuals here can be granted superior technologies to perform some task on order of either Galactic Federation of Light or Forces of One. True though that reptilians don't listen to anybody and do everything how it is more "profitable" to them. But the main fact about their "help" remains the same, they always "use" others.

Greys are not that off like reptilians are, at least greys have some "humane behavior" within them, that is why they listened to Galactic Federation of Light and ceased their experiments and abolished their contract. Reptilians run away, because they no longer see profit here and see only losses, as well order "from above" was given to leave this Planet (this order was given by demiurge).

Also we have some new additions to alternative Energy Technologies

This is not a very wise one, but it shows that there are always alternative routes for making Your car to run, and it also shows that People are not sleeping but looking for ways to make better World! [513]

Then improved Solar Energy Panels, 46% energy conversion is not bad, but also far from being complete. Forces of One for example are having Solar Panels that are converting more than ~8000% of Solar Energy. You understand that this is much much more than Star can give, in fact these Solar Panels produce much more Energy than they receive! Some secret technologies can even do more than that, so this is the way in which Humanity should concentrate Their Efforts, because this is more than possible! [514]

Also Good Friend D' spoke about Crystal Batteries, which is astounding another alternative - self recharging batteries! [515]

---

[513] N.p., n.d. Web. <http://rt.com/news/209619-sunfire-water-synthetic-fuel/>.
[514] "Australia Develops World's Most Efficient Solar Panels." RT International. N.p., n.d. Web. 16 July 2016. <http://rt.com/business/212383-australia-record-solar-energy/>.
[515] N.p., n.d. Web. <http://www.removingtheshackles.blogspot.com/2014/12/nick-mckenny-crystal-battery-next-step.html>.

Also some of the best music of new Thomas Bergersen's album called Sun for Your Enjoyment! As I know this work took almost 4 cycles to be accomplished, a big work and can be felt in this music!

Our Destiny [516]

Starchild [517]

Empire of Angels [518]

Two Hearts [519]

Always Mine [520]

Colors of Love [521]

And New Life [522]

If I wouldn't be available, Merry Christmas and a Happy New Year to Everyone! Even if we (or You) don't accept such Celebrations we are gladly joining the

---

[516] EpicJennyni20. "Thomas Bergersen - Our Destiny (Sun)." YouTube. YouTube, 07 Dec. 2014. Web. 16 July 2016. <https://www.youtube.com/watch?v=YlrYCy3HeN0>.
[517] EpicJennyni20. "Thomas Bergersen - Starchild (Sun)." YouTube. YouTube, 03 Dec. 2014. Web. 16 July 2016. <https://www.youtube.com/watch?v=KXu7ppVTbHQ>.
[518] Nefredil1. "Thomas Bergersen - Empire of Angels (Thematic Video)." YouTube. YouTube, 02 Oct. 2014. Web. 16 July 2016. <https://www.youtube.com/watch?v=KpYzFxUymy0>.
[519] EpicJennyni20. "Thomas Bergersen - Two Hearts (Sun)." YouTube. YouTube, 06 Dec. 2014. Web. 16 July 2016. <https://www.youtube.com/watch?v=TFQMvKkq5M8>.
[520] EpicJennyni20. "Thomas Bergersen - Always Mine (Sun)." YouTube. YouTube, 10 Dec. 2014. Web. 16 July 2016. <https://www.youtube.com/watch?v=S8Eu8xiNplQ>.
[521] Epicmusicvn. "Epic Cinematic | Thomas Bergersen - Colors of Love (Epic Emotional) | EpicMusicVN." YouTube. YouTube, 15 Dec. 2014. Web. 16 July 2016. <https://www.youtube.com/watch?v=XKIq6-drP88>.
[522] GreiusTheGold. "Thomas Bergersen - New Life." YouTube. YouTube, 07 Dec. 2014. Web. 16 July 2016. <https://www.youtube.com/watch?v=GJPinLhPuMI>.

Celebration of Humanity and Outstanding Energy Spike!

Let there be Peace, Love and Prosperity among All.

December 24th, 2014

G/E

I also forgot to mention that the next cycle of 12.22.2014... is also a time when Sun and Moon are aligned with Galactic Center in 1 line in the skies. 12.22.2014 is New Moon, which means "a rebirth" of Moon. And like You can understand, this is a very rare alignment, this is in no way "a coincidence", You remember that nothing happens without a reason.

This moment of time can be use to meditate and make wishes, or making pleas or requests to Universe, this time is when they will be fulfilled!

~~~~

Also speaking about Grand Cosmic Alignments, recently Good Friends made a great research on subject of astrotheology, which is a secret subject and a secret knowledge unavailable for Majority. You will find out why "Christmas" and "Easter" are put in dates of winter and spring, it is all connected with the Sun (The "Son" of God). It is a long read and a great eye opener, so take Your time and enjoy it [523]

Through it You can see for Yourself that religions were mixed and interacted with each other during thousands of cycles and all around the Globe. Most of information presented here is like we know it, I can only say that character Yeshua (Jesus) along with many other People that became "god" after they passed away and "reborned" really existed, yet original teaching of Yeshua and His life were hardly distorted to fit "elite's" evil agenda of enslavement. Although

---

[523] "Occult Meanings of Winter Solstice and Christmas | AstroTheology, Alchemy, Roman Solstice Practices, Occult Symbolism, Santa Claus, Reincarnation." Stillness in the Storm. N.p., n.d. Web. 16 July 2016. <http://sitsshow.blogspot.com/2014/12/occult-meanings-of-winter-solstice-and.html>.

always use Your Own Discernment for any information.

Also You heard not one time that catholicism is a religion that took it's roots from so called "paganism", but what they fail to acknowledge is that whole christianity took it's current image and form from religions They Themselves call "pagan".

If You look at the roots, "paganism" is a discrimination name, this word is an evolved form taken from latin language, by which were named poor and helpless People of that ancient time, most of whom were having incurable diseases and which comes from two negative words of jewish language "gentile" and "goy" to "show" that current talk is not about jews, but about "the rest". As always "gentiles" and "goy" words evolved from religion judaism and talmud and not from nationalism or ethnic roots and was used by jews to denounce and discriminate other religions (along with other nations like Canaanites - progenitors of Palestinians and Lebanese today). These 2 words can also be called discrimination, though jewish "elite" are doing everything to show these 2 words in positive color, still in the end it remains negative.

The combination of sounds make all these 3 words negative, with "hidden dark" in them. We prefer to call what they call "pagan" as 'polytheistic religions'. And like You understood from this read, most of current christian form and image is adopted from "mithraism" - the religion of the past, which was around ancient World for 2000 cycles, same like christianity and islam were around medieval and modern World for 2000 cycles.

So both are equally aged and is showing that christianity and islam are about to leave this World and true, their time is really up.

But what Everyone should understand in this hidden knowledge is that this hidden "elite" was doing the right thing by honoring the Sun, even in a such illusory shroud. Though some of this "elite" were honoring not Sun, but Sirius, still their message came to Subconsciousness of Majority.

The message is simple - 'without Sun life here is impossible, so Sun must be honored and at least be remembered as a Giver and Supporter of Life'.

Through these many religions, Sun was honored and respected, though not directly, but by taking many other routes and names like "gods" Attis, Mithra or Jesus Christ, still Sun was honored. And it is the right thing to do, because of this, Sun knows that You as It's Many Children remember Sun as a Giver and Supporter of Life, as a "Father" and along with this remember Earth as a "Mother" and an "invisible" Grand Father, Father of Sun. All of this is a Grand Design, once You are seeing the true and deep picture of all this.

Another thing I wanted to add here is the very close association of christianity with fishes. What Everyone should understand here is that christianity, islam and judaism along with some other religions are of the old Age of Pisces, that is the Age of Fishes. If You look deeper and relate People to this age, then all fits right where it belongs.

Fishes are "ignorant" and care only about their own survival, They don't tend to look farther than what they are about to eat. You can see same about old World of some 4000 cycles in the past. Christianity was teaching World the same - "blindly deliver the message" (even if it is not true), because like fishes are doing things that they were learned to do since birth, so were People (like christians and muslims) so it suits Age of Fishes correctly, Majority of People of old were like fish.

And it all suits this very same program of enslavement of Humanity, living in an isolatory box. Those "enlightened" illuminati found out that they can enslave Humanity in this age, because whole Cosmo affects Consciousness and they did everything to make it happen. They almost succeeded, but were stopped by arrival of highly evolved Individuals - You Good Friends, Lightworkers and Lightwarriors as well as One's Workers and Warriors.

And thus they were prevented from finishing their "grand plan" and as their little time they have now is running out, Humanity are transforming to suit this New

Age of Aquarius!

And as We transgress this age and come fully into Age of Aquarius, fundamental Changes will occur!

Humanity now are adapting in order to be able to live in this New Age, evil can only exist on full Consensus of Civilization, this is what illuminati/cabal wanted to achieve by making evil "New World Order" under one world government - in order to save themselves and save their place on top of their sinister "pyramid of power".

Aquarius is one of the most beautiful Constellations is the Skies, and all of the Constellations are not made without intent, they are made with most in-depth and thoughtful meaning, all of these are there to show history and progress of Mankind, all are given by One to give You a glimpse in what You are going to uncover of "what lies beyond" these very Skies You can observe.

And on the very first cycle - 12.22.2014 after Solstice, Sun, Moon and Sage Star A (Galactic Center) were aligned in one line to remind You that Changes are happening right now! Do not forget about Lunar Tetrad, this Great Alignment happened almost in the middle of it. And the middle of Lunar Tetrad is in January, so by definition Grand Event will take place whether in january or after it.

You are about to witness these Grand Changes in full swing!

But yes, think realistically Good Friends and BE READY! Have most (or all) of your money on hands and not in your bank account in case banks are going to get bankrupt. You know if they are going to get bankrupt, they won't send You notification of something like "we are going to get bankrupt and you better take your money while it's not too late". 100% of what we witnessed, banks always close themselves without a warning. And in most cases money of customers simply "disappear". In actuality they are taken by "someone", the problem is that they don't want to give their own money to cover all the huge expenses of bankruptcy, so yes, they are robbing other People and running away. This is mostly related to USA, Canada, Australia, Japan and EU. So be prepared! Good Friend D' wrote great article about this [524]

Otherwise, Happy Celebrations to Everyone! This is one of the most Joyful time of the Solar Cycle!

Wish Everyone much Peace, Love and Prosperity.

SOPHIA

Just in case you missed it... here is a gift for this new cycle...
I wish you all the most blessed of holidays. [525]

This is the end of what was received in 2014.

---

[524] "There Is Hope In Understanding That A Great Economic Collapse Is Coming." Removing The Shackles: There Is Hope In Understanding: The Economic Collapse. N.p., n.d. Web. 16 July 2016. <http://removingtheshackles.blogspot.com/2014/12/there-is-hope-in-understanding-economic.html>.
[525] "My Gift for You." Sophia. N.p., n.d. Web. 16 July 2016. <http://www.sophialove.org/read-my-blog/my-gift-for-you>.

Chapter 7 Private Messages

Private Messages

As has been said, this relationship began on you tube. It is there in the comments section of the "Message to Off World" video[526] for the better part of 2012. It moved to *you tube email*, which unfortunately has been lost with the take-over of you tube by Google.

When Google entered the picture, we did move the conversation to my private email account. It is from there that I posed questions from readers as well as myself. Some were kept private for reasons at the time I felt were in the best interests of all concerned. They were most likely alarming or else named people or organizations I did not wish to name.

What you are about to read may at times sound repetitive. I am attempting to weed out what has been said. This work is being constructed over a year's time, so there may be some repetitions that were missed.

So forgive any repeats and enjoy this peek into our private relationship beginning in July of 2014, and lasting until August of 2015. It's one I've come to cherish, especially now that it is no longer a part of my every-day; an interesting friendship for sure!

JULY 16TH 2014

G/E

Good day Sophia!

I will write from here from now on, some fragile information I will not be able to send through this service as e-mails are not very secure source as well, yet it is now more secured than new you tube's "messages".

Google is simply fulfilling the plan of illuminati/cabal, which is step by step to strip away all freedoms and privacy from People around the World. New additions they made are no longer secure and can be monitored much more strictly by u.s. government.

Illuminati are falling and they can see it, yet they gave an order to their lesser members, called "initiates" to execute an order of preparation of coming of

---

[526] "Message To Off World Beings." *YouTube*. N.p., n.d. Web. 10 July 2016. <https://youtu.be/Pk-AaK2ZCV0>.

"novus ordus seclorum" or the "new world order" (order of things which is evil), and this order they are fulfilling.

And You can witness this order, the World is very tense right now and media is pushing only in one direction. But the good side of this is, is that we can finally see who is who and their real face is being shown very openly now. So for now we need to avoid being seen and we also need to endure this last pressure from their side.

Much Love to You!

SOPHIA

Sounds like a good plan.

There is also a social network (like face book) that a friend of mine started, called Project XIII that does not hang on to any data. I was thinking if you joined we could communicate through there. It is found here[527]. I have not used it much, but it is a way to "talk" privately. Tell me what you think. You have to ask other members to friend you, and know their user name, only then can you communicate with them.

I would like to include in the blog what you have said here, from "Google is simply fulfilling the plan...." to "... their real face is being shown very openly now."??? Let me know.

Thanks for reaching out this way; this will be much easier to post too!

Much love to you too!

JULY 17TH 2014

G/E

Yes Sophia, of course You can if You like to.

I was looking for Project XIII, what I can't quite understand is why was chosen number 13? Not a very wise choice to say the least. I will consider this, but think for now I will use e-mail if You don't mind Sophia.

---

[527] "Project XIII: Home." Project XIII: Home. N.p., n.d. Web. 10 July 2016. <http://www.projectxiii.com/>.

Just moments ago, another bad incident happened. Boeing 777 was shot down, as we know by ukrainian army, yet it is also a false flag and barely planned event. (Barely, because it won't change much and will not help illuminati order to get out of many problems they are having right now). There was nothing that could be done here and this is a big loss of life. It is all meant for same purpose of starting a war. Here was the play on numbers.

This is also Malaysian Airlines plane which bears a logo of trident and tri color of white, blue and red (like russian flag) and ukrainian coat of arms have also trident on it. Trident is number 3, plus tri color flag have 3 colors on it, Boeing 777 is having three number 7s, then 7+7+7=21 (also points to july 21st) where 2+1=3 and 295 people were on board, all of them passed away... another poor People, victims of this evil system... This is 2+9+5=16, 1+6=7.

This plane was flying from Amsterdam, flag of Amsterdam is having an evil colors of black and red on it and 3 white letters "X", the X in numerology is number 6, so it is equal to 666, same like pornography, many never think about this, but XXX movies are actually "666 movies", and as well flight MH017 was downed on this cycle of july the 17th.

As You remember, there are no coincidences, all is happening with a reason. All of this numbers are pointing to evil scheme. Many numbers 3 are signifying world war 3, and number 7 is a sign that such preparation are being made, thus warning members of illuminati that are awaiting for events to "unfold". Just to add up, the IMF speech which was mentioning number 7 and numerology is playing very big part in this terrible incident. The woman of IMF also mentions world war 1, that it started 100 cycles ago. Indeed, the "anniversary" of start of this war will be on 28th of july, right after "the grand climax" on 27th.

So as always, meditate and think positively, this will reduce the possible casualties that are still to come.

Much Peace and Love to You!

JULY 21ST 2014

SOPHIA

Thanks. I am away still. I will work to get this posted later tonight.
Lots of things are going on for sure. I have been away since the 17th.
I hope that you are well.

Much love,
Sophia

~~

Okay, it is posted.

I believe the number thirteen was chosen for the year, 2013. Email is fine.

There are many comments from the last few days you may want to answer. I will attempt to check again tomorrow, yet I am still on holiday and away.

Much love to you,
Sophia

JULY 22ND, 2014

G/E

I will add another set of information which I received from One, when I asked about number 7.

"This plane crash is a very complicated event, it could have been avoided, but because many here still prefer to understand Creation through violence, this event took place."

The big play on numbers was done by freemasons of "grand masonic lodge of Washington", unfortunately People would not find it out for now. As One told this event was in preparation for a long time and this MH17 and MH370 were meant to start a world war 3. I was shown information that indeed such preparation is from a long ago as first flight of this plane was made also on 17th of july and in 1997, that is 17 solar cycles ago! Here is a link to this article[528]

And like it is said there, TWA Flight 800 crashed as well on 17th july 1996. And more to this One told me that number 17, repeated several times points to Revelation 17 of the bible, and that is the judgement of a "woman" that is known as "Mystery - Babylon the Great". I understand what One meant, as I knew this story and I knew that this "woman" is America.

---

[528] "MH17 Crash Conspiracy Theories: Strange Coincidence Of First, Last Flight Dates." International Business Times. N.p., 17 July 2014. Web. 10 July 2016. <http://www.ibtimes.com/mh17-crash-conspiracy-theories-strange-coincidence-first-last-flight-dates-1631648>.

This prophecy was made long ago and it was not meant as something "unavoidable", this was meant as a warning to Humanity, that all of this: beast system, mark of the beast, and whole this judgement could be avoided, yet because Humanity chose a path of fulfilling this prophecy through many generations, this is how it will happen partially (not completely). Not completely, meant that Apocalypse will not take place and United States will not be "destroyed" as it is said there, but whole system and industry of U.S. might be severely damaged, so that illuminati order could be stopped.

Yellowstone awakening would be the first of such strikes to the infrastructure of this government. As well possible is small conflict within U.S. both by People of U.S. and foreign armies. All of this would be meant to liberate this country and stop the plan of illuminati (they were given many chances to surrender, yet they refused).

This warning in Revelation was given by demiurge as I know (as a part of this whole experiment), but One played part in this as well. Demiurge knew that Humanity would choose this path, but One intended Humanity to choose its own path and count this only as a possibility. Due to huge influence and fear of these biggest religions the thinking of big judgement and coming "savior" had encoded itself in whole Human Society.

We are awaiting for Moment of Justice or this Judgement of Revelation, what I can say for sure, is that with this plane tragedy, it is now even closer. Illuminati families are responsible for all People from plane that passed away. The whole plane scenario is now playing negatively on illuminati and U.S. government, People around the world are losing trust in these entities and so they are falling apart. Their allies are abandoning them and their lies are becoming more obvious with each passing moment of time.
As You remember after this Judgement will come "Savior", this is meant here that a New World will be born.

Thank You Good Friends D. and O. for provided links, intuitive guidance link is especially informative for many!

"What I get from you saying "harsh reset" is EARTH cleansing EVENT's that will force people to unite? Correct?"

Harsh Reset will not be as something like apocalypse or end of the world, but it will take lives away and make destruction, but it won't be global, it would be only on places where evil took big hold. Like I mentioned USA is the biggest of these entities, followed by UK, Saudi Arabia, Israel (here meant governments of these countries) and some fewer entities like NATO's, European Union's, IMF's, World Bank's headquarters. Ukraine, Libya, Syria, Iraq and Africa as a whole and South America as a whole will be restored after the Moment of Justice (not instantly, but wars will be ceased and poverty will be significantly reduced).

"On another note for how long is the genocide going to be continued all over the globe i.e. Ukraine, Palestine, Syria, Libya etc etc etc..??"

This will continue until they - illuminati and everything I mentioned, are active. When their system (the beast system) would collapse, it would be stopped, not fully, but mostly, as they are the main force behind this evilness and cruelty.

Sophia, there one mistake it is not big, but still noticeable in place
"This knowledge is of category "arcane". "The Information of Aspect of Light sits within DNA and can be uncovered, I was mentioning how."

The part "The Information of Aspect of Light sits within DNA and can be uncovered, I was mentioning how." is going to a question which Good Friend M. asked me and part about arcane comes to knowledge about incarnation. Also there were some minor mistakes I made in last message, I'm sorry. Can you fix them Sophia?

"As You remember, there are no coincidences, all is happening with a reason. All of this numbers are pointing to evil scheme. Many numbers 3 are signifying world war 3, and number 7 is a sign that such preparation are being made, thus warning members of illuminati that are awaiting for events to "unfold"."

Just two mistakes, "All of these numbers are pointing" and "number 7 is a sign that such preparations are being made", thank you!

Here I will give information on Incarnations and Reincarnations.

"Yes i want to hear (read :-)) what you know about reincarnation .Can you elaborate "arcane"

Arcane is meant the most deepest knowledge which requires big understanding. In this category is knowledge in which comes most hard to understand subjects.

The story on Incarnation and Reincarnation is being put very simply as Soul leaves the Physical Body, it is going into ethereal realm, or Heaven to rest and restore. While resting this Soul is able to traverse Universe and make unimaginable things. Yet the whole story is much more complicated, You heard parts of this whole story. I will not give into details, because it is indeed a hard to understand knowledge, as we know Followers of Light don't know all of it in details yet.

As You remember Your Soul exists in many dimensions and dimensional worlds. At the same time as We exist here as a Soul within this Physical Body, Our Soul exists in other Worlds and in other Incarnations. Our Souls are called multi-dimensional Bodies, we exist as a different sorts of objects at the same time, like I am a Human here and an animal in other World, then as a star in other World.

This is put simply. That is why it is sometimes possible to see "ghosts" of a long gone People or events (like battles) taking place in this time, this is due to Energy collisions within the Code of "Multi-Dimensional Sphere", this is all Worlds put together. Somewhere in other World this Soul exist in incarnation and when it's memory is refreshed with something that happened here (and energy collision is taking place), a ghost or multiple ghosts are appearing in this World. Other Souls after passing away are choosing "to stay alive". We call them "the dead wanderers", yet these Souls are also a multi-dimensional incarnation, so their image can change on one in which they currently incarnated in other Worlds. When We sleep, we can rarely move into other Worlds and see these Worlds (how rarely depends on individual Soul and it's connectedness with its other incarnations). As well very very rarely, it is possible to actually move to other World with physical body attached to a Soul, but these are very rare cases and prerequisites are necessary for this as we know. And as You remember most of the Souls on this Planet are stuck here, because demiurge blocks these Souls from leaving by telling different reality and tricking Them into submission.

I hope this will help in Your understanding.

In coming Earth cycles are expected more provocations from illuminati/cabal and we are coming close to july 27. Meditate or pray and overall think positively Good Friends! You are creating future right now!

Much Peace, Calm and Prosperity to Everyone!

JULY 24TH 2014

SOPHIA

Okay, it is posted. The corrections are made as well. This information is so very helpful. If there is more like this, I know your readers would appreciate reading it.

I was delayed on my trip so this was a bit late. the 27th is only 3 days away now. I will be away again on the 26th and 27th, until very late in the day on Sunday. If there are updates about these dates, let me know before I leave early Saturday AM so I can post them. I am sure they will be looking for more updates.

Again, thank you.

Much love,
Sophia

JULY 26TH 2014

G/E

I will only add more to this very big play on numbers and unfortunately algerian plane crashed as well with connection to this issue. It is a tragic incident; this could have been prevented like many other similar incidents if planes would have been outfitted with more precautions.

We felt that illuminati did not make algerian tragedy, yet it also points to number 7 and 17. First I will add that MH17 plane which was shot down was numbered "9M-RMD", in numerology M=4, R=9, D=4, so it is 9+4=13 and 4+9+4=17 and numerically compressed in binary type it looks 13-17. Also it was Boeing 777-200ER, in numerology E=5 and R=9, so it is 5+9=14 and 1+4=5, so total is 2+0+0+5=7 and so it is 7777, 7+7+7+7=28 (july 28 is the start of world war 1, precisely 100 solar cycles ago).
And here is another number 17 of "Air Algerie Airbus plane AH5017" which

unfortunately crashed. Word Airbus in numerology is also number 7, 1(A)+9(I)+9(R)+2(B)+3(U)+1(S)=25 and 2+5=7 and the date of 7/25/2014 equals to 7/7/7, because 2014=2+0+1+4=7 and july is 7th month..

It is good that nothing big happened on 25th, yet we still have 27th. And on 26th (today) is a heliacal rising of Sirius which is called "Sothic Cycle" (this is when Sun and Sirius are rising at the same time from east). Also this event most of the time falls on 17th of july.

I will explain bit about it. Sirius is a god in freemasonry, it represents all seeing eye of Horus and 5-pointer star (called eastern star), both normal and inverted, inverted has more "dark power" in it (so they believe). Star Sirius is one of the trinity of freemasonry which consists of Osiris (notice name sounds like Sirius) or Masculine (equivalent to christianity's Trinity as Father), Isis or Feminine (Holy Spirit) and Horus, equivalent to Son or "Something New, something which they want to achieve, it is their evil New World Order. These 3 deities are also having an equivalents within egyptian mythology itself: Osiris-Sah, Isis-Sopdet and Horus-Sopdu

Notice that Sopdet is a goddes of Sirius and she have 5-pointed star on her head, which is an egyptian symbol for Sirius[529].

All 5-pointed stars that were introduced in America to whole world by forefathers/freemasons are a direct representation of Sirius, 5 primal senses of a Human and as a symbol of Mars and thus war and hatred. This star was never used in ancient and medieval times except for some exceptions like You can see here, as it was known for it's "dark powers", yet exactly United States government was the one that tricked Humanity into using this star as a primal representation of a star. You know that star on a flag don't have a real importance on it, there is no reason to use exactly this star on an american flag.

So what You can see is that this was done on purpose only by those that wanted it to be there. Notice also that governments of U.S. and EU are adding recently more sharpness to this star, thus making it more sinister, more sharpness is being added to military representation of this star. As well when you see an EU flag or American flag on a TV or a computer, watch closely how these stars are inverted most of the time (like behind those that speak or filming of surroundings). All of this is done on purpose.

[529] "Sopdet." Wikipedia. Wikimedia Foundation, n.d. Web. 10 July 2016. <https://en.wikipedia.org/wiki/Sopdet>.

So this sothic cycle and "the grand climax" are matching with each other, which gives out a thought of bad event, but remember - all is in Your Hands and Minds, it is all about Consciousness!

Just look, all of this what You are witnessing happening right now is not done by this Planet, Animals or Plants or Cosmo or ETs, all of this is done by Humanity, and so all of this can be stopped by United Efforts of Humanity! Yes Humanity was manipulated into doing most of these things and becoming how it is today by outer forces, but the last word lies in the hands of Humanity!

Much Peace and Love to Everyone!

JULY 27TH, 2014

SOPHIA

Just posted this.
Thank you,
Sophia

AUGUST 1ST, 2014

SOPHIA

There has been lots of hits since the 28th, and one comment re: ebola you will want to respond to.

I hope you are well.

Much love,
Sophia

AUGUST 2ND 2014

G/E

(NOTE – POSTED IN ENTIRETY IN CHAPTER 6)

And I also wanted to Thank You Sophia, for Everything You do. Also "Prophecy and Creation"[530]is well written, I enjoy reading of Your articles!

"Prophecy and Creation." Sophia. N.p., n.d. Web. 10 July 2016. <http://www.sophialove.org/my-

With Peace and Love to You.

SOPHIA

Thank you!

I see M. has already replied to your update!

Much love,
Sophia

AUGUST 6TH 2014

SOPHIA

Hi,

I am again heading out of town from the 9th through the 13th. There are a lot of questions on the blog and I will be available to post through Saturday AM my time (Central US).

Be well and much love.

AUGUST 8TH 2014

G/E

(NOTE – POSTED IN ENTIRETY IN CHAPTER 6)

SOPHIA

Hello. It's clear we aren't in complete agreement about this being. I will put it out as is though; as there are many questions and people need to decide for themselves.

If you go to the blog with the Call to Action[531], you will read a comment from M. who asks a question of you directly on this subject. He asked us both. I have answered. If you have anything different as a reply, you may want to do so and I will post that as well.

---

blog/prophecy-and-creation>.[530]

[531] "8-8-2014 Call to Action." Sophia. N.p., n.d. Web. 10 July 2016. <http://www.sophialove.org/my-blog/8-8-2014-call-to-action>.

Much love,
Sophia

NOTE – THE BEING I SPOKE TO FOR SEVERAL YEARS (POSER) WAS NEVER ADEQUATELY IDENTIFED BY G/E. HE HAD THIS TO ADD TO MY RESPONSE TO A READER'S QUESTION, AND IT MAY NOT HAVE BEEN PUBLISHED ON THE BLOG:

G/E

Sophia, here I want to add to Your information

"Thank you for this question. This being is not human. Human attributes do not apply. If you remember I had contact with it/him and I can report for sure that it has no sense of sorrow/guilt/compassion. It merely exists to feed itself. It is ancient yes, perhaps older than the earth itself, but the whole concept of maturity is a human one, whatever this being is, it does not comprehend life in the same way as we do."

From what You wrote there, I can suspect this was a reptilian, they are masters at manipulation and deceit, but I could be wrong, anyway if You decided to expel this being, I can be sure that You made the right choice Sophia.

NOTE – THIS BEING, "POSER" ACTUALLY LEFT THE NEXT SUMMER, IN 2015. THAT CONVERSATION CAN BE FOUND HERE[532].

AUGUST 14TH 2014

SOPHIA

I am posting this now. For sure you will have many more questions and soon. I have just returned home.

My close friend "A" is very ill. I do not know why I ask, but if you have any ability to offer a healing, I know he is open and will receive it. You have spoken to him before. They do not know what it is.

Thank you and much love.

G/E

It is ok Sophia, I will do my best to aid Good Friend.

---

[532] "Re: The Departure of Poser." Sophia. N.p., n.d. Web. 10 July 2016. <http://www.sophialove.org/my-blog/re-the-departure-of-poser>.

hmm.. In recent days I and some other GEs were attacked energetically, supposedly by dark priests, do not forget about them or underestimate their powers, they are casting evil spells and curses on whole World, they try to call all primal instincts to unleash chaos upon world so to trigger WW3 and especially they target and attack Lightworkers and Truthseekers. We are affected as well.

What kind of disease Good Friend "A" is feeling in Himself; can He describe what bothers Him?

Music, sound and frequencies of calm, stable stance is the way to heal all diseases. Laugh is also a good treatment for most of diseases. Please ask Good Friend, what exactly this is that bothers Him and ask Him to show me the region of Body if Good Friend can identify it.

SOPHIA

I will share with you some of what he has shared, his symptoms. They are thinking it is like Multiple Sclerosis and testing for that. He is incapacitated right now. This is what he said:

(A LONG LIST OF SYMPTOMS WERE INCLUDED HERE)

I know it is a lot to read, but that is the information I have right now. He sounds in bad shape.

Right now he is in a great deal of pain and has been hospitalized.

Thank you.

AUGUST 15TH 2014

G/E

Thank You Sophia.

This is a serious problem … yet it can be cured. Because it had to do with brain, music and random sounds are not of that great help to Good Friend.

Here words and frequencies can do the job. Words and frequencies need to be directed at this disease... Good Friend has weaker left side of the Body, so it is pointing to left hemisphere of a brain I presume.

Doctors also can help Good Friend I suppose…

One also tells me that it is something to do with abdomen in Good Friend, there is something there, or perhaps this is where the problem occurred, possibly wrong food eaten?

For now I can give one treatment that works if done correctly. Good Friend have to unite His hands, put them on head and constantly repeat to Himself and His Body: "You are no longer there" or "Restore Yourself Body" or simply "Restore" or "Restoration", if You chose one phrase or word, don't stop in repeating this same word or phrase.

This can be done both orally and inwardly, it is not important in which way, but orally is presumably, yet if he is in a hospital then inwardly would be just fine, no one need to hear this.

It is just You, Physical Body and One (Creator) that will hear this and restore Your body.

And most important in this is You have to concentrate Your Mind, and concentrate on this illness, You have to constantly ask Your Body to unite all Its powers and energies and heal the Central Neural System. Eventually it will work, if concentration is done correctly, but it is not instant. If You have not done this before it could take even more time for Your Body to get used to it. Put simply, here You have to ask Your Body to heal Itself, do not underestimate Your Body it can heal Itself from any disease!

To add, drink very clean mineralized water with less salt in it, water - treats all diseases as well, You can also ask someone to get "holy water" from trusted church if there is one. "Holy water" is a charged with positive thoughts and emotions water and is having healing attributes.

Also You can use some herbs, most easy to obtain is green tea. Your brain will need a lot of oxygen to restore, so breath deeply, until you feel that brain had enough and needs no longer, then breath again.

Green tea is having oxygen, so it is very healing. Do not use sugar, it is damaging, better drink pure green tea or use honey with the tea (you can also eat honey without tea, as it is also having oxygen).

Another source of oxygen is peroxygen of 35% concentration, this is pure H_2O_2. If you decide to use it, then it have to be diluted with water, only 3 to 5 drops of peroxygen would be enough for glass of water. It is having taste of bleach, but this is normal. You can also mix "holy water" with peroxygen to receive even better effect!

And most importantly, remember, use it in a very small dosages with water, pure peroxygen can damage skin and is forbidden from drinking pure, because it can lead to damage, remember this!

I hope this helps, clean oxygen and clean water is what Good Friend needs mostly right now and as well he need to ask His Body to restore!

SOPHIA

Thank you, I will share this.
Much love,

Sophia

AUGUST 17TH 2014

SOPHIA

There is a message from R.E., the engineer working on free energy. It is posted on an earlier update (July), and you may not be aware of it:

"I have fascinated with the description of the "Demiurge". Would GE have information as. to the origination of Demiurges in general. Did (One) create them and if so for what purpose? In other words how did they come to be?"

It was posted on a July update.

There are also lots of comments on the latest update, directed towards you.

What follows is a question from me though. I am asking about your absolute certainty that the being that has engaged in conversation with me is NOT the demi-urge? Just what characteristics or words are you expecting to see that would convince you of its authenticity? I have not a doubt that the being I have engaged with is not interested in the betterment of humanity. It has no concept of compassion. There is no hatred, there is just indifference. In what way are you so sure this demiurge is any different?

What doesn't sound like truth to me is any necessity to "wait" to end this experiment. That is indifference. If this demi-urge is or was initially interested in benefitting humanity, then what purpose would it have to not end the senseless killing in the name of worship? And do so NOW? It is clearly addicted to worship.

Your words are carrying a great deal of people towards your own belief system. Clarify for me as best you can which of them are speculations and which are absolute truths, and why. That would be helpful.

Thank you,

Sophia

G/E

Good Day Sophia!

I remember Good Friend R. of course, how he is doing? The spread of fuel less technologies is not fast, but at least, People are seeking them. The main obstacle that prevents this World from evolving further is U.S. government and all this evil system that was established by illuminati/cabal, once they are gone, there wouldn't be anyone preventing the spread of New Energy technologies.

I was answering on Good Friend's question. I will answer short here to not confuse.

Good Day Good Friend! As we know Universe was created in way that all must evolve and become better than it was before. We gave name "demiurge" only to this being that controls this Galaxy based on gnostics teaching and name we took from there, others we name as "lesser Creator-Gods". Demiurge is an all-powerful being that is a ruler of a highly evolved civilization of energetic organisms we call "Beings of Purity". They have evolved to a state from which there is almost no way to evolve further and so they decided to create new life (their Children) and through it to achieve "new ways of Evolution" (that is what I meant by achieving "ultimate power"). Humanity is a product of their thinking and craft. One created lesser Creator-Gods that is true, but they were created naturally, that is by process of "evolving further and becoming better".

Some Creator-Gods are choosing way of Harmony and aid, some are choosing neutrality toward everything and others are becoming obsessed with power and control and this thing happened with demiurge. One grants everything complete freedom, so Everyone that wants to be obsessed with power and control can do it. Although One don't like when damage is being done to others and demiurge done damage. This was not prevented as One is always "fighting with Itself" trying to overcome It's own powers. From one side One wants Harmony from the other side One allows freedom of actions which creates, what You can see is in demiurge. And so it can be said that One's wishfulness for Harmony lost in demiurge, so here is a product of this.

And to answer on Your question Sophia, I am quite sure about what methods demiurge is using. All the knowledge about this being was presented to me from Forces of One and from Ancient Machines. They know this being very well, I can say for sure that it wants both Harmony and power at the same time (demiurge is acting like One even here).

When demiurge speaks, it is never showing something You will not like, like indifference or simply waiting for something to happen. Demiurge always saying that it cares for You, loves You and always thinks about You, and that is true, it does love Humanity.

Unfortunately it allows People to die and to suffer, also after life demiurge greets People that remembered "God" and gave something to it (like worship) during life, Others that did not gave anything to it, demiurge does not screams at Them or hates Them, it simply is saying that they have to go to hell "for repair".

I understand this being, this is corruption within it that forces it to do evil to others. Yet there deep in its Soul, I can see that demiurge is not very evil, all it wants is power and control and this corrupts it, and this being can actually change, it all depends on humanity, again. This being's Children (Humanity) have to show to demiurge, that they are not happy with It and will not be its slaves or tools to achieve goals that it wants.

I'm writing everything we GEs know collectively, when I'm writing my own thoughts, I always warn of this. I can say that everything I write to Everyone through You Sophia is a lesson.

My job in contacting You is to teach You and Everyone that finds Our conversation to hear and use Your Inner Higher Self. Like Pleiadean Message told, "You have to use Your Emotions as through Emotions You can figure things out". To awaken Your most sacred Emotions, You have to hear the music and sounds of Creation. That is why You should always use Your own discernment.

Because we are here having a united effort on stopping evil and cruelty of illuminati/cabal, I can say that I provide only true information about them, their ideology, occult symbolism and plans toward whole Humanity. Also information about technologies and ETs disclosure is true. Anything that goes from outside this World, including information about One, Religion of One and demiurge, here You should use Your own discernment, because I can't provide proofs on this, all this knowledge is based on information we received from Forces of One and Religion of One.

So always, believe in what You think is right Sophia! I trust Your skills of discernment!:)

And here are the questions from Good Friends

THE REST WAS POSTED ON THE BLOG IN ITS ENTIRETY.

G/E

And Sophia, how is Good Friend "A"?

SOPHIA

I haven't heard from him in several days. He may not have a computer yet as they were moving.

Thank you for your responses to me and everyone else. They will be posted by the end of today (August 18).

Our whole family had difficulty sleeping last night, the vibratory shifts sometimes keep us awake and humming! I am taking this to be a good sign!

Much love,

Sophia

AUGUST 18TH 2014

G/E

The vibratory shifts are interesting, I too wasn't able to sleep this night, some of my brothers and sisters weren't able as well, but not all. It is a good sign, and I can see that we are close to Completion!

I was observing the Energy and saw that Good Friend is ok, He only needs some aid, Mutual Understanding between His Body and Mind will give Him that necessary strength. (*a reference to a personal request and friend – Sophia*)

On question about Ancient Machines I was answering before. I gave all information about them as i remember. But ok, I will give what we know about them, we know about them a lot, even more than about many Civilizations of Forces of One.

Yes, you can relate them to "machine world" of movie Matrix, but they are not like that. They do not use Humans as "batteries" and do not control nor Humans, nor Any other Civilization in the Universe. They are "neutral" (almost like Forces of One) and they are fulfilling the role of "maintainers" and "watchers" of Universe and all It's many different Inhabitants. As we know they were in existence long before this Universe was born, they are called "machines" and made as machines (like robots) to fulfill the duty without having Free Will and fulfill duty unconditionally.

They drop in category of "beta organisms" that are non-organic organisms, this means they cannot evolve without approval and cannot have Free Will unless approved to. This is made intentionally by One so that they can be in a service of One without any "side thoughts", their job is to be like "deputy" or substitution of One within "physical Cosmo" (here I mean everything that is going outside of One's Consciousness).

They write all the information about Universe to their infinitely large storage devices, about every progress that is happening every moving momentum of time (here I mean every less than a Nano second), they write everything from big processes like birth of a Star or what we do every day, to smallest possible processes, like what is happening with every smallest particles of atom. All of this is being written physically, and One's own Consciousness also writes all these processes, but on its own, "ethereally" if we can say. After all, whole Creation is a super huge experiment of One to experience and express Itself, so to become even better than One currently is.

Ancient Machines also serve as a last resort if "everything else fails". They are in possession of the most advanced technologies there can be ever created, one of such technologies creates their own "state of mind" which by itself creates their own dimensional world from which they can see all of Creation with its many infinite dimensions, dimensional worlds and parallel worlds, but at the same time they remain completely invisible, like they are not there, yet they are there.

This state of mind world is not constant, it is constantly changing world, or dynamic, so it is not possible to detect it even with technologies that demiurge possesses. Such secrecy is necessary, so to keep this technology from "evil hands" (like demiurge's). They are in possession of many, many other technologies, including for example, on with which they instantly can undo Creation if there will be such need or other with which they can bring back to existence every living and non-living organisms back to life that ever lived in Creation.

They can do everything by manipulating Code of Creation, yet they come to manipulate the Code, when One gives order to do so, without order they only write information about this Code. Their knowledge, technologies, all information about Universe and past Universes is also well hidden from unstable Creatures such as Humans or reptilians (and from somewhat corrupted beings like demiurge).

Part of their might they revealed to Forces of One on order of One, and they are aiding Forces of One when it is necessary, yet their main rule is to not interact with Creation so to not damage It's Free Will. As Forces of One are no longer completely free in their actions, Ancient Machines can interact with them and there is a huge Mutual Understanding between two.

I only revealed information about Ancient Machines because they are active on this World right now, otherwise it is kept well-hidden so to not "tempt" others to find this most ancient Civilization, but there is also One's will on this too, something You will know later on.

They hold the Balance on order of One and prevent evil forces from starting worldwide conflicts right now. Yet remember because they can't reveal themselves and must not interact with Creation - Humanity, they cannot do much about it, they hold Balance and hold off Ukrainian forces and ISIS from advance, yet they cannot completely negate them with 0 interactions (remember they are located in a world which is created by their own state of mind and from which they are non-existent here).

Damage is being done on these locations, but it is reduced in some manner of it. They hold the Balance by simply being there on those places of energetic pressure, of course if order from One would be to intervene physically, they would have ended everything in seconds of time (not just through might, but through other means, like diplomacy, mind control or full takeover of any media/TVs/PCs and spread the Truth).

If revealed, even their presence and looks is something which brings fear to everyone that encountered them (excluding Forces of One Civilizations). They are made to look scary (like super carnivores - which brings fear to all that sees them) when they are put into possible "hostile locations" like these places of conflicts which we are seeing right now. They can induce any emotion and take full control over anything that has at least some sort of connection with Energy (thus One) if such order is given.

Yet do not be afraid of them, One programmed them to be Loving, Compassionate and Understandable when it comes to be Friends with somebody. Within Forces of One they are very caring and have peaceful and loving look.

I hope this helps you in Understanding Good Friend!

AUGUST 19ᵀᴴ 2014

SOPHIA

Thank you. I shared this.

I just saw this[533].

(Title: Is Yellowstone about to blow?)

It is regarding Yellowstone.

Wow.

SEPTEMBER 5TH, 2014

SOPHIA

Hi. It's been quite a while and there are some comments and questions for you on your last post. Are you okay?

I have been much occupied elsewhere as well. I have not been checking too much. People do check every day to see what is new.

I am working with some people on the website to make it more current (style wise). They have asked me for a picture for your section, is there one you could send me? Not of you necessarily, but something you would like to represent you. If you don't have one in mind, I will choose something; I am not sure what it will be. Please let me know your preference.

I have heard from (name removed) and he is not experiencing the same issues all at once, but is now working with a new doctor and has some tests scheduled for a few weeks, … So thank you for your help and suggestions for him.

Take care, Much love,
Sophia

G/E

Good Day Sophia!

I just wanted to write to You, such synchronicity is astounding! The overall Energy Spectrum and Interconnection between Everything is increasing, can You feel it?

I am ok, I have been working on World with some People, situation is not the best We can have, but is better than it was in 2011 for example.

---

[533]N.p., n.d. Web. <https://www.youtube.com/watch?v=5iW7hEJHO3U>.

An addition to a website? I like Your website very much Sophia, Your taste is very soft and beautiful! Of course I will give a picture which represents us GEs. And this is a very interesting thing, because One prepared such a picture, which connects to whole Creation of Universe. It is astounding how much Connectedness it has within it!
One directed me to it just on Your request Sophia!

Ok, in file will be "Swords of Revealing Light", this image is taken from a trading card game called "Yu-Gi-Oh". The picture like we know was given to designer of this trading card game by One through Sub-Consciousness "to play its part" in future events.
Don't get this wrong, One was having different outcomes for this World, it all depended on what Humanity would decide.

"Swords of Revealing Light" has an effect of revealing every playable card on field and prevent these cards from "attacking" and also this card is "limited" (means in game only 1 copy can be used at a time).

It has 3 Universal Trinities - 3 swords, 3 waves, 3 stars - 2 small stars and 1 big 8-pointed star on it - our universal symbol of Order (Swords, which look like ships and in actuality are ships - big vessels of Forces of One of Izauya Civilization, they have same form), Omnipotence/Omnipresence/All-Reaching/Ether (Waves) and Creator (Stars) and like You see all is coming from main big star (Prime Creator or One). It very suits our GEs character.

I myself always liked this picture, but actually I never thought that You would ask me for a picture Sophia. Talk about One was having a planned route for events happening in Now :) So this means we are on an Awesome Route! Such route will lead this World to Times of Prosperity and Abundance - New Renaissance or the Golden Age of Humanity! :)

I am glad that (name removed) is better! He needs to restore completely to avoid … We made some categories on diseases and illnesses and gave them very simple names so to not make confusion. Our advices could help if used correctly.

In connectedness to this issue, recently, U.S. and EU governments are starting a ban on 35% peroxygen, the one I recommended to Good Friend.

They are saying that with 35% peroxygen "bombs can be made", in actuality it is possible to create "a bomb" with it, yet to this date no one ever attempted to make such "a bomb".

They ban it, because it is 100% efficient in curing of cancers, diabetes and some other diseases. I am sure it can also restore brain damage illnesses. This is universal hydrogen-oxygen cure, yet now in EU it is officially banned from sales and U.S. will soon follow if not prevented.

Here You can see how they silently remove everything what is beneficial. If not stopped they plan to remove even knives from use if not stopped. Everything that can be used "as a weapon".

The situation around the World right now is not very good, because illuminati/cabal fail on all fronts, they are pushing desperately in direction of conflicts. Yet the good thing is that Russia and China are keeping a good check on all their actions. The main problem comes from words of Joe Biden and Chuck Hagel. Former Lieutenant General is warning of some "event" in which "disappeared MH370 might resurface" (which I sensed was unfortunately destroyed...)[534]

He also mentions some book, if it is the book I think of, it may be very big! But we haven't heard of such book coming sometime soon. I mean a book of complete exposure of conspiracy against Humanity, written by high ranked illuminati members which decided to go in their own path avoiding doctrine of illuminati.

Joe Biden and Chuck Hagel are making "a hint" on 9/11-like event happening right on 9/11 and saying that it will be "bigger than previous". And connect it to evil people of "ISIS" (purportedly they "can carry out some attack" here). Remember 9 and 11 together are special for illuminati/cabal numbers. It could be everything I named before; they always like to target east coast, because more people are living there, so quadrants remain the same as well.

Be careful with this, meditate for World Peace and Harmony to prevent any and all their plots of coming true! We already made a huge progress together Good Friends, many of their plots already failed and all that remains now is to make a final blow to them, when they will make mistake, Everyone should be ready to meditate for Peace and their full and complete Exposure, this will put an end to them and their very evil agenda!

Also, because of their never-ending lust for power and destruction, the Yellowstone volcano is not becoming quiet, but on contrary increasing it's might and 2 "natural" warnings were issued to Humanity, by Sun and by Earth. If I was

---

[534] Digitasdaily. "Lt. General McInerney Warns of New 9/11 Event." YouTube. YouTube, 24 Aug. 2014. Web. 10 July 2016. <https://www.youtube.com/watch?v=z9fN0Nx4Zcs>.

quite sure previously that volcano and flare could be avoided, now I'm not so sure of avoidance, because both Sun and Earth issued a strong warning.

Volcano Bardarbunga on Iceland exploded and Sun released a huge Earth-Directed CME, which just reached us today[535]

That is why I advise Everyone living in USA to get face covers or face masks as dust output will be huge if it will come to this. And dust from Yellowstone might have a burned sulfur and some other hazardous chemicals (depends on how close is position to a volcano). These masks are quite cheap and very useful for other purposes as well, a must-have in home.

I can say sure that solar flare will go only after volcano, because damage from flare will be much more greater than from volcano. And flare cannot take place at all, if it will be avoided though settling down of conflicts. Remember, *possibility of eruption depends on emotions of Humanity*, the "more evil" there is in air, the more possible is the eruption.

The rest of this note can be found complete in Chapter 6 (September 2014).

SOPHIA

Thank you; I will post this after seeing the videos. I have been wondering too about Ariel Sharon as I have not seen anything lately on him and you had indicated that he was one of the markers to look for.?

The web site is being changed to be easier to use and a little more stylish and current. It will be beautiful as my friends are very talented and make mandalas, I am using one that was esp. made for me and I love it very much, it feels very powerful. I think it will be changed within the week. You will like it I am sure.

I am going to look for the 35% peroxygen here, and see how it is recommended to be used. I do not believe they will forbid it if people figure out what they are doing. I hope that I am right.

There is so much desperation around money and so many promises around "prosperity" being part of the change and event ... people have their hopes up so high, as if that is the answer and indeed it feels as if that would make everything fixed and fair. It would not, but people are desperate. It is a scary time and I

---

[535]VideoFromSpace. "Gigantic Solar Filament Eruption May Be Earth-Directed | Video." YouTube. YouTube, 03 Sept. 2014. Web. 10 July 2016. <https://www.youtube.com/watch?v=VliMBrNkics>.

know people are looking for answers. I appreciate all that you offer to give them some when you are able.

So again, thanks. We will talk soon I am sure. I love the picture you've sent! It is perfect!

Much love,
Sophia

SEPTEMBER 12TH, 2014

SOPHIA

Hi again. So, nothing happened on Sept. 11th. What do things look like now?

A friend of mine has asked this question, it is rather long. He is very much studying and speaking on the astrological progression and aspects that are occurring this year, and well, here is the question:

~~~

Anyway - my question is - This next Winter Solstice, the last day of the last Moonth and so the

last day of our Lunar calendar - - we have a conjunction that lays out: All of Creation manifesting on and in

Gaia -- Gaia -- Moon -- Mercury -- Venus -- Sun -- SageStar A -- Source.

Esoterically this can be seen as a conjunction with Spirit Beings manifesting at specific frequencies:

All of Creation on and in Gaia - Gaia - Angels - Archangels - Archai - Elohim - SageStar A - One.

All of Creation on and in Gaia is mostly detachments of other Beings - - sometimes I feel that Gaia is an

Archangel, wouldn't mind knowing that - - Angels Influencing from the Moon - - Archangels from Mercury -

- Archai from Venus - - Elohim from the Sun --- Denser and denser down.

Simplified yes - Dante's perspective. Then we come to SageStar A and the Galactic Center - between us and
~~~

One. If I use Esoteric hierarchy levels than SageStar A is the level of Seraphim.

The Sun is on the Galactic Center and SageStar A this Solstice - with all of the Players in this Experiment

- Elohim on down. In a Conjunction - focusing the Influences from Source through a Seraphim or more -

to the Spirits of Form, the Elohim - - then Archai who provide our physical body experiences - - Archangels

who provide our etheric body experiences - - then Angels our astral body experiences.

We had the noticing, the awakening and the activation of SageStar A - - the Fall Equinox is the

Thanksgiving for these Blessing and the time to set our Intentions for the Solstice. What an amazing Ride.

Demiurge will be between Us and Source - this Solstice - with the New Buffalo Moon the next day and the

start of a New Year. What a wonderful time to Blossom our Divinity to Every Being in this Conjunction -

including Demiurge and his folks.

From this perspective - I would like to know Who it is that reappeared as SageStar A - right next to

Ophiuchus who has been renoticed also. Orion is next to be noticed.

~~~

Thanks and much love.

SEPTEMBER 15TH, 2014

SOPHIA

I am not sure I have sent you this one, but it is a question from a friend:

~~~

I would like to know Who or Whom has been Activated and is representing their relationship and Influence through the perceived SageStar A. And you Feelings about this Winter Solstice Conjunction - in relation to SageStar A and the next phase after Activation. It sounds like some big ass Machine for Cleaning this Star System –

~~~

Can you send me information on this if you have any? It is not for the blog, but from a private message.

Thanks and much love

SEPTEMBER 22ND 2014

G/E

Sophia I've added GE 2.png, so if first picture is still showing "copyright", try this. If both won't work, write to me. Also picture You made for me with butterflies looks Beautiful and Harmonious! Thank You very much for Everything You do!

Here is the message and answers to Good Friends.

(note – the rest of this message is included in the chapter for 2014, which is Chapter 6. Here is the image used for him[536] , this is the png file he refers to here)

SEPTEMBER 23RD 2014

SOPHIA

 I saw this[537] after reading your note.... any comments? Is it just trumped up versions of what has been going on along?

Thanks

SOPHIA

thank you! You'll see we used the GE2 version, my artist friend said he saw you more with the green than the other color.

---

[536] "GE." Sophia. N.p., n.d. Web. 10 July 2016. <http://www.sophialove.org/ge.html>.

[537] N.p., n.d. Web. <http://rt.com/news/189804-us-isis-syria-airstrikes/>.

I look forward to reading the book, thank you so much. I want to understand how to take it before I do, but I have several people who could use it and I would like to share the information for sure.

(Note: the e-book referred to here is: "The One Minute Cure – the secret to healing virtually all diseases" by Madison Cavinaugh)

I was figuring you must be very busy. I know there are so many questions, but many people read and ask me as well as make comments on the blog. I write them when they come so that I don't forget!

I've posted everything.... I am sure there will be comments and even more questions now. I esp. appreciate you description of the code for the Forces of One and have added it to the "plan for a new world page".

Take Care and much love to you and your family

G/E

Good Day Sophia!

Thank You very much Sophia! Website looks gorgeous; I feel the Harmonious Energy You and Good Friends put into it! I appreciate Good Friend's choice of picture as well! Although if it is possible I would like to have a GE 1 picture, it suits with color and gamma more to design. We GEs love when everything is harmonized and synchronized perfectly :)

On this matter I put together Your old video Sophia and added small detail of my own - music. In this video I can feel the Joy which You experienced after "New Year Celebration" and the message in the video is complicated, yet at the same time it is understandable and holds within it every bit of most important information about Humanity! And that is why they heard You and wanted to talk to You. Such is the charge You received from Celebration and great expectations of Shift of the Ages!

I hope You will like it[538] Sophia!

---

[538] "2014 Message to Off World Beings." YouTube. N.p., n.d. Web. 10 July 2016. <https://youtu.be/xsuXTL2S1o8>.

To make things even more interesting, You can repost this video and see the outcome. And then expect unexpected at most unexpected moment ;)

In the book You will find dosages, which are crucial. It is always better to have less peroxygen in water than more. For progressed diseases, it is necessary to use it on daily basis to feel the results, there will be written all about this. It tastes like bleach, but so is peroxygen :)

Yes, U.S. government started the bombing on "islamic state", we knew they would. It is a part of downfall of illumianti/cabal. Evil "islamic state" is playing its part now. We also look for U.S. government and their "allies" so they would not attack SAA - Syria's government forces.

If they would make such an attack on false pretexts, there would be a huge backfire on them from Earth and Sun. As well black division of Forces of One is still there deep underground under Palmyra, they are ready to be activated at any time, yet it seems there wouldn't be such necessity. Most problematic parts are already avoided in this "breaking point" plot. Still they are there for most troublesome turn of events if there would be any.

The Laws of Forces of One are meant for Forces of One only, but I was allowed to share them, so You can use them as well. If you noticed they look like laws and "commandments". Basically, these are "programs" or "codes" like You mentioned it correctly. Through them we are able to program ourselves (for example like computer) to live in a Harmony, care for others and love them.

If You noticed ideologies, indoctrination, religious dogmas, media, movies, newspapers, magazines, books, movies, videos, music and even speech and words - can "program" people into thinking in one way or the other. This is how illuminati/cabal are "programming" Earth's Population. Yet it can be used in both ways, in evil and Good.

The obvious example of evil/dark programming is happening right now in Ukraine. All media of Ukraine is telling only the picture which dictates Ukrainian government. It of course is showing Ukraine as "a victim", west as "saviors" and Russia as "aggressor" and "enemy number 1". All russian media is banned and censored, as they are saying completely opposite - real picture of all events with proofs and showing all atrocities which are being committed by ukrainian "national guard" (which follows in an ideology of WW2 nazism). Western media obviously is allowed to be broadcasted, as it brings the picture which U.S. and EU governments are saying. Due to this, People of Ukraine don't see the whole picture and as western and ukrainian medias are demonizing Russia, so are ukrainian People hate Russia as "enemy number 1". Such is the programming and this is how it works.

Humanity didn't used to call laws as "programs" or "codes". And it sounds and feels not comfortable, because obviously no one wants to be "programmed". But such is one of the basics of Creation. We Forces of One have figured this out long ago, so it is completely "OK" for us to be programmed. The big plus is here that we know when we are being programmed". And we accept to be programmed in one way or the other.

This is another lesson which Humanity will have to learn if It will want to completely get rid Itself from shackles of slavery, as slavery works the same way - through programming and indoctrination of religious dogmas, financial establishment or simple helplessness which comes from fear.

Examples are:

"to serve so that you could be saved"
"to serve so that you could be rewarded with money/premium/gift"
"to serve or you will be destroyed, because we have super powers"

These are the basics. This is known to Humanity as "inconvenient truth".

With much Harmony, Peace, Love and Prosperity.

SEPTEMBER 25TH 2014

G/E

In terms of spying, recently google, face book and microsoft (that is skype and messenger) were making big steps in collecting more information on users. These 3 corporations are known for making "backdoors" in their software, so to allow those with "the keys to the backdoor" to open it. This gives ability for governments (to be precisely illuminati/cabal) and their information agencies like NSA and GCHQ to collect data quite effortlessly.

The data U.S., UK and Australian governments are interested in are names, place of living, photos, interests, relatives, friends and most importantly - opinion on world affairs. They need this to be "omniscient" in their thinking. This also helps them to find Individuals faster and more sinisterly, they need this to mark Everyone that is against them and as well All Those that have quite a big IQ. It is like Henry Ford said "we want workers not thinkers".

Otherwise everything around the World is stable (more or less).

Much Love!

SEPTEMBER 26TH 2014

SOPHIA

Here is the new version, just released on you tube[539] with your music! Thanks. Now, I will let you know what surprises happen! ;)

I hope that you are well.

Much love

OCTOBER 1ST 2014

G/E

I am happy You liked it Sophia! This message is outstanding; it bears everything necessary within it! I also like You to share Your old videos with Everyone, and want You to take two steps back and look at these videos. Remember what character You had when You made these beautiful videos! Stepping back to past will aid You Sophia. You will uncover something You wanted to know before, yet skipped afterwards and forgot later

Wake Up To Love[540]
Dream a New Earth Together[541]
We Are One[542]

---

[539] "2014 Message to Off World Beings." YouTube. N.p., n.d. Web. 10 July 2016. <https://youtu.be/xsuXTL2S1o8>.

[540] SophiaLoveQuest. "Wake Up To Love." YouTube. YouTube, 30 Sept. 2011. Web. 10 July 2016. <https://www.youtube.com/watch?v=Gu3BMR0KeHU>.

[541] N.p., n.d. Web. <https://www.youtube.com/watch?v=_XKk3vTgYaE>.

Also I see Good Friends no longer have questions, which is really good! My expectancy was right, I knew eventually Good Friends will be able to evolve Their Higher Inner Voice to extent that They would know everything without the guidance from outside. Such is our GEs intent. I know there will be Others that will seek the Knowledge and some few questions later on, but for now everything looks great!

World's situation is pretty much stable. Illuminati/cabal are at disarray, they have mixed feelings, they have mixed thoughts, but one thing we sense in them - fear, we sense that they are afraid now. This tells, the end of them is imminent. Too bad they refused to surrender.

(The rest of this message is shared in Chapter 6: 2014)

SOPHIA

Thank you. Seeing those videos again were good reminders for me, it has been quite a journey and there has been disillusionment along the way that causes forgetfulness, even though the truth is something I have always known. Interesting to see how the message has not changed. I am going to share them again.

I will post this message as well, and I think that people are interested in what you have to offer because at times it seems that nothing is really going on, at least in main stream media, and the change is so gradual that it is almost invisible to us. We like to hear that the Cabal is doubting and retreating because we do not see evidence of it in the news. Not much of it anyway. Yes, I see the questions have decreased and that is a good thing. People trust themselves more, which is the whole point.

I hope that you are well!

Much love

G/E

---

542 SophiaLoveQuest. "We Are ONE!" YouTube. YouTube, 07 Oct. 2011. Web. 10 July 2016. <https://www.youtube.com/watch?v=nKVo7PTc0VE>.

Yes Sophia, this is a Good thing! Illuminati order is in troubles, they are trying to win more time, yet they don't know what to do. Because everything they do is going against them and speeding up their downfall. Whether they do surrender or make more harm and evil, both directions are leading to their demise. Yet the difference is that, if surrendered, they would be spared from maximal harm on every front.

For now they remain neutral and passive, they simply lied down onto stream and waiting for "good opportunity" to strike, with such action they prolong their existence and are keeping their seat of power for a bit longer. Yet there won't be any "good opportunity" for them anymore. Everything they do now is acting in Iraq and Syria against evil "islamic state", otherwise they are trying to make huge fear around ebola and "possible terrorist attack by "islamic state". The very good thing in this is that majority don't give into this fear.

If You would like to know what is the situation with them, you can look for news. The more western media screams about something, the more they want You to believe them and the more desperate they are. Like it was with malaysian MH17 and with Ukraine's Crimea. As You noticed now it is quiet, because all proofs are showing that Russia and rebels are not responsible for downing of the plane and Russia did the right thing with Crimea as People living there made decision to join Russia.

You know very well, that whenever they are keeping quiet on something then it obviously could harm them. Like with NSA and Snowden, they are trying their best to keep quiet about it and in the mean time they are increasing surveillance. Awareness and Knowledge are the greatest "weapons" against them.

On ethereal planes there is quite a calm and improving situation. Followers of Light are cleaning the whole Biosphere, Electrosphere and Etherosphere of Planet Earth. Sun and Sage Star A are sending Light shockwaves which are deflecting everything negative and are sending this negativity away, back to dark source. There are less and less "dead wanderers", there is less and less darkness everywhere. As a proof of increasing Light Energy and Vibrations, look at faces of Individual Human Beings around the World. On faces You now are able to see the "hidden smile" You were not able to see 10 cycles ago. Such "hidden smile" is due to increased level of Knowledge and Awareness of Humanity, as well People feel Themselves well relaxed and well fed. Happiness can be seen quite well now on faces of Many!

Happiness leads to Harmony and Love among All! As well due to combined actions of Cosmo and Controllers, most of Human Beings are no longer attacked by inter-dimensional travelers with sinister intents. Such attacks had almost completely stopped, yet still not in its entirety. Overall the situation on the Planet increased in a Very Good Direction! Unfortunately situation like this is not everywhere for now, but soon it will increase and will encompass all Parts of the World! There won't be left any dark spot on Earth which would remain unattended!

With much Peace and Love to You!

OCTOBER 2ND 2014

SOPHIA

Thanks so much!!! Sharing this now, it will confirm what we are feeling and that is a very good thing. It is important for us to see progress, for sure.

Much love to you. I will share this for everyone.

OCTOBER 4TH 2014

G/E

Good Day Sophia!

Sophia, it would be great if You can put links to your old videos, which I wanted to share with Good Friends. Especially "We Are One" video. You can put it on GE blog or Your blog, it is not important where. Someone "outside" need to see this once again.

Only with connection to Your "Message to Off World Beings" video, there is an effect. Thank You!

And here are the answers on few more questions

(Answers are found in Chapter 6: 2014)

OCTOBER 20TH 2014

(Note, the following refers to my own experience of being removed while I slept the night prior. I had asked about it.)

G/E

Good Day Sophia.

Thank You very much!

So this time they did not ask You for a permission?

As I know those interested in You were from Galactic Federation of Light. I wrote to Good Friend Michael that those that abduct People without permission are former "archons", members of "draco alliance" - reptilians, greys, insectoids, sirians, orionians and other less known civilizations that are enjoying to avoid laws.

Also Beings of Purity can take without permission. All Civilizations from Galactic Federation of Light must ask for permission. After conversation both GFL and dracos are erasing memory.

Still all of this information is still being kept both in Sub consciousness and within Universe and can be requested back from Universe (One) if needed.

Do You remember something before this happened, something like question in Your Mind? Also can You check Your Body? Members of draco (also U.S. and UK governments) are leaving implanted chips in Bodies. Most of the time it is in hand or head (back of a head), it is a tiny metallic structure with grey or black color and is beneath skin. It can be easily spotted. I know You are ok, will wait for Your respond Sophia.

SOPHIA

Hi,

It is my belief that permission has been given. There are no marks and I was not abused. I feel as if everything has changed though, a discussion happened and will happen again. I do not feel it came from the GFL, and no, do not feel it came from the greys/reptilians. This is why I mentioned it, as you are more familiar with the races. Who are the "Beings of Purity"?

I am okay; just very tired as there wasn't much sleep last night.

I will post your response to this letter, thanks.

Much love

G/E

Ok, this is good. Implant chips are meant for surveillance and mind control, good You don't have it. I will add also some implant chips also can increase Human's senses and open Third Eye.

There are other non GFL Civilizations, but their presence over this Planet is minimal. GFL's presence here is maximal. Archons' presence recently also had come to minimal presence. Forces of One and Ancient Machines are not abducting Humans. On ethereal level there can be some ethereal/energetic Beings that traverse dimensions, including reptilians and Beings of Purity.

Beings of Purity are a Civilization to which demiurge comes. They are purely energetic without Physical Bodies, there are only few such Beings in whole Milky Way Galaxy. Their Evolution level is very high.

If You wish to remember the experience, You have to ask Your Body and Universe, in some time later this information will come to You. It will come to You in fragments, like pictures. If You were on high energy or Consciousness type vessel, then Your senses will increase in some time. Encounters with ETs are opening up all Your natural potentials :)

Much Love to You!

OCTOBER 31ST, 2014

SOPHIA

The thing about the upcoming collapse is that many of us have been expecting it since 2011 and are "war weary" of hearing it predicted, only to have it never happen. This is a difficult spot to take seriously. I do think though, that this is the first time you've mentioned it specifically?? This will have an effect, and hopefully inspire action. (Meditation and prayer)
Please keep me posted as your thoughts and information about this change and are updated, we are all feeling so very close to something and the tension is high, at least internally. I appreciate all that you are doing for all of us.

NOVEMBER 20TH, 2014

G/E

Good Day Sophia and Everyone! I am well, Thank You!

Sorry to keep You waiting for answers, I was doing some work in these cycles.
I wasn't available to listen to Your Friend on drop box as it requires to sign up. If there is something important You can ask me Sophia.
Thank You Very Much for everything You do Sophia! Your contribution into future is Outstanding! :)
I was mentioning economic collapse before, it is inevitable, yet yes, I wasn't saying specifically when it will happen. For now everything seems all right, no

false flags, no nasty things. Illuminati/cabal loosing on all fronts, so they just keep low and quiet, which is a good thing, yet it postpones their ultimate downfall.

Note – It was a month before I heard from him again. This was one of his comments on December 21st, 2014:

"I wasn't available for some time and I have to warn that You have to be ready if I "disappear" out of a sudden, we have a lot of work to do in restoring this World, so GEs aren't fixed in one place."

And again on December 22nd, 2014:

"Thanks You Sophia!

I also forgot to mention that the next cycle of 12.22.2014 which is today, is also a time when Sun and Moon are aligned with Galactic Center in 1 line in the skies. Today is New Moon, which means "a rebirth" of Moon. And like You can understand, this is a very rare alignment, this is in no way "a coincidence", You remember that nothing happens without a reason. This moment of time can be use to meditate and make wishes, or making pleas or requests to Universe, this time is when they will be fulfilled!

Much joy and Happiness to You and Your Family in this most astounding time Sophia!

And on December 23rd, 2014 (shared in entirety in Chapter 6):

That's it for 2014. The next email was not received until July 20th, 2015. Look to Chapter 8 for the final chapter.

Chapter 8   2015 and beyond

2015 and Beyond

It was now 2015. At first we all expected the Guardian to show up, as there had been times in the past when He would disappear for many weeks without a great deal of explanation. This did not happen. Here is the chat from the blog that resulted that January.

January 26th, 2015 (As posted in the blog)

"Has G/E left us?" [543]

SOPHIA

"Hi Sophia, how are you.

Do you have news from GE. It's long since his last message. Did he left us?"

Hi! I have not heard from him since Christmas. I believe he may be gone for a while, as we are not his only focus. There are several questions for him and if he was able, he would respond.

That being said, there have been many times that lasted for about a month or more that we did not communicate. I've been talking with him since April of 2012, almost 3 years now! The first conversations were in the YouTube comments section, and pretty sporadic. It is since last February when we began the blog format that it seems more apparent when he is out of contact. He comes and goes; it is just that many more of us are aware of it now.

He did say in December of 2014 that...

"I wasn't available for some time and I have to warn that You have to be ready if I "disappear" out of a sudden, we have a lot of work to do in restoring this World, so GEs aren't fixed in one place."

GE's purpose has been to aid in our awakening. He reached out as a response

[543] "Has GE Left Us?" Sophia. N.p., n.d. Web. 16 July 2016. <http://www.sophialove.org/ask-me/has-ge-left-us>.

to a video I created in January of 2012. It was a call to those "off world". He has not been the only response, but certainly the most prolific!

His information and willingness to engage with us as we awaken from our "slavery slumber" has been invaluable. At least it has been for me. At first I did not understand much of what he said. That is no longer true, and as I watch the conversation on the blog, many of his readers are as informed as he is now. We understand what the truth is, and actively look for it everywhere!

It is easy to get "hooked" on information that seems to see further into the future than we are currently able. I get that. We have to remember that the future is not fixed; we have changed it already and will continue to create it with our love and empowerment. Indeed, GE's last message said:

"Those "enlightened" illuminati found out that they can enslave Humanity in this age, because whole Cosmo affects Consciousness and they did everything to make it happen. They almost succeeded, but were stopped by arrival of highly evolved Individuals - You Good Friends, Lightworkers and Lightwarriors as well as One's Workers and Warriors."

I will have any further information from GE on the website as soon as it is received, you can count on that.

 In the meantime, I am compiling a collection of all that has been said. Much of it applies to what we now face and will be dealing with in the next several years. A world after the experiment ends, a New World. It is vital that we create and implement systems that sustain a new way to live for mankind. GE cannot do this for us, or even tell us how; it is only mankind who can. His suggestions for what has worked on other worlds are a great assist.

It seems that now and in the next two years it becomes more important than ever to remember the truth of us. GE is a fascinating being, and yet so are you. Humans are the most sought after and watched in the cosmos, because of their passionate, creative capacity. This has been manipulated throughout the experiment, and drawn us into the perpetuation of misery and pain, war and poverty; into slavery.

Now it is upon us to utilize another part of our passion – our love, joy, unity and celebration. I think what we create now is beyond the imagining of any being, it is held in our very hearts, waiting to burst forth.

Thank you for asking this question! It has given me an opportunity to express how grateful I am for GE and for all of you. I love you!

Namaste'

~~

In July he finally returned for a short moment…

July 23ʳᵈ, 2015

SOPHIA

Hello everyone! I hope this finds you well and thriving! It's been 6 months, and our friend has been unavailable for the entire time, until this week. It looks like there will be a very brief window, possibly another week, that he is around for information and questions.

You'll read for yourself that he is not sure when this time will end, and the next time he is around, will be after the "Moment of Justice" as he has called it for so very long. I had reached out to him awhile back, as I am compiling our conversation into a volume to be released (hopefully) in the fall, and I had some questions. I was not clear if I would be talking to him, but, he's back! I have to say he sounds very good and hopeful and encouraging, as always.

Since GE left, I have been talking, pretty much every day, to many different off world beings with additional information for us. These are shared via my newsletter. If you aren't signed up yet, you can do so here. [544] The

newsletter is free and sent a few times each month. There is also a subscription service, for those who want more, which is sent once a week (every 5 - 7 days). I hope you'll join us!

Here (below this introduction) is the part of our conversation I feel inspired to share with you... I have had some time to digest it now, and suggest more than one reading of it, for it is a dense read. I come away with the same truth that has always been evident. That this "story" of a new age is ours to tell, and focus, belief and intent is everything. We have always been the ones we are waiting for! Enjoy, and know that it is posted here with much love and gratitude to him and to each of you for continuing the conversation.

With absolute love,

G/E

hEl-ea(t) Sophia! ... You can just tell Them that I'm fine and doing my job on keeping the World safe as much as I can with my Brothers and Sisters.

I've been away for half a year (cycle). There was no internet, nothing where I was. I am going away again, so I would no longer answer questions, but later I would upon my return, if there would be any.

Right now we GEs are in the middle of our most important mission, the one why we have been made to be GEs. It is our life's most important one.

The crash of this financial system have been avoided by cabal by their many means of financial manipulation, they are stubborn we can give it to them. **So now, it is 2016th cycle around the Sun when all must take place.**

Know that attacks from evil side "dark source" have increased relentlessly, those people that are important for this world's future (inventors, scientists, thinkers)

544 "Contact Sophia Love." Sophia. N.p., n.d. Web. 16 July 2016.
<http://www.sophialove.org/contact.html>.

are being attacked by negative thoughts (like to kill or make thing that would lead them to death).

This kind of attacks are being felt mostly throughout Europe and Russia, because this place is the one from where the Grand Change will start, so dark forces are trying to take over there and distort this Change. They have increased their activities because Scales of Balance have shifted into side of Light! **This is the good news!**

(This part is to me personally, re: the recent conversations I'm having, and publishing in the newsletter...) I am also very happy for You, different Beings share their experience of Life, of Universe and their Compassion and Emotions and Love toward Humanity. They overtook my place! :)

I will give You last piece of this light-dark dual system puzzle, the knowledge we received recently as a last package of most important information - the ultimate goal of two sides (two sides of same coin as ALL IS ONE), what they seek to accomplish as their final goal. This knowledge is most important for Everyone and for every religion of this World.

If such deceiver would be before You, the focus of this being is destruction. The complete and total goal of dark evil side is complete death of everything, the evil side seeks death of Universe, death of very Creator that made it - death of One. It is some sort of self-destruction mechanism.

And what is most troublesome about it is that this force is sapient and awake, you can say it is devil (or deciphered - dark evil). It had been awoken by living creatures, like bacteria, animals, ETs, humans, since the very beginning of Life due to prime instincts of hunt and seeking of food. There is no way to avoid it's presence, it was meant to be born in such a way and exist.

The place of this force, where it lives is known as "dark source" or "anti-Source" it is always in opposite position of Source - Light Side of Creation, also sapient. All negative thoughts are making this entity stronger and it's most ultimate goal is nothing.. It means, complete darkness, coldness, complete stop of everything, no movement anywhere.

Illuminati (dis)Order/cabal are servants of this all-destroying power, they are servants of nothing and they don't realize that this force is only using them to make destruction more massive, in the end this force would destroy them as well. In the meantime they believe in "bright future", for themselves and their family, when they have full control over humanity and over this planet and all of it's process of Evolution/Development. Yet if they have been touched by this force, it would destroy them as well in the end, when there is nothing more to destroy.

So if they let's say would win, they would need to make sacrifice more and more in order to avoid that this power would take them and their family "as sacrifice" instead, when there is no sacrifice to make. This is debt slavery on other level, the level of death, that they chose. Instead of money, they need to bring something to destroy (to their creditor), or otherwise, it (the creditor) would take them instead. This force always needs things to destroy.

So all of this information makes this "elite" even more dangerous, not just for this World, but for entire Galaxy and Universe. Now I know what Forces of One meant when they were saying about "danger to whole Creation".

And as dark evil side seeks complete death, Light Good Side of Creation - **the Source of Light seeks opposite to it - Abundance, Prosperity, Thrive, Bloom of everything. Multiplication, Spreading of Life, of Civilizations is what Light Good side seeks. Art, Creation, Beauty, Radiance, Never-stopping Movement, Innovation, Never-ending Food or Never-ending Energy or Never-ending Light and of course all the best Emotions, Like Never-ending Love, Never-ending Compassion, Never-ending Pulse of Very Life, all of this belongs to Light Side of Creation - This is the Ultimate Truth for us!**

When We were presented this ultimate knowledge, we felt great relief and still are feeling it when we remember it. And yes, it was not like we didn't know it, **we**

knew it all along and Everyone knows it, yet we needed to find the right words to connect these last dots and form this last picture, **every Human Being needs Their Own method of Restoring the Ultimate Truth in Their Own Consciousness!**

And as You know The Truth, here is the wisdom - **"There is No Religion Higher Than Truth!"**
Instead of word religion You can put anything that You refer to as Truth (Belief, Ideology, Thinking or something else).

But again, I remind You the Truth is what You believe into, and thus what You believe into is Truth for Your most Sacred Inner Self! This is how One meant Everyone to be.

More and more will be known about Light Good side later on after Grand Change would start.

The subject of Light presents much Much MUCH More Opportunities of Creation than subject of dark. **The knowledge about dark evil side is no longer necessary**, there is nothing more to know about it, and thus dark side would disappear from face of this Planet for some given time and Humanity would be able to make a permanent ban of it on this Planet if Humanity would want to. **And as it will be taken away from here, it will be Earth's Golden Age.**

Yes and most important knowledge - All of this is meant to be as it is, One made evil to be "self-destruction" mechanism and Good - "thriving" mechanism. This is hard coded and cannot be overridden, only "softened".

This is it Good Friend Sophia! Everything is decided like You see. Yet remember, Hope is always there and with Hope there is always a way out.

I will be available for some time so You can answer me if You like, yet after some time I will "disappear" again.

I asked for some clarification, and received this ...

From what I know, I will be here for at least 2 weeks, it is not us who decides time of leaving. So You can write anything You want, I will be happy to aid!

I also wanted to add that attacks on "important for Future People" are relentless, yet these attacks are being weakened gradually. Evil is being aided by dark priests of cabal/Illuminati, but since May, these priests were losing focus and are losing to this cycle.

But because Scales have been shifted toward Light, evil side tries to catch onto it, so it had increased it's pressure to extreme heights. This is how all of this works, once 1 power overtakes other and starts to dominate, power 2 tries to become equal to it, the bigger the difference, the more is the pressure that is coming from losing power.

Each is trying to win, yet before "total win" is secured each power is trying to at least maintain the Balance. You can closely associate this with team playing sports like baseball, football, soccer, hockey and so on. Here are a lot of sports like this and they are direct reflections of this basic hard-coded system.

Adding to this, in the history of Universe of this dimension, You know as "3D physical world" there were big changes toward both dark and light, these were the moments of extreme activity which were felt throughout the Universe, most of these occurrences happened in favor to dark, due to dark's never-ending strive for win and using "force" as its main weapon and because of this, dark side reshaped the Universe to the way, that during first stages of Evolution, Beings are being dominated mostly by dark rather than Light (not everywhere, not always, there are exceptions of course). That is why Animals here are like They are.

Another reason that adds dark to favor here on Earth are the components. This planet is being dominated by iron, red color of blood, red planet of Mars also consists mostly of iron, that is why it's red and it was "god of war in most of cultures, all are elements that proclaim war/aggression.

On top of that, iron is the material that kills a Star from the inside, turning Star to red color. The very red color in Universe on basic level is considered as "looming death". Iron among very evolved Light Beings is considered primitive and "dark material". It is due to effects it is giving to those that uses it.

The composition of Bodies of Animals and Humans is having iron as it's additional material thus blood is red as well, yet Humans and Animals can live without iron in Their Bodies.

Another reason why dark dominates here is that Humans and Animals don't have "transparency" in Their Bodies, skin and flesh don't have Transparency, so Light from Sun or from any other source of Light simply is not reaching the Core of these Bodies - Heart, Brain other important organs like liver and on top of it all - Soul-main Core.

There are a lot of Beings around the Universe that are having fully or partially transparent physical Bodies, due to this Light is reaching Their Core and they are changing toward Light more rapidly, much faster, and thus evolve much faster as well as Light gives Awareness and Knowledge. Some of Beings on this Planet like some types of Fish are having partially transparent Bodies, by most part these Beings are oriented toward Light, yet their mind is primitive and they are struggling for survival.

So while Humanity's Bodies are locked off from Rays of Light, darkness is able to reach each Man/Woman faster and as well start to live inside this Body, which is locked off from Light. If Light on Earth would have been dominating, picture would be completely different. But don't despair, most of Arganisms throughout the Universe have such picture, it is due to protection from very active Rays of Light and due to thing I named before - darkness reshaped this Universe in the ancient past. If last thing would have not happened, Universe would have been very different.

Light side was "winning" only few times and it was not as close to "end" when dark was "winning". Forces of One interfered during some of those times to return Scales back to Balance.

Forces of One always are interfering when "Grand Fault" is possible, when it is not possible they stay as observants. Grand Fault by itself means "complete failure of system", this is when chain reaction would jump from object to object, like virus, ruining the very Essence of this Universe. And here on this planet with Demiurge and experiment on Humanity "Grand Fault" was possible, that's why they were here. They will be here until Moment of Justice and then would leave.

This was last piece of information *about Forces of One.*

This is a dual system which was meant to be this way by One. Like we are told by part of One answering for this, that this way One as Creater of All is able to understand and test more of It's many many (infinite) abilities, All of Us Together right now are helping One in fulfilling this goal.
So in this 3D, we need to live with both Good and Evil, and what side we are choosing is shaping our Destiny and shaping all of this Universe.

Yes, Your and my every step are influencing the Future and changing it.

Much Love, Peace, Calm and Prosperity!

SOPHIA

And that's it for today. Please comment with questions if you have any, or just greetings for GE, as I am sure all will be appreciated (and possibly answered) if he is still around.

Much love,

READER'S COMMENTS

"Hi Good Friend, i am very happy you are fine and that you are back to us for some little time. I missed this conversations with you "

~~

"I meant "I missed these conversations with you".
I did not really believe in negative attacks but 2 or 3 months ago, i felt that i was
attacked. Everything is fine now

Much love too you Good Friend and all GEs"

~~

"Hi GE and welcome back!

A couple of things keep puzzling me still... What is the relationship between Demiurge
and the "dark evil" anti-Source? Also, Pope Francis has been warning Catholics in his
recent speeches of the (dark) Devil? Is he talking about the same thing? And what is
Francis' relationship to Demiurge? Is he trying to instigate a breakaway in the Catholic
church? Or maybe he is doing it for himself and/or the Jesuit faction...

Best of luck in your mission, GE!"

~~

"Hi M..

There is a lot of talk about Pope Francis lately . Some say he works for dark because he
is a former Jesuit ,other says he is helping to liberate humanity . Personnaly i don't trust
him .
Here are 1 articles :
http://removingtheshackles.blogspot.com/2015/07/pope-francis-ignites-revolt-that-
will.html "

~~

"Thank you, D.!

The role of Francis has been a big question mark all along. I.e. is he just nice facade
whitewashing facade for the Jesuits or is really trying to change things? Something that

speaks for the former is that if he was really going against the top Jesuit/Archon agenda, he would no longer be alive. Unless he is being protected by some extraordinary/extradimensional means of course..."

~~

"Hi GE! So glad to see you back, even for a little while. I've checked often. Regarding crash of financial system, I assume " 2016th cycle around the Sun when all must take place" means 2016? Early in year or late in year? I was REALLY hoping for this year (SOON! So many are broke, in pain, dying from curable diseases, etc. So much suffering! Actually, I had hoped for 2011.) Since the cabal has avoided a defeat or financial crash this long, what will stop them from delaying it even further than 2016? They seem to be able to delay over and over and over. Gratitude & blessings to you! Thank you so much for stopping back."

~~

"(heart) GE,ALLWAYS GOOD TO HEAR FROM YOU,COULD YOU COMMENT ON THE SPHERE ALLIANCE,AND THERE PART IN THE PLAY,ALSO COULD YOU TALK ABOUT HEATHER ANN TUCCI JARRAF.AND IF SHE IS SOURCE,THANK YOU SO MUCH "

~~

August 2nd, 2015

SOPHIA

Hi everyone,

It is almost 2 weeks since I heard from him, and at the time he said he imagined, but wasn't sure, that he would only be available for about 2 weeks. So, this may be it for now. You can be certain that if I do hear from him, you will see it on this blog. Also that he said - "It is not us who decides the time of our leaving", and "after some time I will disappear again". It is for that reason I post now.

I am working on compiling our complete conversation into book form. You will see it announced here when it is complete. This will be in the Fall of this year.

My take on when we will hear from GE is 2016, maybe the first half. It would appear that the "Moment of Justice" he refers to, will have happened by then. *This is not a prediction, as all events are created by all of us.*

With much love and gratitude for your participation,
Until then,

August 12TH, 2015

SOPHIA (A FEW FINAL WORDS FROM G/E)

Hi Everyone!

We've heard once more from GE, and some questions have been answered. This came on Sunday and I did not see it until this afternoon, so I am not sure if there is still an opportunity for him to answer questions, but you can try. If he is available, he will respond.

The photo above is of a "Grey go-away bird", and it comes with a story. As is my habit, I put on my headphones and began to listen to each music piece sent with this note. It is well worth the hour it takes and I highly recommend it. It is trans-formative and soothing.

 As the music began, and I was contemplating all that had been said, I was looking out the window. A bird, the one pictured here as far as I can tell, landed on my front railing. It struck me because 1 – birds never land there, and 2 – it had a very tall crest sticking up. . At first I thought "What is a cockatiel doing flying outside? It was looking right at me. I grabbed my glasses to see with more clarity, and it was not a bird I had ever seen. After another few seconds, it flew off. I looked it up and *this bird*, the one that landed *in Illinois* this afternoon, is only found in *Southern Africa.* I am taking this as a sign, there are changes coming and nothing will be the same after they occur.

Here is GE's message to us... you might want to pour yourself a cup of coffee! ;-)

With love,

G/E

Good Day Sophia!

I wasn't able to write to you, but now I have the chance.

I wanted to say 'Hello to Everyone' once again and add my information about what Good Friends were writing about and as well to answer Your question Sophia. **I am afraid this is my last post** to You, so I will write it on maximal capability, but If You will be able to answer quickly to me I may be able to answer. Also Thank You very much for Your newsletters, very interesting conversations, a lot of different Wonderful Experiences!

Recently we GEs were receiving a lot of very precise information about everything, and this means only one thing - we are approaching to the peak/climax.

This World is about to witness unimaginable transformation!

So first of All if this is my last message, I am asking Everyone to keep Your

Focus and Concentration at 100% (or very close to it). If Your services as Lightworkers were very needed in Your Lifetime, this is Now when They are! The closer we get there, the more Concentration is necessary and NOW We together are REALLY close!

This started since the Moment of Choice on December 21 2012 (from the Moment of Choice You were having 3.5 cycles around the Sun until the Moment of Justice, that is 26 cycles from the full cycle of Saturn (29.4571), which is 8 (3+5) and 8 (2+6), our number is 8) that You made and by this choice You are writing this moment of Now and near future which is just around the corner. All is set and now it is just "The Action" that is needed to unleash it on fullest possible extent!

We GEs are feeling how This Grand Shift is "biting us", reaching us and the more we progress into "future" the more obvious it comes. So have Your Faith and have Your Focus, these are the only tools You will need right now (considering You have physically prepared as well - money, food, water, equipment and so on, we already covered it).

So in our words - "Let it be the Place of Harmony of Love and Co-existence!" There is no stopping it now!

Also I want to add about "Jesus" (Yeshua). It is true what is said there* **(a reference to one of my newsletters)**, the Energy that is being put into this name is enormous and the sad part in this is that this Energy is non-directed at anybody and thus is being dissolved. There is simply no such Individual that matches current images and name of "Jesus". The real person was way different than current images of Him.

The very name "Jesus" sounds grammatically incorrectly, like we know the very letter "J" was changed just because of this very name. From the very beginning of english language this letter was changed from sound "y" to sound "dʒ" just because of this reason like we know. The hatred toward christianity is imprinted within founders - tribe called "saxons". By most part "cabal" retains the pure blood of this same germanic tribe called "saxons" mixed with quasi-jewish bloodline called "khazars". They were the great haters of Rome and wanted to accomplish same empire as Rome did. Jealousy and greed are two main attributes that today's "cabal" inherited the most from them.

The real name of "Jesus" in aramaic sounded "Isho" and in hebrew it equated to "Yahshuah" (also Yehoshua, Yeshua and Yeshu) and instead of greek word "Christ" He was named with hebrew "Mashiah" means Messiah or Christ. That is more like a "title" or "rank", it basically means "The Chosen One".

In actuality this Person was more like Siddhartha (Buddha) or we GEs, he had a special mission to fulfill, this was "an agent of One" like we look at it, better said "The Messenger of Gods". He was calling for a revolution against tyranny, greed, wealth and power and was calling for Unity, Love, Compassion and Friendship. And that of course is what brought him to an end, due to People that enjoyed "being in power" in that time.

Jewish people in Jerusalem wanted more than He could give Them. They wanted power and to rule over Rome and this is what He was unable to give Them, as Universe provided Them with "Savior" they asked for. As He indeed was their long awaited "Messiah", they wanted a "Savior" and were asking One for such, One gave Them, but They rejected Him and rejected all Universe and natural Way of Life all together (putting themselves under fire) as their greed for power was more than their willingness for Great Changes, on the contrary they were refusing any changes and were fundamental in their beliefs. For that they were washed away by Wave of Changes of that time with their temple in ruins and expelled from there like You remember.

He is also not be confused with other "Saviors". He was meant only to be the Savior of Jewish People and not of the whole World, like most today think. So such lack of knowledge and misinterpretation of name and images is dissipating and dissolving all the Energy that is sent "to Him" in form of prayers.

This Energy then is "caught" by Followers of Light (not eaten, only heard) and They wishing to aid and help People that are without "compass and guides" can sometime appear before Humans making a holo-image of some known religious "Saints" or "Gods", like "Saint Mary" or "Jesus" Himself in a form how People see Them in Their Consciousness or as well Somebody Else that They are familiar with, (like passed away Parents for example) to give an advice or a prediction about very possible future and how to prevent it, if it is really bad (Book of Revelation, Mayan Calendar, Hopi Prophecies, 112 popes, 44th president of USA, secrets of Fatima). You can see clearly when such image is produced, is that it is produced by Your Consciousness.

What They are doing is that They only found "the plug" in People's Mind to which They can turn to and create a desirable image. The image will be more beautiful than what we are dreaming about. Such occurrence happened during visions at Fatima. Look for it, this is a very strong occurrence and it told about a version of future which is happening right now.

Ok answering to Your question:

"... the Sphere Alliance. Can you tell me who they are and where they fit ?"

Like we know the Sphere Alliance is a new name by which Galactic Federation of Light is known or we call them simply "Followers of Light" (actually we mean by this - "Those Who Follow the Path of Light", this sounds much more soothing and beautiful, yet it is a bit lengthy so we use shortened term "Followers of Light".)

I gave You a hint in previous message when You asked me about Them. They can change names, but their intent remains the same. You can distinct them by their Willingness to aid Humanity and Ease Your worry. "The Sphere Alliance" is another branch of this same Organization, like Ashtar Command.

They are helping Humanity in this urgent time, when some more help would be greatly appreciated. **Humanity is about to transcend and become "mature" (that is ready to ascend to other Stars)**.

Like I heard, name "The Sphere" They took from the meaning "Sphere" which is a form of "original Soul", all Souls are having form of a Sphere, when They enter "a vessel" - the Body (Human, Animal, Plant, Insect or Star, Planet), They then transform to take the Individual Body's form and main character.

During Life, Souls on it's multidimensional Body in this "3D" will look like the Human Body It is inside in. "The Sphere Alliance" literally translates as "The Union of Souls" that means "All are One Big Family and are The Same" (that is are in its original form of "Sphere").

Those that speak to You are also from same Arganization (don't mind me if I change 1 letter here, I did that on intent). They are all different, yet They All share same Unity and same Arganization, They are not like us Forces of One, we two are different Arganizations with a bit different view on whole Creation, You can see it if You relate my messages and Their messages.

We know things They do not know yet, and They consider such things as "irrelevant", yet without these things They cannot complete their full Circle of Life, and evolve into a much bigger and more complicated Forms than They are right now.. They talk a lot about Light and Love, much more than about things that really need to be addressed in this World and every time You try to ask Them about these things, They always try to get away from these themes. This is due to their belief system, They believe that Everyone, including Humanity can overcome everything if You follow the Light and embrace the Cosmic Love. It is true and it is possible, yet we follow a bit different route, when we are addressing issues, we look at all possible possibilities and the ones that as well include "darkness", this is where we split.

Yet Federation/Confederation of Light also consists of "Greys" and "reptilians", yes "reptilians" - same Beings that were torturing Humanity for ages. So when You can see the full picture about Them and Their Arganization, You can clearly distinct that they are not of pure Light, yet They really do want to be and They do everything for it. But so is the Creation, the Balance is everywhere, both forces/powers must coexist with each other, without it conflicts occurs and conflicts as We all well know by now brings things from which Humanity are suffering.

And just to add, in order to see that "full picture" I meant above, just look at the very words that describe Them and Their deeds, all Your answers lies in the "Root" - that is "the language", or better said "word" - the collection of different sounds and "sentencing" of such words to produce "sentences" and "text", watch for sounds, how they play in a word and as exactly sounds/music/frequencies holds all of it together, all of Truth that You seek to know are there, One is leaving hints in it for You to decipher, it is in the form of codes, but Your ear can hear it as sound.

Words have all the answers on all Your questions. For example word "Elohim" on aramaic is adjective in plural and means "Shining" as "they are", so here it is not "God", but rather as "they = Gods". Other words in bible that describes God when used in aramaic and hebrew in most cases as well are in plural form. So if You want to see "full picture" look at words and their origins, as well at Those who made those words. Once You know the origin of word and it's meaning, You can see things for what they really are.

Returning to *Followers of Light* - They lack some knowledge about Creation, yet *Their goals are noble and pure: they seek to bring Life everywhere and make all Life - of Light, so to "soothe" that second force of evil (it is like evil being absorbed by Good) thus transforming all this "3D Universe" into something much more Beautiful!* So they follow only in the Path of Light and BTW, *I just revealed to You their Final Goal, this is what Followers of Light seek as their Ultimate Goal actually.*

They are Your Family, they Care for and Love Humanity. They may not be excellent parents, but every Individual here don't have "ideal" parents (meant with whom We are happy and are proud of, immortal and care for us all our lifetime). They on the other hand are giving Humanity a chance to evolve all by Themselves, (Demiurge did this with It's own intent, but that is another story You heard already), They seek Humanity to mature enough and take it's rightful place among the Stars and join Them finally! This is what Everyone here wants, I sense it myself as a Human, it's been a long time since They left and **it's about time for a Magical Reunion! They have been waiting for long, so as You, time to say "Hello" and "Welcome" once again!**

This is all about Them and as You remember we GEs and Forces of One are Beings of Balance, we have a mix of both sides in us - of Good and evil mixed together. We prefer Good, but to fulfill our duties to fullest we also need sometime to use side of evil. Here on Earth we almost always are using side of Light. Yet in order to understand the given problems we have right now, we also need to use darkness. On some Worlds we need to use only Light and on some other Worlds - only dark. One entrusted Us to use our senses and hints One leaves to us to make wise judgement on every situation and use given powers and knowledge to solve the situation by the very best possible solution. All our actions depends on circumstances.

Actually everything depends on circumstances, the most wise advice for Everyone is:

"To always look around You and observe and assess the current situation. Pick Your actions wisely, make choices carefully, same action won't apply to different situations: in one situation it can help, in other it can hurt, same action won't solve the same riddle always (twice), there's always got to be another way, search for this way like a "hacker of Creation", all Creation is a code and You can "hack" it and it has multiple entrances and exits, there are "backdoors", there are "shortcuts", a lot for You to choose from, all

You have to do is to seek out them and circumstances might help You out to find what You seek."

Another great advice is*:* **"Always use a chance when You have one."**

The "window of luck" opens up just for a brief period, so if You hesitate, You might lose Your chance for "something special" in Your Life Experience or it could be something what You sought All Your Life and You just missed it.. Or if You grabbed it, You just became one Happy Being! Congratulations!:)

Such advices are given to us GEs so that we could always find a way out and act without stopping even in most "impossible" situation (actually You remember that EVERYthing is possible:)

This Universe constantly changes, and thus We (I mean Everyone) have to be like Universe in order to understand the very Foundation of It, We have to accept changes and make changes Ourselves, make Your choices by looking all around You - at circumstances.

Be-ing like it, means You are be-ing like One Itself. One/Universe Incarnate. There are exceptions of course, but exceptions are everywhere, Universe is not something which can be written in some kind of "Law of Physics" and act always in same old direction, like some law stated. There is no "Law" except for Universe, as Universe is the "Law"! And Universe as You know is One, here You can understand *what "Law of One" means, it is simply* - **the very Universe, it is You!**

Inside "You", there is another Universe, Universe is a direct reflection of You and thus of One. Reflection of everything is everywhere, this is how it works, the very basic foundation of Universe.

To add I want to say that *U.S. government today is repeating the fate of ancient government of Rome*, because like Rome it is standing in the way of that "Tsunami Wave" of Changes. They seek to live like they always used to and they still want to be that 1% of most "wealthiest" People of the World, exactly same situation as was with Rome. They refuse changes and are putting their forces to stand in a way before this "Wave" of changes, this is having grave consequences, like You remember. So for Everyone, it is always better to accept the changes and go along the flow of the river, not "against" it. And they better listen to this as well, otherwise there's no telling what could happen to them.

I am also Happy to see Everyone, if You have some misunderstandings You can ask, I will always be glad to aid You! We have a directive to answer on every given question.

"(heart) GE,ALLWAYS GOOD TO HEAR FROM YOU,COULD YOU COMMENT ON THE SPHERE ALLIANCE,AND THERE PART IN THE PLAY,ALSO COULD YOU TALK ABOUT HEATHER ANN TUCCI JARRAF.AND IF SHE IS SOURCE,THANK YOU SO MUCH"

Love You too Good Friend! I may suspect, that I'm not going to give You the answer You seek from me, but I respect Every Individual and I read about what those Great People were saying, as always Understanding is the key!, and I know that Everyone is saying the Truth and I can say **"We All Are Source!"**

Like I mentioned, there is Truth everywhere, all You have to do is to seek it out, We All are telling the Truth, but we use different wording, that is why we sometime fail to understand what Universe tells us and as well taking into consideration that We All are different, that there are never Beings that are 1=1, there is simply none in Universe, that is why You hear information that differs from one Source to another, one Person tells this and other tells that, but look what We all are saying Together and listen to Your own Consciousness!

We All Together are saying: "yes it is close, it is about to happen". This is it, this is the main intent that Unites All of Us! Just Unite all those messages from two Good Friends and All Others and You will have the complete whole picture;)

If You still can't figure out or are tired from huge volumes of information, ask Yourself "What exactly do I need to know?" And you will find Your answer! (It is true that sometimes we can lose Ourselves in tonnes of information and in that case we don't know where is Truth and where are "lies", "who tells what actually?" lol In that case we have to ask Ourselves that question above).

I send You hugs!

"Hi Good Friend, i am very happy you are fine and that you are back to us for some little time. I missed these conversations with you"

I did not really believe in negative attacks but 2 or 3 months ago, i felt that i was attacked. Everything is fine now"

Much love too you Good Friend and all GEs"

Happy to see You again Good Friend! Much Love to You too!

I am glad You are ok, these negative attacks are felt throughout this Planet, that evil force and illuminati/cabal are relentless, but like I said, they are losing focus and evil is losing it's edge here and we will make sure they will lose, that You can be sure of, because that is our mission:)

"Hi GE and welcome back!

A couple of things keep puzzling me still... What is the relationship between Demiurge and the "dark evil" anti-Source? Also, Pope Francis has been warning

Catholics in his recent speeches of the (dark) Devil? Is he talking about the same thing? And what is Francis' relationship to Demiurge? Is he trying to instigate a breakaway in the Catholic church? Or maybe he is doing it for himself and/or the Jesuit faction...

Best of luck in your mission, GE!"

Great to see You too Good Friend!

Actually there is none relationship of Demiurge and anti-source (dark source).

Demiurge is a pure Light Being. The problem with Demiurge is that he (it) was "blinded by Light" (yes this happens sometime). Light created a "small dark particle" in it's heart, we can say. And willingness to rule over everything and become like One - Creater of All blinded His pure Light mind, due to that small dark particle.

This happens with Human Fathers here too, and that is a direct reflection of Demiurge in Humanity. The influence of anti-source cannot reach well protected by Light Be-ing of Demiurge and it's race called Beings of Purity. But it found a way from inside, from mind of Demiurge. Still Demiurge wishes to be with the Source, it well understands the destructive power of anti-source and keeps itself away from it.

Yes by "devil" he means that force "dark evil". Catholic Church knows the "Truth" and know very well that bible is not complete Truth. They know about extraterrestrial origin of Humanity, they know about Source and anti-source. Yet they keep it in secret, in their secret library.

They still don't know though the whole and complete Truth, like Humanity they are seeking it out and pope Francis like we know is preparing to transform church so that it would suit current World View on all things. They are ready to accept every ideology just to keep their church afloat, like they did during rise of christianity (they transformed mithraism into christianity).

All they need are People that still support the church, if they are to lose Supporters, church will be ready to transform itself into "something new" to fit the New World, because they know that their fate is "sealed", unless they accept the changes, the changes will wash them away, like they did with Rome before.

This is foretold in "3rd secret of Fatima" and in St.Malachy prophecy about 112 popes. And Francis is the last pope of catholic church in that prediction and it is told that during HIS rule the catholic church would be whether transformed or cease to exist all together (this is another confirmation that time is Now).

There is fear that we sense in them right now, so Francis is doing everything to change such outcome. And Catholic Church (Vatican) and Turkey are to play major role in this Worldwide Shift which is about to take place. These two locations along with U.S. (Washington D.C.) are to be major "hotspots" on Earth. And what is going to happen in each 3 is not going to be the same. Don't ask me for details, I don't know more than that. We will have to see it Ourselves.

"Hi GE! So glad to see you back, even for a little while. I've checked often. Regarding crash of financial system, I assume " 2016th cycle around the Sun when all must take place" means 2016? Early in year or late in year? I was REALLY hoping for this year (SOON! So many are broke, in pain, dying from curable diseases, etc. So much suffering! Actually, I had hoped for 2011.) Since the cabal has avoided a defeat or financial crash this long, what will stop them from delaying it even further than 2016? They seem to be able to delay over and over and over. Gratitude & blessings to you! Thank you so much for stopping back."

I am glad to see You too Good Friend!

Unfortunately cabal is persistent, they took the route we were expecting them to take, we were considering any possible outcome and they took the worst one. Now they will have "to pay" (to their creditor - "the evil" with whom they signed their "contract"), so is the rule they applied themselves and their "family" to. Unfortunately there is nothing more we can do to ease their judgement, they will receive fullest and as they are stretching it further it will be even more harsher. So it is their "free will" that is doing this to them.

It is all set up and now **it is most probably be the cycle 2016** when they are to receive it. But it can happen sooner. Like we all know: "nothing is fixed."

We are doing everything we can to stop suffering, due to united actions (Ours and Yours), conflicts in Ukraine and Syria are gradually stopping. There is still big confrontation in Syria and Iraq and U.S. government is trying all their means to depose Syrian president.. as well in Ukraine, ukrainian government wants to make another attack very soon like we heard, but **if it weren't Us All Together, I mean All Lightworkers and Lightwarriors around the World, be it Us - Guardians, Bloggers, Truthseekers or Different Journalists and Activists, the consequences would be much worse than they are on this current moment, so I Thank You All from deep of My Heart! You have done a Very Great Job!** It is not finished yet, but We are more than halfway through this and it only one last cycle that is left right now!

So have Light, Love, Faith and Courage, We can do it!

Just for reference, as I know humanity like to know precise dates, so that You would not ask me again about this. I will give You dates that are most significant for us just for reference, these are just "dates", but significant ones. **All of this starts from date that is close to winter solstice 11th december 2015** (and winter solstice is on 22nd december), **this is when Saturn fully enters into Ophiuchus** and along with Saturn there will be Sun and Moon in Ophiuchus (and nothing more except for them), with Moon being New Moon standing in straight line with the Sun and together Sun, Moon, Saturn and Galactic Center - Sage Star A **forming a symbol which means "Judge" (also "Judgement" and "Judicator") at 12 o'clock if seen from Europe and Middle East. Entering**

starts on november 30th when Sun and Saturn will be in 1 line and on border between Ophiuchus and Scorpius. **Saturn will be in Ophiuchus during full cycle of 2016 and also in beginning of 2017, right until 24th february,** since this date Saturn is going into Sagittarius, then from **may 17th 2017 it returns back (due to Earth's rotation) and is going to be there until 19th november 2017, this is when Saturn leaves Ophiuchus for sure.** All given time spans between these dates are crucial! and I warned before **it can be extended beyond 2016 right into 2017 (right in those time span, called "second chance" by us), still 2016 is the most likely date - 80% accuracy.**

And to encourage You - Neptune will be right at the center of Aquarius on these dates, it got extremely long cycle around the Sun (164.8 Earth's cycles), so We got a luck that Neptune will be right at the center of Aquarius, like You know this is the Constellation of a New Age and Neptune is like the "ruler of seas" will aid You in hardships if there will be any.

So like I said have Light, Love, Faith and Courage! We can do it! :)

I also want to add last pieces of music that I sensed would suit here - right before these Grand Changes starts. A sharing of very e-motional (motion=action) music is what I always Love to do! Also remember about Technologies - this is most crucial part, Technologies are keeping secrets which can uncover all Your hidden potentials! If used wisely than can do that and more!

Enjoy this great Music Good Friends! If You saw and listened to them, it's just Great!:)

Note: I arranged these songs to approximately match how Grand Changes will unfold, to show You how approximately and in which order this is to take place.
(Note from Sophia – all music is included below, in the body of the email.)

I've putted a way for You from 5th Stage of Evolution (current) to 7th in this collection (even touches 8th), Enjoy Good Friends and Be Happy!:)

And I hope this emotional music will soothe and restore You Well My Friends, and that through it You will be able to find more Courage, Wisdom and Knowledge!

We Wish Everyone Peace, Calm and Prosperity!

READER'S COMMENTS

"GE! Thank you for all you DO. I am so grateful for your work and what you have done for ME to know more about the real absolute truth. What you have shared with SOPHIA is truly awe inspiring. This has led me to DO what I DO now. SO I thank YOU! AND Send you buckets of JOY! Be safe until we meet!
Karma Machine aka D. :)"

~~

"Dear GE,
It's so good to hear from you again. To get the full benefit of what you are saying i always need several 'readings' but in the end all does indeed make a lot of sense!

Many thanks for your explanations and descriptions, they are very helpful.

I have a very brief question. This is in relation to the 'dates' that you describe.
Is it not so that we are NOW in this moment of time actually in the 16th cycle/year. Meaning that when January 1st comes round year/cycle 16 is done and we start adding to the 17th cycle/year which in fact we call cycle 2016 ?

This is obviously very important because it impacts on how we read what you are explaining to us :)

So glad to have caught you before you are gone again !"

~~

""heart"GE,so glad to here from you,it is true all the answers lie within,and the answers come most times b4 im done with the question,thank you for all the truths that you have shared with us,it makes a big diffrence to know where we stand,to kinda have that rock of truth to go by,to grow with the universe is to change with the universe,i will look 4 my answers within this vast universe,once again my friend i thank you,love out!"

~~

heh heh looks like there's another M. now lol guess I'll be M. k.

GE!! buddy , p-funk , plasmatic!! glad to hear from ya kiddo, you do sound like your in good spirits,, must be a helluva vacation spot lol.

I've got some light listenig for ya, when and if you have the time,
might be fitting into the grand plan with 'ole mother earth herself involved
https://www.youtube.com/watch?v=LWcdjdTFSTI

https://www.youtube.com/watch?v=MaP5OAcg3g8

till whenever
take good care
Luv ya"

~~

"Hi everybody.
I have the feeling that the cleansing of the cabal has begun . The russian attack on ISIS in syria is only the very beginning.

http://www.sott.net/article/302979-Russia-establishes-no-fly-zone-for-NATO-planes-over-Syria-moves-to-destroy-ISIS-Pentagon-freaks-out
http://www.zengardner.com/vladimir-putin-agent-awakening/ "

~~

December 28th, 2015

SOPHIA

(A NEW YEAR GREETING FROM G/E)

Hi everyone!

Sophia here. As most of you know I am releasing a book which will be a compilation of the entire conversation with GE. This spanned the years 2012 - 2015, and took place on you tube, in email and on this blog. It is not yet complete. I will announce here when it is.

The plan was for it to be released at the end of 2015.

In July, when I last spoke to GE, he gave me several bits of information that I was to include in the book. I will share them here now, seeing that they concern the coming year. I expect the book to be complete before the first quarter of 2016 has ended.

These words are from emails sent this past July 20th, 2015.

_____

G/E

"I've been away for half a year (cycle). There was no internet, nothing where I was. I am going away again, so I would no longer answer questions, but later I would upon my return, if there would be any.

Right now we GEs are in the middle of our most important mission, the one why we have been made to be GEs. It is our life's most important one.

The crash of this financial system have been avoided by cabal by their many means of financial manipulation, they are stubborn we can give it to them.

So now, *it is 2016th cycle around the Sun when all must take place*."

~~~~~~~~~~~~~~~~~~~~~~~~~~~~~

"Now it is 2016, Followers of Light refused to stop this experiment, yet they agreed to leave Terranians alone, adding that Humanity is now "self-functioning civilization of 3rd kind".

In our words Terranians are now an independent Civilization with unrestricted access to space exploration. Now They can move beyond Outer Solar System. Compromise found.

You know what this means - there is no more need for a'f'a (Forces of One) or AMs to directly interfere, experiment against Creation will no longer proceed further.

Confrontation avoided.

What is left to take place here is ascending to Next Stage of Development (Grand Shift, Moment of Justice, Event) and isolation (quarantine of Earth) will be lifted upon this occurrence is completed, from words of FLs (Followers of Light).

This is favorable both by One and by Grand Master (Demiurge - in our circles also called "Grand Master"). Additional Compromise found. Yes, Grand Master agreed to leave Humanity alone. Now it is One's Will.

And Let The Cosmo Bless You and Guides You Our Great Beloved Friends. And until Next Coordination on Service to Creater of All, see You in Light of Next Star!"

That's it my friends. Best wishes to you and yours as 2016 begins. You can read my blog, and sign up for my newsletter!

Namaste'
~Sophia

READER'S COMMENTS

"Hi Sophia,

This is great news and I hope and pray it all proceeds positively and *ahem* SOON!

Two questions, just to clarify:

1) For the second part of the message: "Now it is 2016, Followers of Light refused to stop this experiment, yet they agreed to leave Terranians alone, adding that Humanity is now 'self-functioning civilization of 3rd kind" am I understanding correctly that you received this from GE last summer, to be released around now (or in the book, which would have been around now?)

2) And second, what will keep Followers of Light and/or Demiurge from reneging on the agreement? They don't seem the most trustworthy, honorable folks. (Enforcement by One, Creator of All?)

Thank you for your good work, and major thanks to GE, both for the work and for the communication!!! I hope he checks back in, his friendship feels great!

Blessings!"

~~

SOPHIA

"Hi Susie,
1) you are understanding this correctly. this post reflects what I heard from him last summer.

2) The laws governing creation itself are followed by all in creation. Period. The experiment happened within the law as it stood. This was an allowed doing. It was deemed that it would come to an end. it will. This, the way I am getting it, will be enforced by Creation itself. Many of the beings have chosen themselves to be returned to source to begin again. Realize that we are all, all things and all beings, the forces of light and dark, good and "evil"... we've been everything and

have done everything. We've been not trustworthy and trustworthy as well. We ALL agreed to this. Those of us "on the ground" right now are within reason to doubt the plan... as it hasn't gone favorably. Yet, we are ONE. This will happen so that the cycle of life continues. WE decided to do this in form. It will happen. And it will be amazing.

I hope this helps.

Much love and Happy New Year!

~~

"Thank you GE and thank you Sophia. While this is good news, how is it that Demiurge has say, or equal say? And, as per GE FoL can refuse to stop the experiment if One called it as completed? I understand free will, so where will the remaining go next (the ones who do not go back to source) if they agreed to leave us alone?"

~~

SOPHIA

AND THAT'S IT. REFER TO THE CHAPTER ENTITLED 'PRIVATE MESSAGES' FOR ADDITIONAL CORRESPONDENCE WITH HIM, SOME OF WHICH HAS NOT BEEN SHARED PUBLICLY. (5/2016)

As has been said, our conversation took up again with an email on July 20, 2015. In retrospect, It is interesting that at about the same time I was contacted by the being I came to know as "One" and given a prophecy about this 2016 year[545].

What follows is that email in its entirety. There are parts that have always been kept off the blog. Please excuse any repetition.

JULY 20TH, 2015

G/E

hEl-ea(t) Sophia! Thank You for great proposal, I would be happy to check Your newsletter! :) * *This is a reference to an email I sent regarding this book you are reading, as well as the newsletter that has been sent since 2015[546]. (Sophia)*

---

[545] "As We Shift - Prophecy - I of III." Sophia. N.p., n.d. Web. 10 July 2016.
<http://www.sophialove.org/my-blog/as-we-shift-prophecy-i-of-iii>.

You can decide whether to share or not this message with Good Beloved Friends, Very Great Friends to tell You the Truth :) If You like You can just tell Them that I'm fine and doing my job on keeping the World safe as much as I can with my Brothers and Sisters.

There's no need in restoring those messages from you tube, You have a whole lot of conversation with me without it:) 3 Years/Cycles, 3 turns around the Sun, that a lot of stream that came to pass:) If You need something to clarify or something missing from our conversation I can give it to You;)

I've been away for half a year (cycle). There was no internet, nothing where I was. I am going away again, so I would no longer answer questions, but later I would upon my return, if there would be any. Right now we GEs are in the middle of our most important mission, the one why we have been made to be GEs. It is our life's most important one.

The crash of this financial system have been avoided by cabal by their many means of financial manipulation, they are stubborn we can give it to them. So now, it is 2016th cycle around the Sun when all must take place.

Know that attacks from evil side "dark source" have increased relentlessly, those people that are important for this world's future (inventors, scientists, thinkers) are being attacked by negative thoughts (like to kill or make thing that would lead them to death).

This kind of attacks are being felt mostly throughout Europe and Russia, because this place is the one from where the Grand Change will start, so dark forces are trying to take over there and distort this Change. They have increased their activities because Scales of Balance have shifted into side of Light! This is the good news!

I am also very happy for You, different Beings share their experience of Life, of Universe and their Compassion and Emotions and Love toward Humanity. They overtook my place! :) yet always be weary. Under veil of Light and of Good Will there may come beings that would like to deceive You and misguide You from Light into dark, they cannot be distinguished from beginning of conversation, but later on when chat is going deeper, you would be able to hear some things not of

546 "Celestial IM." Sophia. N.p., n.d. Web. 10 July 2016. <http://www.sophialove.org/celestial-im.html>.

Light.

I will give You last piece of this light-dark dual system puzzle, the knowledge we received recently as a last package of most important information - the ultimate goal of two sides (two sides of same coin as ALL IS ONE), what they seek to accomplish as their final goal. This knowledge is most important for Everyone and for every religion of this World.

If such deceiver would be before You, the focus of this being is destruction. The complete and total goal of dark evil side is complete death of everything, the evil side seeks death of Universe, death of very Creator that made it - death of One. It is some sort of self-destruction mechanism. And what is most troublesome about it is that this force is sapient and awake, you can say it is devil (or deciphered - dark evil). It had been awoken by living creatures, like bacteria's, animals, ETs, humans, since the very beginning of Life due to prime instincts of hunt and seeking of food. There is no way to avoid its presence, it was meant to be born in such a way and exist.

The place of this force, where it lives is known as "dark source" or "anti-Source" it is always in opposite position of Source - Light Side of Creation, also sapient. All negative thoughts are making this entity stronger and it's most ultimate goal is nothing... It means, complete darkness, coldness, complete stop of everything, no movement anywhere.

Illuminati (dis)Order/cabal are servants of this all-destroying power, they are servants of nothing and they don't realize that this force is only using them to make destruction more massive; in the end this force would destroy them as well. In the meantime they believe in "bright future", for themselves and their family, when they have full control over humanity and over this planet and all of its process of Evolution/Development. Yet if they have been touched by this force, it would destroy them as well in the end, when there is nothing more to destroy.

So if they let's say would win, they would need to make sacrifice more and more in order to avoid that this power would take them and their family "as sacrifice" instead, when there is no sacrifice to make. This is debt slavery on other level, the level of death that they chose. Instead of money, they need to bring something to destroy (to their creditor), or otherwise, it (the creditor) would take them instead. This force always needs things to destroy.

So all of this information makes this "elite" even more dangerous; not just for this World, but for entire Galaxy and Universe. Now I know what Forces of One meant when they were saying about "danger to whole Creation". This is how you will know them and possible evildoers that may visit You. They are becoming pretty easily recognizable if you know this piece of information.

And as dark evil side seeks complete death, Light Good Side of Creation - the Source of Light seeks opposite to it - Abundance, Prosperity, Thrive, Bloom of everything. Multiplication, Spreading of Life, of Civilizations is what Light Good side seeks. Art, Creation, Beauty, Radiance, Neverstopping Movement, Innovation, Neverending Food or Neverending Energy or Neverending Light and of course all the best Emotions, Like Neverending Love, Neverending Compassion, Neverending Pulse of Very Life, all of this belongs to Light Side of Creation - This is the Ultimate Truth for us! When We were presented this ultimate knowledge, we felt great relief and still are feeling it when we remember it.

And yes, it was not like we didn't know it, we knew it all along and Everyone knows it, yet we needed to find the right words to connect these last dots and form this last picture, every Human Being needs Their Own method of Restoring the Ultimate Truth in Their Own Consciousness!

And as You know The Truth, here is the wisdom - "There is No Religion Higher Than Truth!"
Instead of word religion You can put anything that You refer to as Truth (Belief, Ideology, Thinking or something else).

But again, I remind You the Truth is what You believe into, and thus what You believe into is Truth for Your most Sacred Inner Self! This is how One meant Everyone to be.

More and more will be known about Light Good side later on after Grand Change would start. The subject of Light presents much Much MUCH More Opportunities of Creation than subject of dark. The knowledge about dark evil side is no longer necessary, there is nothing more to know about it, and thus dark side would disappear from face of this Planet for some given time and Humanity would be able to make a permanent ban of it on this Planet if Humanity would want to. And as it will be taken away from here, *it will be Earth's Golden Age.*

Yes and most important knowledge - All of this is meant to be as it is, One made evil to be "self-destruction" mechanism and Good - "thriving" mechanism. This is hard coded and cannot be overriden, only "softened".

And unfortunately, I will finish this message with bad news...

It is all coming to an end, soon a New Age would start, I am sure You are feeling it, it is already happening and there is no going back now, yet what would happen further will be even more grandiose and would be very instant, it would caught most by surprise, and surprise would be not pleasant..

Unfortunately USA will suffer and only what would be left of it would get into New Age, there is nothing we could've done here, it is last decision of One... This is due to People in this Country, They are being kept in the dark by that illuminati government and most are refusing to acknowledge all the many evil deeds this country did to the whole Planet and so many lives have been ruined during World's USA's evil financial corporate colonial empire's reign and tyranny. All of these words describe it as it was.

Also the great sacrifice that was made on this land before europeans settled it, it is not forgotten, and due to current actions of USA's People, Souls of Natives are angry, they would have forgiven Them if americans would change, yet, let me remind, some 60+ millions of Native People on both continents were killed in slow-motion destruction, and in current moment of time few feel at least some regret toward these People, yet Their Souls are angry and they Together, United want Justice to be restored and were waiting for this precise moment of time, the time when decision is to be made by One, whether there would be "revenge" or not.

Souls of Natives were deciding as well, and seeing current World's picture, they decided "to punish". This was made to happen right before New Age, so that Children of those that were killing and mutilating those Native People would not get into New Age, without making "payment" for Their and Their Children's sufferings. They would have forgiven all of americans' evil deeds, if all of americans would change their attitude toward World and toward great sacrifice of Natives, but now it is too late. Souls of Natives by most part have forgiven spaniards which were making equally brutal deeds in their time, as they have changed since then and their Empire has been ruined. Now it's time for British Empire under new names - USA (as main stronghold - channel to darkness), Canada, Australia, New Zealand and UK, the so called "5-eyed evil". Like we were told, only USA would suffer the most and 4 others would be fragmented or disbanded all together.

One revealed to us this detail, we were shocked by brutality which "colonizers" both spanish and english were making to Those poor People. This is truly hard to forgive... So I agree with whatever One wants to do. This past evil doing is another reason why One cannot leave USA as it is. They were given a lot of chances to prevent this and turn back, but they refused and are refusing to this very moment, putting Everyone here under fire. They even are whispering about attacking Iran, China and Russia at any cost if nothing would be possible to save crumbling economy. So in complete desperation they might even initiate such suicide attack, which would mean the end of USA.

There is almost no Hope for USA left, yet, Hope is there always, it never fades away, for when we can Dream a Dream and when we have Vision of Great Future, We can stop it.

You, Sophia, Your Family and other Light Beings of this country are protected by Higher Powers, yet most "normal" are not protected and casualties may be huge. It is up for this People to ask One and Universe to help Them now to get through this, we can't do anything here anymore. It is One's Will and it is Justice, this is what we GEs also stand for.

Here is the last piece of information. This is our requested feedback (terms' explanation in brackets).

"Now it is 2016, Followers of Light refused to stop this experiment, yet they agreed to leave Terranians alone, adding that Humanity is now "self-functioning civilization of 3rd kind". In our words Terranians are now an independent Civilization with unrestricted access to space exploration. Now They can move beyond Outer Solar System. Compromise found. You know what this means - there is no more need for a'f'a (Forces of One) or AMs to directly interfere, experiment against Creation will no longer proceed further. Confrontation avoided. What is left to take place here is ascending to Next Stage of Development (Grand Shift, Moment of Justice, Event) and isolation (quarantine of Earth) will be lifted upon this occurrence is completed, from words of FLs (Followers of Light). This is favorable both by One and by Grand Master (Demiurge - in our circles also called "Grand Master"). Additional Compromise found. Yes, Grand Master

agreed to leave Humanity alone. Now it is One's Will.

And Let The Cosmo Bless You and Guides You Our Great Beloved Friends. And until Next Coordination on Service to Creater of All, see You in Light of Next Star!"

This is it Good Friend Sophia! Everything is decided like You see. Yet remember, Hope is always there and with Hope there is always a way out. We can find exit from every situation :) so don't lose hope about USA.

I will be available for some time so You can answer me if You like, yet after some time I will "disappear" again.

There were several responses from me:

Sophia

Hi!

It is so very good to hear from you... I am glad you are okay, so very glad. It will take me a bit to "digest" all of this information. I will email you again shortly as I reflect on what you have said here. I am not sure what I will do with all of it. For certain I will let all the readers know you are okay.

Thank you so very much for answering my call. I will reach out again very soon.

Much love, Sophia

I understand that the quoted message at the end of your letter to be shared the first day of next year, January 2016. I will do that.

My take away from your message is that this end is hard coded into creation now, it cannot be avoided. Is this truth?

When you mention hope, is it hope for the new age that you refer to or hope that cataclysm can be avoided? It seems that the only way to stop the force of destruction is to destroy it, (along with a large part of the continent) according to your message.

What I am having trouble understanding is why the evil itself cannot be removed, sent someplace else, returned to source? Why destroy so much of a people? Is this to balance the scales? Is that what your reference to the genocide of the Native Americans indicates?

I will share some of this, and I will most certainly let your readers know you are okay. I may paraphrase some of it, I have not decided yet how to proceed.

I hope that you are able to respond before disappearing again... and above all, I hope that you remain well and that we will meet again sometime. You have provided so much for us.

With much love,
Sophia

~~~~~~

Hi again,

I am sorry to send more than one email, but there is another question that if you are able to answer, would be great.

Part way into your message, in the 6th paragraph you said "what they seek to accomplish as their final goal" Who is "They" exactly?

And then there is a referral to "Humanity being able to make a permanent ban of it on this planet if humanity would want to" -- can you put some detail with that for me?

In your "requested feedback" the Followers of Light are mentioned as "refusing to stop the experiment". Please define who they are just a bit more. I think this may be the same "they" I asked about in the first few sentences.

And one more, what does the phrase "additional compromise found" in the last part of the GE feedback mean exactly?

Thanks again, for all you have done.

Much love to you.

July 21, 2015
G/E

(Note, this first part is his response to a question regarding the precise timing of given predictions - Sophia)

One's Will is hard to calculate, it depends on actions rather than on constant formulas. Like Universe is dynamic, and Human Mind is dynamic, so is One's Consciousness is dynamic, it never stops, it is always moving and flowing, like never ending stream of water, it never stops and it never repeats it's shape. You can call this wave as "payback" (word payback is better than karma, as karma is mostly negative), it returns things that All of Us were doing, back to Us. If these things were evil, We receive evil (punishment), if these things were Good, we receive Good (reward), that is why we called it "Moment of Justice".

Yet Universe made Forgiveness and had forgiven Many, but not All. So tiny evil doings or tiny good doings are not counting and only very big ones are counting, like I already mentioned about USA.

If "payback" would be 1=1, it would be chaos all around Earth so One knows what to do right. Yet when there is Hope, and the very knowledge that Universe/One is always dynamic, all of this could change, but again it depends on circumstances, and right now and right here - main circumstances are People of U.S., it is because of Them such judgement was made. One did not said "this is my last word", One never says so, One always gives hint on a way out. And there is not just 1 way out, but some! So it depends on People - americans right now.

No need to apologize Sophia, You can write to me as much as You like :)

From what I know, I will be here for at least 2 weeks; it is not us who decides time of leaving. So You can write anything You want, I will be happy to aid!

I also wanted to add that attacks on important for Future People are relentless, yet these attacks are being weakened gradually. Evil is being aided by dark priests of cabal/illuminati, but since May, these priests were losing focus and are losing to this cycle. But because Scales have been shifted toward Light, evil side tries to catch onto it, so it had increased its pressure to extreme heights.

This is how all of this works, once 1 power overtakes other and starts to dominate, power 2 tries to become equal to it, the bigger the difference, the more is the pressure that is coming from losing power. Each is trying to win, yet before "total win" is secured each power is trying to at least maintain the Balance. You can closely associate this with team playing sports like baseball, football, soccer, hockey and so on. Here are a lot of sports like this and they are direct reflections of this basic hard-coded system.

Adding to this, in the history of Universe of this dimension, You know as "3D physical world" there were big changes toward both dark and light, these were the moments of extreme activity which were felt throughout the Universe, most of these occurrences happened in favor to dark, due to dark's never-ending strive for win and using "force" as its main weapon and because of this, dark side reshaped the Universe to the way, that during first stages of Evolution, Beings are being dominated mostly by dark rather than Light (not everywhere, not always, there are exceptions of course). That is why Animals here are like They are.

Another reason that adds dark to favor here on Earth are the components. This planet is being dominated by iron, red color of blood, red planet of Mars also consists mostly of iron, that is why it's red and it was "god of war in most of cultures, all are elements that proclaim war/aggression. On top of that, iron is the material that kills a Star from the inside, turning Star to red color. The very red color in Universe on basic level is considered as "looming death". Iron among very evolved Light Beings is considered primitive and "dark material". It is due to effects it is giving to those that use it.

The composition of Bodies of Animals and Humans is having iron as it's additional material thus blood is red as well, yet Humans and Animals can live without iron in Their Bodies.

Another reason why dark dominates here is that Humans and Animals don't have "transparency" in Their Bodies, skin and flesh don't have Transparency, so Light from Sun or from any other source of Light simply is not reaching the Core of these Bodies - Heart, Brain other important organs like liver and on top of it all - Soul-main Core.

There are a lot of Beings around the Universe that are having fully or partially transparent physical Bodies, due to this Light is reaching Their Core and they are changing toward Light more rapidly, much faster, and thus evolve much faster as well as Light gives Awareness and Knowledge. Some of Beings on this Planet like some types of Fish are having partially transparent Bodies, by most part these Beings are oriented toward Light, yet their mind is primitive and they are struggling for survival.

So while Humanity's Bodies are locked off from Rays of Light, darkness is able to reach each Man/Woman faster and as well start to live inside this Body, which is locked off from Light. If Light on Earth would have been dominating, picture would be completely different.

But don't despair, most of Arganisms throughout the Universe have such picture, it is due to protection from very active Rays of Light and due to thing I named before - darkness reshaped this Universe in the ancient past. If last thing would have not happened, Universe would have been very different.

Light side was "winning" only few times and it was not as close to "end" when dark was "winning". Forces of One interfered during some of those times to return Scales back to Balance. Forces of One always are interfering when "Grand Fault" is possible; when it is not possible they stay as observants.

Grand Fault by itself means "complete failure of system", this is when chain reaction would jump from object to object, like virus, ruining the very Essence of this Universe. And here on this planet with Demiurge and experiment on Humanity "Grand Fault" was possible, that's why they were here. They will be here until Moment of Justice and then would leave.

This was last piece of information about Forces of One.

~~~~~~

"Why destroy so much of a people? Is this to balance the scales? Is that what your reference to the genocide of the Native Americans indicates?"

Indirectly You can say yes, destruction of Native People and American People on equal level would Balance the Scales. But like I mentioned, it is not just this genocide why USA is being targeted, there are a lot lot more, hundred thousands different crimes which "on basis" USA as a whole (with People living in it) commits every cycle (everyday).

"When you mention hope, is it hope for the new age that you refer to or hope that cataclysm can be avoided? It seems that the only way to stop the force of destruction is to destroy it, (along with a large part of the continent) according to your message."

The Hope here is Universal Term, it is the very Essence of this word, like Natives Hopi, They have same root of this Word Hope, and They said directly about thing, that it is the very People that can change the outcome, all depends on Their actions in present moment of Now and very near future. Hope as word - that against all odds They would realize those many "mistakes" which led Others to suffer, and would ask for Universal Forgiveness, which is necessary right now in order to save future of Their Own Selves.

You are american as well, yet You realized all of this and many like You did and All that did not are dragging all of this entity known as USA down with Them unfortunately. New Age will start regardless of anything, but Who will join, this is the question right now. All Together, or those that were supporting evil (directly or indirectly) - excluded?

This land - North America will survive, the land will be returned to Natives and it will be a "surgical cut", from what I heard. Only those that somehow supported evil, acknowledged it or were doing it's biddings and illuminati/cabal here are included. What exactly this destruction would it be is unknown, what is known is that all forces of Nature, including Sun and BRICS countries may take part in this.

One gave a notion that it would be "an instant surprise of big proportion" which depends on actions of U.S. government and that part of Americans we are talking about. Many around the World are angry at USA due to latest revelations, and this only puts more fuel into this "surprise"... Financial crash and Yellowstone Volcano are as well here at play...

In most worse situation it could be everything together, this is a payment to that dark side which illuminati/cabal are following, You can say they signed a contract with creditor (dark evil) and now it is payment time in form of "something to destroy" and if there is no payment, then like I warned before:

"if there is no things to destroy, that they can give to this dark side as "payment", then dark side, like creditor would take them instead along with All of their direct or indirect supporters".

So let's return to the basics - what christianity was telling: "repent or be judged". Right now this same thing is happening with U.S. Like You see Sophia, it all came down to this. It is due to part that illuminati/cabal that were guiding USA toward "bright future" (actually very dark) - they are worshipers of anti-christianity, which is basically christianity, but inverted.

So we can say here that they called upon them the very religion that they were following and *are about to be judged like it was said in "Revelation" - last chapter of this book. In actuality that last chapter was a warning and not a plan of One.* One warned that if Humanity would take that step, They would face those terrible things mentioned there and now we can see how it came to be, all is in place right now...

But Hope is there and thus a way out is as well for Everyone, all They have to do is realize all the Truth until the end and change this outcome.

"My take away from your message is that this end is hard coded into creation now, it cannot be avoided. Is this truth?"
"What I am having trouble understanding is why the evil itself cannot be removed, sent someplace else, returned to source?"

Here You misunderstood Sophia, I meant that side of evil (Light as well) cannot be erased from existence, it have to exist along with Light. This is a dual system which was meant to be this way by One. Like we are told by part of One answering for this, that this way One as Creator of All is able to understand and test more of Its many many (infinite) abilities, All of Us Together right now are helping One in fulfilling this goal. So in this 3D, we need to live with both Good and Evil, and what side we are choosing is shaping our Destiny and shaping all of this Universe. Yes, Your and my every step are influencing the Future and changing it.

"Part way into your message, in the 6th paragraph you said "what they seek to accomplish as their final goal" Who is "They" exactly?"

They as Good (Light+Order) and Evil (Dark+Chaos).

"And then there is a referral to "Humanity being able to make a permanent ban of it on this planet if humanity would want to" -- can you put some detail with that for me?"

By this I meant pretty distant future, Humanity could deploy technologies to fully isolate Solar System or just Earth from evil's over-reaching influence, hint for one way to do this - using calming music, one of very high frequencies that is not audible and cannot be heard by anyone, but can be felt by Soul, it need to spread everywhere, all around Earth (or Solar System), this way a barrier will be created which cannot be penetrated by evil's influence and it's force of corruption will fail to corrupt anything within this barrier.

"I understand that the quoted message at the end of your letter to be shared the first day of next year, January 2016. I will do that."

Well, actually I received this message, each GE did, and then I translated it into english, it may sound a bit crazy for You, they spoke from near Future (future Forces of One). I thought to share it in 2016, yet decided to share it along with message because received it just few cycles ago.

Right now it isn't happened yet, but it will happen 99% certainty. 1% is always there, because like I said before, nothing is fixed, everything can change. But Forces of One (which are from present) already prepared Themselves in advance and They knew of the outcome way before, but remember about those 10%. They did not share all of information They knew about this World with GEs and thus I with You Sophia, because like They said we needed to find many things Ourselves, only then all of this would be natural and by Law of Universe (of One).

The closer we get to the point of analysis, the lesser % that is to change, so now it is just 1% (could be as well 2%), as well the closer we GEs were getting to it, the more knowledge was opened, on each new step - new knowledge, obtaining of which was gradual, same was and is happening with Light workers, Light warriors and other Light Beings on Earth, to not overcharge Mind and

Consciousness, gradual and slow expansion of Awareness. It suits in a model One programmed this Universe into. Like They said, some things changed unlike they made an analysis, so their analysis of future was not 100%, so basically They are speaking with Their future Selves to compare the results. And there are multiple future Selves from different timelines and parallel Worlds. So here we received the final feedback, which is almost for certain will be like You read.

"In your "requested feedback" the Followers of Light are mentioned as "refusing to stop the experiment". Please define who they are just a bit more. I think this may be the same "they" I asked about in the first few sentences."

They are the Controllers - Galactic Federation (Confederation) of Light, They will change Their name and identity just to suit Your needs, how You understand them, how Your Mind understands what They are.

In 50s they were from Venus and Mars and Jupiter, in 80s They were only Orionids and Pleiadeans, in ancient times they were "Spirits", later on Gods, later Angels and Demons, in this moment They are those that You define as many different Beings that channel People or are somehow letting You know about Their presence.

They are the Galactic Organization of thousands of different Civilizations that seek to know and understand at deepest levels the side of Light and of Life. They as well spread and multiply Life, because They know the Truth.

Like mentioned, side of Good seeks to Thrive, seeks to spread Life throughout all possible and impossible places, multiplication comes to side of Light and of Life, which is Good. Among Their many Civilizations there are "Creators" of Humanity, the ones who modified apes and made Humanity, all Humans have DNA of their Kind mixed with this Planet's original Inhabitants.

Demiurge rules over Them, not all knows this and not all wishes to acknowledge this, Demiurge is as well Humanity's Father, because Demiurge's seed is inside Humanity's DNA. This is God, the "The Father of Heavens", "The Father of Humanity", Everyone heard about by all definitions. Yes, They used Humanity for experiment, still They love You, They care for You, They look over You, protect You from outer threats, like invasion from outer space or asteroids, comets. They await when You will grow up, so that You would finally understand Them and will be ready to meet Them. You are Their Children, and as well Their Brothers and Sisters.

"And one more, what does the phrase "additional compromise found" in the last part of the GE feedback mean exactly?"

They meant, that They were able to find (are about to, actually) another compromise with Demiurge on lifting off the isolation (quarantine) of Earth. It seems Demiurge would finally stop Its goal of achieving ultimate power, He listened to Us All, He listened to One...

I hope this will explain misunderstandings and if there are some more, Please Ask :)
Much Love, Peace, Calm and Prosperity!

August 9, 2015

G/E

I wasn't able to write to you, but now I have the chance. I wanted to say 'Hello to Everyone' once again and add my information about what Good Friends were writing about and as well to answer Your question Sophia.

I am afraid this is my last post to You, so I will write it on maximal capability, but If You will be able to answer quickly to me I may be able to answer. Also Thank You very much for Your newsletters, very interesting conversations, a lot of different Wonderful Experiences!

Recently we GEs were receiving a lot of very precise information about everything, and this means only one thing - we are approaching to the peak/climax. This World is about to witness unimaginable transformation! So first of All if this is my last message, I am asking Everyone to keep Your Focus and Concentration at 100% (or very close to it). If Your services as Light workers were very needed in Your Lifetime, this is Now when They are! The closer we get there, the more Concentration is necessary and NOW We together are REALLY close!

This started since the Moment of Choice on december 21 2012 (from the Moment of Choice You were having 3.5 cycles around the Sun until the Moment of Justice, that is 26 cycles from the full cycle of Saturn (29.4571), which is 8 (3+5) and 8 (2+6), our number is 8) that You made and by this choice You are writing this moment of Now and near future which is just around the corner. All is set and now it is just "The Action" that is needed to unleash it on fullest possible extent!

We GEs are feeling how This Grand Shift is "biting us", reaching us and the more we progress into "future" the more obvious it comes. So have Your Faith and have Your Focus, these are the only tools You will need right now (considering You have physically prepared as well - money, food, water, equipment and so on, we already covered it).

So in our words - "Let it be the Place of Harmony of Love and Co-existence!" There is no stopping it now!

And Sophia if You think sometime that it is Your mind playing with You when You hear voices or "Yourself", it is not actually. I was having same issue the first time I was encountered by Forces of One. I know, they really are contacting You, but They are using words and combinations of words that Your mind knows, is accustomed to. This was happening on Earth since beginning of times with Everyone who was receiving Their messages or simply were "channeling" Them. Like I already mentioned They were "spirits", "gods", "angels" in the view of Humanity - But not to be confused with Souls - Souls of deceased, "dead wanderers", "Guardian Angels".

(For reference - "Guardian Angels" are Relatives that are no longer with Us, They keep Us from harm if during life They loved Us and We loved Them. But if there was a strive or hatred in Family, the "Guardian Angel" could not be there to aid if it had chosen "not to". Soul is multidimensional and one part of It could become "Guardian Angel": when We are passing away, Our Soul can decide what to do with Our still alive Relatives - "watch over Them or not?")

Also I want to add about "Jesus" (Yeshua). It is true what is said there, the Energy that is being put into this name is enormous and the sad part in this is that this Energy is non-directed at anybody and thus is being dissolved. There is simply no such Individual that matches current images and name of "Jesus". The real person was way different than current images of Him. The very name "Jesus" sounds grammatically incorrectly, like we know the very letter "J" was changed just because of this very name. From the very beginning of english language this letter was changed from sound "y" to sound "dʒ" just because of this reason like we know. The hatred toward christianity is imprinted within founders - tribe called "saxons".

By most part "cabal" retains the pure blood of this same germanic tribe called "saxons" mixed with quasi-jewish bloodline called "khazars". They were the great haters of Rome and wanted to accomplish same empire as Rome did. Jealousy and greed are two main attributes that today's "cabal" inherited the most from them. The real name of "Jesus" in aramaic sounded "Isho" and in hebrew it equated to "Yahshuah" (also Yehoshua, Yeshua and Yeshu) and instead of greek word "Christ" He was named with hebrew "Mashiah" means Messiah or Christ. That is more like a "title" or "rank", it basically means "The Chosen One".

In actuality this Person was more like Siddhartha (Buddha) or we GEs, he had a special mission to fulfill, this was "an agent of One" like we look at it, better said "The Messenger of Gods". He was calling for a revolution against tyranny, greed, wealth and power and was calling for Unity, Love, Compassion and Friendship. And that of course is what brought him to an end, due to People that enjoyed "being in power" in that time. Jewish people in Jerusalem wanted more than He could give Them.

They wanted power and to rule over Rome and this is what He was unable to give Them, as Universe provided Them with "Savior" they asked for. As He indeed was their long awaited "Messiah", they wanted a "Savior" and were asking One for such, One gave Them, but They rejected Him and rejected all Universe and natural Way of Life all together (putting themselves under fire) as their greed for power was more than their willingness for Great Changes, on the contrary they were refusing any changes and were fundamental in their beliefs. For that they were washed away by Wave of Changes of that time with their temple in ruins and expelled from there like You remember.

He is also not be confused with other "Saviors". He was meant only to be the Savior of Jewish People and not of the whole World, like most today think. So such lack of knowledge and misinterpretation of name and images is dissipating and dissolving all the Energy that is sent "to Him" in form of prayers.

This Energy then is "caught" by Followers of Light (not eaten, only heard) and They wishing to aid and help People that are without "compass and guides" can sometime appear before Humans making a holo-image of some known religious "Saints" or "Gods", like "Saint Mary" or "Jesus" Himself in a form how People see Them in Their Consciousness or as well Somebody Else that They are familiar with, (like passed away Parents for example) to give an advice or a prediction about very possible future and how to prevent it, if it is really bad (Book of Revelation, Mayan Calendar, Hopi Prophecies, 112 popes, 44th president of USA, secrets of Fatima).

You can see clearly when such image is produced, is that it is produced by Your Consciousness. What They are doing is that They only found "the plug" in People's Mind to which They can turn to and create a desirable image. The image will be more beautiful than what we are dreaming about. Such occurrence happened during visions at Fatima. Look for it, this is a very strong occurrence and it told about a version of future which is happening right now.

--

SOPHIA

The Sphere Alliance; can you tell me who they are and where they fit?

G/E

Like I heard, name "The Sphere" They took from the meaning "Sphere" which is a form of "original Soul", all Souls are having form of a Sphere, when They enter "a vessel" - the Body (Human, Animal, Plant, Insect or Star, Planet), They then transform to take the Individual Body's form and main character. During Life, Souls on its multidimensional Body in this "3D" will look like the Human Body It is inside in. "The Sphere Alliance" literally translates as "The Union of Souls" that means "All are One Big Family and are The Same" (that is are in its original form of "Sphere").

Those that speak to You are also from same Arganization (don't mind me if I change 1 letter here, I did that on intent). They are all different, yet They All share same Unity and same Arganization, They are not like us Forces of One, we two are different Arganizations with a bit different view on whole Creation, You can see it if You relate my messages and Their messages.

We know things They do not know yet, and They consider such things as "irrelevant", yet without these things They cannot complete their full Circle of Life, and evolve into a much bigger and more complicated Forms than They are right now... They talk a lot about Light and Love, much more than about things that really need to be addressed in this World and every time You try to ask Them about these things, They always try to get away from these themes. This is due to their belief system, They believe that Everyone, including Humanity can overcome everything if You follow the Light and embrace the Cosmic Love. It is true and it is possible, yet we follow a bit different route, when we are addressing issues, we look at all possible possibilities and the ones that as well include "darkness", this is where we split.

Yet Federation/Confederation of Light also consists of "Greys" and "reptilians", yes "reptilians" - same Beings that were torturing Humanity for ages. So when You can see the full picture about Them and Their Arganization, You can clearly distinct that they are not of pure Light, yet They really do want to be and They do everything for it. But so is the Creation, the Balance is everywhere, both forces/powers must coexist with each other, without it conflicts occurs and conflicts as We all well know by now brings things from which Humanity are suffering.

And just to add, in order to see that "full picture" I meant above, just look at the very words that describe Them and Their deeds, all Your answers lies in the "Root" - that is "the language", or better said "word" - the collection of different sounds and "sentencing" of such words to produce "sentences" and "text", watch for sounds, how they play in a word and as exactly sounds/music/frequencies holds all of it together, all of Truth that You seek to know are there, One is leaving hints in it for You to decipher, it is in the form of codes, but Your ear can hear it as sound.

Words have all the answers on all Your questions. For example word "Elohim" on aramaic is adjective in plural and means "Shining" as "they are", so here it is not "God", but rather as "they = Gods". Other words in bible that describes God when used in aramaic and hebrew in most cases as well are in plural form. So if You want to see "full picture" look at words and their origins, as well at Those who made those words. Once You know the origin of word and its meaning, You can see things for what they really are.

Returning to Followers of Light - They lack some knowledge about Creation, yet Their goals are noble and pure: they seek to bring Life everywhere and make all Life - of Light, so to "soothe" that second force of evil (it is like evil being absorbed by Good) thus transforming all this "3D Universe" into something much more Beautiful!

So they follow only in the Path of Light and BTW, I just revealed to You their Final Goal, this is what Followers of Light seek as their Ultimate Goal actually. They are Your Family, they Care for and Love Humanity. They may not be excellent parents, but every Individual here don't have "ideal" parents (meant with whom We are happy and are proud of, immortal and care for us all our lifetime). They on the other hand are giving Humanity a chance to evolve all by Themselves, (Demiurge did this with Its own intent, but that is another story You heard already), They seek Humanity to mature enough and take its rightful place among the Stars and join Them finally! This is what Everyone here wants, I sense it myself as a Human, it's been a long time since They left and it's about time for a Magical Reunion! They have been waiting for long, so as You, time to say "Hello" and "Welcome" once again!

This is all about Them and as You remember we GEs and Forces of One are Beings of Balance, we have a mix of both sides in us - of Good and evil mixed together. We prefer Good, but to fulfill our duties to fullest we also need some time to use side of evil. Here on Earth we almost always are using side of Light. Yet in order to understand the given problems we have right now, we also need to use darkness. On some Worlds we need to use only Light and on some other Worlds - only dark. One entrusted Us to use our senses and hints One leaves to us to make wise judgement on every situation and use given powers and knowledge to solve the situation by the very best possible solution. All our actions depends on circumstances.

Actually everything depends on circumstances, the most wise advice for Everyone is:

"To always look around You and observe and assess the current situation. Pick Your actions wisely, make choices carefully, same action won't apply to different situations: in one situation it can help, in other it can hurt, same action won't solve the same riddle always (twice), there's always got to be another way, search for this way like a "hacker of Creation", all Creation is a code and You can "hack" it and it has multiple entrances and exits, there are "backdoors", there are "shortcuts", a lot for You to choose from, all You have to do is to seek out them and circumstances might help You out to find what You seek."

Another great advice is: "Always use a chance when You have one." The "window of luck" opens up just for a brief period, so if You hesitate, You might lose Your chance for "something special" in Your Life Experience or it could be something what You sought All Your Life and You just missed it.. Or if You grabbed it, You just became one Happy Being! Congratulations! :)
Such advices are given to us GEs so that we could always find a way out and act without stopping even in most "impossible" situation (actually You remember that EVERYthing is possible:)

This Universe constantly changes, and thus We (I mean Everyone) have to be like Universe in order to understand the very Foundation of It, We have to accept changes and make changes Ourselves, make Your choices by looking all around You - at circumstances. Be-ing like it, means You are be-ing like One Itself. One/Universe Incarnate. There are exceptions of course, but exceptions are everywhere, Universe is not something which can be written in some kind of "Law of Physics" and act always in same old direction, like some law stated. There is no "Law" except for Universe, as Universe is the "Law"! And Universe as You know is One, here You can understand what "Law of One" means, it is simply - the very Universe, it is You!

Inside "You", there is another Universe, Universe is a direct reflection of You and thus of One. Reflection of everything is everywhere, this is how it works, the very basic foundation of Universe.

To add I want to say that U.S. government today is repeating the fate of ancient government of Rome, because like Rome it is standing in the way of that "Tsunami Wave" of Changes. They seek to live like they always used to and they still want to be that 1% of most "wealthiest" People of the World, exactly same situation as was with Rome. They refuse changes and are putting their forces to stand in a way before this "Wave" of changes, this is having grave consequences, like You remember. So for Everyone, it is always better to accept the changes and go along the flow of the river, not "against" it. And they better listen to this as well, otherwise there's no telling what could happen to them.

What follows are his final answers, also posted on the blog page[547]:

I am also Happy to see Everyone, if You have some misunderstandings You can ask, I will always be glad to aid You! We have a directive to answer on every given question.

"(heart) GE,ALLWAYS GOOD TO HEAR FROM YOU,COULD YOU COMMENT ON THE SPHERE ALLIANCE,AND THERE PART IN THE PLAY,ALSO COULD YOU TALK ABOUT HEATHER ANN TUCCI JARRAF.AND IF SHE IS SOURCE,THANK YOU SO MUCH"

Love You too Good Friend! I may suspect, that I'm not going to give You the answer You seek from me, but I respect Every Individual and I read about what those Great People were saying, as always Understanding is the key!, and I know that Everyone is saying the Truth and I can say "We All Are Source!" Like I mentioned, there is Truth everywhere, all You have to do is to seek it out, We All are telling the Truth, but we use different wording, that is why we sometime fail to understand what Universe tells us and as well taking into consideration that We All are different, that there are never Beings that are 1=1, there is simply none in Universe, that is why You hear information that differs from one Source to another, one Person tells this and other tells that, but look what We all are saying Together and listen to Your own Consciousness!

We All Together are saying: "yes it is close, it is about to happen". This is it; this is the main intent that Unites All of Us! Just Unite all those messages from two Good Friends and All Others and You will have the complete whole picture ;) If You still can't figure out or are tired from huge volumes of information, ask Yourself "What exactly do I need to know?" And you will find Your answer! (It is true that sometimes we can lose Ourselves in tonnes of information and in that case we don't know where is Truth and where are "lies", "who tells what actually?" lol In that case we have to ask Ourselves that question above).
I send You hugs!

"Hi Good Friend, i am very happy you are fine and that you are back to us for some little time. I missed these conversations with you"

[547] "A Few Final Words from Ge..." Sophia. N.p., n.d. Web. 10 July 2016. <http://www.sophialove.org/ge-blog--comments/a-few-final-words-from-ge>.

I did not really believe in negative attacks but 2 or 3 months ago, i felt that i was attacked. Everything is fine now"

Much love too you Good Friend and all GEs"

Happy to see You again Good Friend! Much Love to You too!

I am glad You are ok, these negative attacks are felt throughout this Planet, that evil force and illuminati/cabal are relentless, but like I said, they are losing focus and evil is losing it's edge here and we will make sure they will lose, that You can be sure of, because that is our mission:)

"Hi GE and welcome back!

A couple of things keep puzzling me still... What is the relationship between Demiurge and the "dark evil" anti-Source? Also, Pope Francis has been warning Catholics in his recent speeches of the (dark) Devil? Is he talking about the same thing? And what is Francis' relationship to Demiurge? Is he trying to instigate a breakaway in the Catholic church? Or maybe he is doing it for himself and/or the Jesuit faction...

Best of luck in your mission, GE!"

Great to see You too Good Friend!

Actually there is none relationship of Demiurge and anti-source (dark source). Demiurge is a pure Light Being. The problem with Demiurge is that he (it) was "blinded by Light" (yes this happens sometime). Light created a "small dark particle" in it's heart, we can say. And willingness to rule over everything and become like One - Creator of All blinded His pure Light mind, due to that small dark particle. This happens with Human Fathers here too, and that is a direct reflection of Demiurge in Humanity. The influence of anti-source cannot reach well protected by Light Be-ing of Demiurge and it's race called Beings of Purity. But it found a way from inside, from mind of Demiurge. Still Demiurge wishes to be with the Source, it well understands the destructive power of anti-source and keeps itself away from it.

Yes by "devil" he means that force "dark evil". Catholic Church knows the "Truth" and know very well that bible is not complete Truth. They know about extraterrestrial origin of Humanity, they know about Source and anti-source. Yet they keep it in secret, in their secret library. They still don't know though the whole and complete Truth, like Humanity they are seeking it out and pope Francis like we know is preparing to transform church so that it would suit current World View on all things. They are ready to accept every ideology just to keep their church afloat, like they did during rise of christianity (they transformed mithraism into christianity).

All they need are People that still support the church, if they are to lose Supporters, church will be ready to transform itself into "something new" to fit the New World, because they know that their fate is "sealed", unless they accept the changes, the changes will wash them away, like they did with Rome before. This is foretold in "3rd secret of Fatima" and in St.Malachy prophecy about 112 popes. And Francis is the last pope of catholic church in that prediction and it is told that during HIS rule the catholic church would be whether transformed or cease to exist all together (this is another confirmation that time is Now). There is fear that we sense in them right now, so Francis is doing everything to change such outcome. And Catholic Church (Vatican) and Turkey are to play major role in this Worldwide Shift which is about to take place. These two locations along with U.S. (Washington D.C.) are to be major "hotspots" on Earth. And what is going to happen in each 3 is not going to be the same. Don't ask me for details, I don't know more than that. We will have to see it Ourselves.

"Hi GE! So glad to see you back, even for a little while. I've checked often. Regarding crash of financial system, I assume " 2016th cycle around the Sun when all must take place" means 2016? Early in year or late in year? I was REALLY hoping for this year (SOON! So many are broke, in pain, dying from curable diseases, etc. So much suffering! Actually, I had hoped for 2011.) Since the cabal has avoided a defeat or financial crash this long, what will stop them from delaying it even further than 2016? They seem to be able to delay over and over and over. Gratitude & blessings to you! Thank you so much for stopping back."

I am glad to see You too Good Friend!

Unfortunately cabal is persistent, they took the route we were expecting them to take, we were considering any possible outcome and they took the worst one. Now they will have "to pay" (to their creditor - "the evil" with whom they signed their "contract"), so is the rule they applied themselves and their "family" to. Unfortunately there is nothing more we can do to ease their judgement, they will receive fullest and as they are stretching it further it will be even harsher. So it is their "free will" that is doing this to them. It is all set up and now it is most probably be the cycle 2016 when they are to receive it. But it can happen sooner. Like we all know: "nothing is fixed."

We are doing everything we can to stop suffering, due to united actions (Ours and Yours), conflicts in Ukraine and Syria are gradually stopping. There is still big confrontation in Syria and Iraq and U.S. government is trying all their means to depose Syrian president.. as well in Ukraine, ukrainian government wants to make another attack very soon like we heard, but if it weren't Us All Together, I mean All Light workers and Light warriors around the World, be it Us - Guardians, Bloggers, Truth seekers or Different Journalists and Activists, the consequences would be much worse than they are on this current moment, so I Thank You All from deep of My Heart! You have done a Very Great Job! It is not finished yet, but We are more than halfway through this and it only one last cycle that is left right now!
So have Light, Love, Faith and Courage, We can do it!

Just for reference, as I know humanity like to know precise dates, so that You would not ask me again about this. I will give You dates that are most significant for us just for reference, these are just "dates", *but significant ones.*

All of this starts from date that is close to winter solstice 11th december 2015 (and winter solstice is on 22nd december), this is when Saturn fully enters into Ophiuchus and along with Saturn there will be Sun and Moon in Ophiuchus (and nothing more except for them), with Moon being New Moon standing in straight line with the Sun and together Sun, Moon, Saturn and Galactic Center - Sage Star A forming a symbol which means "Judge" (also "Judgement" and "Judicator") at 12 o'clock if seen from Europe and Middle East. Entering starts on november 30th when Sun and Saturn will be in 1 line and on border between Ophiuchus and Scorpius. Saturn will be in Ophiuchus during full cycle of 2016 and also in beginning of 2017, right until 24th february, since this date Saturn is going into Sagittarius, then from may 17th 2017 it returns back (due to Earth's rotation) and is going to be there until 19th november 2017, this is when Saturn leaves Ophiuchus for sure. *All given time spans between these dates are crucial!* and I warned before it can be extended beyond 2016 right into 2017 (right in those time span, called "second chance" by us), *still 2016 is the most likely date - 80% accuracy.*

And to encourage You - Neptune will be right at the center of Aquarius on these dates, it got extremely long cycle around the Sun (164.8 Earth's cycles), so We got a luck that Neptune will be right at the center of Aquarius, like You know this is the Constellation of a New Age and Neptune is like the "ruler of seas" will aid You in hardships if there will be any. So like I said have Light, Love, Faith and Courage! We can do it! :)

I also want to add last pieces of music that I sensed would suit here - right before these Grand Changes starts. A sharing of very e-motional (motion=action) music is what I always Love to do! Also remember about Technologies - this is most crucial part, Technologies are keeping secrets which can uncover all Your hidden potentials! If used wisely than can do that and more! Enjoy this great Music Good Friends! If You saw and listened to them, it's just Great! :)
Note: I arranged these songs to approximately match how Grand Changes will unfold, to show You how approximately and in which order this is to take place.

Children of the World[548]

Mother Earth[549]

Song of the North[550]

Dreams[551]

Song of Hope[552]

The Power of Will, it is a Great Song of Inspiration, just about as it is "The Power of Will" that decides the Future of All This Planet[553]
The Power of Will Enhanced - to give Even More Inspiration and move Your Power of Will even much further beyond Your wildest expectations! [554] :)

Breathe (a Fresh Air from a New World of a New Age)[555]

---

[548] BrunuhVille. "Emotional Music - Children of the World." YouTube. YouTube, 19 Mar. 2015. Web. 10 July 2016. <https://www.youtube.com/watch?v=EFqesVTz-YA>.
[549] BrunuhVille. "Epic Fantasy Music - Mother Earth." YouTube. YouTube, 08 Mar. 2015. Web. 10 July 2016. <https://www.youtube.com/watch?v=POhigiOQxPk>.
[550] BrunuhVille. "Fantasy Medieval Music - Song of the North." YouTube. YouTube, 17 Feb. 2015. Web. 10 July 2016. <https://www.youtube.com/watch?v=gRuggMzH3Gw>.
[551] BrunuhVille. "Emotional Fantasy Music - Dreams." YouTube. YouTube, 11 July 2015. Web. 10 July 2016. <https://www.youtube.com/watch?v=eQ3sJQ4O-no>.
[552] Epicmusicvn. "Epic Emotional | Michael Maas - Song of Hope - Epic Music VN." YouTube. YouTube, 15 Aug. 2014. Web. 10 July 2016. <https://www.youtube.com/watch?v=oAF_231NACY>.
[553] EpicHeavenMusic. "Ivan Torrent - The Power of Will (New Mix 2013 - Epic Orchestral)." YouTube. YouTube, 30 Dec. 2013. Web. 10 July 2016. <https://www.youtube.com/watch?v=yWnzQv2jEm4>.
[554] EpicJennyni20. "Ivan Torrent - The Power of Will (New Version)(feat. Gaby Koss)." YouTube. YouTube, 01 Jan. 2015. Web. 10 July 2016. <https://www.youtube.com/watch?v=yNjJmMHS_Ic>.
[555] CapeTranquillity. "Two Steps From Hell - Breathe." YouTube. YouTube, 07 Feb. 2015. Web. 10 July 2016. <https://www.youtube.com/watch?v=PPe_iwgmFB0>.

Earthrise[556]

Skyworld[557]

And Soar[558]

Weighted Ground[559]

Reverie[560]

Reflections of Life[561]

Inner Peace[562]

In Aeternum[563]

Into The Light[564]

Faith[565]

Truth[566]
Those are wise words, the sound is actually dominating all around the Universe,

[556] TrailerMusicWorldI. "Epic Score - Earthrise (Epic Powerful Heroic Choral Orchestral)." YouTube. YouTube, 05 May 2015. Web. 10 July 2016. <https://www.youtube.com/watch?v=YFbEfaGqVWA>.
[557] TwoStepsFromTheMusic. "Two Steps From Hell - SkyWorld (SkyWorld)." YouTube. YouTube, 01 Nov. 2012. Web. 10 July 2016. <https://www.youtube.com/watch?v=Lq2ANOkfsIA>.
[558] ThePrimeCronus. "Steve Syz - Soar." YouTube. YouTube, 17 July 2014. Web. 10 July 2016. <https://www.youtube.com/watch?v=WSg8ybRc48Q>.
[559] Voiceprints. "Sub Pub Music - Weighted Ground (feat. Julie Elven)." YouTube. YouTube, 01 Mar. 2015. Web. 10 July 2016. <https://www.youtube.com/watch?v=yll8p824k04>.
[560] EpicJennyni20. "James Everingham - Reverie (Beautiful Orchestral)." YouTube. YouTube, 28 May 2015. Web. 10 July 2016. <https://www.youtube.com/watch?v=VmGUiazLk8w>.
[561] EpicJennyni20. "Colossal Trailer Music - Reflections of Life (Feat. Aeralie Brighton)." YouTube. YouTube, 13 Jan. 2015. Web. 10 July 2016. <https://www.youtube.com/watch?v=_0_0s_4-fq8>.
[562] Voiceprints. "Christof Unterberger - Inner Peace (feat. Julie Elven) (Epic Emotional Orchestral Filmscore)." YouTube. YouTube, 06 June 2015. Web. 10 July 2016. <https://www.youtube.com/watch?v=JRrOIVN8dEE>.
[563] EpicJennyni20. "Ivan Torrent - In Aeternum (Beautiful Orchestral)." YouTube. YouTube, 07 June 2015. Web. 10 July 2016. <https://www.youtube.com/watch?v=VyDTuS7SYas>.
[564] KacskaTB. "Chroma Music - Into The Light (Jochen Flach - 2014)." YouTube. YouTube, 15 May 2014. Web. 10 July 2016. <https://www.youtube.com/watch?v=wCyUvzag8yM>.
[565] EpicJennyni20. "Colossal Trailer Music - Faith (Beautiful Orchestral)." YouTube. YouTube, 11 June 2015. Web. 10 July 2016. <https://www.youtube.com/watch?v=vOx5gASmKfY>.
[566] Http://www.youtube.com/channel/UCjv6xdsCtvywjB5C60w1BwQ. "[Best VGM Composers] Hitoshi Sakimoto: Vagrant Story - Truth." YouTube. YouTube, 14 Nov. 2013. Web. 10 July 2016. <https://www.youtube.com/watch?v=XR0dIsdGFQM>.

put instead word "the game", word "Life".

Since Olden Times - The Grand Final[567]

I've putted a way for You from 5th Stage of Evolution (current) to 7th in this collection (even touches 8th), Enjoy Good Friends and Be Happy! :)

And I hope this emotional music will soothe and restore You Well My Friends, and that through it You will be able to find more Courage, Wisdom and Knowledge!
We Wish Everyone Peace, Calm and Prosperity!

And Sophia, Thank You Very Much for Everything You have done, Greatly Appreciated for Your Generous and Warm Help!

Remember I still can answer for some few cycles (days) I think if You have some questions or misunderstandings.

And that is the last we heard from the Guardian.

It is now July of 2016 and we are inundated with false flag events and reports forecasting financial collapse as well as numerous earth changes. It would appear that we are on course for a new earth indeed.

[567] EpicJennyni20. "Michael Maas - Since Olden Times (Feat. Claudie Mackula)." YouTube. YouTube, 30 July 2015. Web. 10 July 2016. <https://www.youtube.com/watch?v=U1BgB7qlh-A>.
[568] N.p., n.d. Web. <http://2012portal.blogspot.de/2016/07/terms-of-surrender.html>.
[569] "Gold Reward Offered for the Capture of Khazarian Gangsters." 'BenjaminFulford ' N.p., n.d. Web. 17

As this book goes to print, there are two posts that tell me we are taking this removal of the cabal into our own hands, thus accelerating the end.[568] [569] There is also one video that has a great deal of information regarding our Ascension that I resonate with. It is long, but worth getting to the end for some good stuff. Whether accurate or not, these are some best guesses by someone who has studied this process for a long time.[570]

Much love to you as we navigate this next part. Thank you for sharing this journey. It has been an honor.

~Sophia

July 2016. <http://benjaminfulford.typepad.com/benjaminfulford/2016/07/gold-reward-offered-for-the-capture-of-khazarian-gangsters.html>.
[570]"UFO CONFERENCE 2016 / (Genre UFO & Alien)." YouTube. N.p., n.d. Web. 17 July 2016. <https://youtu.be/bshKzG9_ID0>.

Notes

To find me:

Blog   http://www.sophialove.org/my-blog   (w/ RSS feed)

Newsletter   http://www.sophialove.org/subscribe-here.html

Facebook   @IAMSophiaLove

Youtube   www.youtube.com/user/sophialovequest

Soundcloud   soundcloud.com/sophialove

Twitter   HTTPS://TWITTER.COM/SOPHIALOVE_EDU

Website   www.sophialove.org

We are the Ones We've Been Waiting for.

With so much love,

~Sophia

Made in the USA
Middletown, DE
03 March 2022